The St. Vincent Handbook
Directory and Almanac

The St. Vincent Handbook
Directory and Almanac, 5th Edition
©2022 Hobo Jungle Press

Published by **Hobo Jungle Press**
St. Vincent & the Grenadines, W.I.
Sharon, Connecticut, USA

First edition
April 2022

Printed in the United States of America

ISBN #978-1-7331321-8-3
Library of Congress Control Number: 2022934887

The St. Vincent Handbook
Directory and Almanac
5th Edition

Edited by Robert M. Anderson

TABLE OF CONTENTS

FOREWORD

When we first laid eyes on *The St. Vincent Handbook* during the summer of 2021 we knew this was a work that needed to be resurrected for a generation of Vincentians who are, for the most part, unaware of its existence. Aside from the scholarship implicit between its covers, its importance to the historical record of St. Vincent and the Grenadines cannot be overstated.

Like many immigrants (we are originally from the United States and have lived in St. Vincent for 20+ years), we take more than a passing interest in the history and culture of our adopted homeland. It is for this reason that in 2013 *Hobo Jungle Press* re-published the controversial, but nevertheless important account of the Carib wars by Charles Shephard, originally published in 1831 under the title *An Historical Account of the Island of St. Vincent*. That volume has proved to be extremely popular and nine years later it still has a remarkable following. In his introduction to that work, Paul Lewis, a Vincentian with scholarly ties to the island remarked that "while Shephard's 'history' is biased, it is a timepiece and presents the views of the dominant white, colonial, land-holding and administrative class...." Even more important, Lewis says, is "the rich statistical information contained in the appendices".

Similarly, *The St. Vincent Handbook*, which was last updated in 1938, offers a predominantly one-sided view of life in the colony, albeit without the umbrella of slavery; but it, too, is rich beyond measure in statistical information, first person accounts and documentation that attest to the islands' vibrant growth, as well as the gradual recognition of the importance of indigenous culture in the life of its citizens.

It is almost hard to believe that one man, Robert Mowbray Anderson, not only conceived of the "handbook", but brought it to fruition, not once, but five times between the first edition in 1907 and the final edition published in 1938. At nearly 500 pages it is a compendium of island life covering almost two centuries, including accounts of disasters (volcanic eruptions, hurricanes, fires, and more), lengthy communications between the administrators of the island and the Monarchy, names of individuals in public service, tributes to those who served in wars; the list goes on and on. We are humbled by Anderson's tenacity in gathering every bit of information he could get his hands on in order to include it in the handbook.

The book you are currently holding has not been edited in any way from the original 5th edition, save for the use of the Galliard typeface, designed by Matthew Carter and modeled on the work of Robert Granjon, a sixteenth-century "punchcutter" whose typefaces were renowned "for their beauty and legibility" (Wikipedia). A few obscure words have been updated for a generation of English speakers who no longer use Middle English in their speech. The tables and charts have been made easier to read (we hope). The original photographs, some of which were taken by R.M. Anderson, are not included as the originals were not available to us. Beyond that, we have done our best to do justice to the original publication. The cover design is the same as the one used in the first edition. The excerpt by Sir Rupert John in the back of the book gives the reader some insight into the life of Robert Anderson without delving into his personal life. While Sir John's essay was not part of the original handbook, we thought it was important to give credit to the man who made the handbook possible.

We are indebted to Dennis Gaymes, the proprietor of Gaymes Book Centre in Kingstown, St. Vincent, for introducing us to the *The St. Vincent Handbook*. Dennis is a historical book collector *par excellence* and we hope to bring other out-of-print works to a younger generation of Vincentians in the near future thanks to his acumen.

We apologize for the lack of an index, particularly to individuals and scholars who might want to make use of the handbook in their research. While an index was included as part of the original handbook, it was necessary to reorder the pages for this publication and we felt that recreating the index was beyond the scope of this work. A few copies of the original handbook are available in selected libraries for those who deem an index necessary for their work.

— Marc Erdrich & Ruth Boerger, Publishers
Hobo Jungle Press
April 2022

INTRODUCTION

The fifth and final edition of the 1938 *St. Vincent Handbook*, edited by Robert Mowbray Anderson, has long been out of print so the decision to reprint it must be commended. Previous editions of the *Handbook*, first published in 1907, were in 1909, 1911 and 1914. The editor regretted the lapse of 24 years between the fourth and fifth editions and felt that a sixth edition, given its usefulness, demanded a shorter period. He was for whatever reason unable to produce a sixth edition. Understandably, what is presented here is not a new edition, but a reprint of that of 1938.

But who is Robert M. Anderson? R. M. was a man of many parts: editor and owner of *The Sentry* and *Vincentian* newspapers, which became incorporated into one newspaper, *The Vincentian,* that still exists today as the country's oldest newspaper; Chief Government Printer; clerk to the Registrar of the Supreme Court; a photographer of note; a music teacher; founding member of the St. Vincent Music Council; and solicitor. He was also an author, producing two booklets, *Facts on Edinboro*, the community in which he lived and *Notes and Reflections on St. Vincent*.

Anderson's *Handbook* is not a history of the then colony of St. Vincent but a veritable database of information from 1498 to 1937: 1498 being the date when colonial history told us, wrongfully so, that Columbus discovered St. Vincent. It ignored the fact that Columbus never visited St. Vincent and that there were people living here when the Europeans arrived. Anderson wrote this fifth edition at a time when British colonisation was being challenged as was seen with the riots of 1935, but he was indeed, as Rupert John in his book *Pioneers in Nation Building* (see excerpt p. 471) describes him, an "Anglophile", with an interest in the welfare and development of the land of his birth. This edition of the *Handbook* was dedicated to Administrator A. Alban Wright, who appeared to have facilitated his work, "making it possible for the editor to undertake and complete his work." (from the Preface)

The *Handbook* gives a "descriptive sketch" of St. Vincent's topography, geology and climate, with historical notes from 1498. It provides in chronological order, highlights of the years, with different aspects of the colony's history, providing some, like the volcanic eruptions of 1812 and 1902 and the English-"Carib" (sic) war of 1795-1796 in greater detail. It will be extremely useful for tourist guides seeking quick information about dates when certain buildings and sites of historical interest were established: the Central Police Station, church buildings, the Kingstown cemetery, as examples. One can find information about the names and dates of publication of the colony's different newspapers. For cricket lovers, information about the outstanding performances and the departure of Charles A. Ollivierre on May 25, 1900, to join the West Indian cricket team, the first Vincentian to do so, will be of interest.

The editor had tourism very much in mind and reproduced letters written by visitors to St. Vincent, praising its beauty and giving impressions of the colony. St. Vincent has long been described as the "Gem of the Antilles," but do we know how this started? One of the letters praising the beauty of St. Vincent was from W. M. Benedict Reilly of the *Monthly Illustrator*. It states, "We hope the name, 'the Gem of the West Indies' which we have given to St. Vincent is original, for we should like to enjoy the honour of having been the first to call it by a name so appropriate and one which it so richly deserves."

The *Handbook* also carries short pieces on a variety of places of interest: the churches, Botanic Garden, the Carnegie Free Public Library, the secondary schools at that time, the Glen Community School that no longer exists, the Agricultural School, city and towns, the Grenadine islands, the governors and administrators who had served the colony, and names of government officers in the public service, among others. Although dated 1938, the *Handbook* still provides a lot of valuable historical information that could be easily accessed by following the chronology of events.

The reader is informed at the very beginning that the *Handbook* is not an official publication but that the information it contains has been obtained from government and other official records. The governor's office and government offices held the colony's archives and Anderson, through his relationship with the Administrator, was able to tap into them. The only problem for academic research is a lack of identification of sources but it is in any event a point of reference for anyone seeking information about the colony's past.

For many years I have had Anderson's *Handbook* as my close companion, using it as a point of reference and double checking dates on which particular events took place. I recommend it strongly to all persons who need a quick review of the country's past. There is certainly a lot of information stacked into it that will not be easily found elsewhere. The fact that it was considered useful and perhaps necessary, to reproduce the *Handbook* after 84 years does to a large extent point to its importance.

— Adrian Fraser
April 2022

PREFACE TO THE 5TH EDITION

E VERY intelligent person must attach significance to the information supplied in a handbook and therefore will agree that in order, to sustain its usefulness a revised edition should make its appearance within a shorter period than 24 years.

In these days, when school children are given facilities for travelling to distant lands and people of slender means contrive to tour the islands in the Caribbean Sea as eagerly as those who come within the category of "The Tourists", it is an injustice to a colony like St. Vincent to withhold from them the abundant attractions of which they should gain some knowledge.

His Honour A. Alban Wright, the administrator (recently promoted to St. Lucia), fully recognizing the value to the colony of such a publication, and having been associated with work of this description elsewhere, has been considerate in various ways, thereby making it possible for the editor to undertake and complete his task.

It is sad to say that again the editor has been beset by persons whose attempts to thwart his efforts have been unsuccessful. How unfortunate it is for the colony that there are members of the community who aver that they are conscious of nothing in St Vincent worthy of recording as an inducement to tourists and visitors. Notwithstanding this they will not endeavour to take up residence in another place more congenial to their aspirations. It is gratifying, however, to know that noteworthy visitors who have lived in or travelled to larger places have revisited and have honestly given expression to their favourable impressions in regard to St. Vincent.

A few officers in the Government Service could not find it convenient to supply the desired information relating to their appointments, etc., but the hope is entertained that the book will nevertheless be considered interesting.

"St. Vincent tells the world", by the contents of the handbook, in the same way as cities and countries do when they advertise their beauties, charms, merchandise and the like!

Apart from the scenic grandeur and salubrious climate the magnificence of the cluster of little islands known as the Grenadines that are described as "Lilies in a Pond", there are institutions which arrest the attention of strangers:

The Government Cotton Ginnery, with its variety of by-products, has made advancement; the Arrowroot Association sprang into existence in time to stabilize that commodity for the production of which St. Vincent possesses worldwide fame; the Banana Association has been extremely useful in affording instructions and controlling the exportation as stipulated in the contract; the St. Vincent Molasses Export Company Ltd. is zealously preparing for the blending of syrup and the consequent establishment of another industry which will unquestionably prove of vast importance. These represent a few of the numerous items that one can mention; a short note relating to them will be seen on perusal of this little book.

The vigilance and co-operation of the officers of the Agricultural Department have been remarkably advantageous to the development of the staple products of the colony.

In soliciting leniency for the delay in the publication of this book, perhaps it should be mentioned that many items have been inserted at length which originally were intended to be curtailed. For example, the pathetic despatches which were forwarded and received during the Great War on to the triumphant period should be collected in book form. A comprehensive message from His late Majesty the King to the children in the elementary schools of the Empire, and an equally interesting message from the Queen Mother to the girls in the elementary schools of the Empire, both comprise as they do the fabric for Empire building, and should be handed down for the inspiration of the children that are yet to come exactly as expressed. Certain details relating to the profound sorrow occasioned by the passing of His Majesty King George the Fifth should be embodied extensively.

The inclusion within a limited number of pages of what transpired during the eventful years (1914-1937) has indeed presented a difficulty not easily explained.

The editor is grateful to those who have very kindly contributed articles and in other ways rendered assistance. The list of Chief Justices, not hitherto included in the handbook and involving work of great research, was prepared by His Honour G. C. Griffith Williams who occupied the position of Chief Justice from 1935 to 1938.

He is aware of many important subjects not included in this book but craves indulgence for all omissions and errors of which he may be found guilty.

ROBERT M. ANDERSON

Descriptive Sketch of the Island

◆━━∞━━◆━

TOPOGRAPHY AND GEOLOGY

AINT VINCENT, the most beautiful and verdant, the Emerald Isle and the peerless link of the Caribbean Chain, is situated in 13 degs. 10 m. north latitude and 60 degs. 57 m. west longitude, at a distance of 97 miles west of Barbados, 68 miles north-northeast of Grenada, 21 miles southwest of St. Lucia and 170 miles north of Trinidad.

The Island is roughly elliptical in shape; it is 18 miles long and 11 miles broad. The area is 130 square miles and with the addition of that of the Grenadines the total is 150 square miles.

The topography is mountainous; an axial range divides the island longitudinally into two nearly equal parts, which are further subdivided by lateral spurs radiating from the central range outwards to the coasts. Within the Leeward belt, the spurs are steep, sharp-crested and serrated, and the valleys are deep and narrow, whilst within the Windward belt they exhibit flatter, more gently sloping and rounded topography. The northern part of the island is dominated by the Soufriere Mountain (4,084 feet) which is separated from the neighbouring uplands (Morne Garu and Richmond Peak (3,528 feet) by a broad depression. Farther south, the central range rises to 3,193 feet at Grand Bonhomme and to 2,433 feet at Mt. St. Andrew, the most southerly mountain, surmounting the funnel-shaped Kingstown Valley. The hill-ranges radiating from Mt. St. Andrew towards the southeastern coastline enclose an almost mountain-locked basin, known as the Mesopotamia Valley.

The rivers of St. Vincent are short and straight; their upper courses are steep and gorge-like, but their lower reaches broaden out into small delta-shaped alluvial flats, particularly conspicuous on the Leeward side of the island. The more gentle undulating foothills of the Windward belt enclose flat shallow valleys occasionally merging into extensive coastal plains, of which the largest is the low-lying flatland north of Georgetown: (The Carib Country) on the northeast coast.

At altitudes below 700 feet within the Windward belt, the land surface displays a series of conspicuous step-like plateaux, believed to represent the rem-

1

nants of former sea-beaches, which owe their formation to marine denudation, operating during successive periods of a previous epoch of submergency.

In certain areas (for example, the coastal region near Brighton in the southernmost part of the island) as many as four terrace levels or benches may be distinguished, of which the third is very persistent at an elevation of about 200 feet. Further inland in the Mesopotamia Valley, two or three higher terraces may be traced on the hillsides, but they are not so well preserved. The surfaces of the terraces have been greatly eroded, particularly those of the higher levels, and the present-day rivers have cut through the escarpments so as to subdivide the land into rounded blocks, ended in low flat-topped headlands, occasionally capped with the residues of old sand dunes such as occur at Diamond and at Brighton. The Leeward (western) belt exhibits only traces of former coastal benches since marine denudation is usually much less intense along sea borders protected from wind and wave action. Nevertheless, remnants of former terraces may be distinguished in the Leeward bluffs (for example, the sea-cliffs near Barrouallie and Chateaubelair), though not in the interior valleys where intense erosion has removed all signs of their former existence.

The coastline of St. Vincent is not deeply indented. The largest bay is Kingstown Harbour in the southwest on which the chief town is situated. The Leeward coast abounds with steep cliffs where rocky spurs have been truncated by marine denudation, the intervening coast between occupied by inlets lined with pebbly or sandy beaches. The Windward coastline is almost straight, and for the most part devoid of high cliffs.

The interior of the island is nearly inaccessible. A coastal road circumscribes the island, excepting for a section in the extreme north, but there are no roads traversing the main axial mountain range except a track that skirts the Soufriere crater and joins Georgetown and Chateaubelair.

Nowhere better than in St. Vincent can the rapidity with which denudation takes place in a moist tropical climate be studied and exemplified. Excepting on the steepest slopes, where loose accumulations will not rest, the rocks are deeply covered with weathered material, which has either been formed *in situ* or has been carried down by landslips or as rain wash.

The axial mountain ridge is as a whole fairly continuous, at any rate from Mount St. Andrew, which overlooks Kingstown to Richmond Peak, which is a few miles south of the Soufriere. Some of the streams, however, in cutting back the heads of their valleys from opposite sides of the island, have nearly succeeded in meeting across the main ridge and uniting to form a low open channel from side to side of the island.

The whole of St. Vincent is of volcanic origin. There are no marine sedimentaries, and no organic limestones.

2

Although lava flows are not the predominant features of the coast sections, and are far less important than the ash beds—yet it is not to be imagined that these are rare or absent. There are many fine examples of them on both the Leeward and Windward shores of St. Vincent. Their mass is often considerable, as they are frequently 40 feet and sometimes 80 or 100 feet thick, and some, are nearly a mile in length. They are mostly andesites or andesitic basalts, porphyritic, with large crystals of pyroxene, plagioclase felspar, and commonly olivine. On the fresh fracture their dark colour and vitreous lustre often indicate the presence of considerable amounts of a glassy base.

The thickness of these larva flows and the large area they cover are two of the most striking features of the geology of the island. Among the more important examples may be mentioned the lava which outcrops on the south side of Kingstown Bay, that which occurs below Petit Bordel, at Chateaubelair, and that which forms the Black Point, south of Georgetown. On the Leeward coast, near Cumberland, and also near Barrouallie, thick streams of lava may be seen in the sides of the valleys a little distance inland. By the vertical cliffs they form they can be easily traced as they run up the valleys, and it is clear that they are of considerable age; for as they appear on both sides of the stream at the same level, they were at first continuous and have been cut up into separate blocks as the streams deepened their course and worked through them into the softer ashes below. It is this alternation of ash beds with columnar-jointed lavas which yields under the influence of sub-aerial erosion those picturesque and varied effects which make the Island of St. Vincent famous for the beauty of its scenery.

The difference in aspect between the flat-terraced coastal plains in the Windward, and the sharp spurs and deep valleys which, on the Leeward side run right down to the sea, is so striking as to call for explanation. The Windward plains are eroded and cut into by valleys, but these have none of the rugged steepness which makes the Leeward coast so picturesque. The ridges between the valleys are broad and flat-topped with fine fields of sugar-cane, arrowroot and cotton. They differ entirely from the knife-edges which separate the ravines of the higher grounds and the narrow ridges between the deep valleys on the western shore. In some places the low, round-backed hills have rather the appearance of a chalk country in the south of England.

———◆◦◦◆◦———

CLIMATE

In some respects, the climate of St. Vincent is of the hot, moist, equatorial type; in others it is more of a tropical nature. The latitude of the island (13 degs. 10 m,) is sufficiently far north to allow the influence of the northeast trades to be strongly felt during the relatively dry winter, but the northerly swing of the equatorial convectional rains, gives a well-marked, wet summer season. The warm surface waters of the Caribbean have an equalizing effect on the temperature, restricting the annual range to 3.7 degs. F. (Kingstown), but the diurnal range of about 10 degs. is usually sufficiently great to render the nights pleasantly cool, especially as the humidity is comparatively low due to the great porosity of the soil and resultant lack of evaporation of surface water. The absolute maxima and minima recorded are 89 degs. and 60 degs., but temperatures above 87 degs. or below 68 degs. are very rare. The mean annual temperature is 80.1 degs.

Until 1930, the only published meteorological records were those of the Botanic Gardens and the Experiment Station at Kingstown, the former of rainfall alone and the latter of temperature and humidity as well. Since that year, however, there has been a welcome increase in climatological data, and rainfall records are now taken at several stations on either side of the island. Unfortunately, there are gaps in their readings which are therefore of small use for comparative purposes, but six stations have more or less complete records over the last three years.

Detailed examination of the available data of rainfall shows that the average annual precipitation at the recording stations varies from 60 inches to 115 inches, but none of the stations with records for over three years is far removed from the coast. The lowest reading is from a station with an open situation in the extreme south and the highest from an estate in the narrow and steep-sided Buccament Valley on the Leeward side. In general, stations on the Windward coast are drier than those on the Leeward, but examples in relatively open country on the Leeward coast (e.g. Peters Hope) show readings comparable with those of the Windward side. The heaviest recorded precipitation seems to occur in the deeper of the Leeward valleys where the hot, moist airs of summer are trapped and forced to ascend. No records of high level stations are available, but it is obvious to the observer that the precipitation is heavier on the mountains. Not only is the mountain vegetation characteristic of a moister climate, but numerous showers fall there which leave the coasts untouched.

St. Vincent is sufficiently near the equator to show a faint summer double maximum in its rainfall records, but precipitation is well enough distributed for severe droughts to be rare even in the dry winter season (January–July). The majority of years show a well-marked double maximum individually, but the time of its incidence is so variable that it becomes faint in any average. The mean humidity is about 70 (though it may rise to almost 80 in summer) and this, combined with the constant northeast trades and the absence of standing water, renders the winter climate of the island one of the healthiest and most delightful in the West Indies. St. Vincent lies within the hurricane belt, but it is now sixteen years since a severe hurricane visited the island.

4

Historical Notes

1498 / The island was discovered by Columbus on the 22nd day of January. That day, according to the calendar of the Spaniards being St. Vincent's day, it was considered appropriate to name the island St. Vincent.* At the time of its discovery, St. Vincent, like several of the other, small islands, was inhabited by the Caribs, who were very numerous and warlike. The coast was difficult of access and the appearance of the interior was that of a dense forest with many rivers and precipitous ravines.

Possessing these natural means of defence, and abounding with facilities of existence from a fertile soil, the ocean and rivers being well supplied with fish, the forests teeming with large trees peculiarly adapted for canoes, St. Vincent became a chosen residence for that tribe of native who regarded the island as the rendezvous of their expeditions to the continent. They continued in peaceful possession of the island until 1627.

1627 / St. Vincent was included in the Earl of Carlisle's patent which was granted by Charles I, but apparently he did not assert any pretensions to the island.

1643 / M. de Bretigny, on his way to assume command at Cayenne, passed at St. Vincent. The Governor sent to him as a present nineteen goats; in return, biscuit and brandy were given. M. de Bretigny's men wished to remain.

1660 / English and French Sovereigns agree to act of neutrality or treaty. In accordance with this, the Caribs having promised to do all in their power to preserve peace, and to punish any of their countrymen who should break

---

*Saint Vincent was deacon of Saragossa. Gibbon, however, thinks he was attached to a church, either at Evora or Beia, from the circumstance of the adjoining cape being named after him; he lived about the end of the third age, under the Emperors Diocletian and Maximian; he was tortured and put to death by Datianus, the Governor of Spain, January 22nd A.D. 305, who endeavoured to root out Christianity in that country. An account of his sufferings is to be found in *Tillemont Memoires Ecclesiastiques*, Vol. V, Part II 58. See Gibbon, Chap. XVI.

it, were allowed the undisturbed possession of the islands of St. Vincent and Dominica, which were their only places of retreat.

1672 / A new commission was granted to Lord Willoughby constituting him Governor of Barbados, St. Lucia, St. Vincent and Dominica; on his demise Sir Jonathan Atkins was appointed. In spite of these grants no steps appear to have been taken to form a settlement on the island.

1675 / A ship carrying natives from Africa foundered on the coast of Bequia. Those who escaped from this wreck were received by the inhabitants as brethren. The first black men therefore who landed upon this island were as free as the air they breathed. They had indeed escaped from a slaver's bond but when they touched these shores they were the lords of their own destiny. The natives fostered these strangers, and in time they gave to them their daughters in marriage; the tribe which thus sprang up, preserving more of the primitive colour of their fathers than the higher hue of their mothers, was called "Black Caribs" to distinguish them from the aborigines to whom the name of "Yellow Caribs" was given.

1680 / Sir Richard Dutton succeeded Sir Jonathan Atkins.

1685 / On Sir Richard Dutton's departure for England he appointed Colonel Edwin Stede Lieutenant-Governor. The latter, unlike his predecessors, vigorously asserted the rights of the Crown by appointing Deputy Governors for the other islands. He sent Captain Temple to St. Vincent to prevent the French taking wood and water without permission—a practice in which they indulged prior to his assumption, but apparently no attempt was made to occupy or administer the island.

1719 / Following an attack on St. Vincent by the French from Martinique, under the command of Major Paulian, in which the Black Caribs were victorious, many of the inhabitants of that place removed to St. Vincent at the invitation of the Black Caribs.

The French force from Martinique under the command of Major Paulian, landed at St. Vincent, to assist the Red Caribs in driving out the Negroes. He landed without much opposition and began to burn the Negro huts and destroy their plantations, expecting the Indians would attack them from the mountains; they, however, did not assist their allies, and the Negroes, by retreating to the woods in the daytime and sallying in the night, destroyed so many of the French, including their commander, that the survivors were obliged to retreat; they afterward, by persuasion and presents, made peace with both Indians and Negroes.

When the French arrived from Martinique they brought with them their slaves, and the Black Caribs who were shocked at the idea of resembling the slaves brought by the French took refuge in the thickest part of the woods; and in order to perpetuate a visible distinction they compressed so as to flatten the foreheads of all their new-born infants. Upon being refused by the Yellow Caribs a friendly participation in the landed property, they began hostilities against them; and by force brought them to terms resulting in an equal division of the lands on the Leeward coast.

After another war in which they were again defeated, the Yellow Caribs retired to the Windward part of the Island while several fled to the continent and others to Tobago.

1722 / His Majesty King George I made a grant to the Duke of Montague of a few of the West Indian islands including Saint Vincent.

1723 / By virtue of the grant to the Duke of Montague, Captain Uring sailed with considerable armament to take St. Lucia and St. Vincent. When dislodged at St. Lucia by superior force of the French, he sent Captain Brathwaite to try his fate at this island whilst he sailed to Antigua. The Caribs calmly but firmly opposed all propositions made by Captain Brathwaite who departed after an exchange of cordiality.

1730 / The English and French agreed that until their rights to the islands of Lucia, St. Vincent and Dominica were determined the said islands should be entirely evacuated by both nations. Instructions to this effect were consequently issued to the Governor of Barbados.

1735 / By a return made to the Government of Barbados the inhabitants of St. Vincent were estimated at 6,000 Negroes and 4,000 native Caribs, who waged continual war against the Negroes.

1740 / The French, in spite of treaties of neutrality, continued to extend their influence and in this year the exports from St. Vincent were valued at £63,625.

1748 / St. Vincent was again declared neutral by the treaty of Aix-la-Chapelle.

1756 / Hostilities between French and English resumed.

1762 / The expedition which was sent against Martinique under General Monckton and Rear-Admiral Rodney also took this island. The General obtained a grant of 4,000 acres of land in Charlotte Parish called Monckton's Quarter which he sold to Messrs. Gemmels and Baillie for £30,000. Mr. Swinburne had 24,000 acres.

1763 / St. Vincent was ceded in perpetuity to the British Crown without any reservation of the rights of the Caribs. General Robert Melville was appointed first Governor of the island. On October 7th, by Proclamation of

George III, it was announced that Letters Patent were issued creating the Government of Grenada, Dominica, St. Vincent and Tobago. Councils and Assemblies of the representatives of the people were provided for and the Governor authorized to constitute Courts of Justice with the right of appeal to the Privy Council of Great Britain.

1764 / The island of St. Vincent produced 12,000 andouilles (sic) of tobacco, 7,900 cwts. of cocoa, and 14,700 cwts. of coffee.

1765 / The possession by the British of this fine island soon attracted the notice of the colonists in North America, Barbados and Antigua who came in great numbers. Such, however, was the rapacity of the new settlers that they not only solicited and obtained grants of the unoccupied lands but insisted in appropriating also those that belonged to the French and even to the Caribs. The consequence was that such of the French as chose to remain had to purchase their tracts of land for the third time; while the Caribs were so incensed that they broke out into open rebellion. This injustice on the part of the English colonists was the origin of all the Carib wars which subsequently spread such desolation over the island, and cost the mother country such sacrifice of blood and treasure. The task of reducing the Caribs to submission was one of no ordinary difficulty, and its execution was attended with heavy losses on the part of the troops.

1771 / Soon after the appointment of Brigadier-General William Leybourne to be Governor, the planters resolved to carry into execution their lucrative plans; hitherto there was no cultivation beyond the river Coubaimarou; the land granted to General Monckton in that vicinity, proving to be fertile, allotments were eagerly purchased and many enterprising persons induced to obtain the sanction of the Government for other grants of land beyond that boundary; 20,538 acres were disposed of for the sum of £162,854. Disturbance was nevertheless threatened.

1772 / In April, orders were issued from England to send two regiments from North America to assist in reducing the Caribs to due submission, and to adopt other means best calculated to secure the tranquillity of the colony. Sir Charles Green, Bart., Lieutenant of the 31st and John Simon Farley, Lieutenant of the 68th, were employed in this service.

Dr. George Young, who had the care of the Botanical Garden, which was established by Governor Melville, received a Gold Medal from the Society for the Encouragement of Arts for having in that Garden 140 healthy plants of true cinnamon, plants of logwood, turmeric, East India mango, Tobago nutmeg, sesamum [sesame] or oily grain, cassia fistula, vanelloes, anatto, China tallow tree, and many other curious plants.

1773 / Major-General Dalrymple, under whose direction the expedition was carried on, distinguished himself considerably on the occasion, but did not effect the humiliation of the Caribs until the month of February. In obedience to instructions, General Dalrymple made overtures for peace which were joyfully accepted by the Caribs. The Treaty was published in the *Gazette* of 27th February, signed on behalf of His Majesty—W. Dalrymple; and on behalf of the Caribs—Jean Baptiste, Dufont and others. An extensive district of St. Vincent was allotted to them on condition of their laying down arms and acknowledging the King of Great Britain as the rightful sovereign of the island.

The loss of the British on this expedition was 150 killed and wounded, 110 died of disease and 428 were sent to hospital.

The following oath was to be taken by the Caribs:

> *We, A. B. do swear in the name of the immortal God and Christ Jesus, that we will bear true allegiance to His Majesty George the Third, &c., &c., and that we will pay due obedience to the laws of Great Britain and the island of St. Vincent, and will well and truly observe every article of the treaty concluded between His said Majesty and the Caribs; and we do acknowledge that His said Majesty is rightful lord and sovereign of all the island of St. Vincent, and that the lands held by us the Caribs are granted through His Majesty's clemency.*

A silver medal was struck to commemorate the peace which was restored in this year. The Obverse of which is a Bust of King George III in high relief and the Reverse is a representation of the figure of Britannia presenting an olive branch to a naked Carib. The inscription is "PEACE AND PROSPERITY TO ST. VINCENT'S MDCCLXXIII." (This medal is now in the Library.)

1774 / The Lord Chief Justice of the Court of King's Bench pronounced judgment against the Crown as to its right to the 4½% duties demanded in lieu of the duties formerly paid to the French King by the Island of Grenada. These duties were consequently abolished in Grenada, Dominica, St. Vincent, and Tobago.

1776 / Hitherto the island formed a part only of a government which embraced, also Grenada, Tobago and Dominica, but from their increasing importance they were created into separate governments; Valentine Morris Esq was entrusted with the charge of St. Vincent.*

---

*From a narrative of the life of V. Morris, Esq it appears that the island was in want of requisite for defence, consequently, he drew bills on the Treasury which were dishonoured. The holders of bills instituted legal proceedings against him resulting in the sale of his estates in England and the West Indies; also his confinement in the King's Bench Prison. Sometime afterward some of the bills were paid by the Treasury.

In the meantime, Lieutenant-Colonel Etherington of the Royal Americans arrived from Europe with a number of raw recruits; instead of establishing discipline among them and attending to the fortifications, they were constantly employed in clearing an estate on the Wallibou river, about 23 miles from Kingstown, supposed to have been obtained from Chatoyer, a Carib Chief. This fact was known to the French, who were preparing to make an attack. Notwithstanding frequent intimations of impending hostilities Governor Morris remained indifferent.

1779 / On the 16th of June, St. Vincent shared the common fate of most of the British West Indian possessions in that unfortunate war with America. The island surrendered with scarcely a struggle to a small body of troops from Martinique consisting of 450 men only, commanded by a Lieutenant in the French Navy. The terms offered and accepted were similar to those given to Dominica. The forms of the British Constitution however were unaltered, the Council and Assembly continued their sittings and warrants were issued in the name of the King of Great Britain. The Marquis de Bouille, Governor-General of Martinique, appointed Lieutenant-Governors among whom General Du Montet was the first whose conduct was mild and conciliatory.

1780 / On the 10th of October a great Hurricane devastated this and neighbouring islands: Grenada, St. Lucia, and Martinique. The greater portion of the dwelling houses, churches, and other buildings were destroyed.

Admiral Rodney, with the concurrence of General Vaughan, attempted to recover possession, but the French had so established themselves as to render one day's experience sufficient to prove the futility.

1781 / M. Duplessis who superseded General Du Montet, distinguished himself by arbitrary demands of money and supplies for the troops. He was relieved by General Blancheland, a greatly respected officer, whose tragical fate on his return to his native land did not appear to have been merited. (Guillotined at Paris on 17th April, 1793).

1782 / During the administration of General Freydeau, the French Minister of Marine by royal ordinance directed "les Terres incultes vagues et non concedes" to be granted to Mrs. Martha Swinburne a "Dame d'honneur" in the Palace.

1783 / Comte de Tilly, the last French Governor, of whom nothing remarkable is recorded, remained in his appointment until the conclusion of negotiations of the peace of Versailles.

In England, an Act was passed allowing the importation of goods from Europe into the islands of St. Christopher, Nevis, Montserrat, Dominica, St. Vincent, Grenada, and the Grenadines; and of goods the produce or manufacture of the said islands, and of Tobago and St. Lucia from thence into that Kingdom upon payment of the British plantation duties, and to cancel certain bonds entered into for payment of the duties due thereon, for continuing certain temporary acts for the encouragement of trade, etc.

1784 / On the last day of January, possession of the island was restored to to the English, whereupon Edmond Lincoln, Esq, was appointed the Governor. The Assembly voted £5,000 currency for fortifications. Cultivation was extended, extensive sugar works were erected where cotton and tobacco only had been previously ventured, and the Caribs consequently grew happy and contented with their allotments.

1786 / Governor Lincoln died in the Government. An Act of the Legislature was passed regulating matters pertaining to the Assembly. There were 19 members, three for each of five parishes, two for Kingstown and two for the Grenadines. The qualification of members tor the parishes and islands was 50 acres of land in cultivation, or producing an income of £300 a year; and for the town, house of the yearly rental value of £100. For electors a freehold of 10 acres or a house in Kingstown of £20, yearly rental value, or £10 elsewhere.

The Supreme Court for Civil Causes was called the Court of King's Bench and Common Pleas, over which the Chief Justice presided; his salary was £2,000 a year. There were three assistant Judges who were not professional men and acted without salary.

The proceedings were regulated by a Court Act. The Court of Sessions for trial of criminal offences was held twice a year. The Chief Justice was president; the members of Council and Judges sat according to seniority. The Court of Error for Appeal from King's Bench and Common Pleas was composed of the Governor and Council. The Governor was also sole Chancellor; from the last two Courts there was the right to appeal to His Majesty-in-Council.

1787 / In March, James Seton, Esq assumed the Administration. For some time after the island continued in a state of uninterrupted tranquillity.

On the 9th of January, the first Methodist Missionaries landed in St. Vincent and preached in Mr. Claxton's house the same evening. The next evening they preached at Mr. Clapham's, about ten miles from Kingstown, where Mr. Clark the missionary was offered the use of a room for his congregation. The president of the Council gave him permission to preach in the courthouse on Sundays. Six or seven of the soldiers stationed on the island were Methodists. The Negroes considered the Missionaries as men imported for them, and the commencement of the undertaking was considered by the Society exceedingly favourable.

Lord Nelson, who described himself the messenger of bad news, communicated to Lord Collingwood's brother the intelligence regarding the illness and death of his colleague, Wilfred Collingwood. The letter was forwarded from H.M.S. *Boreas* while at Nevis, and was dated May 3, 1787. It contained the following incident:

> *He sailed on Tuesday for Grenada, where I was in hopes, could he have reached Mr. Haines some fortunate circumstance might turn out; but it pleased God to order it otherwise. On Friday, the 21st of April, at ten at night, he left this life without a groan or a struggle. The ship put into St. Vincents, where he was interred with all military honours; the regiment, President, and Council attending him to the grave. It is a credit to the people of St. Vincents which I did not think they would have deserved. Adieu, my good friend, and be assured I am, with the truest regard,*

> *Your affectionate friend,*
> HORATIO NELSON

1789 / From San Domingo the doctrines of the republicanism reached Martinique, to which place the Caribs traded. With the adoption of these principles discontentment arose. The Caribs and their allies, the French, again overran the country, burning the cane fields, plundering the houses, and mercilessly murdering the English colonists.

1790 / Although many persons had joined the Methodist Missionary Society, Mr. Baxter, a preacher, being unable to make any impression upon the Caribs, removed to Kingstown. The French priests at Martinique had persuaded the Caribs that the missionaries were spies sent by the King of England and that the King would afterward send an army to conquer their country. Mr. Baxter endeavoured to convince the Caribs of the falsehood of these reports, but their continued sullenness convinced him that it was high time to hasten out of the country with Mrs. Baxter.

1793 / Three hundred breadfruit plants were landed at Kingstown by Captain Bligh for the purpose of being distributed among the different islands. The *Providence* completed the voyage from St. Helena to St. Vincent in 27 days.

The Assembly passed an Act declaring that no person in the island should in future preach, without first obtaining a licence; and no person was eligible to a licence, but those who had actually resided twelve months on the island. This militated entirely against the itinerant plan pursued by the Methodist missionaries who had been established by that sect in the islands. Though they should continue idle for one year, at its expiration there was no certainty of procuring a licence. On representation by Dr. Coke toward the end of the year, he was informed "that His Majesty in Council had been graciously pleased to disannul the Act of the Assembly at St. Vincent."

1795 / The disturbed state of affairs continued till the arrival of the *Zebra* Sloop-of-War, with succours from Martinique, then the British headquarters.

Arms and ammunitions, were expected from Gaudeloupe. On the night of March 10th the Caribs on the Leeward part under direction of Chatoyer, and those of Windward under Duvalle were to proceed to Kingstown to unite with their French confederates.

The Governor, James Seton, Esq, was a man of cool, steady and determined character. His son of the same name, a Brigade Major, displayed considerable talent. The sugar plantation had extended as far as Byera on the Windward coast, and many small French settlements had been consolidated on the Leeward side, but the state of defence was very defective. The Colonial Militia was the only body of men to afford effectual resistance pending reinforcements from Martinique, then the residence of the Commander-in-Chief.

On 5th March, when information as to insurrection at Grenada was received, an alarm was fired. In the evening, the Militia under arms appeared on the Parade when they were reviewed by the Governor who exhorted them to render their characters worthy of distinction. Mr. W. Greig, a merchant, informed the Governor that he was urged by a Carib to withdraw from this island as his countrymen intended to proclaim war.

On the 7th, the Governor-in-Council requested the attendance of Chatoyer and Duvalle on the following Tuesday. "It is too late, it might have been sent sooner" was the answer. Mr. Irvin, one of the Governor's Aides-de-Camp and proprietor of an estate at Massarica, was sent to speak to the Caribs in that locality and by them to send an order requesting the Chief of Grand Sable to attend the Governor.

March 8th, several gentlemen partook of Maroon Dinner with some of the chiefs. On the Tuesday following, the Caribs, including these chiefs, made an attack, plundering and demolishing the plantations on which they had comfortably resided for more than 10 years. On Sunday evening, information that Caribs at Marriaqua had been ranging the Estate of Mrs. La Croix was received. A detachment of the Militia and a small party of volunteers with some armed Negroes under the command of Brigade-Major Seton and Major H. Sharpe, respectively, were ordered to apprehend the perpetrators. Mr. Dupre, a Swiss of the English party, disguised himself and gained admission into their camps; but before they were completely surrounded, many escaped. Eighteen only were made prisoners.

On the 9th March, James Gerald Morgan, Esq, Capt., of. Windward Militia sent intelligence regarding mediated attack by whole body of Caribs and requested immediate assistance. Lieutenants MacDowall and Hugh Perry Keane commanding a detachment of Militia and volunteers were ordered to reinforce him. Sans Souci Estate was reached during the night, so they waited until the morning. At Bellevue Estate they were told that fire had already been set to the dwelling house on Three Rivers Estate and adjoining cane fields. As they approached, the enemy fired warmly from the cane fields, increasing in number every moment. A variety of circumstances determined them to return to Kingstown without delay. From Massarica river they saw a body of Caribs posted before them on a ridge which commanded the road. When completely exposed to their fire, the Caribs opened a tremendous volley of musketry which was maintained with unabating ardour. While preparing to advance and charge them, they were attacked in the rear by another body of enemy. In this critical and perilous situation, nothing but a retreat in the best manner possible could have been attempted. Thirty-one persons lost their lives. Whites and Blacks abandoned their abode. The Caribs, inflated with success, and encouraged by the prevailing timidity of all descriptions of people, seemed to invoke the demon of destruction to mark their progress. On reaching Dorsetshire Hill they pulled down the British Standard and displayed the flag of the French Republic. The conspirators under Chatoyer, Commander-in-Chief, were quite as active but did not commit such devastations. Chatoyer chose Mr. Kearton's Estate in St. Patrick's Parish for his share.

On Tuesday 10th March, they were joined at Chateaubelair by all French inhabitants in that neighbourhood. Duncan Cruikshank, Alex. Grant and Peter Cruikshank, three respectable white young men were made prisoners and carried along with them to Dorsetshire Hill. The Saturday following, Chatoyer ordered their massacre.

Dorsetshire Hill Was fortified to the best of their advantage. The Governor remained to the end at Berkshire Hill, where necessary fortifications were carried on; a post was likewise established on Sion Hill. In order to prevent the enemy approaching unseen the surrounding cane fields were burnt. The Caribs were frequently seen on Liberty Lodge and Redemption Estates. A small party proceeded as far as Government House which was then on Montrose Estate. All of their positions were within six furlongs from Kingstown. Captain Newton of the Artillery and Major Whytell of the Militia, maintaining the post at Sion Hill, considerably annoyed the enemy and kept them greatly in dread. They ventured to approach within reach when a well-directed shot drove them back. They contented themselves with burning the canes on Arnos Vale and adjoining estates. Captain Campbell with the company of the forty-sixth Regiment arrived from Martinique on Wednesday.

On Thursday, the Sloop-of-war, *Zebra* arrived, and the *Roebuck* on Saturday.

At midnight on the 14th, the party formed at the residence of Mr. Hartley on Sion Hill. Captain Skinner of the *Zebra* was in command and led the van with detachments of sailors and marines from his vessel and from the *Roebuck*.

14

Lieutenants Hilt and Greaves followed with sailors collected from merchants ships in Port. Captain Campbell with the company of the forty-sixth came next while Major Whytell and Captain Farquhar Campbell with detachments of Militia and armed Negroes brought up the rear.

Major Sharpe showed Captain Skinner the road and Mr. Seymour volunteered to be an Advance Guide. In the order named, they ascended the winding and rugged path leading to Dorsetshire Hill unperceived until within eighty yards. The enemy was immediately under arms, raised a most appalling yell, at the same time pouring a brisk and well-continued shower of musketry, which was received, without returning a single shot. When within twenty yards, orders were given to fire a volley and charge. These orders being instantly obeyed, Captain Skinner and Lieutenant Hill mounted the bank and were closely followed by the detachment of seamen; Captain Campbell and Major Leith did the same in another situation. The buildings were stormed, the enemy fled in all directions. Through the darkness of the night many effected their escape. Those who resisted were bayoneted and in about fifteen minutes their fate was determined. Five seamen were killed and Lieutenant Hill and four men wounded. Several of the French and Caribs lay dead on the field, among them being Chatoyer, the Commander-in-Chief of the forces, who was notorious for his cruelty. There was found upon this chief a silver gorget presented to him by His Majesty, then Prince Henry, on his visit to St. Vincent, cruising on the West Indian station. The French were panic-stricken and endeavouring to reach Layou. A goodly number of them, including Dumont, the Secretary of the conspiracy, was intercepted by the Negroes. Not many days after their apprehension, they were hanged; their, bodies towed beyond the harbour and committed to the deep. Twenty-four others found in arms after taking the oath of allegiance were similarly dealt with. Confounded and dismayed, the Caribs retreated to the part of the island assigned to them. The insufficiency of troops and colonial resources rendered impracticable the continuance of this pursuit, which might have resulted in a complete suppression of the enemy.

On the 18th, Colonel Gordon with a detachment of the Northern Regiment marched to the town of Chateaubelair; although effectually protecting all the estates in that vicinity from the plunder to which they were hitherto exposed, it became necessary to burn that town. Besides destroying the upper works and the canes on Wallibou Estate the enemy murdered Mr. Grant the overseer by inhumanly passing his body between the cylinders of the sugar mill.

A spirited Proclamation, dated 20th March, was published by the Governor, wherein he enumerated the barbarities and unjustifiable conduct of the enemy and declared the attack treasonable; also, that he would subject prisoners to the same treatment as that received by his countrymen from them.

The terms of the Proclamation were therefore carried into effect as long as circumstances required such determined conduct.

Recovering from their panic, the Caribs pitched three camps in the neighbourhood of Calliaqua, and on the 21st the most valuable part of the town was burnt. On another occasion, at midnight, in defiance of the guns at Sion Hill, they effected the total destruction by fire of the Sugar Works on Arnos Vale Estate. The Villa, Belmont and Fairhall Estates shared the like fate, and many defenceless Negroes were barbarously murdered.

The arrival at Barbados of the long-expected fleet, was reported on the 30th March; but owing to some delay, no assistance reached the island before 5th April, when two transports arrived from Martinique under convoy of the *Montagu* with the seventy-fourth and forty-sixth Regiments. The soldiers marched straight away to their appointed quarters at Berkshire Hill. Three years residence at Gibraltar had prepared them for this climate.

On the 8th, the ship *Cockrane* (Captain Wiseman) arrived from Liverpool; nine seamen attempting to land at Greathead Bay were surrounded by the Caribs. A party from Sion Hill ventured their rescue but failed. An attack on their camp being determined by the Governor, the following dispositions were made on the 10th: Captain Campbell of the forty-sixth at the head of the Grenadiers to make the attack; Captain Hall with the Light Infantry, and Colonel Lowman of the Militia with his men and a detachment of sailors from the *Roebuck* were to intercept, in different directions, the enemy's retreat to Calliaqua. They marched at about 10 pm and reached their respective destinations at one next morning. The spirited reception of the troops justified the supposition that the enemy had accurate information. Heavy and successive rains during the march damaged the arms of the men, in consequence of which the Light Infantry hesitated after commencing a smart engagement. From an unknown person, the unexpected order to retreat caused such confusion among the Militia and sailors under Colonel Lowman as to result in their return to Kingstown early in the morning. The Light Infantry, the Grenadiers of the forty-sixth and Lieutenant Farquharson with twenty-one men of the third, battalion of the sixtieth, charged the enemy with such bravery that they fled on all sides with the utmost precipitation. The loss of the enemy was considerable, but as they generally carry off their dead, not more than twenty were found. The loss of the English was two killed and a few wounded of the regulars. Of the Volunteer Militia under Capt. William Fraser, Mm. Thomas B. Taylor, Philip Hepburn and John McBroom were killed and Alexander Stewart and Joseph Richardson wounded. The loss was in a measure compensated by the recovery of the sailors who had been taken prisoners. To procure reinforcements, 500 slaves were armed and produced on parade. Brigade Major Seton was their Lieutenant-Colonel. The other officers were appointed from the Militia and a Sergeant from the regulars to each company. They very soon became an active and useful body of men. On the 25th of April two armed schooners sailed from Kingstown with troops under command of Lieutenant Seton. They were reinforced at Chateaubelair with a small detachment of the 46th Regiment, commanded by Ensign Lee. Early in the morning of the 26th, they sailed for the settlement of Duvalle, the Carib Chief. From their brave perseverance every obstacle was surmounted and victory obtained. Twenty-five houses were devoted to the flames, but the loss of 16 canoes and 4 swivels found on the batteries must have rendered the defeat doubly formidable.

The Brigands who survived the storming of the Camps on the 10th of April, together with the Marriaqua and Windward Caribs and those English and French Negroes who joined them, assembled on the Vigie.

On the 7th of May at 9 a.m. about 800 of them in eight distinct columns directed their coasts toward the Camps at Calliaqua, then maintained by the Hon. Captain Molesworth with 100 regulars and nearly as many rangers. Advancing within range, a six-pounder was discharged upon them which occasioned their halting. The enemy, sending a flag of truce, made certain proposals which Captain Molesworth declined with the utmost contempt. The *Alarm* frigate from Kingstown, having arrived at Calliaqua, poured a whole broadside upon the foe. On her repetition of the discharge and landing 130 sailors they scampered away with marvellous speed. During this transaction a detachment of the regulars with a six-pound field piece under Captain Hall took the post on Dorsetshire Hill to effectually secure the safety of the town. With the united efforts of the French troops and the disaffected Negroes and Mulattoes of the island about 300 in number, the Caribs advanced from Orange Grove. After brave resistance, their ammunition being expended, the English troops retired leaving the enemy in possession of the hill.

Early the next morning, a detachment under Lieutenant Colonel Seton ascended unperceived by the enemy. After a short, but sharp conflict the enemy fled on all sides. They were pursued and several taken or killed. The English lost nine killed and 26 wounded. Those of the militia killed were Mm. Seymour Weire, Howard, and Gillies. The enemy had received reinforcement of 110 men from Guadeloupe. In order to induce the Negroes to join them, the Caribs offered liberty, but happily for the inhabitants the proposal, however flattering, was rejected with disdain. A considerable number of the Negroes being well armed opposed them and either gallantly fell or triumphed with their masters.

In consequence of this inflexibility of conduct in the Negroes they became equally the objects of detestation with their owners.

General Sir John Vaughan visited the Island on the 30th May. On his return to Martinique, the headquarters, he sent a reinforcement of Artillery and a quantity of stores which were followed by a detachment of Major Malcolm's corps of Rangers consisting of 100 men who arrived on the 8th June. On the ensuing day, the third Battalion of the sixtieth, 600 men under the command of the gallant Lieutenant-Colonel Ritchie also arrived.

On the 11th of June the troops received orders to march at evening at different periods and in different divisions. Lieutenant Colonel Leighton's division moved from Sion Hill at about 11 o'clock and proceeded without interruption through the town of Calliaqua and along Belmont road. Lieutenant Colonel Ritchie's division moved from Sion Hill at about 2 o'clock, proceeded through Warrawarou Valley on the Fountain Estate. The corps of Rangers commanded by Lieutenant-Colonel Seton moved earlier in the evening and proceeded along the road leading to Calder Works until they reached Calder Ridge when they divided. Major Ecuyer and Major Lieth with a party marched to Augustine's Ridge at the head of Biabou Valley. Captain Martin and Captain Fraser took post on the Bridge at the Carreer Estate in Marriaqua Valley. Lieutenant Col. Seton and Lieutenant Brown took post at the Yambou Pass near to the Mesopotamia works. Lieutenant Col. Prevost and Captain Alves remained at Calder Ridge. About daybreak, Lieutenant Colonel Ritchie's division attacked about 250 Caribs. They immediately fled to Marriaqua. In this expedition the enemy were defeated with great loss and were pursued in various directions. Twenty-three of the enemy were found killed in the forts of whom 16 were whites and about 60 were taken prisoners, among whom was M. Souhallet, the Commander. Lieutenant-Colonel Prevost intercepted and killed many of the fugitives in the retreat through the Calder Estate—not a fourth part of the whole escaped. The British lost Captain Piquet of the Third Battalion, Thomas Clapham, Joseph Preston, and Thomas Taylor of the Militia, also 13 privates killed; 3 Officers and 55 Privates were wounded. After this engagement the troops were employed in scouring the Marriaqua Valley, killing several of the enemy, taking prisoners and destroying their houses. From Augustine's party at his ridge some opposition was met and a few men who imprudently exposed themselves were wounded; before night, however, the Caribs retreated to Massarica. Captain Campbell of the forty-sixth with a detachment remained at Vigie; Lieutenant Colonels Leighton and Ritchie marching therefrom took the route to Marriaqua and joined the other Corps at the works on Carreer where they halted that night. Lieutenant Colonel Prevost's party took post at Calder Hill and Major Ecuyer's remained all night upon Augustine's Ridge.

On the morning of the 13th the whole began their march to the Windward Quarters. One party proceeded through Marriaqua Valley down to Biabou Valley to the high road at the Adelphi Estate, the other gained the high road in different directions by Yambou River and the Calder Road; the whole joined and encamped near the ruin of the dwelling house on Union Estate.

After the arrival of provisions on the morning of the 15th the march was resumed and passing on Bellevue ridge where they halted. Mount Young was reached the next morning; seven men died from fatigue. The Caribs fled precipitately from Mount Young leaving great quantities of corn in their houses. No time was lost in destroying the enemy's petits augres, canoes and houses at Grand Sable. About 200 canoes were destroyed, some larger ones were styled their "men-of-war". Alexander Wiseman, a volunteer in the forty-sixth was killed by the accidental discharge of a musket.

On 23rd June, detachments commanded by Major Ecuyer sailed for Owia on two Droghers under convoy of the *Thorn* Sloop-of-war and arrived on 25th. In the first attempt to land several were killed and wounded. A smart fire from the vessels however drove them off and the party landed without further opposition. Several skirmishes ensued with this party and that at Mount Young, in one of which Captain Schneider of the sixtieth was killed. About this time the evacuation of St. Lucia by Brigadier General Stewart opened easy communication between that Island and St. Vincent.

In consequence of assistance from St. Lucia the affairs of the enemy assumed a new appearance and they took post on a height at the extremity of Wallibou Estate. The guns from the *Thorn* were ineffective but those from the forecastle and quarter-deck of the *Roebuck* greatly annoyed them.

This reconnoitring took place on the 2nd of July and resulted in their removal to Lafond's Hill just above Colonel Gordon's post at Chateaubelair upon which they began to fire but without any effect.

On the 6th a party sailed to reinforce Colonel Gordon and arrived at Chateaubelair the following day. Attempting an attack on the succeeding day, the enemy proved far more numerous than had been expected; supported by a two-pound marmizette (sic), which commanded a narrow pass, they considerably injured the advancing party, who were obliged to retreat. Twenty-three were killed and 45 wounded. Messrs. William Greig and Thomas Grant, both Volunteers, were killed; Lieutenant Moore also died of his wounds.

About this time General Vaughan who died at Martinique was succeeded by Major-General Paulus Æmilius Irving.

Lieutenant Colonel Leighton, having been recalled from Mt. Young on 12th arrived in Kingstown on 14th with the forty-sixth and a detachment of Rangers.

These were embarked on the 16th with three six-pound field pieces and two howitzers; they landed at Troumaca and marched to Bostock Park.

On the 18th, the troops took possession of Fevrier's Ridge which afforded complete command of the enemy's camp. In order to ascertain the range, the party fired one of the guns which alarmed the enemy who silently retreated during the night to the bed of the Morne-a-Garou River.

Two parties pursued them, one of whom opened fire as the enemy were ascending Morne Cochon in Indian files and scrambling among the bushes to get up the hill. Many must have been killed and wounded for they were seem to drop in the bushes. As they got up they commenced fire at the English from behind trees to cover their rear.

On the 22nd, the enemy were discovered marching up the dry ravine toward the pass into Rabacca. Major Leith with a detachment from Musement's Hill was too late to intercept them; an engagement, however, ensued.

23rd—A sloop and a schooner landed at night: 100 men and 10 women from Guadeloupe, with a small mortar and marmizette; the sloop *Le Floreal* was taken by *Thorn*. The schooner was chased to St. Lucia. The troops from Musement's, embarked to take post on opposite side of Morne Ronde, found it impracticable.

31st—A party of 50 consisting of the former French inhabitants, free coloured persons, and Negroes set fire to Mr. Garvin Hamilton's dwelling house, works and Negro houses at Rose Hall, killed about 10 of his slaves and wounded several. They proceeded to Dr. Tait's at Washilabo, burnt all the buildings and inhumanly murdered Mr. Donald Munro, the manager. Major Josias Jackson, fortunately passing in his canoe, landed with his armed slaves, joined some Negroes who had collected together, and headed this party in pursuit of them when proceeding to Colonel Gordon's. The brigands, perceiving them retreated, doing no further damage.

5th August—The party ordered to attack the enemy's camp at Morne Ronde marched at midnight on the 4th; they consisted of 200 of the forty-sixth and 100 of the Rangers under the command of Captain Douglas of the engineers. They took the road to the Soufriere, proceeded along the ridge until they reached the descent leading to the enemy's camp. At half past nine o'clock they were fired upon by the advance picket in ambush, which after some resistance retired and joined the main body then occupying an advantageous position that effectually commanded their camp. A very obstinate engagement ensued, extending beyond an hour. A path was cut on each side of the ridge by which the Rangers got 'round, and as soon as they made their appearance the enemy gave way, running off by the woods toward Duvalle's, abandoning their camp with everything in it and without attempting any further resistance, although their numbers were superior to those opposed to them.

Commandant Massoteau, his Aide-de-Camp and about 20 others were taken prisoners; 16 being found killed. Only a small quantity of cassava and salt was found in the camp. The loss of the detachment was 12 killed and 40 wounded. Dr. Oliver, an Ensign in the Rangers, died of his wounds.

Everything at Duvalle's and Chatoyer's was destroyed, several prisoners taken and many dead bodies found in the ravines.

Posts were established at Morne Ronde and Richmond, and the troops withdrawn and sent to Mt. Young. Mr. William Gray, a volunteer, fell into the hands of the enemy and was, doubtless, immediately sacrificed.

On 17th August, Brigadier-General Myers arrived from Martinique and assumed command. Major Ecuyer was ordered to march from Owia toward Mt. Young which he did, obliging the enemy to retire as he advanced. After waiting three or four days in the open air for the promised junction of the General, he returned to Owia and despatched Captain Law to headquarters to notify what had been done and to receive further orders.

On the night of the 3rd of September, the enemy made an attack on the post at Owia.

During the contest, which lasted for some time, two of the enemy's columns fired on each other; a similar error was also committed by the English troops. Major Ecuyer was overtaken next morning and murdered.

All the officers were missing, but in a day or two they came in. Dr. Baillie was taken prisoner and sent to Guadeloupe but returned in December. The loss, which was considerable, included 4 officers among the 31 killed.

The boats of H.M.S. *Experiment* (Captain Barrett), rescued those who escaped to the rock while others went through the woods of Morne Ronde.

On the 15th of September four vessels from St. Lucia landed 500 men with provisions at Owia. It was consequently deemed expedient to evacuate Mount Young.

About 9 p.m. on the 19th, Lieutenant-Colonel Leighton with troops and artillery marched away leaving their huts illuminated. They reached Sion Hill on the 21st.

On the evening of the 22nd great numbers of the enemy appeared at Marriaqua Valley, and early next morning were posted on Fairbairn's Ridge, having completely cut off communication between Vigie and the town and driven off the cattle from Fountain and Belair Estates. The safety of the Vigie being the object of general concern, Lieutenant-Colonel Ritchie with a party of 300 Regulars and Rangers and 80 mules loaded with supplies were despatched. They kept the high road on to Calliaqua through Pradies, Harmony Hall and

Raguets's Negro grounds until they reached Belmont road at the extremity of Fairhall when they were fired upon by the enemy. When the troops gained the summit of the ridge and obliged the enemy to abandon the galba (sic) fence, Captain Foster of the forty-sixth gave orders for an immediate charge but not an individual obeyed.* The troops most disgracefully gave way just at the moment of victory and fled in different directions, closely pursued by the enemy. The greater part of the provisions fell into their hands; the loss was estimated at about 60 killed and taken prisoners. Had they not found shelter beneath the guns at Fort Duvernette, which were assiduously plied by Major Henry Sharpe, the whole detachment would have been cut off. Colonel Ritchie collected about 30 of the party and retreated to Prospect Estate where he defended himself for several hours against a large body of the enemy who lost many men. At midnight the small party marched to Villa Estate and the next morning took refuge in Fort Duvernette. Colonel Ritchie died from the effects of his wounds and Michael Keane, an officer of the Rangers, was killed in the former action.

Colonel Ritchie's party reached Kingstown on the 25th rendering the situation there less precarious; the old French post on Kelly's Ridge was put in a defensible state and Captain Molesworth was ordered to evacuate Morne Ronde. Two Negro messengers were engaged to carry letters by different routes to the Vigie, one of whom, Thomas Nash, a Ranger, succeeded with great dexterity in getting in on the morning of the 26th. He was rewarded with twenty Johannes and his freedom; the other returned. The same afternoon Brigadier General Myers marched from Dorsetshire Hill with a large detachment and took post at Baker's Estate, now called Cane Hall, opposite to the enemy on Fairbairn's Ridge, but he returned when it was dark. The feint had the desired effect, for the enemy concentrated their whole force on this side. Captain Cope of the sixtieth who commanded the Vigie, conformable to orders so fortunately received, evacuated that post at the early hour of seven, taking advantage of a heavy shower that fell then. They went down to Carapan Estate on to Calliaqua, where boats were awaiting to convey them to Sir William Young's Island and the Rock, whence they were brought to Kingstown next morning. Although several of the posts were strengthened by these men, as also by those from Morne Ronde who arrived on the 27th, yet the anxiety was intense.

The inhabitants continued in this state until the evening of 29th September when H.M.S. *Scipio* and several transports were sighted to Leeward. Owing

---

*In consequence of the stoppage of part of their allowance, dissatisfaction arose among the men. Officers disputed with the committee about their pay and neglected the general discipline, hence this disastrous occurrence.

to calm weather Captain Barrett ordered all the small vessels down to the fleet, consequently several hundreds landed that night. The next day the following were landed—part of the fortieth commanded by Major Marcourt, the fifty-fourth by Lieutenant-Colonel Goddy Strutt and the fifty-ninth by Lieutenant-Colonel Francis Fuller.

Major General Irving also arrived having been appointed to this command by Commander-in-Chief General Leigh. The enemy retired from Fairbairn's Ridge and occupied Vigie. Lieutenant-Colonels Strutt and Leith, with a detachment of 750 men, marched about 10 p.m. on 1st October 'round by Calliaqua, ascended the heights of Calder Estate gaining their situation about 3 in the morning. Generals Irving and Myers, Major Duvernette, Lieutenant-Colonels Fuller and Leighton, with the principal body about 900 men, marched from Sion Hill and Arnos Vale at 2 o'clock proceeding up Warrawarou Valley. On crossing the river, they branched off into different directions. The party journeying by Debuque's, being attacked by the enemy—who were advantageously posted behind trees and bushes—lost a considerable number of officers and men before the enemy were driven off. Another party under similar circumstances was opposed by the enemy. The firing continued furiously the whole day. For reasons best known to the Generals, orders to retreat were given to the different detachments. Meanwhile the enemy made their escape. A non-commissioned officer and about 10 men were maliciously led by a Negro to the Vigie instead of showing the way to town. On perceiving the enemy had fled the Sergeant took possession of the post.

General Irving, on hearing this, ordered a party of Rangers under Lieutenant Kelly to take possession of it. James Kirkwood, somewhat of an eccentric character, having joined the Sergeant and party, considered his possession of the post as paramount and demanded and obtained a receipt. Notwithstanding this, General Irving received the thanks of the Commander-in-Chief and of the Colonial Secretary for his capture of the Vigie.

There was a general state of inactivity for several days after the unfortunate 2nd of October. The fifty-fourth regiment embarked for Grenada, and after remaining aboard for a few days was re-landed on the 10th and stationed at Stubbs.

One detachment marched to Windward, another to Aker's Hill and afterward to Yambou Works. During this suspension the enemy obtained ammunition and other necessaries from St. Lucia and entrenched themselves on Mount Young and Mount William.

On the 18th General Irving, with a party, crossed Colonaire River intending to occupy the north Ridge of Colonaire Vale, but the fire of the enemy from Mount William necessitated an immediate retreat to Bellevue.

Colonel Graham's futile attempt on the 30th October to gain Blackett's Bluff, i.e. a ridge near to Colonaire Pasture, resulted in the loss of 4 men killed and 16 wounded. Adjutant Brown died of his wounds.

About the 22nd October a resolution strongly expressing public opinion with reference chiefly to the inactivity of the army was entrusted to Henry Haffey and Joseph Warner, Esqs, for presentation to Major-General Leigh, Commander-in-Chief of His Majesty's troops in the Windward Islands.

27th October—General Stewart arrived from Martinique to relieve General Myers.

On 30th November, General Irving returned to Martinique and Brigadier-General Stewart assumed command.

On the 8th December there was an engagement of little importance—the enemy retired.

A flying corps of Negroes, subscribed for by proprietors in Marriaqua, Biabou and Yambou for purpose of ranging those heights and woods, were put under command of Mm. Duprey and LaBorde. The former surprised a small party at Greig's Ridge on the 15th and took them prisoners.

On the 11th, 150 of the enemy attacked a party consisting of 18 regulars and rangers and 6 Negroes. This small party gallantly defended itself until reinforcements arrived when the enemy retreated.

1796 / Two soldiers who deserted to escape punishment for provisions they had robbed, communicated the weakness of the main position. At 4 o'clock on morning of 8th January, an attack by enemy was commenced. M. Chenou, a Frenchman from St. Lucia, succeeded in stabbing two sentries and shooting a third before he was taken prisoner by a sergeant. Lieutenant Verity prevented the sergeant putting him to death. Lieutenant Panton was compelled to relinquish the battery. The troops were obliged to stand on their ground and retreat to Bellevue Ridge where Major McLeod was posted. Lieutenant-Colonel Fuller with 200 men marching from Biabou out to the camp, fell in with the enemy and routed them. The troops continued the retreat to Kingstown under difficulties, travelling on Aker's Hill and Calder Heights, thence onward. Simmons and Ashburner, Volunteers, were killed; 16 officers wounded, one taken prisoner and over 135 privates killed and wounded. The series of misfortune gave rise to grave misapprehension.

The arrival of Major General Hunter from Martinique on 12th January inspired considerable confidence. After becoming acquainted with the actual position and state of the army, he brought the whole force to the heights around the town, maintaining the post at the Vigie.

On the 14th the intention of the enemy to attack the Vigie became apparent, whereupon the General issued orders for its evacuation.

The enemy, elated at their success, advanced on Baker's Ridge and fixed picket guard under the redoubt on Miller's Ridge.

On the night of the 18th they fired shots and shells ineffectively.

A large party of Caribs crossed Miller's Ridge and encamped about Bow Wood.

20th—Lieutenant-Colonel Prevost attacked the enemy on Baker's Ridge from Miller's Redoubt; he encountered serious difficulties, was severely wounded in two places and found them strongly posted in large numbers. He therefore retired with the loss of a few men, having done some mischief to the enemy, cutting to pieces the advance picket guard.

Consequent on the gallantry of the Volunteers, of whom Alexander Cruik-shank, Alexander Cumming, George Burgess, John Dalaway and James Campbell were leaders, the Militia was infused with fresh vigour. Major Josias Jackson, with a party of Island Rangers, routed the Caribs who had crossed Green Hill and taken possession of the Bow Wood House. On their retreat they set fire to the house throwing in the dead within their reach. Major Fraser, with reinforcement, assisted incompletely clearing the enemy from that quarter. The English loss was about 50 killed and wounded.

Lieutenant-Colonel Power with 300 men of the sixty-third arrived on the ship *Brunswick* in the height of this day's action. This is the third occasion on which the Colonists were happily relieved of their despondency.

The inhabitants offered bounties and encouragements to the Volunteers; they supported the General in every way possible. Lieutenant-Colonel Haffey was assiduous. Among the officers of the Rangers, who formed body of 300 volunteers, were Lieutenant Colonel Leith, Major Fraser and Captains Alves and Ross. Some of the principal inhabitants with Lieutenant-Colonel Fairbairn enrolled to act as Dragoons.

21st—Major McLeod surprised a picket of the enemy from Miller's Redoubt; they fled precipitately leaving a number of muskets, cartouch boxes and various other articles. Captain Edward French of the Militia, with a small party, also made a spirited attack on the enemy. Subsequently, they began to abandon Baker's Ridge, firing at Dorsetshire Hill and Miller's Ridge the while. Several of these shots reached Kingstown and one fell into the bay—none of which did any damage.

23rd and following day, a six pound field piece at Miller's Ridge so confused them that they moved to Vigie. The dead bodies found at their encampments were numerous. Their wounded were sent to Grand Sable, while others took their place.

17th March—General Abercromby, with his army, arrived at Barbados. On 22nd he sailed on an expedition against St. Lucia and landed there on 27th.

25

The principal Forts were attacked and taken and the island surrendered. This disastrously affected the Brigands of St. Vincent for their main resource of their reinforcements and supplies was cut off.

7th April—Four men deserted to the enemy. One named Bradshaw, promoted by Marinier to a Company, was in command of 200 men to surprise the picket at Arnos Vale. He failed in the attempt, was taken prisoner and hanged the following day.

3rd June—General Abercromby arrived and on the following day the fleet conveyed the troops. The Governor, in a letter to the inhabitants, congratulated them on the circumstance.

7th—The General returned from Carriacou, at which place his presence was required.

9th—The troops having been landed and cantoned at Sion Hill, Cane Garden and Arnos Vale Estates, they marched in the afternoon as follows:

1st column under command of Brig. General Knox	To Marriaqua Valley
2nd column under command of Maj General Hunter	To Calder Ridge
3rd column under command of Maj General Morshead	To Carapan Ridge
4th column under command of Lieut Col. Fuller	To Belmont Ridge
5th colimn under command of Lieut Col. Dickens	Up WarrawarouValley
6th (Reserve) column under command of Lieut. Col. Spencer	To follow the line of march

The foregoing, comprised 3,960 men.

Notwithstanding the separation from the main body of a part of Lieutenant-Colonel Dickens' division, before daylight he gained possession of Louis Patience, an important pass; the Caribs fled, making little resistance. On another engagement, Lieutenant-Colonel Dickens maintained his grounds but lost 3 officers and 51 men killed and wounded.

Between 6 and 7 a.m. Generals Hunter and Morshead began to cannonade the Old Vigie from Calder and Carapan Ridges. The respective distances are about 500 and 300 yards. Lieutenant-Colonel Fuller's division having overcome its difficulties, opened fire on the Old Vigie from the foundation of the old house at Belmont. Consequent on the effect of this, fire orders were issued to storm the post. These were executed at about 2 o'clock with remarkable promptitude. With Colonel Blair of the Buffs and Major Stewart of the 42nd they drove the enemy thence, and continuing succeeded in gaining possession of two other posts.

There was a cessation of firing on both sides until about 5 o'clock when the Artillery was preparing to open, a flag of truce was sent to General Abercromby offering submission. This was previously accepted on the terms of delivery of the posts at Owia, Rabacca and Mount Young with their garrisons. After consulting with the Governor, the agreement was finally concluded the next morning at 9 o'clock. At noon, 460 men marched out, laid down arms, were conducted to Kingstown and straightway embarked on board the vessels in the harbour. The loss of the English was about 40 killed and 141 wounded. The estimated loss of the enemy was not more than half that of the English.

Volunteer Gordon, Captain McLean and Lieutenant Houstan were killed; Captain Douglas of the Engineers died of his wounds.

Sir Ralph Abercromby, in the general orders issued on the occasion, highly commended the officers severally for their good conduct and the men for their intrepidity. He had satisfaction in publicly acknowledging that the success of His Majesty's arms on the 10th proceeded from the information supplied by Major-General Hunter and from local knowledge of the ground communicated by the gentlemen of the colony, who not only pointed out the route but conducted the columns.

14th—Lieutenant-Colonel Spencer, with 700 men, marched out and took possession of Mount William and Mount Young. Lieutenant-Colonels James Stewart and Graham with a party each, took posts respectively at Colonarie and Rabacca. Owing to boisterous weather, Lieutenant-Colonel Gower with his party on H.M.S. *Ulysses* could not land to take possession of Owia.

Pending final conclusion of agreement with respect to surrender at Old Vigie, two companies of Brigands had effected their escape to the vicinity of Mount William. On their way thither, they wantonly destroyed the extensive sugar works on Colonarie Vale.

15th—Force of circumstances having urged the discontinuance of hostilities, the Caribs sent in a flag of truce to Mount Young with proposals. Desfon, Jack Gordon, and Baptiste, three Chiefs, were accordingly conducted by the Dragoons to town. They requested the retention of their lands, but were informed that nothing short of unconditional submission would be attended to. They were, however, allowed until 18th in order to consult with chief of families.

The English could not have accommodated these deceitful and perfidious people, as their religion was to wage inexpiable wars, for in 1769 when the Caribs with their French allies volunteered to Count D'Ennery, then Governor of Martinique, to extirpate the English inhabitants with very little assistance from him, he was shocked at such a savage proposal, and immediately informed the Colonial Government, thereby enabling the prevention of its execution. Victor Hugues, on the contrary, encouraged their ferocious disposition, and excited them to massacre the inhabitants, fixing the night of the festival of St. Patrick for the deed, when the inhabitants were likely to be off their guard. To this may be attributed the destruction of property and cruelties subsequently perpetrated. The Committee of the Planters instructed their

European Agents to represent the expediency of the removal from the island of one or the other. The Government, being convinced of the propriety of such a resolution, directed the removal of the Caribs to Rattan, a small island in the Bay of Honduras.

When the time for their answer had expired the Caribs disappeared from Mount Young. Not being in anyway disturbed, they began to traffic in their usual manner.

24th June—The Governor issued Proclamation declaring martial law at an end.

At a general meeting of the inhabitants attended by the Governor, it was decided that Balliceaux (a corruption of beloiseaux) should be appropriated for the temporary reception of the Caribs. Mr. Campbell the proprietor cheerfully agreed.

13th July—A Colonial Assembly was summoned.

15th July—General Abercromby issued orders for removal of Caribs to Balliceaux. Pursuant thereto, General Hunter requested the attendance of the chiefs, several of whom were escorted to Kingstown and duly notified as to their removal. Four days were allowed. In the event of non-compliance, hostilities were to commence against them.

16th and 17th—Over 600 Caribs came from their camp on the heights and took position about half a mile from Mount William between the English post and the sea.

18th—The son of Chatoyer, in the presence of Lieutenant-Colonel Haffey and his officers, eloquently addressed the attendant Caribs, advising their surrender. He promised to take his family to Colonel Haffey next day, and so set an example.

19th—Colonel Haffey ordered his corps under arms and sent Captains Lander and Munro with two companies each in different directions, himself occupying a portion. To prevent alarm, Captain Lander proceeded alone to persuade the Caribs to submit, but found that upward of 300 had fled to the woods including Chatoyer the Orator. On the enemy retreating toward Colonarie Captain Munro took 102; the total taken amounted to 280.

20th—These were conducted to Calliaqua thence transported to Balliceaux. Lieutenant Laborde of the Rangers, who was sent with a party to Grand Sable to receive the proffered submission, found their houses abandoned and themselves numbering 200 under arms in a convenient little eminence.

They ordered him to withdraw immediately, declaring they would never submit to the English. They did not revolt so much from the prospect of death as from the idea of submission. Owing to the smallness of the party he was obliged to retreat. Lieutenant-Colonel Graham, who had frequently expressed his good opinion of the Caribs and their similar disposition toward him, discovered a large party strongly fortified; with utmost sincerity of friendship they invited him to approach, which he did at the head of his men. When within a few yards a whole volley of musketry was poured around him. He was severely wounded as also an officer of Sauter's Corps and all his party except Mr. Matthews, their guide. The officer fell into possession of the Caribs, who cut him in pieces.

Over 1,000 houses and sundry canoes, the property of the enemy were burned.

6th August—A party of brigands and Negroes belonging to French inhabitants attacked Mr. Gorst's Plantation in Layou, taking him and his overseer Mr. Robert Hares away. The latter escaped and the former was released. This party retreated from the Vigie during the truce, and was under command of Marie Pedra, a black man from St. Lucia, whom they had left five days before on the heights of Colonarie.

8th—Lieutenant Burton with a party of Regulars from Greg's Ridge, joined by Farquhar Campbell and Robert Sutherland, Esqs, marched through Benny and Davis's lands on through Kennedy's Trace until they came to the Ridge which divides Charlotte from St. George's. Having prematurely fired a shot, 40 of the enemy escaped leaving one killed and two prisoners.

Lieutenant-Colonel Abercromby established himself at Duvalle's Settlement, which he found abandoned. Letraille, Delaprade and Jean Toulie, three notorious men, surrendered themselves.

Two prisoners from Balliceaux were sent into the woods to report the treatment they had received, and consequently not a day passed without several persons coming in.

Hippolite, with desperate party, attacked the post at Tourama defended by Major Brown of the 40th with 150 men. After three assaults they retired leaving their commander and two others killed.

During September, efforts to surprise and capture the straggling parties of the enemy were continued. In these, the Rangers distinguished themselves. They passed over the Soufriere and descended by the bed of the Rabacca River, which had a considerable effect on the enemy.

2nd October—Marin Pedre, attended by Moniquet and others, surrendered to Captain McMurdock of the Buffs. Being satisfied with his reception and assurances of security, he sent messages to the different parties, whereupon several hundred persons of all description, surrendered. The most prominent among the chiefs were Thunder Toussaint and Emanuel Duvalle; young Chatoyer were soon afterward added to the number.

26th—The number surrendered were 5,080 men, women, and children.

1797 / 25th February—H.M.S. *Experiment*, Captain Barrett, arrived from Martinique with transports, to convey the Caribs to Rattan. They embarked from Bequia.

11th March—They sailed for their place of destination.

The Spaniards, who had constructed a fort, opposed their landing. They were, however, dislodged with a loss to the English of 5 men killed, and 5 wounded. The Caribs were put in possession of the fort.

Major-General Hunter and Captain Barrett received addresses from the Colonial Legislature for their distinguished services in this eventful struggle. Each was presented with a sword.

The claims of proprietors which formed but a small part of the aggregate loss, amounted to upward of £57,000. The Committee of Expenditure had drawn on His Majesty's Treasury during the insurrection £40,000.

1798 / 2nd March—William Bentinck, Esq, successor of Governor Seton arrived.

15th May—By an address to His Majesty praying for extension of time for repayment of loan, the Council and Assembly stated their expenses and losses, at a strictly moderate computation, exceeded £900,000. Resolutions were submitted for the erection of the courthouse and Goal.

Mr. Samuel Clapham, a part owner of Mount William Estate, was murdered by Caribs near Rabacca, where he had gone on a fishing excursion

By direction of the British Government, several of the remaining Caribs were removed to the Spanish Main; among them was Cuffy Wilson, whose sentence to death was commuted to banishment, for it was alleged he saved the life of Captain McCumming and other prisoners.

Drewry Ortley, Esq, the President of the Council, who administered the Government at intervals, was presented with a piece of plate valued 300 guineas, in recognition of his ability evinced on such occasions. The forts of the island were again ordered to be repaired.

1799 / The corps of Rangers retained for scouring the woods of remaining Caribs were disbanded. Cultivation and other pursuits were resumed.

1800 / The produce of St. Vincent was 16,518 hogsheads of sugar.

1801 / The produce of St. Vincent amounted to 17,908 hogsheads of sugar.

1802 / 11th June—Henry William Bentinck, Esq, who had been appointed Governor, arrived. He granted, during His Majesty's pleasure, 5,260 acres of the Carib lands to different persons who had been actually engaged in the war.

1804 / June—An act was passed declaring that by the late rebellion the Caribs had forfeited all claim to their lands and that they were vested in the Crown.

On Sunday morning, 21st of October, the magazine door in Fort Charlotte was forced open by lightning. Several hundred barrels of gunpowder were in the magazine at the time.

1805 / By an act, passed in May, the remaining Caribs were pardoned on condition of surrender and submission to the laws. They were situated at Morne Ronde, where 230 acres of land were granted them, but they were prohibited from disposing of any or cultivating sugar. The Caribs were sometimes useful in rough weather, assisting to ship sugar from the estates unprovided with wharves, their habits being somewhat amphibious. Mr. Ottley again administered the Government. He died while in office and was succeeded by Robert Paul, Esq, the next senior member of the Council.

1806 / Sir George Beckwith assumed the administration of the Government. He was appointed in 1804 and arrived in the West Indies in 1805 when he commanded the forces in consequence of the death of Sir William Myers.

1807 / In November, Mr. Alexander, the Treasurer, obtained a Treasury warrant to discharge him from payment of £40,000 which the Committee of Expenditure had drawn in Bills on His Majesty's Treasury for expenses rendered necessary during the insurrection.

Colonel Thomas Brown, an English gentleman who had distinguished himself on many occasions and adhered to the sovereign during the American War of independence, was promised 6,000 acres of the Carib lands.

The impolicy of such an enormous grant to one individual was strongly urged from the impossibility of the cultivation being carried on so extensively as it was then, and in view of the corresponding loss to the revenue, Dr. Colquhoun was appointed Agent for the occupants. He succeeded in proving the impolicy of the grant. The lengthy discussions of claims and counter claims were brought to a close in 1809. It was ultimately decided that the Colonel should be granted 1,700 acres. The remainder was sold to the occupants at the rate of £22 10s. per acre of cleared land, exclusive of grants to families of individuals who had suffered in the war. The Colonel received about £25,000 from the purchase money. The remainder was at the disposal of the Government. The land was divided into eight large estates and a great and permanent increase of the revenue was secured.

1808 / On 14th November the appointment of Sir Charles Brisbane to succeed Sir George Beckwith was announced. The former was a Captain in the Navy, who had distinguished himself in the capture of the Dutch Island of Curaçao. Sir George Beckwith was appointed Governor of Barbados.

Sir Charles Brisbane arrived in January, 1809.

1808 / A French planter named St. Hilaire who resided at Mayreau was murdered by his own slaves. His brother from a neighbouring island learned the dreadful event and succeeded in the conviction of the five perpetrators of the foul deed, the principal of whom was executed at Mayreau and four in Kingstown.

During his visit to England on business connected with the appropriation of the Carib Lands, Sir Charles Brisbane represented to Mr. Percival, the Prime Minister, the propriety of appropriating a part of the purchase money toward the building of a Church in Kingstown. The sum of £5,000 was promised and afterward paid.

1812 / The other two years passed on without any particular occurrences until the dreadful eruption of the Soufriere took place. Baron Humboldt states in his personal narrative that it had thrown out flames in 1718 but whence his information was derived has not been satisfactorily ascertained; but that there had been previous eruptions, either from this or some other source, the volcanic formation of the whole island and the different strata of which all the mountains are composed sufficiently indicate, and it appears probable from the events that occurred on the mainland, that some subterraneous communication exists with the continent. After various oscillations of the earth, a dreadful earthquake happened at the Caracas in March, which destroyed the whole of that City, and nine thousand persons lost their lives. The Valleys of the Mississippi and the Ohio were at the same time in a state of commotion. Thirty-two days afterward, on the 27th of April, the eruption burst forth.

Previous to this event, according to the best accounts which are here consolidated, the appearance of this mountain was singularly romantic. The crater was half a mile in diameter and 500 feet in depth; in the centre of this hollow was a conical hill 200 feet in diameter and 300 in height, the lower half of which was fringed with brushwood, shrubs and vines, while the upper was strewed with virgin sulphur. At the base of it were two small lakes, the one sulphurous and aluminous, the other pure and tasteless. From the fissures of the cone a thin white smoke exuded, occasionally tinged with a light blue flame. Evergreens, flowers, aromatic shrubs, and many alpine plants clothed the steep sides of the crater, and from its external base, nearly to the summit, the mountain was covered with an exuberant growth of forest trees.

The first indication was a severe concussion of the earth, a tremendous noise in the air and the bursting forth of a vast column of thick black smoke from the crater. Volumes of sand and favillae darkened the air like a heavy storm of rain and covered the woods, ridges, and cane fields with light grey ashes resembling snow thinly strewed with dust, which speedily destroyed every appearance of vegetation. For three days all these symptoms continued to increase. During this the sun seemed to be in a total eclipse, the sea was discoloured, the ground bore a wintry appearance from the thick crust of the fallen ashes, and the cattle was starving for the want of their accustomed food.

On the 30th at noon, the column of smoke assumed a sanguine hue, rose with a livelier motion and dilated itself more extensively. The noise became incessant with a vibration that affected the feelings and hearing. The Caribs who were resident at Morne Ronde fled from their houses to Kingstown and the Negroes from their work; the very birds were beaten to the ground, overpowered by the sand and stones projected from the mountain. At length, just as the day closed, the flame burst forth pyramidically from the crater. The thunder now grew deafening, and electric flashes, some like rockets, and others like shells, darting in all directions and in all forms, illumined the immense column of smoke which hung over the volcano. In a short time the lava poured out on the northwest side. It was opposed there by the acclivity of a higher point of land, but being driven on by fresh accessions, it ascended and surmounted the obstacle, forming the figure V in a torrent of fire, plunged over the cliff carrying down rocks and woods in its course, and finally precipitating itself into a vast ravine at the foot of Morne Ronde; all this while large globular bodies of fire were exploded from the crater, which burst, and either fell back into it or among the surrounding bushes, which were instantly in a blaze. In about four hours the torrent of lava reached the sea, and shortly after another stream descended eastward toward Rabacca. The island was now shaken by an earthquake (that) was followed by a shower of cinders which fell like hail for two hours, and this was followed by a fall of stones mingled with fire, which continued for an hour.

Many houses were set on fire, many Negroes were wounded, and some were killed, but happily the weight of the stones bore no proportion to their magnitude, or the sufferers from them would have been still more numerous than they were. At length, in the afternoon of the 1st May, the eruption ceased, and the mountain sank gradually into a solemn silence; the volcano however still burned, and on the 9th of June it again gave alarming signs of activity, but nothing more occurred than the throwing up of a quantity of stones and ashes which fell back into the abyss whence they came.

All the former beauty of the Soufriere was of course destroyed. The conical mount disappeared and an extensive lake of yellow coloured water, whose agitated waves perpetually threw up vast quantities of black sand, supplied its place. A new crater was formed on the northeast of the original one and the face of the mountain was entirely changed; many of the adjoining ravines were filled up, particularly Wallibo and Duvalle's. In the former the river, was absorbed for some years, but the gradual accumulation of water burst through the sandy barrier and carried many Negro houses in its progress. Thirty-two slaves belonging to Wallibo Estate were washed into the sea by the torrent.

At Duvalle's, the former settlement of the Carib Chief, a sugar plantation had been established by Mm. Thesiger and Calvelly. The works situated in a valley were entirely covered by the sand and ashes and some hogsheads of sugar remained there calcined to a cinder. The Rabacca river was also filled up and its stream seldom reached the sea except in cases of heavy rains.

It was at first feared that the island would be rendered barren by the ashes which lay on its surface to a considerable depth, but they did not prove so injurious as was supposed. The great danger was famine, but the neighbouring colonies of Barbados, Demerara and Dominica, with a generous promptitude, hastened to supply the island with provisions, and a Committee was appointed by the Council and Assembly for the purpose of purchasing supplies. An investigation of the losses sustained was also made and a petition presented to the Prince Regent; praying for relief was most favourably received. On the case being laid before Parliament the sum of £25,000 was voted for the relief of the sufferers.

It is a wonderful circumstance, although the air was perfectly calm during the eruption, that Barbados was covered several inches deep with the ashes and the inhabitants on the last day of the eruption were terrified by the approach of utter darkness which continued for four hours and a half and then slowly decreased; there also, and in several other islands, the troops were under arms, supposing from the continued noise that the hostile fleets were engaging.

1813 / A tunnel of 250 feet long was cut through Mount Young greatly improving the means of communication, and a stupendous work was afterward undertaken by the owner of Grand Sable estate in cutting another tunnel through the same mountain nearer the sea for the convenience of shipping the produce. The material to be perforated proved to be stone instead of terras as was expected, and 360 feet in length were accordingly blasted by drilling in the solid rock at an expense of about £5,000.

1814 / In an action before the Supreme Court, Mr. Kean contended successfully against the principle that a black man is to be reputed a slave until the contrary is proved. He also succeeded in obtaining from the Court of King's Bench a formal decision that this presumption against freedom and in favour of slavery was not warranted by law.

This judgment was considered as "an occurrence of great importance, because so far as the authority of the court by which it was pronounced extends, it will have the effect of preventing the recurrence of those violations of all natural justice, of the frequency of which every West India newspaper furnishes sufficient evidence.

1816 / Consequent on the insurrection in Barbados in April, martial law was proclaimed on the island for a short time. "Neither on this or on any other occasion, has the slave population of Saint Vincent ever manifested a disposition to enter into political questions, or to claim fancied rights, a certain sign of contentment in their station. While slavery exists, it is no doubt an evil. But the most prejudiced abolitionist must admit that it exists in the island in a very mitigated form."

1817 / The establishment of a registry of slaves was deemed expedient. The Legislature, therefore, passed an Act by which the names, ages and descriptions of all slaves were enrolled; returns were made every three years and copies sent to the General Registry in London at a considerable expense.

A newspaper entitled the *Royal Gazette and Weekly Advertiser* was published by John Drape at his office, No. 25 Kingstown. It must have continued for many years as there are copies for 1833. The motto was "They who conceive that our newspapers are no restraint upon bad men, or impediment to the execution of bad measures know nothing of this country."—Junius.

1818 / The coin known as the Johannes passed by weight at nine shillings the pennyweight and was the most common throughout the islands; each colony mutilating its own by plugs and various marks to prevent exportation so deteriorated the coin that it was called in at a considerable loss and Doubloons came into more general circulation.

1819 / Hurricane causing slight damage to crops on the ground.

1822 / Commercial restrictions imposed on American trade having been removed, her flag appeared in West Indian ports and supplies of lumber and provisions became more abundant; but the demand for colonial produce not being great, a proportion of the payments were made in specie, to the inconvenience of the inhabitants from the loss of the circulating medium.

1824 / On 13th October, Major Champion, who commanded a part of the twenty-first regiment stationed at Fort Charlotte, was murdered by a private named Ballasty. The private who was sentry at the drawbridge loaded his musket with balls and challenged the Major on his return from an evening drive; on receiving an answer in the affirmative, he deliberately fired and shot him through the body.

The unfortunate officer died a few hours afterward.

The Governor promptly summoned a Special Court of Sessions when the assassin was tried, convicted and executed on the drawbridge where the crime had been committed.

1825 / In April, St. Vincent was honoured with the first visit of His Lordship the Bishop of the Diocese of Barbados and the Leeward Islands. His Lordship was sworn an ex-officio member of Council in all the islands comprised in his Diocese; he was also Ordinary when the date of his appointment preceded that of the Governor.

1829 / In November, Sir Charles Brisbane died, having administered the Government for the unprecedented period of 20 years. Few islands have been able to boast of such a lengthened period of tranquility so pleasing and beneficial to the inhabitants.

1830 / An Act for the relief of His Majesty's Roman Catholic Subjects in St. Vincent and its Dependencies was passed whereby such Acts and parts of Acts of this island, as imposed any restrictions or disabilities on Roman Catholic Subjects, were totally repealed.

1831 / 11th August—The colony was visited by a dreadful hurricane which caused much damage to the estates and was attended with the loss of several lives. The greater part of the sugar works and other buildings were destroyed. Nineteen vessels were driven on the shore in Kingstown, several of which were floated again within a week. Seven others were totally wrecked in different parts of the Government. The estimated loss as calculated by the Committee of the Legislature amounted to £163,420 sterling.

1834 / Early in this year, the parliamentary resolutions regarding the abolition of slavery were announced. A system of apprenticeship preparatory to the changed condition was brought into operation from the 1st August, from which date all children under 6 years were declared to be free.

The Magistrates were sent from England with the additional appointment of Protectors of Apprentices; they received instructions from the Home Office. The slaves were addressed by them on the subject of the proposed change of their condition. There was considerable disappointment among many who expected immediate, unconditional freedom. August 1st was nevertheless observed as a general holiday.

In their endeavour to administer justice, the Magistrates incurred the displeasure of several of the proprietors.

1836 / A newspaper entitled the *St. Vincent Chronicle* was published and a pocket almanac of that year was printed at the office *The Chronicle* and published by Mm. Adams and Mitchell.

1838 / May 10th—The House of Assembly met and passed the resolution to abolish the system of apprenticeship from 1st August of the same year.

August 1st—The important day on which hundreds and thousands are made absolutely free and slavery will remain unknown throughout the West Indian Colonies except only in the island of Trinidad. The clergy and preachers in the island had been required by the Lieutenant Governor to have their churches and chapels opened for a general thanksgiving on the part of the newly emancipated. The sight was beautiful, all respectably and even gaily dressed, and when they joined in the psalm in full chorus it was delightful to reflect on the fact that at the very same moment hundreds and thousands were met together in the different islands to pour forth their thanks in hymns of praise to the creator and disposer of all events for the same blessing of unrestricted freedom.

There was a quiet but steady refusal to work for the offered wages; the combination was general and continued for several weeks. Evidently, a few reluctantly consented to labour in the field, accepting the amount offered. With the determination on both sides it became impossible to cultivate the estates; consequently the proprietors offered them for sale in small lots to the black people who readily purchased.

An entire Estate was bought by a few black people who afterward subdivided it, making villages, gardens and in every way endeavouring to render themselves independent.

1839 / An Act was passed for the abolition of currency and the substitution of sterling money in these islands.

1840 / About this year a newspaper entitled the *New Era* was published by Mr. Henry Balasco who was also the printer. The plant was purchased by Mr. Alexander Henry Abbott who printed and published the *St. Vincent Mirror*. The peculiar circumstances connected with the termination of this newspaper are these: The editor severely criticised the conduct of the sailors from H.M.S. *Jasper* on Christmas Day 1858, designating them "uncivilized ruffians". On New Year's Day 1859, a considerable number of the crew landed and demolished the printing plant.

1842 / By Letters Patent under the Great Seal of the United Kingdom of Great Britain and Ireland, bearing date at Westminster 21st August, Barbados, Trinidad, Grenada, St. Vincent, Tobago, and St. Lucia, with their respective dependencies were constituted the Diocese of Barbados.

1843 / On the 30th of November, an Act was passed raising the number of Representatives for the General Assembly to 25, establishing an income qualification and extending the franchise to incomes as well as properties,

1844 / On the 23rd May, the Act to establish and encourage Friendly Societies was confirmed.

1846 / The first introduction of Portuguese labourers was witnessed, a class of immigrants that amounted in a few years to 2,400; they have proved a valuable addition to the general population of the island.

At Carriacou, the newspaper entitled the *Carriacou Observer and Grenadines Journal* was published, and although it consisted of a single sheet, it was considered well adapted as a miscellany to be useful, in accordance with its excellent motto: "True patriotism consists not merely in that love and zeal for one's country which will cause the citizen to arm in defence of her rights and interests, but in an earnest and zealous endeavour to promote the well-being and social improvements of those who from adventitious circumstances are debarred the enjoyment of advantages possessed by their more favoured brethren. He who does this, actuated by the principles of truth and justice, is the true benefactor of his country."

1847 / On 9th February, a resolution passed the House of Assembly for a sum of money to defray the funeral expenses of the late Speaker, the Rev. Nathaniel Struth, and for erecting a testimonial to his memory in Kingstown Church.

April 7th—His Excellency Colonel Reid, Governor-in-Chief, arrived in His Majesty's Schooner *Viper* from Grenada and was sworn in before the Honourable Board of Council.

August 26th—The two Houses of Legislature dissolved by proclamation in consequence of the frequent adjournments occasioned by the non-attendance of sufficient members to form a House of Assembly.

October 9th—Elections for new House of Assembly concluded. The Legislature to meet on the 19th for despatch of business.

1848 / An elegant *Pocket Almanac*, comprising commercial, political, and other useful information, was published. It was compiled by Mr. John Drape, the Government printer, and printed in London by Mr. J. D. Bayley of George Yard, Lombord Street.

1849 / The arrival of liberated Africans was another welcomed accession. The outbreak of small pox in this year committed fearful ravages among the labouring population.

1850 / By an Act dated 12th March, the number of representatives was reduced to 19 as it originally stood.

1853 / Yellow fever broke out, as in several other colonies, and was attended with great mortality especially among the white youths of both sexes.

1854 / The benefit of the Encumbered Estates Act was extended to St. Vincent. The troops were withdrawn. A third epidemic in the form of cholera made its appearance extending its ravages to all classes. The number of deaths from the disease exceeded 2,000.

Sir John Campbell, Lieutenant-Governor, wrote on the character of the people thus:

> *But when we turn to the great body of the native population, it is beyond all dispute that it has been the subject of progressive melioration both moral and physical. In treating of the Negro people as here existing, it must never be forgotten that seventeen years only have now run their course, since they were emancipated from a state absolutely opposed to all improvement, and with this in view I record not only my satisfaction, but a feeling of joyful surprise at the advances made by them during the six years to which my observation and experience have extended. As a general rule, they possess beyond all reasonable question, most of the essential elements of progress, and in a pre-eminent degree, natural intelligence and quickness of perception sharpened by a praiseworthy desire to better their condition, somewhat controlled in action indeed, by the indolence incident to a tropical climate, by the facilities for acquiring a comfortable subsistence, and by dilatory habits thereby accruing.*
>
> *Looking around this country, and considering the extent of land recently acquired by the labouring population and the thriving villages reared by them, any unprejudiced observer must be convinced of the fact of an improved physical condition of the lower orders."*

Adverting to a former feeling of aversion to labour he remarked:

> *I do not believe that any symptoms of aversion to field labour are to be observed, and feel nearly confident that wherever proper relations subsist between the employers of labour and those in authority under them, and the labourers, there is little difficulty in procuring people to work and in retaining them as long as required."*

In relation to intelligence and trustworthiness he remarked:

> *There are several instances of black men being employed as overseers and even as managers upon estates, and I believe that they are found to do their duty well and faithfully, and the extension of education will, I hope, add gradually to the number of this respectable class of the native population.*

1856 / An Executive Council was created, consisting of 10 members, five from the Legislative Council and five from the Assembly.

1858 / The newspaper entitled *St. Vincent Guardian* was published weekly by Mr. James McKay Sutherland at No. 29, Long Lane, Kingstown. The Proprietress was Mrs. Eleanor Maria Kay. Its motto was, "I speak to the People as one of the People." In 1866 Mr. Robert Porter Cropper assumed the editorship and published at No. 39, Bay Street. Mr. Francis Drape succeeded Mr. Cropper in 1867 and published at No. 86, Sharpe Street.

1859 / The Court of Appeal for the Windward Islands was duly inaugurated. The Executive Council was remodelled with the addition of an Administrative Committee selected by the Governor and composed of three members from the Legislative Council and two from the Assembly. This Committee held office during pleasure. Their duties were to assist the Governor in preparing the annual Estimates and in collecting and disbursing the public moneys.

1861 / The first cargo of East Indian labourers arrived. The system of importation although beneficial was of enormous cost to the proprietors.

1862 / By an Act passed in June, the Administrative Committee no longer formed a Board of Audit of Public Accounts, nor were they charged with the care of public buildings; by the same Act they were deprived of their salaries.

The newspaper entitled *St Vincent Witness* was published weekly at No. 73, Middle Street, by Mr. William Henry Stowe who was also the proprietor and printer. The motto was "I'm in the place where I'm demanded by conscience to speak the truth and therefore the truth I speak." There was a temporary suspension and in 1879 the publication was resumed when Mr. William Faber Stowe was printer and publisher and Mrs. Amelia E. Stowe (widow of W. H. Stowe) was the proprietress.

1863 / The Newspaper Act was passed under which Declarations of Proprietors, Publishers, and Printers are required to be made and delivered to the Registrar.

1866 / 26th October—Considerable damage was done by fire to the offices for the Treasurer, Auditor, Inspector General of Police, and Postmaster; Barrack for the Police Force and a lock-up for prisoners; an armoury for the Militia and a Bonding store connected with the Customs Department.

1868 / January 29th—His Excellency the Lieutenant-Governor delivered an address, and in the name of Her Most Gracious Queen, opened the Legislative Assembly under the new constitution. His Excellency then withdrew. The President acknowledged, the compliment paid to him by His Excellency and hoped that by the co-operation of the Honourable Members his earnest endeavours to discharge the duties of the chair would prove successful. A reply to the address was submitted.

Necessity arose for the dissolution of the Legislative Assembly and another was constituted. There were three ex-officio, three nominee, six elected—12, and a casting vote for the Crown.

The *St. Vincent Government Gazette* was published weekly until 1st May 1902 from which date it has been issued fortnightly.

1869 / Publicity given to Her Majesty's sanction to modify the Statutes of the Order of St. Michael and St. George, originally instituted by King George the Third in connection with His Majesty's Mediterranean Possessions, together with such an enlargement of its numbers as will render it available as a reward for distinguished merit or services in any part of Her Majesty's Colonial Possessions.

1870 / At a meeting of the Legislative Assembly held 31st May, a Report on the increased supply of water for Kingstown was presented. The capacity of six available Springs on Richmond Hill Estate was 65,512 and two on Montrose Hill, 19,904 imperial gallons a day. The West India and Panama Telegraph Company requested a subsidy of £1,800 a year for ten years viz. £800 from St. Vincent and £500 each from Grenada and St. Lucia. The surplus of General Revenue was £7,865.

1871 / A proclamation was issued for giving currency in certain colonies to Gold Coins made at Sydney, New South Wales, of the like designs of those approved for the corresponding coins of the currency of the United Kingdom.

A fire brigade composed of members of the police force was organized.

The subscription List for the relief of sufferers by the Fire at Point A Pitre, Guadeloupe, amounted to $1,082.55.

1872 / At an adjourned meeting of the Legislative Assembly, held 26th January, an humble address to Her Most Gracious Majesty Queen Victoria was considered, directed to be engrossed and forwarded in the customary course. The address was expressive of the deep sympathy of the people of St. Vincent with the suffering and anxiety of mind occasioned to Her Majesty and the Royal Family by the late dangerous and prolonged illness of His Royal Highness the Prince of Wales. Sincere congratulations were offered for the happy recovery and heartfelt thanks to that Divine Providence under whose dispensations His Royal Highness' valuable life has been preserved to Her Majesty and to the Nation.

On the 8th May, a despatch from the Earl of Kimberley to Lieutenant-Governor Rennie, dated 5th March, was read at the meeting of the Legislative. Assembly, the second paragraph of which was "I am commanded, to instruct you to convey to the President and Members of the Legislative Assembly in St. Vincent, the Queen's thanks for their kind expressions of sympathy, and to assure you that Her Majesty warmly appreciates the spirit of loyalty to the British Crown and of attachment to the Person and family of the Sovereign, which is displayed in this address."

1873 / In consequence of the contemplated disestablishment of the Anglican Church, two petitions setting forth the alleged claims of the Roman Catholic and Wesleyan Methodist denominations respectively were presented at the meeting of the Assembly on 29th January. That for the former was signed by Thomas Donnelly (RC), Incumbent of Kingstown and Vicar Foran of St. Vincent, and countersigned by F. Joachim Gonin, Archbishop of Port-of-Spain, with eight signatories following. The latter—244 signatories.

The petition from the Anglican Church, showing the fulfilment of the trust imposed on them as the Established Church of the State, was signed by H. H. Parry, Bishop, H. W. Laborde, the clergy, etc. total—8,660 signatories and was submitted at the meeting held 1st April.

The Committee appointed to ascertain specially the number of persons possessed of the franchise who signed the respective petitions reported as follows:

The petition of the Roman Catholic Body appeared to have the signatures of four persons possessed of the franchise; that of the Anglican 105; and that of the Wesleyan Methodist 5.

From the Registrar-General's returns the following facts were shown:

Baptisms by Anglican Ministers	61 %
Wesleyan Methodist	34 %
Roman Catholic	5 %
Marriages, by Anglican Ministers	56 %
Wesleyan Methodist	34 %
Roman Catholic	10 %

With reference to the foregoing His Excellency embodied the following in his remarks on the subject:

The Colony has hitherto maintained a State Church at great expense and has passed laws obliging that Church to afford its ministrations either absolutely free or at certain specified rates. This Church has therefore been pointed out to the people as the one favoured by the Government, as the one to which all have contributed, and consequently as the one on which all have claims—and it would be the strongest possible argument against the maintenance of any special Church if with all these advantages the Anglicans had not performed a far larger proportionate share of religious rites than the Ministers of other persuasions. The result of the table of baptisms, marriages, and burials merely gives proof that the Anglican Ministers have attended to their duties and this fact is readily admitted.

A striking circumstance is observed in the fact that Mr. Laborde, temporarily administering the Government, introduced to the Assembly the Bill for disestablishing the Anglican Church of which body his brother was the chief representative.

The troops, which in consequence of representation had returned to the colony and stationed at Fort Charlotte in 1868, were finally withdrawn. During that period the colony paid £4,000 a year toward their maintenance.

A newspaper entitled *St Patrick and St. David's Parish Magazine* was issued. This title was afterward changed to the *St. Vincent Church Magazine*. It contained general information regarding the Anglican Church as well as current topics relating to the colony, etc. It was edited by the clergy and printed by Mr. W. H. Stowe at the office of *The Witness*.

1874 / In compliance with application £140 was voted for the West India Encumbered Estates Court as St. Vincent's contribution in respect of the years 1872 and 1873, during which transfers of property were effected by means of the court, the beneficial operation of which resulted in facilitating the restoration of cultivation, inducing greater enterprize and causing addition to the revenue of the colony.

The commissariat store at Edinburgh was converted to a Colonial Hospital. £900 expended proved insufficient, consequently a supplementary vote of £400 was taken.

1875 / On Friday the 29th January, His Lordship Bishop Mitchinson was formally installed in St. George's Church, Kingstown as Bishop of St. Vincent and its dependencies,

24th August (St. Bartholomew's Day)—After an impressive service in the beautiful parish church and a procession of the clergy and the congregation, the almshouse at Calliaqua was formally opened in the presence of Lieutenant-Governor and Mrs. Dundas. His Excellency delivered an address after which the benediction was pronounced by the Rural Dean. "Blessed are the merciful for they shall obtain mercy" was the text deeply impressed on the minds of all.

The first step toward this object was a bazaar in Kingstown on 3rd and 4th June, 1873, organised by Mrs. Smith (wife of the Rev. E. Leslie Smith, Perpetual Curate of the Parish). By this effort £155 was realized and expended partly in the purchase of a property in Calliaqua and in repairs to the building thereon. The application of the Curate for £120 to complete payment and effect improvement was not entertained by the Legislative Assembly, but £50 was granted "to be applied for the relief of paupers, lepers, etc."

On the 9th of September, unusual and destructive rain fell. In a few hours Kingstown was inundated: 6 vessels were driven ashore in Kingstown, including a brigantine, three of which were successfully floated soon afterward. Seven lighters belonging to T. F. Linley, Esq, were dashed to pieces; three houses were swept into the sea; the cemetery at the Roman Catholic church yard was washed away; damage was done to the Kingstown Water Works; the catch, pipe and main pipes were carried away and service pipe broken. The jetty also sustained damage and the piles of lumber along Bay Street were considerably demolished. The mails from the steamer were conveyed to and from the boat by means of ropes. The roads in the neighbourhood were cut into furrows.

The beautiful valley of Marriaqua, with the village Mesopotamia containing the homes and the holdings of an industrious people, was almost a wilderness. Their homes, arrowroot grounds, small cane fields, the simple machinery by which they prepared their produce, were in many cases utterly destroyed, and worse, the inundation in this district caused lamentable loss of life.

At Queensbury and at Buccament Valley, a house was overwhelmed by an avalanche of earth and rocks. Of the inmates, five perished and two sent to Hospital. £300 was voted for immediate relief by means of small loans without interest and £500 for repairs to roads.

The destruction at other parts of the Government was also of a serious nature and appalling tales are associated with the loss of lives.

His Excellency John Pope Hennessy (CMG), Governor-in-Chief of the Windward Islands arrived on the 29th December and at 1:30 p.m. the oaths of office were administered with the usual formalities.

The commodious Police Barracks, commenced in 1873, was completed.

1876 / Heavy rain on 1st and 2nd January was more destructive in St. David's Parish than elsewhere. The Caribs and others living at the base of the Soufriere and at Morne Ronde were the greatest sufferers. Down the steep sides of the mountain the water came in torrents sweeping everything before it; large rocks that were thought immoveable came rolling down the banks.

The roar of the water was fearful, being heard high up on the hills for several minutes before they saw the real cause of the noise. The women and children yelled with fright. The three ravines in the neighbourhood became wild watercourses and thus continued for two nights and a day. Several fled to Chateaubelair where they lodged in the church's schoolroom and were attended by the townsfolk. The Lieutenant-Governor sanctioned small weekly allowances.

The water unearthed a considerable amount of "Soufriere Coal", large logs of locust and other wood which were burnt at the time of the eruption of 1812 and which 64 years had failed to decay.

Rev. G. F. Bourne, the Anglican minister in that parish, thanked Mr. Lindo, the Wesleyan preacher, for his kind assistance in connection with the sufferers.

An Act to alter and amend the political constitution of this island and its dependencies passed 5th August 1875, was confirmed by Her Majesty. The Legislative Assembly was thereby abolished and provisions made for the constitution of a Legislature for this Government.

With the consent of the Most Reverend Father in God, Archibald Campbell, Lord Archbishop of Canterbury, Primate of all England and Metropolitan; and approval of the Right Reverend John Mitchinson, D.D., Bishop of the Church of England in the island of Barbados, Her Majesty was pleased to command by Warrant dated 28th November, that after the 1st January 1877, the island of Grenada, St. Lucia, St. Vincent and their dependencies be separated from the Diocese of Barbados.

The *Saint Vincent Gazette* purporting to be a newspaper of St. Vincent was printed by Mr. T. R. N. Laughlin at No. 6 Chacon Street, Port-of-Spain, Trinidad. The Agent was Mr. H. S. Thornhill, of No. 3 North River Road, Kingstown, St. Vincent.

The *Mail News and Adviser*, also the *St. Vincent Gazette* and *Planter's Magazine* were printed and published by Mr. John B. Proudfoot at No. 74 Long Lane, Kingstown. They contained commercial information and subjects of interest to agriculturists respectively.

1877 / Letters Patent dated 30th May were issued providing for the constitution of an Executive Council composed of the officers discharging the functions of Colonial Secretary, Attorney General and Treasurer and such other persons lawfully appointed thereto. The unofficial members were The Hons. John Hercules-Hazell, David Cowie, David Kennedy Porter, Archibald Gerald, and Robert Suckling Cheesman. The Legislative Council was composed of the aforesaid officers of the Government, the Hons. John Hercules Hazell, David Cowie and Robert Suckling Cheesman.

1878 / The first meeting of the Legislative Council was held at the courthouse in Kingstown on Saturday, the 26th January. There were present His Excellency Lieutenant-Governor Dundas (CMG); His Honour G. Trafford, Chief Justice; the Hons. The Colonial Secretary, Attorney General, Treasurer, J. H. Hazell and R. S. Cheesman. The oath of Allegiance was tendered by the Chief Justice and subscribed in succession by the members. After declaring the Legislative Council of St. Vincent duly opened, His Excellency delivered a lengthy speech in the course of which he remarked:

The late Legislative Assembly of St. Vincent by a unanimous, and in my opinion a wise decision resolved that the circumstances of the colony required an alteration in its constitution, and they placed in Her Majesty's hands the framing of a new Legislature.

In compliance with the desire of the Legislative Assembly, and in exercise of the power conferred by an Act of the Imperial Parliament, the Queen has granted a new constitution to St. Vincent, the particulars of which have just been read to you. With us, therefore, as the Legislative Body under the new Constitution, rests hereafter the responsibility of legislating for this Island.

I need hardly remind you that this is no light responsibility. The interests of nearly forty thousand people are in our keeping: We must protect every class. From the highest to the lowest, from the wealthiest to the poorest, all interests must be jealously guarded by us.

Brief as the period is since I issued my commission appointing the gentlemen who were to be the unofficial members of this Council, death has suddenly deprived us of the valuable services of one of them (D. Cowie, Esq). A diligent and successful Planter, a just and considerate employer of labour, a genial, kindly, and upright man, an honest and loyal Councillor, is not easily repaired.

Among the important matters referred to for their consideration were the encouragement of steam navigation on our coasts for which a subsidy has been granted; the erection of a new Hospital; the proposition of the West India and Panama Telegraph Company for amending the Act granting them a subsidy.

In reply to His Excellency's speech the honourable members remarked they did not underestimate, or lightly assume, the responsibilities as members of the Legislative Council. It would always be their care, in framing laws for the good government of the people, that the interest of all classes would be considered.

Agreement was entered into between the Lieutenant-Governors of Tobago and St. Vincent for the transportation of prisoners under sentence or order of imprisonment penal servitude to and from the respective colonies.

1879 / In the humble address to Her Most Gracious Majesty Queen Victoria, from the Legislative Council on the occasion of the death of Her Royal Highness the Grand Duchess of Hesse, Princess Alice of Great Britain and Ireland, Her Majesty was assured that "Though the people of this colony are but few, and the island a small and remote dependency of Your Empire we feel sure that Your Majesty has no colony where the winning virtues of Her Royal Highness have become more familiar than in this."

A prospectus from the Trustees of "The Alice Memorial Fund" was laid before members of the Legislative Council. It was intended to perpetuate the memory of the late Princess by the extension and support of an institution at Darmstadt, which bore her name as having been founded by her: Alice Hospital. Any remaining funds were to be devoted to the orphanages of Darmstadt in which the Princess Alice also took much interest. £50 was voted as a contribution from this colony.

An attempt to revive masquerading, which was prohibited, gave rise to a disturbance. Several of the policemen were wounded; nearly every respectable male in Kingstown was sworn a Special Constable. H.M.S. *Blanche,* telegraphed for, arrived from Barbados after peace had been restored.

A newspaper entitled the *Advertising Sheet*, published by Mr. John B. Proudfoot superseded the *Mail News and Advertiser*.

1880 / 16th March—His Excellency George Dundas, Esq (CMG), Lieutenant-Governor of this colony died at Government House. His Excellency Major Strahan (CMG), Governor-in-Chief of the Windward Islands, arrived on the 17th and assumed administration of the Government, The funeral, which was of a military character was attended by officers and men of H.M.S. *Griffon*. Holy communion was administered to the bereaved widow and a few of her friends by the Ven. H. W. Laborde, Archdeacon; the remains were interred in the chancel after the firing of volleys.

At a meeting of the Legislative Council held Saturday 20th March, His Excellency Major Strahan (CMG), referring to the sad event said, "I feel confident that I only re-echo the feeling of the Council and of the whole community in deploring the death of Lieutenant-Governor Dundas, and in expressing heartfelt sympathy with her who above all others had opportunities of appreciating among his many fine qualities, the kindly and affectionate nature which endeared him to all who knew him."

Subscriptions amounting to $280.93 were remitted to that place on behalf of the sufferers by the flood at St. Kitts.

The salary of the Lieutenant-Governor ceased to be paid from Imperial Funds after 31st March.

An interesting pamphlet entitled *Precis of Information* concerning the colony of St. Vincent, West Indies, prepared by George Dundas, Esq (CMG), late Lieutenant-Governor of this island, was printed at the office of the *Government Gazette*.

1881 / The Kingstown Cemetery was opened for the burial of the dead from the 1st February, rules for the government thereof having been made on the 21st January.

1882 / 25th January—Letters Patent passed under the Great Seal of the United Kingdom, dated 6th September 1880, was published, superseding those of 30th May 1877, and making effectual and permanent provision for the office of Governor and Commander-in-Chief of the Windward Islands.

Particulars regarding the establishment by His Royal Highness the Prince of Wales of a Royal College of Music were duly published. Referring to the extension of the enterprise His Royal Highness was pleased to express that "Her Majesty's Colonial Subjects have indeed already shown that the possession of musical talent exists among them in as great a degree as in any other nation; for they may claim with pride that they have produced one of the most accomplished vocalists of the present day.

"I have the more confidence in making this appeal from the readiness and public spirit which the Colonies have always evinced to promote every object tending to strengthen the ties that now so happily unite us."

1883 / 7th April—Colonel William Crossman (RE, CMG), and George Smith Baden-Powell, Esq, Royal Commissioners, with their Secretary, Charles Alexander Harris, arrived on the H.M.S. *Dido*. Inquiries were made into the public revenues, expenditure, debts, and liabilities of the Islands of Jamaica, Grenada, St. Vincent, Tobago, and St. Lucia, and of the Leeward Islands.

1884 / A telegram dated 29th March, having announced the sudden death of His Royal Highness the Duke of Albany, the members of the Executive and Legislative Councils forwarded to Her Majesty the Queen an address of condolence, expressing sincere hope that strength will be given to Her Majesty to bear the heavy affliction. Her Majesty's thanks for the expression of sympathy were duly communicated. The celebration of Her Majesty's birthday, having been deferred by direction, Thursday the 26th June, was appointed for its observance in this colony.

Convention between the Post Office Department of the United States of America and the post offices of the several islands constituting the Government of the Windward Islands, ratified.

A local exhibition in connection with the International Forestry Exhibition, Edinburgh, was held at the police barracks, Kingstown, on 17th, 18th and 19th April.

The prizes awarded St. Vincent at the International Exhibition were:
Silver Medal —For collection of Exhibits
Bronze Medals—For basket work and fibrous substances, and "dug-out" or boat.
Diplomas—For foods, drugs, spices, and forester's or squatter's hut.

Sir Joseph Hooper of Kew Gardens negotiated with the Hon. William Russell, Representative of St. Vincent, for procuring a collection of exhibits from this Colony for the Museum at Kew.

1885 / In connection with resolutions submitted to the respective Legislative Councils of Grenada, St. Vincent, St. Lucia, and Tobago, regarding their union as recommended by the Royal Commissioners, a public meeting was held in Kingstown, on the 20th January, to which delegates were sent in from all the small towns and some of the villages in the colony to express the opinions of the people with regard to the union of the four islands.

At the meeting of the Legislative Council held 20th February, the following resolution was submitted:

> *Resolved that the Unofficial Members do, unanimously but respectfully, beg to inform Lord Derby that they declined to adopt the principles of Union as shadowed forth in His Lordship's Resolutions, and that in doing so, they represent fully the wishes of the people of St. Vincent.*

14th April—The Lieutenant-Governor informed Honourable members at meeting of Legislative Council that he had received a despatch stating that Her Majesty's Government had decided not to press further, at present, the proposal for uniting the four lesser Windward Islands into a single colony.

At the same meeting a resolution was passed tendering thanks to the Hon. William Russell for the great trouble and interest taken and economy exercised on behalf of the colony in connection with the Edinburgh Forestry Exhibition.

1886 / The Local Exhibition in connection with the Colonial and Indian Exhibition, London, was held on Tuesday and Wednesday, 2nd and 3rd February. The prizes exceeded £50, the highest being £5 awarded to Miss L. Huggins for essay on the colony.

Commenting on the exhibition in London, *The Times* of August 23rd remarked, "The St. Vincent court is a crowded one, but thanks to the well-arranged catalogue, it is easy to find what one wants, which is more than can be said of some of the other West India courts." Many of the numerous articles were then favourably described.

Printed documents were received from Sir A. J. Adderley (KCMG), Executive Commissioner for the West Indies and British Honduras, in connection with Indian Exhibition, London, giving particulars of various meetings held at the suggestion of His Royal Highness the Prince of Wales in reference to the continuation of the Exhibition. Soon afterward the Commissioner wrote, "I have now the pleasure to state that Mr. G. D. Harris who has assisted me in this administration, and who has generously placed £120 at my disposal for the publication of the *West Indies and British Honduras Handbook*, has promised to give me £500, which sum should enable me to administer this section of the Exhibition for a year without a call on you for a pecuniary grant.

Monday, 16th August—There was a terrible cyclone which caused the loss of four lives and did enormous damage generally, rendering 2,000 persons homeless.

The weather on Sunday 15th was all that could be desired. The barometer stood at its usual height—29.75 and there was no indication of approaching change.

At 5.40 a.m. on Monday the wind began to blow in gusts from north and west, the barometer then registered 29.40 and was still falling. When it was six o'clock, 29.20 being registered, the fury of the cyclone suddenly burst upon Kingstown and neighbourhood.

For more than an hour the tempest raged, rushing from all points of the compass. The magnificent trees in the Botanic Gardens were uprooted—many with their heads pointing south and others due north. Soon after 7 o'clock as the cyclone passed on, the barometer registered 29.70. Torrents of rain continued to fall while the wind blew heavily from northeast until noon.

The homeless and wounded people from the country districts having become too numerous for the colonial hospital, the cathedral was opened for temporary accommodation. Lieutenant Governor Gore convened a meeting of the principal gentlemen and appointed Committees. The courthouse was utilized for accommodating the sufferers, upper floor for women and children, and the lower for men. Food was distributed by a committee appointed for that purpose, but from the following day the work was entrusted to Sergeant-Major Jackson, Sergeant Payne and Corporal Vincent.

The use of Government buildings in the districts for shelter and distributing centres so reduced the number of people at the courthouse —492, that on the morning of the 23rd the building was entirely vacated.

Mr. George Durrant, the Town Warden of Kingstown, reported the number of houses damaged to be 253, of these 199 to a slight degree, 33 of a serious nature and 21 totally destroyed; the loss estimated to exceed £2,600.

In the Kingstown District (exclusive of City of Kingstown), Mr. Kingdon reported 101 houses severely injured, 87 completely destroyed and many others much damaged. Calliaqua District—Mr. VanHeyningen computed 443 houses destroyed and 222 damaged and that rations had been given to an average of 600 persons. In the town of Calliaqua, the Warden reported 21 houses destroyed and 28 damaged. Windward District—32 houses blown down and 22 damaged; the wharves of Rabacca and Georgetown suffered greatly from the surging of the sea.

Leeward District—Mr. Hughes reported 10 houses destroyed or damaged in Buccament Bay, 13 at Cane Grove Estate, four at Penistons, five at Hope

Village, two at Queensbury, whilst at Kearton's Bay and Hill there were five. At Akers Hill five huts were blown down.

Mr. Watkins reported that in Bequia two houses were blown down and the Mill points of Union Estate torn away.

The buildings at the fort suffered: the Royal Artillery quarters, occupied by Mr. Brisbane and family, were almost demolished and that gentleman, in attempting to save his life, was killed by the falling roof. The residence at Ross Castle was too shaken to admit of repair and the doctor's quarters at Low Point was completely wrecked. The shelter at the Cemetery was blown down. Twenty-seven of the enormous Palm trees which formed the beautiful grove at Arnos Vale were thrown across the road.

There was considerable damage to Estates' Houses, buildings and crops, churches, chapels, schools, roads, etc.

The people throughout the colony, with commendable fortitude, proceeded forthwith to re-erect their fallen houses and to effect repairs wherever practicable.

Telegrams and Resolutions expressive of sympathy from the Legislatures of the neighbouring colonies were promptly forwarded, and from the following places the respective amounts were voted:

Barbados	£500
Trinidad	£250
Grenada	£250
St. Lucia	£100
Antigua	£100

Shortly after one month of the disaster £400 was received on account of subscriptions collected by the Lord Mayor; £250 from Sir A. J. Adderley, including a donation of £25 from the Right Hon. E. Stanhope, Secretary of State for the colonies; £100 collected by Mr. McAdam of Antigua; £20 by Mr. Bennett of St. Lucia; and £65 by Archdeacon Hutson of Grenada.

Mr. D. K. Porter of this colony, ex-member of Executive Council, placed the munificent donation of £500 at the disposal of the Government; £50 from Porter & Co., and £25 from His Excellency Walter J. Sendall, the Governor-in-Chief.

In compliance with the joint wish of the Lord Mayor and Sir A. Adderley (KCMG), Mr. Stanhope brought the case of the sufferers to the notice of the Queen, whereupon Her Majesty was graciously pleased to contribute £100.

On Sir A. Adderley's list, which contained many names, etc., appeared prominently H.R.H. the Prince of Wales (KG), our late King, £50. The total was £341 15. Mrs. Sendall collected £70 11. The total from all sources was £3,514 19 2.

Sir A. J. Adderley (KCMG), was untiring in his efforts to achieve success in whatever undertaken for which the Legislature recorded heartfelt gratitude.

The number of cases relieved were 1,905 at a total cost of £3,485 14 11. The available funds could only suffice about one-half of the actual losses; a distribution accordingly took place upon a basis of 50 per cent of estimated damage, one-fifth in money and the remainder in building material. The Resident magistrates performed this task, assisted in the Calliaqua District by the Revs. H. A. Melville, and William Hutchinson, and by Mr. Edward Brown; in the Kingstown District by Mr. F. H. Watkins and the Rev. J. S. Hughes; in the Town of Kingstown by the town warden.

The following appeared in *Illustrated London News* of 25th September:

> *St. Vincent, fruitful of arrowroot, cocoa, and sugar, claims a special paragraph by reason of the disaster that has recently befallen this beautiful island. The hurricane, which devastated St. Vincent on the 16th of August, destroyed numbers of cane-fields and about 600 houses and seven churches, and left 2,000 people homeless. The city of Kingstown, so delightfully situated in a bay that has been compared to the Bay of Naples, has manfully done what it can to succour the sufferers. But the colonists are in sore need of help. Realising this, Sir Augustus Adderley has, with characteristic thoughtfulness, caused collecting boxes to be placed in the West India Court, in order that visitors may subscribe to lessen the misery that prevails in St. Vincent. Finally, one cannot leave this fascinating court without warmly thanking Mr. J. McCarthy for his uniform kindness and courtesy as guide, philosopher and friend.*

August 29th—There was a total eclipse of the sun in connection with which an expedition was sent to the West Indies. Many persons ascended the hills for the purpose of observing the phenomenon.

A committee was appointed by His Excellency the Governor to report upon the laws relating to the mode of raising revenue in the colony and with a view to establish, as far as practicable, a uniform customs tariff and rate of excise duty in the, islands of the Windward Group.

The following formed part of the records of a meeting of the West India Committee held 27th May:

St. Vincent—The petition praying for a constitution similar to that of Jamaica, whereby the people may have control over taxation and expenditure and a legitimate share in legislation through their elected representatives, has been presented to the Lords by the Earl of Dunraven, and to the Commons by Mr. Baden-Powell, M.P.

A Newspaper entitled *The Sentinel* was edited by Mr. Thomas Wells Durrant, who was a joint proprietor with Mr. William Jones Durrant. Mr. James A. Stowe was the printer and publisher. Two years afterward Mr. Benjamin E. Gaskin succeeded Mr. Stowe.

1887 / Wednesday, January 12th—A Public Meeting was held at the courthouse, Kingstown, under the presidency of His Excellency the Governor, at which Mrs. Sendall presented the 48 Diplomas, each accompanied with a commemorative Medal, awarded by His Royal Highness the Prince of Wales as Executive President of the Colonial and Indian Exhibition, London, to the following members of the Local Committee, in recognition of their services, and to Exhibitors:

> The Hon. Alfred Kingdon, Chairman
> The Hon. F. B. Griffith
> The Hon. Captain Denton, The Hon. Sandford Arnott (MD)
> The Hon. William E. Hughes
> C. E. Clarke, Esq
> P. F. Huggins
> T. B. C. Musgrave, Esq, Secretary.

The following Resolutions were unanimously adopted at the meeting:

That the thanks of the exhibitors be tendered to the Hon. Alfred Kingdon and the other members of the exhibition committee for the indefatigable exertions in promoting the objects of the Exhibition and making it conducive to the interests of the Colony;

That this meeting desires to convey to Sir Augustus Adderley (KCMG), the best thanks of the community of St. Vincent for the important services which he has rendered to the colony in his capacity as Royal Commissioner for the West Indian Section of the Colonial and Indian Exhibition of 1886;

That this meeting desires to record on behalf of all classes of the community of St. Vincent their sense of the deep interest in the welfare of the colonies evinced by His Royal Highness the Prince of Wales as the original promoter of the Colonial and Indian Exhibition of 1886; and

That His Excellency the Governor be requested to convey to His Royal Highness this expression of their sentiments of loyalty and gratitude;

That this meeting desires to convey its sincere thanks to His Excellency the Governor for presiding and to Mrs. Sendall for so kindly presenting the diplomas and medals to the exhibitors at the Colonial and Indian Exhibition. It further wishes to record its appreciation of the deep interest His Excellency and Mrs. Sendall have evinced in the welfare of the Colony.

An address from the Legislative Council in connection with Her Majesty's Jubilee contained the following paragraph:

> *That Your Majesty's Dominions may be wedded ever more and more closely into an impregnable Empire; that Your Majesty may long live to receive the homage and love of a loyal people; and that every blessing may attend one so favoured of Heaven as we deem Your Majesty to be, is the sincere*

prayer of Your Majesty's devoted Servants and loyal subjects in this Your
Colony of St. Vincent.

Sir Henry Holland, the Secretary of State for the colonies, who was commanded so to do, directed His Excellency the Governor to convey Her Majesty's thanks for the address and her sincere appreciation of the expressions of loyalty contained therein.

An Ordinance was passed to provide for the observance of the 21st day of June as a Public Holiday in celebration of the 50th Anniversary of Her Majesty's accession to the Throne. A special service was held at St. George's Cathedral; His Excellency the Governor, the members of Councils, and public officers were in attendance. The parcel of land known as The Parade Ground, used for the purposes of recreation, was designated Victoria Park in commemoration of the event, and several trees were planted by Mrs. Sendall and other ladies during the function. Subscriptions were received to supplement which the Legislature voted £30. A dinner was given to the poor of the island, arrangements for which were entrusted in Kingstown to a Committee composed of the Chief Justice, Chairman, the Hons, Henry A. Hazell and Charles J. Simmons, and the town Warden; for the out districts, the respective police magistrates.

The inmates of the hospital and asylums were served with a special dinner.

An address was presented to Walter J. Sendall (CMG), expressing appreciation of the able and courteous manner in which His Excellency conducted the deliberations of the Council, and for the great interest evinced in the welfare of Saint Vincent.

The Hon. W. E. Hughes in seconding the motion to present the address remarked:

> *One great reform His Excellency had introduced into the Legislative Council, which did not exist in former Councils, which the Unofficial Members highly appreciated: he had removed the locks from official lips in the Council, he had let free their consciences, and with freedom of thought he had granted them freedom of speech; this permission had been of great assistance to the Unofficial Members, and he had no doubt, a help also to His Excellency.*

His Excellency said that his duties as Governor brought him into constant communication with the Official Members of the Council and he gladly bore testimony to their efficiency as Public Officers.

The assistance rendered by the Unofficial Members could not be over estimated, and it would be difficult to find a more capable and useful legislative body for so small a Colony.

> *I shall always remember my sojourn in St. Vincent with feelings of pride and satisfaction; and I shall cordially welcome any opportunity of renewing*

with you those labours which have been so pleasant to myself, as they have, I hope, been productive of benefit to the best interest of the Colony."

1888 / 9th June—H.M.S. *Icarus* arrived from Grenada conveying His Majesty King Ja Ja, ex-King of Opobo, Sunday Ja Ja and one servant. An ordinance was passed authorising the reception and detention of certain political prisoners.

The financial depression of the colony evoked extensive suggestions for retrenchment.

An address was presented to His Honour Captain Denton, Administrator, offering congratulations for the appointment to Colonial Secretaryship of Lagos and expressing opinion of the diligence, steadiness and efficiency with which he gratuitously discharged the duties of Colonial Secretary and Administrator.

His Honour was gratified to find that his efforts to do his duty met with appreciation. He regretted leaving St. Vincent where he had sojourned for nearly eight years, and would always look back with pride and pleasure to the position he had held in the Council. He thanked members for the ready help and cordial assistance which they had at all times rendered him.

1889 / 1st January—Tobago was separated from the Windward Islands Government and united with Trinidad.

11th March—A Colonial Silver Wedding gift was presented to Their Royal Highnesses the Prince and Princess of Wales as reported in the following extract from the *Court Circular*:

> *Marlborough House, Monday—Lady Knutsford attended at Marlborough House this afternoon, and presented to the Prince and Princess of Wales the present, which had been subscribed for by the several Colonies and Dependencies of the Crown to commemorate Their Royal Highnesses' Silver Wedding.*
>
> *It consisted of a clock and candelabra together with twelve large wall lights fitted for electric lights.*
>
> *Lord Knutsford, Secretary of State for the Colonies, and Sir Frederick Young, Treasurer of the Fund, were present.*

Their Royal Highnesses repeated the expression of their warm acknowledgements for this handsome present, which had at the request of the donors, been selected by the Prince himself.

The clock and candelabra occupy the whole of the mantelpiece in the great saloon at Marlborough House, and the electric wall lights are arranged round the walls and fully light the apartment.

It will, no doubt, be satisfactory to those who contributed to know that their gift will be in constant use, reminding Their Royal Highnesses of the kind feelings and loyalty which prompted it.

1st June—The Graham Wing of the Colonial Hospital, erected from funds bequeathed by James Graham, Esq, who died 17th May 1877, was declared by His Honour J. Choppin, the Administrator, to be open for the admission of patients in the presence, and with the concurrence of the Members of the Committee of Management. Patients to be treated gratuitously.

Applications for admission to be made to any of the undermentioned gentlemen, who severally had the disposal of the number of beds set opposite to the their names:

His Honour the Administrator	1 Bed
Messrs. D. K. Porter & Co.	4 Beds
The Honourable W. E. Hughes	1 Bed
The Honourable H. A. Hazell	1 Bed

1890 / The Botanic Garden, practically abandoned for nearly 60 years, was re-established and Mr. Henry Powell, from the Royal Gardens, Kew, who arrived on May 14, appointed curator.

October 29th and 30th—A local exhibition was held at the courthouse, Kingstown, from which exhibits were forwarded to the Jamaica exhibition 1891. The prizes awarded at the local exhibition amounted to £110. $15.00 was awarded to Mr. J. C. Trimmingham for a handsomely inlaid Table of native workmanship, composed of over 5,000 pieces of 30 different kinds of woods, which was purchased for Government House. $10 to Mr. E. M. Brown of Belair for a Polo Cart which the Administrator purchased.

Over 2,000 persons attended the Exhibition; the grand collection, covered a space exceeding 3,000 square feet; the decoration of the room was charming.

The Executive Committee composed of

The Hon. G. Smith, Q.C., Chairman
The Hon. Charles. J. Simmons
P. F. Huggins, Esq
Lewis Porter, Esq
James Campbell, Esq
T. B. C. Musgrave, Esq, Secretary.

There was also held on the 30th an agricultural show at the market place, the prizes in connection with which exceeded £55.

Mr. William Crumpton D. Proudfoot published *St. Vincent Commercial News*. This was intended to resuscitate the *Advertising Sheet* which was published by his father, Mr. John B. Proudfoot, in 1879.

1891 / 28th February—His Majesty ex-King Ja Ja and one servant left the Colony for Barbados on H.M.S. *Pylades*. An extract was published from the *Jamaica Post* giving a graphic description of the St. Vincent Court at the Jamaica Exhibition:

> *This should prove one of the most attractive Courts in the Great Show. On entering from the main building, the first to catch the visitor's eye are three hexagonal columns in a row; the centre one being fitted with some choice samples of the celebrated St. Vincent arrowroot and cassava starches, and those on either side containing samples of muscovado* [unrefined sugar] *and crystalized sugar, nutmegs (shelled and unshelled), mace, raw cocoa, and prepared chocolate. There are also several small boxes containing samples of tobacco and cigars, native grown and made. The exhibits contained in these columns are all of choice selections, first class quality and tastefully arranged.*

Every particular class of exhibit was favourably commented on.

The *Colonial Standard and Jamaica Despatch* in its review of the Exhibition referred thus to the St. Vincent Court.

> *One of the most interesting Courts at the Exhibition is that of the little island of St. Vincent. Due regard being had to its size, 140 square miles, and its population 47,000, it is doubtful whether any other part of the world has in comparison contributed so much to our exhibition. There is no part of Jamaica, of similar extent, which has sent up so many and varied exhibits as St. Vincent has. The list of the exhibits fills seven or eight pages of the official catalogue. The court is in the charge of Mr. T. B. C. Musgrave, a nephew, we learn, of the late Sir Anthony Musgrave, who was for several years Governor of Jamaica. Mr. Musgrave has compiled a pamphlet giving an historical and descriptive sketch of St. Vincent in which the most interesting and important facts as to its history, geological formation, productions, resources, revenue, social condition, &c., are brought together and narrated in a concise, graphic, lucid style.*

At a meeting of the Legislative Council the Administrator said with reference to the Exhibition, "It was gratifying to know that Mr. P. C. Cork the Commissioner of the Windward Islands at the Jamaica Exhibition in his report stated that the St. Vincent Courts were universally acknowledged to be the most interesting tropical courts in the Exhibition, and that a Diploma of Honour, the highest award (only given in cases of especial excellence) had been awarded to the general collection and arrangement of the exhibits."

Besides the above, St. Vincent had been awarded three other Diplomas of Honour, 23 Gold, 13 Silver and 6 Bronze Medals. The satisfactory results obtained at this exhibition, were admittedly due to the ability, exertions and zeal of Mr. Musgrave and to the good taste displayed by him in arranging the exhibits to whom the thanks of the Government and those of the entire community are due. An honorarium of £50 was voted by the Legislature in recognition of Mr. Musgrave's services.

The six Caribs who arrived at Jamaica after Mr. Musgrave, occupied a hut in the Industrial Village of the exhibition grounds. They caused additional attraction, as visitors constantly enquired for the two pure Caribs who in turn showed them round the Courts, then on to the making of baskets in the Hut, at which the other four were daily engaged. The sum realized from their work amounted to £23.

His Excellency Sir Henry and Lady Blake often visited the courts and always evinced great interest in the work of the Caribs. Lady Blake distributed among them six very fine cutlasses with nickel-plated blades and handles of horn.

Additional instructions were issued authorising the appointment of an extraordinary member to the Executive Council on any special occasion.

The introduction of an ordinance to enable the Chief Justice of St. Vincent to hold the office of Chief Justice of Grenada or St. Lucia met with general disapproval, which almost culminated in a riot. The inhabitants being strongly opposed to the union considered the move preliminary to confederation and became somewhat excited at the apparent determination on the part of the Government.

H.M.S. *Buzzard* arrived on the night of the 19th November from St. Lucia. The boat with Captain Browne was left at Cane Garden Point; the ship steamed to the opposite point of the harbour when the inhabitants were attracted by the searchlights to the lower portion of the town, thereby facilitating the landing of the Captain in the other direction.

Stones were, however, thrown at the carriage in which he drove and it is believed the Captain was struck for the crowd pursued him to Government House.

The Hon. Henry A. Hazell was erroneously suspected to have gone to Grenada to confer with His Excellency. He arrived on the R.M.S. *Solent* on the 20th and was landed under escort of officers and men from the ship-of-war who marched on both sides of his carriage to Sion Lodge.

His Excellency Sir W. F. Hely-Hutchinson arrived on Coasting Steamer *Exe* on 20th.

At the meeting of the Legislative Council held on 21st November, His Excellency said he had instructions to introduce the ordinance and he would do so, but intended to submit the objections of the unofficial members.

On the motion for the introduction of the Bill, Mm. MacDonald, Simmons and Hazell voted against; His Excellency was aware that Mr. Smith, who was not present, was equally opposed. The official members, as a matter of course, voted in favour.

A vote of thanks to Captain W. J. H. Browne, R.N., and another to officers and men; and of £20 to be divided among the sailors of H.M.S. *Buzzard,* were duly passed.

The streets were thronged and shouts of "no confederation" came from every direction and every class. The vigilance of the officers and men assisted by the police fortunately averted that which would otherwise have remained a blot in the island's records.

The agitation gradually subsided and on 26th His Excellency departed on H.M.S. *Buzzard*.

In a despatch from Lord Knutsford to Sir W. Hely-Hutchinson dated 22nd December, His Lordship stated that while he still considered the measure would be beneficial to the colony, he did not regard its enactment as a matter of sufficient importance in the public interest to be effected in the face of the unanimous opposition of the unofficial members of the Legislative Council, especially as their objection appeared to be shared by the inhabitants of the colony generally. The Administrator was instructed to proceed no further with the bill.

A comprehensive pamphlet compiled by T. B. C. Musgrave, Esq, in connection with the Jamaica Exhibition was printed in that island and was entitled *Historical and Descriptive Sketch of St. Vincent*.

In this year the *St. Vincent Sentry* superseded *The Sentinel*. This newspaper is published at the present time by Mr. J. E. Sprott.

1892 / 14th January—With feelings of the deepest regret His Excellency announced the lamented death of His Royal Highness Prince Albert Victor Christian Edward, Duke of Clarence and Avondale (KG), which took place at 9.30 a.m.

The Governor felt sure every member of this loyal community united in feelings of the deepest and most respectful sympathy with Her Most Gracious Majesty the Queen and Their Royal Highnesses the Prince and Princess of Wales in the sad bereavement sustained, and joined in the heartfelt national regret of the untimely fate.

Wednesday the 20th being the day fixed for the funeral, the public offices were closed and minute guns fired from 11 o'clock a.m. to correspond with the hour at which the funeral service was appointed to commence at Windsor Castle.

His Excellency the Governor, accompanied by members of Councils, heads of departments, and other public officers, proceeded from Government Office to St. George's Cathedral where a special funeral service was held at 11 a.m. The sacred edifice was appropriately decorated, the service intensely impressive, whilst the accommodating space was entirely occupied.

An address of condolence from the Legislative Council to Her Majesty the Queen touching the death of His Royal Highness Prince Albert Victor was duly submitted, in which the following paragraph appeared:

THE SYMPATHY WITH YOUR MAJESTY, WITH THE DECEASED PRINCE'S AF-
FLICTED PARENTS, AND WITH THE PRINCESS TO WHOM HIS ROYAL HIGH-
NESS WAS SO SOON TO HAVE BEEN UNITED, IS ESPECIALLY HEARTFELT
AND UNIVERSAL. THE SUDDEN AND CALAMITOUS EXTINCTION OF THE HOPES
WHICH WERE CENTRED IN THE DECEASED PRINCE ADDS TO THE SORROW OF
THE NATION, AND BY NONE IS THAT SORROW MORE DEEPLY FELT THAN BY
YOUR MAJESTY'S LOYAL SUBJECTS IN ST. VINCENT.

In addition to the expression of Her Majesty's deep sense of the loyalty and affectionate sympathy evinced by her subjects in every part of her Empire on the sad occasion, the undermentioned official telegram was received:

THE PRINCE AND PRINCESS OF WALES ARE ANXIOUS TO EXPRESS TO HER
MAJESTY'S SUBJECTS WHETHER IN THE UNITED KINGDOM, IN THE COL-
ONIES, OR IN INDIA, THE SENSE OF THEIR DEEP GRATITUDE FOR THE
UNIVERSAL FEELING OF SYMPATHY MANIFESTED TOWARDS THEM AT A TIME
WHEN THEY ARE OVERPOWERED BY THE TERRIBLE CALAMITY WHICH THEY
HAVE SUSTAINED IN THE LOSS OF THEIR BELOVED ELDEST SON.

IF SYMPATHY AT SUCH A MOMENT IS OF ANY AVAIL, THE REMEMBRANCE
THAT THEIR GRIEF HAS BEEN SHARED BY ALL CLASSES WILL BE A LASTING
CONSOLATION TO THEIR SORROWING HEARTS, AND, IF POSSIBLE, WILL
MAKE THEM MORE THAN EVER ATTACHED TO THEIR DEAR COUNTRY.

Among the votes passed at a meeting of the Legislative Council were £341 0 11 for expenses in connection with the Jamaica Exhibition; £164 4 8 toward purchase and fitting out of a revenue cruiser; £250 for establishing telephone communication in and about Kingstown, and £500 for extension to Georgetown. A loan was subsequently raised for further extension and to refund general revenue.

In a report on the Zoology and Botany of the West India Islands the following was noted:

> During the past year Mr. F. Du Cane Godman (FRS), has continued to employ a collector in the island of St. Vincent, and owing to the valuable assistance thus afforded to the Committee, it has been possible to complete the exploration of this island. The collections in Zoology are very extensive, and those in botany extend to the whole of the phanerogams and the vascular cryptograms. No expense has been incurred by the Committee in regard to any of these collections in St. Vincent.

1893 / In March a public library was opened, but used as a free reading room until April, when subscriptions at the rate of 1/6 per quarter were demanded. £100 was granted annually for the upkeep until 1896; it was then reduced to £25. £75 was voted for the salary of librarian and an additional £100 for repairs to the building and providing necessary fittings.

8th March—The General Board of Health appointed by Commission held the first meeting, convened by proclamation, at the courthouse.

In view of the precautions taken in Europe and elsewhere against the cholera, the Government thought it desirable to revive the general and several local boards of health under the Act of 1865. No. 1 District was subdivided and assigned respectively to the inspection of members. The local boards were duly appointed and considerable interest bestowed upon all matters pertaining to sanitation. £100 was placed at the disposal of the General Board of Health by the Legislature.

The jetty at Chateaubelair was formally opened for traffic by His Honour Captain Maling who, in the presence of a large assembly, expressed the hope that the establishment of coastal steam communication would soon be an accomplished fact.

In an address to Captain Irwin C. Maling the members of Council referred to the re-establishment of the local botanical station, the lighting of Kingstown, the Kingstown and Georgetown water works, and telephonic communication, among the other improvements as being associated with his administration. His Honour was congratulated on the eminently satisfactory financial condition of the colony.

His Honour, sincerely thanked Honourable Members for the address and concluded as follows:

> *I need hardly say that I cannot leave a colony in which I have been so happy and in which I am so deeply interested without carrying home that interest with me, and I shall bear away with me the best and kindest feelings towards every class of the community.*

On 29th June a public meeting was held at the courthouse to present a farewell address to His Honour Captain Maling. There was a large attendance and at the close of the impressive proceedings the police band played the familiar tune of *Auld Lang Syne*.

12th September—There was a terrific thunderstorm during which the residence of Mr. Learmond of Kingstown Park, was struck by lightning. There was slight damage in every room and one of the family rendered insensible.

A planters club was organized in Kingstown under the management of Mr. C. Belling. It was intended mainly for the convenience of members visiting the town, affording facilities for friendly meetings and the interchange of ideas.

The Right Reverend Doctor Enos Nuttall was appointed Primate of the Anglican Church in the West Indies.

An epidemic broke out in the Grenadines during the month of October; consequently Dr. Bruce-Austin proceeded to Clifton at Union Island. He arrived there with Mr. Butler, a dispenser, at 8 a.m. on 31st October when 43 persons suffering from influenza and bilious remittent fever were attended to and prescribed for. One hopeless case succumbed. On the next day, 63 persons were administered to at Ashton; November 2nd, 59 at Mayreau, and the same number at Canouan on the 4th. Foodstuffs and medical comforts were promptly dispatched from Kingstown. Four deaths occurred subsequently at Canouan.

1834 / 25th June—His Excellency transmitted a telegraphic message of congratulation to Her Majesty the Queen on the birth of a son to Their Royal Highnesses the Duke and Duchess of York. Her Majesty's thanks for the cordial expressions were duly received. A resolution was also passed by the Legislative Council for which Her Majesty's appreciation was notified.

Lectures were given by Dr. Bruce-Austin on "Aids for first Help to the Injured".

There was always an appreciative audience. His Honour Colonel Sandwith was often present and on one occasion His Excellency was in attendance.

Sir Vincent Barrington, the Deputy Chairman of the Saint John Ambulance Association, while at Government House during the short interval of the steamer's stay, expressed delight at the enterprise, made suggestions as to division of classes and appointed Dr. Newsam examiner. It is to be regretted that before certificates could be obtained the valuable instructions were discontinued.

The accidental drowning on 27th June of three of the members of the Eton cricket team on their way to Barrouallie was the cause of very painful excitement. Mr. William M. Donawa was a useful member in the community and commanded the esteem of all who knew him. As Chief Government Printer his loss was keenly felt, his musical talent rendered him an acquisition in various ways, notably: organist of St. George's Cathedral for several years and a prominent member of the Orchestral Society. At the time of this lamentable occurrence he was Secretary of Court "Morning Star" A.O.F. in the welfare of which Society he evinced great interest.

Mm. Edward Quow and Alfred Stokes, other victims, although of humbler stations in life, were much respected for their gentility.

The places of business being closed, the attendance at the interment was unprecedented. The processions met at the Cathedral gate and after the ceremony the enormous concourse extended thence to the cemetery, preceded by the Kingstown Orchestra.

Casualty Hospitals at Barrouallie, Chateaubelair, and Georgetown were opened. Immediately afterward their utility was strikingly illustrated.

Owing to the financial outlook of the colony, the proposal of the General Concessions Syndicate Limited for establishing an Hotel and a Steamship Service could not be entertained, but the dire need was generally admitted.

1st November—The postage rate on letters between this Colony, Grenada, and St. Lucia was reduced from 2½ d. per half ounce to 1d. In 1891 the postal rate was reduced from 4d. to 2½ d., with the result that in 1893 the number of letters rose from 1,158 in 1890 to 1,816 while the decrease in receipts was 7s. 8d. only.

24th December—A fire occurred at 8.10 p.m. at Dalrymple's Establishment. It commenced in the grocery and from there communicated to all the other departments. There was deep sympathy for Mr. Dalrymple and his employees. The fire brigade was commended for the work done under the able direction of Mr. Laborde.

1895 / 25th February—Cricket match against the first English team touring the West Indies. For the English Mr. Lucas, with 22, alone obtained double figures, and the innings closed for 63. When stumps were drawn St. Vincent had compiled 139 for the loss of nine wickets; A. Holder, 32; V. Richards, not out, 26; T. Osment, 19; C. Simmons, not out, 16; and F. W. Griffith, 11, were the principal scorers. The match thus ended in a victory for St. Vincent by a wicket and 76 runs.

The customs tariff was revised so as to compensate for the suspension of export duty. It was in substance a return to the scheme of duties existing prior to the McKinley Tariff Treaty.

An extensive report by Professor J. B. Harrison (MA, FCS, FGS), Government Analyst of British Guiana, on the state of the sugar industry of Saint Vincent, was published. A very high opinion was formed regarding the purely manual cultivation of the estates visited. The fields were in a state of high tillage and kept in excellent order as regards weeds, etc., a state that might be termed garden cultivation. No improvement could be suggested upon the methods of working up the land.

The aquatic sports afforded considerable enjoyment on Wednesday afternoon, 28th August. An awning was erected on the Kingstown jetty and the police band was in attendance. There were races for decked and undecked sailing boats, rowing boats (including Moses boats). The swimming race was very interesting, and then the most successful event of the afternoon—the greasy pole—came on while most of the competitors came off.

There was a terrific thunderstorm on Friday night the 6th of September, and at 4.15 on the morning of the following day a loud crash startled the inmates of the telephone exchange, who, rushing from their apartments, beheld the switchboards on fire and the house filled with suffocating smoke.

Their vigilance averted what might otherwise have been very disastrous. One switchboard was irreparably damaged; the other only slightly so was speedily repaired by Mr. McLeod, the supervisor, and at 10 a.m. of the same day all the subscribers were in communication.

During a thunderstorm on Sunday the 15th September the flagstaff at Fort Charlotte was shattered and an iron rail near the magazine was struck by lightning. A house in the Bay Street in Kingstown sustained damage and two dogs lying on the steps thereof were killed by the vivid lightning. The face of an inmate was scorched by a piece of the burning timber. The mills of Belvedere and Choppins estates were slightly damaged and the deck of the sloop *Rosetta* was also scorched.

In consequence of excessive rain on Tuesday night 17th several rivers were flooded, the Mesopotamia bridge was destroyed, a few houses washed away and five lives were lost.

In Kingstown a portion of a wall was thrown down and water poured into several houses and shops. A part of the Buccament bridge was destroyed and extensive damage done in the Cumberland district. The Caribs from Morne Ronde interviewed Canon Branch of Barrouallie for purpose of submitting their perilous condition to the Government. There was a rent or crack in the hill which overhung their village.

On Sunday night 17th November the Sloop *Viper* was wrecked on a reef to the Windward of Carriacou. One male, four females and three children were drowned. The disaster caused a panic among the sympathetic inhabitants of that place whose characteristic hospitality was eagerly extended to the survivors.

1896 / 24th January—The Governor telegraphed expression of sympathy to Her Majesty the Queen on behalf of the Windward Islands on the death of His Royal Highness Prince Henry of Battenburg for which Her Majesty's thanks were duly communicated.

A commission was appointed to enquire and report on the incidence of land tax, export tax, etc. The first meeting was held at the Courthouse on 20th June, and weekly sittings thereafter, of which public notice was given.

The report, which was of considerable length, comprised recommendations regarding the condition of roads and means of communication in the interior; the exodus of the labouring population; the want of markets; cheap money for assistance to small landowners; and various important suggestions.

On the morning and night of Saturday 28th October there was a flood of considerable magnitude whereby 25 lives were lost and extensive damage done to property in nearly every quarter save Kingstown and its immediate vicinity. Several houses were swept into the sea, a few of which bore the occupants away. Of 3,000 cocoa trees three years old, many bearing, on an estate in the Leeward District, nine were left, and of 500 to 600 nutmeg trees, none remained. It was said that the estate Windsor Forest is gone in the sea.

Eleven deaths at Sandy Bay were caused by a landslip; nine bodies were discovered, five at Mount Young, two at Mount Bentinck and one each at Waterloo and Rabacca made total loss of life in the Carib Country 20.

Acres of cane were washed away, thousands of cocoa and nutmeg trees destroyed; there was widespread devastation of provision grounds and incalculable destruction of livestock. The general appearance presented wonderful evidence of the extent and violence of the disaster. Generous contributions were received for the relief of the suffering and destitute.

Mm. William Patrick and Henry Cork were awarded medals and certificates by the Royal Humane Society for rescuing four persons from destruction by the floods at the risk of their own lives.

His Excellency Sir Charles Bruce (KCMG), in his address to the Legislative Council on 30th November referred to his views respecting the creation of a peasant proprietary and certain resolutions he had received relative to immediate construction of roads and bridges to afford employment to the masses and so prevent the emigration, and among others that the people should have a voice in the government of their country by being allowed to return at least eight representatives to the Legislative Council. In conclusion His Excellency expressed the hope that members would associate themselves with him in an earnest desire to cooperate for the public good, labouring without partiality or prejudice, in a spirit of equal sympathy with all classes of the people.

1897 / 1st January—The duties of Colonial Treasurer were added to those of Administrator and Colonial Secretary.

Under the patronage of His Honour the Administrator and Mrs. Thompson, athletic sports were held at Victoria Park on New Year's Day. There was excellent weather and every event was attractively amusing, especially the pony race with egg and spoon.

11th February—Urgent representations having been made regarding the critical position of the sugar industry, Her Majesty the Queen was pleased to order a special enquiry as to the condition and prospects of the West Indian sugar growing colonies and on this day the Royal Commissioners composed of Sir Henry Wylie Norman, (GBC, GCMB, CIE), Sir Edward Grey, Baronet, (MP), and Sir David Barbour (KC, SI), with the Secretary Sydney Olivier, Esquire, (BA), accompanied by Dr. Morris, Assistant Director of the Royal Gardens, Kew, arrived on H.M.S. *Talbot* from Grenada.

14th February—Lord Hawk's cricket team arrived on R.M. Coasting Steamer *Taw* from Grenada. In the Cricket Match on 15th they defeated the local representatives. His Lordship was bowled in the first innings by Richard Ollivierre's 2nd ball to him before he could make a single run, but in the 2nd innings he made 51. P. F. Warner scored 156 in the 2nd innings. The total scores were: English team 141 and 287; the home team, 154 and 136. A prize bat contributed by ladies of the island was presented to Hedley Hiven for scoring 62 runs, the highest among the local team. T. Layne, who was next, played beautifully for 58.

On Monday 3rd May, Mr. Charles John McLeod, Barrister-at-Law, was tried for contempt of court. He was defended by the Honourable A. Wellesley Lewis of Grenada and Mm. James McCombie Salmon, L. T. Augier McVane, and John William Girad of St. Lucia. The Hon. C. Ormond Hazell, Acting Attorney General, and Mr. Conrad Simmons acted as *amici curioe*. The proceedings were of considerable length and of a sensational nature. At the conclusion of the trial Mr. McLeod was committed to the prison in Kingstown for 14 days by His Honour G. P. St. Aubyn, the Acting Chief Justice.

10th June—A cyclone of moderate velocity passed over this island; at 11 a.m. there was a thunderstorm. Three lives were lost; also one of the five vessels which encountered the storm at sea. At Georgetown, the roof of the building used for the telephone exchange and post office was blown off, the Anglican School destroyed, the house of Mr. Antrobus smashed by a falling tree and several huts damaged. There were minor damages at different parts of the Windward District.

An ordinance was passed to provide for the observance of the 21st June as a public holiday in celebration of the 60th Anniversary of Her Majesty's Accession to the Throne. The congratulatory address which was submitted in due course assured Her Majesty, among other things, that "Although the little group of Islands which forms this colony is but a small unit of the mighty realm which is blessed with Your Majesty's beneficent rule, its inhabitants are second to those of no section of the Empire in their loyalty to Your Throne and Person, and in their appreciation of those noble qualities of heart and mind which endear Your Majesty to each one of the many peoples and communities who acknowledge you as their Sovereign."

Her Majesty's cordial thanks for congratulations and good wishes were tendered in the customary manner.

The following telegraphic message from Her Gracious Majesty the Queen was also received: "From my heart I thank my beloved people. May God bless them."

His Excellency the Governor sent the following: "Grenada joins her Sister St. Vincent in felicitations, joy, and devotion on Happy Anniversary."

His Honour the Administrator replied: "In loyal devotion to our Beloved Queen and in rejoicing on this glorious day St. Vincent unites with her sister colony."

20th and 21st June—The official celebration comprised a Thanksgiving Service at St. George's Cathedral at 11 o'clock a.m. on Sunday 20th. His Honour the Administrator, members of Councils, the staff of public officers, and several Societies formed in procession from the courthouse and marched to the cathedral with police in line on both sides preceded by their band.

On the following day the Administrator received members of councils, public officers, ministers of religion and the leading members of the community at the Council Chamber in the courthouse, Kingstown, at 11.30 a.m.; at 12 o'clock noon there was a royal salute and *feu de joie* fired by the police force in the courtyard. His Honour then proceeded with those present to the police barracks, where doles of 2/- were given from public funds to 200 poor persons.

On the evening of the 22nd large beacon bonfires were lighted at Dorsetshire Hill and on prominent places at Georgetown, Barrouallie, Chateaubelair and Bequia. The other islands of the Grenadines were similarly illumined extending to and including Grenada.

Saturday 26th—His Excellency Sir Alfred Maloney (KCMG), held a full dress Levee at the courthouse in Kingstown at 12 o'clock noon.

The members of the Executive Council, in an address to His Honour Edward Rawle Drayton, Esq, recorded their sense and esteem of the zealous care and eager anxiety evinced by him during his brief administration, earnestly hoping that Her Majesty's Government would promote His Honour to a sphere which would enable the expansion of that administrative power which they had witnessed with admiration.

After referring to the critical condition of the affairs of this charming colony and the hope entertained, His Honour thus concluded: "I thank you, Gentlemen, most sincerely for the kindly sentiments you have expressed and for your many acts of kindness to me, both official and private, and I assure you that the friendships I have formed and the labours that I have shared with you in St. Vincent this year have made it one of the most satisfactory periods of my life."

Letters Patent were published authorizing the Senior Member of Executive Council of Grenada to administer the Government of the Windward Islands during the absence of the Governor or other officer having a prior right, or if there be no person in the Windward Islands so appointed.

On Tuesday 14th December Kingstown was enlivened by the keen interest taken in the election at the courthouse of representatives to constitute a board for the town of Kingstown. The successful candidates were Mm. A.

H. Spence, David McDowall, J. G. W. Hazell and Dr. Bruce-Austin. After the announcement by Mr. George Durrant, the Town Warden, the members, with the exception of Mr. J. G. W. Hazell who was unavoidably absent, gave expression to the warm appreciation of the confidence reposed on them. The nominated members were Mm. T. R. Nairn, E. St. J. Branch, Helon E. Ollivierre and John M. Joseph. The first meeting was held on Wednesday 29th when Mr. J. G. W. Hazell was elected Chairman.

1898 / Mr. W. Cradwick, Superintendent of the Hope Gardens, Jamaica, was appointed by the Secretary of State for the colonies to assist the Government in considering what land would be best suited for the establishment of a Peasant Proprietary Body.

Vice Admiral Sir John Fisher, after an inspection, expressed himself as highly pleased with the police guard of honour on the occasion of his landing at the Kingstown jetty. He had no idea St. Vincent could produce so fine a guard and that it was the best police guard of honour he had seen in the West Indies.

On 15th August His Honour the Administrator forwarded and received the following telegrams: "St. Vincent sends congratulations to Grenada on the celebration of the anniversary of her discovery" and "Grenada returns thanks for congratulations."

St. Vincent, having undergone in common with other sugar growing colonies the trying financial depression resulting from the failure of the staple industry, planters were looking forward hopefully for a propitious turn of the tide. Stimulated by the efforts of the Government to foster the establishment of minor products through the Crown Lands Allotment Scheme, several of the large proprietors and ambitious small settlers turned their attention to cocoa cultivation. With all the potentiality with which the fertile soil of the country is blessed, it responded to efforts of the cultivators, and never was there fairer promise of an approaching era of prosperity than the luxurious plantations of growing cocoa, some near bearing, presented on many of the best estates in the colony. But, in the midst of a delightful dream which cheered the hearts of all classes, the angel of death appeared in the character of an appallingly destructive hurricane on the morning of the 11th September, utterly devastating the island, driving away every fond hope which was cherished for its industrial resuscitation, and casting its inhabitants deep down into the slough of misery and despond. Meteorological indications of the storm were not wanting. Since the 6th the standard Mercurial Barometer at the Botanic Garden, 203 feet above sea level, had been lower than usual, the readings ranging from 29.926 at 3 p.m. on the 6th to 29.838 at 3 p.m. on the 10th. At 5:55 on the following morning the reading was 29.724. The wind at this time was blowing in fitful gusts from N and NW. The Barometer continued to fall slowly until 10 a.m. when it was 29.539, and yet still falling. The force of the storm was then in alarming evidence, the terrific wind dealing destruction on every side and striking the inhabitants with mortal fear.

The following vivid description of the catastrophe is extracted from *The Sentry* of the 23rd September, the publication of which paper was suspended until that date, the editor having received a severe injury in the hurricane, and the widespread confusion and sadness rendering the immediate collection of reliable reports almost an impossibility.

> *The hurricane lasted six hours with an interval of fifty-five minutes during which the barometer remained steady at 28.509 keeping the awe-stricken population in a suspense as frightful as the fury of the storm; and whilst the trembling, bewildered populace who had escaped death or serious injury during the first attack of the angry winds wandered to and fro seeking what they deemed the safest shelter, the seas arose still more dreadfully and the storm clouds burst with a vehemence that gave to each individual one common thought: that this was the last of St. Vincent and its 40,000 inhabitants. The hurricane is passed, but today, 12 days after it occurred, the affrighted people have not yet recovered from the shock of the dreadful catastrophe, and the colony is stunned from the terrible blow. Since that dreadful day that will never fade in the history of this island, there has been a suspension of trade in anything else but what contributes to the relief of the 30,000 of sick and destitute that are like helpless children depending on the Government for food, clothing and shelter. The deaths recorded are 205, but as this does not include all those from inland villages, the missing, or crews of ships lost, the estimated loss of life to the present is 300. The mortality is being daily augmented: the old, some of the wounded, and infants dying from the late exposure and suffering.*
>
> *We will not venture to depict the panic which the terrible hurricane created in Kingstown. The dreadful noise of the stormy waves spending their force against the buildings on the Bay Street and flooding the cross streets, tossing boats and lighters, particles of the wrecked latrines and slaughter house on the muddy foam almost in the centre of the Town like straw, the frightful clashing of galvanized sheeting, the clatter of tiles and slates dashed by the winds against the walls, the constant noises of falling houses, the flashes of lightning, the rumbling of thunder—all this and more—the shrieks of affrighted women and children, the moans of the wounded gave a never-to-be-forgotten experience to the people of Kingstown on Sunday 11th of September. The loss of property in Kingstown although considerable, cannot be compared with the out villages. This we believe is not because the storm was less violent here, but fortunately the houses are more compact and the buildings are mostly of brick and stone. Nearly all the fragile tenements have been demolished and the others more or less damaged; but there is hardly a roof in town of slate, galvanized iron or shingle which has not been perfectly stripped or greatly damaged. In few cases substantial wall buildings have crumbled.*

69

*Two of these are the Public Library and Lawlor's Store. The central ward of
the Colonial Hospital has been unroofed and the walls partially demolished.*

The destruction by sea bereft the colony of nearly all the craft. The sloops
Sylvia, Water Witch, Pioneer, Falcon, and *Whisper* were lost; *May Queen, Carib*
and *Eli* driven ashore; schooner *Rising Tide* was driven out of the harbour
and Captain Lotmore, who attempted to overtake it, perished with the crew.
Schooner *Ocean King* capsized to the Windward of this island and three of
the crew were rescued near St. Lucia. At Bequia the sloop *Relief* went ashore
and schooner *Petrel* became a total wreck. The ship *Loando,* 1,446 tons, the
barque *Lapland,* 582 tons and the barquentine *Grace Lynwood,* 599 tons were
driven from Carlisle Bay, Barbados, on night of the 10th and arrived on the
shores of the Windward District within 4 hours. In their nautical experience
the captains averred they never encountered so terrific a storm and believed
the velocity of wind, at certain intervals, to have been at 100 miles an hour.
All lives were saved but vessels wrecked.

The Government are doing all that possibly can be done for the relief of
distress and suffering. As early as the 13th, food was sent to the country districts for distribution and temporary sheds began to be erected to house the
homeless. All in authority, or of any position, willingly spent themselves in
relieving the distressed. The Governor came up from Grenada, and with the
Administrator visited the various centres in the town and country districts
and saw what was being done. Besides the relief in food, all willing to work
were employed in clearing streets and roads of the giant trees (some near a
century old) which blocked them.

Nevertheless, hundreds of injured and dying from all parts of the island
were conveyed to the wards, whereupon, it became necessary to provide for
the extraordinary number of patients. Mr. Osment and Mr. Kernahan constructed a rough covering of galvanized roofing on the upper floor of the
building in order to make the lower floor habitable. The wards presented the
appearance of a battlefield, wounded and mangled lying about in all directions, writhing and moaning in agony. The wards being overcrowded a few
marques from St. Lucia were pitched in the Hospital Yard, besides which a
ward was fitted up at the police barracks and placed under the care of Dr.
Austin. Besides the good work performed by this medical officer one thousand cases were attended to by the energetic and sympathetic Surgeon, Dr.
Newsam, who was ably assisted by Dr. Whiteman of Grenada and Mr. Cyril
Durrant, then a medical student on a visit to his parents.

October 5th—His Excellency Sir A. Moloney, Lady Moloney and Private
Secretary arrived on H.M.S. *Intrepid.*

Subscriptions received for hurricane relief fund to 13th October, 1898 amounted to £13,746; to 25th October, £15,175; to 8th November, £22,627; 17th, £23,080.

The following are mainly from the Report of His Honour H. L. Thompson, Administrator, to Sir A. Moloney, the Governor:

Immediately after the storm the most pressing necessity was the care of the injured and the bulk of this work fell upon Dr. Newsam, the colonial surgeon, at the Colonial Hospital in Kingstown, and of his untiring devotion to duty during that trying time I cannot speak too highly.

For several days the Colonial Hospital was like the "cockpit" of an old ship after an engagement, and Dr. Newsam with the Hospital Staff and the many volunteer assistants he had, worked in the most heroic manner to relieve the misery and distress around them.

We were fortunate in having the presence in Kingstown of Mr. Durrant a young medical student who was on a visit to his friends and Mr. Turpin who had had some medical experience. Both these gentlemen rendered invaluable assistance.

Dr. Whiteman came from Grenada and remained until the end of September when Dr. Pollonais arrived from Trinidad. These performed valuable services in the Hospital.

In Barrouallie Dr. O'Neale with the policemen stationed there, faced a scene which is hard to realise, until assistance could be sent. In the remains of his own house Dr. O'Neale improvised a temporary hospital where all possible care was bestowed upon the sufferers.

At Chateaubelair, Dr. Durant from Grenada did good work and was transferred to the Windward side of the island where his kindness, courtesy, and care were much appreciated by all classes.

Mr. Neverson, the dispenser at the pauper asylum, and Mr. Learmond who was specially engaged, were exceptionally useful as dispensers on the Leeward coast.

Mr. Huggins, the Revenue Officer at Chateaubelair, was most energetic and received able and loyal assistance from the Rev. A. J. Cocks, the Wesleyan Minister at that place.

Lieutenant F. Owen-Lewis, His Excellency's Aide-de-Camp, who was good enough to take charge of relief work in the Cumberland District was exemplary; by his tact and kindness he soon gained the confidence of the people.*

The work in Layou and neighbourhood was entrusted to Mr. Miles Phillips, the Acting Inspector of Schools, who was very energetic.

In Georgetown, Mr. Isaacs, the Acting Magistrate, took timely and active steps to cope with the situation. He was loyally assisted by the Rev. B. A. Queeley, Ms. Gray, Garrett and E. M. Beach.

Soon after his arrival from Grenada, Mr. Musgrave was put in charge of a large country district. His thorough knowledge of the island and people facilitated his good work. He was assisted by the Revs. H. E. Gresham and E. M. Johnson; also by Mm. Alexander Smith, Hadley and Snodgrass.

The Chairmanship of the local committee in Kingstown devolved on Mr. Wells Durrant who showed considerable tact, discretion and powers of organisation and management.

Rev. J. McLuckie was in charge of the refugees who occupied the Presbyterian Church. It was admirable to see the crowds following him in prayers from the first day.

Mr. Rice and the Rev. D. Duffus successfully coped with the relief work at Bequia.

The services of Mr. Laborde and police force were especially reported on but His Excellency was reminded of the splendid work done by Mr. Laborde in organizing the purchase and distribution of food and other supplies to the various stations. Elymas John, one of the constables, lost his life from actual overwork.

His Excellency's attention was drawn to the services of Mr. F. W. Griffith, Chief Clerk in the Government Office, who was unremitting in his work from early in the morning until late at night. If there was not someone able to deal with the people as Mr. Griffith did there would have been far more discontent, for they daily surrounded the Government Office.

Conspicuous among the many gentlemen who rendered valuable assistance were the Venerable Archdeacon Turpin, Mm. Spence, (Chairman, Kingstown Board) Coull and Conrad Simmons.

The Administrator gratefully acknowledged, in addition to generous help from neighbouring colonies, the ready manner in which officials were placed at the disposal of this Government. From Grenada there were Mr. Musgrave,

---

*Lieutenant Owen-Lewis of the Bombay Light Infantry was Lady Moloney's brother. He was shot on 24th November 1899 in the Transvaal during a reconnaissance with an armoured train. Deep sympathy was felt for his relatives by the people of this island to whom he had endeared himself.

Dr. Whiteman and Dr. Durant; from St. Lucia, Mr. T. Dyer, (who did excellent work at Barrouallie) and from Trinidad, Dr. Pollonais, two trained Nurses and Mr. Murphy, Superintendent Sergeant.

His Excellency recorded his appreciation of the great work of public relief performed by Mrs. Thompson, the Administrator's wife, and her willing band of lady assistants, which all others must view with respectful admiration.*

The Administrator, Mr. Thompson, showed undoubted administrative ability and it was a very gratifying duty of His Excellency to give him the first place as regard to the value of his exceptional and distinguished public services.

Contributions to hurricane relief fund to 31st December 1898 amounted to £28,187. 16. 11. and the unexpended balance in Treasury £9,216. 10. 8.

On behalf of people of Windward Islands His Excellency forwarded telegram expressing heartfelt sympathy to Her Majesty, Their Royal Highnesses the Prince and Princess of Wales and rest of Royal Family on distressing news of death of Her Majesty the Queen of Denmark. Her Majesty's appreciation of the message of condolence was duly conveyed.

Intimation was received regarding the establishment of a school of tropical medicine at the Albert Docks Branch Hospital of the Seamen's Hospital Society, at which the Medical Officers of the colonies would be given special instruction in the treatment of tropical diseases. Any material, no matter how much or how little, bearing on tropical pathology would be acceptable.

A small weekly newspaper entitled *The Rambler* was issued in conjunction with *The Sentry*.

1899 / On the 17th February, the Governor sent a telegram to the Secretary of State for the colonies on behalf of people of the Windward Islands offering to Her Majesty the Queen, Their Royal Highnesses the Prince and Princess of Wales and the rest of the Royal Family, sincere condolence and heartfelt sympathy on distressing news of death of His Royal Highness Prince Alfred of Saxe-Coburg-Gotha. The answer was received on 21st and conveyed Her

---

*Her Majesty the Queen evinced appreciation of Mrs. Thompson's exemplary works of charity displayed in this island by giving sanction to her enrolment as an Honorary Associate of the Order of St. John of Jerusalem in England. The Order, which was incorporated on the 14th May 1888 (with addenda 1888 and 1890), has Her Majesty as the Sovereign Head and Patron, H.R.H. the Prince of Wales (KG), as Grand Prior, H.R.H. the Duke of York (KG), as Sub-Prior, H.R.H. the Duke of Connaught (KG), as Bailiff of Egle and His Grace the Archbishop of York as Prelate. The distinction is conferred on ladies recommended to the Chapter General of the Order as having performed heroic deeds.

Majesty's cordial thanks for kind sympathy of people of Windward Islands with Herself and Royal Family in their sorrow.

Another telegram on behalf of people of Windward Islands was forwarded on the 17th February by the Governor to the French Government conveying expression of profound sympathy on occasion of death of the President of the Republic.

On Wednesday afternoon 22nd February the Steam Yacht *Maria* arrived with the undermentioned distinguished visitors: Sir Cuthbert Quilter, Bart., M.P., Lady Quilter, Sir Neville Lubbock (KCMG), Mr. and Mrs. Miller, Mr. P. Quilter, Mr. U. Quilter, Dr. Mason, and Mr. Muter. On the 23rd His Honour the Administrator, and a few of the principal proprietors were invited to a conference on board the yacht. Sir Cuthbert Quilter then explained the object of his visit to the colony, namely to enquire into the conditions of agriculture, to inspect the lands available for cane cultivation and on the request of Mr. Chamberlain to report on the prospects of a central factory. A lengthy discussion ensued during which the gentlemen expressed the desirability of a central factory being erected in this island. Sir Cuthbert Quilter was emphatic in his observation that cooperation and unity on the part of the landowners must not be wanting, as the cooperative principle was the only one on which central factories could be established with any hope of success in these small islands.

The visitors accompanied by the Administrator were taken to the Carib Country by Mr. Porter on the 24th for purpose of viewing the site suggested for erection of the factory. They were highly pleased with the scenery and climate of the island and also spoke in terms of praise of the courtesy and civility of the people generally. They took their departure on Sunday 26th.

Among his notes on the islands visited Sir Cuthbert Quilter asked, "Why should not St. Vincent have a chance of prospering and adding to the trade of the Empire as much as Central Africa, where the conditions are nothing like so favourable?"

The sad news of the death of the Right Reverend Bishop Bree, on Sunday 26th February in England, was somewhat surprising, latest intelligence being that His Lordship was gaining strength. There was a memorial service at St. George's Cathedral on Sunday, 12th March. The altar was draped and decorated in a manner befitting the occasion and on the Bishop's Chair were placed two beautiful wreaths of white roses. *Hymns for the Dead* were sung; the solemn strains of the *Dead March in Saul*, effectively rendered on the organ during the service, inspired an awful gloom and filled the mind with loving thoughts of the departed one. The Venerable Archdeacon Turpin selected for his theme, "Death", and during his discourse made touching reference to His Lordship's exemplary career.

16th May—The Most Reverend Enos Nuttall, (DD), Bishop of Jamaica and Archbishop of the West Indies, arrived for purpose of attending the synod. A conference was held on the same day.

The synod of the Diocese of the Windward Islands was held in St. George's Cathedral on Wednesday the 17th and Thursday the 18th. There were present:

The Most Reverend Enos Nuttall (DD), President

The Archdeacon of Grenada	The Rev. G. A. I. Frederick of St. Vincent
The Archdeacon of St. Vincent	The Rev. D. Duffus of St. Vincent
The Rev. Canon Arthur of Grenada	The Rev. W. H. Mayers of St. Vincent
The Rev. F. F. C. Mallalieu of Grenada	The Rev. R. J. Clarke, of St. Lucia

The Lay Representatives were

T. J. Otway, Esq, Grenada	J. G. Coull, Esq, St. Vincent
E. E. Hughes, Esq, Grenada	*Acting Registrar*
The Hon. C. J. Simmons, St. Vincent	His Honour J. B. Walker, St. Vincent
H. A. Hazell, Esq, St. Vincent	*Chief Justice, Acting Chancellor*

Important resolutions were passed and suggestions made in addition to extensive discussions on general matters relating to the Diocese to be forwarded to England.

His Grace occupied the Pulpit at the Cathedral on Wednesday evening the 17th and preached on I. Thess. IV. 1.

The following Telegram was transmitted on 11th August:

THOMPSON TO ADMINISTRATOR LEEWARD ISLANDS,

ST. VINCENT DEEPLY SYMPATHISES WITH LEEWARD ISLANDS AND ESPECIAL-
LY MONTSERRAT IN THE CALAMITY WHICH HAS BEFALLEN THEM. REGRET
THAT FINANCES OF THE COLONY WILL NOT JUSTIFY A VOTE IN AID OF
DISTRESS AND FEAR THAT RECENT LOSSES FROM A SIMILAR MISFORTUNE
WILL INTERFERE WITH PRIVATE SUBSCRIPTIONS. LATTER HAVE BEEN ASKED
FOR AND WILL BE FORWARDED IF RECEIVED.

Musical and other entertainments were organized on behalf of sufferers in the Leeward Islands. The large attendances at the courthouse and at the several places of worship coupled with numerous subscribers on lists throughout the colony proved the general sympathy of a people who were themselves sufferers. The total amount collected was about £130 in addition to sums forwarded direct by ministers of religion.

During his visit to the mother country a series of questions were put to Sir Alfred Moloney by a representative of the "Commerce" regarding the Windward Islands. His Excellency thought it a great mistake to rely upon one crop in any island, and the soil of the West Indies being so fertile there was no necessity to do this. With reference to the West Indian Negro, "I have always taken the view that we owe a great deal to the Negro, and personally I am of opinion that the coloured people of the West Indies should be treated in a thoroughly liberal way. They are good workers, and if the Negroes are accorded proper respect and consideration, they should make good workmen and I hope good citizens."

Monday, 11th September, was observed as a day of general supplication. The Merchants having voluntarily closed their establishments for two hours, the Administrator directed that Offices of the Government be closed from 11 a.m. to 1 p.m.

Touching sermons were preached recalling the awful distress which prevailed on that date a year ago. All the places of worship in the colony were filled to overcrowding.

At the last meeting of the Legislative Council for the year, held 27th December, Mr. MacDonald on behalf of the unofficial section congratulated His Honour Mr. Thompson on the able manner in which he had conducted the affairs of the Government especially in reference to the laborious and difficult period immediately following the hurricane of 1898. The Honourable Member referred to the cordial relations which had always existed between His Honour and the unofficial members of the Council from his first assumption of the Government. The remarks were endorsed by the other unofficial members present.

The Attorney General then said, "On behalf of the Official Members of the Council, Sir, I desire to express concurrence with the remarks of the Unofficial Section. Full opportunity has been afforded me of forming an idea of the nature of the duties it had fallen to your lot to discharge. I can only say a debt of gratitude has been incurred by the people of St. Vincent. They are powerless to discharge their obligation but we hope a sovereign power will reward your services and so satisfy it." His Honour the Administrator thanked the members for their kind and gratifying remarks.

1900 / Successful efforts were made to avert the closing of the branch of Colonial Bank, contemplated in consequence of insufficient business.

Subscriptions from the general community were collected for presenting in a permanent shape an illuminated address to Mr. and Mrs. Thompson. The draft address was presented here but the piece of silver with the inscription was beautifully mounted, framed, and forwarded direct by an English firm to Mrs. Thompson's London address. It was placed on an easel in a prominent position in the drawing room.

Besides contributing to the list, the people of Belair Estate presented as a souvenir, a miniature satin banner on a silver rod, with pathetic lines printed in gold dedicated to Mrs. Thompson. The printing was handsomely embroidered with forget-me-nots (the work of Father Putz).

In his sermon at the Cathedral on Sunday 11th February, the Venerable Archdeacon Turpin made sympathetic references to the approaching departure of Mr. and Mrs. Thompson and eulogized the good works they had performed during their sojourn here.

The patriotic concert on Wednesday 20th, and the special musical Service in the Cathedral on Sunday 24th December 1899, followed by a public meeting on the Wednesday thereafter, were the earliest movements in connection with the Soldiers, Widows and Orphans Fund, indicating the loyalty which characterizes the people of St. Vincent. On February 16th the sum of £200 was remitted for the Lord Mayor's Fund through the Crown Agents for the colonies as the first instalment. The subscription lists presented a remarkable feature, containing, as most of them did, numerous small contributions from hundreds of labourers and others in humble walks of life.

A further remittance of £32 was paid to the British Empire League Fund for the assistance of sufferers belonging to or connected with the colonial forces taking part in the war in South Africa. Appreciation of the loyal and patriotic spirit shown by the people of St. Vincent was again expressed.

At the meeting of the Legislative Council held 7th February, Mr. MacDonald presented an address to His Honour the Administrator on behalf of the members of the Council. The address was expressive of the deep appreciation of His Honour's work and his untiring efforts to improve the condition of St. Vincent during the period of his administration.

After referring to the kindness, courtesy and assistance he had received, His Honour thus concluded: "I thank you for your kind reference to my wife and can assure you that we shall always look back with pleasure to the five years we have spent in St. Vincent which, in spite of the misery and suffering we have had to witness, have been made happy years by the kindness of all classes and the generous manner in which you have now referred to us will be not least pleasant recollection of our stay."

In the *Government Gazette* of 15th February, the Administrator and Mrs. Thompson expressed their great appreciation of the honour that had been done to them by the presentation of an address from the people of St. Vincent, their thanks for the support and consideration they had received during their stay in St. Vincent and the wish for happiness and prosperity to the colony and to every individual in it.

On 27th February the following telegram was despatched by His Excellency to the Right Honourable the Secretary of State:

"People of Windward Islands rejoice over victory of Empire's arms", to which the Secretary of State replied:

"I cordially appreciate assurance of sympathy in the success of Her Majesty the Queen's forces, contained in your telegram of 27th February, sent on behalf of Her Majesty's loyal subjects in the Windward Islands."

22nd March—The St. Vincent Volunteer Rifle Association had its first drill at the police barracks.

1st April—The residential building of the proprietor of Richmond Hill Estate was burned between 4 and 5 a.m. Owing to its position the town was illumined by the flames. The remains of a body, supposed to be that of Mr. William Smith, were found among the ruins.

A special telegram dated 4th April supplied information from a Brussels despatch that a man fired a revolver at the Prince of Wales when leaving the railway station in a train en route to Copenhagen.

With reference to the futile attempt to assassinate the Prince of Wales, congratulations of the Government and people of the Windward Islands were tendered, and the appreciation and thanks of Her Majesty the Queen and Their Royal Highnesses the Prince and Princess of Wales, for the loyal sentiments indicated in His Excellency's despatch of 25th May were conveyed.

16th May—His Lordship Bishop Swaby, who arrived yesterday, was installed in St. George's Cathedral at 11 a.m.

On 19th May the Administrator sent the following telegram to His Excellency:

> ST. VINCENT DESIRES TO OFFER TO HER MAJESTY'S GOVERNMENT HEARTY CONGRATULATIONS ON THE RELIEF OF MAFEKING.

On that day there was great rejoicing on receipt of intelligence of the relief of Mafeking. Flags were hoisted at Fort Charlotte and at almost every house in Kingstown and vicinity. A Royal Salute was fired near the Kingstown jetty whilst the bells of the Cathedral, Methodist Chapel and Roman Catholic Church, joining, pealed forth a merry noise. In the afternoon there was a monster demonstration in Victoria Park by a large procession carrying illuminated mottos and patriotic inscriptions.

On the 22nd May the Administrator received the following reply: "Loyal congratulations on relief of Mafeking from Grenada and St. Vincent highly appreciated."

Mr. C. A. Ollivierre, the St. Vincent representative, left the colony on 25th May to join the West Indian Cricket Team for England. The jetty was thronged with spectators to wish him *bon voyage*. He was presented with a purse, contents of which were contributed by his many friends and well-wishers, also with a congratulatory and encouraging letter. From Barbados he communicated his thanks with the assurance that nothing on his part would be wanting to make his selection satisfactory.

On Tuesday 5th June the long expected news of Lord Roberts' entry into Pretoria was received with wild enthusiasm by all sections and classes of the community. There was an unsurpassed outburst of loyalty and patriotism. Crowds cheered Lord Roberts and the army, others sang patriotic songs, whilst many with flags and banners marched along. The school children of the Anglican, Methodist and Roman Catholic denominations preceded by the Venerable Archdeacon Turpin, Rev. Mr. Darrell and Father Putz, paraded the Town.

Night came only to change the scene and make it more interesting. At the Mission House illuminated pictures were exhibited, and at the windows of Mr. N. B. Cropper, appropriate words, among the many being, One Flag, One Fleet, One Throne.

The procession of "rough riders" on the following day was so attractive and interesting that the entire population of the town and suburbs came out to behold it. There were over 40 horsemen in suitable attire following bicycles tastefully decorated with our national colours. Among the representatives of the leading business houses were Mm. J. G. W. Hazell and J. H. Simmons.

The Rev. A. Moss (MA), son of Mrs. Eliza Moss of this island, who is Vicar of Ladywood, Birmingham, arrived on 12th June on a visit to his relatives. His soul-stirring sermons preached in St. George's Cathedral will ever live in the memory of the numerous hearers who were comprised of every denomination.

Regardless of recognition by the Government, Wednesday 13th June was fixed by the loyal inhabitants as an independent holiday in honour of Lord Roberts' entry into Pretoria.

About 60 "rough riders," the cricketers, porters with hand and donkey carts fitted as for ambulance and the Kingstown Orchestra assembled on Victoria Park. After the formation the band played the National Anthem.

The procession then paraded the town to the inspiring music of the orchestra wending their way through the dense crowd to be met in every street.

The riders proceeded to Calliaqua at which town they were reinforced. The party galloped jubilantly to the Church where the bell pealed forth its pious approbation of the event.

They returned to Kingstown, and after recess proceeded to Government House where three cheers were given for Her Majesty the Queen, the Administrator, Mrs. Drayton and Mr. J. G. W. Hazell, followed by singing of the National Anthem. Returning to Kingstown they assembled opposite the Government buildings where three cheers were given for Lord Roberts after which the singing of the National Anthem brought the jubilant demonstration to a close.

The houses in Kingstown were all appropriately decorated. The Patriotic Concert at the Courthouse at 8 p.m. was in every way a success.

2nd July—A Branch of the Savings Bank was opened at the office of the Assistant Treasurer in Georgetown and one at the office of the Revenue Officer in Chateaubelair.

Upon receipt of intelligence of the assassination of the King of Italy the Administrator forwarded the following telegram to His Excellency the Governor: "St. Vincent has heard with horror of the dastardly crime in Italy. I beg that in your telegram you will include the expression of our sympathy with the Italian Government and Royal Family."

28th July—S.S. *Ocamo* of the Pickford & Black line was the first that called here in pursuance of the new contract.

30th July—His Royal Highness the Duke of Saxe-Coburg and Gotha, Duke of Edinburgh (KG), second son of Her Majesty the Queen, expired at the Castle of Rosenau, near Coburg at 10 o'clock p.m. to the great grief of Her Majesty and of all the Royal Family.

His Honour Edward Drayton, Administrator and President of the Legislative Council submitted an humble address to Her Majesty the Queen on behalf of the inhabitants of the Colony. It contained expression of sorrow at the sudden death of Her Majesty's beloved son, His Royal Highness Prince Alfred, Duke of Edinburgh and of Saxe-Coburg-Gotha, and embodied the following paragraph: "Your Majesty's loss will be deeply sympathised with throughout the Empire, but in no part thereof more warmly than in your West Indian colonies, where the visit of the lamented Prince in 1861 is still remembered with pleasure and affection."

The following telegram was received from the Right Honourable the Secretary of State for the Colonies: "I am commanded by Her Majesty the Queen to thank you and people of Windward Islands for sympathy with Her and Royal Family on death of Duke of Edinburgh."

1st October—Georgetown and Chateaubelair declared ports of entry under the provisions of "The Customs Ordinance 1900".

The following telegrams were despatched and received respectively by His Excellency the Governor:

ON BEHALF OF PEOPLE OF WINDWARD ISLANDS TENDER LOYAL AND HEART-FELT SYMPATHY WITH HER MAJESTY THE QUEEN AND ROYAL FAMILY ON LAMENTABLE DEATH OF PRINCE CHRISTIAN, WHOSE LIFE IT IS FELT IS AN ADDITION TO THE SACRIFICE MADE FOR THE COLONIAL EMPIRE.

HER MAJESTY COMMANDS ME TO CONVEY THANKS TO PEOPLE OF WINDWARD ISLANDS ON BEHALF OF HERSELF AND ROYAL FAMILY FOR KIND EXPRESSION OF SYMPATHY FOR DEATH OF PRINCE CHRISTIAN.

On Monday 29th October, His Excellency Sir Alfred Moloney formally opened the agricultural school. The large and appreciative gathering represented all classes of the community. Lengthy and interesting addresses were delivered, principally by His Excellency Mr. Drayton (the Administrator) and the Rev. J. H. Darrell. The police band was in attendance and there was a guard of honour.

31st December—Commencing at 11.40 p.m., 19 minute guns were fired from Fort Charlotte, while the Church Bells in Kingstown were tolled, to mark the end of the nineteenth century.

A newspaper entitled *St. Vincent Times* was published by Mr. Joseph B. Bonadie. (It is published at the present time.)

1901 / On 23rd January His Honour the Administrator received a telegraphic despatch from the Right Honourable the Secretary of State for the Colonies conveying the mournful intelligence that Her Most Gracious Majesty, Victoria, Queen of Great Britain and Ireland, and Empress of India, expired at Osborne, in the Isle of Wight, at half past six o'clock yesterday afternoon.

The Administrator immediately telegraphed:

THE PEOPLE OF ST. VINCENT BITTERLY LAMENT THE DEATH OF THE BEST
AND GREATEST OF BRITISH SOVEREIGNS. RESPECTFULLY WE TENDER TO
HIS MAJESTY THE KING AND THE ROYAL FAMILY THE ASSURANCE OF OUR
LOYALTY AND DEEP HEARTFELT SYMPATHY.

To which the Right Honourable the Secretary of State for the Colonies replied:

HIS MAJESTY COMMANDS ME TO VERY GRATEFULLY ACKNOWLEDGE ON BEHALF
OF HIMSELF AND THE ROYAL FAMILY KIND MESSAGE OF SYMPATHY ON THE
DEATH OF THE QUEEN AND ASSURANCE OF LOYALTY FROM THE PEOPLE OF
ST. VINCENT.

The orders for general mourning were that all persons were expected to put themselves into deepest mourning from 28th January; that after the 6th day of March, half mourning should be worn until the 17th day of April.

On Saturday 26th, at noon, the accession to the throne of His Majesty, King Edward the Seventh, was proclaimed with the usual formalities at the Courthouse in Kingstown, in the presence of the leading members of the community.

February 2nd, the day for the funeral, was proclaimed for observance in this Colony as a day of mourning and humiliation for the grievous loss sustained by the Nation in the death of Her late Majesty of glorious memory, whose mortal remains were committed to their last resting place at Frogmore near Windsor.

Memorial Services were held in all the churches and chapels of the Colony. In compliance with general directions the officials assembled at the Courthouse at 11 a.m. and proceeded to the Cathedral in the order following:

The Police band (playing a dead march), Chief of Police in command of Police Guard, His Honour the Administrator, His Honour the Chief Justice, Members of Executive and Legislative Councils, Ministers of Religion, Foreign Consuls, Public Officers, Legal and Medical Practitioners, the Kingstown Board, the Freemasons, Representatives of the Press, Merchants, and

Planters, etc. The Foresters, Church of England and other Friendly Societies and Carriages. The places of worship, Courthouse and several business establishments were draped in black for several weeks.

The following telegram from the Secretary of State for the Colonies was published for general information:

HIS MAJESTY COMMANDS ME TO TRANSMIT FOLLOWING MESSAGE TO YOU FOR PUBLICATION:

TO MY PEOPLE BEYOND THE SEAS—THE COUNTLESS MESSAGES OF LOYAL SYM-PATHY WHICH I HAVE RECEIVED FROM EVERY PART OF MY DOMINIONS OVER THE SEAS TESTIFY TO THE UNIVERSAL GRIEF IN WHICH THE WHOLE EMPIRE NOW MOURNS THE LOSS OF MY BELOVED MOTHER. IN THE WELFARE AND PROSPERITY OF HER SUBJECTS THROUGHOUT GREATER BRITAIN THE QUEEN EVER EVINCED A HEARTFELT INTEREST; SHE SAW WITH THANKFULNESS THE STEADY PROGRESS WHICH UNDER A WIDE EXTENSION OF SELF-GOV-ERNMENT THEY HAD MADE DURING HER REIGN; SHE WARMLY APPRECIATED THEIR UNFAILING LOYALTY TO HER THRONE AND PERSON AND WAS PROUD TO THINK OF THOSE WHO HAD SO NOBLY FOUGHT AND DIED FOR THE EMPIRE'S CAUSE IN SOUTH AFRICA. I HAVE ALREADY DECLARED THAT IT WILL BE MY CONSTANT ENDEAVOUR TO FOLLOW THE GREAT EXAMPLE WHICH HAS BEEN BEQUEATHED TO ME. IN THESE ENDEAVOURS I SHALL HAVE A CONFIDENT TRUST IN THE DEVOTION AND SYMPATHY OF THE PEOPLE AND OF THEIR SEVERAL REPRESENTATIVE ASSEMBLIES THROUGHOUT MY VAST COLONIAL DO-MINIONS. WITH SUCH LOYAL SUPPORT I WILL WITH GOD'S BLESSING SOL-EMNLY WORK FOR THE PROMOTION OF THE COMMON WELFARE AND SECURITY OF THE GREAT EMPIRE OVER WHICH I HAVE NOW BEEN CALLED TO REIGN.

(SIGNED) EDWARD R. AND I.

WINDSOR CASTLE

4th FEBRUARY, 1901

In the address to the King's Most Excellent Majesty by the members of the Executive and Legislative Councils on behalf of themselves and the people of this colony, the following paragraph was included:

IN THE MIDST OF OUR SORROW WE DERIVE MUCH CONSOLATION FROM THE KNOWLEDGE THAT THE THRONE HAS PASSED TO A MONARCH WHO IS SO UNI-VERSALLY BELOVED AND HONOURED BY THE NATION. WE MOST HUMBLY AND RESPECTFULLY TENDER OUR CONGRATULATIONS ON YOUR ACCESSION, AND IN ASSURING YOUR MAJESTY OF OUR LOYALTY AND DEVOTION TO YOUR THRONE AND PERSON, WE PRAY THAT A LONG AND PROSPEROUS REIGN AWAITS YOUR MAJESTY, ON WHOM MAY EVERY GOOD GIFT BE BESTOWED BY THE ALMIGHTY.

DATED AT THE COUNCIL CHAMBER

KINGSTOWN, 30th JANUARY, 1901

(SIGNED) EDWARD DRAYTON, ADMINISTRATOR

ORMOND HAZELL, ATTORNEY GENERAL

E. D. LABORDE (ME, LC)

D. A. MACDONALD(ME, LC)

G. ANTON (MLC)

F. C. WELLS DURRANT (MLC)

JAMES H. DARRELL (MLC)

With reference to the address, the Secretary of State for the colonies communicated that he had received His Majesty's commands to convey to the

Executive and Legislative Councils of St. Vincent, and through them to the people of the Island, an expression of his deep gratitude for their sympathy and for the assurance of their loyalty to His Throne and Person.

In an address to His Honour Edward Rawle Drayton, after referring to his administrative skill and industry, the members of the Legislative Council thus concluded, "In bidding you a reluctant farewell we express the sentiments of the entire community that you will shortly receive that promotion in the Service to which the admirable work you have done for St. Vincent eminently entitles you. Our best wishes for the future happiness and prosperity of Mrs. Drayton, yourself and family will follow you wherever you go."

His Honour was deeply touched and gratified by the handsome terms in which the Rev. Mr. Darrell, in the moving address, referred to his administration of the Government, and after expressing regret to leave St. Vincent for whose inhabitants he had inevitably developed a strong attachment, continued to say, "For myself and my wife, to whom you have been kind enough to refer, I may say we will regard our two visits to St. Vincent as white mile-marks on our way through life, to be looked back upon with affectionate remembrance."

At the meeting of the Legislative Council held 24th January, His Honour the Administrator and members of the Council referred to the bitter grief of the whole British nation consequent on the death of beloved Queen Victoria.

The members of the Kingstown Board also gave expression to sincere and dutiful condolences on the sorrowful occasion of the decease of His Majesty's Noble Mother, Her Most Gracious Majesty Queen Victoria. The address was signed by E. D. Laborde, Chairman; J. H. Darrell, David McDowall, John M. Joseph, R. E. Harold, Frank W. Griffith, T. R. Nairn, C. H. Biddy.

Major-General Foord Hilton, who, accompanied by his A.D.C., passed here on 15th February en route to Barbados, inspected the Police Force drawn up in the Barrack Yard and afterward saw the Fire Brigade at practice. He was highly pleased with the manner in which the men went through their drill and the general efficiency they displayed, and subsequently communicated the same to His Honour the Administrator. The press congratulated the Honourable E. D. Laborde and Sergeant-Major Beale.

Mr. W. K. Morrison, bee expert, paid a visit of 14 days' duration, from 30th March, during which time he inspected all parts of the island with a view to inaugurating a bee-keeping industry. He reported there ought to be no difficulties in securing a fair crop of honey in St. Vincent, even by amateur bee-keepers; there are some very fine situations in St. Vincent for large apiaries, where the conditions are very favourable; there is no lack of honey producing plants in St. Vincent and it is only a question of knowledge to get very large yields of honey therefrom.

14th May—His Excellency Sir R. B Llewelyn (KCMG), left the colony; His Hon. E. J. Cameron arrived, and having taken the oaths, assumed aministration of the Government on the 15th.

A consignment of 15 complete moveable comb hives with other necessary bee-keepers' supplies arrived by Schooner *Racer* on 27th June for the Curator, Botanic Station. The industry was then established.

In a circular dated 8th August, the Right Honourable the Secretary of State for the colonies communicated the melancholy intelligence of the death of Her Imperial Majesty the Dowager Empress and Queen Frederick of Germany and Prussia, Princess Royal of Great Britain and Ireland, Sister of His Majesty the King. Her Imperial Majesty expired on the 5th instant to the great grief of His Majesty and of all the Royal Family.

20th August—There was a terrific Southwesterly gale which swept into Kingstown Harbour with disastrous results. The schooner *Racer*, purchased by Mm. John H. Hazell Sons & Co. to replace the *Petrel* which they lost in Hurricane of 1898, was driven firstly against the jetty to which extensive damage was done, and then ashore.

The *Leonora* was beached almost in the Bay Street with little damage.

The *Condor* was tossed about, capsized and ultimately dashed on the shore bottom upward.

The *Hilda*, 135 tons English register, built in Nova Scotia, was trading between this and neighbouring islands for several years. The admired schooner was in docks for eight weeks and after an expenditure of over $800 became a hopeless wreck. It was, however, insured.

Hopes were entertained of the *Flirt* until the *Hilda* was dashed against it. Mr. T. F. Linley, the owner had just sustained a similar misfortune in connection with the *Relief*.

The hull of the *Carib* was slightly damaged and in effecting repairs the sloop was converted into a schooner.

The *Lady Bird* Revenue Cruiser, was driven ashore at Mayreau and became a total wreck. The *Doris* of Carriacou was also destroyed.

D. K. Porter and Co's. wharf and crane were demolished, several of their lighters and the warehouse considerably damaged.

The Town Board was commended for the speedy and effective manner in which the Bay Street was cleared, and the police for their vigilance in preventing plunder.

The gale at Canouan was severe and did much damage to cultivation. On the following day there was an awful thunderstorm, vivid lightning and heavy downpour of rain.

On receipt of intelligence at Trinidad Sir Alfred Moloney telegraphed, "Most anxious to learn extent of damage done. Trust no loss of life. Heartfelt sympathy to all. Can I help?"

The following telegraphic correspondence respecting the attempted assassination of the President of the United States was passed:

```
(SEPT. 7) GOVERNOR TO BRITISH AMBASSADOR, WASHINGTON,
ON BEHALF OF INHABITANTS OF WINDWARD ISLANDS BEG YOU TO TENDER
DEEPEST SORROW AT OUTRAGE AND SINCERE SYMPATHY. EARNESTLY HOPE
FOR RECOVERY.
BRITISH AMBASSADOR, WASHINGTON, TO GOVERNOR,
UNITED STATES GOVERNMENT GRATEFULLY ACKNOWLEDGE YOUR MESSAGE AND
DESIRE ME TO CONVEY TO YOU THEIR HEARTFELT APPRECIATION OF SYMPA-
THY THEREIN CONTAINED. (SEPT. 9)
```

15th October—Miss Rachael Paterson, the first European matron for the colonial hospital, arrived. Not only has the colony benefited by the services of a highly qualified nurse but was somewhat fortunate in the selection of one exemplary in every respect.

On Sunday 3rd November, the Rev. Benjamin Samuel, a native of this island, occupied the pulpit at the Cathedral during evensong and made a pleasing impression on his numerous friends and well-wishers. He left the colony on the 8th to assume his appointment in British Honduras.

Proprietors and others interested in the production of arrowroot held meetings on 13th, 20th and 27th November to discuss the position of the industry and to endeavour to arrive at the best means to ensure remunerative prices. It was agreed that the shipments be curtailed and a minimum price fixed.

This being the first celebration of the Christmas Festival during the present reign, it was deemed opportune to further express good wishes of the people of St. Vincent toward Their Majesties the King and Queen. The following was transmitted for publication on the morning of 25th December:

```
SENTRY, ST. VINCENT, TO DAILY TELEGRAPH, LONDON,
A GOLDEN SUNSHINE ILLUMINES THE CHRISTMAS MORN. DEVOUT RELIGIOUS
CELEBRATIONS. SPECIAL DINNERS PROVIDED FOR POOR AND INFIRM. IN
LOYAL DEVOTION WE TENDER OUR NOBLE KING AND QUEEN CONGRATULATIONS
ON THIS THE FIRST CHRISTMAS OF THE REIGN; REJOICING TO FORM PART
OF THE GREAT BRITISH EMPIRE OVER WHICH WE TRUST THEY WILL LIVE
LONG TO RULE.
```

1902 / Private contributions from St. Vincent to the National Memorial to Queen Victoria amounted to £15 4 8.

The following telegrams were transmitted between the Right Honourable the Secretary of State for the Colonies and His Excellency the Governor early in the month of March:

85

Contributions from St. Vincent to the fund for the women's memorial to Queen Victoria amounted to £18 5 6.

All other local events of the memorable year 1902 fade into comparative insignificance in view of the great eruption of the Soufriere on the 7th of May in that year. This phenomenon, which coupled with an almost simultaneous outburst of Montagne Pelee, Martinique, and which seem to evoke sympathetic action in every other volcano, attracted to St. Vincent the attention of the civilized world and created matter for the investigation and study of the greatest scientists in Europe and America. Although the pages of history record an eruption of the Soufriere in 1812 giving evidence of the possibility of another volcanic catastrophe someday overtaking the island, yet this generation had seen nothing but beauty and loveliness in the pearly-green sheet of placid water which perpetually lay in a crater whose natural adornments not even the most phlegmatic beholder could fail to admire, and not even the most enthusiastic writer could satisfactorily describe; a picture which no artist's brush could effectively depict. The Soufriere was regarded by natives as well as by visitors as the grandest dowry of St. Vincent—the most beautiful sight in the West Indies. No one cherished the slightest suspicions of evil lurking under the serene water of the crater, and notwithstanding numerous earth tremors in 1901 and anon in early months of 1902, no happier bands of holiday-makers ever gathered on the summit of the Soufriere than those which spent the Easter Holiday of 1902 there and noticed the uncommon beauty of the crater, with its rapidly changing surface rivalling the beauty of the rainbow, and sometimes covered with a sheet of loam, as if the volcano had even then been in a quiet state of ebullition.

About a fortnight prior to the eruption of the 7th May, the people of the Leeward villages adjacent to the mountain were alarmed by the frequency and increasing severity of earthquakes, and on the 7th May these premonitions were accompanied by subterranean noises and grumblings like distant thunder. The inhabitants, then being alarmed by the awful news which arrived from Martinique on the 3rd relating to the eruption of Mount Pelee and the destruction of the plantation Guerin and loss of many lives, could no longer regard the indications of local volcanic activity with indifference.

Terrified by the severity of the shocks at Morne Ronde, the Caribs fled to Chateaubelair for safety. By 1 o'clock on the afternoon of the 6th there could be no doubt that the Soufriere was in eruption, as from then clouds of steam

86

could be seen at Chateaubelair and Wallibou issuing at unequal intervals from the old crater; and the shocks became more conspicuously connected with the mountain, as they were only experienced in that neighbourhood. The people of the Windward districts—from a point of view where the upper parts of the mountain were obscured by thick trade wind clouds—were in blissful ignorance of what was being witnessed by the Leeward residents, and even in Kingstown the citizens were more concerned with the fate of fellow colonists in Martinique than with the behaviour of our own volcano—not dreaming that on the morrow 2,000 souls would be swept into eternity by the deadly emission of the erupting Soufriere. The best record of the progress of the eruption is contained in the notes written by an eyewitness, Mr. T. M. Mac-Donald, who viewed the crater from the dwelling house at Richmond Vale from 6 p.m. on the 6th until he was obliged to flee for his life to Chateaubelair at 2 p.m. on the day of the great eruption. His notes were published in the *Sentry* of 16th May and reproduced from the local paper in the report on the Eruptions of the Soufriere and Mount Pelee by Dr. Tempest Anderson (MD, BSC, FGS), and Dr. John S. Flett (MA, DSC, FRSE).

After recording minor discharges and incidents indicating the activity of the volcano, Mr. MacDonald tells what occurred between 7:30 p.m. on the 6th and 6 p.m. on the 7th when the volcano had completed its terrible work of destruction of life and property, and reduced the Carib country—the verdant fields of which demonstrated the agricultural wealth of the island—into a vast graveyard in which 2,000 bodies were buried under banks, nay, even hills of ejectamenta. Mr. MacDonald's account, in part, runs thus:

> At about 6.30 p.m. (6th) a greater discharge of vapour took place, with flame along the whole rim of the crater, forming a red, sparkling line between base of column of vapour and rim of crater, accompanied by a loud noise. At intervals of about two hours during the night similar discharges to the preceding took place, and at midnight flames were seen from Chateaubelair round the rim of the crater.

> No further observation was noted at Richmond Vale House till shortly after 6 a.m. on the 7th, when a discharge took place with the usual column of thick vapour, but beneath this was a much shorter column of almost dense black, and of a heavier nature, as it quickly subsided back into the crater. This was the first appearance noted of what was probably solid matter being erupted, the white vapour being no doubt vapour of water only. At about 7.40 a.m. an enormous high column of white vapour was ejected, and it may be here mentioned that these tall columns rose in a very short space of time—say, about a minute—to heights of about 30,000 feet and over, by comparison seven or eight times the height of the mountain (nearly 4,000 feet). Outburst took place now at shorter intervals, and at about 10:30 a.m.

the eruption became continuous, enormous volumes of vapour reaching to a very great height.

11:10 a.m.—At this time there was thunder and lightning, showers of black and heavy material could now be seen thrown outwards and falling downwards from the column of whitish vapour, associated with loud noises and more violent outburst. From the commencement the Old Crater seemed to be the scene of activity, but at times it seemed as though some of the discharges proceeded from what is known as the New Crater, a little northeastward from Chateaubelair. The area of the escape of vapour seemed now to be extending in a direction corresponding with Morne Ronde (westward).

11:15 a.m.—Thunder and lightning still continuing, and associated each time with a more violent outburst from crater.

11:35 a.m.—Discharge still violent, and Old Crater apparently the great centre of activity, enormous volumes ascending in curling and whirling waves, those beneath forcing those above higher and still higher; the colour of the vapour now assuming a darker shade—white changing to light grey, and low, rumbling noises audible.

11.40 a.m.—The edge of the Old Crater was quite distinct, but was belching out over the whole area. Flash and peal were continuous. The contour of the whole mountain was unaltered, and vegetation still remained fresh and green, with one enormous pillar of vapour overhead.

12:25 p.m.—Small vents seemed to be formed on slopes near old road facing Richmond Vale, and jets of vapour emitted from them; then a more violent outburst, which seemed to be extending the crater westward, with dense black upheavals and rumblings.

12:35 p.m.—It seemed as if slope to left of old road up Soufriere had formed into fissure, as vapour was issued from small vents, and at 12:40 p.m. these fissures were unmistakable, and discharges from crater were extended to Windward.

12:50 p.m.—Enormous outburst through vent or front of mountain; as far as could be ascertained, the mountain being largely enveloped in vapour, etc.

1 p.m.—There was tremendous roaring, stones being thrown out to Windward thousands of feet high.

1:15 p.m.—Activity seemed shifting to Windward and Wallibu River Valley direction, the eruption continuing unabated in violence.

1:25 p.m.— Still further extensions of activity in the direction of Wallibu River and Morne Garn to right of old road.

1:30 p.m.—Violent action to right, with heavy falls of streams of fine matter and black stones.

1:32 p.m.—Violent to left also, with showers of blackish material. A minute afterwards volumes of vapour covered the whole area.

1:50 p.m.—There was a black outburst to right, and showers of large and small stones shot eastward and downwards with tails of fine, black matter following. These stones issuing from interior of enormous column of vapour, thousands of feet above the mountain. Some large stones were also seen falling from thousands of feet up on face of column to westward, and some were also seen falling from Windward side.

1:55 p.m.—Rumbling. Large black outburst with showers of stones all to Windward, and enormously increased activity over the whole area. A terrific huge purplish and reddish curtain advancing up to and over Richmond Estate. At this stage left Richmond Vale House and hurried into and pushed off boat a few minutes after 2 p.m. Saw vapour as we rowed hard across Chateaubelair Bay, coming down to sea level past Richmond Point. Sea peppered all round with stones, one of which, about a cubic inch, fell inside the boat in which were 11 persons. The huge curtain referred to was advancing after the racing boat, which never seemed likely to get out of range of it or the falling stones, which latter varied from the size of one's fist downward. All in the boat felt that their end was near, and someone cried out, 'We are all done for—head for shore!' This was done, and the boat beached between Petit Bordel and Rosebank. Got on to public road, where streams of people were hurrying along, all anxious to get to some place of safety. The lightning and thunder at this time was terrific, and there were noises inland. Everything seemed to point to a general break-up both on land and on sea. Fortunately, the writer found a stray horse at Rosebank, which he mounted without a saddle and rode slowly along after the rest of the party. On reaching Troumaca Hill the bulk of the party refused to face the descent into the ravine, fearing darkness seen advancing from eastward.

Small stones were coming down all the time in a continuous shower, and Troumaca stream was thick from ashes. At Cumberland a saddle was obtained, and the journey to Wallilabou continued in bodily comfort. Reached the last-named place about 6 p.m. and found everything covered with dust from the eruption nearly one-eighth of an inch thick, and small stones had also reached there.

From Kingstown the volcanic clouds rising and spreading in awful majesty toward the zenith, were witnessed with mixed feelings of fear and admiration of this stupendous work of nature whilst the roaring, rumbling, cannonading noise of the angry elements added to the grand solemnity of the scene. It was about 11 a.m. when the signs of the eruption were clearly visible in town, and as the day proceeded the activity rapidly increased until the awe-inspiring cloud of ashes and scoria had spread over the whole island, obscuring the light of the sun and necessitating the lighting of lamps at 4 p.m. A boating party left Kingstown in the course of the day with the intention of proceeding to a point enabling them to view the erupting volcano. They had a narrow escape from the fringe of the terrible black cloud which was emitted *at the climax of the eruption and which destroyed everything in its track on both sides of the mountain.*

The following graphic description of that cloud is from the pen of the late Rev. J. H. Darrell who was one of the party:

We were rapidly proceeding to our destination when an immense cloud, dark, dense and apparently thick with volcanic material, descended over our pathway, impeding our progress and warning us to proceed no further. This mighty bank of sulphurous vapour and smoke assumed at one time the shape of a gigantic promontory, then a collection of twirling, revolving cloud-whorls, turning with rapid velocity, now assuming the shape of gigantic cauliflowers, then efflorescing into beautiful flower shapes some dark, some effulgent, some bronze, others pearly white, and all brilliantly illumined by electric flashes. Darkness, however, soon fell upon us. The sulphurous air was laden with fine dust that fell thickly upon and around us discolouring the sea; a black rain began to fall, followed by another rain of favilla, lapilli, and scoriae. The electric flashes were marvellously rapid in their motions, and numerous beyond all computation. These, with the thundering noise of the mountain, mingled with the dismal roar of the lava, the shocks of earthquake, the falling of stones, the enormous quantity of material ejected from the belching craters, producing a darkness as dense as a starless night, together with the plutonic energy of the mountain, growing greater and greater every moment, combined to make up a scene of horrors.

The late Dr. Christian Branch, who was in the same boat, was similarly impressed and thus described the scene:

The island to the north of us and northeast was now covered with a mighty black pall of smoke, perhaps two miles deep, and the smoke column was now a vast shapeless blackness. Then began the most gorgeous display of lightning we could conceive. All around us and above, so near, that several times I saw it between us and the cliffs not 200 yards off. It was still bright daylight with us, but the whole atmosphere quivered and shimmered with wavy lines intersecting each other like trellis work. We were encircled in a bristling ring of fiery bayonets. It was too stupendous to terrify; one could only marvel and feel nervous. A few stones plumped in the sea around us, and then fell pretty thickly. There were light pebbles for the most part, and only these fell in the boat. A nasty shower of mud followed the lightning, and then a long shower of gritty sand. After this, a fog of fine dust descended, and it got darker and darker, until we could with great difficulty see the shore and points along which we steered.

The fall of dust and pumice stone began in Kingstown at 2 p.m. and the panic created by the eruption was increased by this phenomenon. The uneducated quaked with fear; and with regard to many whose knowledge of history permitted it, the fate of ancient Pompei came before them and terrifying thoughts of a repetition of history haunted the mind. Doors and windows had to be closed. Hardly a living object was now seen on the mud-covered

90

streets, and these circumstances coupled with the thick darkness accompanied by the dismal roar of crater and thunder created an experience which can only be felt, not described. But in the next two hours the fall of dust abated and with the clearing atmosphere hearts became lighter and persons again ventured out in search of news of the out districts.

On the return of the adventurous boating party to Kingstown at 5:30 that evening, they were greeted at the landing place by a crowd representing all classes, eager to learn something of the Leeward district, for long ere then telephonic communication with Chateaubelair had been cut off; and these were men who had come from the scene of the great catastrophe. The story of their providential escape and of the appalling spectacle they had witnessed was profoundly interesting, but it intensified the citizens' concern with respect to the fate of those who were living within the zone of the crater's deadly blasts.

On the northern and eastern sides of the volcano, the premonitions of danger were not observed on the previous day and the settlers on the Carib Country Estates were not aware of the seriousness of the volcanic disturbance until the very Wednesday morning when the rumour reached Georgetown from Chateaubelair relating to the terrifying activity of the mountain, and when the rumbling sounds and flashes which hitherto had been mistaken for mere thunder and lightning, followed by earth tremors increasing alike in their duration and severity, struck the people with deepest anxiety and apprehension. Their fears of approaching danger were confirmed at about 10 a.m. when direct news from eye-witnesses told of the appalling activity of the Soufriere. But then the eruption developed with such rapidity as to render the flight of those who resided on the estates practically adjacent to the mountain, an impossibility.

The report of Drs. Anderson and J. S. Flett, who gathered their information two months after the catastrophe—when the terrible excitement was over and when statements of facts and personal experiences were obtainable from survivors—contains the following intensely interesting record:

> In the Carib Country, work in the fields had stopped, and in the sugar works—though they were full of people—no sugar making was going on. Everyone was watching the progress of the eruption in mingled fear and admiration. Small stones began to fall after mid-day, and about half past one in some places there were showers of hot scalding mud. The cattle, horses and mules were mostly out grazing, but nearly all the people had gathered into the more substantial buildings, the managers' houses or the stores and cellars attached to the sugar works, though many were in their huts in the villages adjoining the estates. Some had been struck with falling stones, but as yet probably no one was killed, and but few injured.
>
> Then, with a loud roar at 2 o'clock, the great convulsion came. Those who were in the open air saw the huge black cloud rolling down the moun-

tain in globular, surging masses. They fled into the houses and shut the doors. Onward it rushed with a loud rumbling noise and filled with lightnings. Any who were in the open air perished at once. Many of the Negroes' huts were so densely crowded with people, that there was hardly standing room. At Lot 14 the manager and his wife and family had shut themselves up in rum cellar below the house, and firmly closed all doors and windows. They had a terrible experience, but they survived. All of those in the house itself or in the Negro village were killed. It will be understood that as the tropical houses are so built as to secure free entrance of air, it is almost impossible to close them up securely, and the suffocating blast reached the interior and stifled all who were there. All the animals in the fields also perished.

At Rabaka (sic) many who were prevented from fleeing to Georgetown by the floods of hot water in the river had gathered in the manager's house. In one large room there were fifty people. When they saw the dark cloud coming, they firmly shut all the windows—fortunately they were substantial and well glazed and everyone in this room was saved. They felt the heat most intense. It was quite dry, and there was a very strong and irritating odour of sulphur. Some fainted, but all survived. The overseer told us that from the window he saw the black cloud rolling on towards them; when it reached the house there was darkness, and a sharp fall of stones on the roof. The cloud rolled down upon the sea below the house, and when it struck the water, it was 'filled with fire'.

It seemed then to rebound from the surface of the sea and return towards the building, and at this time the wall of a ruined sugar store was knocked down, probably by lightning, as nothing else was overturned. It was when the cloud returned from the sea that the suffocating feeling was experienced. Perhaps this was because it took a little time for the noxious gases to penetrate to the interior of the house. Practically all who were in the Negroes' huts or in the open air perished.

At Orange Hill there was a large substantial stone-built rum cellar, which, by the orders of the manager, was left open to afford a refuge for any who wished to avail themselves of it. About seventy crowded together there. The windows were not shut, but they were small and faced the sea, so that the blast did not directly strike them. One man stood by the door holding it ajar, to admit any who fled from the huts in the village. Forty were in the cellar, and all were saved. Thirty were in the passage leading into the cellar, and they were all killed. None of those survived who remained in the labourers' huts, or were fleeing to and fro about the yard in abject terror. Many shut themselves up in a store with a galvanized iron roof. All died, and were found buried in sand with the roof collapsed and fallen upon them. In the under storey of the manager's house thirty people died. The manager himself, Mr. Fraser, was found dead on his verandah; his wife's body was lying at the foot of the steps leading up to it. They seem to have been overcome as they were returning from the cellar where they had at first taken refuge. We were told that Mr. Fraser complained that the densely packed crowd of Negroes made the atmosphere unbearable, and returned to his house to get some fresh air.

At Turema, the fatal cloud did its deadly work quite as effectively. All who were in the manager's house, estimated to number thirty-five, were killed. One woman survived for three days, and was found by the first search parties who went out from Georgetown. She begged for water to drink; they gave her some, and returned to make arrangements to have her taken to the relief hospital, where she died shortly after her arrival. In the 'Great House,' or Mansion House, four were killed in the kitchen, where the windows and doors had not been effectively closed; two shut themselves up in another room, closing all apertures as thoroughly as possible, and they survived. All who were in the villages or fields perished, without exception.

In Overland village the loss of life was terrible; hundreds were killed. In one small shop by the roadside, in a room perhaps 15 feet square, eighty-seven bodies were found. When we saw this place the ash around was dotted with little hummocks, under each of which lay a heap of bodies, but everything was decently interred, and contrasted strongly with the charnel heaps of bleaching skeletons we saw later on in St. Pierre. One man whom we interviewed had lived in this village; in his house seven died, but four or five survived. When they saw the black cloud coming down, they shut up all doors and windows as tightly as possible. As the hot cloud approached, it was red at first, but changed into black before it passed overhead; the heat was dreadful, and the lightnings very vivid. The air smelt very strongly of sulphur, and their throats were dry and parched. Some burst into spasmodic coughing from the irritant sulphurous acid and fine dust in the air. Many cried out for water, but in a few seconds the suffocating feeling prevented articulation. Then several threw up their hands and fell dead. Others collapsed, but lingered in some cases for an hour or more. Those who survived state that in a few seconds it would have been all over with them. But the air began to clear, there was a slight breeze off the sea, and the windows on that side were thrown open, and, with a sense of great thankfulness, they inhaled again deep breaths of cold pure air. Here, as at Rabaka, those who were watching the cloud state that as it struck the surface of the sea it flashed with fire. One man showed us where the back of his fore-arms had been severely burned by hot mud or ash which came down with the black cloud. The parts of his body covered by clothes were protected, but his shirt sleeves were rolled up, and his arms below the elbows were bare.

At Orange Hill, Turema, and Lot 14, there were large herds of cattle, horses, and mules. Every animal on these estates perished. Some were suffocated or burnt extensively; others had apparently been struck by lightning. They were all in the fields or in open pens, and not one survived. It does not appear, however, that before the great outburst, which took place at 2 o'clock, they had shown any peculiar restlessness, as if they were aware of the impending doom. At Windsor Forest the cattle had that forenoon been in a state of trepidation, and had fled to the shore, where they ran up and down, bellow-

93

ing loudly. Probably this was because earth tremors and subterraneous noises were more common and more pronounced there than in the Carib Country.

At Wallibu, about 12 o'clock, there was a loud sharp noise accompanying an outburst of steam, and the earth shook. The house dogs ran out into the open air howling with terror. On the Windward estates, however, it seems that the dogs remained at the houses and hid themselves, but did not run away or endeavour to escape.

Over the northern shore of the island, the dark cloud descended also, but there its velocity was less, and the devastation it produced much less considerable than in the valleys on the south of the mountain.

Thus, at Fancy and Owia the loss of life and property was considerably less than in other Estates in that District. Many of the deaths there were supposed to be caused by lightning.

All the facts relating to this eruption including scientific opinion clearly demonstrate that although the estimated loss of life in St. Vincent was 2,000 compared with 40,000 at Martinique, yet the eruption of the Soufriere was quite as violent as, if not more than, that of Mount Pelee; for, had St. Pierre been situated at Wallibou, its destruction would have been just as complete.

The profound sympathy of the neighbouring colonies and the American Government was evinced by the abundance of foodstuffs, clothing and other requisites which came as timely relief for the intense sufferings, resulting from widespread bereavements and from bodily injuries which many received from falling stones, or among those who survived the electric shocks and burns from the hot ash which fell in the neighbourhood of the volcano.

10th May—His Excellency Sir R. B. Llewelyn arrived from St. Lucia on H.M.S. *Indefatigable*. The ship brought a large quantity of supplies from Trinidad.

The coasting steamer *Wear* arrived on the 11th from St. Lucia with water etc., the *Taw* from Grenada, on the 13th, conveyed Dr. Orford with appliances for medical aid. The R.M.S. *Esk* from Barbados on the same day brought similar relief; five men of the Royal Army Medical Corps with Major Wills in command also arrived. The American steam boat *Potomac* and subsequently the U.S.S. *Dixie* arrived on their missions of charity. On the whole, the spontaneity with which friends and kindred from all parts showed their tangible sympathy elicited the lasting gratitude of the people. The Mansion House Fund rose rapidly to £42,000 in a fortnight after the catastrophe and continued to rise by leaps and bounds until it was closed at £59,669 17 3.

Minor eruptions of the crater and in the Wallibou River continued at near intervals for months after the great outburst of 7th May. Some of these were witnessed by Dr. P. A. Jagger, of Harvard University and U.S. Geological Survey, Cambridge, Mass., U.S.A., who, with two colleagues, Dr. E. O. Hovey, American University of Natural History of New York, and Mr. G. C. Curtis,

U.S. Geological Survey of Boston, were the first party of scientists to visit the crater after the eruption, they having made a successful ascent of the mountain on the 31st May. Their experience and observations were reported in the *Sentry* of 6th June in which issue also appeared a map of the island after the eruption, a crippled landscape showing the devastated area with remarks thereon by a local contributor. On June 10th Drs. Tempest Anderson and John S. Flett arrived and as a result of their visit and very careful investigation, their very exhaustive and interesting report has been published, and is available. Among the great benefits the inhabitants received from the visits of these American and English scientists, respectively, was the complacency of mind which resulted from the assurance that persons residing outside the volcanic zone, which did not extend as far as Georgetown or Chateaubelair, were not in immediate danger of any eruption of the Soufriere. Hence later ejections of steam clouds and even sand became less alarming and the inhabitants were better able to admire these grand demonstrations of nature.

But on the night of the 3rd September, the Soufriere again assumed a condition which brought terror to the stoutest hearts. Fortunately, it was unattended by fatality, but the *Sentry* of 5th September, in its leading article, thus gives eloquent expression to the emotion which every beholder of the awfully magnificent phenomenon felt:

> *The lurid shimmer that lit up earth and sea and sky as the molten mass in the crater rose higher and yet higher forced up by the exploding steam far down beneath, ever nearer and nearer to the lip of the crater, the reflection of which was like the fires of hell; the twining serpent-like flashes that darted hither and thither athwart the trembling sky, and anon flashed nearer and nearer to the panic-stricken city of Kingstown with such a wild and terrible irresponsibility in their flight as to raise the worst fears in all hearts as the power of the monster threw up white hot masses of matter that ignited the air in their flight as does a meteor; the globular bursting masses of flame that seemed to rend the very heavens, caused doubtless, by the ignition of the sulphurous gas-laden clouds by the burning matter hurled up by the volcano; the accompaniment afforded by the roar of the mountain like the thunderous roll of miles of surf, ever broken by a dire bubbling as of the thousand cauldrons of some fell Walpurgisnacht; all this made up a scene which one can only feel, not describe. Many were the fears openly expressed as the black cloud of smoke (continuously embroidered, alas, with flame) rose further and further, enwrapping more and more of the heavens in its velvety grasp till it rested like an awful pall on the city, that it would descend until those beneath perished by the dioxidisation of the air, or more miserable, were consumed by*

the bursting masses of sulphurous flame. But it mercifully grew less and less dense until it faded away altogether in the direction of the volcano.

In its detailed account of the phenomenon the *Sentry* of the same date gives publicity to the following impressions of a valued correspondent who viewed the scene from Belair:

From this elevation we were enabled distinctly to observe the movements in the locality of each of the electric displays en evidence *for by midnight it was plainly discernible that detonations and their accompanying flashes of light were proceeding from two distinct centres—one northeast of our position well marked since the eruption of May 7th as 'La Soufriere', the other due north at a point in the direction of Martinique. Thus were we face to face with the awful sublimity of a scene in which two volcanoes were involved, and each participating. Anticipatory of evils undefined and yet to come, we weary watchers gazed upon the monotony of flash and report until 1:30 a.m., when the spasmodic and convulsive character of the expulsions betokened a change. A change for that never-to- be-forgotten roar of continuous retching, wrenching sound as if with mighty effort the giant strove to disgorge himself. By 2 a.m. all sounds were blended into this one prolonged methodical out-pouring roar; immense in its intensity as of a huge Niagara.*

On a background of black cloud, the lightnings reflecting, played, be-traying in their positions the electric evolution of each volcano. Upon this sable screen may (Gustav) Doré have found depicted copy enough to have produced all the lurid effect for a picture of the last day. *Crowding on and creeping around the scene from N. to E. circled a deep black pall pregnant, perhaps, with sufficient "mephitic gases" to annihilate a population, the course of this deadly cloud was watched by us with jealous care, its spreading movements effectively discerned by the natural "search lights" all at hand, while we kept the naked light of a candle close in readiness to determine by its flicker the faintest approach of the deadly carbonic.*

After an hour and at about 3 a.m. the sounds became less methodical, and more of the nature of explosions and louder in the direction of Martinique, (here again we were able to prove the relative positions of the eruptions). This change provoked an increase in the grandeur of this appalling spectacle. Lurid meteors shot in showery sprays over the hillsides and in the intervals between the stunning thunder peels one was sensible of the crisp crackle of electricity tingling to the fingertips the nerves at high tension. The labourers in overwhelming fear deserted their thatched cottages and came trooping into the yard, huddling down under the galleries for cover. The howling of the village dogs and the lowing of the cattle in pens, evinced the effect on even the poor beast.

On occasion when the lightning present was pictured in one upsurging wave of flames, men realized how slight are the limitations between time and eternity. All this I have endeavoured to portray, no language however magnificent or exalted by metaphor and poetical fervour could ever present in its proper terrors to the mind.

His Excellency the Governor received and transmitted the undermentioned telegrams:

FROM THE RIGHT HONOURABLE J. CHAMBERLAIN, M.P.
SECRETARY OF STATE FOR THE COLONIES,
I AM COMMANDED BY HIS MAJESTY THE KING TO EXPRESS HIS DEEP REGRET
AT THE CALAMITY WHICH HAS BEFALLEN THE ISLAND OF ST. VINCENT AND
HIS SYMPATHY WITH THE SUFFERERS AND THE BEREAVED IN THAT COLONY.

TO THE SECRETARY OF STATE FOR THE COLONIES,
THE GRACIOUS MESSAGE FROM HIS MAJESTY THE KING HAS BEEN COMMU-
NICATED TO THE PEOPLE OF ST. VINCENT BY ME AND TO THE SUFFERERS
IN HOSPITAL. ALL CLASSES DEEPLY TOUCHED BY KIND SYMPATHY OF HIS
MAJESTY THE KING.

Countless messages of sympathy, telegraphic and otherwise, were received from various parts of the civilized world, and the generous contribution which amounted approximately to £75,000 marked the sincerity of the expressions.

Tents were pitched in the Hospital grounds and a special ward deputed to the injured. The late Dr. C. W. Branch, Medical Officer in charge of the colonial hospital, ably coped with the increased duties devolved upon him. The members of the hospital staff, including those who were detailed for duty at Georgetown, creditably administered to the sufferers.

The following are extracts from a despatch of the Right Honourable the Secretary of State for the Colonies to His Excellency the Governor:

...TO MAJOR WILLS, TO DOCTORS HUTSON, BOWEN, ORFORD AS WELL AS
TO DOCTOR DURRANT AND NURSE PATTERSON, THE THANKS OF THE COLONY
ARE DUE FOR THEIR EFFORTS TO RELIEVE THE INJURIES AND SUFFERING
CAUSED BY THE ERUPTION; AND I GLADLY APPROVE THE GRATUITIES WHICH
YOU PROPOSE TO GIVE TO DOCTORS HUTSON AND BOWEN....
...YOUR DESPATCH NO. 89 OF THE 18th OF JULY, GIVES A REPORT OF
THE WORK DONE BY THE LADIES' RELIEF COMMITTEE IN THE MATTER OF
CLOTHING, BANDAGES, ETC., AND I WILL ASK YOU TO CONVEY TO LADY
LLEWELYN AND THE LADIES WHO WORKED WITH HER MY APPRECIATION OF
THEIR ADMIRABLE EFFORTS FOR THE RELIEF OF SUFFERING AND DISTRESS.

A public meeting was held at the Court House on 15th October at which interesting speeches were made. There was scarcely standing room in the building. Among other things a protest was unanimously adopted against the compulsory emigration scheme contained in the Governor's Minute; and an appeal for the appointment of an officer to execute the commission which Mr. Ashmore was selected to fulfil.

Captain Arthur Young (CMG), Chief Secretary of Cyprus who was select-ed to deal with relief work rendered necessary by the eruptions, arrived on the 12th November. Himself and his Clerk, Mr. C. N. Rice, attended to the arduous task from early in the morn until late at nights. The efficient manner in which he discharged the difficult duties evoked favourable comments generally and in the press. His recommendations were adopted and that for the revision of the system of land tax has resulted in a substantial increase to the colony's revenue.

The Right Honourable the Secretary of State for the colonies noted with pleasure Captain Young's testimony to the good work done by the Administrator and by Mm. Kernahan, Powell, Rice, and Preston.

A largely attended public meeting was held at the Court House on 6th March to discuss the proposed abolition of the office of Chief Justice, and on 14th a deputation of influential gentlemen presented the resolution protesting against any scheme to that effect or tending to lower the status of the colony. Consequent on the communication from His Excellency the Governor, another representative meeting was held on 5th April when further resolutions were adopted.

At a meeting of the Legislative Council held 29th April, His Excellency Sir R. B. Llewelyn formally announced the death at St. Lucia on the 28th of Sir Harry Thompson (KC, MG). The following resolution was thereupon moved and seconded by the Honourables D. A. MacDonald and Conrad J. Simmons respectively:

> *Resolved—That this Council having heard with deep regret of the death of Sir Harry Thompson, a former Administrator of the Colony, wishes to place on record its high appreciation of his qualities both in public and private life, and its recognition of the good work he did, and to convey to Lady Thompson its sincere and deep sympathy and that also of the community with her in her great loss, and to assure her that Sir Harry Thompson will long be remembered here as a good, honest and upright man who did his duty to the Government and to his fellow men.*

The following telegrams were respectively transmitted to and received from Lady Thompson:

ST. VINCENT'S PEOPLE TENDER DEEPEST SYMPATHY IN YOUR BITTER BE-
REAVEMENT—GOD COMFORT YOU
MY HEARTFELT THANKS TO YOU AND PEOPLE OF ST. VINCENT IN MY TER-
RIBLE GRIEF.

A Memorial service was held at the Cathedral on Tuesday afternoon 29th. The places of business were closed in time to enable the employees to attend. The officiating ministers were the Venerable E. A. Turpin and the Rev. G. Paterson. There were present His Excellency Sir R. B. Llewelyn and family, His Honour E. J. Cameron, the officials, the police and a large congregation.

Despite the extreme suffering and grief prevalent in the colony elaborate preparations were made for the observance, on the 26th and 27th June, of the coronation of Their Majesties the King and Queen. The sorrowful intelligence of His Majesty's illness was another pang to the hearts of a truly loyal people whose anguish was already intense.

Owing to an interruption in the cable, a telegram was received from His Excellency the Governor about 7:30 a.m. by sailing boat from St. Lucia, as follows:

> IT IS WITH THE DEEPEST REGRET THAT I HAVE TO INFORM YOU THAT I HAVE RECEIVED THIS MORNING THE FOLLOWING OFFICIAL INFORMATION: THE KING IS SUFFERING FROM PERITYPHLITIS. HIS CONDITION ON SATURDAY WAS SO SATISFACTORY THAT IT WAS HOPED THAT WITH CARE HIS MAJESTY WOULD BE ABLE TO GO THROUGH THE CORONATION CEREMONY, BUT ON MONDAY EVENING A RECRUDESCENCE BECAME MANIFEST, RENDERING A SURGICAL OPERATION NECESSARY TODAY. THE CORONATION CEREMONY IS THEREFORE POSTPONED.

Instead of the proposed Thanksgiving Service, prayers of intercession were offered in the different churches, and the day was devoted to solemn supplication. At the Cathedral an appropriate and impressive sermon was preached by the Rev. D. Duffus, Rector of the Grenadines, from verse 1, Psalm LI.

Consequent on the anxiety experienced on the occasion of the serious illness of His Majesty the King the following telegraphic correspondence was entered into:

> ADMINISTRATOR, ST. VINCENT, TO GOVERNOR. SENT 26th JUNE,
> ST. VINCENT HAS HEARD WITH PROFOUND SORROW THE PAINFUL INTELLIGENCE OF THE ILLNESS OF HIS MAJESTY THE KING, AND DESIRES TO BE ASSOCIATED WITH ANY EXPRESSION OF REGRET BEING SENT FROM THE WIND-WARD ISLANDS.

> SECRETARY OF STATE FOR THE COLONIES TO GOVERNOR. RECEIVED 26th JUNE:
> REFERRING TO MY TELEGRAM OF THE 24th JUNE OPERATION ON HIS MAJESTY THE KING SUCCESSFULLY PERFORMED AND THIS MORNING'S BULLETIN STATES THAT CONSIDERING ALL THE CIRCUMSTANCES HE IS PROGRESSING FAVOURABLY.
> ALL THE CORONATION FESTIVITIES IN LONDON HAVE BEEN ABANDONED EXCEPT THE KING'S DINNER TO THE POOR AND OTHER CHARITABLE ENTERTAINMENTS; YOU SHOULD ADOPT SIMILAR COURSE.

> GOVERNOR TO THE SECRETARY OF STATE FOR THE COLONIES 28th JUNE:
> YOUR TELEGRAMS OF THE 23rd AND 24th JUNE RECEIVED THE 26th JUNE CONVEYING INTELLIGENCE OF SERIOUS ILLNESS OF HIS MAJESTY THE KING. DEEPEST SORROW FELT THROUGHOUT WINDWARD ISLANDS WHICH I BEG MAY BE COMMUNICATED TO THE MEMBERS OF THE ROYAL FAMILY. FESTIVI-

TIES STOPPED AS FAR AS POSSIBLE BUT OWING TO BREAK IN CABLE AND
DELAY IN TRANSMISSION THIS WAS ONLY PARTIALLY PRACTICABLE.

SECRETARY OF STATE FOR COLONIES TO GOVERNOR. RECEIVED 29th JUNE:
REFERRING TO MY TELEGRAM OF THE 25th JUNE, BULLETIN THIS MORN-
ING STATES THAT HIS MAJESTY THE KING IS OUT OF IMMEDIATE DANGER
THOUGH HIS RECOVERY MUST NECESSARILY BE PROTRACTED.

SECRETARY OF STATE FOR THE COLONIES TO GOVERNOR. RECEIVED 3rd
JULY:
I AM DESIRED BY HER MAJESTY THE QUEEN AND HIS ROYAL HIGHNESS
THE PRINCE OF WALES VERY GRATEFULLY TO ACKNOWLEDGE ON BEHALF OF
THE ROYAL FAMILY YOUR TELEGRAM OF THE 28th JUNE, EXPRESSING THE
SYMPATHY OF THE PEOPLE OF THE WINDWARD ISLANDS ON THE ILLNESS OF
HIS MAJESTY THE KING.

SECRETARY OF STATE FOR THE COLONIES TO GOVERNOR. RECEIVED 4th
JULY:
REFERRING TO MY TELEGRAM OF THE 28th JUNE, HIS MAJESTY THE KING
IS REPORTED TO BE MAKING STEADY PROGRESS IN EVERY RESPECT. THE
WOUND, THE DRESSING OF WHICH HAS AT TIMES CAUSED CONSIDERABLE
PAIN, IS NOW LESS TROUBLESOME AND BEGINNING TO HEAL. HIS MAJESTY
THE KING'S COURAGE AND PATIENCE HAVE CALLED FORTH THE GREATEST
ADMIRATION. HER MAJESTY THE QUEEN HAS BEEN IN CONSTANT ATTENDANCE
IN THE SICKROOM, WHERE THE UTMOST QUIET IS ENFORCED. HIS MAJES-
TY THE KING SEEING NO CORRESPONDENCE AND BEING APPROACHED ON NO
AFFAIRS OF STATE OR BUSINESS, I DO NOT PROPOSE TO TELEGRAPH AGAIN
UNLESS AN IMPORTANT CHANGE OCCURS.

On Saturday 9th August was held the solemnization of the Coronation of
Their Majesties King Edward and Queen Alexandra. The Administrator, ac-
companied by the officials and other gentlemen of the community preceded
by the Police and their band, and the Foresters marching to the music of the
Kingstown Orchestra, formed in procession from the Court House to the
Cathedral where a large congregation gathered.

The sacred edifice was appropriately decorated; there was a magnificent
arch at the gate surmounted by the Royal Standard.

Services were also held at the other places of worship at each of which the
attendance was large.

At the close of the Services a royal salute was fired at the Market Square.

His Honour the Administrator and Mrs. Cameron held an "At Home" at
Government House from 4 to 7 p.m.

The Legislature voted £50 for Coronation celebration expenses.

The following is the text of a letter which His Majesty the King was graciously pleased to address to His people on the occasion of Their Majesties'
Coronation:

TO MY PEOPLE,

On the eve of my Coronation, an event which I look upon as one of the most solemn and important in my life, I am anxious to express to my people at home and in the Colonies and in India my heartfelt appreciation of the deep sympathy which they have manifested to me during the time that my life was in such imminent danger. The postponement of the ceremony owing to my illness caused I fear much inconvenience and trouble to those who intended to celebrate it, but their disappointment was borne by them with admirable patience and temper. The prayers of my people for my recovery were heard, and I now offer up my deepest gratitude to Divine Providence for having preserved my life and given me strength to fulfil the important duties which devolve upon me as the Sovereign of this great Empire."

EDWARD R. and I.
BUCKINGHAM PALACE
8th August, 1902

The total expenditure to 31st December in connection with Soufriere Eruption Fund amounted to £29,822 3 5.

1903 / There was an excursion around the island on Tuesday 13th January when a considerable number of the influential section of the community availed themselves of the opportunity offered to view the landscape of renown and the effect produced by the eruptions. The police band was in attendance. As soon as the R.M.S. *Solent* distanced the shore the attractive scenery commanded the attention of the appreciative assembly and so it continued with increased admiration.

Although the sea was boisterous and the wind high yet the picturesqueness of the island afforded ample compensation and rendered the event memorable.

The other excursion to Martinique is one that will not be forgotten for many a year. On Saturday night the 24th January the R.M.S. *Esk* steamed from Kingstown Harbour with 250 persons, among whom were represented all the branches of society and commerce. In the early morn of the next day the passengers were greeted with the charming appearance of St. Lucia. From Castries with its surrounding magnificent fortifications 175 tourists embarked. Passing at Fort-de-France to obtain permission to visit St. Pierre sufficient time was allowed to view the grandeur of that city and its immediate vicinity.

At 3 p.m the ship moored in the harbour of St. Pierre. After admiring Mount Pelee and its majestic prominence the party landed to behold the inconceivable destruction of a city that was considered by many the most beautiful and fashionable in the West Indies. The desolated ruins, the vast amount of ejecta, the number of charred bones, added to the general weird appearance of everything around and combined to produce a feeling of intense solemnity.

The time for embarkation had arrived and a few had actually reached the ship when the volcano noiselessly emitted a dense, effervescing cloud which was providentially kept from the transporting spot by a light breeze. The marvelous velocity with which it descended, the rapidity of its development, the electricity displayed and the consciousness of suffocation resulting in death caused a frantic confusion among the panic-stricken collection of inhabitants from St. Lucia and this colony in their endeavour to avert the horrid doom which befell the citizens of St. Pierre on the eventful 8th of May 1902.

Mr. Alexander Porter died at his residence at Kingstown Park House on 14th February. He arrived in this island in 1868, was a partner in the firm he served in 1874, and so continued until the death of his uncle in 1892 when he became senior partner, possessing more realty in the island than any other individual.

On 14th May publicity was given to the suggestion of Sir Daniel Morris regarding the possibility of starting experiments on a moderate scale with the view of testing how far the soil and climate of St. Vincent are suitable for producing cotton. The adaptability of the soil to this industry and the fostering care of the Department of Agriculture for the West Indies, have enabled St. Vincent to produce a quality so excellent as to successfully compete with all others in the market and thereby become prominent in the commercial world.

July—A collection of local products including attractive samples of arrowroot, cocoa, kola, cassava, farine, two cases of cassava cakes, 31 specimens of bitterwood cups, also a charming selection of photographic views of the island by Mr. J. C. Wilson, were forwarded to the Toronto Exhibition per S.S. *Oruro*.

The *Toronto World* favourably commented on the display of the resources of the British West Indies at the Fair, held 12th September. "It is the tropical richness that is displayed and everything is necessary to the everyday consumption of the people of the Dominion."

The following telegram from the Right Honourable the Secretary of State for the Colonies was substituted for one previously transmitted:

```
BRUSSELS SUGAR CONVENTION. ALL SUGAR IMPORTED INTO UNITED
KINGDOM AFTER 31ST AUGUST MUST HAVE CERTIFICATE OF ORIGIN. THIS
DOES NOT APPLY TO SUGAR WHICH HAS BEEN USED IN PREPARATION OF
SUCH ARTICLES AS BISCUITS, CHOCOLATE, JAM, PRESERVE FRUIT, AND
CONFECTIONERY. ALL SUGAR IMPORTED INTO SIGNATORY STATES REQUIRES
CERTIFICATE OF ORIGIN, BUT HIS MAJESTY'S GOVERNMENT DOES NOT YET
KNOW WHAT THESE STATES MAY REQUIRE WITH REGARD TO ARTICLES IN THE
PREPARATION OF WHICH SUGAR MAY BE USED. MAKE THIS KNOWN AT ONCE,
AND TAKE SUCH ACTION AS MAY BE NECESSARY.
```

The despatch from the Secretary of State for the Colonies advising the transmission of a new public seal for the colony was published in October. The old seal was returned in order to be defaced in privy council.

The total expenditure from Soufriere Eruption Fund to 31st March was £34,340 19 3; to 30th June, £39,111 14 10; to 30th September, £43,055 3 5; and to 31st December, £43,544 8 2 when the available balance was £29,430 3 5.

1904 / His Excellency the Governor was pleased to select the following gentlemen to represent the Windward Islands at the Quarantine Conference held at Barbados on 25th April: for Grenada, The Honourable Edward Rawle Drayton (CMG), Colonial Secretary of Grenada; for St. Vincent, Christian William Branch, Esq (MB, CM); for St. Lucia, William Low, Esq.

The Conference was held from 25th April to 6th May inclusive and passed the following resolution upon which the proceedings were based:

> *That in view of the development of medical science it is possible, and in the interest of trade and communication necessary, to discard some of the restrictions which have in the past been thought essential in the British West Indian Colonies for guarding against the introduction of infectious and contagious diseases, and to substitute precautionary measures of a different nature.*
>
> *That such measures as may be adopted in lieu of the existing systems should be uniform; and,*
>
> *That such measures may most conveniently be embodied in a Convention to be adopted and adhered to for a term of years by the several Colonial Governments represented at this Conference.*

The Convention was accordingly published.

An Agricultural Show, under the auspices of the Imperial Department of Agriculture, was brought to a successful issue on 10th March. There was a large variety of interesting exhibits in the 10 classes, the excellent preparation of which rendered competition extremely keen. Admirers of horses and other stock were gratified in visiting the stalls, etc., erected on the attractive grounds of the Agricultural School. It was numerously attended, the weather was excellent, and the music of the Kingstown orchestra delightful. In the presence of His Honour E. J. Cameron, the principal gentlemen of the colony, the ladies, children and others in attendance, the prizes were presented by Sir Daniel Morris.

On Wednesday 6th April, ginning operations were commenced at the new Cotton Factory erected at Richmond Hill, at a cost of £2,000. It is the largest and most effective in the West Indies, a three-storied building, 90 feet long, 27 feet wide, with a 12-foot verandah. There is a lower basement floor, a ginning floor and a cotton loft.

9th April—His Excellency Sir R. B. Llewelyn (KCMG), invested the Honourable Edward Daniel Laborde with the insignia of the Imperial Service Order.

There was a police guard of honour, and the Kingstown orchestra was in attendance.

The function was held in the yard of the Courthouse and at the doorway, which was tastefully decorated, the ceremony was performed. There was a large and representative gathering indicative of the high esteem in which Mr. Laborde is held. His Excellency expressed great pleasure in presenting to one of the sons of this island the Badge of the Imperial Service Order. It was desirable that the investiture of Mr. Laborde should take place in St. Vincent as it was more for services done here that he had been honoured by His Majesty the King.

His Excellency the Governor was pleased to nominate the following Committee to consider and report upon the various suggestions for the utilization of the balance of the Eruption Fund which were made at the meeting at the Courthouse presided over by His Excellency on Monday the 11th April: Charles J. Simmons, Chairman; Joseph B. Bonadie, P. L. Frederick, S. S. Garrett, J. G. W. Hazell, Thomas Kydd, J. D. McCoy, David Marks, J. G. Morgan, F. A. Richards, Alexander Smith, and J. F. Sprott.

Two interesting meetings were held and on Tuesday 7th June. The report of the sub-committee was approved and left with the Chairman to be forwarded in the proper course to His Excellency the Governor.

The Cricket Match played on Victoria Park between the Eton C.C. and the Kingstown C.C. on the 23rd and 24th May was perhaps more eventful than any other contest of the national game for which this colony has gained reputation. The tournament for the magnificent silver cup offered by the late Alexander Porter was brought to a close in consequence of the overwhelming defeat of the Kingstown C.C. The trophy therefore became the absolute property of the Eton C.C. Thirty-eight and 93 were the respective totals for the Kingstown C.C. For the loss of 8 wickets Eton scored 423 when their innings were declared closed. R. Ollivierre compiled 202 for the Eton. The highest score for the Kingstown was 24 contributed by M. Hughes.

His Honour E. J. Cameron proceeded to England on six months' leave of absence on 3rd June. A large number of ladies and gentlemen gathered on the jetty to bid farewell; there was a police guard of honour and on embarkation a salute of 15 guns was fired.

On the following day the Honourable E. D. Laborde (ISO), assuming the acting appointment of Administrator of the Colony, took the customary oaths at Government Office in the presence of a brilliant representative gathering of ladies and gentlemen. A police guard of honour was formed in Egmont Street facing the building and on completion of the ceremony a salute of 15 guns was fired. His Honour addressed the audience and among other things expressed warm appreciation of the general good feeling toward him which the large attendance indicated.

On 16th June a meeting was held to discuss the proposals for organizing a Volunteer Reserve Corps. Several expressed their willingness to be enrolled and subsequently the formation was effected. The Honourable Conrad J. Simmons was appointed president and on 7th July there was a rifle practice at the range at Richmond Hill.

In response to an invitation of His Honour E. D. Laborde, Administrator, a meeting composed of gentlemen interested in agriculture was held at the Government Office on 25th July. Important matters relating to the cotton industry were discussed and resolutions unanimously adopted for organizing a cotton growers association,

The Convention for the Exchange of Postal Money Orders between the United States of America and this colony was done in duplicate and signed respectively at Washington on the 29th July and at Grenada on the 31st August by H C. Payne, Postmaster General of the United States and R. B. Llewelyn, Governor.

The convention between the Post Office Department of the Dominion of Canada and the Post Office Department of this colony concerning the exchange of Money Orders was done in duplicate and signed at Ottawa, Canada, on 5th September and at Grenada, on 3rd November by W. Mulock, Postmaster General of Canada, and R. B. Llewelyn, Governor of the Windward Islands, respectively.

October—An important notice was issued to cotton growers to the effect that a special sum was allotted to St. Vincent by the British Cotton Growing Association to be expended in connection with emergencies which may arise during the growth of that year's cotton crop.

Sir Daniel Morris (KCMG), accompanied by Mm. E. L. Oliver and Richard Stancliffe, the deputation from the British Cotton Growing Association, arrived on the S.S. *Orinoco* on Saturday morning the 12th November. A meeting was held at the cotton factory for the purpose of affording the deputation an opportunity of conferring with the local cotton growers and other gentlemen interested in the industry. Sir Daniel Morris, addressing the meeting, spoke in complimentary terms of the considerable progress this island had made in the cotton in industry, although introduced only 15 months ago. Mr. Oliver explained the object of their visit to the West Indies and expressed his admiration of the local ginnery, which he considered the best appointed of all he had seen in these islands.

A small weekly newspaper was started by Mr. Joseph B. Bonadie in conjunction with the *St. Vincent Times* but was discontinued after a few months.

1905 / In the month of February announcement was made regarding the decision of his Majesty's Government to withdraw all the British infantry stationed in the West Indian colonies.

Port Royal, Jamaica, to be no longer retained as a naval base, but both that place and the coal depot at St. Lucia to be reduced to cadres on which the expenditure in time of peace would be small, but in time of war could be developed according to necessity. Stock of coal to be kept at both ports for the use of His Majesty's Service.

The West Indian colonies to be visited as heretofore every winter by a naval squadron and a fast cruiser to be permanently stationed in West Indian waters. This was subsequently carried into effect.

The annual agricultural show under the auspices of the Imperial Department of Agriculture was held at the agricultural school on 9th March. There was a larger number of exhibits of common vegetables, economic and staple products, and stock presented, than hitherto. Sir Daniel Morris was present in the colony principally for the occasion.

Lord Brackley's cricket team arrived on 14th March. Keen interest was taken in every detail and the visitors accorded a hearty welcome. In addition to the attendance of the reception committee the Kingstown orchestra, playing at the landing place, greeted them with the familiar air, *See the Conquering Hero Comes*. In the first innings the visiting team scored 147: Hayes 76, Burn 17, Capt. Wynyard 12. The local team responded with 250: R. Ollivierre 99, H. Ollivierre 45, T. Layne 38, were among those who made double figures. The visitors then scored 77 for the loss of four wickets. Although admitting the arrangement that the return match should commence the day after the conclusion of the first and despite the entreaty of Capt. Vanloo and other local gentlemen, His Lordship declined to complete the match.

Congratulatory telegrams were received as follows:

```
FROM GRENADA—GOVERNOR LLEWELYN TO CAPTAIN VANLOO,
WELL DONE! WISH YOU COMPLETE SUCCESS TODAY.

FROM GRENADA—VINCELONIANS TO VANLOO,
ACCEPT HEARTY CONGRATULATIONS.

FROM SAN FERNANDO, TRINIDAD—COUNTRYMEN TO VANLOO
ACCEPT HEARTY CONGRATULATIONS.
```

A return match was commenced on 17th. The Island team scored 230: T. Osment 82, H. Ollivierre 47 and H. Brown 37, were among the principal contributors. His Lordship's eleven compiled 210: Thompson 85, Foley 23.

The following telegrams were received from Grenada and St. Lucia respectively:

VINCELONIANS TO VANLOO,
HURRAH! SPLENDID! HEARTY CONGRATULATIONS. PROUD OF YOU ALL.

AND LABORDE TO VANLOO,
BEST CONGRATULATIONS FOR THE ST. VINCENT TEAM.

April—In connection with the sales of Saint Vincent cotton the vice-president of the British Cotton Growing Association stated that the shipments of Sea Island Cotton, from Mm. J. H. Hazell Sons & Co. and Mr. C. J. Simmons, sold at an all-round price of 17 pence a pound "are quite the best cotton grown under the auspices of the Association." He added, "Judging from the cotton that has been received this year from the West Indies I should say that you have some of the best cultivators in the world. Everybody who comes into these rooms and sees the samples of cotton recently received goes into ecstasies over them."

Early in May, telegraphic communication was received intimating the decision of His Majesty's Government to discontinue the contract with the Royal Mail Company. Adverse opinion from all the colonies was submitted. The Elder Dempster tender was once favourably considered then rejected and ultimately no contract was entered into. The steamers of the Royal Mail Company however continued to ply but the changes of the route rendered the Service inconvenient to several of the colonies.

Announcement was made in June that His Majesty the King was graciously pleased to approve of the appointment of His Honour Edward John Cameron, Administrator of the colony, to be a Companion of the Most Distinguished Order of St. Michael and St. George.

An interesting ceremony was held at the police barrack yard on 21st August in connection with the presentation to Mr. Samuel Hurley of the Imperial Service Medal. There was a representative gathering, a police guard of honour, and the attendance of the Kingstown orchestra. His Honour E. J. Cameron delivered an impressive address reviewing the services of the ex-constable which extended over 49 years. His Honour felt it his duty on Mr. Hurley's retirement to bring his name and his long record under special notice. It afforded His Honour great satisfaction that His Most Gracious Majesty the King, who has ever an eye to the reward of faithful service in his vast Empire, without distinction of class, creed or colour, has been pleased to award to Mr. Hurley the decoration presented.

His Honour also addressed a few words to the non-commissioned officers and men of the police force and expressed his desire to publicly congratulate them on the hard and good work they had done under the direction of Mr. Griffith, the Acting Chief of Police.

An extraordinary *Gazette* dated 12th September contained the opinion of His Majesty's Government that having regard to the conditions, prospects and geographical proximity of Grenada and this Colony, it would be to the advantage of both colonies if they were united. The opinions and wishes of the inhabitants of both colonies were desired, and after sufficient time and full consideration had been given it was proposed to introduce a resolution into the Legislative Council in the month of December the text of which was:

> *That this Council having had under its consideration the notice published in the Government Gazette under date of 12th September last is satisfied that it would be to the advantage of both Colonies that the Colony of Grenada should be united to the Colony of St. Vincent so as to form one Colony to be called the Colony of Grenada and St. Vincent; that the Colony so constituted should be governed by one Governor and have a common Executive and Legislature and a common purse; that the traffic and intercourse between the two islands with their dependencies should be absolutely free and that, as far as local circumstances may permit, there should be a uniform system of laws and taxation throughout the united Colony; that for the carrying out of these proposals a humble address be presented to His Majesty the King praying that His Most Gracious Majesty will be pleased to take such steps as may be necessary to effect the union of the two Colonies.*

A preliminary meeting of gentlemen, representing all interests and districts of the colony, was held at the courthouse on 9th October for the purpose of appointing a committee to organize public meetings in order to arrive at the wishes of the inhabitants respecting the proposed union of Grenada and St. Vincent. The Venerable E. A. Turpin, Archdeacon, was appointed Chairman and Mr. R. S. Cheesman, Secretary. After a lengthy discussion it was unanimously agreed that the proposed union was inexpedient. It was therefore decided that a public meeting be held at an early date for final consideration. A number of popular and representative gentlemen were elected to organize meetings in all the districts of the colony.

Resolutions were adopted regarding the unconstitutional formation of the Executive and Legislative Councils and the disapproval of the Land Acquisition Bill.

A large number of persons representing all classes of the community attended the meeting of Legislative Council held on 8th November. The Honourable Conrad J. Simmons was of opinion that no legislation should be proceeded with until the receipt of the reply from the Secretary of State for the colonies regarding the constitution of the council. There were many outbursts of applause during the Honourable Member's speech in opposition to the introduction of "The Land Acquisition Bill". His Honour E. J. Cameron, the Administrator, explained the circumstances which rendered it necessary to introduce the bill, but Mr. Simmons, adhering to his opinion, entered a protest and respectfully applied for and obtained permission to retire from that sitting of the council. The audience then loudly exclaimed. "We protest against the constitution of this council. Adjourn and constitute it." After a brief pause the words were repeated with greater emphasis. His Honour the Administrator adjourned the council and rising from his chair addressed the people in his personal capacity, expressing regret at the scene which he considered unseemly. He declared that coming here to labour amongst the people of St. Vincent as Administrator he had tried his best to protect the interest of the colony, and it pained him to see a gathering of leading men of the island making a demonstration which it was impossible for him to appreciate.

A public meeting was held at the courthouse on 10th November for considering the result of district meetings on that behalf and the general opinion with respect to the proposed union of Grenada and St. Vincent. The Kingstown orchestra, preceded by a large banner marked "No Confederation! No Union with Grenada!" led the gathering crowds from all parts of the island to the yard of the courthouse. As many as could be accommodated forced themselves into the building to hear the deliberations and eloquent speeches of the movers, seconders and supporters of the resolutions. Under the Presidency of the Venerable E. A. Turpin, Archdeacon, the proceedings were commendably dispassionate. There was much enthusiasm and a remarkable concentration of the wealth and strength of the population.

The expression of opinion desired by the Government was uttered with unanimous voice midst great acclamation and recorded in the following resolutions:

Moved by Mr. E. A. Richards, seconded by Mr. W. C. Forde and supported by Messrs. A. Nicholas and C. O. Hazell (KC), (unanimously carried),

> *That the inhabitants of the Colony of St. Vincent present at this Meeting having fully considered the question of the union of St. Vincent and Grenada and the Resolution which the Government has notified that it purposes to introduce into the Legislative Council in the month of December next, are satisfied that the union of St. Vincent and Grenada would be to the grave disadvantage of St. Vincent and the inhabitants do not wish the union.*

Moved by Mr. J. E. Sprott, seconded by Mr. J. B. Bonadie and supported by the Honourable C. J. Simmons. Mm. J. G. Morgan, J. Cruikshank, P. F. Huggins, J. G. W. Hazell, A. H. Spence, J. Walker, and F. W. Motley (unanimously carried),

> *That the inhabitants of this Colony present at this Meeting are of the opinion and wish that the Government of the Colony of St. Vincent should be constituted a separate Government directly responsible to the Crown as*

prayed for in the Petition of the inhabitants of the Colony of St. Vincent to the Secretary of State for the Colonies bearing date April 1902.

After a hearty vote of thanks to the chairman followed by the singing of the national anthem the happy meeting was brought to a close.

The band then led the people with a brilliant quick march to the Government Offices where they exclaimed, "No union but separation," and jubilantly sang again the national anthem. They proceeded through the town and dispersed shortly afterward.

On Wednesday 15th November, long before the hour for holding the public meeting, enthusiastic crowds composed of residents from every district in the island arrived in Kingstown. Several processions, with music of rural bands including mounted peasants and overseers, paraded the town with banners, "No union", "No confederation", etc., until the Kingstown Orchestra appeared, then the enthusiasts merged into a monster procession. Arriving at the courthouse the band played the national anthem, in which thousands of voices joined.

The following gentlemen appointed a Committee to express the adverse opinion of the inhabitants were in attendance:

The Venerable E. A. Turpin, the Honourable Conrad J. Simmons, Mm. Ormond Hazell (KC), G. R. Corea, T. M. MacDonald, E. A. Richards, J. E. Sprott, J. B. Bonadie, S. S. Garrett, E. M. Beach, J. DeSilva, R. Morris, F. D. Rice, David Marks, R. Falby, Alexander Smith, Charles Layne, James Providence, J. G. Morgan, F. B. McConnie, John Jackson, J. A. Davy. H. L. Ellis, J. M. Joseph, T. Kydd, P. I. Frederick, James Gould, Samuel Dick, Horatio Boucher, and William Dougan.

The undermentioned officials attended with His Excellency Sir R. B. Llewelyn: His Honour E. J. Cameron, Administrator; His Honour P. M. C. Sheriff, Chief Justice; the Honourable T. D. Tudor, Attorney General; J. B. Kernahan, Land Commissioner; and Mr. C. N. Rice, Chief Clerk in the Governor's Office.

In the course of his address, His Excellency informed the gentlemen that the decision of the Government with regard to the proposed union was based upon the advantages to both colonies likely to arise thereby.

Several gentlemen expressed their views in the negative. After a discussion of considerable length Mr. Davy, desiring to show the difference of the votes, said, "All opposed to union please stand," whereupon 27 of the 30 present stood with upraised hands and exclaimed, "No union".

His Excellency again assured the gentlemen that neither he nor the Secretary of State for the colonies had any desire to force the proposal against the wish of the inhabitants. He had seen the demonstrations against union, and

110

he had documents which he would forward to the Secretary of State for the colonies and they would undoubtedly be given due consideration.

The meeting having concluded, the eager throng awaiting results filled the market place and crowded before the gate of the courthouse. Comparative silence prevailed until a member of the committee shouted "No union", "Three cheers for St. Vincent!" Thence started a demonstration of a magnitude unparalleled in the history of St. Vincent. The Kingstown orchestra played the national anthem; the people sang themselves hoarse.

The Governor and party retiring from the courthouse were hemmed in the crowd and thus proceeded, under the banner "We want separation" to Government Office, where His Excellency raised his hat in recognition of the loyal demonstration and excellent behaviour.

1906 / A meeting of the Cotton Growers Association was held at the courthouse on 18ᵗʰ January, at which His Honour E. J. Cameron, the Vice President, presided. There was a large attendance and among the several important matters considered and decided was the extension of the usefulness of the association to general agriculture and commerce. The name was therefore changed to the Cotton Growers Association and Agricultural and Commercial Society.

On 16ᵗʰ February there were three severe shocks of earthquake, one at 1:40, one at 3 and one at 5:45 p.m. They were somewhat general in the West Indies but at St. Lucia the frequency and violence continued for a considerable period to the terror of the inhabitants.

The following minute from His Excellency the Governor was published in extraordinary *Gazette* dated 19ᵗʰ February:

> *Governor to Administrator, St. Vincent,*
>
> The Secretary of State for the Colonies has authorised me to announce that the proposal for the Union of Grenada and St. Vincent was made solely upon public grounds with every regard to the interests of the two Colonies. The manner in which it was set forth clearly indicated that there was every intention to consult the wishes and interests of those concerned and as the scheme has not been favourably received it will not be pressed at the present time.
>
> The people of St. Vincent should bear in mind that their establishments have of late years been largely maintained by grants from Imperial funds and the Imperial Government has therefore an additional special right to speak as to the future of the constitution of the Island. (Intld.) R. B. (LL), 8. 2. 06.

Two letters were received on 26ᵗʰ and 27ᵗʰ February respectively by the Venerable E. A. Turpin, Archdeacon, as chairman of public meeting acknowledging receipt of petition to His Majesty the King respecting the constitution of the Legislative Council, that reference had been made to the Secretary of State for the colonies, and that His Lordship had already instructed the Governor on the subject matter of the address.

The annual agricultural show was held at the agricultural school buildings on 7th March. The exhibits were not so numerous as expected, although this indicated the lack of active interests of all producers in the island and did not adequately demonstrate the general development of local products; yet there was vast improvement in the scientific study of agriculture and in the various industries encouraged by the Imperial Department of Agriculture.

The addresses of His Honour E. J. Cameron and Sir Daniel Morris were exceedingly impressive, interesting and instructive.

The distribution of the prizes was postponed to a subsequent date; at the completion of the distribution of diplomas His Honour the Administrator called for three cheers for Sir Daniel which were heartily accorded. The Commissioner tendered his thanks and bade goodbye.

His Honour E. J. Cameron, Administrator, presided, and Sir Daniel Morris was present at an important meeting at the Cotton Growers Association and Agricultural and Commercial Society held at the Courthouse on 4th April. The prizes in connection with the agricultural show of 7th March were distributed. They included two Silver medals presented by Sir Alfred Jones for the best sample of cotton produced locally in accordance with stipulated conditions and on the recommendation of Mr. Thomas Thornton. A.R.C.S. on the staff of the Imperial Department of Agriculture:

Class 1. Grand Sable Estate, Mm. J. H. Hazell, Sons & Co., first prize and silver medal; Calder Estate, Mm. John H. Hazell Sons & Co., second prize.

Class 2. Golden Vale, Miss Huggins, first prize and medal; Rutland Vale, Mr. A. M. Fraser, second prize.

In order to encourage good cultivation of the allotments on the Land Settlement Estates, the Government offered prizes for competition among the allottees. A notice in Government *Gazette* of 26th April contained the amounts and particulars relating thereto.

At a meeting of the Cotton Growers Association and Agricultural and Commercial Society held 2nd May, unanimous expression was given to the society's appreciation of the good work of the Imperial Department of Agriculture and the following resolution passed:

> *That this Association and Society gratefully records its appreciation of the great work which has been and is being done in the West Indies by the Imperial Department of Agriculture, and the signal success that has attended*

112

it in this Colony prominently exemplified by this island's cotton having taken the premier place in quality;

That the members of this Association and Society, believing that the continued success and further improvement and extension of the cotton industry and agriculture generally in this Colony depends on the continuance of this work, His Majesty's Government be respectfully asked to maintain the Imperial Department of Agriculture for the West Indies;

That the foregoing resolution be forwarded in the regular course to the Lords of the Treasury, the Secretary of State for the Colonies and the West India Committee.

Government Notice No. 63 of 4th May contained the appointments of John Gregg Windsor Hazell, Esq and John Gemmel Porter, Esq to be unofficial members of the Legislative Council.

Mr. Richard Ollivierre, the St. Vincent representative on the West Indian Cricket Team to visit England, left the colony on 12th May. As a rapid scorer he is considered second to none in the West Indies. His display as an all-round cricketer elicited commendation; he upheld his reputation and that of the colony whose cricket is admittedly excellent.

On his return to the colony 13th September, he was accorded an enthusiastic reception and on 26th was presented with a purse as a token of the people's appreciation of his creditable performances in England. The function, which was conducted on Victoria Park after a cricket match, was attended by a large number of gentlemen and several ladies, the Kingstown orchestra being also in attendance. His Honour W. S. Shaw, the Chief Justice, in presenting the purse, made a felicitous speech in which he referred to the unavoidable absence of His Honour the Administrator.

A fire occurred at Diamond Estate Sugar Works, the property of C. J. Simmons, Esq, at about 12:30 p.m. on Tuesday 15th May, destroying the building, a large quantity of produce, and seriously injuring the machinery, which was one of the most costly in the island. Sergeant John H. Leslie, the excise officer on duty, and Mr. Ebenezer Pollard the coppersmith, engaged in effecting certain repairs, were both extensively burnt. The latter died on the evening of the 15th and the former on the following evening.

The evidence afforded no indication of neglect or malicious intent on the part of any person but that the cause of the explosion was purely the result of an accident.

The inter-colonial service of the Royal Mail Steam Packet Company, discontinued in June, was resumed in August.

October—The chairman of the Kingstown Board received a reply to his letter of 14th September intimating Mr. Andrew Carnegie's consent to give £2,000 for the erection of a Free Library building in Kingstown.

The British Cotton Growing Association awarded to Mr. Alexander Smith and Mr. Charles Layne the two gold medals presented by Sir Alfred Jones for the most successful producers of Sea Island Cotton in St. Vincent with respect to the crop for 1905. The judges, in arriving at their decision, took into consideration the following particulars:

(a) the acreage actually planted in cotton; (b) the number of pounds of cotton shipped; and (c) the prices received for each shipment. At the meeting of the Cotton Growers Association and Agricultural and Commercial Society held 5th December, His Honour E. J. Cameron, presiding, congratulated both gentlemen and expressed his appreciation of each one's energy and enterprise with respect to the cultivation of Cotton.

1907 / 8th January—At the meeting of the Kingstown Board, the Deputy Chairman presented a communication received that morning from Mr. Bertram, Secretary to Mr. Andrew Carnegie, acknowledging the receipt of the Board's letter dated 12th December, 1906, and conveying the information that Mr. Carnegie had instructed his cashier, Mr. R. A. Franks, Home Trust Company, Hoboken, N.J., to arrange payments on the library building as the work progresses, to the extent of £2,000. The board thereupon decided to proceed with the structure without delay.

9th January—Mm. Oliver, Hutton and Shelmerdine, cotton experts and representative of the British Cotton Growing Association of Manchester, England, arrived on S.S. *Ocamo* on a commercial visit; Mr. Buttenshaw, representing Imperial Department of Agriculture, accompanying them.

14th January—Mm. Hutton, Oliver and Shelmerdine attended the meeting of the Cotton Growers Association. In the course of his address, Mr. Hutton, the Vice President of the British Cotton Growing Association, remarked that the cotton he had seen on several of the estates here was the best he had seen in his life; he advised planters to use their best efforts to maintain efficiency of labour.

Mr. Oliver also spoke interestingly with regard to the value placed on Sea Island Cotton, its present popularity, and its bright future prospect. He exhibited specimens of beautiful laces made of St. Vincent cotton and spoke encouragingly in general, impressing on the members that there was no fear that the market would be glutted and assuring them that even if St. Vincent produced 1,000 bales of unstained cotton annually, a ready market at remunerative prices would be found when shipped to the British Cotton Growing Association.

17th January—In reply to the telegram of welcome, which the inhabitants of this Island forwarded to His Excellency the Governor on the day of his assumption of the administration of the Government of the Windward Islands, the following was received by His Honour the Administrator:

PLEASE CONVEY TO INHABITANTS OF ST. VINCENT HEARTY THANKS FOR
THEIR GOOD WISHES.

17th January—In consequence of intelligence regarding the terrific earthquake at Jamaica on the 15th, His Honour the Administrator forwarded the following telegram:

ADMINISTRATOR, COUNCILS, PEOPLE OF ST. VINCENT, WISH TO EXPRESS
DEEPEST SYMPATHY WITH INHABITANTS OF JAMAICA IN THE TERRIBLE
CALAMITY WITH WHICH THE ISLAND HAS BEEN STRICKEN.

On 20th, the reply from His Excellency the Governor of Jamaica was received:

DEEPLY GRATEFUL FOR SYMPATHY.

19th January—At the meeting of the Legislative Council His Honour the Administrator alluded to the disaster and moved the following resolution:

That this Council desires to record the deep sorrow and regret with which it has received the intelligence of the terrible calamity which has befallen the Island of Jamaica in the destruction of the Town of Kingston by earthquake and the resulting serious loss of life, and extends on behalf of the people of St. Vincent to the inhabitants of Jamaica its very great and sincere sympathy.

The Honourable Conrad J. Simmons on seconding the motion remarked that St. Vincent's sympathy was all the more full and sincere having regard to the serious troubles she had herself lately passed through. The resolution was then unanimously adopted.

Before the end of January, the subscription list circulated by the St. George's Cathedral Sabbath School together with another by the Misses Richards in aid of suffering children in Jamaica realized £18. 16. 5, of which £10. 1. 0. was remitted by the Venerable Archdeacon Turpin to His Grace the Archbishop of Jamaica. Material purchased for £8. 3. 6. was made up, and in addition to several parcels of clothing received from ladies enabled the committee to forward four cases of relief clothing. Several other movements in aid of the sufferers were organized and remittances made from time to time.

15th April—Arrival of His Excellency Governor Williams. His Excellency, who was accompanied by Lady Williams, Miss Deane, Lieutenant Deane (ADC), and Mr. Fitz-Herbert, private secretary, received a grand reception in lauding. His Excellency subscribed to the usual oaths of office in the Council Chamber at the courthouse and afterward delivered an eloquent speech. His Excellency created a very favourable impression on the people. The party left the same evening for St. Lucia.

24th May—Empire Day. The celebration consisted of the following:

Procession of Church Lads Brigade, members of the I.O.G.T., Day and Sunday School Children of the Anglican preceded by the Kingstown orchestra; divine service at St. George's Cathedral conducted by the Venerable E. A Turpin, Archdeacon; march past on Victoria Park by the brigade, saluting flag in column and in half companies to the appreciation of a large and representative assembly; eloquent address by His Honour E. J. Cameron (CMG), Administrator, in the course of which he explained the motto, "One King, One Flag, One Fleet, One Empire" and the watchwords "Responsibility", "Duty", "Sympathy", "Self-sacrifice"; as a result of Mr. W. C. Forde's subscription list on that behalf the children enjoyed their refreshments at the Anglican school house whilst the brigade camped out on the park. A free patriotic concert after a special session by members of "Star of Hope" Juvenile Temple I.O.G.T. brought the memorable proceedings to a close. The Biabou, Marriaqua, Evesham, and Stubbs Sunday schools of the Wesleyan connection assembled at Mt. Coke where they sang and feasted, the only regret being the absence, through illness, of the Rev. McI. Darrell, the promoter.

The estimated value of the 700 bales of Sea Island Cotton ginned at the Central Cotton Factory, up to 31st May, was £28,000.

2nd June—Mr. J. R. Bovell (FLS, FCS), arrived from Barbados for the purpose of inspecting and reporting on the Carib Country for the information of Sir Daniel Morris (KCMG), the Imperial Commissioner of Agriculture for the West Indies, to whom the question of restoring the water supply of the district through the Carib Canal and of further fostering the re-establishment of cultivation in that part of the island by the expenditure of a portion of the eruption fund thereon was referred for his consideration and recommendations.

Mr. Bovell acknowledged that he fully enjoyed the trip; his visit to the Carib Country being both interesting and delightful. The weather was excellent, and after his daily inspection of the uncultivated area, he was fully requited by the salubrious climate.

Mr. Bovell also expressed his appreciation of the hospitality extended toward him by the proprietors and other people of the Windward district.

4th June—R.M.S. *Esk* arrived, incidentally renewing the Royal Mail Inter-Colonial Service for a term of three months.

12th August—An interesting Lecture entitled "Diseases, Their Causes, Etc." was delivered by Dr. C. W. Branch to the members of the Church Lads Brigade at the Anglican school house. In the course of his lecture the Doctor produced tubes in which bacilli were germinated and also demonstrated the act of planting such bacilli in tubes.

9th September—The first *Illustrated Handbook of St. Vincent* was published.

11th September—Foundation stone of the Carnegie Free Library laid.

A police guard of honour was formed facing the building. At 4 p.m. the Kingstown orchestra playing the Masonic march, followed by His Honour D. T. Tudor as principal officiating Past Master, accompanied by Dr. C. H. Durrant, Worshipful Master with the Brethren of St. George's Lodge No. 2616 in full Masonic dress, came in procession. A Masonic oration of considerable length by His Honour D. T. Tudor opened the proceedings. His Honour referred in glowing terms to the generosity of Mr. Andrew Carnegie of Skibo Castle of Scotland; the Rev. G. Paterson offered solemn prayer; the ode *Prosper the Art* was sung by Mr. Adolphus Richards, the brethren joining in the chorus, during which the stone was lowered by stages; the dainty silver trowel used on this unique occasion was presented to Mrs. Tudor by Dr. C. H. Durrant, Worshipful Master, who delivered a pithy address; Mrs. Tudor in a pathetic manner expressed sincere thanks; Mr. J. E. Sprott, Chairman of the Kingstown Board, then thanked His Honour and Mrs. Tudor for their cordial co-operation, the Freemasons for the unqualified success of the memorable function, and the representative gathering for their attendance—a manifestation of the people's high appreciation of Mr. Carnegie's munificent gift. The Masonic version of the national anthem was then sung.

A letter from the Imperial Commissioner of Agriculture for the West Indies to the Administrator, written at Toronto and dated 14th September, contained the following information regarding the West Indian Exhibits at the Canadian National Exhibition, viz:

> ...*The Exhibit from St. Vincent was one of the most interesting of any, and proved well worthy of the island. It consisted of a fine series of arrowroot from Mm. MacDonald Bros., Simmons, J. H. Hazell & Co., J. E. S. Richards, and others. The specimens of fine Sea Island Cotton were characteristic of the produce of St. Vincent, and were much admired....*

> ...*The samples of sugar from Mm. Simmons and Corea gave evidence that St. Vincent was still a producer of this commodity as also of White Rum. The cassava starch exhibited by Mm. J. H. Hazell & Co. and Mr. I. Stephens led to enquiries as to the possibility of this starch being produced on a large scale.*

> ...*Another starch from St. Vincent was prepared from the Sweet Potato by the Agricultural Department. The samples of cocoa produced at St. Vincent were regarded as equal to good West Indian sorts, and it is evident that there is a good future for this product. There were several samples of nutmeg and mace, all of good commercial quality. There was one sample of Cinnamon and one of Honey; the latter from the Agricultural School. There was also one sample of Vanilla from Mr. P. F. Huggins. Taken altogether the exhibits from St. Vincent had been carefully selected and packed and they were presented in excellent condition.*

> ...*As shown in the Visitors' Book, a large number of merchants and others visited the West Indian Exhibit and it was admitted that this was one of*

the most interesting of the various sections of the Canadian National Exhibition.

P.S. Since the above was written, I am informed that the West Indian Court at the Canadian National Exhibition has been awarded the distinction of a Gold Medal; and that Diplomas of Merit have been awarded to the separate exhibits from the Colonies concerned in recognition of the excellence of the productions contributed by them.

16th December—The produce and manufactures of the colony exported by R.M.S. *Esk* comprised 179 bales of Sea Island Cotton, 923 barrels of arrowroot, 65 bags of cocoa, 16 casks of sperm oil, 41 barrels of divi-divi (dye wood), one case of turtle shell and 8 parcels of sundries at a total moderately estimated value of £7,500.

1908 / In April, the Government having renewed the subsidy to the West India and Panama Telegraph Company, general telegraphic intelligence was posted and otherwise supplied as heretofore. The colony was deprived of this source of information regarding political and other matters from April 1906.

30th May—At the meeting of the Legislative Council, extensive deliberations ensued in connection with the restoration of the Carib Country. Mr. J. R. Bovell of the Imperial Department of Agriculture who visited the locality in June 1907, having reported to the Government that much of the Carib Estates was capable of profitable cultivation, the proprietor the Honourable J. G. Porter proceeded at considerable expense to re-erect buildings, mills, etc. The undertaking far exceeded this gentleman's expectation, especially as serious difficulties arose in respect to the directing of the course of the canal, the divergence of which rendered cultivation and manufacture an impossibility.

After expending £3,100 with liabilities of £400, Mr. Porter applied for a loan of £5,000 in addition to the free grant of £1,600 previously obtained from the Government.

The Right Honourable the Secretary of State for the colonies declined the granting of £5,000 from the Eruption Fund but agreed to a loan of that sum from floating balance of the General Revenue.

Every member present spoke on the subject of the restoration of the Carib Country.

The net surplus funds of the colony, after the repayment to the Imperial Treasury of the final sum of £700 amounted on 31st March, approximately, to £5,600. It was therefore a matter of serious doubt to His Excellency the Governor whether he could recommend to the Secretary of State the suggested loan from those funds.

After much correspondence the decision arrived at was considered unsatisfactory by Mr. Porter who abandoned the operations and ultimately disposed of all his Estates and other property in the Island. The discontinuance of business carried on by the firm of D. K. Porter & Co. and the withdrawal from circulation of the money necessary to be expended for the restoration of the Carib Country affected the prosperous condition of the colony to some extent.

The annual Report of the Registrar-General of Jamaica in respect of the year 1907 included the most recently received vital statistics of a few of the other British West Indian colonies and thus supplied a comparison of an interesting character. The healthiest West Indian islands appeared to be St. Vincent and St. Lucia with death rates at 15.4 and 19.4 per thousand, respectively; Grenada followed with a death rate of 24.5, Trinidad 25.9, Jamaica 26.2, Antigua 27, British Guiana 27.4, and Barbados 28.9.

In October, the announcement was made of the retirement of Sir Daniel Morris (KC, MG). During his tenure of office as Commissioner of Agriculture for the West Indies Sir Daniel Morris was indefatigable in his exertions to revive and extend the prosperity of the West Indies and has therefore won the sincere affection of the people. In consequence of his untiring efforts on behalf of St. Vincent, Sir Daniel Morris is regarded in this island as a genuine friend; it is gratifying to know how warmly the people appreciate the numerous acts of kindness he has done for them and the deep gratitude felt throughout the colony.

On the announcement of his resignation the London Times of 11th October contained the following:

> Not only to the West Indies, with which his name will be chiefly connected, has Sir Daniel Morris done distinguished service, but also to the agricultural needs and progress of the Empire. In 1877 he was appointed Assistant Director of the Royal Botanic Gardens, Ceylon, and after a thorough investigation of the coffee disease, was able to recommend the cultivation of tea, which has since proved such a valuable substitute. On the recommendation of Sir Joseph Hooker, he was transferred to the Directorship of Public Gardens and Plantations at Jamaica in 1879, and while acting in that capacity paid visits, at the request of the Government, to Trinidad, Grenada and British Honduras, to report upon various industries. In 1883, at the request of Lord Derby he was even sent so far afield as St. Helena and reported upon its agricultural resources....In 1886, after manifold services in Jamaica, which were repeatedly acknowledged by the authorities, he was appointed by Lord Iddesleigh, Assistant Director of the Royal Gardens, Kew. In 1896 he was nominated by Mr. Chamberlain as Scientific Advisor to the West India Royal Commission. That Commission made many recommendations for the benefit of the West Indies, but it is safe to say that the only one which proved of practical or lasting value to the West Indies was the establishment of the Imperial Department of Agriculture.

In moving a vote on his behalf in the House of Commons on August 2, 1898, Mr. Chamberlain said,

The recommendations of the Royal Commission were twofold. In the first instance they suggested that a special Department of Agriculture should be established, dealing with all questions of economic plants and Botanic stations in all the islands, and we propose to adopt that suggestion, and that this establishment should be placed under the direction of Dr. Morris, Assistant Director at Kew, who is marked out, as I think anyone who knows anything of Kew will admit, by special qualifications for an important position of this kind. Not only has he all the scientific and other knowledge in the possession of the authorities at Kew, but also special acquaintance with the West Indies, and if those other industries are to be successful there is no one more capable of doing it than Dr. Morris.

It is with the greatest regret from a West Indian point of view, writes the West India Committee circular,

that we have to announce the retirement of Sir Daniel Morris from the Imperial Department of Agriculture for the West Indies over which he has presided with such distinguished ability since 1898. Since that year Sir Daniel Morris has organized a strongly staffed scientific department with experimental agricultural stations on the islands within his immediate purview, which has done much to raise the level of West Indian agriculture and has been of the greatest service to agriculturists of all descriptions. Though the active jurisdiction of the Department does not, as yet, extend beyond Barbados, the Leeward and Windward Islands, the larger colonies have also benefited by it. With the revival of the Cotton Industry of the West Indies the name of Sir Daniel Morris will always be particularly associated, and his gift of organization has been demonstrated by the successful establishment by him of the Agricultural Conferences, which have done so much towards bringing the leaders of agricultural science and practice in the West Indies together under the most favourable conditions for the interchange of ideas and results. We are glad to be able to add that, although Sir Daniel is retiring from the position of Commissioner of Agriculture on November 30th next, in the West Indies, he is not retiring into private life, as there is every reason to believe that a sphere of even more extended usefulness will shortly claim his services."

1909 / On 13th January, a meeting of the Cotton Growers Association and Agricultural and Commercial Society was held at the courthouse. With reference to the cotton conference held under the auspices of the British Cotton Growing Association in August last the Honourable Conrad J. Simmons alluded to efforts that are being made by that association to encourage the growing of cotton in the West Indies. He moved the resolution for a vote of thanks to the association for all they had done. This was seconded by the Honourable J. G. W. Hazell. These two gentlemen also respectively moved and seconded the vote of thanks to the Royal Mail Steam Packet Company for conveying the delegates at a reduced rate. The question of implemental tillage and the scarcity of labour, among other things, were discussed.

1st February—The Free Public Library was formally opened by His Honour Anthony DeFreitas, Acting Administrator, in the presence of a large and appreciative audience. The police, under command of F. W. Griffith, Esq, marched to the music of the Kingstown orchestra for the purpose of forming the guard-of-honour.

On the arrival of His Honour at 4:30 p.m. the police "presented arms" whilst the orchestra played the national anthem, the Acting Administrator having taken his seat to preside on the occasion. Mr. W. C. Forde, Chairman of the Kingstown Board delivered a lengthy address which was explanatory and interesting.

In his opening speech His Honour referred to the laying of the foundation stone by his friend Mr. Tudor, the Attorney General of St. Vincent when Acting Administrator in September 1907; and to the formal opening by himself, another Attorney General Acting Administrator for a short time. He hoped that the continuity of lawyers in connection with the establishment of this Library would prove a good omen. After commenting on the generosity of Mr. Carnegie and other matters to which Mr. Forde alluded in his address, His Honour said, "With the expression of my hope and expectation that the people of the colony will use it for their moral and mental culture, I now declare this Free Public Library open."

Mr. J. E. Sprott and the Rev. F. Ellis, Members of the Kingstown Board, also made interesting speeches.

Lieutenant Janies Campbell of H.M.S. *Brilliant*, who arrived on that ship on 6th February, manifested great interest in the island. He is a grandson of the late Sir John Campbell (Bart.) of Ardnarmurchan, Scotland, who was an esteemed Governor of this island and from whose despatches extracts appear in the historical notes for 1854. The Lieutenant visited St. George's Cathedral, read the inscription over the spot where the remains of his beloved grandfather were laid and obtained photographs of the interior of the edifice, etc., in which he said his father and relations would be extremely delighted.

8th March—Public Telegrams announced the appointment of His Honour E. J. Cameron to be Administrator of St. Lucia and of the Honourable C. G. Murray, 3rd son of the 10th Lord Elibank, to succeed him as Administrator of this Colony.

At the meeting of the Legislative Council held 13th March, it was resolved to invite Sir Rubert Boyce (KT, MR, FRS), the yellow fever specialist, to visit St. Vincent when touring the West Indies. He arrived on the 5th April and on the 8th at the courthouse, Kingstown, delivered a lecture on mosquito-borne diseases which was illustrated by lantern slides.

There was a meeting of the Cotton Growers Association and Agricultural and Commercial Society held on the 14th April, at which the Honourable J.

G. W. Hazell thanked Administrator Cameron for the interest he had evinced in the cotton industry and matters agricultural. He also congratulated him on his appointment to St. Lucia. His Honour replied in suitable terms.

The last meeting of the Legislative Council over which His Honour E. J. Cameron presided before departing to St. Lucia was held on the 16th April. After considering the despatch from the Secretary of State for the colonies and a minute from the Governor relating to the colonial estimates the usual discussion ensued. Then the Honourable Conrad J. Simmons, senior member of the Legislative Council reviewed in highly complimentary terms the manner in which His Honour administered the Government. An address from the members of the council was read by the clerk in which the Administrator was assured, "As your good work in St. Vincent has brought Your Honour promotion to St. Lucia, so we look forward to your administration of the affairs of that Colony leading to your further promotion and thus fulfilling our wishes for a successful career for you."

In replying, the Administrator thanked the members sincerely for the expressions of appreciation and goodwill contained in the address, which he highly valued and, after speaking on different subjects, His Honour said,

> In conclusion I desire to assure you that I shall ever retain a very kindly feeling for, and take a true interest in the welfare of this most beautiful island of St. Vincent--where I have lived and served so long, and which I know so well--that I shall always be desirous to advance that welfare should the occasion arise; and that I earnestly hope and pray for the island's continued well-being and that of its people.

There was an inspection of the Volunteer Reserve by His Honour E. J. Cameron at the courthouse Yard on 28th April. Mr. Richards, who was in command, presented an address to the Administrator on behalf of the corps, Mr. Cameron complimented the corps for the improvement and smartness of its appearance and tendered sincere thanks for the address.

24th May—Empire Day. The celebration consisted of a parade of the Church Lads Brigade and an inspection by His Honour Anthony DeFreitas, Acting Administrator, who was accompanied by the Venerable E. A. Turpin, Archdeacon; F. W. Griffith, Esq, Chief of police; The Honourable W. C. Hutchinson, Acting Treasurer; the Honourable J. B. Kernahan; Dr. C. W. Branch; and other prominent Government officials. The brigade under command of Captain R. M. Anderson executed the March Past in a very creditable manner. The company and physical drills with rifles were smartly performed under the command of Lieutenant R. A. Horne and to the music of the Kingstown orchestra. The Administrator complimented the brigade on its efficiency.

26th May—The Honourable C. Gideon Murray and the Honourable Mrs. Murray arrived.

27th May—His Honour the Honourable C. Gideon Murray took and subscribed the oaths of office in the presence of a representative audience at the courthouse, Kingstown. The guard-of-honour was composed of the volunteers, the police, the church lads brigade, and the boys brigade, all of whom in full uniform marched from the police barracks in admirable order behind the Kingstown orchestra.

The Administrator thus addressed the meeting:

> *Ladies and Gentlemen, I desire to thank you on behalf of Mrs. Murray and myself for the very cordial reception that you have given us to St. Vincent. We were both extremely sorry that we were unable to arrive in the Colony in time to take part in the Empire Day celebration.*
>
> *This is indeed a proud occasion in my life. It is one of those occasions which every man remembers and which he marks down in his life's diary as a red letter day. By direction of His Majesty, I have been sent to this beautiful and fertile Colony of St. Vincent, an island rich in historical associations, and one of the oldest of the British West Indian Colonies. I have been sent to this island to administer the Government for a few years and to guide the destiny of her people. This I will attempt to do to the best of my ability. (Cheers)*
>
> *Assuming the administration of this Government, I follow in the footsteps of an able, prudent and successful Administrator, Mr. Cameron—a gentleman who has justly earned your gratitude for the manner in which he has led you out of, what I may describe, a slough of despond created by the eruption of 1902-03, and into I may say, the land of Beulah—the land of all good things.*
>
> *Ladies and Gentlemen, my experience in other parts of His Majesty's Dominions has taught me that no administration can be successful except it be based on a synthetic understanding between the government and the people. This understanding it will be my earnest endeavour to cultivate and to maintain, and in doing so with the object of advancing the colony's welfare, I feel sure I will receive your loyal and whole hearted support. (Cheers)*
>
> *Ladies and Gentlemen, this colony must progress. This community must prosper. But this can only be done by your cooperation. (Cheers). I certainly cannot do it alone. We must work together. Unity is strength.*
>
> *In conclusion, I must again thank you for the very kind and hearty welcome you have accorded my wife and myself to our new home. (Prolonged cheers)*

In the interim Report made to the Administrator by Sir Rubert Boyce on his visit to the colony appeared the following:

> *There is no evidence to show that the yellow fever originated in St. Vincent. On the contrary, the very fact that the fever did not spread shows that*

there was a very small volume of infection, such as might readily have been introduced from without.

But, however it originated, the practical lesson to be learnt is that it was promptly dealt with by energetic measures and that in consequence it remained confined to a small area and did not spread all over the island. For this, the health authority is to be heartily congratulated.

I visited the colonial hospital and examined the very excellent temporary isolation room which had been constructed for yellow fever cases.

I visited the quarantine station and inspected the observation station and the yellow fever screened hospital. Both are excellent and efficient and have been economically prepared and constructed.

In conclusion, I beg to congratulate the health authority for having acted upon the most recent teachings against mosquito-borne diseases and for having brought in practical measures to diminish the mosquito pest. And I beg to thank you personally for the help you have given me to enable me to get through my work expeditiously.

I wish also to thank Drs. C. Branch and Durrant, with whom I have been constantly associated in my work and who are keenly alive to the impor tance of modern prophylactic measures.

12th June—Dr. C. W. Branch, the medical officer of the Kingstown district in charge of the colonial hospital, died at his residence in Kingstown. By his death the colony lost an energetic, skilful and sympathetic officer, whose unexcelled devotion to duty endeared him to every section of the community. His memorable services were not confined to professional duties; in his unassuming and sincere manner he interested himself in everything progressive and likely to be of benefit to the colony. He was buried with Masonic honours on the 13th and numerous persons attended the funeral to pay their last tribute of respect.

The first meeting of the Legislative Council over which His Honour the Honourable C. Gideon Murray presided was held on 16th June. An address of welcome was presented by the Honourable Conrad J. Simmons on behalf of the Council, to which His Honour replied. The Honourable Mrs. Murray attended the meeting and showed keen interest in the deliberations of the Council.

His Honour the Honourable C. G. Murray presided at a meeting held at the courthouse on 21st July, when the St. Vincent Race Club was inaugurated under the patronage of His Excellency the Governor of the Windward Islands. Accepting the Chair to which he was unanimously appointed His Honour referred to the desirability of reviving the sport of racing, which in former years contributed so largely to the enjoyment and recreation of the people of St. Vincent. On behalf of the people, he recorded an expression of gratitude to the proprietor of Brighton Estate for his generous permission for the use of a race course there for three months of every year.

The following resolution of the Legislative Council together with a reply thereto was published in an extraordinary issue of the Government *Gazette* dated 9th August:

RESOLUTION

> *That this Council is of opinion that the time has arrived when the Colony of St. Vincent should recognize her obligations to the Mother Country in respect to Imperial Defence, and with that object should vote annually and pay unconditionally into the Imperial Treasury an amount approximating to one per cent of the Revenue of the Colony as a contribution towards the Imperial Navy;*
>
> *That while the Council is fully aware that the amount would be infinitesimal in comparison with the large sum expended yearly by the Imperial Government on the upkeep of the Navy, the principle involved is the practical acknowledgment of a debt of gratitude for assistance and protection afforded in the past and present and of Loyalty to His Majesty the King.*

REPLY

> *His Majesty's Government desire to thank the Legislative Council of St. Vincent for their unconditional offer of one per cent of the revenue of the Colony as a contribution to the Navy. His Majesty's Government highly appreciate the patriotic desire of the Council to assume a share of the Imperial burden and cordially welcome the assistance offered but in present circumstances, more particularly as the whole question of Imperial defence is under examination by the conference now assembled in London, they would prefer to postpone for the present the actual consideration of particular offers of support such as this which is so generously made by St. Vincent.*

13th October—His Excellency Sir James Hayes Sadler and Lady Sadler having arrived at Grenada the following cablegram was forwarded: .

THE PEOPLE OF ST. VINCENT WELCOME YOUR EXCELLENCY AND LADY SADLER TO THE WEST INDIES.

To which His Excellency replied,

THANK PEOPLE OF ST. VINCENT ON BEHALF OF LADY SADLER AND SELF FOR VERY KIND MESSAGE OF WELCOME.

27th October—His Excellency Sir James Hayes Sadler (KCMG, CB), arrived in the afternoon from Grenada. There was a police guard-of-honour at the landing place whence His Excellency proceeded to the courthouse in the yard of which there was another guard-of-honour composed of the Volunteers and the church lads and boys brigades. The Kingstown orchestra was also in attendance. The Council chamber was decorated and many persons gathered there to witness the ceremony of the taking of the oaths by His Excellency. An address of welcome was presented to the Governor by the Honourable Conrad J. Simmons. In reply His Excellency expressed very great pleasure to meet under such auspicious circumstances his friend the Honourable C. Gideon Murray, the Administrator, and his charming and hospitable wife. The Governor complimented the Administrator for the good and valuable services he had rendered the colony since his assumption of the administration, adding that although Mr. Murray's sojourn here has been short, it is long enough to prove his ability as an Administrator and to show the people that he has their truest and best interests at heart.

9th November—The Administrator forwarded the following telegram to His Excellency the Governor:

ST. VINCENT DESIRES TO BE ASSOCIATED IN ANY TELEGRAM OF LOYAL CONGRATULATIONS TO HIS MAJESTY ON HIS BIRTHDAY.

In celebration of His Majesty's birthday there was a review on Victoria Park of the local forces comprised of the volunteers, the police and the church lads brigade. After certain evolutions they were drawn up in the centre of the park when the spectators who had come from far and near gathered round to behold the march past.

The Kingstown orchestra played the national anthem to announce the arrival of the King's Representative. His Honour reviewed the forces and returned to the saluting base after which the march past was performed whilst the Band played *The Grenadiers March*. In the course of his speech His Honour said,

> *Today is a day upon which we are all glad to gather together in order, as his subjects, to testify to our feelings of loyalty, respect and admiration, for His Most Gracious Majesty King Edward the Seventh. I know that I voice the sentiment of every one present, and indeed of the whole of the Colony—man, woman and child—in offering loyal congratulations to His Majesty on his Birthday....I thank you on behalf of His Majesty for your loyal salutations.*

The following is an extract from the report of Brigadier General J. W. A. Marshall, the Officer Commanding the Troops at Jamaica, relating to his inspection of the Windward Islands Defence Forces:

> *St. Vincent. Volunteers—One Officer, 25 other ranks.*
>
> *The local volunteer corps, which was being brought into existence at the last inspection, turned out in full strength, with the exception of two men sick, and was well clothed and equipped. The progress of this corps has been very rapid considering the short time they can give to military exercises. They were put through some Company and squad drill which was performed satisfactorily. They were exercised in advance and rear-guard formation, and extended from the former on arrival in the open, into open formation on the range, and in conjunction with a body of the police, developed an attack with ball cartridge.*

1910 / 1st January—His Honour the Administrator formally opened to traffic the new jetty in Kingstown that is constructed partly of concrete and partly of steel and iron. It is of T shape and its approach from the street to the concrete gangway is 60 feet long and 16 feet wide; the gangway is supported by three massive concrete piers at a distance of 21 feet apart; 88 feet from the shore the steel work is connected with the concrete and the gangway continues 70 feet beyond until the T is formed which gives a further length of 30 feet with a width of 45 feet. The entire length of the Jetty is 248 feet.

The Administrator was accompanied by the Honourable Mrs. Murray and Miss Greenwood.

After being saluted by the guard-of-honour whilst the orchestra played the national anthem, His Honour moved on toward the gate of the Jetty and there received the key from Mr. Osment the officer under whose supervision the work was executed. He then delivered an address which elicited enthusiastic applause. His Honour said he might be regarded as optimistic, but, he assured them it was not by pessimism and lethargy that the colony would progress, it was only by optimism and energy we would most likely succeed. The Administrator then declared the jetty open, and whilst he led the procession through the gates toward the promenade (which was gaily decorated), the orchestra played *Rule Britannia*. Soon afterward the aquatic sports commenced.

13th January—The first edition of *The Guide Book to St. Vincent* compiled by the Honourable Mrs. C. Gideon Murray was published. This is prominent among the many striking features of the Honourable Mrs. Murray's active interest in the welfare of the colony. The great demand for copies of the book is gratifying evidence of its usefulness.

On the 26th January the first ordinary general meeting of the shareholders of the St. Vincent Agricultural Credit and Loan Bank Limited was held at the lecture hall of the Free Public Library.

Their Highnesses Prince and Princess Liechtenstein arrived 21st February on a visit to the Administrator and the Honourable Mrs. Murray. His Highness is Austrian Military Attaché, London. The visitors left the colony on the 27th.

28th February—A meeting pursuant to the Royal Commission was held at the courthouse. The Commissioners were received by guard-of-honour composed of the volunteers and the police. The grounds were crowded with spectators as most of the business houses had suspended operations. The Commission sat from shortly after 10 o'clock on to 1:15 p.m. Among the witnesses examined were Mr. Francis W. Griffith, Supervisor of Customs; Mr. W. N. Sands, Agricultural Superintendent; and Honourable C. J. Simmons, Honourable D. A. MacDonald, Mm. G. R. Corea, James E. Richards, and C. E. F. Richards representing the planting and mercantile sections of the community. The commission, after the adjournment of the inquiry, repaired to the library where an excellent display of the colony's products was made.

At 2 p.m. the Commissioners sat to luncheon, the guests at which were fully representative and numbered 60. At the head of the table sat His Honour the Administrator, supported on his right by Lord Balfour, Chairman of the Commission, and on his left by Sir J. Dickson-Poynder; the other seats of honour being occupied by Sir Daniel Morris and other gentlemen of the commission, Chief Justice Shaw and the Honourable Members of the Executive and Legislative Councils. The toasts were *The King* proposed by the Administrator, *The Commission* by the Administrator, Sir J. D. Poynder replying and *The Chairman* by Lord Balfour, the Administrator replying. Mm. Sardine and Taylor contributed a delightful musical programme during the proceedings on piano and violin, respectively.

A dinner was given at Government House in honour of the commissioners and the captain and officers of H.M.S. *Melpomene.*

On his arrival 2nd May, His Excellency Sir James Hayes Sadler (KCMG, CB), was accorded a hearty welcome by His Honour the Administrator and all the prominent officials. There was a guard-of-honour composed of the volunteers and police. The meeting of the Legislative Council held the 4th of May, being the first over which His Excellency presided, the Honourable Conrad J. Simmons, on behalf of the Council, extended a cordial welcome to the Governor. His Excellency heartily thanked Honourable members and assured them that it is a great pleasure and satisfaction to him to be associated with such an able and broad-minded body of gentlemen in the Legislature of this colony and to feel that he had their loyal cooperation and support.

The following notice was published in the Government *Gazette* of 7th May:

> *It is with the profoundest sorrow that the Governor and Command-er-in-Chief of the Windward Islands announces that a telegram was received from the Secretary of State for the Colonies this morning conveying the mournful intelligence that His Most Gracious Majesty, Edward, King of Great Britain and Ireland and of the British Dominions beyond the Seas and Emperor of India, passed away in Buckingham Palace at 11.45 last night.*

On the same day the Governor, being in St. Vincent telegraphed:

THE MOURNFUL NEWS COMMUNICATED BY YOUR LORDSHIP'S TELEGRAM OF LAST NIGHT HAS BEEN RECEIVED WITH THE PROFOUNDEST SORROW BY ALL COMMUNITIES OF THE THREE COLONIES OF THE WINDWARD ISLANDS, WHO RESPECTFULLY TENDER THEIR MOST HEARTFELT AND LOYAL SYMPATHY TO THE ROYAL FAMILY.

9th May—There was a gathering of the inhabitants representing all classes and creeds at the courthouse at 4:30 p.m. for the ceremony of proclaiming King George's accession to the Throne. The guards of the volunteers and of the police with the orchestra supplied the military aspect. After the signing of the Proclamation His Excellency the Governor requested the Registrar of the Supreme Court to read the document which Mr. Robert E. Noble did in an effective manner. The guards presented arms and the band played the national anthem amidst the royal salute of 21 guns. Then His Excellency leading, the people joined him in one consent in saying with heart and voice, GOD SAVE THE KING! LONG LIVE THE KING!

The oath of allegiance was then administered and the proceeding brought to a close.

A telegram conveying the reply from the Secretary of State for the Colonies was received 11th May:

> HIS MAJESTY THE KING COMMANDS ME TO EXPRESS TO THE INHABITANTS OF THE WINDWARD ISLANDS HIS MOST SINCERE THANKS FOR THEIR MESSAGE OF SYMPATHY WITH THE ROYAL FAMILY IN THIS HOUR OF SORROW.

A special meeting of the Legislative Council was convened on 14th May. His Excellency the Governor, the Honourable C. G. Murray, and the Honourable D. MacDonald, representing the unofficial members of the council, in the course of three eloquent speeches paid fitting tribute to the incomparable Edward VII, of blessed and glorious memory. An address of sympathy and loyalty to His Majesty King George V, signed by the Councillors, was read by the Clerk and finally entrusted to His Excellency for transmission.

20th May—A day of mourning. Memorial services were held in the several churches throughout the island and its dependencies. In Kingstown the official service was held at St. George's Cathedral; the officiating clergy being the Venerable Archdeacon Turpin, Rev. R. J. Laurie, who preached the sermon, (from Job, Chapter 1. Verse 21); the Rev. G. Paterson, the Rev. H. E. Gresham, and the Rev. D. Hadley. The official procession was formed at the courthouse and proceeded to the cathedral in the following order: Kingstown municipal band, police guard, volunteer reserve guard, church lads and boys brigade, His Honour the Administrator (in civil service uniform), His Honour the Chief Justice (in his robes of office), members of the executive council, members of the Legislative Council, ministers of religion, foreign consuls, public officers, legal and medical practitioners, The Kingstown Board, journalists, merchants and planters, the Freemasons, the foresters and friendly societies, carriages—a most imposing and impressive display.

The Government *Gazette* of 25th May contained the undermentioned telegraphic message from His Majesty the King:

> TO MY PEOPLE BEYOND THE SEAS
>
> THE INNUMERABLE MESSAGES OF KINDNESS FROM MY LOYAL SUBJECTS BEYOND THE SEAS HAVE DEEPLY TOUCHED MY HEART AND HAVE ASSURED ME THAT I HAVE IN FULL MEASURE THEIR SYMPATHY IN THE GREAT TRIAL WHICH HAS BEFALLEN ME AND THEM, THAT MY SORROW IS THEIR SORROW, AND THAT WE SHARE A COMMON LOSS. THE HAPPINESS OF ALL HIS PEOPLE THROUGHOUT HIS DOMINIONS WAS DEAR TO THE HEART OF MY BELOVED FATHER. FOR THEM HE LIVED AND WORKED, IN THEIR SERVICE HE DIED,

AND I CANNOT DOUBT THAT THEY WILL HOLD HIS NAME IN GRATEFUL RE-
MEMBRANCE.

I AM NOW CALLED TO FOLLOW IN HIS FOOTSTEP AND CARRY ON THE WORK
WHICH PROSPERED IN HIS HANDS. AS A SAILOR I HAVE BEEN BROUGHT
INTO CONSTANT TOUCH WITH THE OVERSEA DOMINIONS OF THE CROWN, AND
I HAVE PERSONALLY REALIZED THE AFFECTIONATE LOYALTY THAT HOLDS
TOGETHER MANY LANDS AND DIVERSE PEOPLES IN ONE GLORIOUS FELLOW-
SHIP. NINE YEARS AGO, I TRAVELLED THROUGH THE EMPIRE ACCOMPANIED
BY MY DEAR WIFE, AND HAD THE LATE KING LIVED WE SHOULD TOGETH-
ER AT HIS EXPRESS WISH HAVE VISITED SOUTH AFRICA IN THE COMING
AUTUMN TO OPEN THE FIRST PARLIAMENT OF THE SOUTH AFRICAN UNION,
THE LATEST AND GREATEST EVIDENCE OF THAT PEACE AND HARMONY WHICH
MY FATHER EVER LOVED TO PROMOTE. IT WILL BE MY EARNEST ENDEAVOUR
TO UPHOLD CONSTITUTIONAL GOVERNMENT AND TO SAFEGUARD IN ALL THEIR
FULNESS THE LIBERTIES WHICH ARE ENJOYED THROUGHOUT MY DOMINIONS,
AND UNDER THE GOOD GUIDANCE OF THE RULER OF ALL MEN I WILL MAIN-
TAIN ON THE FOUNDATIONS OF FREEDOM, JUSTICE AND PEACE THE GREAT
HERITAGE OF THE UNITED BRITISH EMPIRE.

In a despatch from the Secretary of State for the Colonies the following
intelligence was conveyed:

WINDWARD ISLANDS

DOWNING STREET,

SAINT VINCENT 7TH JUNE, 1910.

NO. 28.

SIR,

I HAVE THE HONOUR TO ACKNOWLEDGE THE RECEIPT OF YOUR DESPATCH
SAINT VINCENT NO. 45 OF THE 12TH ULTIMO, REPORTING THE RECEIPT OF
THE NEWS OF THE DEATH OF HIS LATE MAJESTY KING EDWARD VII AND THE
PROCLAMATION OF THE ACCESSION OF HIS PRESENT MAJESTY KING GEORGE
THE FIFTH IN SAINT VINCENT.

I HAVE TO INFORM YOU THAT THE DESPATCH HAS BEEN LAID BEFORE THE
KING WHO WAS MUCH TOUCHED AT LEARNING OF THE SORROW AND WIDE-
SPREAD MOURNING WITH WHICH THE NEWS OF HIS LATE MAJESTY'S DEATH
HAS BEEN RECEIVED THROUGHOUT THE COLONY.

                                    I HAVE, &C. CREWE.
                         GOVERNOR, LIEUTENANT COLONEL
        SIR J. HAYES SADLER, (KCMG), C.B., &C., &C., &C.

9th June—Union Island, a dependency of St. Vincent, was purchased by
the Government for the purpose of allotting small parcels to residents of that
place.

1911 / At the meeting of the Legislative Council held on Tuesday, 24th
January, the Administrator, in the course of his lengthy and interesting speech,
announced that during the preceding year the last of the public debt, for
which the Colony was directly responsible, had been paid off. There was a
floating surplus of £6,000 and a permanent investment of £25,000.

On Wednesday, 8th February, Mrs. Shaw distributed prizes to pupils of the
Grammar School. In his address His Honour W. S. Shaw, Acting Administrator, expressed regret for the unavoidable absence of the Administrator and

the Honourable Mrs. Murray. He congratulated the pupils and referred in complimentary terms to the qualification of the headmaster. At the conclusion of this function there was the unveiling of portraits of Their Majesties the King and Queen. Mr. Shaw again delivered an appropriate address and, as the veil was drawn aside and the pictures exposed, the company sang the national anthem.

8th February—The 2nd ordinary general meeting of the St. Vincent Agricultural Credit and Loan Bank Ltd. was held. The directors' report in respect to the preceding year was unanimously adopted. The balance sheet showed 1,261 shares were sold for which the sum paid was $630.50; the total liabilities amounted to $670.61 and the assets to $835.89, yielding a profit of $165.28. A dividend of 12% was declared.

The business of the Wesleyan Methodist Synod was commenced on the 6th and continued to the 11th February. The investigation of the affairs of the different circuits unmistakably proved the progress that is generally observed.

15th February—There was held the first meeting of the committee appointed by the Administrator to make recommendations respecting the manner in which the coronation of Their Majesties the King and Queen should be celebrated in the colony.

The scheme conceived by Lady Sadler and the Honourable Mrs. Murray was successfully carried into effect. The humblest woman in the community was afforded an opportunity, of which many availed themselves, to contribute to the sum required for procuring a gift for Her Majesty the Queen from the women of St. Vincent. From small contributions £38 8 0 was received by Mrs. W. S. Shaw, who was appointed the Honorary Treasurer. The gift was a parasol and represented the work of Miss McDonald, Miss Kate McDonald, Miss Ethel Durrant, and Miss Leila Durrant, all of whom are natives of this island. It was exhibited at the free public library from March 14 to 18.

A message from the Queen was conveyed to the Honourable Mrs. Murray to the effect that Her Majesty will be graciously pleased to carry the parasol at one or other of the functions of the coronation.

16th March—His Honour the Administrator presented Miss M. E. Webster, nurse-matron of the colonial hospital, with the medal of the Colonial Nursing Association for five years of meritorious service.

Mr. Frederick Fenger of Boston, Mass., arrived alone in his boat from Grenada via the Grenadines. The boat is a canoe yawl named *Yakaboo*, 17 feet long and 3 feet 3 inches wide carrying two bat wing sails. He left Kingstown for Chateaubelair on the 22nd on his way to St. Lucia.

The Synod of the Diocese of the Windward Islands was held in the Cathedral Church of St. George on 30th and 31st March and on 1st April. There were present

His Lordship, The Bishop of Barbados and Windward Islands (President)

Clergy:
- The Venerable The Archdeacon of St. Vincent,
- The Rev. Canon C. Arthur, Grenada
- The Rev. J. Bascom, St. Lucia
- The Rev. H. E. Gresham, St. Vincent
- The Rev. G. A. I. Frederick (BA), Grenada
- The Rev. J. Henderson Bell (BA), St. Vincent
- The Rev. George Paterson (L.TH)
- The Rev. E. E. Giles, Grenada
- The Rev. D. Hadley (L.TH), St. Vincent
- The Rev. G. A. Taylor (BA), Grenada
- The Rev. R. J. Laurie (BA), St. Vincent
- The Rev. A. F. Mandeville (L.TH), Grenada

Laity:
- The Worshipful A. W. Lewis, Chancellor
- Hon. J. G. W. Hazell, St. Vincent
- P. F. Huggins, Esq, St. Vincent
- His Honour W. S. Shaw, St. Vincent
- C. A. Hadley, Esq, St. Vincent
- F. W. Reeves, Esq, M.A., St. Vincent
- A. Abbott, Esq, St. Vincent
- J. C. Date, Esq, Grenada
- J. R. Bertrand, Esq, Grenada
- D. R. Dyce, Esq, Grenada
- J. Martin, Esq, Grenada

The Rev. B. A. Samuel, Rector of Bocas del Toro (Panama) in the Diocese of British Honduras, was present as visitor.

The canons were revised and resolutions passed to consider what steps might be taken toward securing a separate Bishop of the Windward Islands. It was desired to impress upon the several church councils the necessity for

(a) providing a Fund to afford relief to clergymen in case of breakdown, and

(b) making arrangements for a scheme by means of which the lives of the clergy might be insured.

His Lordship expressed great pleasure in announcing the collation of the Rev. J. R. Bascom to the stall of St. Aidan, and of the Rev. H. E. Gresham to that of St. Patrick.

2nd April —A census was taken of St. Vincent and its dependencies. The colony was divided into five districts, to each of which there was a commissioner who appointed enumerators for the subdivisions of the respective districts. The computation proved the population to be 41,877 (males, 18,345 and females, 23,532); St. Vincent, 38,372; Bequia, 1,557; Union Island, 1,074; Canouan, 498; Mayreau, 224; Mustique, 114; Balliceaux and Battawia, 38. In the towns (exclusive of suburbs) Kingstown, 4,300; Georgetown, 551; Calliaqua, 431; Layou 441; Barrouallie, 1,240; Chateaubelair,

719. The natives of St. Vincent numbered 36,283; Grenadines, 3,299; St. Vincent (East Indian parents) 263; Trinidad, 223; Barbados, 848; Other British West Indies, 536; British North America, 6; United Kingdom, 87; Foreign West Indies, 30; Europe, 11; Madeira, 65; United States of America, 6; South America, 22; India, 114; Africa, 61; other places, 18; not described, five. In regard to religions there were Anglicans, 19,932; Wesleyans, 16,096; Roman Catholics, 3,405; Presbyterians, 1,033; others, 961; Non-Christians, 62; not described, 388. Percentage of Births, St. Vincent and Grenadines, 95; other West Indies, 4; Other Places, 1.

4th April—Shooting for the cup offered by His Excellency Sir James Hayes Sadler for annual competition of the constabulary of the Windward Islands, the St. Vincent police scored 567; on the 5th, St. Lucia scored 564, and on the 6th Grenada scored 533. The Cup was formally presented by the Administrator to the officers, non-commissioned officers and men of the Force drawn up for the occasion at the Barrack Yard on the 15th. His Honour heartily congratulated them and conveyed His Excellency's congratulations.

24th May—Members of the St. Vincent Rifle Club shot for and won the cup generously offered by Mr. David Slinger of Grenada for competition of similar clubs in the islands of Grenada and St. Lucia. The scores were St. Vincent 674, Grenada 640 and St. Lucia 561.

2nd June—There was a parade of the local forces on Victoria Park to celebrate His Majesty's birthday. The volunteers and police marched past His Honour W. S. Shaw, Acting Administrator; many persons had assembled for the occasion. The evolutions, *feu de joie*, and royal salute were creditably executed, and the music of the Kingstown orchestra and volunteer band enhanced the delightfulness of the ceremony.

His Honour requested the chief of police to convey to the forces his appreciation of the excellent manner in which they had acquitted themselves.

20th June—His Honour the Administrator accompanied by Mr. T. Osment, the Leeward Warden, and Mr. G. B. Pease (ADC), visited Barrouallie and formally declared, in the presence of a large gathering of people, the new water-service of that town open. The spring is situated at Pierre Hughes near the town; it is protected by a covered concrete catch pit, and the water is conveyed by 1½ inch pipe to a reservoir, the capacity of which is 10,000 gallons. The main from the reservoir to the town is of 1½ inch pipe distributed along the principal streets by standpipes erected at regular distances with half-inch taps.

On 21st June, the Administrator telegraphed to His Excellency the Governor :

COUNCILS AND INHABITANTS OF SAINT VINCENT DESIRE TO BE ASSOCIATED WITH ANY TELEGRAM OF LOYAL CONGRATULATIONS TO THEIR MAJESTIES THE KING AND QUEEN UPON THEIR CORONATION.

22nd June--The Coronation of Their Majesties King George V and Queen Mary was celebrated throughout the colony. The decorations at the cathedral, the churches, the institutions, the Government buildings, the streets, and private residences were extensive and beautiful. The care bestowed in the preparation of each was an indication of sincere loyalty and patriotism.

At 8 o'clock in the morning there was a review on Victoria Park of the local forces, the church lads brigade, and boys brigade, all under command of the chief of police (mounted). The municipal band and the volunteer band were in attendance.

After performing various evolutions the Administrator inspected them and then a *feu de joie* was fired.

Additional drills were accomplished after which they creditably marched past His Honour the Administrator who was attended by Mr. G. B. Pease, the Aide de Camp. They were then "drawn up" for the purpose of listening to the lengthy, appropriate and impressive speech which His Honour the Administrator delivered to the hearing of hundreds of people.

The attendance at the Coronation services held at different places of worship was large, especially was it so at the cathedral where the Administrator and the Honourable Mrs. Murray with all the members of the councils attended. The Venerable E. A. Turpin's sermon was one worthy of the great festival and the grandeur and solemnity of the entire service deeply impressed the congregation.

The official procession moved from the cathedral westward along lower Grenville Street to Tyrrell Street around Victoria Park, then eastward up Long Lane to the market, thence turning to the Bay Street marched up to Sharpe Street and down Granby and Halifax Streets to the courthouse yard. A salute was fired and the municipal band played the national anthem. The Administrator then said aloud, "God save the King" "Long live the King," etc., each of which was repeated by the people with enthusiasm. The proceedings were concluded with three cheers for His Majesty the King and three more for Her Majesty Queen Mary.

During the evening the people were numerous on the streets, admiring the magnificent illuminations of private residences most of which displayed very appropriate mottoes. A beautiful bonfire was lit on Fort Charlotte, and at 8 p.m. thousands of persons assembled along the beach to behold the pyrotechnic display prepared by the Government Coronation Committee.

23rd June—The demonstration of friendly societies and school children was uncommonly grand. Their artistic banners, flags and regalia were attractive. Their procession through the town was headed by the municipal band but there were also the volunteer band and other bands. When they arrived at Victoria Park, they sang the national anthem and patriotic songs. There the Administrator addressed them—a body of loyal adult and juvenile subjects of Their Gracious Majesties. This ceremony was brought to a close with repeated cheers for His Honour the Administrator and the Honourable Mrs. Murray. There was an official reception and a ball at Government House in the evening.

24th June—A meeting of the Legislative Council was held at the courthouse when an address to His Majesty the King was unanimously adopted.

The stock trough erected jointly by the Government and the Kingstown Board in the market square was formally declared open by the Administrator and the Honourable Mrs. Murray. In the course of His address, His Honour referred to the special pleasure it would afford His Majesty to know that such an humane act was done in commemoration of his coronation, for the King is particularly fond of animals and leaves nothing undone to contribute to the comfort of those in the royal stables, which include some of the finest horses not only in the British Empire but of the world.

In the smaller towns the commemoration was equally enthusiastic. The ringing of joy bells, the services, processions, treats, firing of guns, fireworks were all accomplished with credit to the various committees and individuals who undertook the supervision.

Three hundred twenty-five new shillings with the King's head as the effigy were distributed among the poor throughout the colony especially to those who were recipients of the Government poor relief. The ministers of religion and other gentlemen to whom the duty was entrusted delivered a short address at each place and the people were thankful for the appropriate gift and were delighted at the kind remembrance.

The following letter from the King was received by the Secretary of State for the Home Department for transmission:

BUCKINGHAM PALACE, 29th JUNE, 1911, TO MY PEOPLE,
NOW THAT THE CORONATION AND ITS ATTENDANT CEREMONIES ARE OVER, I
DESIRE TO ASSURE THE PEOPLE OF THE BRITISH EMPIRE OF MY GRATE-
FUL SENSE THAT THEIR HEARTS HAVE BEEN WITH ME THROUGH IT ALL. I
FELT THIS IN THE BEAUTIFUL AND IMPRESSIVE SERVICE IN THE AB-
BEY—THE MOST SOLEMN EXPERIENCE OF MY LIFE—AND SCARCELY LESS IN
THE STIRRING SCENES OF THE SUCCEEDING DAYS, WHEN MY PEOPLE HAVE
SIGNIFIED THEIR RECOGNITION AND THEIR HEARTFELT WELCOME OF ME
AS THEIR SOVEREIGN. FOR THIS HAS BEEN APPARENT, NOT ONLY IN THE
LOYAL ENTHUSIASM SHOWN IN OUR PASSAGE TO AND FROM WESTMINSTER AND
IN THE PROGRESSES WHICH WE HAVE MADE IN DIFFERENT DISTRICTS OF
LONDON, BUT ALSO IN THE THOUSANDS OF MESSAGES OF GOODWILL WHICH
HAVE COME TO ME ACROSS THE SEAS FROM EVERY PART OF THE EMPIRE.
SUCH AFFECTIONATE DEMONSTRATIONS HAVE PROFOUNDLY TOUCHED ME, AND
HAVE FILLED ME AFRESH WITH FAITH AND CONFIDENCE. BELIEVING THAT

THIS GENEROUS AND OUTSPOKEN SYMPATHY WITH THE QUEEN AND MYSELF IS UNDER GOD, OUR SUREST SOURCE OF STRENGTH, I AM ENCOURAGED TO GO FORWARD WITH RENEWED HOPE. WHATEVER PERPLEXITIES OR DIFFICULTIES MAY LIE BEFORE ME AND MY PEOPLE, WE SHALL ALL UNITE IN FACING THEM RESOLUTELY, CALMLY AND WITH PUBLIC SPIRIT, CONFIDENT THAT UNDER DIVINE GUIDANCE THE ULTIMATE OUTCOME WILL BE TO THE COMMON GOOD.

GEORGE R.I.

The following despatch was received from the Right Honourable the Secretary of State for the Colonies:

WINDWARD ISLANDS, DOWNING STREET,
GRENADA (GENERAL). 30th JUNE, 1911
NO. 94.

SIR, I HAVE THE HONOUR TO ACKNOWLEDGE THE RECEIPT OF YOUR DESPATCH NO. 105 OF THE 15th OF MAY, WITH REFERENCE TO THE GIFTS SUBSCRIBED FOR BY THE WOMEN OF GRENADA, ST. LUCIA AND ST. VINCENT FOR PRESENTATION TO HER MAJESTY THE QUEEN ON THE OCCASION OF THEIR MAJESTIES CORONATION.

THE GIFTS, TOGETHER WITH THE ACCOMPANYING ADDRESSES, WERE PRESENTED TO HER MAJESTY AT BUCKINGHAM PALACE ON JUNE 19th. MR. D. S. DE FREITAS AND MRS. DE FREITAS ATTENDED AT THE PRESENTATION ON BEHALF OF GRENADA, AND MRS. SHERIFF ON BEHALF OF ST. LUCIA.

I AM COMMANDED BY HER MAJESTY TO SAY THAT SHE WAS PARTICULARLY PLEASED WITH THE PRESENTS AND TO CONVEY HER GRATEFUL THANKS TO THE CONTRIBUTORS FOR THEIR EXCEEDINGLY KIND GIFTS.

I HAVE, &C.,
L. HARCOURT, GOVERNOR
LIEUTENANT-COLONEL SIR J. HAYES SADLER, (KCMG, CB)
&C., &C., &C.

The appreciation of Their Majesties the King and Queen was also conveyed in despatches from the Right Honourable the Secretary of State for the Colonies:

WINDWARD ISLANDS DOWNING STREET
GRENADA (GENERAL) 11th JUNE, 1911
NO. 100.

SIR, I HAVE THE HONOUR TO ACKNOWLEDGE THE RECEIPT OF YOUR TELEGRAM OF THE 22nd OF JUNE, TENDERING TO THEIR MAJESTIES THE KING AND QUEEN ON THE OCCASION OF THEIR CORONATION THE CONGRATULATIONS OF THE COUNCILS AND COMMUNITIES OF GRENADA, ST. LUCIA AND ST. VINCENT.

YOUR TELEGRAM HAS BEEN LAID BEFORE THE KING AND I REQUEST THAT YOU WILL MAKE KNOWN IN THE COLONY UNDER YOUR GOVERNMENT THAT THEIR MAJESTIES GREATLY APPRECIATE THIS LOYAL MESSAGE AND COMMAND ME TO EXPRESS THEIR SINCERE THANKS TO THEIR SUBJECTS THROUGHOUT THE WINDWARD ISLANDS.

I HAVE, &C.,L. HARCOURT, GOVERNOR
LIEUT-COLONEL SIR J. HAYES SADLER,(KCMG, CB), &C., &C., &C.

16th August—A reception meeting was held at the Wesleyan Church, Kingstown, on behalf of the Rev. Henry Haigh, the President of the Wesleyan

Methodist Conference. He was accompanied by the Rev. W. Hudson-Smith, Mr. G. H. Clapham, Mrs. and Miss Haigh, and Mrs. and Miss Hudson-Smith.

26th December—The shooting competition of the volunteers of the Windward Islands for the cup offered by His Excellency Sir James Hayes Sadler resulted in victory for the corps of St. Vincent. The scores were Grenada, 523, St. Lucia, 553, and St. Vincent 575.

1912 / 1st January—Robert E. Noble, Esq, the legal assistant was appointed Acting Attorney General of St. Vincent.

This appointment was for several years held by the Attorney General of Grenada.

15th January—At the meeting of the Legislative Council, Mr. F. W. Griffith was appointed to represent St. Vincent at the conference to be held at Ottawa. Mr. J. G. W. Hazell was appointed to accompany him as commercial advisor.

17th January—Mm. J. W. McConnel and W. Marsland, delegates of the British Cotton Growing Association to the Agricultural Conference at Trinidad, visited St. Vincent. The Honourables C. J. Simmons and J. G. W. Hazell and Mr. W. N. Sands were appointed a committee to expedite the business of the visitors.

20th January—There was a meeting of the Cotton Growers Association, etc., at which His Honour the Administrator extended a hearty welcome to Mr. McConnel, who afterward delivered a lengthy and interesting speech.

31st January—The speech day of the Grammar School was observed. The audience included the Administrator, the Honourable Mrs. Murray, the Chief Justice, Mrs. Shaw, the parents and guardians of pupils. A farcical sketch entitled, "Maria", was satisfactorily performed by the pupils. After the prizes were distributed by the Honourable Mrs. Murray, His Honour the Administrator delivered an excellent speech. At the conclusion, Mr. Reeves the headmaster expressed thanks and called for the customary cheers for the Administrator and the Honourable Mrs. Murray to which the pupils heartily responded.

18th February—A large congregation attended the morning service at the Church of Scotland. An impressive ceremony was performed after divine service when the Rev. Wallace Smith was presented with a valedictory address and a purse.

21st February—At a meeting of the women's guild held in the Church of Scotland, the Honourable Mrs. Murray, President of the guild, presented the Rev. Wallace Smith, on behalf of the ladies of the guild, with a handsome deck chair made of local mahogany on which was an inscription on silver plate. A valedictory address accompanied the gift.

21st March—His Excellency Sir James Hayes Sadler's challenge cup, won by the St. Vincent volunteers at the shooting competition was presented by the Administrator with hearty congratulations from the Governor to Captain Richards. The three cups which are being competed for annually by rifle clubs of the Windward islands are now in the glass case at the free public library, St. Vincent.

Since the inauguration of the peasant land settlement scheme at Union Island a comparison, which reveals the significant change among the inhabitants, has been included in the Commissioner's report:

> In 1909-1910, the year immediately preceding the purchase of this dependency by the Government, the number of cases on the criminal side from Union Island alone, which were brought up for hearing before the Commissioner, amounted to 60. In the year 1910-1911, the year of acquisition, this number was reduced to 25, while during the year 1911-1912, crime would appear to have almost reached the vanishing point, since for the period under review, only 6 cases have been lodged for hearing.
>
> If any proof were needed in confirmation of the truism that possession of land results in making men respectable and law abiding citizens, it is to be found at Union Island where in 2 short years, a community of 1,800 people, who had long borne an unenviable notoriety in this island for misbehaviour of all kinds, has been transformed into one of peace and harmony, which will bear favourable comparison with any place of its size in the West Indies.

Toward the close of the business of the Legislative Council on 25th March, the members recorded their appreciation of the invaluable services Mr. W. S. Shaw has rendered this colony during his sojourn here as chief justice. As an acknowledgment of their indebtedness to him for the arduous work he undertook and successfully accomplished in the revision of the laws of the colony, they unanimously voted an honorarium of £50. Mr. Shaw thanked the members for their kind consideration and promised to obtain out of this generous gift a souvenir as from the Legislative Council of St. Vincent.

His Honour Walter Sidney Shaw presided at the Supreme Court of Judicature for the last time on the 26th March. There were present the Honourable R. E Noble, Acting Attorney General, the Honourable C. J. Simmons and Mr. T. W. S. Garraway, representing the legal practitioners and many other persons. At the conclusion of the cases, Mr. Noble addressed the chief justice in reference to His Honour's departure from the colony after successfully discharging the combined duties of chief justice and of magistrate of the first district. He also gave expression to his appreciation of the ability, the legal acumen, and the absolute impartiality that marked Mr. Shaw's administration of the law. He wished His Honour farewell, adding that the loss to this colony would be a great gain to the people of British Honduras.

Mr. Simmons endorsed the sentiments that were so well expressed by Mr. Noble and added that a pleasing feature of Mr. Shaw's presidency over the local courts was the uninterrupted harmony that existed between the Bench and the Bar since his assumption of the office.

Mr. Garraway supported the tribute paid His Honour by the preceding speakers and alluded to the important work which Mr. Shaw had done in revising the laws of this colony which would greatly facilitate the administration of justice.

Mr. Shaw said he regretted to leave St. Vincent where he had made many friends, whose memory he would ever cherish. His duties on the bench had been often lightened by the help he received from the members of the bar and by the cordial relations that have existed always between them. He regretted that counsel did not appear oftener in the local courts to give their valuable assistance in arriving at the ends of justice. He sincerely thanked all the gentlemen for their good wishes to him and to Mrs. Shaw who is equally sorry to leave St. Vincent, in whose welfare she was deeply interested, and assured them that they both would never forget the good people of this island.

As His Honour R. E. Noble, Acting Chief Justice, presided for the first time over the Supreme Court in its Summary Jurisdiction on 23rd April, Mr. T. W. S. Garraway, barrister-at-law, in a speech offered on behalf of the legal profession his respectful congratulations. The Honourable Conrad J. Simmons endorsed Mr. Garaway's remarks.

The Acting Chief Justice said he was gratified by the kindly expressions. It would be nothing short of affectation to pretend that he was not pleased at his selection for the post, which he would endeavour to fill with satisfactory results to the colony.

25th April—The first West Indian needlework exhibition was held at the lecture hall of the free public library from this date to the 4th May. Needlework from Trinidad, Tobago, Grenada, Union Island, Bequia, St. Vincent, St. Lucia, Martinique, Barbados, Guadeloupe, Montserrat, Antigua, Saba, Anguilla, St. Kitts, Nevis, Tortola, Anegada, Puerto Rico, and Cuba were exhibited. His Honour the Administrator, accompanied by the Honourable Mrs. Murray, Mr. Norman Lamont of Trinidad and Mr. Herbert Ferguson of Grenada, arrived at 4.30 p.m. They were received by Mr. Walter Grant, the chairman of the library committee, who conducted them to the exhibition hall.

In his speech of considerable length, His Honour expressed pleasure at seeing such a representative gathering for it signified that all sections of the community take an interest in a movement which should prove of immense benefit to the fine needle workers of this colony and which should inspire them in the future to greater efforts in the perfecting of their productions.

His Honour made reference to the pages of West Indian history in order to realize how true the old saying is that, "Time is the great teacher and healer of all." That instead of the strife and the struggle, the bloodshed and the battle of one hundred years ago we have today that *entente cordiale* which permits the two powerful combatant nations of those days to live in amity both at home and in these colonies.

On behalf of Mrs. Murray, His Honour publicly extended to the self help association, the workers and others who interested themselves in this and in the other islands, sincere appreciation for their hearty support.

Mr. Lamont, in response to the Administrator's call, said he had pleasure in the opportunity afforded him to attend an exhibition of such an exquisitely fine collection of articles and expressed his appreciation of the happy thought to conceive the idea, and the enterprise that enabled them to bring it to a successful issue. He observed the peculiar characteristic of St. Vincent to lead the other islands in progressive movements. St. Vincent led in the presentation of a coronation gift to the Queen, in contributing to *Titanic* disaster fund, in offering to contribute to the upkeep of the navy. Its recuperative powers are remarkable—there is another lead in the question of West Indian unification and now in this exhibition. Toward the conclusion of a delightful speech, Mr. Lamont paid a tribute to the Administrator and to Mrs. Murray for the excellent work they are doing for the revival of this colony's prosperity. St. Vincent was in the position of the Cinderella among the sister islands. Since the coming of her prince with his wand and her fairy godmother with the glass slipper, this West Indian "Cinderella" was made happy and charming and was being admired as the belle of the ball.

Mr. Ferguson delivered a short but amusing speech in the course of which he referred in highly complimentary terms both to Lady Sadler and to Mrs. Murray as "born organizers" and to the interest they are showing respectively in the welfare of Grenada and St. Vincent.

Mr. Walter Grant congratulated Mrs. Murray on the success of the exhibition and assured her that the library committee would be pleased at all times to place the hall at her disposal, particularly for such laudable purposes.

The winners were then called by Mrs. Murray and the prizes were presented by the Administrator.

In a Circular issued by the Honourable Mrs. Murray at a subsequent date, two suggestions were submitted for the earnest consideration of other West Indian Colonies: 1) That a similar exhibition should be held annually and in turn in the different Colonies of the West Indies at a specified time; and 2) That a central association be formed to which shall be affiliated such self help and home industries associations of the British West Indies as care to join with the object of creating a British West Indian fine needlework industry on cooperative lines, and of assisting the workers to profit by their needlework, not only by local sales but also by sales in Canada promoted by means of systematized advertisement and through appointed agents and depots in that dominion.

The St. Vincent Trained Nurses Association was organized with the object of promoting the interest and raising the standard of general efficiency of the nurses and midwives of the colony. The wife of the Governor of the Windward Islands is president; the wife of the Administrator of St. Vincent is senior vice president; the wife of the Chief Justice and three other ladies resident in the island are also vice presidents. The management devolves on a committee of nine members. The members consist of certified nurses or midwives. Residents of St. Vincent or the Windward Islands interested in nursing are eligible to become subscribers, the entrance fee being 2/6 and the yearly subscriptions 1/-. Lectures will from time to time be given by medical members of the association and other qualified persons.

There are three classes:

Class A includes nurses and midwives who hold 2nd class certificates from the medical board but who have had no training, and who have had at least three years' experience and can produce recommendations as to work and character from a Medical Practitioner or some person of standing able to form an opinion;

Class B includes nurses and midwives who have had some hospital experience or who hold 1st class certificates from the medical board; and

Class C includes nurses and midwives who have had hospital training and have successfully passed an examination by the board of examiners appointed by the committee of the association.

1st June—The Office of Treasurer was separated from that of Administrator and Mr. W. C. Hutchinson was appointed Treasurer of the colony.

At the meeting of the Legislative Council held on 4th June, an address of condolence to His Majesty the King and the Royal Family on the death of King Frederick of Denmark was moved and unanimously carried. His Honour remarked that King Frederick was a good king and his subjects were devoted to him. As subjects of another good king we can truly sympathize with them.

His Majesty's birthday was celebrated in the customary manner on 7th June. The review of the local forces by His Honour the Administrator was the principal public ceremony. The police and volunteer efficiently marched past the Administrator after the usual inspection and the firing of the *feu de joie*. Head dress was removed and three hearty cheers were given for His Majesty the King.

His Honour commended the men for the excellent display and at the conclusion of his address expressed the wish that they would steadfastly maintain such discipline and unflinching devotion to duty as was necessary to constitute the defence of a country.

He thanked the forces on behalf of His Majesty the King for their loyal attendance at the review.

On 25th October, His Honour Robert Blair Roden was accorded a hearty welcome on his assumption of the duties of Chief Justice and Magistrate of the First District. Mr. R. E. Noble the Acting Attorney General assured His Honour of the cooperation of the bar and expressed on behalf of the people of this colony their gratification at his appointment.

Mr. T. W. S. Garraway endorsed the sentiments expressed by Mr. Noble and extended his personal congratulations to His Honour.

The Chief Justice, in reply, said he was deeply sensible of the courtesy shown him in so kindly welcoming him to this colony. He acknowledged that he spent a very pleasant time in this island when he had the honour to act as Chief Justice; and it was the remembrance of that enjoyment and of the great kindness shown him by the public of St. Vincent that made him look forward with gladness to his return to this colony. The maintenance of good relations between bench and bar was essential to the efficient administration of justice and he was delighted to observe that such relations existed here.

28th October—His Excellency E. J. Cameron (CMG), Acting Governor of the Windward Islands, arrived from St. Lucia. He was accorded an official reception on landing at 8 a.m. After inspecting the guard composed of the volunteer and the police he proceeded to the council chamber and subscribed to the oaths. His Excellency delivered an address and expressed his thanks for the hearty welcome mentioning the pleasure he felt in taking this opportunity to visit St. Vincent.

The Acting Governor reviewed the volunteers and police in Victoria Park on the 30th. His Excellency said he was quite pleased with their appearance. Head dress was removed and three cheers given to His Excellency.

The first cricket contest in St. Vincent between teams of Grenada, St. Lucia and St. Vincent respectively, for the cup generously given in 1910 by His Honour P. C. Cork, Administrator of St. Lucia, was held.

1913 / January 14th—At the meeting of the Legislative Council the Customs Preferential Duties Ordinance 1913 was passed. This ordinance gives effect to the Canada-West Indian Preferential Tariff Agreement that was signed at Ottawa on the 9th of April, 1912. The Honourable E. R. Noble, the Acting Attorney General, reviewed the circumstances relating to the conference at Ottawa and congratulated the Honourable F. W. Griffith, the local delegate; also the Honourable J. G. W. Hazell, his commercial advisor, for the important and valuable services they performed for this colony at that conference.

25ᵗʰ—Mr. Richard Ollivierre left the island to represent St. Vincent in the cricket rest matches to be played at Barbados, Trinidad and British Guiana against the M.C.C. Team.

27ᵗʰ—Opening of the Grammar School in its new quarters at the experiment station by His Excellency Sir James Hayes Sadler, who was accompanied by Lady Sadler; His Lordship Dr. W. P. Swaby, the Bishop of Barbados and of the Windward Islands; His Honour R. B. Roden, the Chief Justice (then acting Colonial Secretary), and Mrs. Roden. A review of the work of the school for the last four years was given by the headmaster, who also spoke of the ability of his newly appointed assistant, Mr. J. E. Blackman (BA), (Dunelm), who holds a second class honours certificate. He also mentioned that the number 45, with which the school was re-opening, was larger than had ever been attained in the history of the school. His Excellency paid a tribute to the headmaster's energy and zeal, and gave an interesting speech on the wider ideals of education, both scholastic and athletic. His Lordship congratulated Mr. Reeves, and said that he had known both the masters of the school for many years, and was convinced that in them St. Vincent had two zealous officers. Prizes were then distributed by Lady Sadler, who added two for general improvement and good conduct. The surroundings of the new school are such as to induce both mental and physical improvement in the pupils.

February 13ᵗʰ—His Honour the Administrator and the Honourable Mrs. Murray arrived from England. In addition to the customary formalities of official welcome there was an extraordinary assembly on the jetty and along the street while the enthusiastic cheers of the people made the demonstration exceedingly impressive.

24ᵗʰ—The following message from His Majesty the King to the people of his West Indian colonies was delivered by Her Highness Princess Marie Louise of Schleswig-Holstein at Barbados on the occasion of the opening there of the inter-colonial needlework exhibition:

> The King has charged me with a message to you. He desires me to express to you and through you to all the inhabitants of his West Indian Dominions the interest which he takes in their welfare. He has watched their progress with sympathy, and it has been a great satisfaction to him to see that of recent years the British West Indies have recovered from the period of depression which they met with so much patience and fortitude. His Majesty has noted with pleasure the many signs of permanence in that recovery and looks forward confidently to a bright future for the West Indian colonies.
>
> Although many years have elapsed since he was in the West Indies, the King retains the pleasantest recollections of his cruises in these waters, and of the happy times enjoyed by him on the several occasions of his visits to the islands.
>
> Throughout their chequered history these colonies have been distinguished for their loyalty. This Island of Barbados, one of the oldest of them,

has never suffered the foot of an invader and has ever been steadfast in its fidelity to the Throne.

His Majesty is glad that a member of his family should from its soil convey to his people in Barbados and all the other West Indian Colonies his sincere wishes for their happiness and prosperity.

At the inter-colonial needlework exhibition held at Barbados and which was formally opened by Her Highness Princess Marie Louise, the Honourable Mrs. Murray's prize of £2 for St. Vincent work was won by Miss A. Campbell, the exhibit being a night dress case done in shadow work. A prize of 10/- presented by the Queen's College girls was won by Miss Olive Wall of St. Vincent for a baby's robe. Mrs. Murray's prize of £3 for work in all the colonies except Barbados and St. Vincent, was awarded for an embroidered robe from St. Lucia. Among the general prizes for fine white embroidery, St. Vincent won the first and Trinidad took the second place.

26th—Her Highness Princess Marie Louise of Schleswig-Holstein (a first cousin of His Majesty the King) arrived on a visit to His Honour the Administrator and the Honourable Mrs. C. Gideon Murray. As soon as Her Highness reached the jetty the municipal band played the national anthem. A deputation of girls was next graciously received by Her Highness; they were Veronica Noble, who presented to Her Highness a beautiful bouquet, Violet Hazell, Audrey, Joyce, Leonie Hutchinson, Gertrude Dun, Eileen Osment and Kathleen Durrant. His Honour R. B. Roden, the Chief Justice, the Venerable E. A. Turpin, Archdeacon, members of the executive and legislative councils, and their respective wives were then presented to Her Highness by the Administrator. After inspecting the guard-of-honour formed by the volunteers and police on the jetty, Her Highness proceeded on the carpeted portion on both sides of which numerous persons, who had obtained admission by tickets, made their loyal obeisance. The members of the Kingstown Board awaited Her Highness at the entrance of the jetty from the shore and the Chairman, Mr. Walter Grant, having been presented to the Princess, read an address of welcome. Her Highness in reply said,

I thank you very much indeed for your kind address, and I return you thanks also for the hearty welcome you have given me on my arrival in this beautiful island. I am very pleased with the admirable decorations and I recognize all the trouble you have taken to show your pleasure at my arrival. I am sure I shall be most happy amongst you.

There was a mounted escort under command of Captain Adolphus Richards. Her Highness gracefully responded to the respectful salutations of the innumerable people who assembled on both sides of the entire route to Government House. The decorations of the jetty, the public buildings, the stores, the streets, and private residences were extensive and exceedingly attractive.

144

Miss Hawkes (lady-in-waiting) and Mr. Benyon (equerry) also arrived with the Princess.

28ᵗʰ—Her Highness the Princess visited the historic citadel at Fort Charlotte and was entertained at the cottage there by His Honour the Chief Justice and Mrs. Roden.

March 3ʳᵈ—H.M.S. *Aeolus* arrived.

A memorable meeting of the Legislative Council was held at the council chamber, courthouse. Her Highness Princess Marie Louise attended. There was a large and representative audience including civil and naval officers. The volunteers and police under the command of the Honourable F. W. Griffith formed a guard-of-honour from the gate to the main entrance of the courthouse.

In his speech His Honour the Administrator said,

> *Honourable Gentlemen of the Legislative Council, before proceeding with my customary review of the affairs of the colony, it is my very agreeable duty to give expression to the great gratification evinced throughout the colony at the honour bestowed upon St. Vincent by the visit of Her Highness Princess Marie Louise of Schleswig-Holstein during this month. On behalf of the colony I extend to Her Highness a loyal and hearty welcome and wish her a happy sojourn amongst us. If indeed anything were necessary to emphasize our pleasure at her visit, it would be the knowledge that Her Highness is a near relative of our reigning Sovereign King George the Fifth and is the grand-daughter of that great and revered Queen Victoria, whose name is associated with some of the brightest deeds and pages in the history of our Empire.*
>
> *Her Highness is the bearer of a message of greeting from His Majesty the King to his West Indian subjects. That message, so graciously worded, delivered by Her Highness a few days ago, is an additional proof of the keen personal interest that His Majesty evinces in the welfare of the inhabitants of his West Indian colonies. In St. Vincent His Majesty's words have touched the hearts of the people and have been received with universal feelings of loyalty and enthusiasm. I am glad therefore to be able to announce to you that Her Highness has graciously consented to convey personally to His Majesty the humble gratitude of all his subjects in the colony of St. Vincent and its dependencies, for his generous and sympathetic message and to express to His Majesty the loyal devotion which they bear to His Throne and Person.*

After prolonged cheers Mr. Conrad J. Simmons, thus addressed the meeting:

> *Sir, I have the honour to move the adoption of the very able and interesting address, to which we have had the pleasure of listening today, and, on behalf of the unofficial members of this Council, to join in the loyal and hearty welcome which has been extended to Her Highness Princess Marie*

Louise of Schelswig-Holstein, whose gracious presence here on this occasion will ever remain a bright chapter in the history of this colony.

We respectfully wish Her Highness enjoyment of health, and a happy holiday in St. Vincent, a colony which, though one of the smallest in His Majesty's Dominions Beyond the Seas, nevertheless provides a home for nearly 50,000 as loyal subjects as can be found anywhere in His Majesty's vast Imperial Empire.

And we, his subjects unite in heartfelt gratitude to our King for his kindly thoughtful message which we have received through Her Highness. We are truly happy to know that the assurances of our loyalty and devotion will be conveyed personally to His Majesty by Her Highness.

Sir, it gives me much pleasure to welcome you and Mrs. Murray back to St. Vincent, and you Sir, to the head of this table after your short but well-earned holiday. In expressing this pleasure I know that I am associated not only with those present this morning, but also with all the inhabitants of this colony who have had the good fortune to share the fruits of your successful administration, to which yet another year has been added.

We congratulate you on your administration of the affairs of this Government, and pray that your efforts in the future may meet and surmount any setback to the cotton industry or otherwise, and relying on Divine Providence, we confidently look forward to the continued prosperity and progress of St. Vincent.

Mr. J. G. W. Hazell, seconded the motion and repeated the common wish of the inhabitants that Her Highness would enjoy her stay here and, returning home, carry with her pleasant reminiscences of her holiday.

The motion was carried and the Administrator, after thanking honourable members, adjourned the meeting.

After the meeting of the Legislative Council, an excursion party accompanied Her Highness on H.M.S. *Aeolus* toward the Leeward portion of the island where, in addition to the grandeur of the scenery, the rocky cliffs standing out in bold relief and the many ridges that reached the coast indicate the geological history of the Island through the action of the sea and therefore present a picturesqueness that distinguishes St. Vincent from any other West Indian island.

The Princess was accompanied by His Honour the Administrator, His Honour R. B. Roden, Chief Justice, Mrs. Roden, Miss Hawkes (lady-in-waiting) Honourable E. Fielding (visitor) Honourables J. G. W. Hazell and F. W. Griffith, (members of council) Mr. Whinyates (private secretary to the Administrator) and Mr. Benyon (equerry).

4th—Her Highness Princess Marie Louise planted a tree in the botanic garden and remarked that she hoped to come back some day to see how the tree has grown.

His Honour the Administrator and the Honourable Mrs. Murray, gave a garden party at Government House.

10th—Her Highness proceeded to visit the Leeward district where every village, and out-town vied with each other in the arches erected for the occasion and otherwise in the decorations which, although somewhat rustic, were attractively pretty. The party was comprised of Her Highness Princess Marie Louise, His Honour the Administrator, the Honourable F. W. Griffith and Mr. T. Osment. The Honourable Mrs. Murray and Mr. Benyon accompanied them to Camden Park and returned to Government House. The people assembled at the roadway of the different settlements and plantations along the route and loyally greeted the distinguished visitor.

On the arrival of the party at about 9 a.m. the town wardens of Layou presented Her Highness with an address read by the Rev. G. Paterson to which an appropriate reply was given. The residents of the town were complimented for the display of loyalty. Photographs of the town and of the Anglican church there were also presented to the Princess.

At Barrouallie, an address was read by the Rev. R. J. Laurie and a reply graciously given. After admiring the decorations there, the party went to Wallilabou where they were entertained by the Honourable D. A. MacDonald.

Cumberland was reached at about 4.30 p.m. after crossing the remarkable Belle Isle Hill. Here too an address was read by Mr. N. Blencowe and presented and a reply given.

After another short ride the thickly-populated Village of Coulls' Hill was met. The people were joyful in welcoming the Princess and their decorations were commendable.

The scene of loyal demonstration in which school children were conspicuous at the Village of Troumaca was uncommonly impressive. The party arrived there at 6 p.m.; the address was read by Mr. T. W. Clarke, the headmaster of the Government school at that place.

The party then rode on to the Government Rest House at Belmont where they were received by Mr. W. N. Sands and Miss Hawkes who journeyed by sea.

11th—In the afternoon Her Highness, accompanied by the Administrator and Mr. Griffith, visited Chateaubelair. The villagers on the way loyally greeted the Princess. On the hill at Sharpe's Estate the road was spanned by an arch on which were the words "Welcome to Her Highness." There were several arches in the town under which the party passed and when they arrived at the police station, 500 persons joyfully sang the national anthem. An address of welcome was read by the Rev. C. G. Errey and by him presented to the Princess. Her Highness replied pathetically and alluded to the interview with His Majesty on the eve of her departure from England and his sympathetic message to the people of this island. Her Highness expressed admiration of the town lying beneath the scenery of the great Soufriere and of the tastefulness of the decorations arranged in her honour. Four bouquets were presented by little girls of the town. The party then proceeded to Richmond Vale and returned to Belmont by way of Schwartz and Palmyra roads.

12th—Her Highness visited the famous Falls of Ballaine by boat and landed to view the devastated area at the base of the Soufriere. The party returned to Belmont in the evening.

13th—Her Highness returned to Kingstown arriving at Government House in the evening. The Honourable D. A. MacDonald again had the honour of entertaining Her Highness at Wallilabou.

17th—Her Highness Princess Marie Louise undertook the journey to the Windward district. The party consisted of Her Highness, His Honour the Administrator, the Honourable Mrs. Murray, Mrs. Harrington-Stuart, (Mrs. Murray's sister) Miss Hawkes, (lady-in-waiting) Mr. Benyon (equerry); the Honourable Everad Fielding and Mr. Clowes (visitors) the Honourable E. W. Griffith (Chief of Police) Mr. W. N. Sands (Agricultural Superintendent) and Mr. R. C. Otway (Windward Warden). There was a continuous display of decorations along the route and the people assembled at various places to behold the distinguished visitor and to demonstrate their loyalty to Her Highness. Mr. A. Antrobus read the address at the town of Calliaqua. Accepting the kind offer of the Proprietor, Mr. G. R. Corea, the party stayed for a few hours at his house at Sans Souci Estate.

When at Georgetown the carriages were within view, a salute was fired at that place and the bells of the Anglican and Wesleyan churches there rang the merry peals. There was a platform constructed of tropical palms, festooned with flags and decorated with pots containing luxuriant ferns, flowers, etc. It was carpeted and the carpet extended to the centre of the street where Her Highness alighted from the carriage. On the arrival of the party at 4:30 p.m. the children of the Government school, supplemented by the numerous people there assembled, sang jubilantly the national anthem. As Her Highness approached the platform, Miss Rita Beach and Master Vincent Beach advanced and each presented a bouquet. Then followed several children, representing all classes, each respectfully presenting a bouquet that Her Highness gracefully accepted.

J. M. Gray, Esq (JP), a town warden, who was then presented by His Honour the Administrator, read the following address:

Georgetown, St. Vincent
March 17th, 1913.
Her Highness Princess Marie Louise of Schleswig-Holstein.

May it please Your Highness, on behalf of the inhabitants of Georgetown and the Windward district, we humbly tender Your Highness a loyal and hearty welcome to this part of the island which is of some historic significance in the annals of St. Vincent.

We highly appreciate the honour Your Highness bestows upon us in this visit and venerate you as a near relative of our Sovereign Lord King George the Fifth and also as a Grand-daughter of Her late Majesty Queen Victoria, of glorious memory, whose many acts of clemency to this and other West Indian Islands remain as laurels in our hearts.

We know by the many kind acts Your Highness has performed that you are keenly interested in the welfare of His Majesty's subjects, and your visit today gives us further assurance of your good-will towards them.

The message from His Majesty the King, conveyed and delivered through you at Barbados, is a great solace to us, and we are most grateful to you for having graciously consented to convey personally to His Majesty our humble gratitude for his sympathetic message.

We sincerely hope that Your Highness' visit to this island will prove interesting to you.

Reiterating our veneration to Your Highness, we are Your Highness' most obedient Servants,

J. M. Gray (JP), S. S. Garrett, C. J. Arthur (MD, JP),
S. C. Telfer, (Town Wardens); Rev. A. J. Cocks (Wesleyan Minister),
Rev. B. A. Samuel, (Rector) W. H. Beach, E. M. Beach,
G. V. Ballantyne, Frank Child.

Her Highness in reply made the following impromptu speech with remarkable eloquence:

I desire to thank you most sincerely for the kindly words contained in the address which has just been read. It is impossible for me to convey to you how deeply I appreciate your welcome. All along the picturesque road that we have travelled over since leaving Kingstown early this morning, I have been greeted with unfailing enthusiasm and loyalty.

I have been deeply touched by the cordiality of my welcome not only in this town but in every portion of St Vincent which I have visited and the memory of the care and trouble bestowed upon the erection of the beautiful arches and decorations in Kingstown and all along the routes that I have passed over, will ever remain dear to me.

I came to these historic and beautiful West Indian Islands—if I may so describe myself—the King's messenger, for he entrusted me with a message to you his people beyond the Seas: a message of goodwill and affection to prove to you the keen interest he takes in all that concerns your welfare; and I shall return to England as your messenger to take back to the King the undying love and loyalty of the people of St. Vincent to his Person and his Throne, of which I have had such overwhelming proofs in every part of your lovely island. He will be glad to hear of the happy days I have spent amongst you, and I know it will rejoice his heart to hear that this district that suffered so cruelly during the terrible eruption is showing signs of renewed prosperity.

I pray earnestly that this new era of prosperity which has dawned for St. Vincent under the able and wise guidance of your much, and justly so-beloved Administrator, may ever increase more and more in the future.

It has been my good fortune to visit many parts of His Majesty's vast Empire, but St. Vincent will ever hold a special place in my heart, and I shall always treasure as a valued and precious memory all the loyalty and affection with which you have surrounded me.

The Administrator then said:

Your Highness, Ladies and Gentlemen, it would appear redundant on my part to add anything after the charming, graceful speech just delivered by Her Highness in reply to the address from the Town, and indeed I have refrained from breaking silence on the similar occasions which have presented themselves at the various towns and villages which I have visited in company with Her Highness during the past ten days. But today we may claim to have come to the end of our tour 'round St. Vincent and in Georgetown the premier small town of the colony I cannot desist from breaking that silence. On behalf of the colony I desire to extend to Her Highness our thanks for her gracious condescension in enabling, by means of a somewhat arduous tour, such a great part of the community personally to see her. For there is probably no other lady in St. Vincent who has travelled the whole way on horseback from Kingstown to the foot of the Soufriere on the Leeward Coast, traversing our rugged but gorgeous valleys in such manner as indicates that in Her Highness is personified that fortitude of her race and spirit of endurance for which our Royal Family today is famed and indeed has long been renowned.

As His Majesty's representative in this island I have been gratified to witness the signs of loyalty and enthusiasm with which Her Highness has been greeted wherever she went and it requires no words of mine to emphasize the eloquent passages in which she has acknowledged these testimonies in the various speeches which she has made.

It is not unusual for the visit of a distinguished person to be associated with an act which will give gratification to the community at large and in that way to create the visit a living memory. I am glad to be able to inform you that Her Highness has graciously consented to allow her name to be associated with an act which I feel sure will give very great pleasure to the people of this district and indeed many others outside of it. Before me there stands one who has for nearly 70 years devoted himself unselfishly and ungrudgingly to the interest of Georgetown. I refer to Mr. Simon Solomon Garrett. I know of no one in St. Vincent who has served the community with greater disinterestedness, and I have therefore much pleasure in announcing in the presence of Your Highness that I have this day appointed Mr. Garrett to be a

Justice of the Peace of this colony. In entrusting to him the duties of that office I am aware that I can place them in no more loyal nor safer hands. (Cheers)

Since my return from England it has come to my notice from more than one source that a great deal of dissatisfaction is caused in Georgetown by the regulation which prohibits fishing from the Georgetown jetty. By some chance the subject happened to arise whilst Her Highness was present. Being a keen fisherwoman or at any rate her lady-in-waiting is, she at once interceded on behalf of the Georgetown fishermen. Whereupon having sympathy with the plaint and considering the regulation an unduly harsh one, I decided to mark Her Highness' visit by the announcement which I now make that from henceforth, under certain necessary restrictions, fishing will be allowed from the Georgetown jetty. (Cheers)

Your Highness, once more I thank you for your presence here today and for the keen personal interest evinced by you in the affairs of St. Vincent which has led you to make a comprehensive tour of the colony. As the King's messenger you have conferred upon the colony a great honour by your visit and we trust that Your Highness may bear away very pleasant memories of it.

Mr. S. S. Garrett who is a town warden of Georgetown, gave expression to his sincere gratitude for the honour conferred on him on such an auspicious occasion as this and after thanking Her Highness and His Honour he solicited and obtained Her Highness' permission to present to her a collection of beautifully chased cups and bottles which he made of native-grown Lignum Quashie.* Her Highness graciously accepted them with admiration and thanked him.

After three cheers were cordially given for Her Highness the party descended the platform and visited the hospital, the reading rooms, the Anglican and Wesleyan churches, and the jetty. The temporary residence in this district was the house of the proprietors of the Grand Sable Estate.

18th—Her Highness, accompanied by the Administrator and a few others of the party, rode through Lot 14 Estate to the base of the Soufriere mountain in the morning and in the afternoon they visited Mt. Bentinck and Langley Park Estates, Dickson's Village and the extensive ravine at Rabacca.

19th—The Princess and party rode through the picturesque valleys on to the mountain at the back of Grand Sable Estate. In the afternoon a visit was paid to the Government school (Mr. E. E. King, Headmaster.) An address was presented and the children recited and they sang patriotic songs. Her Highness delivered an instructive discourse and concluded by impressing on

---

*Ed. note: Most likely Quassiae Lignum, more commonly known as quassia wood or bitter wood.

the children their duty to God and the King. The party then drove to the "Carib Country" where many persons had gathered to pay their obeisance. They were entertained at tea by Mr. Frank Child the representative of the proprietor, Mr. W. H. Barnard. At Grand Sable house later in the day His Honour the Administrator administered the oath of a Justice of the Peace to Mr. S. S. Garrett in the presence of Her Highness and the party; for which purpose the Princess' own Bible was used.

20th—Maundy Thursday. The Princess, the Honourable Mrs. Murray, and Miss Hawkes (lady-in-waiting) attended divine service at Holy Trinity Church, Georgetown, and received the Holy Eucharist which was administered by the Rev. B. A. Samuel, the rector.

The royal visitor and party bade farewell and left for Kingstown, responding with gracious bows as they drove pass hundreds of people who came to witness their exit. They travelled by way of Mesopotamia or the Marriaqua Valley.

23rd—The Princess visited the volunteers at their camp at the Carenage and evinced considerable interest in the entire arrangement. The scenery there is charming, the seascape and the landscape are superb. Introducing to Her Highness the volunteers drawn up, His Honour the Administrator made an excellent speech than which there could be none more suited to the occasion. The Princess was pleased to test the night-firing device and secured a hit on the target to the joy of all ranks present. The Honourable Mrs. Murray who also accompanied the Princess participated in the pleasure afforded by the well-organized encampment. When Her Highness and party were about to embark all ranks turned out and lined the route extending to the police boat. The fife and drum band played *Auld Lang Syne* and the march past of the Argyll and Sutherland Highlanders.

25th—There was an impressive and edifying ceremony at the colonial hospital in connection with the distribution of prizes and certificates. Her Highness Princess Marie Louise attended with His Honour the Administrator, the Honourable Mrs. Murray and other guests from Government House. After having been shown through the different wards by Dr. C. H. Durrant, the royal visitor and those who accompanied her entered the spacious ward which was elegantly decorated for the occasion.

The Honourable Mrs. Murray, senior vice president of the St. Vincent Trained Nurses Association delivered a lengthy and interesting address in which allusion was made to the real interest and sympathy Her Highness has always shown in regard to the great work of alleviating suffering and trying to cure disease; Her Highness being a Lady of Grace of the Most Ancient and Distinguished Order of St. John of Jerusalem is closely associated with the duties devolving on those who help the sick and the suffering. The First

Prize was a beautiful medal offered by Lady Hayes Sadler, the wife of His Excellency the Governor, and the president of the St. Vincent Trained Nurses Association; the second prize and the certificates for nurses gaining 50 per cent, and above were offered by the committee of the association. The examination papers were set by Miss Gardner the matron of the Grenada hospital. The vice president announced that Her Highness has graciously consented to the building shortly to be erected for the accommodation of nurses being designated "The Princess's Wing".

Sister Webster, nurse matron of the hospital and honorary secretary of the association, read the report relative to the results of the examination. There were 13 Candidates: three at Grenada, two at St. Lucia and eight at St. Vincent. The winner of the first prize was Nurse Luenda O'Neill of St. Vincent who obtained Lady Sadler's medal for 96 marks of a maximum of 100. Nurse O'Neill approached Her Highness who graciously pinned on the medal and presented a prize from the association and a certificate in class C. The second prize was awarded to Nurse Emerine E. J. White of St. Vincent who advanced toward Her Highness for its acceptance and for a certificate. The Princess then presented six certificates in class C. to Nurses Arrindell, Grant, Felix, Aikens, Ash, and Thompson. After each presentation the Princess shook hands with the respective nurses. These certificates are awarded to successful candidates of examination by the board of examiners both in midwifery and general nursing.

Her Highness said,

> It has been a great pleasure and happiness to me to come here this afternoon to go over this hospital; and I am delighted with all I have seen; and am glad to hear of the proposed improvements and extensions. I do not think I should have regarded my visit to St. Vincent as complete, if I had not found a hospital to go over, as hospitals and nursing are subjects in which I am particularly interested.
>
> Mrs. Murray very kindly referred to my interest in women's work, and I think I may say that I am prepared to give all the time, health and strength I possess to furthering anything and any work that tends to their welfare, and to the alleviation of suffering and distress. (Applause).
>
> There is such an enormous field open to us women. There is so much work in this world which we women have to do and which is waiting to be accomplished by us; and above all things, nursing. Among the many professions in the world that are open to women, I do not think there is one more beautiful or which contains such possibilities of the true ideal of self-sacrifice and self-denial in life as that of a nurse. Whether you be a hospital nurse or a private nurse or a district nurse, your work is the same, your duty is the same, and your aims are the same; but in all things, even in the best and greatest things in life, we have to pay a price in return; and you nurses, in return for having the privilege of doing this great work, should remember

153

that you must give your whole heart to your work, and that it is a work of absolute self-denial and self-sacrifice. Nursing does not only consist of looking after your patients or preparing their meals, or taking their temperatures, or giving medicines, or the mere daily routine that goes on in the wards; there is an infinite amount more that a nurse has to perform and which a nurse who really has her work at her heart can do. Think of the sympathy you must give not only to the sick persons themselves, but also to those who are in anxiety around them! Think of the comfort you can be and all the help you can afford! Think of the enormous amount of anxiety and trouble you can relieve! I suppose sickness is the same all the world over, and I know, from experience in my own home, how comforting it is when there is sickness to have a nurse in the house, and the way that we turn and look to her for support. You come to nurse the patient back to life, but very often you are giving your life in return for the life you are saving for us. Do not get discouraged even if sometimes the work seems monotonous. Always keep the highest ideals before you and remember that the best thing in life is to be a true woman with a woman's loving, sympathetic and understanding heart.

It has been a great pleasure and happiness to me to give you your certificates, and especially Lady Sadler's medal, and I congratulate all of you most heartily and sincerely upon the excellent work for which these Certificates are a reward.

The music of the Orchestra enlivened the proceedings which were exemplary.

26th—Her Highness Princess Marie Louise of Schleswig-Holstein and her party consisting of seven persons, together with the Honourable Mrs. Murray, Mrs. Harrington-Stuart and Mr. G. Whinyates, sailed on R.M.S. *Balantia* for Antigua.

31st—The Princess passed from Antigua on her way to Grenada, Trinidad and British Guiana, thence to England. During the stay of the ship in port Her Highness and a party rode to the hill at Cane Garden Estate where the magnificent view of the harbour equalizes that from Fort Charlotte in the opposite direction.

The party afterward proceeded to Government House from which place Her Highness and the Administrator drove to the jetty. Many persons waited there to witness the embarkation of the Royal Visitor whilst many gathered along the streets and others from windows clustered for a farewell glance.

April 23rd—The Honourable F. W. Griffith, chief-of-police, etc., left the colony to fill the appointment of Treasurer of Antigua and Federal Treasurer.

28th—His Honour the Honourable C. Gideon Murray left the colony for Trinidad.

30th—The following telegraphic messages were transmitted:

```
FROM ACTING ADMINISTRATOR TO PRINCESS MARIE LOUISE,
ST. VINCENT SENDS YOUR HIGHNESS LOYAL AND AFFECTIONATE GREETINGS
ON YOUR DEPARTURE FOR ENGLAND AND WILL EVER RETAIN HAPPY MEMORIES
OF YOUR VISIT TO THIS COLONY.
RODEN, ACTING ADMINISTRATOR
30th APRIL, 1913
GOVERNMENT HOUSE,
BARBADOS, 30th APRIL, 1913
DEAR MR. RODEN,
I CANNOT TELL YOU HOW TOUCHED AND DELIGHTED I WAS TO RECEIVE SUCH
A KIND FAREWELL MESSAGE FROM DEAR ST. VINCENT, AND AM WRITING
TO THANK YOU MANY TIMES FOR THE CHARMING THOUGHT OF WISHING ME
GODSPEED. I SHALL ALWAYS TREASURE AND VALUE THE HAPPY MEMORIES OF
THE DAYS I SPENT AMONG YOU ALL IN YOUR BEAUTIFUL ISLAND AND ABOVE
ALL THE LOVE AND LOYAL AFFECTION WITH WHICH I WAS SURROUNDED, AND
WHICH I PRIZE MORE THAN I CAN EXPRESS IN WORDS.
                                        YOURS VERY SINCERELY,
                                               MARIE LOUISE
```

In his Report dated 30th April, G. Whitfield Smith, Esq, the Commissioner of the southern Grenadines, remarked that "It is gratifying to be able to report satisfactory progress in every direction at Union Island. The financial position of the Land Scheme is of a most hopeful character and one may anticipate with almost certainty that it will work out to a successful conclusion."

May 1st—Mr. James A. Vanloo, died at his residence at Kingstown. The reputation for cricket St. Vincent achieved and maintained is principally due to the untiring energy the popular "Captain Vanloo" evinced for many a year.

Notice given of the selection of the Belair Estate for the establishment and location of small holders under the provision of The Land Settlement Ordinance 1899.

7th—His Honour the Honourable C. Gideon Murray returned from Trinidad.

22nd—A lecture entitled "Plague and its prevention in special relation to rat destruction and Sanitation" was delivered by Dr. St. John Brooks at the lecture hall of the Carnegie Library, Kingstown.

June 6th—His Majesty's birthday was celebrated by the firing of guns at noon and a review of the volunteers and the police at Victoria Park in the afternoon under the command of Lieutenant Fraser and Mr. J. F. H. Otway, the acting chief of police, respectively. The Kingstown orchestra and the volunteers band were in attendance. His Honour the Administrator delivered an address.

The Honourable J. G. W. Hazell, Member of the Legislative Council selected as delegate to the Canadian-West Indian Steamship Service Conference to sit at Trinidad.

The Delegates were:

His Honour T. Lawrence Roxborough (CMG), St. Kitts-Nevis
The Honourable Dr. W. K. Chandler (CMG, MA, LLD), (Barbados).
The Honourable Adam Smith, Trinidad
The Honourable W. D. Auchinleck, (ISO), Antigua
The Honourable J. C. Macintyre, Dominica
The Honourable H. Ferguson, Grenada
The Honourable E. W. Laborde (ISO), St. Lucia.
The Honourable J. G. W. Hazell, St. Vincent
Russell Garnett, Esq (FR) British Guiana
J. McI. Reid, Esq, British Guiana

The deliberations were conducted at the Red House and extended from 10th to 16th June; nine resolutions were passed.

18th—Major J. A. Meldon, 4th Battalion, Dublin Fusiliers, arrived to assume the duties of chief of police of this colony.

20th—The annual meeting of the St. Vincent Trained Nurses Association was held at the court house. Mrs. R. B. Roden, a vice president, conducted the proceedings and in the course of an interesting address referred with regret to the absence of Lady Sadler, the president, and the Honourable Mrs. Murray, the senior vice president. Miss Webster, the honorary secretary, read her report on the transactions during the past year. Mrs. J. F. H. Otway, the honorary treasurer read the financial report and spoke appropriately and encouragingly to the members. His Honour the Administrator addressed the meeting and concluded by alluding, regretfully, to Miss Webster's approaching departure. His Honour hoped that the colony would find in her successor one as able and as zealous as she has been. Votes of thanks were moved by Dr. Arthur and Dr. Hughes, respectively, for His Honour the Administrator and Mrs. Roden. Prizes were then distributed by the Administrator to the most successful midwives of the preceding year.

24th—Mr. Charles James Simmons died at his residence at Bentinck Lodge, Kingstown. He was a native of this island whose services to the Government extending over 25 years have been of great value, principally as a member of the Assembly and of the Executive and Legislative Councils. The funeral ceremony was intensely solemn and the large attendance represented every section of the community.

At the opening of the Supreme Court of Judicature in its summary jurisdiction His Honour R. B. Roden, Chief Justice, expressed the sympathy of the court toward the Honourable Conrad J. Simmons, a member of the bar, for the loss he had sustained in the death of his father.

28th—Mr. Robert Suckling Cheesman died at his residence in Kingstown. He was an unofficial member of the Legislative Assembly and in that capacity he attended the first meeting of the Legislative Council under the new constitution which was held at the court house on Saturday 26th January, 1878.

In the prosperous condition of his life he was among the most prominent gentlemen in the island and under reversed circumstances he resided here with exemplary contentment.

July 2nd—The first annual police sports were held under the patronage of His Honour the Administrator on Victoria Park. At the conclusion of the events His Honour congratulated the competitors and Mr. J. F. H. Otway who organized the meeting when he acted chief of police. His Honour took the opportunity to welcome Major Meldon as the new chief of police and commandant of the local forces assuring him that he would find here excellent material upon which he could impress his military knowledge. His Honour then called upon Mrs. J. G. W. Hazell to distribute the prizes.

15th—A general meeting of the St. Vincent Arrowroot Growers and Exporters Association was held at the court house. A resolution was passed stipulating the minimum price of 3¼ d. per lb. for the unsold portion of arrowroot in respect to the crop of 1912-13 and the entire crop of 1913-14.

20th—At Holy Trinity Church, Georgetown, in the presence of a large congregation the Rev. B. A. Samuel dedicated a beautiful altar service book, the valued souvenir of Her Highness Princess Marie Louise of Schleswig-Holstein. In the course of his address, illustrative of the honour conferred on the church and the community generally the rector said, "The book is England's weapon, and through its donor we cannot but feel that we are brought in closer touch with our Sovereign and the Empire."

The inscription in gold letters reads

Presented to Holy Trinity Church,
Georgetown, St. Vincent,
by MARIE LOUISE, Princess of Schleswig-Holstein, March, 1913.

In Her Highness' handwriting:

In Memory of Maundy Thursday, March 20th, 1913,
From MARIE LOUISE, Princess of Schleswig-Holstein

24th—A sharp shock of earthquake was felt about 4.30 a.m.

29th—At the meeting of the Legislative Council the following resolution was moved by His Honour the Honourable C. Gideon Murray, Administrator, seconded by the Honourable J. G. W. Hazell and unanimously adopted:

Be it resolved that this Council has learnt with sincere regret of the death of Mr. CHARLES JAMES SIMMONS who for so many years took such a prominent, active and useful part in the deliberations of the Executive and Legislative Councils of St. Vincent and desires to place on record its deepest sympathy with his family and relatives upon the great bereavement and to testify to the immense loss which the colony has sustained by his death.

The Honourable Conrad Johnson Simmons then replied:

> *Sir, On behalf of those to whom sympathy has been so graciously extended by the resolution which has just been passed, I beg leave sincerely to thank you, Sir, the Honourable Mr. Hazell, the Honourable the Acting Attorney General, and the other members of this Council for the kindly thought which prompted the resolution, and for the generous references to the services which my late father was always so happy to render to this colony, the land of his birth. May I be allowed to add that I have been and am very deeply touched by, and shall always gratefully remember, the many evidences of recognition of those services.*

H.M.S. *Aeolus* arrived. In addition to the social entertainments at Government House and elsewhere the programme arranged for the enjoyment of the visitors consisted of a dance by the Cinderella Club, tennis tournaments, golf, and matches in cricket, shooting and football. The cricket match was remarkably exciting; it resulted in a tie and Captain Hotham of the ship's team elicited the sympathy of the spectators who admired his sportsmanlike but futile manoeuvres to score the one run required to win.

August 1ˢᵗ—H M.S. *Aeolus* left for St. Lucia.

4ᵗʰ—The ceremony of the opening of the new jetty and water service in the town of Layou was conducted by His Honour the Administrator. On his arrival His Honour was presented with an address by the Rev. G. Paterson. A guard-of-honour formed by volunteers and police awaited the Administrator. In his speech His Honour congratulated the townsfolk for their achievements and alluded to Mr. A. M. Fraser who generously allowed the use of the spring, which enabled the Government to effect the improvement. The Administrator then opened a tap, drew a glassful of water, drank, and declared the service open. His Honour the Chief Justice, who, when Acting Administrator, had assisted in furthering the scheme, made some appropriate remarks. The capacity of the reservoir, which is constructed of reinforced concrete, is ten thousand gallons, supplying at present ten half-inch taps in the town.

6ᵗʰ—The annual exhibition of the Home Industry Presentation Association was held at the court house.

September 16ᵗʰ—A general meeting of the St. Vincent Arrowroot Growers and Exporters Association was held at the court house when the following resolution was unanimously passed:

> *Resolved, that the minimum price for estates arrowroot and other arrowroot for the remainder of the 1912-13 crop shall on no account be lowed or raised below or above the minimum price of 3¼ d. per lb. fixed at the meeting of the Association on the 15ᵗʰ July, 1913.*

At the meeting of the Legislative Council held on 6ᵗʰ October the following resolution of sympathy was passed unanimously:

> *Be it resolved that this Council having learned with deep sorrow of the deaths of the Right Honourable Sir Walter Hely-Hutchinson, (PC, GCMG) and*

Sir Alfred Moloney, (KCMG), who both at different times held the position of Governor and Commander-in-Chief of the Windward Islands and in that capacity administered for several years with great ability the affairs of this colony, desires to place on record and to express its sincere sympathy with Lady Hely-Hutchinson and Lady Moloney in their great grief and in the irreparable loss which they have sustained."

8th—The Honourable Mrs. C. Gideon Murray, arrived from England and was accorded a hearty welcome. There was a large assembly of ladies and gentlemen.

12th—Harvest Festival Services were held at St. George's Cathedral. The Rev. R. J. Laurie, (BA), Rector of the Parishes of St. Patrick's and St. David's occupied the pulpit at 11 a.m. and the Rev. R. G. Barrow, (L.Th.), Assistant Curate for the Grenadines and a native of this island, preached to an exceedingly large congregation at evensong.

14th—Under the patronage of His Honour the Administrator and the Honourable Mrs. C. Gideon Murray, there was a musical and dramatic entertainment at the court house on behalf of the Anglican church. Congratulations are due to Mrs. Roden for the contrivance and for the success achieved.

15th—A consignment of Needlework comprising embroideries, laces, and crochet, the value of which is £114, was forwarded to Canada by the St. Vincent Needlework Association.

22nd—The following telegrams were despatched and received respectively by the Administrator on the occasion of His Excellency Sir James Hayes Sadler's return to the Windward Islands:

TO THE GOVERNOR.
EXECUTIVE (AND) LEGISLATIVE COUNCILS SEND GREETING OF WELCOME TO YOU AND LADY SADLER ON YOUR RETURN.
FROM THE GOVERNOR.
PLEASE THANK EXECUTIVE (AND) LEGISLATIVE COUNCILS FOR MOST KIND GREETINGS.

29th—The Fifth annual Race Meeting organized by the St. Vincent Turf Club was successfully accomplished at Brighton.

November 6th—The Honourable Mrs. Murray presented the three cups won at the race meeting held at Brighton on the 29th October, 1913. The ceremony was performed at the free public library at 3.30 p.m. There were present His Honour the Administrator, His Honour R. B. Roden, Chief Justice, and a considerable number of ladies and gentlemen. A police guard-of-honour under the command of Major J. A. Meldon was in attendance.

The Administrator's Cup was won by The Honourable Conrad J. Simmons's pony "Sir Daniel"; the Bequia Cup was won by Mr. E. M. Beach's pony "Roslin"; and the Capello Cup was won by Mr. W. H. Beach's pony "Rita" in respect to the first of the races to be run for it.

159

15th—Mr. Wycliffe Rose, Director of the Rockefeller International Sanitary Commission arrived on a visit for the purpose of ascertaining if the conditions in St. Vincent would justify a campaign in the colony in regard to Ankylostomiasis. It has been decided that St. Vincent be included in this sanitary campaign organized in consequence of a donation of $1,000,000 by Mr. John D. Rockefeller who desires the fund to be devoted toward the amelioration of the sufferings of humanity.

17th—At the annual Speech Day of the Grammar School, which was observed at the court house, Acts I and IV of Shakespeare's *As You Like It* were creditably performed by a few of the pupils.

Addresses were delivered by His Honour the Administrator, the Honourable Dr. Francis Watts, Imperial Commissioner of Agriculture, and Mr. F. W. Reeves, (MA), the Headmaster. The literary entertainment was highly appreciated by the large and representative audience.

The Honourable Mrs. Murray gracefully distributed the prizes, after which votes of thanks were moved by Mr. Reeves to the Honourable Mrs. Murray, His Honour the Administrator, and the Honourable Dr. Watts for each of whom three times three hearty cheers were given by the pupils. At the request of the Administrator three "hurrahs" were shouted for Mr. Reeves, the Headmaster, and three more for Mr. Blackman the Second Master.

18th—There was a theatrical performance at the court house under the auspices of the Honourable Mrs. Murray in aid of the St. Vincent needlework industry. It was in every respect remarkably successful. The plays were *Don't Let the Lady Go* and *Playing the Game*.

An interesting report on the Sea Island Cotton growing competition for small holders was published on 27th November. The competition was arranged in two classes:

Class I. The best Sea Island Cotton cultivation of not less than 1 acre on a small holding over five but not exceeding ten acres.

Class II. The best Sea Island Cotton cultivation of not less than ½ acre on a small holding not exceeding five acres. There were 39 entries: 21 in Class I and 18 in Class II. It was remarked,

> *This being the first competition of its kind held in St. Vincent a good deal of pioneer work has had to be done; still a satisfactory measure of success has been attained.*
>
> *The advice and assistance of the Agricultural Officers were at all times welcomed, and the addresses of the Agricultural Superintendent were listened to with very keen interest and attention.*

December—At the meeting of the Legislative Council held on 2nd December, over which the Honourable C. Gideon Murray presided, His Honour formally moved the following resolution:

Be it resolved that this Council being of opinion that the time has now arrived when the mail and passenger service between Kingstown and Georgetown should be conducted by a Motor Car Service in preference to the present mode of conveyance by horse and trap, thus enabling an increase of transport facilities for both mails and passengers on the Windward Coast, and being of the opinion also that such mail service should be inaugurated and operated by the Government at the expense of the Colony; now therefore this Council agrees to vote a sum not exceeding £400 for the capital expenditure in the establishment of such a service and to provide from year to year commencing with the financial year 1914-15, such funds for its maintenance as may be found necessary.

The following reply from Lady Hely-Hutchinson was received by the Administrator and published in Government *Gazette* of December 11:

147 St. James' Court
Buckingham Gate, S.W.
November 5th, 1913

Dear Sir,

I am desired by Lady Hely-Hutchinson to thank you for your letter of October 7th forwarding a Resolution of deep sympathy passed by the Legislative Council.

Lady Hely-Hutchinson begs that you will be so kind as to convey her sincere thanks to the members of the Council and to say that she is much touched by their kindly remembrance. I am, dear Sir,

Yours faithfully
M. E. Beale

1914 / His Honour the Honourable C. Gideon Murray delivered an extensive and interesting address at the Legislative Council held on 2nd February in the course of which he referred to the completed reinforced concrete bridges on the Windward road and to the bridge over the New Adelphi River, nurses quarters and residence for the Chief Justice in course of progress and regretted the new road out of Kingstown by Richmond Hill had proved a bigger undertaking than anticipated chiefly owing to the rocky nature of the ground along the line of the route. After commenting on the outstanding proposed expenditure for the year the Administrator concluded by saying, "I now have the honour to declare open this session of the Council and to pray that a Divine Providence may bless its labours and direct its energies for the continual advancement of the moral and material welfare of the inhabitants of the Colony."

Mr. Hazell begged to move the adoption of His Honour's most lucid and instructive address. The various improvements in public works, building of bridges, etc., which were proposed were most gratifying to those of us who

161

had constantly to make use of the tedious 22 miles of road through the Windward part of the island. The works recently undertaken by His Honour would he hoped remain permanently as monuments to his memory, after his most successful tenure of office and while he guided the destinies of our island home.

Mr. MacDonald said he had much pleasure in seconding the motion and in thanking His Honour for his interesting and instructive address. Where praise was due it was right to bestow it, and he must therefore add to what had been said by Mr. Hazell.

He would first, as representing the agricultural section of the community, thank His Honour for his expressions of sympathy with cotton growers over the loss they had sustained, and hoped with him that in the end it would be found that the loss was not so disastrous as had been expected.

He would thank him for the interest he took in agriculture and for the experiments which were being made by the Government with the object of introducing other products, instead of sticking principally to arrowroot and cotton, which were precarious and subject to weather conditions. The lime industry which was being tried should prove of considerable benefit.

We were also indebted to His Honour for his good work in the matter of improving the position of arrowroot, for initiating the scheme, and for his continued interest and advice. The roads and bridges would be lasting memorials of his work, and the water supplies which he had laid down in the small towns were much appreciated by the inhabitants. He thought that he was to be congratulated for his introduction of the Motor Car Service, and it was very gratifying that this island, the smallest in the Government, should take the lead in this respect.

The undertaking of all these works by His Honour only proved how sleepy and lethargic we had been in the past, and showed what could be done by a man possessed of energy, enterprise and ability. Our thanks were due to him, and we hoped that while he remained with us he would enjoy good health which would enable him to carry out and perfect other schemes.

The motion was then put and adopted unanimously. The following reply from Lady Moloney was received by the Administrator and published in the Government *Gazette* of 19th February:

> S.S. Cloutsham
> In the Adriatic
> January 14th, 1914
>
> Dear Sir: I must apologize for not having acknowledged before this the Resolution of sympathy of the Legislative Council of St. Vincent.
>
> It reached me in November but I was suffering from nervous exhaustion, and unequal to any effort. Will you kindly express to the Members of the Leg-

islative Council my regret at not being able to reply sooner, and at the same time express to them my heartfelt thanks for their kind tribute to the memory of my beloved husband, and sympathy with me in my overwhelming sorrow.

Sir Alfred and myself always retain a happy and affectionate memory of St. Vincent, from whose people we received nothing but kindness. We often spoke together of the period which we spent on the island after the terrible hurricane of '98, a time of stress and sorrow which I trust may never return to the Colony.

In my loneliness and desolation, it has comforted me to know that we are not forgotten in St. Vincent.

With renewed thanks to you and all the members of the Legislative Council, I am,

Yours faithfully,
Frances Moloney

Negotiations were entered into for the purchase from Mrs. Charles Simmons of Lot 102 in Kingstown for the premises of the general post office at the price of £700. The resolution of the Council in connection therewith was published in the *Gazette* dated 16th April.

The following resolution regarding the Ankylostomiasis Campaign was passed at a Meeting under the presidency of His Honour R. B. Roden, Acting Administrator, and published in the *Gazette* of 25th June:

Be it resolved that this Council in view of the great benefits "likely to accrue to this Colony through the generous provision made for the eradication of hook worm disease by the Rockefeller Foundation of the International Health Commission pledges itself to provide the necessary funds for the carrying on of the campaign as follows:

1. Providing for expenditure under all heads, the amount to be recovered from the Commission

2. Providing for the salary of one Field Assistant including travelling expenses, probably £50

3. Providing for the cost of drugs, accounting and audit estimated at 40

4. Providing for suitable accommodation for office purposes estimated at 40.

The Medical Officers of the colony will be asked to bring to the notice of the special staff such cases as come before them, and it is believed that the campaign of the Commission will have a valuable effect in educating the people in the necessity for simple sanitary precautions.

Notification by proclamation published 4th August, that owing to the state of public affairs and the demands upon His Majesty's Naval Forces for the protection of the Empire an occasion has arisen for ordering and directing that the Royal Naval Reserves be called into actual service.

In the Government *Gazette* (extraordinary) of the 7th August, a proclamation dated 5th August announcing that "a State of War exists between Us and the German Emperor" was published setting forth the law and policy with regard to trading with the enemy.

September 21st—At a meeting of the Legislative Council held on 14th, instant the following Address of Loyalty to His Majesty the King, and resolution approving of the expenditure of £1,000 on the purchase of St. Vincent Arrowroot as a gift to the Mother Country for the use of His Majesty's Forces and of £1,000 as a contribution to the Prince of Wales' National Relief Fund, were unanimously passed.

Address To His Majesty The King.

> *To His Most Excellent Majesty George the Fifth by the Grace of God, of the United Kingdom of Great Britain and Ireland, and of the British Dominions beyond the Seas, King, Defender of the Faith, Emperor of India:*
>
> *May it please Your Majesty, the Legislative Council of Your Majesty's loyal Colony of St. Vincent, moved by the deepest feelings of affection and duty, desire on behalf of the people of St. Vincent at this time of great trouble and anxiety in the history of the British Empire to humbly tender to Your Majesty the assurance of their Loyalty and attachment to Your Majesty's Throne and Person.*
>
> *Your Majesty's faithful and loyal subjects in St. Vincent earnestly pray that the righteous war now being waged by our beloved Mother Country against Germany and Austro-Hungary may by the blessing of God and the valour and determination of Your Majesty's Forces by land and sea speedily be brought to a successful issue.*
>
> *Dated at the Council Chamber in Kingstown, St. Vincent this 14th day of September, 1914*
>
> *R. B. Roden, Acting Administrator of St. Vincent*
> *W. C. Hutchinson, Treasurer, etc.*
> *John G. W. Hazell, Member, Executive and Legislative Councils*
> *Cyril H. Durrant, Medical Officer, Kingstown District*
> *Duncan A. MacDonald, Member, Executive and Legislative Councils*
> *J. B. Kernahan, Member, Legislative Council*
> *C. de S. Dunn, Chief of Police*
> *H. P. Hazell, Member, Legislative Council*

RESOLUTION

> *Whereas this Council has, on behalf of the People of Saint Vincent adopted an Address of Loyalty to His Majesty the King, on the occasion of War against Germany and Austro-Hungary:*
>
> *And Whereas it is the expressed desire of the People of Saint Vincent to make a gift to the Mother Country for the use of His Majesty's Forces, and to contribute towards the relief of persons in the British Isles who are dependants*

of men at the front, and of those who suffer from unemployment caused by interruption and dislocation of trade and industry, or are otherwise plunged into poverty and distress in consequence of War.

Be it resolved that this Council hereby approves of the expenditure from the General Revenue of the Colony of a sum of £1,000 for the purchase of Saint Vincent Arrowroot as a gift to the Mother Country for the use aforesaid, and of a sum of £1,000 as a contribution to the Prince of Wales' National Relief Fund.

At the conclusion of the meeting the Acting Administrator despatched the following telegram to His Excellency the Acting Governor:

LEGISLATIVE COUNCIL TODAY PASSED LOYAL ADDRESS AND VOTE OF £2,000 FOR THE PURCHASE OF ST. VINCENT ARROWROOT FOR HIS MAJESTY'S FORCES AND CONTRIBUTION TO PRINCE OF WALES' FUND. ASK FOR SANCTION OF YOUR EXCELLENCY AND SECRETARY OF STATE FOR COLONIES. PLANTERS WILL ADD 250 BARRELS ARROWROOT AND PRIVATE SUBSCRIPTIONS ARE BEING MADE TO PRINCE OF WALES' FUND.

On the 18th instant His Honour received the following reply from His Excellency:

WITH REFERENCE TO YOUR TELEGRAM OF 14th SEPTEMBER FOLLOWING TELEGRAM HAS BEEN RECEIVED FROM SECRETARY OF STATE FOR COLONIES. ST. VINCENT LOYAL ADDRESS WHEN RECEIVED WILL BE DULY LAID BEFORE HIS MAJESTY. HIS MAJESTY'S GOVERNMENT APPRECIATE HIGHLY PATRIOTIC SPIRIT SHOWN BY COLONY AND GENEROUS GIFTS BY LEGISLATURE ON BEHALF OF PEOPLE, BY PLANTERS, AND PRIVATE CONTRIBUTORS. PLEASE TELEGRAPH IN DUE COURSE EXACT AMOUNT OF ARROWROOT AND OF SUBSCRIPTIONS AND YOUR PROPOSALS AS TO TRANSMISSION OF FORMER.

The following extracts from a despatch from the Secretary of State for War was published on 9th October:

...The transport of the troops from England both by sea and by rail was effected in the best order and without a check. Each unit arrived at its destination in this country well within the scheduled time.

The concentration was practically complete on the evening of Friday, the 21st ultimo, and I was able to make dispositions to move the Force during Saturday, the 22nd, to positions I considered most favourable from which to commence operations which the French Commander-in-Chief, General Joffre, requested me to undertake in pursuance of his plans in prosecution of the campaign.

November 7th—The despatch from the Secretary of State for the Colonies acknowledging the receipt of an address of loyalty passed by the Legislative Council of St. Vincent included the following paragraphs:

...The address has been duly laid before the King and I have it in command to request you to convey to the Legislative Council an expression of

165

His Majesty's high appreciation of the loyal assurances given on behalf of the people of St. Vincent.

...I take this opportunity to acknowledge the receipt of your telegram of 13th October, and to explain that my telegram of the 12th October was sent under a misapprehension as to the sum which it was intended to devote to the purchase of arrowroot. I have no desire to disturb the arrangements originally made and the Crown Agents for the Colonies have accordingly been instructed to place the £1,000 worth of arrowroot at the disposal of the Admiralty and War Office in equal proportions, and to pay to the Prince of Wales' National Relief Fund £1,000 from St. Vincent funds as contribution on the part of the people of the Colony.

22nd—Sir John Roche Dasent (CB), died at his residence, Ascot Heath House, England. He was the owner of Montrose House in this island where he enjoyed his holiday every winter.

28th—The following telegram received from the Secretary of State for the Colonies was published:

```
I AM ABOUT TO LAY BEFORE PARLIAMENT FURTHER CORRESPONDENCE RE-
GARDING THE MUNIFICENT GIFTS WHICH HAVE SO FAR BEEN OFFERED FROM
THE VARIOUS PARTS OF THE EMPIRE AND BEFORE DOING SO I DESIRE ON
BEHALF OF HIS MAJESTY'S GOVERNMENT AGAIN TO EXPRESS THEIR DEEP
GRATITUDE TO ALL WHO HAVE SO GENEROUSLY AND IN SUCH DIVERSE WAYS
BOTH PUBLICLY AND PRIVATELY CONTRIBUTED TO THE REQUIREMENTS
OF HIS MAJESTY'S GOVERNMENT AND THEIR ALLIES FOR PURPOSES OF
ALLEVIATING THE DISTRESS CAUSED BY THE WAR AND BRINGING IT TO A
SUCCESSFUL ISSUE.
```

In Govt. *Gazette* of December 10, His Honour the Administrator directed publication of a letter from the Crown Agents for the colonies containing information "that the 720 barrels of arrowroot which have been forwarded from the colony as a gift for the use of His Majesty's Forces have been placed at the disposal of the War Office and the Admiralty in equal proportions in accordance with instructions received from the Secretary of State."

1915 / 7th January—The Proclamation of the King dated 5th November, extending to the War with Turkey the Proclamations and Orders in Council then in force relating to the War with Germany and Austro-Hungary was published.

On the same day announcement was made that His Majesty the King was graciously pleased to appoint His Excellency G. B. Haddon-Smith, Esq, (CMG), Governor and Commander-in-Chief of the Windward Islands, to be a Knight Commander of the Most Distinguished Order of St. Michael and St. George.

14th—Intimation appeared in the Government *Gazette* that Dr. F. Watts (CMG), the Imperial Commissioner of Agriculture endeavoured to discover whether any market could be found for West Indian Sea Island Cotton in the

United States and through the kindness of Mr. N. C. Pearson of the *India Rubber World* he was placed in communication with the West Roylston Manufacturing Co., Easthampton, Mass.

21st —There were published copies of the supplement of the *London Gazette* of 27th November, 1914, containing a despatch from Field Marshal Sir John French recounting the operations of the field force under his command throughout the battle of Ypres-Armentieres and another supplement of the 4th December, 1914, containing a despatch from Field Marshal Sir John French covering one from Major-General A. Paris relating to the operations round Antwerp from the 3rd to the 9th October, 1914.

The following letter from Lieut.-Colonel Sir James Hayes Sadler (KCMG, CB), was published in *Gazette* of 18th February:

Bailey's Hotel, S. W.

19th January, 1915

Sir, I would ask you to accept yourself and to convey to the Legislative Council of St. Vincent Lady Hayes Sadler's and my most grateful thanks for the very kind message of sympathy for us in the loss of two sons killed in action tendered to us in their Resolution of the 22nd December, 1914.

I have, etc.,

J. Hayes Sadler

His Honour, The Administrator, St. Vincent

An interesting Report by Mr. W. N. Sauds of the agricultural department who was appointed Commissioner of St. Vincent for attending the International Rubber and Tropical Products Exhibition which was held at the Royal Agricultural Hall, Islington, London, from June 24th to July 9th, was appended to the *Gazette* dated 18th February. It contained among others the following paragraphs:

The exhibits from St. Vincent arrived in excellent order and comprised samples of arrowroot, Sea Island and Marie Galante cotton; cacao; sugar; coconuts; Bengal beans; pigeon peas; cassava chips, cassava starch; peanuts and honey. These were supplemented by a number of large photographs of the cotton industry of St. Vincent the work of the writer, and 2 bales of Sea Island cotton, one of 'ordinary fine' and one of 'superfine'. Mr. Brown, for the Arrowroot Growers and Exporters Association, brought a large number of ¼ lb. packets of 'No Wyta' arrowroot to be displayed and distributed free of cost. He also had a gas cooking range installed and arranged for a lady demonstrator and her assistant from Marshall's School of Cookery to be present each day to demonstrate the different methods of using arrowroot in the preparation of cakes, biscuits, blanc-manges, etc.

I cannot conclude this report without expressing my deep indebtedness to Mr. E. A. Aspinall and the staff of the West India Committee for their invaluable help and assistance and also to Mr. E. H. Brown who represented the St. Vincent Arrowroot Growers and Exporters Association.

A beautiful silver cup given by the British Cotton Growing Association was won by Mr. Alexander Smith of this island for his display of Sea Island Cotton at the International Tropical Products Exhibition held at Islington.

22nd February—The Honourable Mrs. Murray, wife of the Administrator was presented with a diamond star and address by the ladies of the colony and on 25th with selected samples of needlework made by the ladies of the St. Vincent needlework industry.

In the *Gazette* of 18th March notice was given to the effect that St. Vincent was made a centre for the Cambridge local examinations.

20th March—John Gregg Windsor Hazell died. To his memory a font is erected at the Botanic Gardens, and was formally opened by His Honour the Administrator on 19th May.

21st March—St. Vincent No. 1 (Kingstown) troop of boy scouts assembled at the police barracks to make their scout pledge.

19th May—His Honour the Honourable C. Gideon Murray attended at Carnegie Library when members of the Kingstown Board presented a farewell address. (See page 163). There was a guard-of-honour and the municipal band was in attendance.

The Govt. *Gazette* (extraordinary) of 19th May consisted of the following notice:

> *The Administrator, the Honourable Gideon Murray, desires at the close of his administration of the Government of the Colony of St. Vincent and its Dependencies hereby to extend to all Public Officers in the service of the Government his grateful appreciation of the loyal and zealous manner in which they have worked and cooperated with him and supported him during the six years that he has had the honour to administer the Government. He has during that time, he knows, made a great call upon their energies and services and he gladly takes this opportunity to acknowledge and thank them for the ready and willing way in which they have invariably responded.*

The following addresses were published in the *Gazette* of the 22nd May.

From the Legislative Council, Council Chamber, Saint Vincent
27th April, 1915

To His Honour, The Honourable Gideon Murray, Administrator
Your Honour;

> *We the Members of the Legislative Council of this Colony, on behalf of ourselves and the People of St. Vincent, desire to express our regret at your departure, and at the same time we beg to assure Your Honour that the good*

and valuable works that you have executed during your term of office will be a lasting testimony of the able services you have rendered the colony.

We know the trying time you have had to face since the outbreak of war, and can assure you that we highly appreciate the able manner in which you have conducted the administration of the colony during these months. On departing from our shores, you leave behind a record second to none, and we are sure that our sister colony is securing the services of one whose first thought is for the advancement of the colony under his administration. We express the hope that your promotion to St. Lucia is only a step to a higher position on the Government ladder and we assure you that we will always look with pleasure on your advancement until the top rung of the ladder is attained.

We, on behalf of ourselves and the people of this island, beg to convey to the Honourable Mrs. Murray our high appreciation of the valuable assistance she has always so readily extended to all classes of the community, and we trust that you will both be spared to enjoy a long and prosperous life.

A. C. Vincent Prior, Duncan A. Macdonald
W. C. Hutchinson, Cyril H. Durrant
Conrad Simmons, F. A. Corea, E. F. Richards

Mr. Murray replying, among other things said he was extremely touched by the words that had fallen from honourable members. He also wished to say how very sincerely he appreciated the sentiments expressed in the address with which they had presented him; sentiments for which he was grateful and which he would esteem the more because whenever he looked at them, pleasing recollections would be brought back by the motto and the views of St. Vincent which had been so artistically reproduced in the border of the address.

It was very difficult on such an occasion to express one's innermost feelings. He looked back on his six years in St. Vincent as years which had brought him into contact with men and affairs which were of considerable pleasure and of advantage to him in the career which was before him. He had gained much experience here, which, would be useful in the years before him, but first and foremost, he prized and would always remember the number of friends he had made in this colony.

The credit for the work that he had been able to perform in St. Vincent was due largely to the help he had received from others. He had received abundant support and hearty cooperation from every department of the Government and this he gratefully acknowledged. The assistance accorded him by both official and unofficial members of the council, and also that which he had received from everyone in the colony whether it came direct from the public or from the press, greatly encouraged him to pursue his work. He would say that whatever good he had done in St. Vincent had been accomplished in an atmosphere of cordiality and such success as had marked his six years administration in St. Vincent was due to the maintenance of that harmony without which progress would have been impossible.

On behalf of Mrs. Murray he thanked them sincerely for their kind allusions to her in the address, which she would deeply appreciate. He had no hesitation in affirming that more than half the work he had been able to accomplish here was due to the able assistance he had received from her. She shared with him the greatest regret in leaving the colony. The affairs of the island, its social life, and the sincerity of their friends, had so interwoven themselves into their lives that whilst naturally gratified at the idea of promotion, to leave St. Vincent caused them the greatest feelings of regret. Mrs. Murray and he would always look back on their sojourn in this island as amongst the happiest years of their lives; and they would ever be grateful for the manner the people received them when they came here as strangers, and for the many kindnesses all classes had offered them in every direction. He took this opportunity also of thanking the Council for their generous treatment of Mrs. Murray and himself in providing conveniences at Government House which had added much to the comforts of their home.

In conclusion, he stated that they had special gratification in the knowledge that although leaving St. Vincent, their new home would only be 50 miles away. They would look forward with pleasure to the occasions when, passing here, they would see the friends they had left behind them in St. Vincent. And the fact that His Majesty the King had honoured him with the dormant commission to administer the Government of the Windward islands during the absence of the Governor, still retains for him a link in his association with this colony. Closing, he repeated his thanks for the address and their good wishes.

To each of the other addresses His Honour replied in a similar manner.

From the Kingstown Board

His Honour
The Honourable Gideon Murray,
Administrator of St. Vincent, &c., &c.

Sir; On behalf of the citizens whom we, as members of the Kingstown Board, have the honour to represent and for ourselves, we desire to convey to Your Honour an expression of our profound sense of the loss we are about to sustain in your departure from this colony to assume the administration of the Government of St. Lucia.

In the past six years during which you have laboured in St. Vincent, experiencing, in common with the inhabitants, the anxieties and difficulties that have marked the course of that period, the community have recognized in your administration admirable traits of your own disinterestedness, zeal and sincerity; and we, being entrusted with the management of the affairs of Kingstown, have had special opportunities of appreciating Your Honour's eagerness to promote the social and commercial well-being of the colony.

The relations existing between the Government and the board during your administration have been of uninterrupted cordiality; and many of the improvements accomplished or recently commenced in Kingstown with a view to furthering its sanitary efficiency and facilitating domestic conveniences, are largely due to the encouraging assistance we have received from the Government, financially and otherwise, through Your Honour's influential recommendations.

We desire to add to this brief appreciation of Your Honour's successful administration, our grateful acknowledgment of the lasting good which the Honourable Mrs. Gideon Murray has done for the women of Kingstown in founding and promoting the St. Vincent fine needlework industry, whose depot is at our free public library. This is only one of the many beneficial schemes which will, we hope, continue to develop and remain for many years to come as monuments of your united solicitude for St. Vincent's progress.

Sir, you are leaving this colony at a critical period, and this fact deepens our regret to bid you good-bye; but we desire to assure you that, whatever fortune the future may disclose, our goodwill for you will remain unchangeable: Your Honour and Mrs. Murray's name and memory will remain indelibly engraved on the tablets of the grateful hearts of the people of St. Vincent.

We remain, Sir, Yours faithfully, J. Elliott Sprott, W. C. Forde
H. P. Hazell, W. Grant T. Osment, J. M. Joseph
H. McDowall, J. B. Bonadie

From the Small Towns

Saint Vincent, 17th May, 1915
To His Honour,
Lieutenant-Colonel the Honourable Gideon Murray, Administrator,
&c., &c., &c.
Sir,

Before Your Honour's departure from this colony to assume your new appointment at St. Lucia, the town wardens, on behalf of the inhabitants of the parishes of this colony which our respective towns represent, beg to place on record their deep gratitude to Your Honour for the many benefits which not only our towns, but the parishes, have derived through your keen interest in our affairs.

Your Honour has not spared your energies in furthering the development of this island, and, when we review the five years of your able administration, we see that all humanly possible has been done for our advancement. We do not wish to specialize but we ask that Your Honour permit us to make mention of a few of the many important works which your efforts have accomplished to our lasting benefit:

171

(a) The Bridges along the Windward Highway and over the Mesopotamia rivers make it possible for us to have a motor car mail and passenger ice to the important centres of the Windward District, thus furthering its development.

(b) The water supplies to Barrouallie, Layou and Calliaqua have resulted in improved sanitary conditions in these towns and consequently in greater comfort to their inhabitants.

(c) The loan to Georgetown has given the wardens the opportunity of carrying out long desired improvements to the second important town of this colony.

(d) The small bridges at Dicksons, South Rivers and Petit Bordel facilitate, to a very great extent, traffic in these parts.

(e) The jetties at Georgetown and along the Leeward coast and also at Bequia have been of the greatest benefit to shippers of produce throughout the colony and especially those of the Carib country.

These and the many other advantages which the colony has gained under your able administration will always remain to us as permanent tokens of Your Honour's zeal and anxiety for our welfare, and we beg to assure you, Sir, that we part with you with sincere regret knowing full well that it will be most difficult to fill your place both officially and in our hearts.

We beg leave, Sir, to include the Honourable Mrs. Murray in this farewell address. Her sympathy with the gentler sex of this island has endeared her to all of us. There has not been a deserving case which has not met with the consideration it merited, and her many kindly acts will ever be remembered by all.

We tender you both our best wishes for your future, and may you both be spared with health and happiness for many years to come. May God's richest blessings be poured on you wherever you may go.

We have, etc.

H. A. Allen, David A. Dennie, and Charles G. Errey, Town Wardens of Chateaubelair	Rupert C. Otway, Warden of the Windward and Leeward Districts
H. A. Allen, G. O. Walker and George Paterson, Town Wardens of Layou	W. Ernest Davis, Assistant Warden
Arthur S. Antrobus and A. Dougan, Town Wardens of Calliaqua	S. S. Garrett (JP), J. M. Gray (JP), and S. C. Telfer, Town Wardens of Georgetown
F. D. Rice and R. G. Barrow, Town Wardens of Bequia	H. A. Allen, A. F. Mandeville, James Gould and Henry Huggins, Town Wardens of Barrouallie

From the Inhabitants of Union Island

Union Island, St. Vincent,
15th May, 1915
To His Honour, The Honourable Charles Gideon Murray,
Administrator of the Island of St. Vincent and its Dependencies

Sir, We the undersigned on behalf of the inhabitants of Union Island do beg to approach Your Honour on the eve of the severance of Your Honour's official connection with this island.

It is our desire to have placed on record the deepest feeling of regret we feel in losing Your Honour as our Administrator. Words cannot adequately express our gratitude for all the benefits we have received from Your Honour's able and efficient administration.

While other places have to be thankful to Your Honour for many benefits accruing from a thoughtful and judicious administration, Union has everything to be grateful for.

We may be permitted to state here under various heads some of the improvements, etc., effected during Your Honour's regime.

To begin with agriculture: At a glance a person who had seen the island in 1911, and who would now inspect the fields of cotton, potato and corn cultivated by the allottees, and observe the regular and methodical arrangement pursued, would at once be convinced that old methods are giving way to a more scientific and profitable order of things.

In the department of livestock, the people today can boast of over 80 head of cattle, and sheep rearing has supplemented the former cherished goat-rearing.

There are also in evidence a few good strains of Indian and Toggenberg goats, the woolless African sheep, a young zebu bull.

Poultry also forms one of the chief industries, the following varieties being handled: Rhode Island, Plymouth Rock, Leghorn. And it is a fact of no little significance, that fowls and turkeys were this year shipped to Trinidad in large quantities, thus enabling many persons to realise money wherewith to pay taxes and other dues.

Under the head General Improvement may be mentioned the cleaning and enlarging of the two principal ponds; putting a cock to the Ashton cistern, and repairing the spouting to it; and the digging of a well at Clifton. Roads have been repaired, and one can safely ride from Clifton to Ashton on the darkest night; culverts being put where a gutter had previously existed. The old Cotton House on the bay is being repaired, and the Clifton House roof looked after. Ashton and Clifton can boast of cottages paying a house tax of fifteen shillings per annum, thereby increasing the tax roll from £30, of old, to £100.

The morale of the inhabitants is all that could be desired. The general behaviour of the people has so improved, that it is not too much to say that the

173

good done them by Your Honour has made an abiding impression on their minds, as mirrored in the abstention from law whenever possible. Criminal cases are few, and far between.

Surely all this bears eloquent testimony to the sympathy shown and the interest taken in our welfare by Your Honour.

Although pained at having to part with Your Honour, we are glad to know that in the translation is Your Honour's promotion.

In conclusion, we wish Your Honour all prosperity in his new sphere of labour, and with Mrs. Murray, long life and happiness; assuring Your Honour that wherever located, Your Honour has the best wishes of the people of this island.

We have, etc.

Herbert Jones	Mary Scrubb	
Richard Mulzac	Rosalin Robinson	Priscilla Samuel
J. S. Archer	Alexander Stewart	Edward Hutchinson
John G. Clouden	Emanuel Stewart	Frederick Mahon
Aaron Adams	William Ambrose	T. McTaire
Isaac John	Nelson Roome	C. Alexander
Robert Douglas	Angelina Harvey	William Scrubb
Job Simmons	Rose Pope	George Wells
Caroline Hutchinson	John Scrubb	William Wells
Queen George	Primus Ramage	

From the Arrowroot Growers' and Exporters' Association

Saint Vincent Arrowroot Growers' and Exporters' Association,
St. Vincent, BWI
15th May, 1915
Sir,

In view of your approaching departure from St. Vincent I am directed to convey to Your Honour the grateful thanks of the Arrowroot Growers and Exporters for the very great interest you have shown in the arrowroot industry during your administration of the Government of this colony; and on their behalf to wish you and Mrs. Murray continued happiness and prosperity.

The above was expressed at a special meeting of the Arrowroot Growers and Exporters Association on the 28th ultimo, when the following resolution was unanimously passed:

Resolved that this meeting desires to record the grateful thanks of the Arrowroot Growers and Exporters in St. Vincent to the Honourable Gideon Murray, Administrator, for the unswerving, helpful interest he has shown in the work of the St. Vincent Arrowroot Growers and Exporters Association, the promotion and organization of which was due to His Honour's initiative; and that, in view of His Honour's approaching departure the secretary *convey to him this association's best wishes for His Honour's and the Honourable Mrs. Murray's future health and prosperity."*

I have, etc.,

J. Elliott Sprott, Secretary
His Honour, The Honourable Gideon Murray, Administrator

31st May—Anthony DeFreitas, Esq, appointed Chief Justice of the colony by virtue of a commission under the hand of the Administrator and the public seal of the colony.

15th June—His Honour Reginald Popham Lobb (CMG) arrived in the colony.

The following telegram was published in *Gazette* of 9th August:

```
HIS MAJESTY THE KING COMMANDS ME TO EXPRESS HIS SINCERE THANKS
FOR THE LOYAL MESSAGE OF HIS COLONIES OF THE WINDWARD ISLANDS AND
HIS GRATIFICATION FOR THEIR ASSURANCE OF SUPPORT OF THE COMMON
CAUSE.
```

The following resolution was embodied in Council Paper No. 6 of 1915

Be it resolved that this council, after considering the telegram of the 21st of July from the Secretary of State for the Colonies communicating the proposal of the Army Council to raise a West Indian Contingent for active service on certain conditions there indicated, unanimously accepts that proposal in principle on behalf of the people of St. Vincent, and at the same time desires to express its great satisfaction that the colony has been afforded the opportunity of thus fulfilling its earnest and long felt desire to take its part in upholding by force of arms the just cause in defence of which His Majesty is now engaged.

His Excellency the Governor cabled on 19th September prior to the departure of the St. Vincent Contingent:

```
PLEASE WISH ST. VINCENT CONTINGENT FROM ME GOD SPEED AND GOD'S
PROTECTION UNTIL THEIR SAFE RETURN.
MY CONGRATULATIONS TO THE PEOPLE OF ST. VINCENT ON THEIR BRAVE
LADS.
```

5th October—Following telegram received from Secretary of State for Colonies:

```
HAVE PLEASURE TO ANNOUNCE SAFE ARRIVAL GRENADA AND ST. VIN-
CENT CONTINGENTS. HIS MAJESTY'S GOVERNMENT DESIRE TO TAKE THIS
OPPORTUNITY OF CONVEYING THEIR HEARTY THANKS AND CONGRATULATIONS
TO THESE COLONIES ON THE EFFORTS WHICH ARE BEING SO SUCCESSFULLY
MADE TO RENDER EFFECTIVE AID IN THE COMMON CAUSE.
DESIRE TO ADD MY PERSONAL CONGRATULATIONS.
```

The Government *Gazette* (extraordinary) of 23rd October comprised the following message from His Majesty the King:

Buckingham Palace
23rd October, 1915
To my People.

At this grave moment in the struggle between my people and a highly organized enemy who have transgressed the laws of nations and changed the ordinance that binds civilized Europe together I appeal to you.

I rejoice in my Empire's efforts and I feel pride in the voluntary response from my subjects all over the world who have sacrificed home, fortune and life itself in order that another may not inherit the free Empire which their ancestors and mine have built.

I ask you to make good these sacrifices.

The end is not in sight. More men and yet more are wanted to keep my armies in the field and through them to secure victory and enduring peace.

In ancient days the darkest moment has ever produced in men of our race the sternest resolve.

I ask you men of all classes to come forward voluntarily and take your share in the fight.

In freely responding to my appeal you will be giving your support to our brothers who for long months have nobly upheld Britain's past traditions and the glory of her arms.

GEORGE R.I.

The following telegrams which were transmitted by the Secretary of State for the Colonies and the Governor were published on 30th October:

From the Secretary of State for the Colonies

October 29--His Majesty the King met with an accident, fortunately not serious, while inspecting his troops in the field yesterday. His horses, excited by the cheers of the troops, reared and fell. His Majesty was severely bruised but after a fair night his general condition improved; temperature 99.2, pulse 75, no complications.

From the Governor of the Windward Islands

His Majesty the King's loyal subjects of the Windward Islands have heard with great regret of the accident to their King and express the fervent hope that His Majesty the King very soon will be restored to good health and they pray God that His Majesty will be spared to rule over them for many years.

Subscriptions to the Red Cross Fund in response to Lord Lansdowne's Special Appeal amounted to £97. 7. 11½; a detailed list appeared in Gazette dated 9th December. The following letter from the Crown Agents for the Colonies was also published then:

Whitehall Gardens,
London, S. W. 26th October, 1915
Sir,

In reply to your letter No. 837 of 15th September, requesting us to purchase for each man of the St. Vincent Detachment of the West Indian Contingent a wooden pipe, a tobacco pouch filled with tobacco, and a metal match box, I have the honour to inform you that these articles were ordered from The Army & Navy Cooperative Society Ltd. at a total cost of £8 8 9, and despatched to Seaford Camp on 13th October. A copy of a letter from the officer commanding the contingent reporting the distribution of the gifts is enclosed. No commission is being charged on this transaction.

I have, etc.,

(Sgd.) P. Ezechiel, for Crown Agents
His Honour, The Administrator, etc., etc., etc., St. Vincent

A message from His Majesty the King was published on 24th December:

Another Christmas finds all the resources of the Empire still engaged in war and I desire to convey on my and on behalf of the Queen a heartfelt Christmas greeting and our good wishes for the New Year to all who on land and sea are upholding the honour of the British name.

In the officers and men of my Navy on whom the security of the Empire depends I repose in common with all our subjects a trust that is absolute.

On the officers and men of my armies whether now in France, in the East, or in other fields I rely with an equal faith confident that their devotion their valour and their self- sacrifice will under God's guidance lead to victory and an honourable peace.

There are many of their comrades now alas in hospital and to these brave men also I desire with the Queen to express our deep gratitude and our earnest prayers for their recovery.

Officers and men of the Navy and of the Army, another year is drawing to a close as it began in toil bloodshed and suffering but I rejoice to know that the goal to which you are striving draws nearer into sight.

May God bless you and all your undertakings.

1916 / His Honour R. Popham Lobb in *Gazette* of 19th February, invited volunteers to enlist in the second St. Vincent contingent and mentioned that volunteers for enlistment in the second St. Vincent Contingent are now required. The contingent will number 50 men and of these 12 have already been selected. Applicants for the remaining vacancies, whether they have already applied in writing or otherwise should apply *in person* to the acting chief of police at the police barracks, Kingstown, between the hours of 10 a.m. and 4 p.m. on Wednesday the 23rd February, 1916.

The minimum standard of height is 5 feet 4 inches and chest measuring 30 inches and men who are below either of these standards should not apply.

No candidate will be accepted unless he has good eyesight and is free from physical defect and disease, and preference will be given to single men without dependants.

This is the only notification on the subject which will be issued. No recruiting meetings or other special means of attracting volunteers have hitherto been necessary in order to fill the ranks of the St. Vincent contingent and they will not be necessary now, for the loyal spirit which has always animated the colony needs no such incentives.

The first contingent were a body of men who would do credit to any country and I have no doubt that the response to His Majesty's call to service will enable St. Vincent to do its duty by sending a second contingent equally as good.

The following telegram was despatched by His Excellency the Governor to the Right Honourable the Secretary of State for the Colonies:

THE LOYAL SUBJECTS OF HIS MAJESTY THE KING IN THE WINDWARD ISLANDS HAVE HEARD WITH THE DEEPEST SORROW OF THE DEATH OF FIELD MARSHALL EARL KITCHENER AND THE OFFICERS AND MEN OF H.M.S. HAMPSHIRE AND DESIRE ME TO CONVEY TO YOU THEIR SINCEREST SYMPATHY AT THE SAD LOSS. THEY ALSO WISH YOU TO EXPRESS TO THE RELATIVES OF THE BRAVE OFFICERS AND MEN WHO SO NOBLY GAVE THEIR LIVES FOR THEIR KING AND COUNTRY AT THE BATTLE OF JUTLAND THEIR PROFOUND GRIEF IN THEIR BEREAVEMENT.

HADDON-SMITH
7th JUNE, 1916

The reply appeared in *Gazette* of 3rd August:

The following despatch from the Right Honourable the Secretary of State for the Colonies is published for general information.

31st July 1916
Windward Islands.
Grenada (General) Downing Street,
No. 96, 23rd June 1916

Sir, I have the honour to acknowledge the receipt of your telegram of the 7th June expressing the sympathy of the people of the Windward Islands in the losses sustained in the naval action off the coast of Jutland and in the loss of His Majesty's Ship Hampshire with Earl Kitchener and his staff.

A copy of your telegram has been laid before His Majesty the King.
I have, etc.,

A. Bonar Law, Governor
Sir G. B. Haddon-Smith (KCMG)

The Government *Gazette* (Extraordinary) of 10th August comprised the following notice.

178

The following telegram from the Right Honourable the Secretary of State to His Excellency the Governor is published for general information:

His Majesty the King commands me to express his sincere thanks to the people of the Windward Islands for their loyal and patriotic message on the occasion of the second anniversary of the declaration of war.

Collections in aid of the Red Cross Fund amounted to £132; the statement of sums received and the sources were published on 18th November.

On the same day particulars relating to clothing for the wounded were published:

It was decided (1) to open a subscription list to provide garments for sick and wounded soldiers and sailors; (2) to invite regular monthly contributions of three pence and upwards; (3) to accept contributions of clothing, materials or finished garments; and (4) to accept offers of voluntary work.

It is requested that all contributions, whether monthly subscriptions, clothing material or finished garments, and the names of volunteer workers be sent to Mrs. Popham Lobb at Government House who will be glad to give information regarding the nature of the materials and the size of the garments.

It was announced on 14th December that the number of volunteers for enrolment in the third St. Vincent contingent of 50 men has so far exceeded requirements that 71 men have been selected. The strength of the contingent will therefore be increased to 100 men.

Robert A. Hudson, Esq, Chairman of the finance committee in letter dated 20th November 1916 stated:

I am desired by the finance committee to add that they would be under obligation if, when transmitting the receipt to the Government of St. Vincent you could ask that our warm and grateful thanks should be conveyed to the people of the colony for the generous help they send to us in our work for the sick and wounded.

Another Christmas message from His Majesty the King was made public in *Gazette* of 25th December:

CHRISTMAS DAY, 1916

I send you, my sailors and soldiers, hearty good wishes for Christmas and the New Year. My grateful thoughts are ever with you for victories gained, for hardships endured and for your unfailing cheeriness. Another Christmas has come around and we are still at war. But the Empire, confident in you, remains determined to win. May God bless and protect you.

At this Christmastide the Queen and I are thinking more than ever of the sick and wounded among my sailors and soldiers. From our hearts we wish them strength to bear their sufferings, speedy restoration to health, a peaceful Christmas and many happy years to come.

GEORGE, R.I.
Published by His Majesty's Command,
R. Popham Lobb, Administrator

1917 / On 12th February an extraordinary issue of the Government *Gazette* appeared with the following notice from His Honour R. Popham Lobb:

> *In the midst of a war which will decide the fate of the Empire and its peoples it is fitting that public and private festivities should be deferred until the peace and security which the colony enjoys are no longer being purchased with the lives of those who are daily fighting and dying for us.*
>
> *Under ordinary circumstances the celebrations held in the Carnival season would take place during the present month.*
>
> *Such displays however are repugnant to the general feeling of the community as being unseemly and incongruous at such a time.*
>
> *The Administrator therefore trusts that those who had intended to participate in these festivities will respect that feeling and refrain from a course of conduct which would be foreign to the traditions and discreditable to the good name of St. Vincent.*
>
> *The services of His Honour the Honourable C. Gideon Murray having been lent to the war office it was notified in the Gazette of 20th February, that His Honour R. Popham Lobb, (CMG), was appointed to succeed him as Administrator of St. Lucia and that His Honour Anthony DeFreitas, Chief Justice etc. would act as Administrator of this colony.*

The enclosure to a letter from the Honorary Secretary of the National Committee for relief in Belgium was given publicity in *Gazette* of 21st June:

> *19th May 1917*
>
> *In view of the fact that the United States Government has generously assumed all financial responsibility for the work of the commission for relief in Belgium, it has been decided that the National Committee for Relief in Belgium will suspend its appeals to the public in the British Empire. Any monies received after June 1st will be held to provide for emergencies now unforeseen in connection with relief in Belgium.*
>
> *This course of action is in accordance with the suggestion made by Mr. Hoover, Chairman of the Relief Commission, who is now in Washington, and has the approval of His Majesty's Government and the Belgian Minister.*
>
> *During the existence of the committee over £2,400,000, subscribed throughout the British Empire for the relief of our oppressed allies in Belgium, has passed through its hands. The second annual meeting will be held at the Mansion House on June 15th, when opportunity will be taken to ex-*

press gratitude to those committees and individuals who have co-operated
with such marked devotion in the work of the national body.
Signed on behalf of the National Committee:

W. H. Dunn, Lord Mayor of London, Chairman
Randall Cantaur, Francis Cardinal Bourne
John Brown, Moderator, Church of Scotland
W. B. Selbie, President, Free Church Council
J. H. Hertz, Chief Rabbi, W. A. M. Goode, Hon. Secretary

By virtue of a Dormant Commission published on 2nd August, His Honour R. Popham Lobb (CMG) was appointed to administer the Government of the Windward Islands in certain events.

The Right Honourable the Secretary of State for the colonies transmitted the following telegram from Sir Douglas Haig:

```
OUR ARMIES IN FRANCE, DRAWN FROM EVERY PART OF THE BRITISH EM-
PIRE, BRING TO THE FOURTH YEAR OF THE WAR A STEADY CONFIDENCE
JUSTIFIED BY THEIR PAST ACHIEVEMENTS. UNFALTERING IN THEIR RES-
OLUTION TO COMPLETE THE TASK TO WHICH THEY HAVE PUT THEIR HANDS
THEY WILL FIGHT UNTIL THE ENEMY IS FINALLY OVERTHROWN.
```

The report for the year ended 31st March in respect to the ankylostomiasis campaign which was appended to the Gazette of 16th August, disclosed:

Census	5,702
Examined	5,669
Positive to *Ankylostomum duodenale*	2,791
Negative to *Ankylostomum duodenale*	2,878
Treated for *Ankylostomum duodenale*	2,620
Cured of *Ankylostomum duodenale*	2,169

Educational Work	Number	Attendance
Lectures to Schools	8	937
Public Lectures	4	1200

On 30th August mention was made of the activities in regard to the West Indian Flag Day, thus:

With reference to Notice No. 137 in the *Gazette* of the 5th July, 1917, the Acting Administrator is very pleased to be able to announce that a successful West Indian Flag Day was organized in Kingstown on the 1st August by a ladies committee consisting of Mrs. C. J. Simmons (Chairman), Mrs. J. H. Aikman, Mrs. N. B, Cropper, Mrs. W. C. Hutchinson, Miss A. McKie, and Mrs. J. E. Sprott, by whose indefatigable work and efficient organization the sum of £210 4 4 was collected, which has been transmitted to the honorary secretary of the West Indian Contingent Committee at 15 Seething Lane, London, E.C.3.

The following telegram from His Excellency the Governor also appeared therein:

```
WITH REFERENCE TO YOUR TELEGRAM 4th AUGUST HIS MAJESTY'S LOYAL
SUBJECTS OF THE WINDWARD ISLANDS REQUEST ME ASK YOU CONVEY TO SIR
DOUGLAS HAIG THEIR CONFIDENCE IN AND ALSO THEIR ADMIRATION FOR
THE BRAVE ARMY HE COMMANDS AND TO ASSURE HIM THAT THEY ARE DETER-
MINED TO DO THEIR DUTY AS A PART OF THE GREAT EMPIRE IN PROVIDING
THEIR QUOTA TO HELP THE COMMANDER-IN-CHIEF TO COMPLETE HIS TASK
WHICH ALTHOUGH DIFFICULT IS ASSURED OWING TO THE DETERMINATION
AND VALOUR OF THE OFFICERS AND MEN UNDER HIS COMMAND.
```

A message from His Majesty the King was published in *Gazette* (extraordinary) of 18th October:

Buckingham Palace.

During the last twelve months I have had constant opportunities for witnessing afresh both at home and in Flanders the great work of mercy carried out by the united efforts of the Red Cross Society and the Order of St. John of Jerusalem in England. In every theatre of the war regardless of distance discomforts or danger the task of alleviating pain and suffering and of ministering to those in need is performed with unparalleled devotion by the men and women who have taken service under the Red Cross. The prompt and unstinted provision of medical and general stores and comforts is an all-important work and one of the main responsibilities undertaken by the Joint Committee. In Hospitals and convalescent homes, hospital trains, motor ambulances, and launches, our sick and wounded, as well as those of our Allies, are I know indeed grateful for the aid and cooperation which the joint societies bring to the medical services of the armies; nor have the needs of the prisoners of war been forgotten in the allocation of your funds. I trust therefore that there will be no falling off of generous financial support on the part of anyone at home and in the Dominions overseas, without which this work cannot be maintained. During the War, I have had great satisfaction in sending to the Joint Committee on the 20th of October, a donation of £5,000. This year for the Our Day collection on the 18th of October it is a pleasure to me to contribute £10,000 to mark my appreciation of what has been achieved by the Red Cross Society and the Order of St. John of Jerusalem in England in the past and my deep sense of the importance of continuing these achievements in the future.

GEORGE R.I.

Again, on 6th December another announcement from His Majesty the King was made.

To my People

The world-wide struggle for the triumph of right and liberty is entering upon its last and most difficult phase. The enemy is striving by desperate assault and subtle intrigue to perpetuate wrongs already committed and stem the tide of a free civilization. We have yet to complete the great task to which more than three years ago we dedicated ourselves. At such a time I would call *upon you to devote a special day to prayer that we may have the clear-sight-edness and strength necessary to the victory of our cause. This victory will be gained only if we steadfastly remember the responsibility which rests upon us and in a spirit of reverent obedience ask the blessing of Almighty God upon our endeavours. With hearts grateful for the Divine Guidance which has led us so far towards our goal let us seek to be enlightened in our understanding and fortified in our courage in facing the sacrifice we may yet have to make before our work is done. I therefore hereby appoint 6th January the first Sun-day of the year to be set aside as a special day of prayer and thanksgiving in all the churches throughout my Dominions and require that this Proclama-tion be read at the services held on that day.*

GEORGE R.I.

An event of historic importance was made known on 12th December by the following notice in the Government *Gazette*:

The following telegram from the Right Hon. the Secretary of State for the Colonies to His Excellency the Governor is published for general informa-tion:

OFFICIAL NEWS DECEMBER 10th, JERUSALEM HAS SURRENDERED TO GENERAL ALLENBY ON DECEMBER NINTH AFTER SUCCESSFUL OPERATION BY OUR ARMY IN PALESTINE AGAINST ENEMY POSITIONS WHICH ENCIRCLED HOLY CITY. BRITISH OFFICIALS ACCOMPANIED BY BRITISH, FRENCH, ITALIAN AND INDIAN MAHOMEDAN GUARDS ARE ON THEIR WAY TO SAFEGUARD THE CITY AND THEIR HOLY PLACES. I AM CONFIDENT THAT THIS GREAT HISTORICAL EVENT WILL BE HAILED WITH SATISFACTION THROUGHOUT THE EMPIRE.

1918 / A letter from the West Indian Contingent Committee to His Hon-our the Acting Administrator was published in Govt. *Gazette* of 3rd January:

The West Indian Contingent Committee
15 Seething Lane, London, E.C. 3,
25th October 1917

Sir, We beg to thank you for your letter 1014 of August 28th, which only came to hand this month, informing us that the West Indian Flag Day on behalf of the West Indian Contingent Fund was organised by a ladies com-mittee, and held in Kingstown on August 1st, and advising us of the despatch of £210 4s. 4d. the net amount collected, to us through the Crown Agents for the Colonies.

2. We have now duly received this amount and shall be obliged if you will kindly convey to Mrs. C. J. Simmons, Mrs. J. H. Aikman, Mrs. N. B. Cropper, Mrs. W. C. Hutchinson, Miss A. McKie and Mrs. J. E. Sprott, our very cordial thanks for their efforts which have proved so successful.

We would further ask you to convey to the public and press and to all con-cerned our thanks for making West Indian Flag Day in St. Vincent a success.

Adding Our Thanks To You Personally, We Have, Etc.,

Everard Im Thurn, Chairman
Algernon E. Aspinall, Honourable Secretary

An extract from a report from the General Officer Commanding in Chief, East African Force, to the Secretary, War Office, relating to the Detachment, British West Indies Regiment up to 15th June 1917 appeared in *Gazette* of 11th April:

> *This Detachment landed in East Africa from Egypt on 6th August, 1916, and has served on lines of communication from Korogwe to Wami River and Mikesse to Rufiji and is still employed on the latter section.*
>
> *It was originally intended that this detachment should reinforce the 2nd Battalion West India Regiment but it has acted throughout as a separate unit.*
>
> *The chairman of the finance committee of the British Red Cross Society forwarded the following letter to His Honour R. Popham Lobb:*

The Order Of St. John Of Jerusalem In England
The British Red Cross Society, Joint War Committee.
83, Pall Mall, London, S.W. 1.
7th February 1918

OUR DAY, 1917

> *Sir, We have received through the Crown Agents a remittance of £36 9 9, the response from the colony of St. Vincent sent by you in reply to our appeal. Our official receipt has been sent to the Crown Agents.*
>
> *I am desired by the Joint War Committee of the British Red Cross Society and the Order of St. John to convey to you, and through you, to the inhabitants of St. Vincent our warm gratitude for the generous help you send to us and for the interest you take in the cause of the sick and wounded.*
>
> *I am, etc.,*
>
> *Robert. A. Hudson, Chairman of the Finance Committee*
> *R. Popham Lobb, Esq (CMG) Administrator and Colonial Secretary*
> *St. Vincent, Windward Islands*

From the General Officer Commanding Mesopotamia Expeditionary Force, came a reply which appeared in *Gazette* of June 20th:

> *In reply to your No. 33891, dated 9th June, 1917, I have the honour to report that 397 non-commissioned officers and men of the British West Indies Regiment are serving with this force.*
>
> *They are employed in the following capacities:*

Motor Boat Drivers	*101*
Guards	*81*
Clerks	*71*
Carpenters	*23*
Camp Police	*16*
Blacksmiths	*12*
Fitters	*11*
Telephone Operators	*6*
Miscellaneous duties	*76*

These non-commissioned officers and men have been of great value to the force; they have performed their duties in an efficient manner and to my entire satisfaction. The majority of them have been on service for a year, and they have been especially welcome as representatives of such a distant portion of the Empire.

(Si.) F. S. Maude, Lt. Gen., etc.

The *Gazette* (Extraordinary) of 6th July comprised a telegram:

The following telegram has been sent by His Excellency the Governor to the Right Honourable the Secretary of State for the Colonies:

HIS MAJESTY'S LOYAL SUBJECTS OF THE WINDWARD ISLANDS ASK YOU KINDLY TO CONVEY TO THEIR MAJESTIES THE KING AND QUEEN THE DUTI-FUL AND RESPECTFUL CONGRATULATIONS OF THE PEOPLE OF THESE ISLANDS ON THIS THEIR MAJESTIES' SILVER WEDDING DAY ASSURING THEM OF THEIR STEADFAST DEVOTION TO THE CROWN AND THEIR EARNEST PRAYER THAT IT MAY PLEASE GOD TO PRESERVE THEIR MAJESTIES IN GOOD HEALTH TO REIGN OVER THE EMPIRE FOR MANY YEARS.

HADDON-SMITH

A Message from the Prime Minister of England to His Excellency the Governor was delivered in the *Gazette* of 15th August:

Message from Prime Minister of England on the fourth anniversary of the War:

The message which I send to the people of the British Empire on the 4th anniversary of their entry into the War is HOLD FAST. We are in this war for no selfish ends. We are in it to recover freedom for the nations which have been brutally attacked and despoiled and to prove that no people however powerful can surrender itself to the lawless ambitions of militarism, without meeting retribution swift, certain and disastrous at the hands of the free nations of the world. To stop short of victory for this cause would be to compromise the future of mankind. I say HOLD FAST because our prospects of victory have never been so bright as they are today. Six months ago, the ruler of Germany deliberately rejected the just and reasonable settlement proposed by the Allies. Throwing aside the last mask of moderation, they partitioned Russia, enslaved Romania and approached the seizure of supreme power by overwhelming the Allies in a final and desperate attack. Thanks to the invincible bravery of all the Allied armies it is now evident to all that the dream of universal conquest for the sake of which they wantonly prolonged the war can never be fulfilled. But the battle is not yet won. The great autocracy of Prussia will still endeavour by violence or guile to avoid defeat and so give militarism a new lease of life. We cannot seek to escape the horrors of war for ourselves by laying them up for our children. Having set our hands to the task we must see it through till a just and lasting settlement is achieved. In no other way can we ensure a world set free from war. HOLD FAST!

D. Lloyd George
August 4th, 1918

With reference to telegram of 6th July, the Right Honourable the Secretary of State for the Colonies forwarded a Despatch which appeared in *Gazette* of 12th September:

Windward Islands, Grenada (General)
Downing Street,
26th July 1918
No. 70.

> *Sir, I duly laid before Their Majesties the King and Queen your telegram of the 6th July, conveying the congratulations of the inhabitants of the Windward Islands on the occasion of Their Majesties' silver wedding: and I have it in command to inform you that Their Majesties were much pleased to receive this evidence of the loyalty and goodwill of the people under your government.*

> *I Have, etc.,*

> *(Sgd.) Walter H. Long, Governor*
> *Sir G. B. Haddon-Smith (KCMG)*
> *Etc., Etc., Etc.*

The letter from the chairman of the finance committee of the British Red Cross Society to the Crown Agents was published in the *Gazette* of 10th October:

Chairman of Finance Committee
British Red Cross Society to Crown Agents
83, Pall Mall, London, S.W. 1.
14th August 1918

> *Gentlemen, I have to thank you for your letter of 12th instant covering cheque value £85 representing contributions from St. Vincent as under:*

Amount collected by the sale of roses, etc.	*£51 12 11½*
Proceeds of entertainment organized by Mrs. Conrad Simmons	*£33 7 0½*

> *I beg to hand you herewith our official receipts and to ask if you will be so good when transmitting the same to St. Vincent to ask if the Governor will kindly hand them to the proper quarters, with an expression of the warm thanks of the British Red Cross Society and Order of St. John for this further practical evidence of the sympathy and interest shown by our friends in St. Vincent in our efforts to alleviate the sufferings of our sick and wounded comrades in the field.*

> *Yours faithfully, etc.,*

> *(Sd.) Robertt. A. Hudson, Chairman of Finance Committee*

The *Gazette* (Extraordinary) of 1st November comprised the following telegram:

The following telegram from the The Right Honourable the Secretary of State for the Colonies to His Excellency the Governor is published for general information:

OCTOBER 31ˢᵗ. THE FOLLOWING ANNOUNCEMENT WILL BE MADE IN HOUSES OF PARLIAMENT THIS AFTERNOON. SOME DAYS AGO GENERAL TOWNSHEND WAS LIBERATED IN ORDER TO INFORM THE BRITISH ADMIRAL IN COMMAND IN THE AEGEAN THAT THE GOVERNMENT OF TURKEY ASKED THAT NEGOTIATIONS SHOULD BE OPENED IMMEDIATELY FOR AN ARMISTICE BETWEEN TURKEY AND THE ALLIES. A REPLY WAS SENT THAT IF THE GOVERNMENT OF TURKEY SENT FULLY ACCREDITED PLENIPOTENTIARIES, VICE ADMIRAL CALTHORPE WAS EMPOWERED TO INFORM THEM OF THE CONDITIONS UPON WHICH THE ALLIES WOULD AGREE TO A CESSATION OF HOSTILITIES AND TO SIGN AN ARMISTICE ON THOSE CONDITIONS ON THEIR BEHALF. TURKISH PLENIPO-TENTIARIES ARRIVED AT MUDROS EARLY THIS WEEK AND AN ARMISTICE WAS SIGNED BY ADMIRAL CALTHORPE ON BEHALF OF THE ALLIED GOVERNMENTS LAST NIGHT AND COMES INTO OPERATION AT NOON TODAY. IT IS NOT POSSIBLE AS YET TO PUBLISH THE FULL TERMS OF THE ARMISTICE BUT THEY INCLUDE THE FREE PASSAGE FOR THE ALLIED FLEETS THROUGH THE BOSPHORUS TO THE BLACK SEA, THE OCCUPATION OF THE FORTS ON THE DARDANELLES AND THE BOSPHORUS, NECESSARY TO SECURE THEIR PASSAGE, AND THE IMMEDIATE REPATRIATION OF ALL ALLIED PRISONERS OF PAR.'

And the *Gazette* (Extraordinary) of 11ᵗʰ November announced:

The following telegram from the Right Honourable the Secretary of State for the Colonies to His Excellency the Governor is published for general information:

ARMISTICE WITH GERMANY SIGNED 5 O'CLOCK THIS MORNING.

Then followed the telegram from His Excellency the Governor:

HIS MAJESTY'S LOYAL SUBJECTS OF THE WINDWARD ISLANDS BEG TO REQUEST YOU TO TENDER HIS MAJESTY THEIR RESPECTFUL CONGRATULA-TIONS ON THE VICTORIOUS CESSATION OF HOSTILITIES WHICH HAS BEEN ACHIEVED BY THE GALLANTRY OF HIS MAJESTY'S FORCES AND THE UNITY AND STEADFASTNESS OF THE PEOPLE OF THE BRITISH EMPIRE AND ALSO ON THE RESOLUTE CONDUCT OF THE WAR BY HIS MAJESTY'S GOVERNMENT WHEREBY THE HONOUR AND INTEGRITY OF OUR GREAT EMPIRE HAS BEEN PROTECTED AND MAINTAINED.

HADDON-SMITH

The despatch from the Secretary of State for the Colonies was duly published:

Windward Islands, Grenada (General)
Downing Street, 21ˢᵗ November 1918
No. 116

   Sir, I have the honour to inform you that your telegrams of the 11ᵗʰ and 13ᵗʰ November, sent on the occasion of the signing of the Armistice, have been laid before His Majesty the King, who has commanded me to convey to the people of the Windward Islands his warm appreciation of their messages of loyalty and congratulation.

   I have, etc.,

(Sgd.) Walter H. Long
Governor, Sir G. B. Haddon-Smith (KCMG)
Etc., Etc., Etc.

On 21st November a telegram from the Right Honourable the Secretary of State for the Colonies to His Excellency the Governor was published. It was read in the churches throughout the colony on Sunday the 17th.

> *Now that the war has been brought to a victorious conclusion I desire on behalf of His Majesty's Government to express to the people of the Windward Islands our high appreciation of their constant support of the effort of the Empire whose battles they have shared by land and sea and of their generous response to the calls on them.*

The following message from Her Majesty the Queen was forwarded to His Excellency the Governor for publication:

> *A few months ago at the height of our anxiety and strain, I sent a message in the name of the women of our lands to our men fighting for us across the seas. Now in an hour of thankfulness and hope I should like to give a message to the women of the Empire.*
>
> *During the war they have been given the high privilege of service, they have risen to the great opportunity and have proved their courage, steadfastness and ability.*
>
> *I have been allowed to watch and appreciate their work in many parts of the country and my heart is full of admiration and gratitude for what I have seen.*
>
> *I earnestly trust that though the thrill and glamour of war are over the spirit of self-sacrifice and helpfulness which it has kindled will not wane in the coming days. A new era is dawning upon the world, bringing with it many difficulties, fresh responsibilities and serious problems to be faced. Parliament has secured for the whole country greater opportunities of more thorough and varied education, but it will depend upon the parents whether these opportunities are used to the full.*
>
> *We all rejoice that plans are afoot for bringing to an end the existence of such bad and crowded housing as makes home life almost impossible.*
>
> *Today more than ever the Empire needs her daughters, for in the larger world of public and industrial work women are daily taking a more important place.*
>
> *As we have been united in all our work, whether of head or hands, in a real sisterhood of suffering and service during the war, let us go on working together with the same unity of purpose for the resettlement and reconstruction of our Country.*
>
> *MARY, R.*

The good wishes of Their Majesties the King and Queen were telegraphed by the Right Honourable the Secretary of State for the Colonies:

```
BUCKINGHAM PALACE. ANOTHER CHRISTMAS HAS COME ROUND AND WE ARE
NO LONGER FIGHTING. GOD HAS BLESSED OUR EFFORTS. THE QUEEN AND
I OFFER YOU OUR HEARTFELT GOOD WISHES FOR A HAPPY CHRISTMAS AND
MANY BRIGHTER YEARS TO COME. TO THE DISABLED SICK AND WOUNDED WE
```

SEND A SPECIAL GREETING PRAYING THAT WITH RETURNING HEALTH YOU
MAY BE COMFORTED AND CHEERED BY THE VISION OF THOSE GOOD DAYS OF
PEACE FOR WHICH YOU HAVE SACRIFICED SO MUCH.

GEORGE, R.I.

1919 / 25th December 1918—At a parade of the St. Vincent volunteers and police at the courthouse on the 22nd March, the Administrator, on behalf of His Excellency the Governor-in-Chief, presented to His Honour Anthony DeFreitas the insignia of an Officer of the Order of the British Empire, to which he was appointed by His Majesty the King for services rendered in St. Lucia at the outbreak of war.

Fifteen returned men of the St. Vincent contingents of the British West Indies Regiment received the war chevron and in the case of Private Nathaniel Laidlow the silver badge for service overseas.

His Honour also handed to Mr. S. F. Leigertwood, senior assistant to the assistant for cotton research, the certificate of the Imperial Department of Agriculture Intermediate Examination in Practical Agriculture.

The following government notices were comprised in the extraordinary *Gazettes* of 29th June and 3rd July, respectively:

> The signing of the Treaty of Peace will be received with deep thankfulness throughout the British Empire. This formal act brings to its concluding stages the terrible war which has devastated Europe and distracted the world. It manifests the victory of the ideals of freedom and liberty for which we have made untold sacrifices. I share my people's joy and thanksgiving and earnestly pray that the coming years of peace may bring to them ever increasing happiness and prosperity.

> Government Office
> 29th June 1919

By the KING
A PROCLAMATION

GEORGE, R.I.

> Whereas it has pleased Almighty God to bring to a close the late widespread and sanguinary war in which we were engaged against Germany and her Allies, we therefore, adoring the Divine goodness and duly considering that the great and general blessings of peace do call for public and solemn acknowledgement, have thought fit by and with the advice of Our Privy Council to issue this Our Royal Proclamation hereby appointing and commanding a general thanksgiving to Almighty God for these His manifold and great mercies be observed throughout Our Dominions on Sunday, the 6th day of July; and for the better and more devout solemnization of the same, we have given directions to the Most Reverend the Archbishops and the Right Reverend the Bishops of England to compose a form of prayer suitable for this occasion to be used in all churches and chapels and to take care for the timely dispersing of the same throughout their respective dioceses; and to

189

the same end we do further advertise and exhort the general assembly of the Church of Scotland and all spiritual authorities and ministers of religion in their respective churches and other places of public worship throughout the United Kingdom of Great Britain and Ireland and in all quarters of Our Dominions beyond the seas to take part as it may properly behove them to do in this great and common act of worship and we do strictly charge and command that the said public day of thanksgiving be religiously observed by all as they tender the favour of Almighty God and have the sense of His benefits.

 Given at Our Court at Buckingham Palace this first day of July in the year of Our Lord one thousand nine hundred and nineteen and in the tenth tear of Our Reign.

GOD SAVE THE KING

In the *Gazette* of July 3, the following telegram was published:

NOW THAT PEACE HAS BEEN SIGNED I DESIRE ON BEHALF OF HIS MAJES-TY'S GOVERNMENT TO THANK THE MEMBERS OF THE COLONIAL SERVICE FOR THEIR WORK DURING THE WAR AND TO EXPRESS OUR APPRECIATION OF THE DEVOTION TO DUTY WHICH THEY HAVE SHOWN DURING ALL THESE TRYING YEARS. NOT A FEW, I FEAR, HAVE SUFFERED IN HEALTH OWING TO THE EXCEPTIONAL STRAIN AND ALL HAVE BEEN EXPOSED IN A GREATER OR LESS DEGREE TO SERIOUS PRIVATIONS. BUT IN A TRUE SPIRIT OF PATRIOTISM THESE HARDSHIPS HAVE BEEN CHEERFULLY BORNE. BY ENSURING THE GOOD CONDUCT OF THE ADMINISTRATION THROUGHOUT THE WAR IN ALL HIS MAJ-ESTY'S POSSESSIONS, THE MEN WHO HAVE REMAINED AT THEIR POSTS HAVE CONTRIBUTED, NO LESS THAN THOSE WHO HAVE FOUGHT IN THE FIELD, TO THE GREAT NATIONAL EFFORT WHICH HAS RESULTED IN VICTORY.

JULY 2ND.

A Proclamation by the King was made public on 5th July:

By the KING

A PROCLAMATION

GEORGE, R.I.

 WHEREAS *a definite Treaty of Peace between Us and the Associated Governments and the German Government was concluded at Versailles on the 28th day of June last: in conformity thereunto we have thought fit to command that the same be published in due course throughout all Our Dominions: and we do declare to all our loving subjects our will and pleasure that upon the exchange of the ratification thereof the said Treaty of Peace be observed inviolably as well by sea as by land and in all places whatsoever: strictly charging and commanding all our loving subjects to take notice hereof and to conform themselves thereunto accordingly.*

 GIVEN *at our Court at Buckingham Palace this first day of July in the Year of our* LORD *One thousand nine hundred and nineteen and in the tenth Year of our Reign.*

GOD SAVE THE KING

190

PEACE CELEBRATIONS
Programme

The official day for the Peace Celebrations is Saturday, 19th July. As the northward mail arrives on that day, which is also the market day for people from the out-districts and the Grenadines, permission has been given for the stores in Kingstown to remain open for the convenience of the public on the 19th instant, and Thursday and Friday, the 24th and 25th instant, have been declared public holidays.

The peace bonfires at Cane Garden Point, Dorsetshire Hill, Mount St. Andrews, Fort Charlotte, Fancy, Bequia, Union Island, Canouan, and Mayreau, will be lit at 8 o'clock p.m. on Saturday the 19th instant.

Thursday, the 24th July: Every invalided soldier will be given five shillings, and a grant of two shillings will be given to the destitute poor throughout the colony except in Kingstown.

A special meal will be provided for the inmates of the Thompson Home and for the patients at the hospital, pauper and leper asylums and the Yaws Hospital, and for the prisoners in the jail.

A parade of the local forces and returned soldiers will be held at Victoria Park in conjunction with a procession of school children at noon. In the afternoon, the children of the schools in Kingstown, Lowmans, Questelles, and Sion Hill will be entertained in the grounds of the court house, and later on they will be taken to a cinematograph show at the Electric Theatre. A meal will be provided in the Market Square at 4 p.m. for all the poor of the district.

Friday the 25th July: The programme of sports to be held in the Victoria Park will be issued later.

OUT-DISTRICTS

Arrangements have been made through the school managers for the entertainment of all the school children in the various districts including the Grenadines, and a sum of money has been placed at the disposal of the wardens of each of the small towns, including Bequia, for expenditure on purposes connected with the celebrations.

Another telegram from the Secretary of State for the Colonies was published on 26th July:

```
JULY 12TH. BLOCKADE OF GERMANY RAISED AS FROM TODAY. MINERAL
LICENCE BEING ISSUED BY BOARD OF TRADE AUTHORIZING SUBJECT TO
REMAINING UNITED KINGDOM PROHIBITIONS IMPORT AND EXPORT TRADE
BETWEEN UNITED KINGDOM AND GERMANY. TERMS OF LICENCE WILL BE COM-
MUNICATED TO YOU LATER. PROHIBITED EXPORT LIST C BEING ABOLISHED
AND EXPORTS TO HOLLAND AND SWITZERLAND MAY BE CONSIGNED DIRECT TO
IMPORTERS INSTEAD OF TO SOCIETE SUISSE DE SURVEILLANCE. CONSIGN-
```

191

A captured German machine gun obtained from the War Trophies Committee and presented to St. Vincent by the West India Committee as a trophy of the Great War has been placed at the Carnegie Free Library.

A message from the King was made public on 10th November:

6th November

> *I am commanded by His Majesty the King to send you for immediate publication the following message which is addressed to all the peoples of the Empire:*

> *To ALL MY PEOPLE, Tuesday next, the 11th November, is the first anniversary of the armistice which stayed the worldwide carnage of the four preceding years and marked the victory of right and freedom. I believe that my people in every part of the Empire fervently wish to perpetuate the memory of that great deliverance and of those who laid down their lives to achieve it.*

> *To afford an opportunity for the universal expression of this feeling it is my desire and hope that at the hour when the armistice came into force, the eleventh hour of the eleventh day of the eleventh month, there may be for the brief space of two minutes a complete suspension of all our normal activities. During that time except in the rare cases where this might be impracticable all work should and all locomotion should cease so that in perfect stillness the thoughts of everyone may be concentrated on reverent remembrance of the glorious dead.*

> *No elaborate organization appears to be necessary. At a given signal which can easily be arranged to suit the circumstances of each locality I believe that we shall all gladly interrupt our business, pleasure, whatever it may be, and unite in this simple service of silence and remembrance.*

> *GEORGE, R.I.*

1920 / An investiture was held by Sir George Haddon-Smith (KCMG), Governor and Commander-in-Chief of the Windward Islands, at the court house, Kingstown, on the 12th February at 5 p.m.

A guard of honour of the St. Vincent police and volunteers, under the command of Captain R. J. Paul, Trinidad constabulary, acting chief of police, was mounted in the courtyard.

After inspecting the guard, His Excellency, who was accompanied by Lady Haddon-Smith and attended by Mr. C. N. Rice, private secretary, proceeded to the council chamber and there invested Miss Annie McKie, who was presented by Lady Haddon-Smith, with the insignia of the fifth class of the Most Excellent Order of the British Empire.

The ceremony was attended by the Colonial Secretary, His Honour the Chief Justice, heads of departments and other government officials, leading representatives of the community, and by a large number of ladies and gentlemen.

Lord Milner's circular despatches of the 1ˢᵗ September and 10ᵗʰ October 1919, transmitting copies of Admiralty Fleet orders regarding the award of the British War Medal and the Victory Medal, were all published in the *Gazette* of 26ᵗʰ February.

The extensive and interesting report of the Tropical Agriculture College committee was published in *Gazette* of 1ˢᵗ March.

The following telegrams in connection with the visit of His Royal Highness the Prince of Wales were published in the *Gazette* of 1ˢᵗ April.

```
HIS ROYAL HIGHNESS THE PRINCE OF WALES,
H.M.S. RENOWN:

HIS MAJESTY'S LOYAL SUBJECTS OF THE WINDWARD ISLANDS RESPECTFUL-
LY BEG TO TENDER TO YOUR ROYAL HIGHNESS A HEARTY WELCOME TO THE
WEST INDIES, AND TO EXPRESS THEIR DEEP APPRECIATION OF THE KIND
THOUGHT THAT HAS PROMPTED YOUR ROYAL HIGHNESS TO INCLUDE IN YOUR
TOUR THESE ANCIENT AND LOYAL PARTS OF HIS MAJESTY'S DOMINIONS.
THE PEOPLE OF GRENADA HAVE HEARD WITH JOYFUL GRATITUDE THE DECI-
SION OF YOUR ROYAL HIGHNESS TO HONOUR THEIR ISLAND BY A VISIT AND
DESIRE ME TO ASSURE YOUR ROYAL HIGHNESS OF A LOYAL AND SINCERE
WELCOME.
                                              HADDON-SMITH
                                            24ᵗʰ MARCH 1920

GOVERNOR HADDON-SMITH,
25ᵗʰ MARCH 1920
THE PRINCE OF WALES GREATLY APPRECIATED THE LOYAL MESSAGE WHICH
YOU HAVE FORWARDED FROM THE PEOPLE OF THE WINDWARD ISLANDS AND
LOOKS FORWARD TO HIS VISIT TO GRENADA VERY MUCH.
                       COLONEL GRIGG, H.M.S. RENOWN
```

Captain E. C. Kennedy of H.M.S. *Constance,* in letter dated 28ᵗʰ March 1920, wrote from Montserrat:

> *On behalf of the officers may I thank you and all those who so very kindly helped to make our stay at Kingstown such a pleasant one.*
>
> *We enjoyed our two days very much and hope we may have another opportunity of visiting St. Vincent and of returning some of the hospitality that was shown us.*

Dr. E. Greaves began his lectures at the Carnegie Hall on tropical hygiene, etc., on 8ᵗʰ June.

A special service was held at St. George's Cathedral ON Wednesday, 25ᵗʰ August, at 3 p.m. on the occasion of the handing over for safe custody of the flag and shield presented to the British West Indies Regiment by the League of the Empire.

His Honour S. J. Thomas, Acting Administrator, and Miss Thomas attended at Grenada on the occasion of the visit of His Royal Highness the Prince of Wales and were the guests of His Excellency Sir George Haddon-Smith (KCMG) and Lady Haddon-Smith.

Staff of His Royal Highness The Prince of Wales
Rear Admiral Sir Lionel Halsey (KCMG, KCVO, CB) Chief of Staff
Lieutenant Colonel E. W. M. Grigg, (CMG, CVO, DSO, MC)
    Grenadier Guards, Political Secretary
Sir Godfrey J. V. Thomas, Bart., Private Secretary
Captain Dudley B. N. North (RN, CMG, MVO) Naval A.D.C.
Captain Lord Claude N. Hamilton (DSO, MVO)
    Grenadier Guards, *Equerry*
Captain Honourable Piers W. Legh (MVO, OBE) *Equerry*
Paymaster Lieutenant-Commander Arthur C. A. Janion (RN, OBE)
Sub-Lieutenant Lord Louis F. A. V. N. Mountbatten (RN)

The following address from St. Vincent was read by His Honour S. J. Thomas, Administrator of St. Vincent on 24ᵗʰ September:

His Royal Highness, Edward, Prince of Wales.

May it please Your Royal Highness,

The people of the colony of St. Vincent ever loyal to the Throne desire to be allowed to add their welcome to Your Royal Highness.

They would have rejoiced to have renewed to Your Royal Highness the loyal welcome demonstrated to Your Illustrious Father, His Majesty King George the Fifth, at that time Duke of York.

They are moved with deep regret at your not being able to visit their beautiful island home, on account of the sickness recently prevalent there, to the risk of infection from which it would not have been just to subject Your Royal Highness.

In the awful war forced on the British People and now by the grace of God brought to a triumphant issue, you have deservedly attained great renown. To the laurels of war you are now adding those of peace.

It is well known how greatly Your Royal Highness has at heart the well-being of all the peoples of the Empire. Your presence in the sister colony of Grenada emphasizes the solicitous care which is felt by His Majesty the King for the prosperity of the colonies and the welfare of their communities.

It is only right to mention therefore that as far as possible by means of land settlement and other schemes the interests of the poorest classes in St. Vincent have been considered. By the introduction of Sea Island Cotton and a system of Government purchase, considerable prosperity has been made available without distinction to all cultivators of the soil. The new encouragement given to the growing of sugar canes should also further an additional source of prosperity to the colony. As the finances of the colony permit, every endeavour will be made to further additional beneficial schemes for the ame-

lioration of the conditions of all classes and especially in this connection must be mentioned such matters as education and public health.

Your journey has taken Your Royal Highness to the ends of the world and though you may have noticed differences of climate and possibly of other conditions, there can have been no difference in the loyal feelings evidenced to yourself and to the Royal Family of which you are so notable a scion.

Will Your Royal Highness be pleased to accept the assurance that a welcome of equal warmth awaits you should Your Royal Highness at any future time be able to visit St. Vincent.

S. J. Thomas, Administrator, N. C. Ruggles, Attorney General
D. Hadley (MEC), Cyril H. Durrant (MLC)
Vernon J. Richards (MLC), W. C. Hutchinson Treasurer
Lewis L. Punnett (MEC, MLC), J. Elliott Sprott (MLC)
Alex. M. Fraser (MLC)

His Royal Highness the Prince of Wales made the following reply:

Your Honour,

I very much appreciate the spirit which has prompted the people of St. Vincent and the southern Grenadines to send an address of welcome to be presented to me here. It was a matter of very keen regret to me to have to abandon my projected visit to the island of St. Vincent. I beg you to convey to all its residents my great disappointment that I cannot receive this address in St. Vincent itself, and my most cordial thanks for the affectionate loyalty by which it is inspired.

I am glad to hear that the island is making good progress in all matters relating to education and public health, and that so much new prosperity has been brought within the reach of all cultivators of the soil. I shall always take a deep interest in its welfare, and I send to its government and people my best wishes for their future well-being and happiness.

EDWARD P.

The celebration of the centenary of St. George's Cathedral on the 6th September was an event of historical importance. Sunday 5th being the eve of the festival, appropriate hymns were sung at evensong. The preacher Rev. C. Culpan took as his text the first sentence of the Lord's Prayer.

On Monday morning at 5 o'clock there was Sung Eucharist; the Rev. B. A. Samuel was the preacher. Being a native of St. Vincent, conversant with the history and other affairs of St. George's Cathedral for 40 years, he was able to introduce many interesting facts in his discourse whilst reviewing the mission in this colony. His text was taken from the 145th Psalm, v. 4, "One generation shall praise Thy name unto another." The music was described as being exquisitely solemn and charming.

The procession comprised the surpliced choir and clergy, the several societies, associations and guilds of the cathedral. His Honour the Administrator, members of the executive and legislative councils, government officers, members of the church and parochial councils, the Kingstown Board, the Freemasons, The Ancient Order of Foresters, The Independent Order of Odd Fellows, all with magnificent banners. His Honour S. J. Thomas, the Chief Justice, wore his ermine gown. The police under Major Tough produced the military aspect and the municipal band contributed greatly to the unprecedented enthusiasm which pervaded the entire city of Kingstown.

This immense procession wended its way to the cathedral for Matins. The officiating clergy were The Venerable Archdeacon C. Downie, Canon H. E. Gresham, Revs. B. A. Samuel, G. A. I. Frederick, C. Culpan, S. Coleman, and V. Armstrong of St. Vincent, and the Rev. E. Dash, Rector of St. Andrews, Grenada. Archdeacon Downie occupied the pulpit and preached to the large congregation from Gen. 28, v. 17. "This is none other but the House of God and this is the gate of Heaven."

At Evensong Rev. Dash preached from St. Paul in his Epistle to St. James: "Even so faith if it hath not works is dead." There were other services on different days of that week when instructive sermons were preached.

There was a bazaar on Wednesday 8th at the court house, the proceeds of which amounted to £213 7 9½; then there was a variety entertainment of a high standard on Wednesday 15th.

These efforts constituted the basis for the cathedral centenary fund which the Archdeacon confidently expected would reach £1,500 before its close.

The Right Honourable the Secretary of State for the Colonies transmitted the following telegram:

```
11 OCTOBER. HIS MAJESTY THE KING HAS ADDRESSED TO ME THE FOLLOW-
ING LETTER. ON THE RETURN HOME OF THE PRINCE OF WALES, I WOULD
ASK YOU TO EXPRESS TO MY REPRESENTATIVES IN AND TO THE PEOPLE OF
THOSE DOMINIONS AND COLONIES WHICH HE HAS VISITED MY HEARTFELT
APPRECIATION OF THE UNIVERSAL AFFECTION AND LOYAL ENTHUSIASM
EVINCED TOWARDS HIM THROUGHOUT HIS TRAVELS. THESE WARM-HEART-
ED SPONTANEOUS MANIFESTATIONS OF REGARD FOR OUR ELDEST SON HAVE
DEEPLY TOUCHED THE QUEEN AND ME. WE HAVE FOLLOWED WITH PRIDE AND
ADMIRATION THE TRIUMPHANT SUCCESS OF HIS MISSION AND ALL THE MORE
SO WHEN WE RECOGNIZE THAT THESE HAPPY RESULTS ARE CHIEFLY DUE TO
HIS OWN PERSONALITY, TO THE BUOYANT AND GENIAL SPIRIT IN WHICH HE
HAS PLAYED HIS PART, TO THE SENSE OF DUTY AND TO THE UNSTINTING
MANNER IN WHICH HE HAS GIVEN OF HIS BEST. THIS AND HIS PREVIOUS
TOUR HAVE GIVEN HIM SPECIAL OPPORTUNITIES TO GAIN A KNOWLEDGE
OF OUR OVERSEAS DOMINIONS AND COLONIES AND TO BECOME PERSONALLY
ACQUAINTED WITH THEIR PEOPLES. MAY SUCH MUTUAL INTERCOURSE CREATE
FRESH TIES OF CONFIDENCE AND DEVOTION BETWEEN THE THRONE AND
THE GENERATIONS PRESENT AND FUTURE OF THE GREAT LANDS AND THUS
PROMOTE THE UNITY, STRENGTH AND PROSPERITY OF THE EMPIRE. TO MY
SON THE WIDE AND HAPPY EXPERIENCE HE HAS EARNED WILL EVER BE A
PRICELESS POSSESSION.
```

The following telegrams from the Secretary of State to the Governor were published for general information.

IT HAS BEEN DECIDED THAT ON THURSDAY, 11th NOVEMBER, BEING THE
SECOND ANNIVERSARY OF THE ARMISTICE, CENOTAPH IN WHITEHALL SHALL
BE UNVEILED BY THE KING AND THAT AS PART OF THE CEREMONY ON THAT
DAY THERE SHALL BE BURIED IN WESTMINSTER ABBEY AN UNKNOWN BRITISH
WARRIOR WHOSE BODY SHALL BE TAKEN FROM AMONGST THOSE BURIED IN
FRANCE. EVERY PRECAUTION WILL BE TAKEN TO PREVENT HIS IDENTITY
BEING KNOWN. COFFIN WILL BE BROUGHT TO CENOTAPH WHERE IT WILL BE
MET BY THE KING ATTENDED BY REPRESENTATIVES OF THE WHOLE EMPIRE.
THERE WILL BE SHORT SERVICE AT CENOTAPH CONSISTING OF SINGING
OF HYMN, "O GOD OUR HELP IN AGES PAST" AND THE LORD'S PRAYER.
THIS SERVICE WILL BE SO TIMED THAT UNVEILING OF CENOTAPH TAKES
PLACE ELEVEN A.M. EXACTLY AFTER WHICH THERE WILL BE TWO MINUTES
SILENCE FOLLOWED BY "LAST POST." WREATHS WILL THEN BE LAID BY HIS
MAJESTY, THE PRIME MINISTER, AND REPRESENTATIVES OF THE EMPIRE.
FUNERAL PROCESSION THEN WILL PROCEED TO ABBEY WHERE FUNERAL SER-
VICE WILL TAKE PLACE, BODY BEING BURIED IN A GRAVE IN THE NAVE OF
THE ABBEY. IT IS PROPOSED THAT JUST AS LAST YEAR THERE SHOULD BE
DURING THE TWO MINUTES SILENCE COMPLETE SUSPENSION OF ALL NORMAL
BUSINESS WORK AND LOCOMOTION THROUGHOUT THE UNITED KINGDOM THAT
THOUGHTS OF ALL MAY BE CONCENTRATED ON REVERENT REMEMBRANCE OF
THE GLORIOUS DEAD.

MILNER

1921 / From 1st January the medical officer of Carriacou ceased to be the medical officer of the St. Vincent Grenadines comprised in the No. 6 Medical District.

A despatch from the Secretary of State for the Colonies relating to the establishment of the Tropical College of Agriculture was published on 5th May. It mentioned among other things, that a site had been selected at St. Augustine, Trinidad. The concluding paragraph was,

> The contributions so far assured amount to £52,100 towards the establishment of the College and about £13,000 a year towards the cost of its upkeep. It must be recognised that the latter figure is decidedly inadequate for the maintenance of the College on the scale contemplated in the Committee's report, but it may be anticipated that the revenue will be increased, not only by further contributions, but also automatically in consequence of the growth of the revenue of the contributing Colonies. The question of obtaining further contributions from industrial sources is one that will shortly be considered by the Committee.

In a lengthy despatch published 28th July the Secretary of State for the Colonies emphasized:

(a) The danger of over-estimating revenue

(b) The financial risk of budgeting for deficits to be met out of accumulated balances

(c) The desirability of taking advantage of periods of prosperity to build up substantial reserves against the possibility of future lean years.

From Census Report

The total number of persons living in St. Vincent and its dependencies on the night of Sunday, 24th April 1921, was 44,447, an increase of 2,570, or 6.14 per cent as compared with the census of 1911 which was 41,877.

The following table shows the population as determined by estimation and by enumeration.

Estimated 1911	Census 1911	Estimated 1921	Census 1921	Difference between Estimation and Enumeration	Decrease per cent by Estimation	Increase per cent Enumerated
54,374	41,877	53,937	44,447	9,490 or 21.35%	437 or .80%	10 years 6.14%

The town of Kingstown in 1911 had a population of 4,300, of which ships in the harbour yielded 194, leaving the true number of population 4,106. This year's census, 3,836, shows a decrease of 270 or over 7%, while the country populations have increased by 1,800 and the Grenadines 610. Unlike the census of 1911 the number of persons enumerated in the harbour of Kingstown was nil, as there was not a single ship in port on the morning of April 25th, 1921.

The following table serves to show the populations of the several towns.

Towns	1921			1911		
	Males	Females	Totals	Males	Females	Totals
Kingstown	1,518	2,318	3,836	1,754	2.546	4,300
Georgetown	362	427	789	217	334	551
Calliaqua	136	231	367	194	237	431
Layou	140	192	332	190	251	441
Barrouallie	513	658	1,171	602	638	1,240
Chateaubelair	326	425	751	307	412	719
Totals	2,995	4,251	7,246	3,381	4,635	7,682

The following telegram from the Secretary of State for the Colonies to the Governor was published for the information of Sea Island Cotton Growers:

APPLICATIONS FOR ADVANCES UPON GINNED SEA ISLAND COTTON ACTUALLY
IN THE COLONY SHOULD BE MADE IN WRITING TO THE COLONIAL SECRE-
TARY, GOVERNMENT OFFICE.
OCTOBER 22ND. I HAVE ARRANGED WITH THE EMPIRE COTTON GROWING
COMMITTEE THAT A SUM OF £10,000 SHALL BE PLACED AT DISPOSAL OF
COLONIAL GOVERNMENT IF REQUIRED FOR PURPOSES OF MAKING ADVANC-
ES UPON SEA ISLAND COTTON ACTUALLY IN ST. VINCENT AT A RATE NOT
EXCEEDING 1/3 PER LB. ON FIRST QUALITY, AT LOWER RATES FOR LOWER
QUALITIES, INTEREST 7%. YOU ARE AUTHORIZED TO PUBLISH THIS AND TO
MAKE ADVANCES ACCORDINGLY AT YOUR DISCRETION AFTER SUITABLE EXAM-
INATION OF COTTON BY AGRICULTURAL SUPERINTENDENT AND EXECUTION OF
NECESSARY DOCUMENTS. OWNERS MUST UNDERTAKE NOT TO EXPORT COTTON
ON WHICH ADVANCES HAVE BEEN MADE UNTIL ADVANCES HAVE BEEN REPAID
EXCEPT TO BRITISH COTTON GROWING ASSOCIATION AFTER NOTIFYING CO-
LONIAL GOVERNMENT. ASSOCIATION PREPARED TO ENTERTAIN APPLICATIONS
FOR SIMILAR ADVANCES UPON COTTON IN THIS COUNTRY.

Sir Edward Davson's proposals regarding the establishment of a Conference or Council of the West Indian Colonies were given publicity in the Government *Gazette* of 29th November.

On 31st December it was made known that Major Wood has approved of
the provisional appointments submitted to him for interviews with the following deputations on the undermentioned subjects:

1. Citizens' Committee (a) Representative Government
                        (b) Economy in Administration
                        (c) Federation
                        (d) Primary Education

2. Interim Committee of Management St. Vincent Chamber of Agriculture and Commerce

   (a) Agricultural and Commercial Development

   (b) Adoption of the elective principle for the Legislative Council

3. Directors of the St. Vincent Agricultural Credit and Loan Bank

   (a) Loans to peasants

   (b) Extension of the peasant proprietary system

4. Committee of Estate Owners

   Revival of sugar cane cultivation

| 1922 / | **Report on Major Wood's Visit** |

Major the Honourable Edward Wood, Parliamentary Under Secretary
of State for the colonies met several deputations in the council chamber on
Thursday, 12th January, representing different interests in the colony. All of
them, we understand, received a sympathetic hearing, and their points were
carefully noted. At the end of his interviews, Major Wood was met by a very
large crowd of representative citizens in the courtyard, which waited patiently

to hear a word from the lips of the under secretary. His Honour the Administrator, R. Popham Lobb, introduced Major Wood and told the gathering that two things were represented by the presence of the party standing before them, and those two things were the colonial office and His Majesty's Navy. The Navy had been seen frequently in these parts but the colonial office had never been in St. Vincent, and the presence of Major Wood, representing the colonial office, was a happy augury and would certainly do some good for the island even though the visit was short.

Major Wood then addressed the crowd and assured them of the pleasure he had in paying a visit to their beautiful island though short it was. His pleasure was deepened by the warmth and cordiality of the welcome which he had received on landing and on all possible occasions since. He was glad to have a chance of speaking to them. He was able to say from his travelling that St. Vincent was not less warm in its spirit of loyalty to the King than anywhere else. He had come to visit strangers, but he did not feel he was among strangers.

Many referred to England as the mother country. He could assure them that she has the same feeling for these colonies as a mother has for her children. When he returned to England, he would tell the people of England, and also His Majesty, that none is more loyal to the throne than the people of St. Vincent. The people of England he said, were not likely to forget the help which St. Vincent had given during the war, which help had been written in letters of gold on the battlefields and on the seas. The British Empire, he said, stood for the strongest influence for peace and justice, the best instruments for the working of the human race. All the members of the Empire should stand together and work for their mutual prosperity, and they should think of the British Empire as a big partnership of which they were all partners. He will tell the English people that the heart of St. Vincent beats soundly and that they might trust St. Vincent for help in solving the problem now before them.

Captain England of the H.M.S. *Valerian* next addressed the crowd. He said he felt it a great privilege in having to bring Major Wood to St. Vincent. He was also pleased to be able to come around to show the flag, and this was a very pleasant duty. He would like to have had some of the English people on board his ship who had never travelled, to hear *Rule Britania* played by their band in welcoming Major Wood to their island. The welcome to Major Wood he thought was wonderful. He then thanked the community for the hospitality shown his men and the men of the Navy generally.

The party then drove off to the Carnegie hall where a fashionable lunch had been provided by the citizens committee. After the luncheon, they drove through the agricultural districts of the island.

The party consisted of Major Wood, Parliamentary Under Secretary of State for the colonies, Mr. Ormsby Gore, Member of Parliament, and Mr. Wiseman, Principal Clerk of the Colonial Office.

The Honourable W. C. Hutchinson, Colonial Treasurer, was appointed to act as Administrator in consequence of the absence on leave of His Honour R. Popham Lobb (CMG) for three months from 11th May.

Princess Mary's acknowledgment of the receipt of the casket and of an address from the people of St. Vincent and the Southern Grenadines was published in the *Gazette* of 11th May.

Buckingham Palace
3rd April 1922
Dear Sir George Haddon-Smith,

I shall be very much obliged if Your Excellency will be so kind as to forward the accompanying letter signed by the Princess Mary to Mr. R. Popham Lobb, Administrator of St. Vincent.

Yours very truly,
Edward Wallington
Treasurer to H. M. the Queen

Buckingham Palace
His Excellency, Sir George Haddon-Smith (KCMG)
Government House, Grenada
To the People of St. Vincent, Bequia, and the Southern Grenadines.
Your Excellency,

I thank the people of St. Vincent and its Dependencies very sincerely for the casket of native wood and their address of congratulation on my marriage, which you have been good enough forward on their behalf.

I am much touched to hear of the great interest they have taken in my work for social welfare and for children.

I much appreciate the allusions to Lord Lascelles, whose family, I fully realize, has long been associated with the West Indies, and we both are most grateful for the expression of good wishes for our future happiness.

I can assure the donors that I shall cherish their gift as a pleasing souvenir of their affection and regard.

MARY

A telegram from the Governor to the Secretary of State for the Colonies and the reply of His Royal Highness the Prince of Wales were published in the *Gazette* of 11th July:

FROM GOVERNOR TO SECRETARY OF STATE FOR THE COLONIES, LONDON.

PLEASE CONVEY TO HIS ROYAL HIGHNESS THE PRINCE OF WALES THE RESPECTFUL AND ALSO SINCERE CONGRATULATIONS OF THE PEOPLE OF THE WINDWARD ISLANDS ON HIS SAFE RETURN FROM HIS EASTERN TOUR THE PEOPLE OF THE WINDWARD ISLANDS ALSO SEND THEIR LOYAL WISHES TO HIS ROYAL HIGHNESS ON THE OCCASION OF HIS BIRTHDAY, AND EXPRESS

THEIR FERVENT HOPES THAT HIS ROYAL HIGHNESS WILL BE SPARED TO THE BRITISH EMPIRE FOR MANY YEARS.

From Edward P. to Governor, St. George's, Capital Windward Islands.

PLEASE CONVEY TO PEOPLE OF WINDWARD ISLANDS MY GRATEFUL THANKS FOR THEIR TELEGRAM OF GOOD WISHES.

The Captain of H.M.S. *Repulse* forwarded the following message

> *To Governor from Captain of* Repulse*:*
>
> *On leaving St. Vincent I desire to express to Your Excellency and Lady Haddon-Smith, His Honour the Administrator and all in St. Vincent the hearty thanks of myself and all officers and men of* Repulse *for the great time and hospitality with which we have been received in St. Vincent. We will never forget this charming visit to your beautiful island.*

His Honour R. Popham Lobb (CMG) recorded his appreciation of the work of the civil service in the Government *Gazette* of 7th November, as follows:

> *On relinquishing the Government of St. Vincent, the Administrator wishes to place on record his grateful appreciation of the work of the civil service during his tenure of office and to express to public officers and subordinates of all grades his personal thanks for the good and loyal service which they have given to the colony.*
>
> *Their work is the more praiseworthy because it has been performed under exceptional and trying conditions which date from the outbreak of the War and to a great extent still continue, imposing also a heavy strain upon officials whose remuneration in many instances, should be greater than it is, did the resources of the colony permit.*
>
> *Willing and efficient service under such conditions implies a sense of public duty which is a real asset to the colony, and the Administrator has every confidence that the same standard of performance will be maintained under his successor.*

The following letter from the Secretary for Examinations, Cambridge University, to the local secretary and the detailed report of the winner of the St. Vincent Scholarship for the current year are published for general information:

> *24th November 1922, University of Cambridge*
> *Local Examinations and Lectures Syndicate*
> *Syndicate Buildings, Cambridge*
>
> *Sir, I have the honour to acknowledge the receipt of your letter of 29th July, enclosing a copy of the School Ordinance 1921 relating to the St. Vincent University Scholarship. The conditions under which the Scholarship is to be awarded have been carefully noted, and we have today telegraphed that*

*the best claim is that of candidate Index Number 224—P. E. McI. Clarke, who satisfied the required conditions.**

I have, etc.,
A. H. Nanson Sewell, W. M. Lopey, Esq
Grammar School, St. Vincent

The following resolution was passed at the meeting of the Legislative Council held on the 4th November:

Be it resolved that this Council places on record its deep and sincere appreciation of the valuable services rendered by Mr. Popham Lobb, to this colony and of his conscientious devotion to the welfare and interest of the people of the colony during the period of his administration.

1923 / The undermentioned gentlemen were appointed a general committee by the Administrator to arrange for the participation of this colony in the British Empire Exhibition to be held at Wembley in April 1924:

> His Honour J. Stanley Rae, Chief Justice (Chairman)
> The Honourable W. C. Hutchinson (ISO), Colonial Treasurer
> The Honourable J. E. Sprott
> The Honourable A. M. Fraser
> The Honourable Rev. E. A. Pitt
> W. M. Grant, Esq
> A. DaSantos, Esq
> T. Jackson, Esq, Agricultural Superintendent, (Secretary),
> Assistant Secretary, V. D. Archer, Esq

The committee had power to add to their numbers.

The following sub-committee or executive committee have been appointed:

> T. Jackson, Esq, Agricultural Superintendent
> W. M. Grant, Esq
> Secretary, V. D. Archer, Esq

The sum of £400 was voted for expenditure in connection therewith.

---

*The first St. Vincent scholar pursued studies in medicine at Queen's University, Ireland, where the Degrees MB, ChB and BAO, were conferred upon him. He then entered into practice in Belfast, Ireland. In 1937 he obtained the Degree of DPH in Belfast and afterward the Degree of DTM and H at the University in Liverpool, England.

His brother, the late Leon McIntosh Clarke DDS, when a lad in 1915 was the St. Vincent boy scout representative at the International Tournament at British Guiana and there won the Gold Cup being the first prize for swimming 75 yards and back, he won the Scroll of Honour, being the second prize for ¼ mile swimming race and the Silver Spoon mounted in gold, being the second prize for the long distance dive.

His Honour Robert Walter, Esq (CMG), arrived in the colony on 1st May and assumed the administration of the government by virtue of a commission.

The Government *Gazette* of 15th May contained the following announcement of the death of Mrs. Field:

The Administrator announces with deep regret the death on the 12th instant of Mrs. M. F. Field who for the past thirty years served both government and the public loyally and faithfully in the capacity of operator of the central telephone exchange.

In the *Gazette* of the 2nd June it was notified that His Majesty the King was graciously pleased to approve of the bestowal of the Imperial Service Order on the Honourable W. C. Hutchinson, Colonial Treasurer of this colony.

His Honour the Administrator issued a commission on 7th June appointing James Stanley Rae, Esq to be Chief Justice of the Colony.

The following messages from Their Majesties the King and Queen to the children in the elementary schools of the Empire on Empire Day, 1923, were published for general information.

The King's Message
To the children in the elementary schools of the Empire

On this day my people in all parts of the world join to celebrate their unity and to draw closer the common ties which hold them together.

Each of our many peoples has its own life to live, each has its own work to do; yet all are members of one family, sharing their sorrows and joys.

You have learned how the Empire was built up by brave and wise men and women in the past. It is only by courage, wisdom and unselfishness that it will endure. It is a great inheritance. Your fathers and forefathers made it. Its future welfare and good name are, under the providence of God, in your hands.

Do not think of it as a thing far away from you. Everyone of you counts, and what you do and learn now will decide how far you will be able to play your part worthily when you grow up.

Get knowledge, be brave, honourable, and kind, thinking of others before yourselves, and always play the game. So will you fit yourselves to hand down this community of free nations to your children and grandchildren as a great instrument for justice, peace and goodwill, which will deserve the respect and esteem of mankind.

The Queen's Message
To the girls in the elementary schools of the Empire

On this day of memory and hope, which is also the birthday of good Queen Victoria, this is my message to you, the daughters of our worldwide family of nations and peoples.

Think always of what you can do to make your homes happy and how you can best prepare yourselves to make happy homes for the generations of children which will follow you. In our vast Empire there are many kinds of homes and many different customs. The home which fosters clean minds and kind hearts is God's Temple, and the spirit of the good home, whether it be rich or poor, is one of the best things in the world. You can learn many lessons at school which will help you to become wise and useful citizens of the British Commonwealth; but you can learn and practise nothing better for yourselves and all members of the great British family than the simple lessons of love, kindness and unselfishness, which in cloud or sunshine are the strength and beauty of life.

At the meeting of the legislative council held on 25th June the following address of welcome was presented to the Administrator by Mr. Sprott on behalf of the Council:

Legislative Council Chamber, St. Vincent, 25th June 1923
To His Honour, Robert Walter (CMG)
Administrator of St. Vincent and its dependencies.

Sir, Before proceeding with the business of the day, we desire to place on record a welcome to Your Honour as President of this council and to express our hope that your period of office in this colony will be marked by pleasant personal experiences and will constitute a brilliant chapter in the records of your official career.

We assure Your Honour of our confidence in your ability to afford us helpful guidance in all our deliberations and, on our part, we shall always endeavour during discussions to maintain pleasant relations between the president and members.

In common with other parts of the Empire, this colony is now passing through a period of economic stress. The cloud of financial depression may not be as heavy over St. Vincent as it appears in some of the neighbouring colonies, yet the affairs of this Government require watchful care and the ex-

ercise of true economy, and in this direction our best services will be constantly offered with the common purpose of promoting the colony's welfare.

We trust that Divine Providence will help Your Honour with wisdom and with health and strength to pursue your purpose in the right course and that your efforts may be rewarded by a fair measure of success.

Charles E. L. Cox, J. Elliott Sprott, W. C. Hutchinson
L. Punnett, Geo. H. Steven, Alex. M. Fraser, Alfred G. Hazell

His Honour then read a lengthy and interesting reply appended to *Gazette* of 21ˢᵗ August.

At a meeting of the Legislative Council held 12ᵗʰ October, the Honourable J. E. Sprott delivered a lengthy address on the retirement of His Excellency Sir George Haddon-Smith after which the following resolution was unanimously passed:

Be it resolved that this council, in view of the impending retirement of His Excellency Sir George Basil Haddon-Smith, places on record its appreciation of the valuable services rendered by His Excellency to this colony during his term of office as Governor of the Windward Islands, and gives expression to the high esteem and regard which it entertains for His Excellency and Lady Haddon-Smith, and also extends to His Excellency upon his retirement from the public service the sincere hope and prayer that he may long live to enjoy his well-earned leisure.

After careful consideration of the proposal of a closer union between Trinidad and the Windward Islands, the Right Honourable the Secretary of State for the Colonies communicated his conclusion which was published in *Gazette* of 27ᵗʰ October:

Downing Street, Windward Islands
Grenada (General), 20ᵗʰ August, 1923

Sir, I have the honour to acknowledge the receipt of your despatch of the 2ⁿᵈ April on the subject of closer union between Trinidad and the Windward Islands.

After careful consideration I have come to the conclusion that at the present time it would be useless to pursue any of the schemes for the amalgamation of these colonies. I do not however wish this opinion to be regarded as a final rejection of these schemes and I should be prepared to re-open the matter at a later date if this course proved to be desired by public opinion. I would therefore suggest that in order to give public opinion the opportunity of forming a correct judgment on the matter the whole correspondence should be published, subject to such revision as may be thought desirable and also to the consent of both Governors.

Sir S. H. Wilson has intimated his agreement to this proposal and I have requested the officer administering the government, Trinidad, to consider in what respects the correspondence will require revision prior to publication and to forward his suggestions for your concurrence.

A similar despatch has been addressed to the officer administering the government of Trinidad, and I am furnishing him with a duplicate of your despatch Grenada (General) of the 2nd April, which although it should be included in the correspondence to be reviewed, has not apparently yet been communicated to him.

I have, etc.,

(Sgd.) Devonshire, Governor

Sir G. B. Haddon-Smith (KCMG)

Etc., Etc., Etc..

1924 / The Duke of Devonshire directed that the following letter dated 12th January be forwarded to His Excellency Sir George B. Haddon-Smith:

Downing Street
12th January 1924

Sir, I am directed by the Duke of Devonshire to inform you that he has received your despatch Grenada General No. 182 of the 29th October forwarding resolutions passed by public bodies in Grenada and minutes of proceedings in the Legislative Council on the occasion of your relinquishing the administration of the government of the Windward Islands.

The Duke of Devonshire has read with much pleasure these tributes to your administration, which covers a period of nearly nine years and entailed exceptional responsibility owing to the war and the resulting economic difficulties. His Grace recognises that you served during the whole of this period with ability, determination, unremitting zeal and careful regard to the instructions of himself and his predecessors. He desires to record his high appreciation of your distinguished public services, not only in the Windward Islands but throughout a long career in the colonies.

A copy of this letter is being communicated to the officer administering the Government of the Windward Islands for publication locally.

I am, etc.,

H. J. Read

Sir George Basil Haddon-Smith (KCMG), His Excellency Lieutenant-Colonel W. B. Davidson-Housten (CMG) Acting Governor and Commander-in-Chief of the Windward Islands travelled from St. Lucia by air on 10th March, arrived at 10.45 a.m., took the prescribed oaths at the courthouse in the presence of His Honour the Chief Justice and the Executive Council and flew away to Grenada for a similar purpose at 1.45 p.m.—a typical flying visit!

The telegram intimating the proposed changed in constitution of the Legislative Council was published in the *Gazette* of 24ᵗʰ March:

21ST MARCH. HAVE MUCH PLEASURE IN INFORMING YOU THAT HIS MAJESTY THE KING IN COUNCIL HAS THIS DAY MADE ORDER-IN-COUNCIL PROVIDING FOR REFORM OF CONSTITUTION GRENADA, ST. LUCIA AND ST. VINCENT. I AM CONFIDENT THAT THE INTRODUCTION OF THE ELECTIVE INSTITUTION AS CONTEMPLATED BY THE ORDER WILL MAKE FOR THE BETTER GOVERNMENT OF THESE ANCIENT AND LOYAL COLONIES AND WELL-BEING OF THEIR INHABITANTS.

On the arrival at Grenada of His Excellency Sir Frederick Seton James (KBE, CMG) the Administrator forwarded the following telegram:

ST. VINCENT SENDS HEARTY AND LOYAL GREETINGS TO YOU AND LADY JAMES AND WISHES YOU A PROSPEROUS AND PLEASANT TERM OF OFFICE.

His Excellency arrived in St. Vincent on 1ˢᵗ October and took the prescribed oaths in the presence of the Executive Council. The following address was presented to His Excellency the Governor:

Council Chamber, Saint Vincent, 1ˢᵗ October 1924
To His Excellency Sir Frederick Seton James (KBE) (CMG)
Governor and Commander-in-Chief of the Windward Islands.
May It please Your Excellency,

We, the members of the Legislative Council, for ourselves and on behalf of the people of St. Vincent and its dependencies, have the honour to offer Your Excellency a hearty welcome to this colony; and to assure you of our desire to do all that lies in our power to assist you in the performance of the important work involved in the administration of this Government.

We desire to pay you all the honour and respect due to the representative of His Majesty the King, our devotion to whom is unsurpassed throughout the worldwide Empire.

We earnestly hope that in your efforts to keep this colony in the march of progress which is the inspiring watchword of the British Empire, you will be crowned with success; and, so long as the honour falls upon us, as your councillors, to advise and to support you in measures aiming towards advancement, we should do so with the utmost sincerity and zeal.

That your health and that of Lady James may be preserved throughout the term of your administration of the Windward islands, and that you may find your task easy and enjoyable, is the wish of your Councillors.

(Signed by members of council.)

20ᵗʰ October—Effect was given to the separation of the posts of Headmaster of the Grammar School and Inspector of Schools.

In Government *Gazette* of 21st October, it was notified for general information that the St. Vincent Scholarship was awarded to Mr. Ardon B. Brereton.*

On 27th October the Administrator appointed a war memorial committee comprising The Honourables J. E. Sprott (Chairman) A. M. Fraser, W. M. Grant, and J. M. Richards and M. S. Hampton, Esqs. The committee was authorized to collect subscriptions to supplement the grant of £250 from general revenue.

The sad announcement of deaths by the Administrator was made in *Gazette* of 30th October:

> The Administrator has to announce with deep regret the death of Miss Annie McKie (MBE), who has been identified for so many years with charitable work in this island. The Administrator feels that the colony has lost a very highly esteemed and respected member of the community, who to the very end of her long life devoted herself so actively to good works.

> The Administrator has to announce with deep regret the death of Mr. Walter Carden Hutchinson (ISO), who served in the public service of the colony faithfully and conscientiously for many years and who throughout his career showed deep devotion to the best interest of the colony.

> In Mr. Hutchinson's death the colony has lost one of its best servants, and the Administrator feels the loss of a personal friend.

> The public offices will be closed to the general public from 2.30 p.m.

The Honourable J. E. Sprott at the meeting of the Legislative Council held on 27th November, after referring to the valuable services rendered respectively, moved the following resolutions:

> Be it resolved that this Council place on record its recognition of the loss sustained by the community in the death of the late Mr. W. C. Hutchinson (ISO) and extend to the widow and children of the deceased sincere sympathy in their bereavement.

> Be it resolved that this Council record its sense of the loss sustained by the colony in the death of Miss Annie McKie (MBE), a much esteemed member

---

*Dr. Brereton prosecuted studies in Medicine at the University in Edinburgh, Scotland. He accepted the appointment as Government Medical Officer at Dominica then joined the Medical Service of the Windward Islands. He was selected to become qualified as a Radiologist and proceeded to England in 1936 where he obtained the Degree of DMR and E at Cambridge; he is now a Medical Officer and the Radiologist of the Colony.

of the community who devoted herself to charitable works and rendered valuable services as Trustee and Secretary of the Thompson Home for many years.

1925 / The inaugural meeting of the new Legislative Council was held on 13th May and presided over by His Honour Robert Walter (CMG). The members were:

> Neville Harry Turton, Attorney General
> John Felix Hamilton Otway, Acting Colonial Treasurer
> Stanley Branch, Colonial Surgeon
> James Eliott Sprott, Nominated Member
> Alexander Murdoch Fraser, Elected Member for Leeward
> Walter MacGregor Grant, Elected Member for Kingstown
> Joseph Milton Gray, Elected Member for Windward

The prescribed oath was administered to His Honour the Administrator by His Honour the Chief Justice and to Honourable Members in order of precedence by the Administrator who read the following message from His Excellency the Governor:

> *I greatly regret that it has not been possible for me to open in person the Legislative Council under the new constitution granted by His Majesty the King to St. Vincent. I extend a hearty welcome to Unofficial Members especially elected members of Council and trust that the Government with their assistance derived from their knowledge of the people's wants will be able to work to the best interests of the colony and its people. Governor-in-Chief of the Windward Islands.*

His Honour then delivered a lengthy and interesting address. In one paragraph His Honour said:

> *....The New Council starts, as I indicated on December 1st last, with a satisfactory bank balance; it behoves us while keeping prudent reserves, while distinguishing between what is desirable and what is essential, to exercise a spirit of practical idealism in expending the revenue of the colony to the best advantage in the best interests of the people. I rely upon Honourable Members of this Council with their accumulated knowledge of local conditions to assist the Government to the utmost in the prudent disposal of our revenue and a just and equitable incidence of taxation.*

Concluding Remarks.

> *You will see from the sketch I have tried to give you that we have a multiplicity of problems, economic, social and moral, before us; problems which no single man can hope to solve. As Moses said, "How can I myself alone bear your cumbrance and your burden and your strife?" or as a witty modern prelate put it, "The Administrator has to drive the coach; his critics are always urging him to upset it."*

> *Our problems require the wholehearted cooperation of the best minds in the colony with a single and pure desire to promote the true interests of the people. Remember that the millennium has taken many years in coming and*

that the new Council with the best intentions in the world will not be able to turn this dear little island into a Paradise.

Economic and material prosperity is no doubt a desirable thing but what is essential in this mechanical, money-loving world is a sober, God-fearing, law-abiding, hard-working people. I should like to see the Government of this colony broad-based upon the trust and affection of the people and our deliberations based upon mutual confidence rather than mere captious criticism.

The solution of our difficulties will rest largely on the manner in which we approach them. We must try to discriminate between the merely desirable and the essential and between what may be expedient and what is right, and strive to stick to the right through thick and thin. Progress comes from dissatisfaction and renewed effort.

> *The common problem, yours, mine, everyone's,*
> *Is not to fancy what were fair in life*
> *Provided it could be, but finding first*
> *What may be, then find how to make it fair*
> *Up to our means.*

Let us aim at practical idealism and remember always that we simply cannot get on without God. Let us also remember that the universe works slowly:

> *Let no man think that sudden in a minute*
> *All is accomplished and the work is done;*
> *Though with thine earliest dawn thou shouldst begin it*
> *Scarce were it ended in thy setting sun.*

And now I invite Honourable Members and all present here today to join with me in invoking the assistance, guidance and blessing of Almighty God on all the deliberations of this Council in regard to all matters and measures that may be dealt with in this Chamber and in praying that all our decisions and measures may tend to the true and eternal welfare of this Colony and its inhabitants.

I now declare the first session of the new Legislative Council open.

The Honourable member for Windward replied at length to the Administrator's address.

On 20th May the Administrator in Government *Gazette* (extraordinary) announced with deep regret the death of the Honourable James Elliott Sprott, Nominated Member of the Legislative Council and the Chairman of the Kingstown Board. His Honour added that "Mr. Sprott's death will be a serious loss to the political and civic life of the community in which he took so deep an interest", and he personally feels the loss of a valued councillor with whom his relations have always been most cordial.

A resolution of loyalty to His Majesty the King was forwarded by the Administrator and in due course the following despatch was received:

Downing Street, 22nd May 1925
Windward Islands, St. Vincent
No. 24

> *Sir, I have it in command from His Majesty the King to acknowledge the receipt of your telegram of the 11ᵗʰ of May, and to convey to you his high appreciation of the assurances of loyalty expressed in the Resolution passed by the New Legislative Council of Saint Vincent on the occasion of its opening.*
>
> *I have, etc.,*
>
> *L. S. Amery, Governor,*
> *Sir F. S. James (KBE, CMG) Etc. Etc., Etc.*

At the meeting of the Legislative Council held on the 26ᵗʰ May, the Administrator in his reference to the services of the late J. E. Sprott remarked:

> *Whatever people's opinion of Mr. Sprott might be—and a man in his position was bound to have some political opponents—it would be conceded by all that the late Honourable Member was zealous in the service of his country and did his best according to his light. Mr. Sprott passed away at the early age of 54, passed to a region where*
>
> > *Envy and calumny and hate and pain,*
> > *And that unrest which men miscall delight,*
> > *Can touch him not and torture not again!*
>
> *and for all we knew he might be looking down on us at this moment and might be interested in our doings. He left behind him a widow and five children to whom the warm sympathies and condolences of all will go forth. Mr. Sprott himself had been spared a long and trying illness; for those he left behind him remained the burden and the grief.*

The Administrator then moved the following resolution:

> *Be it resolved that this Council place on record its sense of the loss sustained by the untimely death of the late Honourable J. E. Sprott, Nominated Member, and that an expression of this Council's deep sympathy be forwarded to his sorrowing widow and family in their heavy bereavement.*

On 15ᵗʰ October Mr. Arnold Morgan Punnett was appointed a nominated member of the Legislative Council *vice* the late Mr. J. E. Sprott.

Princess Mary honoured the West Indian Pavilion of the British Empire Exhibition Wembley on 30ᵗʰ October with a visit and spent nearly half an hour inspecting the exhibits in which she appeared to take much interest. She was presented with two Sea Island Cotton handkerchiefs by Mr. Ernest Brown (St. Vincent) and a bouquet of roses by Miss McDougall in the Jamaica Court.

In *Gazette* of 12ᵗʰ December, His Honour announced the death of Mr. Henry Snagg, Justice of the Peace of Canouan.

1926 / His Excellency Robert Walter (CMG), Acting Governor and Commander-in-Chief of the Windward Islands, who was granted three months' vacation leave to be followed by five months' leave of absence, on 13th July availed himself of the opportunity of saying *au revoir* to the warm-hearted people of beautiful St. Vincent and of wishing them all possible prosperity.

Consequent on the departure of His Excellency the Acting Governor His Honour James Stanley Rae was appointed on 15th July to act as Administrator.

His Honour Herbert Fergusson (CBE), Administrator of Grenada, assumed the administration of the Government of the Windward Islands on the 15th July.

The following telegram was forwarded by the Acting Administrator:

27th SEPTEMBER. COLONY OF SAINT VINCENT SENDS DEEPEST SYMPATHY FOR SUFFERERS AT TURKS AND CAICOS ISLANDS AND ASK GOVERNMENT ON THEIR BEHALF TO ACCEPT GIFT OF £150 TO AID IN THEIR IMMEDIATE WANTS. AMOUNT CABLED TO YOU THROUGH BARCLAYS BANK.

On 4th October the telegram from the Commissioner of Turks Island was published:

PEOPLE OF TURKS AND CAICOS ISLANDS EXPRESS DEEP GRATITUDE FOR SYMPATHY AND ASSISTANCE FROM ST. VINCENT.

PHILLIPS

In *Gazette* of 12th October it was made known that the St. Vincent scholarship was awarded to Mr. James P. E. Cropper.[*]

1927 / The following telegraphic communication between the Governor and the Administrator was published in the Government *Gazette* of 16th May.

Telegram received from the Governor (at St. Lucia) on 15. 5. 27. 15th May.

VERY DISASTROUS FIRE OCCURRED AT CASTRIES NIGHT OF 14th TO 15th MAY. IMPOSSIBLE AT PRESENT TO ESTIMATE LOSS. MANY HOMELESS. WOULD WELCOME ANY FINANCIAL ASSISTANCE FROM PEOPLE OF ST. VINCENT.

Telegram despatched to the Governor on 16. 5. 27.

16th MAY. WITH REFERENCE TO YOUR TELEGRAM OF 15th MAY, ST. VINCENT IS PROFOUNDLY GRIEVED AT SHOCKING TRAGEDY WHICH HAS FALLEN UPON HER SUFFERING SISTER ISLAND. PLEASE CONVEY TO THE PEOPLE OF ST. LUCIA THE ASSURANCE OF OUR DEEPEST SYMPATHY IN THIS TERRIBLE DISASTER. I AM CABLING £250 FROM THIS GOVERNMENT WITH THE APPROVAL OF THE LEGISLATIVE COUNCIL AND I AM TAKING STEPS TO APPOINT RELIEF COMMITTEE. DO YOU REQUIRE FLOUR, POTATOES OR CLOTHING?

Further telegrams appeared in *Gazette* of 23rd May:

Telegram received from the Governor (at St. Lucia) on 17. 5. 27.

---

*Entered McGill University, Montreal, Canada and obtained degree of BSc in Electrical Engineering in 1931, and that of EE in Civil Engineering in 1933.

17th MAY. WITH REFERENCE TO YOUR TELEGRAM OF 16th MAY YOUR MESSAGE
IS BEING COMMUNICATED TO THE PEOPLE OF ST. LUCIA AND I DESIRE ON
THEIR BEHALF TO THANK YOU FOR THE SYMPATHY EXPRESSED BY SAINT
VINCENT AND ALSO FOR THEIR MOST GENEROUS GIFT OF £250. WILL WIRE
YOU LATER RE FOOD AND CLOTHING REQUIREMENTS.

Telegram received from the Governor (at St. Lucia) on 17. 5. 27.

FURTHER TO MY TELEGRAM OF 17th MAY, FLOUR, POTATOES AND CLOTHING
WILL BE MOST ACCEPTABLE.

GOVERNOR

Eight certificates of honour with Medals were awarded to St. Vincent. Four were obtained in 1924 and four in 1925.

The following is a copy of a resolution moved in Legislative Council by the Honourable the Attorney General and seconded by the Honourable Member for Kingstown:

Be it resolved that the Legislative Council of St. Vincent desire to place on record its sincere appreciation of the valuable work done for the benefit of the colony by the chairman of the British Empire Exhibition Committee, His Honour Mr. Justice Rae, the Secretary of the Committee, Mr. T. P. Jackson, the London representative, Mr. Ernest Brown and the members of the local committee, viz., the Honourable A. M. Fraser, the Honourable W. M. Grant, A. DaSantos, Esq, and Conrad Hazell, Esq

And be it further resolved that an honorarium of £50 be paid to Mr. Ernest Brown and an honorarium of £25 to Mr. T. P. Jackson in recognition of their valuable services.

And be it further resolved that an honorarium of £5 be paid to Mr. V. D. Archer, Assistant Secretary of the Committee.

Passed the Legislative Council this 4th day of May, 1926.

The following are some extracts from the West India Committee circular:

Duke and Duchess of York visited St. Vincent Court.

The Queen visited St. Vincent Court.

The exhibit of Sea Island Cotton in the St. Vincent exhibit reminded the Queen of the gift of a parasol with lace made from St. Vincent cotton presented to Her Majesty by the colony on the occasion of the Coronation.

Mr. Amery, Secretary of State for the Colonies, visited the St. Vincent Court on July 28th, 1925. Mr. Amery having stayed in St. Vincent some years ago as the guest of the Master of Elibank, then Mr. Gideon Murray was *especially interested in the section. He was received in the St. Vincent Court by Mr. Ernest Brown.*

It can be truthfully said that St. Vincent is one of the best commercial exhibits in the Pavilion.

Her Royal Highness (Princess Mary) was pleased to accept two Sea Island pocket handkerchiefs in the St. Vincent Section.

When one considers the space which St. Vincent occupied in the pavilion, it must be admitted that good use has been made of it and the exhibit is a credit to all concerned.

Mr. E. Brown received letters of congratulation on the St. Vincent exhibit both from the Prince of Wales and the Duke of York.

Report on St. Vincent arrowroot by Mr. J. Ellis Barker appended to the report on the representation of St. Vincent at the British Industries Fair and the Ideal Home Exhibition:

I have given a thorough trial to St. Vincent arrowroot and find it pure and of excellent quality. Arrowroot consists of carbohydrates in the most digestible form. It is therefore an ideal food for invalids, and mixed with heated milk or with milk and eggs, one can perfectly combine the carbohydrates with the fats and proteins of the milk, or of the milk and eggs.

St. Vincent arrowroot should be generally used. If it is a perfect invalid food, it is of course equally perfect as a food for daily use. It makes excellent biscuits, cakes, sweet dishes, cheese dishes, etc., of every kind, and the fact of its being an Empire production should add to its attractiveness.

I myself was greatly benefited by taking milk thickened with arrowroot in convalescence many years ago. By mixing the St. Vincent production with milk, milk becomes more digestible because it cannot form clots or a solid curd in the stomach when taken in this form. Those who cannot easily digest milk should strengthen it with St. Vincent arrowroot and they will be surprised at the result.

It is an extraordinary thing that people treat arrowroot as if it were only a sick room food. Oysters and champagne, chicken and milk are sick room foods, too, but they are not sick room foods only. I imagine the writers of the cookery books are to blame, and if your friends want to popularise their stuff they should bring out a little print of four pages or so, headed 'Stick this into your cookery book,' with gummed edges to induce people to do so.

1928 / *Gazette* (Extraordinary) of 5th April contained the appointment for the Legislative Council:

> *Mr. A. M. Punnett, Nominated*
> *Mr. A. B. C. DaSantos, elected for Windward*
> *Mr. A. M. Fraser, elected for Leeward*
> *Mr. W. M. Grant, elected for Kingstown*

Willoughby Bullock, Esq, arrived in the colony on 15th April and assumed the duties of Chief Justice.

The first meeting of the new legislative council was held on 23rd May under the presidency of His Honour Robert Walter (CMG).

The prescribed oath was administered to His Honour the Administrator by His Honour the Chief Justice and to the Honourable members in order of precedence by the Administrator.

The following members were present:
> *William Edgar Howard-Flanders, Acting Attorney General*
> *John Felix Hamilton Otway, Colonial Treasurer*
> *Stanley Branch, Chief Medical and Health Officer*
> *Arnold Morgan Punnett, Nominated Member*
> *Alban Bertram Conway DaSantos, Elected for Windward District*
> *Alexander Murdoch Fraser, Elected Member, Leeward District*
> *Walter McGregor Grant, Elected Member, Kingstown District*

Before proceeding with the business His Honour read the following telegram from His Excellency the Governor:

> REGRET VERY MUCH I SHALL NOT BE ABLE TO OPEN THE NEW COUNCIL IN PERSON. I WELCOME BOTH THE OLD AND NEW MEMBERS TO NEW COUNCIL AND I AM SURE THAT THEIR LABOURS WILL BE ALWAYS IN THE BEST INTERESTS OF THE COUNTRY AND PROVE PRODUCTIVE OF PROSPERITY AND HAPPINESS.

His Honour extended hearty welcome to the members and delivered his address in the course of which he requested the members to remember those great and noble words of Mr. Baldwin: "There are four words of salvation for this country and the whole world and they are Faith, Hope, Love, Work" and he said, "Shall I add that the greatest of these is Love?"

The Honourable Member for Kingstown replied.

His Honour Robert Walter (CMG), Acting Governor and Commander-in-Chief of the Windward Islands, was granted leave; consequently His Honour Herbert Fergusson (CBE), Administrator of Grenada, etc., assumed the administration of the Government of the Windward Islands and His Honour Willoughby Bullock assumed the administration of this Government on 4th August.

His Honour R. Walter (CMG) on board S.S. *Inanda* 4th August telegraphed:

> MR. AND MRS. WALTER DESIRE TO EXPRESS GRATIFIED APPRECIATION OF SPLENDID SEND OFF AND KINDNESS SHOWED THEM BY WARM-HEARTED ST.

VINCENT DURING THEIR SOJOURN. ALL POSSIBLE HAPPINESS AND PROSPER-
ITY TO ISLAND.

The Acting Administrator replied:

YOUR KIND MESSAGE MUCH APPRECIATED AND YOUR DEPARTURE REGRETTED
BY ALL. ST. VINCENT WISHES YOU GOOD LUCK AND GOOD HEALTH

In *Gazette* of 15th October it was notified for general information that a scholarship was awarded to Mr. Newton S. Nanton.*

A telegram signed Dawson of Penn and Stanley Hewit described illness of His Majesty the King in *Gazette* dated 30th November.

The *Gazette* of 1st December containing the following telegram from His Excellency the Governor to the Secretary of State for the Colonies was published for general information:

30th NOVEMBER. YOUR TELEGRAM OF 29th NOVEMBER ON THE SUBJECT OF
HIS MAJESTY'S ILLNESS, DESIRE ON BEHALF OF WHOLE PEOPLE OF THE
WINDWARD ISLANDS AND MYSELF AS GOVERNOR TO CONVEY TO HIS MAJESTY
OUR GREAT REGRET FOR HIS MAJESTY'S ILLNESS AND OUR MOST SINCERE
WISH THAT HIS MAJESTY MAY SPEEDILY RECOVER.

JAMES, GOVERNOR

A short meeting of the legislative council was held on 21st December when, in consequence of the illness of His Honour Willoughby Bullock, the Acting Administrator, The Honourable W. E. Howard-Flanders, the Attorney General presided.

The Attorney General said that His Honour Willoughby Bullock desired him to express his great regret at his inability, through illness, to be present today. In accordance with His Honour's request to be relieved of his duties as Acting Administrator, His Excellency the Governor had arranged for the Honourable N. Julian Paterson of Grenada to take over the administration of the Government. He understood that Mr. Paterson would arrive on Sunday, the 23rd December, on the S.S. Canadian *Skirmisher*.

At the meeting of the Legislative Council held on 27th December, His Honour N. Julian Paterson (KC) Acting Administrator expressed regret at having to inform Honourable Members of the Honourable W. E. Howard-Flanders' illness in consequence of which it had been necessary for him to appoint Mr. Hosten to take his place.

The Honourable member for Kingstown said that on behalf of the council and the people of St. Vincent he desired to extend a hearty welcome to His

*The Honourable N.S. Nanton, entered King's College, London University, where he pursued studies in Law and obtained the degree of LL.B. He was called to the bar of the Inner Temple. After returning to the colony he acted as Magistrate of the Second District. He is now in practice at the local bar and an elected member of the legislative council

Honour as Acting Administrator. He could assure Mr. Paterson that it was very welcome news to the people of St. Vincent to learn that he had been appointed to act as Administrator. For some months past there had been great dissatisfaction here over the administration of the Government and the unofficial members of the council had in mind to send a telegram to the Secretary of State for the colonies, through the Governor, asking for someone to be sent to be Administrator as they felt that they had no Administrator. When, therefore, it was known that the Governor had appointed Mr. Paterson to act as Administrator, public feeling had been allayed. He felt that as a West Indian His Honour would have a better knowledge of affairs than a stranger to these colonies could have and he was confident that his administration of the Government would prove beneficial to St. Vincent.

The Acting Administrator said that he thanked the Honourable Member very much for the welcome extended to him on behalf of the Council and the people of St. Vincent; it was very encouraging.

There would no doubt be lots of questions and problems confronting him and he could assure Honourable Members that he would do his best.

There was the following telegraphic correspondence in Gazette dated 24th December:

FROM GOVERNOR TO ACTING ADMINISTRATOR
BEST WISHES TO YOURSELF AND THE PEOPLE OF SAINT VINCENT FOR
CHRISTMAS AND THE NEW YEAR.

FROM ACTING ADMINISTRATOR TO GOVERNOR
MANY THANKS FOR GOOD WISHES FOR CHRISTMAS AND THE NEW YEAR TO THE
PEOPLE OF ST. VINCENT AND MYSELF. WE BEG TO RECIPROCATE THE SAME
TO YOUR EXCELLENCY AND GRENADA.

1929 / His Honour Major H. W. Peebles (DSO, OBE), the newly appointed Administrator of the colony, arrived on 3rd April. The Governor being in residence in St. Vincent, Major Peebles officiated as colonial secretary.

The Honourable member for Kingstown on 16th April extended hearty welcome to His Excellency Sir F. Seton James (KBE, CMG) Governor and Commander-in-Chief of the Windward Islands on the first occasion on which he presided over a meeting of the Legislative Council. He sought permission to offer hearty welcome to Major Peebles also. His Excellency thanked the Honourable Member for the welcome extended to him on behalf of the unofficial members.

A message from His Majesty the King expressive of thankfulness for his recovery and the reply sent by His Excellency the Governor were published in the *Gazette* of 24th April.

In the *Gazette* of 4ᵗʰ June, it was announced that His Majesty the King was pleased to appoint His Excellency Sir Frederick Seton James (KBE, CMG) to be a Knight Commander of the Most Distinguished Order of St. Michael and St. George.

On 18ᵗʰ June, a notice in Government *Gazette* announced the appointment of Mr. F. A. Corea to be an unofficial member of the executive Council as from the 15ᵗʰ.

A Thanksgiving service for the recovery of His Majesty the King was held in all the churches throughout the colony on Sunday, the 7ᵗʰ July.

Later in the month telegrams were received supplying information of the King's illness and condition consequent thereon.

The synod of the Diocese of the Windward Islands, the first to meet since the election of a separate bishop for the islands nearly three years ago, opened its sessions with a service in St. George's Cathedral at 8 p.m. on Thursday, 24ᵗʰ October when the sermon was preached by Bishop Vibert Jackson, Archdeacon of Grenada, and closed its deliberations with another service in the same church at 8 p.m. on Tuesday, 29ᵗʰ, at which His Lordship the Bishop of the Diocese addressed the congregation informing them of the synod's decisions.

The Administrator, His Honour Major H. W. Peebles (DSO, OBE), Patron and Chief Scout of St. Vincent, presided at an interesting meeting which was held at the Carnegie Library on 28ᵗʰ November for the purpose of hearing the experiences gained by Mm A. V. Sprott, J. Otway and A. D. Duncan, the St. Vincent representatives who attended the World's Jamboree held at Arrowe Park, Birkenhead, England.

1930 / On 24ᵗʰ December the customary Christmas greetings were telegraphed from governor to Acting Administrator and vice versa.

Government *Gazette* (Extraordinary) of 21ˢᵗ March comprised the following telegrams:

ADMINISTRATOR TO GOVERNOR
20ᵗʰ MARCH. ON BEHALF OF MYSELF, COUNCILS AND PEOPLE OF ST. VINCENT, I DESIRE TO OFFER SYMPATHY TO YOUR EXCELLENCY ON INJURY SUSTAINED AND TO EXPRESS THE HOPE THAT YOUR EXCELLENCY WILL MAKE A SPEEDY RECOVERY.

GOVERNOR TO ADMINISTRATOR
PLEASE ACCEPT ON BEHALF OF YOURSELF, COUNCILS AND PEOPLE OF ST. VINCENT, MY SINCERE THANKS FOR YOUR KIND MESSAGE OF SYMPATHY

WHICH I CAN ASSURE YOU I APPRECIATED MORE THAN I CAN EXPRESS IN
WORDS.

JAMES, GOVERNOR

The commission appointing James Henry Jarrett, the Acting Chief Justice to act as Administrator was published in Government *Gazette* of 14th May.

The Acting Administrator's activities were exceptional. He visited the hamlet of Edinboro, made extensive enquiries in the presence of the superintendent of public works, the road engineer and other public officers regarding the dilapidated commissariat building and represented its condition along with recommendations which must have been comprehensive and convincing.

The vast improvement at Edinboro at the present time was made possible as the result of his intervention.

The following messages appeared in the *Gazette* of 23rd May:

His Excellency Sir Frederick Seton James (KCMG, KBE)
Governor of the Windward Island
S.S. Ingoma

> *On behalf of the civil service, Councillors and inhabitants of the Windward Islands I wish you and Lady James Godspeed. The progressive and active policy carried out by you during your six years as Governor has borne fruit of which you must justly be proud and will be a standing memory of advancement and progress. It is our earnest hope that you may make a speedy recovery to complete health.*

Peebles

Peebles Acting Governor
Grenada

> *I have received your telegram of 22nd. Please convey to civil Service, Councillors and inhabitants of the Windward Islands my grateful thanks for the message which you have sent. I greatly appreciate the sympathy expressed for my recovery to health.*

Governor

His Excellency Sir F. S. James (KCMG, KBE) Governor and Commander-in-Chief of the Windward Islands being absent on leave the Honourable H. R. R. Blood, who assumed the duties of Colonial Secretary of Grenada on 5th June, assumed the administration of the Government of the Windward Islands on the 6th June.

The Honourable A. B. C. DaSantos, at a meeting held 10th June, extended hearty welcome to His Honour J. H. Jarrett, Acting Administrator and assured His Honour that he could confidently rely on members of Council for support.

His Honour in reply expressed his deep appreciation for the kind words of welcome from both sides of the Council and the ready offer of assistance which had been made. It was his desire that in the short time at his disposal he might accomplish something of real benefit to the island and its people and he was glad to be able to say that even already he had received definite proof of the genuineness of the offers of assistance.

In the Government *Gazette* (extraordinary) of 5th August the following sad announcement was published:

> The Acting Administrator has to announce with deep regret the death of Mr. Frederic William Reeves (MA), who served in the public service of the colony faithfully and conscientiously for many years and who throughout his career showed deep devotion to its best interests.
>
> In Mr. Reeves' death the colony has lost one of its most valued servants.

The following telegrams in connection with the recent hurricane in Dominica were published for general information on Sept. 8th:

```
ACTING GOVERNOR, WINDWARD ISLANDS
TO GOVERNOR, LEEWARD ISLANDS, 5. 9. 30
I HAVE RECEIVED FIRST ACCOUNT OF SERIOUS DISASTER TO DOMINICA AS
A RESULT OF RECENT HURRICANE. I ASK YOUR EXCELLENCY TO CONVEY
TO INHABITANTS OF THAT ISLAND THE SINCERE SYMPATHY OF MYSELF
AND PEOPLE OF THE WINDWARD ISLANDS AND OUR DESIRE TO RENDER ANY
ASSISTANCE THAT LIES IN OUR POWER.
                                        DOORLY, ACTING GOVERNOR

GOVERNOR, LEEWARD ISLANDS
TO ACTING GOVERNOR, WINDWARD ISLANDS, 6. 9. 30
VERY GRATEFUL YOUR TELEGRAM DATED 5th SEPTEMBER. SHOULD BE GLAD
TO RECEIVE ASSISTANCE FOR THE SUFFERERS. LATEST REPORTS INDI-
CATE THAT WIDESPREAD DESTRUCTION PEASANTRY HOUSES. RESTORATION
ESTIMATED ABOUT £10,000. GROWING CROPS DEVASTATED. SUBSCRIPTIONS
MIGHT BE FORWARDED DIRECT TO THE ADMINISTRATOR OF DOMINICA.
```

His Excellency Sir Thomas Alexander Vans Best (KBE, CMG), Governor and Commander-in-Chief of the Windward Islands, arrived in Grenada on 25th September and assumed the administration of the Government of the Windward Islands, whereupon the Acting Administrator forwarded the following telegram:

```
ON BEHALF OF MYSELF AND THE PEOPLE OF ST. VINCENT I OFFER YOUR
EXCELLENCY A VERY HEARTY WELCOME ON YOUR ARRIVAL IN THE WINDWARD
```

It was notified for general information in *Gazette* of 21ˢᵗ October that the St. Vincent scholarship was awarded to Mr. Arnott Samuel Cato.*

At the meeting of the Legislative Council held on 22ⁿᵈ October the Honourable W. M. Grant, elected member for Kingstown, considered it desirable to place on record the appreciation of the colony for the assistance received from the Colonial Development Fund, and he therefore moved the following resolution:

> *That it be placed on record how fully this Council appreciates the assistance given to the colony by the Imperial Government through the Colonial Development Fund in order to permit of those necessary improvements to be carried out which otherwise could not now be carried out owing to the lack of the necessary funds.*

The undermentioned Government notice was published in the *Gazette* of 1ˢᵗ November:

> *His Excellency the Governor desires to express his great pleasure at the arrangements made for his official reception on the 23ʳᵈ instant and to convey his thanks and appreciation to all the officers concerned.*
>
> *His Excellency further desires that his appreciation may be conveyed to the officers and men of the guard of honour which received him and to the units of boy scouts and girl guides which were in attendance on his landing.*

1931 / His Majesty the King was graciously pleased to approve the appointment of N. J. Paterson, Esq (BA, KC), as an Officer of the Most Excellent Order of the British Empire (Civil Division).

Ransley Samuel Thacker, Esq, arrived in the colony on the 16ᵗʰ January and assumed the duties of Chief Justice.

The population of St. Vincent on the night of Sunday, the 26ᵗʰ April 1931, was 47,961 an increase of 3,514 or 7.91 per cent on the census of 1921 when it was 44,447.

The following table shows the population as determined by estimation and by enumeration.

---

* Mr. Cato pursued the study of medicine at Edinburgh, Scotland, obtaining the Degree of MB and ChB. He is now a medical practitioner in the island of Barbados.

Estimated 1921	Census 1921	Estimated 1931	Census 1931	Difference between Estimation and Enumeration	Decrease per cent by Estimation	Increase per cent Enumerated 10 years
53,937	44,447	53,706	47,961	5,745 or 11.98%	231 or .43%	7.91%

The following table shows the population of the several towns as compared with the census of 1921.

Towns.	1931			1921		
	Males	Females	Totals	Males	Females	Totals
Kingstown	1,720	2,549	4,269	1,518	2,318	3,836
Georgetown	421	522	943	362	427	789
Calliaqua	147	279	426	136	231	367
Layou	149	193	342	140	192	332
Barrouallie	569	698	1,267	513	658	1,171
Chateaubelair	327	434	761	326	425	751
Totals	3,333	4,675	8,008	2,995	4,251	7,246

The inaugural meeting of the Legislative Council was held at the Council Chamber on 20th May.

His Honour Major Herbert Walter Peebles (DSO, OBE), Administrator, escorted by His Honour Ransley Samuel Tacker, Chief Justice, and the Reverend Canon A. H. Barlee (MA), Chaplain, entered the Council Chamber at 11 a.m. and took his seat at the Council table.

Prayers were read by the chaplain.

There were James Reali Gregg, Attorney General, ex officio member; John Felix Hamilton Otway, Colonial Treasurer, ex officio member; Stanley Branch, Chief Medical and Health Officer, nominated official member; Arnold Morgan Punnett, nominated unofficial member; Alexander Murdoch Fraser, elected member, Leeward District; Agostinho DaSilva, Elected Member, Kingstown District; and Frederick Augustine Corea, elected member, Windward District

The prescribed oath was then administered to His Honour the Administrator by His Honour the Chief Justice and by the Administrator to Honourable members in order of precedence.

Among other things His Honour said, "I offer a hearty welcome to the two new elected members and I welcome back those old members who gave me their cooperation and considered counsel during the last session."

The Honourable F. A. Corea, elected member for Windward, replied at considerable length.

1932 / The *Gazette* of 3ʳᵈ September contained the following notice:

> *His Honour Major H. W. Peebles (DSO, OBE) Administrator, having left the Colony for Grenada this morning on duty, the Honourable J. F. H. Otway, Colonial Treasurer, etc., under Clause 21 of the Letters Patent, as Senior Resident Member of the Executive Council, has taken the prescribed oaths and assumed the administration of the Government.*

An announcement appeared in the *Gazette* of 4ᵗʰ October that the St. Vincent scholarship was awarded to Mr. Patrick Denniston O'Neill Crichton.*

On 25ᵗʰ October Messrs. Robert M. Anderson and Ebenezer Dimcan sailed on the *Lady Drake* for Dominica having been chosen as delegates to represent St. Vincent at the West Indian Conference which met in the city of Roseau on the 28ᵗʰ October. Any political achievement in the constitution may reasonably be attributed to this conference.

1933 / A public meeting was held at the Council chamber courthouse in Kingstown on 10ᵗʰ January when His Honour Major H. W. Peebles, the Administrator on behalf of the people of St. Vincent, extended hearty welcome to the Closer Union Commission, the personnel of which consisted of Sir Charles Fergusson, Chairman, and Sir Charles Orr (both of whom served in the capacity of Officer Administering the Government, the first named in New Zealand and the second in the Bahamas). The secretary was Mr. McNeil Campbell on the permanent staff of the Colonial Office, London. The shorthand writer was Mr. M. W. Gilkes of Trinidad who travelled by Pan American airplane to join them at Antigua. His Honour assured the commissioners that small as this colony is, they can rely on its unswerving loyalty to the crown; it has pride in being part and parcel of the Commonwealth of Nations.

The chairman in reply alluded to the interpretation of the terms of reference, "To examine on the spot the possibilities of closer union between Trinidad, the Windward and the Leeward Islands or some of them."

Wednesday 11ᵗʰ was observed as Education Day and the teacher's association held a conference at Georgetown. The Honourable J. H. Otway, Colo-

---

*Mr. Crichton entered the University of Edinburgh, Scotland and began his studies in medicine but in consequence of continued ill health he was compelled to return to the West. Indies. He is now engaged in the Government Service.

nial Treasurer, made a brilliant opening address. The Honourable F. A. Corea and the Rev. E. S. M. Pilgrim (MA) also delivered encouraging addresses.

In its issue of 4th February, *The Vincentian* recorded the presentation of a beautiful silver cup by the St. Vincent Athletic Club of New York, U.S.A. awarded to that club by the New York Cricket League. Mr. R. T. Samuel, to whom the trophy was sent as a gift to their "native isle", caused it to be deposited in the showcase of the Carnegie Library in Kingstown.

On behalf of the inhabitants the editor tendered sincere thanks and quoted the following lines:

> *There's a strange something, which without a brain*
> *Fools feel, and which e'en wise men can't explain,*
> *Planted in man, to bind him to that earth*
> *In dearest ties, from whence he drew his birth.*

Prior to the departure of His Honour Major W. H. Peebles (DSO, OBE) many functions were held and addresses presented. His Honour left the island on the *Lady Drake* on the 23rd February.

The report on the Education Commission which toured Trinidad and Tobago, the Windward and Leeward Islands as far back as November 1931, was released by the various governments concerned on 19th April.

His Honour Arthur Francis Grimble (CMG, MA), Administrator, arrived on 6th July accompanied by Mrs. Grimble and three daughters.

His Honour went to the Council chamber where the oaths were taken before His Honour H. J. Hughes, Acting Chief Justice, in the presence of the Honourable members of Council and numerous persons who occupied the chamber to its utmost capacity.

The Honourable F. A. Corea for himself and on behalf of the unofficial section of the Council welcomed His Honour to the colony and assured him of their loyal support. He extended his welcome to Mrs. Grimble and the Misses Grimble and hoped that their stay in the island would be greatly enjoyed, that when in course of time His Honour is given promotion they will all have happy reminiscences of St. Vincent.

Mr. S. DeFreitas, Acting Attorney General, for himself and on behalf of the official section endorsed the welcome and good wishes of the Honourable F. A. Corea.

His Honour, in a very lucid style addressing the Honourable members of Council and the ladies and gentlemen of St. Vincent, said he thanked them from the bottom of his heart not only for himself but also on behalf of his wife and family for this unexpected but marvellous and cordial welcome accorded them. It was the habit of kind-hearted people, he said, not to realise fully the extent of their kindness. He did not desire to leave the hall without making them feel how deeply their courtesy and welcome had gone.

An address from the Representative Government Association was presented to the Administrator.

At the meeting of the Legislative Council held on 19th October, the Honourable A. M. Punnett expressed great pleasure in extending for himself and on behalf of the unofficial members a very hearty welcome to His Honour and to Mrs. Grimble and daughters. He expressed the hope that during His Honour's administration much would be achieved for the public benefit and that his deliberations with the Council at all times would be directed toward the welfare of St. Vincent.

The Honourable member for Leeward endorsed the expressions of welcome made by Mr. Punnett and added that he hoped His Honour's stay in St. Vincent would be a happy and enjoyable one.

His Honour the Administrator in reply said that it was just a little over three months since he had received on arrival at St. Vincent what he had then described as a wonderful welcome. His Honour said that (on that occasion) he had told them that on stepping ashore, he was at once enveloped in a most friendly atmosphere. That immediate friendliness had made a deep impression upon him; his three months' association with the people of St. Vincent had done nothing but confirmed his conviction of its sincerity. He knew that with such a spirit abroad, it would be impossible for him not to work in harmony with the Council and the people. His Honour said that no matters pertaining to the welfare of St. Vincent would ever fail to engage his deepest concern. He would eagerly look to the Council for such advice as would assist him to further the progress of the island. His Honour again thanked the Honourable Members for their welcome.

1934 / The following telegram from the Acting Governor and that from Governor of British Guiana were published on 6th February:

```
TO GOVERNOR, BRITISH GUIANA
DESPATCHED FROM ST. LUCIA ON 15th JANUARY, 1934
I DESIRE TO OFFER TO YOUR EXCELLENCY AND PEOPLE OF BRITISH GUIANA
THE MOST SINCERE SYMPATHY OF THE INHABITANTS OF THE WINDWARD
ISLANDS ON THE LOSS OF LIFE AND DAMAGE TO PROPERTY AND CROPS
OCCASIONED BY THE RECENT FLOODS.
                                        DOORLY, ACTING GOVERNOR

FROM GOVERNOR, BRITISH GUIANA
RECEIVED AT ST. LUCIA ON 16th JANUARY 1934

ON BEHALF OF THE PEOPLE OF THIS COLONY I DESIRE TO THANK YOU FOR
THE EXPRESSION OF SYMPATHY CONTAINED IN YOUR TELEGRAM OF THE 15th
OF JANUARY. I AM GLAD TO SAY THAT THERE HAS BEEN NO LOSS OF HUMAN
```

LIFE THOUGH DAMAGE AND LOSS OF LIVESTOCK AND FOOD PROVISION HAS
BEEN VERY HEAVY.

GOVERNOR

At the meeting of the Legislative Council held 8th March, the following resolution was moved by the Acting Attorney General and seconded by the Treasurer.

> Be it resolved that this Council, having considered the report of the Closer Union Commissioners together with the Secretary of State's announcement in this connection and Estimates of Expenditure, is of opinion that effect should be given to the report subject to such modification as may seem necessary or desirable to the Secretary of State.

Dr. P. J. Kelly (CBE, MB, BS), Medical Commissioner, held an enquiry at the public health office in connection with the organization of the medical service in St. Vincent from 1st to the 9th May.

The following persons were nominated to become First Members of the St. Vincent Banana Association with effect from the 8th June 1934, for the purposes defined in subsection (3), Section 19, of the Banana Ordinance 1934:

The Honourable F. A. Corea	C. B. Sayles Esq, J.P.
The Honourable A. M. Punnett	G. MacDonald, Esq
The Honourable A. DaSilva	
E. M. Beach, Esq	G. Robertson, Esq
J. L. Punnett, Esq	A. G. Hazell, Esq

The Honourable C. B. Sayles was appointed the first president.

At the adjournment of the meeting of the Legislative Council held 8th June, The Honourable nominated unofficial member said that for himself and on behalf of the other unofficial members of the Council he wished to say how deeply they regretted His Honour's departure to Grenada to assume the acting appointment of Administrator of that colony. It was but a short time since His Honour's arrival in Saint Vincent, and during that time he had shown a spirit of sincere interest in the welfare of the colony and had allowed no opportunity to pass for securing some benefit to, or improvement on, conditions in the colony. The Honourable Member said that it was clear that St. Vincent could ill afford to lose His Honour at this moment, but that we could only now hope for his speedy return. The Honourable Member wished His Honour and family a very happy time in Grenada.

His Honour in replying said that he thanked the Honourable members from the bottom of his heart for their expressions of regret at his departure. It was for him a very sad and also a very happy moment, happy because he had succeeded in getting through the ordinance which had been before them today and from which he hoped much benefit to the colony would be derived; sad, because he was leaving.

227

He was (His Honour said) just beginning to learn something of conditions in St. Vincent and becoming more and more interested in them. In the small efforts he had made to secure some benefit for the people, he had met with marvellous cooperation, both from those here present, and from other members of the community. His Honour said he had never dreamt of receiving such outstanding loyalty, devotion and cooperation in so short a time. He thanked them all for their valuable assistance and said he looked forward to coming back to St. Vincent.

Consequent on the departure from Grenada of His Honour H. R. R. Blood (CMG), Colonial Secretary and Administrator of Grenada, who was promoted to Sierra Leone, His Honour Arthur F. Grimble (CMG) was appointed to act as Colonial Secretary and Administrator of Grenada from 10th June, and the Honourable J. F. H. Otway, Colonial Treasurer of St. Vincent, was appointed to act as Administrator of St. Vincent.

There was an historical event on 22nd July when at Divine service, 9 a.m. Messrs. Frederick Layne, a native of this island, Edward O. Buxo, a native of Grenada, and Wellington Cooper, a native of the Bahamas, all students at Codrington College, Barbados, were ordained in St. George's Cathedral by the Lord Bishop of the Windward Islands.

Observance of Centenary of Emancipation

The first day of August was proclaimed a bank holiday for the purpose of celebrating the Centenary of Emancipation in the British West Indies. Thanksgiving services were held in the churches and in other places of worship; Friendly Societies and other recognized organizations observed the memorable event in various ways. The Mesopotamia branch of the Representative Government Association held a meeting there at which eloquent addresses were delivered by ministers of religion and other speakers from Kingstown and elsewhere. The function of the Kingstown Anglican School was presided over by His Lordship the Bishop. There were several addresses in addition to the creditable contribution by the children. The Watch Night service for which preparation was made by the Methodist Synod of the Barbados-Trinidad District was conducted in Kingstown, by Rev. F. Lawrence. The weather was quite unfavourable and the night dark, but the large Kingstown church was packed at an early hour and the service was worthy of the great occasion. The Rev. Lawrence carried his congregation back to that eventful night, when a great nation was making its exodus from a land of slavery to the country out of sight where freedom awaited them. They little dreamed that under the dire load of their affliction an interest was being taken in them.

Behind the scene was God, "I have seen I have seen the affliction of my people" and He came swiftly to their deliverance, a deliverance as thorough and complete as when He commissioned Moses to lead His Israel into the promised land.

His Lordship Vibert Jackson (DD) was the preacher at the cathedral at 9 a.m. and selected his text from, Gal. 3, 28 (RV), "There can be neither Jew nor Greek; there can be neither bond nor free; there can be no male and female, for ye are all one man in Christ Jesus." From this a graphic and instructive sermon was preached.

The Rev. A. C. Johnson, Rector of St. Paul's, Calliaqua, and chaplain to the Lord Bishop, preached an interesting sermon from Psalm 126, v. 4, "The Lord hath done great things for us already, whereof we rejoice." With the varied experience gained in different colonies where he laboured, he depicted in his eloquent style the advancement made within the century.

At the Roman Catholic church in Kingstown the sermon preached by Rev. Fr. John Van der Plas was also very interesting.

His Honour the Acting Administrator announced with the deepest regret on 14th August, the death of Mr. William Erling Dolly, late Superintendent of Works, and added that Mr. Dolly was a loyal and conscientious officer through whose death the colony had lost a most valued servant.

In Government *Gazette* of 11th September, it was notified that Mr. Alric Benedict DaCosta was awarded the St. Vincent scholarship.*

At the meeting of the Legislative Council held on 18th October, the Secretary of State's despatch relating to the Scheme of Closer Union was laid.

His Honour A. F. Grimble (CMG) returned from Grenada on 22nd October and resumed the administration of the Government.

The Dormant Commission appointing His Honour A. F. Grimble (CMG) Administrator of St. Vincent to administer the Government of the Windward Islands in certain events was published in *Gazette* of 31st October.

At the meeting of the Legislative Council held 9th November, the following constituted a part of the proceedings:

The Honourable Nominated Unofficial Member said that for himself and on behalf of the other Unofficial Members, it gave him very great pleasure to welcome His Honour back to St. Vincent. They all missed him for the short time he was absent, and they were glad to have him back again. The Honourable Member said that he wished also to congratulate the Treasurer, Mr. Otway, on the able manner in which he had conducted the affairs of the Government while acting as Administrator.

---

*Mr. DaCosta is pursuing studies in medicine at the university in Edinburgh, Scotland.

The Honourable Member for Leeward said that he endorsed the expressions of welcome to the Administrator, and the congratulatory remarks to Mr. Otway made by the Honourable Nominated Member.

The Administrator expressed gratitude for the welcome back that had been given him. He had certainly enjoyed being in Grenada, although it had given him a heartache to leave St. Vincent. He had learned a good many lessons of West Indian administration in Grenada which he hoped now to be able to apply to the advantage of St. Vincent. His Honour referred to the willingness of the Grenadian peasant classes to make sacrifices for the education of their children. It was that spirit, and the resultant leavening of the masses with a higher standard of education and culture, which had made Grenada the economic, social and political capital of the Windward Islands. St. Vincent was very far behind in this respect and would remain so until the mass of the people was ready to take to heart the lessons of their sister colony. His Honour said that this was not an expression of reproach, but a plain statement of fact made in the hope that St. Vincent would seize the opportunities of advancement, which a few far-seeing Vincentians saw ahead of the island. The main effort must come from the people if the best was to be made of those opportunities; and the people could do no better than emulate the example set by the Grenadian peasant in sacrificing everything for the advantage of his children. Concluding his remarks, His Honour said he wished to take this opportunity of thanking Mr. Otway for the able manner in which he had carried on the administration while he was in Grenada, and also the Honourable Members of Council for their assistance during his absence.

The following motion, notice of which had been given at a previous meeting, was made by the Administrator:

> That the official majority should be abolished; that only those officials whose presence is necessary for the conduct of business should sit as Members of the Legislative Council; that an unofficial majority should be created with elected as well as nominated members on the definite understanding that (in addition to his existing power of veto) the Governor would be empowered at any stage to carry any measure which he considered necessary in the interest of public order, public faith, or other essentials of good government.

1935 / The first Health Week within the Government of St. Vincent was conducted at Union Island on 2nd February for which Dr. Reginald Austin, the Medical and District Officer of the Grenadines, successfully developed considerable enthusiasm among the inhabitants of the dependency.

The following letter was published by His Honour's direction:

H.M.S. Nelson *at St. Vincent*
7th February 1935

> *Sir, With the departure of H.M.S.* Nelson *may I convey to you and to the inhabitants of St. Vincent the appreciation and thanks of myself, the officers and men of H.M.S.* Nelson *for the enthusiastic welcome and generous hospitality which has been extended to us on all sides.*
>
> *The visit has been a very real pleasure to all of us, and for myself, I much regret that the forthcoming termination of my appointment precludes any possibility of my again bringing the home fleet to your friendly island. However, I hope my successor will still continue to do so.*
>
> *In saying goodbye we all wish you and your island a full measure of success, prosperity and happiness.*
>
> *I have the honour to be*
> *Sir, Your obedient servant,*
>
> > *Cork & Orrery, Admiral*

His Excellency Sir Selwyn MacGregor Grier (CMG), Governor and Commander-in-Chief of the Windward Islands, arrived at Grenada on the 20th February and assumed the administration of the Government of the Windward Islands. His Honour the Administrator thereupon forwarded the following telegram

> FOR MYSELF AND ALSO ON BEHALF OF PEOPLE OF ST. VINCENT I EXTEND TO YOUR EXCELLENCY AND LADY GRIER A MOST HEARTY WELCOME TO THE WINDWARD ISLANDS, AND EARNESTLY HOPE THAT YOUR ADMINISTRATION WILL BE ONE OF ABUNDANT SUCCESS.

His Honour George Cyril Griffith Williams arrived on 22nd February and assumed the duties of Chief Justice.

The Coming-of-Age Jamboree was opened on 20th April by the Administrator. Contingents from neighbouring islands participated. Every event on the programme was successfully carried out.

Special posting stamps of four denominations were issued from 6th May in connection with the celebrations to commemorate the 25th anniversary of His Majesty's accession. They continued in use until 31st December.

The celebration of His Majesty's Silver Jubilee occupied the 6th, 7th and 8th of May. On the 6th there were official procession, ceremonial Thanksgiving services, review of the local forces, distribution of King's Silver Jubilee medals, reception at Government House, and bonfires on prominent points surrounding Kingstown; on the 7th, dinner for the poor throughout the colony, gymkhana on Victoria Park, display of fireworks in Kingstown, bonfires elsewhere; on the 8th, treat and outing at Edinboro for children of primary schools; general decorations of Kingstown with flags and bunting by day and illuminations by night.

The following telegram from the Right Honourable the Secretary of State for the Colonies to His Excellency the Governor was published for general information on 11th May:

WITH REFERENCE TO MESSAGES OF LOYALTY SILVER JUBILEE, I HAVE RECEIVED THE FOLLOWING TELEGRAM FROM SECRETARY OF STATE FOR THE COLONIES BEGINS. YOUR TELEGRAMS OF MAY 1st AND MAY 3rd CONVEYING LOYAL MESSAGES TO HIS MAJESTY THE KING ON THE OCCASION OF HIS SILVER JUBILEE HAVE BEEN LAID BEFORE HIS MAJESTY WHO DESIRES THAT AN EXPRESSION OF HIS SINCERE APPRECIATION AND THANKS MAY BE CONVEYED TO YOU TO LEGISLATIVE COUNCILS OF GRENADA SAINT LUCIA AND SAINT VINCENT AND TO PEOPLE OF WINDWARD ISLANDS FOR LOYAL MESSAGES ENDS. GOVERNOR.

The enclosure in a circular despatch containing the text of the address which the Secretary of State for the Colonies delivered to His Majesty the King was published in the *Gazette* dated 23rd July:

On behalf of all Your Majesty's subjects in the many lands of your Colonial Empire, I offer you, Sir, their loyal and heartfelt congratulations.

Many of these countries are well known to Your Majesty personally, and the proud memory of your own visits, Sir, has been renewed by those of members of your family, whom they have rejoiced to honour. Throughout these distant lands, your Jubilee has been celebrated, and Your Majesty's own message has been heard. Infinite in their variety of race and creed and rule, the peoples of these lands are one in personal devotion to Your Majesty and in loyalty to Your Throne. Everywhere they are mindful of the wise and gracious solicitude with which you have ever watched over their interests and promoted their welfare, a solicitude in which Her Majesty the Queen has conspicuously shared. It is their earnest prayer that Your Majesty may long be spared to continue Your high imperial task.

The Honourable C. B. Sayles as the first chairman submitted an interesting report to the first annual general meeting of the Banana Association in which he remarked:

It is my privilege to present to you the first annual report on the working of the Association.

In June last year a contract was entered into with the Canadian Banana Co. Ltd., by your association to purchase on certain terms all the Gros Michel bananas grown in the island of St. Vincent for a period of five years commencing 1st January 1936. This contract is renewable for a further period of five years so that growers are assured of a definite market for their produce for some time to come. The terms of the contract to purchase are: for a count bunch of 9 hands 50c.; 8 hands 37½c.; 7 hands 25c.; and for 6 hand bunches where the company so elect to take them 12½c. will be paid.

I am definitely satisfied that the making of new and reconditioning of old roads is a matter of paramount importance in relationship to the banana

232

industry and unless these are provided the industry cannot progress and a
wonderful opportunity for the further development of the colony will be lost.

Presentation to Hon. J. H. Otway
at meeting of Legislative Council 21ˢᵗ October

Before proceeding with the Order of the Day, His Excellency presented to the Honourable J. H. Otway, Colonial Treasurer, the Badge of an Officer of the Civil Division of the Order of the British Empire together with the relative Grant of Dignity. In presenting the badge and warrant on behalf of His Majesty, His Excellency reminded the Council that Mr. Otway's official career in the Windward Islands embraced a period of 38 years, whereof thirty had been spent in the service of St. Vincent. There were few officers who, during so long an official career as Mr. Otway's, had maintained so high and consistent a standard of loyalty and devotion to duty. By his unwavering adherence to such high principles, he had upheld the dignity of the service to which they both had the honour to belong. It was for this reason, His Excellency concluded, that he now had the honour to present him with the insignia of the Order which His Majesty the King had been pleased to confer on him.

Disquietude developed into rioting in Kingstown on the morning of Monday, the 21ˢᵗ day of October. The meeting of the Legislative Council was in progress under the presidency of His Excellency Sir Selwyn Grier, when a crowd gathered at the entrance to the courthouse and afterward entered the yard. They comprised the labouring class and those in the humbler stations of life, all of whom lost control of themselves and indulged in a disgraceful conduct which until then was foreign to St. Vincent.

There was no member of the intelligent class anywhere near these frantic persons who could exercise any restraint; they were, to all appearances, without the advice of anyone who could impress upon them the adoption of a constitutional process; but they vented their fury after the manner of a revolutionary party which unfortunately several from this island who have been forced to travel in search of work doubtless have concluded is worthy of imitation.

At the meeting of the Legislative Council held on Friday, the 18ᵗʰ, the bill for an ordinance to amend further the Customs Duties Ordinance was introduced. The objects and reasons of the Ordinance were to abolish the surtax, to alter the mode of ascertaining *ad valorem* duties and to impose a revised custom tariff.

His Excellency addressing the Council on 28ᵗʰ October said,

Honourable Members of Council, before adjourning this meeting, I feel that I must make some reference to the deplorable events of the past week.

The causes of the riot which took place on the 21ˢᵗ of this month are still obscure but it has been brought to my notice that possibly one contributory cause was a misunderstanding of the Government's policy in introducing the measure which we have just passed into law.

I have been informed that in Georgetown and in other outlying districts and probably in some of the retail shops of Kingstown itself, shopkeepers made advances in the prices of essential commodities which were quite unjustifiable on the facts as we know them, but which may have been and probably were due to a complete misunderstanding of Government's intention. Now, it is well known to all of us that the type of shopkeeper to whom I refer could not have seen, or if they saw it could not have understood, the schedules attached to the Ordinance, and I regard it as probable that information of a very misleading character was given to them. I have no doubt that in the course of the investigations which are now in progress, more light will be thrown on this matter.

I feel however that there is another cause to which I must refer and that is the unfortunate spirit of racial antagonism which has been engendered by the Italy/Abyssinian war, a war which we all deplore and about which everyone of us feels strongly.

I sincerely trust that for the future, the people of this colony of whatever race or creed will remember that they are one and all citizens of the British Empire with the same rights, privileges and responsibilities which that citizenship entails.

My information is that unwise speeches have been made in this colony, speeches which have been misunderstood and may have added to the racial feeling to which I have referred. I trust that those who have in the past made speeches of this character will realise that it is incumbent upon them to avoid exciting public feeling amongst ill-informed people. If they fail to realise this, steps will have to be taken to deal with them.

As regards the question of unemployment, I find it difficult at the moment to say much. Where there is genuine unemployment and this Government with its very limited resources is able to provide work, that work will be provided.

But the salient feature of the recent disturbance is that the actual rioting was caused by a gang of men and, I am afraid, some women drawn in the main from the outskirts of this town who cannot claim to be genuine workers at all. I am informed by those who saw that crowd that many of them have records well known to the police of this colony and it is, I think, a source of satisfaction to us all that throughout the colony as a whole, very few of the genuine workers—of the peasants who obtained their living by cultivating their plots of land and of the labourers on the estates—were in any way affected. These people went about their normal business as peaceful and law-abiding citizens.

It has been brought to my notice that the liberty of the press and of speech has on occasions been abused in the past, and I am not prepared to permit further abuse of that liberty. If necessary, and the matter is under consider-

ation now, I shall summon this Council together and invite it to pass legisla-
tion which will give the Government increased powers to deal with those who
make it their business to foment trouble.

The situation which exists now is one which makes it essential that the
Government should prevent any further misrepresentation and abuse calcu-
lated to intensify that bitterness of feeling.

Let us now do our best to set aside all animosities and work together to
restore peace, law and order. But to make our efforts effective there must be
good will and mutual understanding.

The following telegraphic correspondence was transmitted on 24th December:

```
FROM GOVERNOR TO ADMINISTRATOR
I DESIRE TO OFFER TO YOU AND THE PEOPLE OF ST. VINCENT BEST WISH-
ES FOR A HAPPY CHRISTMAS AND A PROSPEROUS NEW YEAR.
GOVERNOR WINDWARD ISLANDS

FROM ADMINISTRATOR TO GOVERNOR.
FOR MYSELF AND ON BEHALF OF THE PEOPLE OF ST. VINCENT I HEARTILY
RECIPROCATE YOUR EXCELLENCY'S CHRISTMAS AND NEW YEAR WISHES.
ADMINISTRATOR
```

1936 / The delegates of the West Indian Sea Island Cotton Association assembled at the Council Chamber courthouse in Kingstown on Thursday, 2nd January, for their 3rd annual general meeting. His Honour A. F. Grimble, in extending welcome to them, delivered an address. The President, Mr. G. A. Jones, Commissioner of Agriculture, also delivered an address.

In the course of the Commissioner's address he said,

Gentlemen, the Association is to be congratulated on the marked im-
provement which has taken place in the Sea Island Cotton market since we
last met and more especially since the association was first formed.

The visit arranged by the advisory committee for the then Secretary of
State for the Colonies, Sir Philip Cunliffe-Lister, to inspect an exhibition of
Sea Island Cotton goods held in the Regent Street branch of Austin Reed's,
brought further publicity and resulted in keen competition between the large
retailers. Radio talks by Sir Algernon Aspinall timed at about the same time
as Sir Philip Cunliffe-Lister's visit further stimulated interest.

The Government *Gazette* (extraordinary) dated 21st January consisted of mournful intelligence:

It is with deep sorrow that the following telegram received today from His Excellency the Governor of the Windward Islands, is published for general information:

PROFOUND REGRET TO INFORM YOU THAT HIS MAJESTY KING GEORGE
THE FIFTH PASSED AWAY JUST BEFORE MIDNIGHT.

On the 22nd January, the Proclamation of the Accession and Allegiance to His Majesty King Edward VIII was read at the courthouse in the presence of a large and representative assembly.

Circular January 22nd, 1936. My telegram No. Circular January 21st.

HIS MAJESTY THE KING EDWARD VIII WAS DULY PROCLAIMED AT THE
ACCESSION OF THE COUNCIL HELD YESTERDAY AND ON HIS PROCLAMA-
TION MADE FOLLOWING DECLARATION: THE IRREPARABLE LOSS WHICH THE
BRITISH COMMONWEALTH OF NATIONS HAS SUSTAINED BY THE DEATH OF HIS
MAJESTY, MY BELOVED FATHER, HAS DEVOLVED UPON ME THE DUTIES OF
SOVEREIGNTY. I, KNOWING HOW MUCH YOU AND ALL MY SUBJECTS WITH, I
HOPE I MAY SAY, THE WHOLE WORLD FEEL FOR ME IN MY SORROW, AND I
AM CONFIDENT IN THE AFFECTIONATE SYMPATHY WHICH WILL BE EXTENDED
TO MY DEAR MOTHER IN HER OVERPOWERING GRIEF.

WHEN MY FATHER STOOD HERE 26 YEARS AGO HE DECLARED THAT ONE OF
THE OBJECTS OF HIS LIFE WOULD BE TO UPHOLD CONSTITUTIONAL GOVERN-
MENT. IN THIS I AM DETERMINED TO FOLLOW IN MY FATHER'S FOOTSTEPS
AND TO WORK AS HE DID THROUGHOUT HIS LIFE FOR THE HAPPINESS AND
WELFARE OF ALL CLASSES OF MY SUBJECTS.

I PLACE MY RELIANCE UPON THE LOYALTY AND AFFECTION OF MY PEOPLE
THROUGHOUT THE EMPIRE AND UPON THE WISDOM OF THEIR PARLIAMENTS TO
SUPPORT ME IN THIS HEAVY TASK AND I PRAY THAT GOD WILL GUIDE ME
TO PERFORM IT.

At the meeting of the Legislative Council held 22nd January, the Administrator addressing the Honourable Members of Council said that the death of our beloved Sovereign, King George the Fifth, at Sandringham on the night of the 20th January was announced to them as citizens and subjects yesterday. The Executive Council on the same day passed a resolution expressive of its sorrow for the loss that His Majesty, the Queen Mother and the whole Empire had suffered, and of its continued humble loyalty and devotion to the Throne of England and the Head of the Royal House of Windsor. It was his solemn duty to convene them today for the purpose of confirming to them the sad news which they have already heard as citizens, and of asking them, as the representative of Government and people of St. Vincent, what message they desired to be conveyed to His Majesty, of sympathy for the loss of His Royal Father, of sorrow for the passing of a loved and noble king, and of loyalty to the throne and person of the new sovereign.

His Honour said he understood that the Honourable Member for Windward proposed to move a Resolution of sympathy.

The Honourable F. A. Corea, Elected Member for Windward, then moved a resolution of sympathy, and in doing so said he was sure that in moving this resolution they had the whole-hearted support of all members of the community who felt the deepest sympathy for the members of the Royal Family in their great loss, he would say, in the Empire's great loss. The late lamented

King had by his particularly sympathetic manner, by his exemplary Christian life and by that atmosphere of family life in which he lived, endeared himself to his people. Moreover, owing to the modern facility for speaking across the seas, His late Majesty, by being able to speak to his people in the different parts of his Empire from his home, had brought about a still closer affection between himself and them.

It could truly be said of him that he came to be regarded as a father rather than a King.

The Resolution moved by the Honourable Member is as follows:

> Be it resolved that we, the Members of the Legislative Council of Saint Vincent, on behalf of the Government and people of the colony, do respectfully tender to His Majesty through His Excellency the Governor of the Windward Islands an expression of our profound sorrow at the grievous loss suffered by His Majesty, the Queen Mother, the Royal Family, and the whole Empire in the death of our beloved Ruler, King George the Fifth; and that we most humbly assure His Majesty of our constant loyalty to His Throne and Person and pray that God may bless His Majesty with health and happiness and vouchsafe Him a long and prosperous reign.

With the rest of the British Empire, St. Vincent mourned the loss of her beloved King George V who passed away to his rest on January 20. In accordance with notice published by His Honour the Administrator, the different sections of the community representing the professions, and occupations, societies, and the like assembled at the courthouse at 8 a.m. on Tuesday, 28th January, preparatory to attending the memorial services in Kingstown corresponding with the funeral of His late Majesty King George V.

The mournful procession was formed there in order given in the Government *Gazette*. It comprised the largest number ever seen in St. Vincent, and the dense crowd that occupied the entire sidewalk from the courthouse to the Cathedral displayed conduct of reverence that reflected great credit upon that class of the inhabitants.

His Honour the Administrator Arthur Francis Grimble (MA, CMG) attended together with The Honourable J. H. Otway (OBE), Colonial Treasurer, Major H. Grist, Chief of Police, and many other Government officials and their wives and members of their families. In addition, there were representatives of the Kingstown Board, the legal and medical professions, contingents of the St. George's Friendly Society, the Freemasons, the foresters, the volunteers, the constabulary, nurses, Girl Guides, and Boy Scouts. The ample seating accommodation of the cathedral was fully taxed by the congregation which was estimated at 2,400. Mr. T. D. Hampson, Assistant Secretary of the West India Committee, who was on a visit also attended with the Administrator.

As the officials were conducted to their places, the cathedral organist (Mr. W. H. Lewis) played *Dead March* from *Saul* (Handel), and at the close of the service, *Marche Fanebre* (Mendelssohn).

The service was conducted by the Venerable H. G. Pigott (MA), Archdeacon of S. Vincent, who followed the order in leaflet which was specially prepared for the occasion. The sermon was preached by the Rev. Fr. R. H. Hatch, Rector of the Cathedral Parish, and the lesson read by the Rev. Fr. I. M. Yerbury. Other clergy present were Rev. Canon Samuel; the Rev. Fr. W. E. Evans; the Rev. Fr. A. C. Johnson; the Rev. Fr. G. A. I. Frederick (BA), the Rev. Fr. F. E. Layne (LT) and the Rev. E. O. Buxo (LTh)

The following telegram received by His Excellency the Governor at Grenada on 29th January 1936 from the Secretary of State for the Colonies was published for general information.

NO. 17.

I HAVE LAID BEFORE THE KING YOUR TELEGRAM DATED 21st JANUARY, 22nd JANUARY, 23rd JANUARY, AND YOUR TELEGRAM OF 24th JANUARY, TRANSMITTING ON BEHALF OF THE GOVERNMENT AND PEOPLE OF GRENADA, ST. LUCIA AND ST. VINCENT MESSAGES OF CONDOLENCE WITH HIS MAJESTY AND QUEEN MARY AND THE ROYAL FAMILY ON THE DEATH OF KING GEORGE AND THE ASSURANCE OF DEVOTION TO THE CROWN. I AM COMMANDED BY THE KING TO CONVEY TO YOU AN EXPRESSION OF SINCERE GRATITUDE FOR THESE KIND MESSAGES OF SYMPATHY AND HIS DEEP APPRECIATION OF LOYAL SENTIMENTS BY WHICH THEY ARE ACCOMPANIED.
4th FEBRUARY, 1936

Sir John L. Maffey (KCMG, KCB, KCVO), Permanent Under Secretary of State for the Colonies, accompanied by Lady Maffey, His Excellency Sir Selwyn MacGregor Grier and Lady Grier, arrived in the colony on Monday afternoon, 17th February. There also arrived on H.M.S. *Dundee* Mr. J. B. Sidebotham, the Secretary to Sir John Maffey, and Lieutenant-Commander C. D. Melbourne (RN), the A.D.C. to the Governor.

His Honour A. F. Grimble (CMG), Administrator, and Mrs. Grimble attended to receive the distinguished visitors and His Excellency the Governor and Lady Grier; members of the Executive and Legislative Councils, of the Kingstown Board; Government officers and other influential members of the community were also in attendance on the jetty.

Although the time at his disposal was extremely limited Sir John and Lady Maffey went through Mesopotamia over the identical route followed by the late King George V and like his late Majesty, passed along the Vigie of historic fame and journeyed on to the Yambou Pass which the late King said was the best thing of the kind he had seen out of Switzerland.

On Tuesday, 3rd March, a meeting of the Kingstown Board was specially convened to present a farewell address to His Honour A. F. Grimble. Regret was expressed at His Honour's approaching departure and congratulations were offered for His Honour's promotion to the Governorship of Seychelles islands.

On Wednesday, 4th March, at 11 o'clock a.m., the Members of the Legislative and Executive Councils met at the council chamber for the purpose of presenting an address to the President His Honour Arthur Francis Grimble (CMG). After His Honour had taken his seat the address was read by the Honourable A. M. Punnett, the Nominated Member, and supported in an able speech by the Honourable F. A. Corea, Member for Windward. The Honourable H. A. O'Reilly, Attorney General, on behalf of the official side of the table, in choice language and flowing delivery, paid glowing tribute to the Administrator's achievements during his term of office. The Administrator then replied.

With voice tremulous at times with suppressed emotion, he thanked the Honourable Members for their kind remarks about him in their valedictory address. He stressed his love for the island which began from his first impression of it. He knew he would love the island and the people whose kindly acts and many courtesies had taken hold of his heart and the hearts of his people.

On Thursday, the 5th day of March, at 9 o'clock in the morning, His Honour A. F. Grimble, wife and family, left these shores by the S.S. *Inanda*, en route for his new appointment as Governor-in-Chief of the Seychelles islands via England. On board the *Inanda* on his way to St. Lucia was the Governor-in-Chief Sir Selwyn Grier, who thus had an opportunity of bidding personal farewell and having some final conversations with the departing Administrator.

The Office of Registrar was separated from that of Attorney General on 9th June and Mr. G. Elmore Edwards, Barrister-at-Law, was appointed Registrar of the Supreme Court.

On Thursday, 18th June, news was received announcing that the synod at Grenada had elected The Venerable H. N. Vincent Tonks, Archdeacon of Grenada, to the Bishopric of the Windward Islands; consequently, the Cathedral bells pealed and service was held. This consisted of the announcement followed by the *Te Deum* and prayers for the Bishop-Elect. The service was closed after the singing of hymn 355.

On 22nd June it was announced that the King has been graciously pleased, on the occasion of His Majesty's birthday, to give directions for the following promotion in the Most Distinguished Order of Saint Michael and Saint George, to be an Additional Member of the Second Class or Knight Commander of the said Most Distinguished Order, His Excellency Sir Selwyn MacGregor Grier (CMG), Governor and Commander-in-Chief of the Windward Islands.

The King has been graciously pleased, on the occasion of His Majesty's birthday to approve of the award of the Medal of the Civil Division of the Most Excellent Order of the British Empire to John Walter Bailey, Corporal, St. Vincent Police Force, for meritorious service.

Miss Sheila MacDonald, youngest daughter of Mr. Ramsay MacDonald who is a personal friend of His Honour A. Alban Wright, Administrator, and Mrs. Wright, arrived on 8th August to spend a few months with the Administrator and his family. During her stay in St. Vincent she endeared herself to all with whom she came into contact.

The *Gazette* of 24th October contained the notification of the award of the St. Vincent scholarship to William Landreth Cummings.*

By Proclamation dated 7th December 1936 and published in the Government *Gazette* of the following day, it was proclaimed that the Trinidad Currency Notes Ordinance 1936 would come into operation on 1st January 1937.

The telegram of the abdication of His Majesty King Edward VIII dated 10th December was published in Government *Gazette* (extraordinary) of 11th December. His Honour the Administrator on that day forwarded the following telegram:

11th DECEMBER 1936

AT A MEETING OF THE EXECUTIVE COUNCIL HELD THIS MORNING THE KING'S MESSAGE WAS READ AND COUNCIL UNANIMOUSLY ADVISED THAT I SHOULD ASK YOUR EXCELLENCY TO TRANSMIT TO THE SECRETARY OF STATE FOR COMMUNICATION TO HIS MAJESTY THE FOLLOWING:

ON BEHALF OF MYSELF AND THE PEOPLE OF THE COLONY OF SAINT VINCENT I DESIRE TO EXPRESS BOTH OUR PROFOUND SORROW THAT HIS MAJESTY HAS FELT COMPELLED TO LAY DOWN THE BURDEN OF HIS SUPREME OFFICE AND ALSO OUR SYMPATHY AND OUR HUMBLE AND HEARTFELT WISHES THAT HE WILL ENJOY LONG LIFE, HEALTH AND HAPPINESS. WE ALSO WISH AN ASSURANCE TO BE CONVEYED TO HIS MAJESTY THAT THE DEEP LOYALTY AND AFFECTION OF THE PEOPLE OF SAINT VINCENT ALWAYS ACCORDED TO HIS MAJESTY WILL BE EXTENDED IN FULL MEASURE TO HIS LAWFUL SUCCESSOR.

In the presence of a large and fully representative gathering in the yard of the courthouse the following Proclamation was read by the Honourable H. A. O'Reilly, Attorney General, on behalf of the Administrator, the Chief Justice, the Members of the Executive and Legislative Councils, and the Chairman of the Kingstown Board.

Whereas by an Instrument of Abdication dated the tenth day of December instant, His former Majesty King Edward the Eighth did declare His irrevocable determination to renounce the Throne for Himself and His Descendants, and the said Instrument of Abdication has now taken effect, whereby the Imperial Crown of Great Britain, Ireland and all other His

---

*Mr. Cummings proceeded to Edinburgh, Scotland to pursue the study of medicine .

former Majesty's Dominions is now solely and rightfully come to the High and Mighty Prince Albert Frederick Arthur George:

We, Arthur Alban Wright, Administrator of the Colony of Saint Vincent; George Cyril Griffith Williams, Chief Justice; Harry Allan Oswald O'Reilly, Attorney General; John Felix Hamilton Otway, Treasurer; Archibald Guelph Holdsworth Smart, Senior Medical Officer; Frederick Augustine Corea, Percy Wilfred Verrall and Clifford Bertram Sayles, Members of the Executive Council; Arnold Morgan Punnett and Agostinho DaSilva, Members of the Legislative Council; and Walter Henry Richards, Chairman of the Kingstown Board, all of the said Colony of Saint Vincent, therefore, do now hereby with one voice and consent of tongue and heart, publish and proclaim, that the High and Mighty Prince Albert Frederick Arthur George is now become Our only lawful and rightful Liege Lord George the Sixth, by the Grace of God, of Great Britain, Ireland and the British Dominions beyond the Seas, King, Defender of the Faith, Emperor of India;

To whom we do acknowledge all Faith and constant obedience, with all hearty and humble affection, beseeching God, by whom Kings and Queens do reign, to bless the Royal Prince George the Sixth with long and happy years to reign over us.

Given under my hand and the Public Seal of the Island of Saint Vincent, at Kingstown, Saint Vincent, this twelfth day of December, One thousand nine hundred and thirty-six.

C. Griffith Williams, P. W. Verrall, A. O'Reilly, C. B. Sayles,
J. H. Otway, A. M. Punnett, A. G. H. Smart, A. DaSilva,
F. A. Corea, Walter H. Richards

At the meeting of the Legislative Council held on 12th December, the Administrator said that he did not propose to speak today on the swift and unexpected march of events which, in circumstances unparalleled in our history, had to our profound sorrow deprived the Empire of a King blessed in such full measure with the great qualities of Kingship, a King who both as Prince of Wales and Monarch had never spared himself in the service of the Empire, a King whose devoted and loyal subjects we all of us had been proud to be, and who would always carry with him the good wishes and the deep affections of his former subjects.

Today it is our joyful duty to proclaim His Majesty King George VI as King and Emperor. His Honour said that we were happy to know that in the person of our new King we had a Ruler who would more than uphold the high and glorious traditions associated with the Monarchy, and Her Gracious Majesty the Queen had already won her way deeply into the hearts of all the peoples of the Empire.

His Honour further said that it was now his privilege to move the following Resolution:

Be it resolved, that we, the members of the Legislative Council of Saint Vincent, on behalf of the Government and people of the colony, do most humbly assure His Majesty of our constant loyalty to His Throne and Person, and pray that God may bless Their Majesties the King and Queen with health and happiness and vouchsafe them a long and prosperous reign.

The Honourable A. M. Punnett, Nominated Unofficial Member, seconded the motion adding that it gave him very great pleasure to do so.

In the course of his address to the Legislative Council on 15th December, His Honour said, among other things:

I arrived in St. Vincent in June and took over the reins of Government from the Honourable J. H. Otway (OBE). Mr. Otway had administered the Government of the colony since the previous March, when His Honour Mr. A. F. Grimble (CMG), my predecessor in the post of Administrator, left St. Vincent on well-deserved promotion to the post of Governor of the Seychelles.

I should like to take this opportunity of recording my grateful appreciation not only of Mr. Otway's most efficient services as Acting Administrator, but also of the manner in which he placed his extensive knowledge and experience of local conditions at my disposal and of the valuable assistance and advice afforded to me by him in the difficult task, which confronted me on my arrival, of taking up the administration of a colony with the needs and problems of which I had small acquaintance.

My six months residence in St. Vincent has enabled me to assess the value of the work performed by my predecessor. He never spared himself in advancing the interests of the colony and its inhabitants. During his tenure of office, the colony made marked progress, and I feel sure that he has carried with him to his new sphere of work the good wishes of all responsible members of the community.

St. Vincent is slowly recovering from the effects of the depression, and the future of the agricultural industry now appears to be much brighter than it has been for some years. It is expected that the value of exports during 1936 will be about £20,000 more than during the year 1935.

Finally, I should like to thank the members of this Council, and all my advisors, official and unofficial, for the valuable help that they have always afforded to me and for the wise counsel which they have so readily put at my disposal. The elections which will take place in March or April of 1937, may mean that fresh faces may be seen round this table when the newly elected Council first assembles in the coming year. To those now members of this Council who will not then be present here I would say farewell. I look forward to welcome those new members who may be successful at the forthcoming elections and I trust that the new Constitution, which marks a definite political advance in St. Vincent, will also mark the beginning of an era of increased prosperity and contentment for the people of this colony.

The telegram from His Majesty the King dated 12th December, was published in *Gazette* of 16th December:

242

CIRCULAR, DECEMBER 12th. PROCLAMATION OF HIS MAJESTY KING GEORGE
THE SIXTH WAS SIGNED AT THE ACCESSION OF COUNCIL TODAY. IMMEDI-
ATELY AFTER SIGNATURE OF PROCLAMATION HIS MAJESTY WAS PLEASED TO
MAKE THE FOLLOWING DECLARATION:

YOUR ROYAL HIGHNESSES, MY LORDS AND GENTLEMEN:

I MEET YOU TODAY IN CIRCUMSTANCES WHICH ARE WITHOUT PARALLEL IN
THE HISTORY OF OUR COUNTRY. NOW THAT THE DUTIES OF SOVEREIGNTY
HAVE FALLEN TO ME I DECLARE TO YOU MY ADHERENCE TO THE STRICT
PRINCIPLES OF CONSTITUTIONAL GOVERNMENT AND MY RESOLVE TO WORK
BEFORE ALL ELSE FOR THE WELFARE OF THE BRITISH COMMONWEALTH OF
NATIONS.

WITH MY WIFE AS HELPMATE BY MY SIDE, I TAKE UP THE HEAVY TASK
WHICH LIES BEFORE ME. IN IT I LOOK FOR THE SUPPORT OF ALL MY
PEOPLES.

FURTHERMORE, MY FIRST ACT ON SUCCEEDING MY BROTHER WILL BE TO
CONFER UPON HIM A DUKEDOM AND HE WILL HENCEFORWARD BE KNOWN AS
HIS ROYAL HIGHNESS THE DUKE OF WINDSOR.

At the meeting of the Legislative Council held on 16th December, His
Honour the Administrator addressed the members of Council and other persons who assembled there:

Ladies and Gentlemen,

*This day marks another step in the political progress of St. Vincent and
I trust marks also the beginning of an era of increased political contentment
and of added prosperity in the history of the colony of St. Vincent.*

*The birth of the new Constitution, which the new Order in Council
promulgates as from Friday, means the death of the old Constitution which
has been in existence since April 1925.*

*The Constitution of 1925 differed from its predecessor of 1885 in that
under the former, His Majesty granted to the colony a measure of representation by election to the Legislative Council, whereas under the Constitution of
1885, all the unofficial members were nominated members.*

*We can certainly look back with satisfaction and I think with pride on
the achievements of the Legislative Council during the last 12 years, and on
behalf of the Government I thank the members both of the Council which
will be dissolved on Friday and of former Councils for the public service which
they have rendered in such full measure and for the assistance so unstintingly
given by them at the deliberations of the Council. The people of this island
owe a debt of gratitude to the several individuals who have so worthily filled
the position of elected members of this Council.*

*His Majesty has now thought fit to bestow a further measure of rep-
resentation on the people of the colony. An increase has been granted by the
new Constitution of from 3 to 5 in the number of elected members and from
1 to 3 in the number of nominated unofficial members, making an aggregate total of 8 unofficial members in the persons of the Administrator, the
Attorney General and the Treasurer.*

I pray that God may guide the new Councillors, whoever they may be, in their efforts to further the interest of the colony of St. Vincent and of its people.

The Attorney General then read the Proclamation which dissolved the Council on the 17th December.

Telegraphic correspondence was conducted by His Excellency the Governor and His Honour the Administrator.

FROM GOVERNOR TO ADMINISTRATOR
I SEND TO YOU AND THE PEOPLE OF ST. VINCENT BEST WISHES FOR A
HAPPY CHRISTMAS AND A PROSPEROUS NEW YEAR.

GOVERNOR WINDWARD ISLANDS

FROM ADMINISTRATOR TO GOVERNOR
ON BEHALF OF MYSELF AND THE PEOPLE OF ST. VINCENT I THANK YOUR
EXCELLENCY FOR YOUR GOOD WISHES FOR CHRISTMAS AND THE NEW YEAR
WHICH ARE MOST HEARTILY RECIPROCATED.

ADMINISTRATOR, 28th DECEMBER 1936

1937 / It was announced in *Gazette* dated 1st February that the King was graciously pleased to give directions for the appointment of His Honour Arthur Alban Wright (BA), Administrator of St. Vincent, to be Companion of the Most Distinguished Order of St. Michael and St. George.

In the *Gazette* of 27th February, it was notified that the King had commanded the Secretary of State for the Colonies to request His Excellency the Governor of the Windward Islands to convey to the Legislative Council an expression of his sincere appreciation of the sentiments of loyalty and devotion to the Throne contained in the resolution passed by the Council and forwarded on the 12th December, 1936.

In *Gazette* of 16th March, it was notified that Lieutenant Harold John Hughes was appointed to represent the St. Vincent Volunteer Force at the Coronation of His Majesty on 12th May.

The following is an extract of a letter received by the Administrator from the Captain of H.M.S. *Dragon* thanking the inhabitants of St. Vincent for their hospitality during the ship's visit.

Dear Mr. Wright,

May I take this opportunity of recording on behalf of all of us on the Dragon sincere thanks for the generous hospitality offered to us during our short but most enjoyable visit to your beautiful Island.

Yours sincerely,

M. Johnson

At 9:20 a.m. on 6th April, His Excellency the Governor entered the Council Chamber and stood at his seat.

The Clerk of Councils read first the Proclamation convoking the Legislative Council, and then the names of the Members of the Council which are as follows:

Ex Officio Members	Arthur Alban Wright, Administrator
	Harry Allan Oswald O'Reilly, Attorney General
	John Felix Hamilton Otway, Colonial Treasurer
Nominated Members	Arnold Morgan Punnett
	Alexander Murdoch Fraser
	William Alexander Hadley

Elected Members

George Augustus McIntosh, Kingstown Electoral District
Newton Smith Nanton, North Windward Electoral District
Alphaeus Caleb Allen, South Windward Electoral District
Herbert Fitz-Allan Bryan Davis, Leeward Electoral District,
Donald Cuthwin McIntosh, Grenadines Electoral District.

The prescribed oaths were then taken by each member of the Legislative Council above mentioned, and also by the Clerk of Councils in the presence of His Excellency the Governor.

The Honourable A. M. Punnett, addressing His Excellency, said that it seemed so short a while since the Members of the old Council had the pleasure of welcoming His Excellency and Lady Grier to St. Vincent on their first visit to this colony, and now the Members of this Council had, with deep regret, to bid them both farewell.

On behalf of the Nominated Members of the Legislative Council and of the inhabitants of St. Vincent and its dependencies, the Honourable Member expressed the hope that His Excellency's health would rapidly improve and that His Excellency and Lady Grier would enjoy many happy years at home. He wished them both *bon voyage*.

His Excellency the Governor delivered a lengthy address in the course of which he said,

> *I have come here today to welcome you at the first meeting of a new Legislative Council, which, as you well know, differs in important respects from previous Legislative Councils in St. Vincent.*
>
> *This Council is a direct result of recommendations made by the Closer Union Commission which visited these islands in 1933.*
>
> *The main events in 1936 and the activities of the various Government departments during 1936 were dealt with by His Honour the Administrator in his address to the Legislative Council on the 15th of December of last year. I ask Honourable Members therefore to study that address, and I on my part propose merely to supplement it with a few remarks on subsequent events.*
>
> *Today I find myself in the position of welcoming and at the same time saying farewell to this Council. It had been my hope that I should be able to*

identify myself with the work of the newly constituted Councils of the Windward Islands but failing sight has made this impossible.

The future progress of this colony depends on a coordinated effort to make the best use possible of its resources and on a spirit of cooperation with the administration.

The Honourable Member for Kingstown replied.

Announcement was made on 17th April that Alfred Gregg Hazell, Esq, was appointed as the representative of St. Vincent to attend the Coronation in lieu of the Honourable Arnold Morgan Punnett who would not be able to attend. Mr. Hazell laid the wreath for St. Vincent on the Cenotaph on the 14th May. In doing so in his official capacity it may well be remembered that his brother William is included among those for whom the honour was then paid.

On 22nd April, it was announced that Mr. M. Byron Cox was appointed to act as Magistrate, Second District, in the place of Lieutenant Hughes.

On the 7th May His Honour the Administrator telegraphed hearty welcome to His Excellency the Governor:

```
FOR MYSELF AND ALSO ON BEHALF OF THE PEOPLE OF ST. VINCENT I
EXTEND TO YOUR EXCELLENCY AND MRS. POPHAM A MOST HEARTY WELCOME
TO THE WINDWARD ISLANDS. YOU HAVE THE BEST WISHES OF ALL IN THIS
COLONY FOR A HAPPY SUCCESSFUL AND PROSPEROUS PERIOD OF ADMINIS-
TRATION.
```

And in the *Gazette* of 11th May appeared the reply:

```
WITH REFERENCE TO YOUR TELEGRAM 16, PLEASE ACCEPT AND CONVEY TO
PEOPLE OF ST. VINCENT THE SINCERE THANKS OF MY WIFE AND MYSELF
FOR THE KIND MESSAGE CONVEYED IN YOUR TELEGRAM 7th MAY.
```

The following telegrams despatched by His Honour the Administrator to the Secretary of State for the Colonies conveying loyal messages from St. Vincent to Their Majesties the King and Queen on the occasion of their Coronation, were published on 18th May:

```
FOLLOWING MOTION MOVED BY ME AND SECONDED BY HONOURABLE F. A.
COREA, SENIOR UNOFFICIAL MEMBER OF EXECUTIVE COUNCIL, WAS PASSED
WITH ACCLAMATION AT 10 A.M, TODAY IN JOINT SESSION OF EXECUTIVE
AND LEGISLATIVE COUNCILS OF ST. VINCENT. GRATEFUL IF YOU WOULD
PLACE THIS BEFORE HIS MAJESTY:
WE THE MEMBERS OF THE EXECUTIVE COUNCIL AND OF THE LEGISLATIVE
COUNCIL OF ST. VINCENT, HAVING MET TOGETHER IN JOINT SESSION ON
THE EVE OF HIS MAJESTY'S CORONATION, SUBMIT OUR HUMBLE DUTY AND
OF THIS COLONY AND OF ALL THE KING'S FAITHFUL IN THIS COLONY TO
CONVEY TO HIS MAJESTY KING GEORGE SIXTH AN EARNEST ASSURANCE OF
THE UNSWERVING DEVOTION AND LOYALTY OF THE INHABITANTS OF ST.
VINCENT TO HIS MAJESTY'S THRONE AND PERSON. WE PRAY THAT THEIR
GRACIOUS MAJESTIES THE KING AND QUEEN ENJOY A LONG, HAPPY AND
PEACEFUL REIGN, THAT THEY AND ALL THE MEMBERS OF THE ROYAL HOUSE
MAY BE RICHLY ENDOWED WITH EVERY DIVINE GIFT AND BLESSING, AND
THAT HIS MAJESTY'S ACCESSION TO THE THRONE MAY MARK THE BEGINNING
```

OF AN ERA OF ADVANCEMENT IN THE STRENGTH, UNITY AND GLORY OF THE
EMPIRE AND IN THE PROSPERITY AND CONTENTMENT OF ITS PEOPLES.

Telegram sent 10th May 1937

RESPECTFULLY REQUEST THAT FOLLOWING RESOLUTION PASSED BY THE
KINGSTOWN BOARD TODAY BE PLACED BEFORE THEIR MAJESTIES:

BE IT RESOLVED THAT THIS BOARD AS REPRESENTING THE CITIZENS OF
KINGSTOWN, THE CHIEF CITY OF THE ISLAND OF ST. VINCENT IN THE
BRITISH WEST INDIES DESIRE TO CONVEY TO THEIR MAJESTIES KING
GEORGE THE SIXTH AND QUEEN ELIZABETH ON THIS THE OCCASION OF
THEIR CORONATION, THE DEEPEST ASSURANCE OF THEIR LOYALTY TO THEM
AND TO THE THRONE AND THEIR SINCEREST WISHES FOR A LONG, HAPPY
AND PEACEFUL REIGN, AND THAT A COPY OF THIS RESOLUTION BE SENT TO
THEIR MAJESTIES.

ADMINISTRATOR

Telegram sent 11th May 1937

AT REQUEST OF SAINT VINCENT WORKINGMEN CO-OPERATIVE ASSOCIATION,
I FORWARD A COPY OF A RESOLUTION OF LOYALTY TO THEIR MAJESTIES
PASSED BY THE ASSOCIATION TODAY.

BE IT RESOLVED THAT THE MEMBERS OF THE SAINT VINCENT WORKINGMEN
COOPERATIVE ASSOCIATION ON THIS GRAND EVENT OF THEIR MAJESTIES
CORONATION DO HEREBY DECLARE TO KING GEORGE SIXTH AND QUEEN
ELIZABETH OUR UNSWERVING LOYALTY AND DEVOTION AND PRAY THAT EVERY
BLESSING WILL ATTEND THEIR MAJESTIES AND ALL THE MEMBERS OF THE
ROYAL FAMILY; THAT HIS REIGN MAY BE LONG, PEACEFUL AND EVENTFUL,
AND MAY THE EMPIRE BE CONNECTED BY A STRONGER AND MORE POWERFUL
TIE THROUGH THE INFLUENCE AND PATTERN OF THEIR MAJESTIES EXEMPLA-
RY LIVES.

ADMINISTRATOR

The following address was delivered by the Right Honourable the Secretary of State for the Colonies to His Majesty the King on behalf of the
Colonial Empire, at a reception held at Buckingham Palace on Tuesday, the
11th May.

> *Sir, On behalf of the fifty-five million people of Your Majesty's Coloni-*
> *al Empire, I beg to offer their loyal devotion to Your Majesty's Person and*
> *Throne. The peoples of your Colonial Empire live scattered among all the*
> *continents and oceans of the world. They differ in race, language, creed, and*
> *tradition. But today they are at one in tendering with deep sincerity their*
> *loyal greetings to Your Majesty and to Her Majesty the Queen, and in offer-*
> *ing their fervent prayers that Your Majesties may long continue to perform*
> *your high and onerous duties, and that you and your children may be blessed*
> *by Almighty God with every happiness and prosperity.*

The following telegram despatched by His Excellency the Governor of the
Windward Islands to the Secretary of State for the Colonies was published for
general information:

ON BEHALF OF THE WINDWARD ISLANDS I WOULD ASK YOU WITH MY HUMBLE
DUTY TO THE KING TO CONVEY AN HUMBLE EXPRESSION OF CONGRATULATION
AND LOYALTY TO THEIR MAJESTIES KING GEORGE VI AND QUEEN ELIZA-

BETH ON THE OCCASION OF THEIR CORONATION AND AN ASSURANCE OF THE
DEVOTION TO THE THRONE WHICH LIES DEEP IN THE HEARTS OF THEIR
SEVERAL PEOPLES.

GOVERNOR OF THE WINDWARD ISLANDS

12th May—Coronation celebration. Official Procession, review of local forces, treats for poor of small towns and Government institutions, at home at Government House, fireworks.

13th—Treat for school children, sports at Victoria Park, pageant

There were floats and one decorated car, namely, a float representing the world—a globe 8 feet in diameter: The British Empire in gold, and other parts of the world in silver.

"St. George and the Dragon"

"Columbus at the Court of Spain"

"Pax et Justitia"

The Girls High School's float was very elaborate and beautiful in design. It represented the British Empire with Britannia at the top.

"Emblems of the Empire"

"Flags of the Empire"

John H. Hazell Sons & Co Ltd., was the only firm represented in the pageant procession. The good taste and keen insight with which this float was produced explains why John H. Hazell, Sons & Co. Ltd. have flourished through 92 years.

18th—Dinner for the poor

His Excellency H. Popham (CMG, MBE), Governor and Commander-in-Chief of the Windward Islands, took the prescribed oaths on the 26th May and left for St. Lucia the same day.

His Honour A. Alban Wright (CMG), Administrator, held a levee in honour of the birthday of His Majesty the King at the Council Chamber, Kingstown, on Wednesday, 9th June, after the parade of the local forces on the Victoria Park.

The following telegraphic correspondence between the Governor and the Secretary of State was published for general information on 15th June:

From Governor to Secretary of State

> JUNE 9th. GRATEFUL IF FOLLOWING MESSAGE MAY BE CONVEYED TO HIS
> MAJESTY. ON BEHALF OF PEOPLE OF WINDWARD ISLANDS I SUBMIT OUR
> HUMBLE DUTY AND SINCERE GOOD WISHES ON THE OCCASION OF YOUR MAJ-
> ESTY'S BIRTHDAY.

From Secretary of State to Governor

> FOLLOWING TELEGRAM HAS BEEN RECEIVED FROM THE SECRETARY OF STATE
> FOR THE COLONIES. YOUR TELEGRAM 81 HAS BEEN LAID BEFORE THE KING

WHO DESIRES AN EXPRESSION OF HIS SINCERE THANKS FOR THE MESSAGE
CONTAINED THEREIN MAY BE CONVEYED TO YOU.

The following telegraphic correspondence between the Governor and the Secretary of State was published for general information on 15th July:

GOVERNOR TO SECRETARY OF STATE

19th JUNE—CHIEF TOWN OF THE ISLAND OF BEQUIA PREVIOUSLY WITHOUT DISTINCTIVE NAME, NAMED BY ME PORT ELIZABETH YESTERDAY WITH DUE CEREMONIAL. TOWN BEFLAGGED AND GREAT ENTHUSIASM. CITIZENS OF THE TOWN UNANIMOUSLY REQUESTED THAT THE FOLLOWING MESSAGE SHOULD BE SENT TO THE SECRETARY OF STATE FOR THE COLONIES:

CITIZENS OF THE CHIEF TOWN OF BEQUIA, ST. VINCENT GRENADINES, FORMALLY NAMED TODAY PORT ELIZABETH HUMBLY BEG TO OFFER AFFEC-TIONATE GREETINGS TO HER ROYAL HIGHNESS PRINCESS ELIZABETH.

GRATEFUL IF MESSAGE COULD BE CONVEYED WITH MY HUMBLE DUTY TO THE KING.

GOVERNOR

SECRETARY OF STATE TO GOVERNOR

YOUR TELEGRAM HAS BEEN LAID BEFORE THE KING. HIS MAJESTY HAS BEEN PLEASED TO GIVE RETROSPECTIVE APPROVAL TO THE NAMING OF THE CHIEF TOWN OF THE ISLAND BEQUIA AFTER PRINCESS ELIZABETH.

THE KING HAS ALSO COMMANDED ME TO REQUEST YOU TO CONVEY TO THE CITIZENS OF THAT TOWN AN EXPRESSION OF HIS THANKS FOR THEIR MES-SAGE TO HER ROYAL HIGHNESS PRINCESS ELIZABETH.

SECRETARY OF STATE

The following telegraphic correspondence between the Governor and the Administrator was published for general information:

I SEND TO YOU AND THE PEOPLE OF ST. VINCENT BEST WISHES FOR A HAPPY CHRISTMAS AND A PROSPEROUS NEW YEAR.

GOVERNOR WINDWARD ISLANDS

FROM ADMINISTRATOR TO GOVERNOR

YOUR TELEGRAM 81 MUCH APPRECIATED AND HEARTILY RECIPROCATED BY ME AND PEOPLE OF ST. VINCENT.

ADMINISTRATOR

Contributions Written for and Letters Relating to the St. Vincent Handbook

<hr>

THAT BEAUTIFUL GREEN ISLE

Far away from chilly climes,
In waters deep and blue,
A necklace of gems is strung,
'mongst which an emerald of
wond'rous hue.

To call it a glistening emerald, the island of St. Vincent, is not in the least bit exaggerating, for that is just what I thought it looked like when I had my first glimpse of the island from the deck of the steamer, early one morning in the month of August.

It was a refreshing morning and the sun was casting its sparkles on the water, throwing them far up into the hills. I could see there was a compact, clean looking little town—seemingly on the water's edge and, glancing upwards, I remember exclaiming admiration at the view before me. The tall palm trees silhouetted against the almost clear sky, the mass of hills and mountain peaks covered with an abundance of vegetation of various shades of green, the bright flowering trees scattered here and there blending so beautifully with the deep blue sky, a few large houses perched up proudly here, and some smaller dwellings there, all with their gaily coloured roofs, made, indeed, a vivid picture.

I have now resided in St. Vincent for a few years and I have seen many, if not all, of its beauty spots. Of these there are many all over the island and were I asked to name the most beautiful, I would not know which to choose.

The good roads make motoring very enjoyable and I think I am correct in saying the drive along the Windward coast is the most popular. One can drive for over 23 miles on an excellent road this way, past rugged coastal scenery where the huge rocks and massive boulders remind one so much of bits of Devon and Cornwall. It is at this portion of the coast that the deep blue Atlantic Ocean sends her rollers—topped with pompous white horses—bounding over and over unceasingly. It is really glorious to watch them. Then, passing on, we drive through large well-kept arrowroot estates, fields of sugar cane, healthy cotton fields and shady groves of coconut palms, now and again getting more sea views on the way.

On still further, we come to the spot where the car must be left behind and, by arrangement, horses are there to meet us, for I am thinking now of one of the most wonderful points in the island called Owia (once a favourite home of the Caribs but where only a mere handful of the pure native Caribs can now be found). To reach Owia, we mount our horses and travel (repeatedly with our hearts in our mouths) along narrow precipices, up hills and down, crossing Bloody Bridge—a scene in days gone by, as depicted by its name, of fierce battles between the Caribs aided by the French against the British—on through picturesque country reaching Owia, one of the highest points in the island. This is a privately owned estate where valuable arrowroot is grown, a pretty little hamlet with its quaint church. We can see the lights of St. Lucia from Owia on a clear night.

The Caribbean Sea washes the shores of the Leeward coast. Magnificent scenery greets us all the way as we journey over hill and down dell, through tiny villages, and oft-times passing items of interest, especially attractive to historians.

Returning from our enjoyable drives, we have still another of God's marvelous works to admire and that is the gorgeous sunset. On almost all the three hundred and sixty-five days in the year, eventide brings St. Vincent a sunset that is the envy of many an artist, so full is it of brilliant hues. Many people have been fortunate enough to catch a glimpse of the "green ray" as the sun dips his head to say goodnight and disappears, as it were, into the great beyond.

Very interesting is the old fellow, Soufriere, standing 4,048 feet high, which erupted in 1902, towering up in the centre of the island like a giant guarding his children around him (who have not, fortunately, inherited the father mountain's fiery temperament). A drive to the base and then a climb to the crater of this volcano, makes a pleasant few hours out.

Arrowroot, St. Vincent's chief export, is an interesting study. To be shown over one of the well-kept factories, seeing the different processes of washing and drying, then to endeavour to discern the various grades of this useful and valuable product, is very edifying indeed.

The Sea Island Cotton grown in this island is of the best quality and is being used very extensively now in the textile trade.

Sugar here, too, is a very important industry. Indeed how many edibles and drinkables are derived from that tall, somewhat slender stalk called cane!

A great asset to St. Vincent is the Aquatic Club, with its spacious dance hall, card room and verandahs. The fact that the furnished bungalows adjoining the club are practically never vacant, is recommendation for them in itself.

With the recently equipped En Pension, run by a local lady, where one can always rely on a nice cool rest at night and where the cuisine is of the best,

252

coupled with the few already well established commercial hotels here, and the long-hoped-for golf course with first class hotel thereon (which it is whispered is now coming to St. Vincent) this island should be one of the most popular health resorts in the West Indies. The climate is a very healthy one, particularly in the months of November to April. The cool breezes then really make one feel it is good to be alive!

Margery S. Sayles, 3.9.37

St. Vincent is one of those delightful places which are small enough to offer the curious traveller quite intimate friendship, yet which are not so small as to exhaust all their charms under the first hurried glance of the passerby.

It must be understood that to come to know St. Vincent well, energy is needed and the ability to undergo minor discomforts of roughish travel. Although the coast road is good, the broken nature of the country prevents its becoming a luxury highway leading to all the selected beauty spots of the island. Indeed, one of the well-frequented ways, that leading from coast to coast by way of the Soufriere crater, is a footpath, used not nearly so much as a means of seeing a most magnificent view as a means of conveying fish to market. That is significant. You cannot avoid enjoying the beauties of the place even in the course of the daily routine because everywhere is attractive. Still, it would be a pity to rest content with casual acceptance of the very lovely scenes. If you want to sense the spirit of the early adventurers, if you like seeking a more personal contact with the delights of fresh places, you must away into the bush and the highlands, wandering along narrow by-paths past tiny houses and patches of cultivation, or clambering up steep slopes amongst the trees and flowers, alert for the sight of the St. Vincent parrot or the rare sound of Soufriere bird. And give thanks as you go that you need not fear for snakes or other such evils. Probably nothing more than an ant, or, at the most, a scorpion, will come to disturb you.

As regards life on the island, since the character of the population is not very complex, it is quite possible for the onlooker to gather a rough acquaintance with conditions. Passing through the little villages and the towns, you can peep at the different types of houses, you can inspect the day's washing being scrubbed in the rivers, watch the goats, cows and pigs, all part of the domestic circle. Or you can stroll along the highroad early on Saturday morning, to meet all the people as they troop to market and to hear (if you are sufficiently acclimatized to the West Indian voice) their gay back-chat.

Again, for those who are interested in the relationships between peoples and the politics of a country, St. Vincent affords an excellent chance for observation, since here you have all the many problems of government and organization concentrated in its small community of people. How far the policies pursued are being successful, the visitor can spend many an interesting and argumentative hour trying to decide.

Agriculture is the mainstay of the island, and no traveller should leave without obtaining an impression—if time permits—of the cycle of crops, of the anxieties attendant on the caprices of wind, rain and sun, of the field and factory work on the estates, of the smallholding labour.

Certainly St. Vincent has much to offer. Passing tourists will enjoy its scenery and its bathing; they may admire the cleanliness of Back Street, the dance floor at the Aquatic Club. But it is to the lingering guest, the person who is inquisitive about the island, that the really worthwhile St. Vincent discloses itself.

Sheila Macdonald

———◆◆∞◆◆———

The island of St. Vincent is one of the most pleasant spots I have ever spent a holiday in. The first year I visited it, I spent two months there. The time passed far too quickly and a longer period was my aim in subsequent years. A more delightful place for anyone from England to spend the winter I cannot imagine. The climate is equable, never too hot nor too cold, the days are days of sunshine, there are no sudden and treacherous blasts of intense cold such as occur on the Mediterranean coast. There are no dangerous snakes or other reptiles such as are found in many tropical places. Kingstown, the capital and principal port, looks always as clean and bright as a new pin and apart from being picturesque, set as it is in a crescent of hills covered with foliage, is a credit to the administration and town authorities; Kingstown is a port and capital of which any community can feel proud.

The Aquatic Club at Villa, set on the shores of a bay enclosed by Young's Island, affords ideal bathing, and the Villa bungalows along this shore are charming residences for visitors staying a month or more.

Though small the island is, so mountainous and rugged in the interior that there is much to be seen and many spots to be visited. The air of these higher localities is as bracing as that of the Surrey or Sussex Downs on a clear summer day.

There are so many beauty spots it is difficult to mention them all without omitting one of importance; but no one should fail to visit the Buccament and Mesopotamia Valleys, the Soufriere, Falls of Balaine and the Three Rivers.

Further, it is not only St. Vincent that is beautiful, but the same is true of the two dependent isles Bequia and Mustique which have white sand beaches to bathe from and glorious scenery. Those English people who attempt to escape from the cold of an English winter by staying in the south of France or in Italy, would find that St. Vincent offers all and more than either of these countries, that life is as easy and comfortable and the people hospitable and courteous.

St. Vincent has a history well worth studying; it passed through turbulent times some hundred and fifty years ago; it won through them. There had been ups and downs in the prosperity of the island as in that of other countries, the courage of the population has pulled them through such bad times as have occurred. The aim of the British Empire is individual freedom and progress combined with law and order. That aim I feel sure the people of St. Vincent keep in view and I have been struck by the pride the people take in their island, by the care of the administration for the welfare of the people, the work of the religious and educational authorities and the work also of the experts in agriculture. These things combined with an appreciation of the fact that without law and order there can be no real progress will go far to make St. Vincent one of the brightest dependencies of the Crown.

H. Lethbridge Alexander (Major-General)

———◆◆∞◆◆———

After a most delightful holiday of two and a half months in the West Indies, from many points of view the most delightful I have ever spent, I am once more on the water speeding back to Para to tell my friends all about it.

So much has happened in that short time, so many places have been visited, so many acquaintances made, so many of nature's marvels explored, that I can see it is going to be no easy matter to recount my experiences fully and adequately.

Not least among these experiences are the human interests which my visit has occasioned. The warmest friendships have been established in every island where I had the privilege of sojourning for a few days, and I shall live in the pleasurable anticipation of renewing as many of them as possible at no very distant date. In these sunny lands, friendships are made speedily and easily if you show a friendly front, and mine—let the cynic say what he will, and do his best or his worst in endeavouring to prove that such bonds must necessarily be evanescent and fleeting—have come to stop.

Now I am going to run the risk straight away of offending someone who may hereafter chance across these lines in Barbados or Trinidad, in Grenada, St Lucia, or Martinique (the extent of my travels), by foregoing all claims to originality, and weakly adopting a view already expressed by certain other misguided individuals in regard to *the* gem of the Antilles, and to the precise spot which this jewel of the coronet should adorn in its Caribbean setting.

255

All I can say is that the charms of St. Vincent are simply bewitching, and if anyone should complain that my judgment is warped please point to those jumbie trees which mark your harbour front at Kingstown, and lay the blame there. In their midst must the stranger land if he comes at all, so of course he is at once spell-bound.*

I think Sir Fredrick Treves must have been aware of their ensnaring influence when he visited the West Indies, for in his "Cradle of the Deep," aglow with interest as it is, there is a chapter missing, a most important chapter, and it ought to occur in the neighbourhood of Grenada and St. Lucia about page 109.

I regard your *Handbook* (1914) as a wonderful production; it teems with interest and variety, and its compilation has evidently been attended with an immense amount of diligent research. I have not yet had time to read everything, but have been deeply interested in such passages as the following:

The geography and geology of the island, the accounts of the hurricane of 1898, and the eruptions of La Soufriere in 1812 and 1902 in the "Historical Notes," the "Places of Interest," the letters of appreciation etc., the "Grenadines."

Where is the vulcanologist, even the interested amateur like myself, who will not take the trouble to scramble up the shrubby slopes of La Soufriere, and photograph its furrowed brows and mile-broad crater lake?

As this feat is so easy of accomplishment, and today so devoid of risk to life and limb, may I point to the desirability of keeping the tracks which lead to the summit from the dry river beds of Wallibou and Georgetown open, and cleared by the more frequent and generous use of the cutlass and a box of matches?

And may I further suggest the pictorial insertion in your *Handbook* of a few views of this majestic volcanic pile, surely a wonder of the world even now in its state of perfect quietude?

"What else did you do, besides climbing volcanoes?" asks a friend. My reply is that I was more than fully occupied with interests for the whole of my too brief stay of a fortnight. I yachted and trawled for fish; I boated in Kingstown harbour and off the Leeward rocks of Bequia and caught fish, or missed them or saw them caught by others. They were nearly always hungry, and so was I, especially for fresh fish, full worthy of the frying pan. I stayed at the Crichton Hotel with great comfort, a minimum of expense and made there a number of delightful friends. I bathed at the "quarry" and Young's Island, and wherever and whenever the opportunity of a swim in these magically trans-

---

* Few of these trees are now to be seen.

parent and delicious waters presented itself. I collected corals and shells, sea fans and sponges, cinders, samples of rock and volcanic ejecta as mementos of my visit for friends in Para. I added but a few insects to a large collection of lepidoptera, but the single record of *Madoryx oielus*, a rare hawk moth, which seemed abundant on *Tecoma entaphylla*, the Whitewood, made up largely for the insular and necessarily limited entomological fauna of the island. I visited the schools, talked to the children and did my humble best in acceding to the kindly expressed wish of Archdeacon Turpin that I would assist him at the Sunday services in St. George's Cathedral. I was driven in a trap to Mesopotamia, in another to Villa for the inspection of Fort Duvernette, taken up to see Fort Charlotte, the asylum and the Yaws Hospital, housed for two nights in the isle of Bequia, put up at Chateaubelair and Rutland Vale, motored to Georgetown, conveyed on horseback to see the Carib country and the desolation caused by the eruption of 1902, rowed for four hours on end in a great dugout canoe along the perfectly enchanting Leeward coast, conducted about on foot by all and sundry to see sights, pay a call or purchase something, and was entertained generally by all sorts of kind people. Such, in brief outline, was the way I enjoyed life to the full, and to St. Vincent do I hope someday to return.

In conclusion I want to make reference to that brilliantly expressed letter of appreciation from Miss Mabel Dearmer in your *Handbook*. I endorse every word she says and corroborate every detail from personal experience. Her wit is admirable and happy. "Here," says she, "in St. Vincent, 'every prospect pleases,' and man is—perfectly delightful."

Miles Moss (MA, FZS, FES),
Chaplain of the Anglican Church, Para, Brazi
l

◆━◆━∞━◆◆━

When Columbus, weary from the pains and the perils of interminable ocean, sighted at last the happy islands, it is said that he had in his mind, not only the dream of great wealth—rivers that ran gold, cities "garnished with all manner of precious stones," but actually the belief that he had found at last the end of man's desire, the earthly paradise, the veritable Garden of Eden with the Tree of Life still standing in its midst. And to the traveller, with the fog and murk, the mud and drizzle of a London November yet in his mind, this is not, after all, such a wild surmise. Why not? In St. Vincent the sun is always shining, the sea is always blue and the trees green—and what a green!—"changing and iridescent like a peacock's neck," says Kingsley, "til the whole island, from peak to shore seems some glorious jewel—an emerald with tints of sapphire and topaz hanging between blue sea and white surf below, blue sky and white cloud above."

Personally, I am convinced that Columbus was right. That has been the gigantic discovery of my visit to St. Vincent (made possible by the kindness of His Honour the Administrator and the Honourable Mrs. Murray), and I am still a little dazzled.

It takes the English nation at least 400 years to grasp an idea, therefore we are now ripe for the discovery of the sanity of Columbus: but once having realized our fact, whatever it may be, it then becomes a part of our creed and ineradicable—we are ready to stake our existence on its truth. But how wonderful to be the first to realize it! Still I can find no other explanation of the existence of St. Vincent, for here "every prospect pleases" and man is— perfectly delightful. From the brown friendly faces, with flashing smiling eyes and teeth, that meet him on the jetty, to the kindly white ones whose hospitable welcome has become a byword, the stranger, looking round, feels that he has met with friends and, unaccountable as it may seem journeying from so far, he is at home. And later, after the first delight of landing, he is almost bewildered by the prodigality of Nature in the earthly paradise. Accustomed to the ceaseless cry of the London unemployed, whose keenest experience is hunger, and whose deepest wisdom is the knowledge of cold, frozen limbs and hearts, and lives—the empty cupboard and the fireless hearth—the traveller now finds a land where food is to be had for the plucking, trees bearing the bread of the people, magic seas in which the fish leaps to be caught. Here black babies sit by the roadside sucking sugar cane, while at home white babies suck the empty lids of condensed milk tins. Here, food, warmth, clothing, (but there is little need of clothing in the Garden of Eden!) are provided comparatively for nothing. The earth is so fertile that Aaron's rod stuck into it at any point would blossom and bear fruit. Smiling fields of cotton and arrowroot testify to the general prosperity. Wooded mountains, fertile valleys, rushing streams, and here and there a village dotted amid the green make up the happy island discovered 412 years ago. Here it is at last! We know it now! Here is the earthly paradise to which people who suffer from illness or boredom, or riches, or overwork may come and winter and find health and peace. What an escape from London in November! What a heavenly rest cure!—and how much cheaper is the return ticket than the fees charged at a nursing home! If only it were known! If only the secret were common property!

But the rush of the people that I picture would considerably alter the life of St. Vincent. A large hotel would be necessary to accommodate them, perhaps two. That is inevitable. With time the face of the country must change, but, given care and foresight, the change need not necessarily be for the worse.

258

I have exceeded the limit of my space but must yet add a postscript. I can imagine some resident reading my words and finding them over enthusiastic. "There is a volcano here," he might say. "There are hurricanes, and the lives of the poor are not so rosy as you picture them."

That is true, for the fact remains that this paradise, although a paradise, is still an earthly one and therefore imperfect, but to the visitor wintering here, it is the heavenliness rather than the earthliness which will be the most apparent. He will drop his burden, whatever it may be, and return home renewed in mind and in body.

And I hold to my own opinion; I am on the side of Columbus.

Mabel Dearmer
Government House, St. Vincent, 1910

The Salvation Army
27, Edward Street,
Port-of Spain, Trinidad, B,W.I.
January 24th, 1938

Dear Mr. Anderson,

At the conclusion of five very happy days spent in your charming island, I gladly send you a note. I shall not soon forget the impression made upon me when the Lady Nelson *sailed into the Harbour and I saw your beautiful Harbour lying at the foot of majestic mountains. I was agreeably surprised at the spacious and clean streets of Kingstown as well as the general air of solidarity of the buildings. In the country the cheerfulness of the peasantry is most marked, whilst the cool equable climate is a revelation.*

With kindest regards and best wishes, yours sincerely,

Geo. J. Robinson, Brigadier S.A.

After leaving the fairy green island of Grenada, with its miniature harbour with deep water right up to the quay and laid out by nature as if with a view to the most charming scenic effect, one steams in one of the excellent new ships of the Royal Mail Intercolonial Service over a sea of all shades of blue and purple past the numerous islands of the Grenadines each standing out boldly in its loneliness and together forming a chain of unsurpassed wild beauty to the fine island of St. Vincent.

259

As one approaches the island the beautiful bay of Kingstown opens out before us with the town lying snugly along the shore presenting almost an Italian appearance with its red brick and tiled houses. Behind the town rise range above range of wooded hills culminating in mountain peaks in the centre of the island often hidden by the clouds.

In few regions is the country so broken and bounteous nature has clothed the fertile soil, where not cultivated, with forests to the very hill tops. Every here and there the cultivation spreads up the steepest slopes to the tops of the ridges and the far-famed cotton and arrowroot of St. Vincent bear witness to the fertility of the soil and the ease with which it is cultivated.

There are many delightful climbs among the mountains and one of the most interesting expeditions that every visitor to the island should make is to that wonder of the world, the Soufriere volcano, from the edge of whose crater 3000 feet above the sea level you look down 1800 feet to the apple-green lake a mile across. This great opening to the earth's centre where vast forces are stored up to break out, spreading devastation all round, is truly awe-inspiring. The botanist will be interested in studying the way in which nature is clothing again the sides of the mountain laid bare by the eruption of 1902. At first lichens, then coarse grasses, and finally stately tree ferns stand out from an undergrowth of begonias and lycopodium.

To reach Chateau Belair, a little hamlet from whence the start is made to the Soufriere, a row of 18 miles must be taken along the coast on the Leeward side of the island, every yard of which is full of interest and of beauty as each headland is rounded and new bays open out to view.

A visitor will find here the genial hospitality for which the West Indian islands are so well known, and it is hoped shortly he will feel that he need not trespass on this unduly when a new hotel is open for visitors.

George Carrington

———◆∞◆———

No one in England sympathises with those who leave the motherland to take up their residence in the West Indies at all events from a health point of view, for it is well known that the climate in these parts is well suited to Europeans. At the same time, some islands undoubtedly are less salubrious than others. There need be no apprehension as to St. Vincent which has been termed "the gem of the Caribbean Sea," for the climate during half the year is delightfully fresh and cool and even during the warm season is quite healthy on account of the pleasant breezes which temper the heat. Fears may perhaps be entertained on other accounts. It is true that there have been great upheavals of nature connected with the eruption of La Soufriere, and that occasional hurricanes have played havoc with the island; but consolation may be derived from the thought that not only are these visitations few and far between, but that their approach is heralded by certain unmistakable warnings. No English family therefore need scruple to settle down in St. Vincent, and mothers may be quite sure that their children's health is not likely to suffer. Perhaps to some parents it may be a pang to notice how soon the rosy cheeks of their children lose their colour and give way to pale white faces. This however is no sign of detriment to the children's constitution, and so long as they are permitted to walk out in the Botanical Gardens or Agricultural School in the early morning and in the cooler portion of the afternoon they will not suffer any diminution of vigour. The scenery of St. Vincent is picturesque. Its rugged mountains and luxuriant growth can best be appreciated by those who take the trouble to mount ponies and look down from the many elevations which command views of the smiling valleys and large cotton or sugar plantations which lie below on all sides. Riding opportunities are abundant and the ponies to be hired in the colony are sure-footed animals well adapted to the climbs demanded of them.*

Kingstown is the chief town of St. Vincent. At the back of its quiet little harbour are plenty of pretty residences, and some way behind on a slight elevation from the shore can be discerned Government House. Here the Administrator resides and his home is the centre of the island's social life.

The Law Courts are a fine spacious building facing the public square and here justice is administered without fear or favour by the Chief Justice of the island. In a room on the upper storey of this building the Legislative Council meets to transact the business of the colony.

Local government also has its own special work in the island and since its inception the Kingstown Board has won golden opinions by the zeal with which it has promoted all that makes for the better improvement and sanitation of the town. It was through the instrumentality of its chairman that Kingstown obtained the munificent offering of a free Free Library from that prince of generosity, Andrew Carnegie. What the benefit of reading is to those who share the quiet life of an English colony can readily be imagined. St. Vincent has suffered from several visitations but there are not wanting signs of general improvement.

It is a little striking that despite all that has occurred, there is but little destitution and poverty which cannot be met by the Chief Relieving Officer. This speaks volumes for the industry of the natives who are simple folk and well-contented to work for what in the mother country would be considered very low wages. It is curious to watch them on a Saturday when they come to

---

*Motor cars and buses have now superseded ponies.

dispose of their produce and make their purchases for the coming week in the market place. My own impression of them is that they are a quiet, law-abiding and civil people. A striking characteristic is the fervour with which they conduct their religious services in their own homes. On a Sunday evening, nearly every house passed seems to have its own little coterie of hymn-singing worshippers. They seem to prefer this quiet form of service to the public churches. Yet the cathedral, the Wesleyan and the Catholic clergy are all active and have large congregations.

A very welcome and encouraging gleam of hope for Vincelonians (sic) has been occasioned by the general praise bestowed on the quality of the cotton grown in the island. Sir Daniel Morris the agricultural expert did not hesitate to inform the British Cotton Growing Association that this superiority was accounted for by the natural conditions of the soil of St. Vincent. This no doubt explains the superiority which commands for the cotton of St. Vincent a higher price than is given for any other kind grown in any other portion of the British Empire.

Robert E. Noble

———————————◆∞◆◆———————————

Health Is Better Than Wealth

It is like a dream that I am again in this beautiful land of my nativity to spend what has been termed "a well-earned furlough."

After nine years' residence in Central America, where I administered to the spiritual needs of the Anglicans, I was, indeed, glad to come and to bring with me my wife and child, especially as the former, like myself, was in ill health wrought by malarial fever contracted in the place where I laboured.

It was gratifying, on arrival in June 1910, to take up residence under the roof of my old home at Victoria Park where, within four weeks, the climatic influence unmistakably asserted itself and brought about a remarkable improvement in the condition of our health. I was then encouraged by all interested to visit and reside in almost every notable health resort the island so richly affords, and certainly with my little family by my side, I availed myself of every opportunity. I ascended the mountains, roamed in the valleys, and enjoyed the balmy breeze of the sea as I rowed along, enchanted by the magnificent scenery.

I can now entirely appreciate and endorse the numerous expressions of opinion pertaining to the unsurpassing salubrity of the climate of St. Vincent to which island many visitors have applied their own familiar names, indicative of their admiration and gratitude, which are by no means misnomers.

Rev. (now Canon) Benj. A. Samuel

I had not landed at St. Vincent an hour before I felt convinced that I was among the kindest and most hospitable people I had ever met. The week I spent in the island was one of the brightest of my life and I hope to return again some day.

The scenery of St. Vincent is as beautiful as any of the ten islands I visited in the Caribbean Sea. The bathing at The Villa was greatly enjoyed by Mr. Staucliffe and myself. The trip in a canoe to Chateau Belair and Peters Hope was in every way delightful. The keen intelligence of the chief planters made the mission of Sir Daniel Morris and myself on behalf of cotton growing intensely interesting and made the success of that industry in St. Vincent an absolute certainty. I made friendships there which I hope may prove lifelong.

I must not forget the delightful day spent at Argyle.

E. L. Oliver

To anyone who knows the West Indies it is a cause of wonder that so few English tourists should come to see them. The beauty of these gorgeous islands must be seen to be believed. The wealth of colour on land and sea and in sky is indescribable; even the pen of a Ruskin would fail.

Tourists from Britain flock to the Canary Islands so that in Las Palmas alone there are four large English hotels, besides numerous native establishments all more or less catering for visitors; yet the Canaries are not to be compared with these islands of the Caribbean.

No doubt some who would come here are deterred by fears of excessive heat and raging fevers. They may purge their minds of all such fears. Of St. Vincent at least I can speak from experience. I came to it from a cold Scotch spring and have remained during the hottest months of the year. My health was never better; I have not known a day's discomfort, much less sickness in the six months of my stay. The climate from Christmas to May is described as ideal by those who know it. I have no experience of that season but can testify that what are considered the worst months leave little to be desired in point of weather. Always the heat is tempered by cooling breezes.

There are many attractions for the tourist. If he knows anything of his country's naval history, his pulse will quicken as he sails over seas where gallant fights were fought and memorable victories won. If he has an eye for nature's beauties, he will see some of the most gorgeous and magnificent scenery in the world—valleys that are like vales of paradise—little picturesque villages in palm-fringed sandy bays which are like pages out of a romance. He may ride or drive, fish, bathe, boat under conditions which are simply perfect. A month in St. Vincent would be a never-to-be-forgotten memory of delight.

Yacht-like sailing craft of from ten to fifty tons ply between the islands and carry passengers. The adventurous can taste the delights of whale fishing in the season. The neighbouring cays can be explored; there are mountain peaks for the climbers, and the "Soufriere" with its grand lake crater.

As for accommodation, there is a good hotel in Kingstown with a most moderate tariff, while in nearly all the smaller towns there is a rest room for travellers, where for a shilling or two, one can get a spotless and comfortable bed.*

It is a safe thing to say that any tourist who does try the West Indies will be glad that he did so.

Rev. W. S. Provand

Knockdolian, Colmonell, Ayrshire
4th November 1913
Mr. Robexrt M. Anderson
Dear Sir,

If I had time to spare it would interest me very much to write a little about my impression of St. Vincent. But I am too busy.

St. Vincent was the first of the beautiful West Indian Islands in which I stayed in the early months of 1911, and the hospitality of His Honour the Administrator and of the Honourable Mrs. Murray, together with the kindness of every one whom I met not only made my visit to St. Vincent itself most enjoyable but enabled me to appreciate much more fully what I saw afterwards in the other islands. St. Vincent undoubtedly leads the world in cotton growing. I was told also that it holds the first place in the world as a producer of arrowroot—a wonderful record for so small an island.

The beauties of the island can perhaps be described by others. They are far beyond the power of my pen.

I can only hope that at some date not too far in the future I may have another opportunity of repeating the visit made to St. Vincent which was certainly the most interesting as well as the most enjoyable visit I ever paid.

Yours truly,

John W. Mcconnell

<hr>

*There are now two hotels in Kingstown, also boarding houses; The New Guest House at McKie's Hill near the Murray Road; bungalows at Villa and Edinbobo, besides bay houses.

Visit of Princess Marie Louise

*Princess Marie Louise of Schleswig-Holstein is very much a royal personage. She is a granddaughter of Queen Victoria, a monarch whose extraordinary goodness and attachment to her people will ever be amongst the most pleasing memories associated with the British Empire. She is also a first cousin of our reigning Sovereign, King George V, who day by day proves that he will walk directly in the footsteps of a father who proved the most popular Sovereign of modern times. The life of Princess Marie Louise has not been without trials, but their only effect seems to have been to strengthen the simple trustful nature inherited from her illustrious grandmother. In consequence, she enjoys a popularity which innate sympathy never fails to win. Her kindness finds its outlet not only in Court society, but in the direct ministration of deeds of mercy to the London poor. It is well known that she is personally interested in a home or settlement of the East End workers of England's mighty metropolis, and that her visits to the denizens of this overcrowded part of London are frequent and the delight of many a poor artisan seamstress.

She has now shown the natives of St. Vincent (themselves an unaffected, homely people) that her heart finds a warm corner none the less for the native population of all His Majesty's colonies. Herself a capital horsewoman, Princess Marie Louise has been able to make acquaintance with the people of St. Vincent in their surroundings, both on hill and in dale, and to sympathise with their simple agricultural life. At the outset, the idea of sojourning with Honourable Mrs. Murray was entirely a personal matter. Later on, when the Princess was given to understand how valuable would be a visit of one month's duration to a colony like St. Vincent, and how enthusiastically she would be received as a royal personage by the loyal inhabitants of the island, another thought occurred to Her Highness. The West Indies form so valuable a portion of the King's Empire that the chance of visiting one island thus afforded made it easy to obtain access to the other colonies in the Caribbean group.

As soon as King George became acquainted of his cousin's intention, he at once, with his strong grasp of political thought, perceived that through the personality of the Royal Princess, the door became open for himself as Sovereign to enter largely into the welcome and loyalty certain to be aroused by such a visit. He accordingly emphasised his royal pleasure at the projected tour and deigned to send, by the voice of his cousin, a very special message of greeting to all his West Indian subjects. Then it came to pass that the projected

---

*This contribution appeared by permission in the *Barbados Weekly Illustrated* paper (April 19 and 26, 1913).

visit to the Administrator of St. Vincent had a more far-reaching result than was originally intended. The honour of entertaining for the greater period so distinguished a guest fell by good luck to one of the ablest Administrators at the time doing work in the King's West Indian colonies.

The Honourable C. Gideon Murray, brother of Lord Murray of Elibank, has undoubtedly been most successful in his direction of St. Vincent. For three years he has displayed an energy and enterprise in dealing with the practical needs of St. Vincent which are beginning to show there its own brave harvest of achievement. When he assumed the reins of Government, the finances of St. Vincent were at low ebb and commerce was depressed, but now under his regime a substantial surplus is secured and the island marches bravely on the road to prosperity. Mr. Murray has been aided in his efforts by a charming wife whose social zeal in uplifting St. Vincent has merited the praise of all. It was, indeed, a veritable triumph, and one well deserved, when so popular a hostess was able to secure, and that for a whole month, so illustrious a guest at Government House as Princess Marie Louise. In the past, visits of royalty to St. Vincent have been few and far between. It is true that King George V himself landed in the island many years ago in the company of his much lamented brother the Duke of Clarence. This was in 1880 when both princes were naval officers on board the *Bacchante*. Once, also on a certain fleeting occasion in the sixties, the late Duke of Edinburgh weighed anchor in the harbour of St. Vincent. Both royal visits are now memories of long ago. When it was known that for a whole month a royal personage was to remain as a guest of Government House, the news seemed to the Vincelonians too good to be true.

The first island in the West Indies to be reached from England by the Princess was Barbados, and the fervent citizens of that enthusiastically loyal colony were naturally proud of the fact that Her Highness first set foot on their strand. At Barbados the Princess Marie Louise first experienced what a West Indian greeting could be, and it was here that she delivered the first of her many speeches and conveyed for transmission by cable to the whole of the West Indies the King's most gracious message.

There are those who have not hesitated to call King George V an orator. Certain it is that the words used by His Majesty have in them at times the ring of true eloquence and what Shakespeare calls, "The power to stir men's blood." King George V is known to be an expert in his knowledge of his own colonial possessions, and his people are aware that his interest and love of the Empire are not one whit less than that manifested by his late Imperial father. Everyone also knows that the Sovereign has publicly recalled pleasant recollections still clinging to him of the days spent on the *Bacchante* when cruising in the West Indian portion of the British Dominions as a naval officer.

266

In the gracious message delivered by the Princess Marie Louise, these notes of the King found adequate expression. George V made a graceful allusion to the extreme interest with which he had noted how successful of recent years his West Indian colonies had emerged from commercial depression and expanded their trade. St. Vincent is assuredly a good example in point. Until a few years back, this island was begging an Imperial grant in aid. Now she is self-supporting and her trade is increasing by leaps and bounds. The King assured his people that he knew full well West Indian loyalty to be of sure and certain quality, and expressed satisfaction that a member of his own family should be reciprocating to his own people the expression of his own personal regard as their King and Emperor. It is superfluous to say with what rapturous applause the message was greeted or to add that the building in which the exhibition of needlework was held, and the streets of Barbados were alike crowded and alive with masses of zealous loyal subjects. The Governor of Barbados (Sir Leslie Probyn) said tactfully in his reply that the Sovereign had expressed nothing in the message which all Barbadians did not already know only too well, but nevertheless all hearts could not fail to be deeply touched at being the recipients of so truly regal a message.

On reading the public telegrams of that evening, the people of St. Vincent could hardly await with patience the coming of the Princess on the 24th February with its opportunity of showing a loyal response. It will be long before the scene presented on the Kingstown jetty on the occasion of the landing of Princess Marie Louise is forgotten in St. Vincent. When the *Berbice* hove in sight, the crowd collected on the beach was of thick dimensions, every official in readiness and the guard of honour in its place, all and everyone being on the keen edge of excitement. There came boom of a rocket as a royal salute, and then Princess Marie Louise, accompanied by the Administrator, stepped ashore. At once Her Highness was presented with a beautiful bouquet by Miss Veronica Noble, a diminutive little lady of four and a half years of age, to whom she returned her grateful thanks by a kiss. The band struck up the national anthem, a royal salute of arms was given a moment later, and the members of Legislative and Executive Councils and their wives were personally presented to the Princess, who had moved to the end of the jetty to receive an address of welcome from the Kingstown Corporation. In simple, unaffected language, Princess Marie Louise returned her acknowledgments expressing a lively anticipation that she would find pleasure in the beautiful island she had come to visit. Her Highness must have felt extremely gratified at the royal welcome afforded. The town had been gaily decorated with bunting, and her drive en route to Government House was taken under gracefully constructed arches and past long lines of enthusiastic Vincelonians, who cheered themselves hoarse with loyalty. After a few days interval the inhabitants of St. Vincent saw once more in public view their royal visitor.

The Attorney General of the Colony (Honourable Robert E. Noble) formally greeted Her Highness at the court gate when, after passing the guards of volunteers and police and listening to the strains of the national anthem, she was escorted by the Chief Justice (His Honour Robert Blair Roden) to the Legislative Chamber. Here in the presence of a closely packed assembly the Administrator read his speech aloud.

He began by offering a warm welcome to the Princess and predicted that Her Highness' visit would be some consolation for the rather bad cotton season to which the island had recently been subjected. He alluded to the improvement in the arrowroot productive profits of the colony and was able to show a handsome surplus accruing from the past year to the revenue.

On the whole, His Honour said the colony had undoubtedly prospered in 1911-1912, and the time had surely arrived when St. Vincent might with safety launch forth into schemes for its material betterment without fear of incurring serious debt. The speech was listened to with genuine interest.

Mr. Murray was succeeded by the Honourable Conrad J. Simmons, who respectfully wished Her Highness enjoyment of health and a happy holiday in St. Vincent—a colony which he said, though one of the smallest in His Majesty's Dominions beyond the seas, nevertheless provided a home for nearly 50,000 as loyal subjects as could be found anywhere in His Majesty's vast Imperial Empire.

On the following day, a garden party at Government House was given in honour of the Princess by the Administrator and the Honourable Mrs. Murray. About 120 persons received the honour of a special invitation. On this interesting occasion the Princess shook hands with each guest as he or she was presented by Mrs. Murray, and later in the afternoon Her Highness signalised the social event by planting a mahogany tree in the Botanic Gardens which adjoin Government House. The simple kindness and courtesy shown by the Princess placed all at their ease and contributed especially to make this garden party a most memorable and delightful social function in St. Vincent.

Princess Marie Louise being of an energetic temperament and her host one to enjoy much the opportunity of showing his distinguished guest some of the romantic beauty of this island, rides were judiciously arranged by which Her Highness could reach the most beautiful scenes of St. Vincent.

The Leeward District—perhaps the most picturesque portion of the colony—was first essayed. Everywhere, when once it was known that the Princess was adopting so simple a method of seeing Vincelonian scenery, warm interest was shown amongst the inhabitants.

Each little village on the coast or mainland where it was known that Her Highness would be likely to pass became the scene of decorative display, whilst almost a general holiday seemed to be taken as though by common consent. The native population appeared most eager to greet the Princess with their humble tokens of loyalty. Lowmans Village, Camden Park (where small huts had been constructed to house the many sufferers from the terrible eruption of 1902), Layou, a picturesque small town on the Leeward coast, Barrouallie, Troumaca on the Hill were all in turn passed by the Princess and her cavalcade of equestrians. It might be most said that one grand triumphal progress marked Her Highness' route and such a demonstration of simple loyalty was manifested as would have done credit to any English colony.

The Princess passed under palm-leaved arches, and amid a brave display of bunting and at every one of the little towns and hamlets an address of welcome was read.

To all these tokens of esteem the Princess invariably replied in simple and kindly words. At length Chateau Belair was reached, the majestic but terrible mountain of La Soufriere loomed into sight. A great gathering of about 500 persons had collected at the Police Court to attest their sense of the honour done them by the Princess' visit and here again a speech was accorded.

Once the Leeward side of St. Vincent had been honoured by the Princess, it would manifestly have been an invidious thing had not another journey to the Windward District been organised. Accordingly, a further riding expedition was formed, and once again on the other side of the island the native population was afforded its opportunity of manifesting heartfelt attachment to the Throne. The route taken to Windward was from Kingstown direct to Georgetown; but this implied that progress had to be effected through the interesting towns of Calliaqua, Bridgetown, and Colonarie, before the halting stage of Grand Sable was reached by the Princess.

The simple decorations, the loyal zeal, the enthusiasm of the crowds, the touching emotion of the native population all along the route to Georgetown baffle description. They are all alike indescribable. The Princess very naturally was not a little moved by what she witnessed. She promised over and over again these humble natives that she would assure the King in person, so soon as she returned to the Mother Country, of the depth and strength of Vincelonian loyalty. Everywhere, the Princess responded to addresses of welcome. Her simple, sweet thanks won golden opinions and will endear her to the memory of all. Her Highness can never forget the scenes through which she passed, The tropical scenery of St. Vincent filled her with admiration. The weather proved propitious and her trip an unqualified success.

Princess Marie Louise returned to Government House on 20th March, quite enchanted with her outing. Easter Sunday was reached three days later, but even then it was impossible for Her Highness to be quietly restful when she received information that the Volunteers had actually gone into camp for their annual March and looked forward to being inspected by her. On Easter

Sunday afternoon Princess Marie Louise rode out with the Administrator to enkindle, as she alone could, the islanders' martial enthusiasm by praise for the brave fellows belonging to the volunteer and police force, to whom St. Vincent looks for protection in the event of invasion or outbreak of riot.

The last public act of the Princess in St. Vincent was to preside at a meeting held in the Colonial Hospital at Kingstown for the purpose of personally presenting with medals those nurses who had successfully secured prizes for competency in their art. Her Highness, in a most graceful speech, betrayed her own genuine enthusiasm for the nursing profession—the highest vocation as she styled it open to womanhood. A new wing for the use of nurses is shortly to be added to the Colonial Hospital, which is to bear the name of the Princess Marie Louise Wing in her honour.

When at length the 26th March arrived and her month's visit was up, it could truthfully be said that the Princess had left no stone unturned to show her genuine interest in St. Vincent. On her departure Her Highness spoke most delightfully of the effect which the beautiful grandeur of St. Vincent's scenery had aroused in her, and also most gratefully of the warmth of the reception everywhere. To use a simple expression, the Princess Marie Louise seemed to have taken to St. Vincent as heartily as St. Vincent had taken to her. At length the last day of her visit dawned. When she left Kingstown in the evening, the jetty was brave with lights and was a grand spectacle. The crowd with its splendid enthusiastic farewell left nothing to be desired in the consistency of loyalty which had been kept up from the first to the last. With genuine regret people returned to their homes hoping that the Princess would be induced to honour the island with a second visit at no distant date. How much the feeling of loyalty has been awakened and the moral good done by such a visit as this cannot be measured. Time will show the result to be strikingly beneficial to the colony.

Honourable R. E. Noble

———◆◇◆———

There are in St. Vincent as in the other West Indies many signs of occupation by savage peoples before the settlement. The old stone chisels are commonly called "thunderbolts" and are now believed to have fallen in thunderstorms from the sky. This idea is almost general through the world wherever stone implements are to be found and the memory of their use has faded. Even among the present Caribs of St. Vincent there is no knowledge of the origin and meaning of these stone objects, though they were in use less than 150 years ago.

These antiquities in the Lesser Antilles are commonly spoken of as Carib, but they must represent also the relics of other preceding races, though it has not been possible yet or attempted to differentiate them in this sense. In St. Vincent we have picture rocks or petroglyphs, stone implements, shell implements, and pottery. A few interments have been found, but these unfortunately have not been observed and described by responsible persons.

Petroglyphs—There are here both types described by Everard im Thurn in Guiana—the shallow and the deeply cut.

On the left hand of the Petit Bordel ravine high up among the bushes, on a small rock cliff are several shallow cut or rather scratched figures, of more or less human shape. The spot is difficult of access and the figures hard to trace.

In the middle of the glebe field, above the village of Barrouallie, is a small rock with a fine petroglyph. It represents a human face surrounded by a halo of thirteen rays. It is probable this may be a solar symbol, and the rays refer to the thirteen lunar months in the year.

On the right bank of the Layou River, not far from the point where the high road leaves the stream, is a massive boulder known locally as the "markstone", which bears on its smooth, water-worn surface a large figure with a human face. It is one of the finest petroglyphs in the West Indies.

In a cave in the left cliff of the Buccament valley near the sea, are several faces cut on the rocks.

On the extreme point of land on the Villa Estate, overlooking the northern strait between the mainland and Youngs Island, is a small petroglyph very much weathered, and hard to get at and find. It faces towards Youngs Island and is about 10 feet above sea level.

On the right bank of the Yambou River as it flows through the gorge are two picture stones which are very good specimens. Any native from the village of Mesopotamia nearby would direct a visitor to the spot. These two petroglyphs may be visited on horseback or in a light trap from Kingstown (now by motor car).

The only picture rock within easy reach of the town is that at the Villa*

Stone Implements—The relics of this class found in the Antilles belong to the period of polished stone, and no finer work of this kind is to be found anywhere in the world. It is characterized by the beautiful finish and often the elaboration of shape and ornamentation of the objects. Polished kelts or stone chisels of green stone or dark blue trachyte are common, and splendid specimens of axe heads may be obtained cheaply. The buyer can safely trust

---

*At Colonarie Estate, also near a stream not far from the buildings, there are artistic Carib inscriptions on the surface of a large stone.

any stone implement offered to him. The present labourers have neither the knowledge nor the patience to fake such articles. Occasionally a broken or bruised specimen is rubbed up, but this naive attempt to improve is easily detected.

None of the worked mullers of rubbing stones, so common in St. Kitts, are found in St. Vincent. Until recently the forms known were: (1) axe heads, plain and ornate, simple and winged; (2) kelts of all sizes; some petaloid, oval like the kernel of an almond, others of the Scandinavian type with straight sides, others again of aberrant shapes; (3) a few stone knives, sacrificial knives so-called; (4) banner stones, curious and elaborately shaped objects, some of large size, probably of symbolic meaning; (5) perforated sinkers or spindle whorls; (6) a very few stone bowls, one very elaborately carved in a geometric pattern.

The researches of the Rev. Thomas Huckerby, however, have brought to light a number of interesting domestic implements, which as is natural for tools intended for common use, show far less care and elaboration in shape and finish. Mr. Huckerby has identified the forms known to antiquaries as lap stones and querns, i.e. large slabs on which grinding and rubbing was done; ironing stones, large unshaped stones with under surface worn by use; small smooth stones used in polishing pottery; hammer stones; and some which he thinks were molds on which pottery was modelled. Numbers of these have been found together in a cache buried at a depth of several feet. This association pointed out their significance and confirmed his previous surmises with respect to forms he had collected. Mr. Huckerby's collections have been enthusiastically received and his opinions endorsed by scientists in Germany and the United States.

Shell Implements—Very few of the kelts of conch shell, so common in Barbados and some of the other islands, have been so far recognized in St. Vincent.

Pottery—It has been long known that curious pottery vessels and fragments, recognized to be of Amerindian work, may be found in Balliceaux, a small cay south of St. Vincent. After experience of aboriginal pottery in other islands, the writer some years ago hunted up and located a site of an Amerindian village on which fragments of pottery may be found in Petit Bordel valley, and since, a similar site in the neighbourhood of Biabou. Broken pots with incised patterns and modelled ornaments and some fragments with painted patterns have been collected. Fragments representing heads of various beasts and grotesque human faces are turned up in Mustique, a cultivated island south of St. Vincent.

These are, apparently, decorations of vessels. The object, however, may have had a symbolic or religious meaning.

272

Mr. Huckerby has been quite successful in the search for pottery, and certain sites, like that referred to at Petit Bordel, have yielded a number of fragments. A few pieces are complete enough to show the original size and form of the vessels.

The study of these relics shows us that the Amerindian islanders were a people well advanced in the neolithic (polished stone) period of culture. They were warlike, yet devoted to artistic decoration requiring patience and application. They well understood the potter's art as far as the processes of hand modelling and coiling went, but they knew nothing of the potter's wheel. They employed several colours both as slips and for painted patterns on their pot ware. No example of chipped flint has been found, though as in other West Indian Islands, rough flint flakes are common in association with the other refuse on the sites of their villages. They could drill hard stone and make keen edged tools without the use of flint.

Dr. C. W. Branch

A Prediction

That belt of islands known as the West Indies has been likened to a string of pearls set in a sapphire sea. None can doubt that the choicest gems are to be found in the Windwards. The late Sir Frederick Treves it was who dubbed the three largest of them *The Three Lovelies*, and had he been familiar with the Grenadines, most certainly they would have been *The Little Lovelies*. Whether large or small, authors and travellers have speculated times without number as to which is the fairest isle of them all and yet a consensus of opinion is hard to come by.

There are those who give the palm to that Antillian gem, St. Vincent. It was in 1498 that Columbus discovered her. Who knows but that ere 1948 she may be rediscovered? I predict that those lovers of island homes and island pursuits, the erstwhile discoverers of Muskoka, one day will herald with joy the finding of a gem whose Naples-like bay is but a prelude to her glories within.

V. W. L.

273

EXTRACTS

From *The Vincentian*

That Beautiful Green Isle

Some incidents linger always in one's memory and one of the most prominent in mine is the morning we anchored in the bay of Kingstown, St. Vincent, British West Indies.

The sun was shining brightly in the deep blue sky, flecked with white clouds, and a few of a nimbus character, and being around 6 o'clock it was ideally cool.

I went on deck as soon as I could, and there I beheld a beautiful picture, the background of which was formed by hills and mountains covered with vegetation of many different hues of green and brown, bright flower-bearing trees mingled with coconut and palm trees. Pretty houses and bungalows dotted here and there looked down upon the clean little town of Kingstown.

I rooted out my friend and travelling companion and we decided to go ashore and have a look around. In about ten or fifteen minutes we were alighting from the rowing boat which brought us from our ship, and stepping on to the jetty we were soon advised that the best thing to do was to take a car and see some of the island. Our ship, we were informed, was to sail about midday, so our time was very limited, but we made the most of the short time we did have and saw quite a lot.

This little paradise is well worth a visit, not one of a few hours, but a visit extending over three or four months or longer. I am not speaking now from the impressions I gained during that drive my friend and I took but from knowledge gained during a four months holiday, because we decided to return to St. Vincent the following year.

The climate is a healthy one; there is nearly always a beautiful and refreshing breeze blowing, day and night, and during the cool months, which are from, say November to April, the climate is ideal.

The roads are in very good order, which enables one to enjoy to the full the many picturesque drives in various parts of the island. The one I have in mind at the moment is from the capital town of Kingstown to the next little town of Georgetown. This takes one almost the entire distance of about 23 miles along the Windward Coast, affording scenery which reminds one so much of days spent in Devon or Cornwall—stretches of rocky coast upon which the deep blue Atlantic Ocean sends her rollers, tipped with white horses bounding over and over, unceasingly.

Then, let us take a drive to the other side of the island (the Leeward) and we will be greeted with an entirely different type of scenery. We face the Caribbean Sea this side, but before we reach the coast we pass through fields of arrowroot (the island's chief product, of course) through sugar estates, over hills commanding glorious views from every point, and through beautiful green valleys fringed with groves of coconut palms and all kinds of tropical fruit trees.

We took one of the little seaside bungalows on the Windward Coast, which are available for a very moderate sum per month to visitors, and we were thus able to enjoy as much sea bathing as we wished.

Yes, I think when able, I shall pay that Green Isle another visit for there is no better place for a thoroughly peaceful and restful spell than St. Vincent.

M.S.S.

Jottings on the Grenadines

The exquisite scenery, salubrious climate and soothing breeze are attractions second to none. The Grenadines invite the people to their enchanted shores to sojourn awhile in an atmosphere of romance. A voyage through the Grenadines is an income of pleasure and satisfaction that will last through a lifetime.

On a fair day, after leaving Bequia in a southerly direction going from island to island, there is much to delight the eye as throughout the entire route you are surrounded by the charm, mystery and scenic glory of a fabled land. Wonder succeeds wonder as your tour reveals islands of unparalleled fascination. These isles—which lie like an emerald necklace—present a never-to-be-forgotten sight, as the mountain peaks of St. Vincent and Grenada—which are situated at each end—look down on them as if smiling with complacency. When viewed in an easterly or westerly direction they are unrivalled and can easily be placed among the chief beauty spots of the world.

Do not for one moment think the scenery of the Grenadines dies away when the sun sets. Oh no! Nature is not so unkind. During a moonlit night, when all is still and hushed into silence and the moon lets forth her light from a cloudless sky, the beauty increases. What the sunlight hides the moonlight reveals. And as the traveller's eyes range in fanciful imagination, he is at a loss for words to express himself, and growing curious at the sight, he finds himself as though he were in dreamland, only to be aroused from his lethargic state by a voice saying, "These are fairy isles miraculously broken off, cast adrift and are here seen floating on turquoise sea."

The sea is ideal for bathing and other aquatic sports. The pearly-white, sandy beaches make the water attractively transparent and invigorating, and give it enough interest to enchant the conchologist.

Anonymous

275

A Visitor's Impressions of St. Vincent

I have enjoyed my stay here immensely. My health has improved, which condition I attribute chiefly to the rejuvenating influences of the breezes, the continuous scenic beauty, and the pleasing surroundings in which it was my good fortune to share with others in need of nature's invaluable gift—health.

You ask my impressions of the sanitary condition of St. Vincent—well! I have not been able to see very many of your villages, but I have seen a great deal of Kingstown, your chief town, and as a sanitary inspector from Trinidad—which is reputed to have the most up-to-date public health system in the West Indies, I can say that the sanitary condition here is surprisingly good.

As one walks along your streets, the striking cleanliness of your drains from yards and wherever situated, the almost total absence of unsightly and offensive accumulations of refuse, your clean yards particularly in the slum quarters and your up-to-date systems for the ultimate disposal of city refuse give the explanation why so small a number of flies is seen around their favourite resorts, a few being markets, retail shops, bake houses, barrack yards and dumping grounds. It also shows appreciation of education along sanitary lines by the citizens. I hope that I will be able to revisit St. Vincent in the near future when I shall enjoy more fully its salubrious climate.

Of course, I will do my best to induce those of my friends who may be contemplating a holiday, whether for health or pleasure, to make St. Vincent their first and last port of call.

F. Collymore, Sanitary Inspector
Couva, Trinidad, B.W.I.

The Editor
The Vincentian
Arnos Vale, St. Vincent
19th April 1937

> *Dear Sir,*
>
> *The following will give some idea of my impressions which you are at liberty to publish.*
>
> *Of all the West Indian Islands I have visited during the past 6 years, I find St. Vincent undoubtedly the healthiest and most congenial climate.*
>
> *The fresh sea breezes make the tropical heat easily bearable by Europeans. The town is clean and well-ordered, and even the largest of this group of is-*

lands would do well to imitate the width and layout of Grenville Street with its prolongation including Halifax, Granby and Tyrrel Streets.

The amenities of the Aquatic Club make sea bathing delightfully easy and pleasant, and the scenery especially in the Mesopotamia Valley and on the Leeward Coast is superb.

Yours truly,

L. V. Haysman

⟶◆∞◆⟵

From "Notes and Reflections on St. Vincent"

St. Benedict's College (1937)—We are all greatly indebted to you for the welcome and great deal of kindness you extended to us during the three weeks we spent in St. Vincent, a holiday we finally considered too short. The best indication that both masters and boys had a really enjoyable holiday among you all is the fact that everyone is quite determined to revisit the island. The beautiful memories of our first landing on your hospitable shores; of the fine impression made on us by the neatness to Kingstown during our first drive from the Bay to Edinboro; of visits to places of great interest, in which St. Vincent certainly abounds, such as the Soufriere, the Dry River, the Spa; and above all, what puts all these in the shade, of the happy hours spent in the company of the Vincentians themselves, a people unbeaten in hospitality. All these memories still live in our hearts, and in some way or other communicate themselves to the other college boys and relatives who did not make the trip, so that these have already made up their minds to choose St. Vincent for their holidays next year.

After five weeks, the boys are still talking of the tour as freshly as they did one or two days after we landed. It has done the college a great deal of good. The boys have returned to work with a spirit which I can only attribute to the holiday in your pleasant island. Now we know why so many Trinidadians have been anxious to go to St. Vincent, and the best we can do is to encourage anyone proposing a visit to a W.I. isle to make it the Land of Arrowroot. Not only in the town, but in the distant country districts as well, the people are very kind and entertaining. How can we forget the enjoyable half-day we spent at Barrouallie!

Again, I must say we shall return some day. But so many San Fernandians are also keen on the trip that they will need a San Fernandian quarter.

Anonymous

⟶◆∞◆⟵

Notes of His Majesty the late King George V
from his cruise on HMS *Bacchante* when His Majesty
and the late Prince Albert Victor visited St. Vincent in the year 1880

Feb. 7th—This island has a more peaked appearance than any other we have seen; all the lower peaks are wooded and evidently volcanic.

Feb. 8th—Church this morning under the awnings on the quarterdeck, after which Archdeacon Laborde called, and young Mr. Cowie...

Feb. 9th—At 2 p.m. four of us landed and, having been met by Mr. Cowie on the pier, rode out by Bolton Tower to his house at Belvidere. The road first climbed the hills behind the town and then wound down to the south coast of the island, from which pretty views of the Grenadines, Bequia and the rest constantly present themselves. After passing under a long and lofty grove of palm trees that reminded us of that at Codrington College at Barbados, "their tall immoveable pillar stems looking the more immoveable beneath the toss and flicker of the long leaves as they wake out of their sunlit sleep and rage impatiently for a while before the mountain gusts and fall asleep again", we came down to the beach by the curious little island of Duvernette in the offing, with its steep rocky sides and little hut on the top amid its greenery, where a captain in the 10th Hussars selected to live happily alone for a considerable period, and which now is sometimes used as a lazaretto...

On to the road to Kingstown, from which, however, we turned off to the right and so went up Dorsetshire Hill, at top of which there are remains of an old fort now dismantled and used as a school. It commands, as from the summit of a natural amphitheatre, a sweeping view over the whole of the bay below and of Kingstown with its parallel streets stretching at our feet and of the two branches of lower hills which embrace it on either side. Down to the 6 o'clock officer's boat after a most enjoyable ride. In the evening we landed again and went up to Government House to a dance, which poor Mr. Dundas (the Lieutenant Governor) who is in very ill health, gave. He got up on purpose to welcome us but soon afterward retired to bed leaving Mrs. Dundas to do the honours. The house is entirely of wood, and one of the most prettily situated in the West Indies among its grove of nutmeg and palm trees but in rather a dilapidated condition. A new one is about to be built. The garden is the first botanical one established in the West Indies. This is the last dance we shall have in the West Indies, as Lent begins in two days' time.

On 10th—A cricket match was played between the *Bacchante* and the Saint Vincent Club in which the former was defeated—68 and 84 respectively.

At 2 p.m. we landed with three shipmates and went for a ride with Archdeacon Laborde, who is one of the oldest inhabitants of the island. We went through the town and had a look at the cricket match. The party rode to the

Leeward or western side of the island and returned just in time to get off by the 6 o'clock boat.

Feb. 11th—Landed at 9.30 a.m. with the Commander, Roxby, Burrows, and Murray and rode right across the centre of the island, going first up by Belair into the Marriaqua Valley and over the summit. Here we had a lovely view of the distant islands away to the south, as well as of the uplands in the centre of the island, their valleys and rolling hills all of course feathered over with verdure.

The Captain overtook us after luncheon, riding with the Archdeacon. We then came down and went through the Yambou Pass, which is the best thing we have seen of the kind out of Switzerland.

Feb. 12th—Though it is a pouring wet morning, the Archdeacon came on board to say goodbye before we started. We lay to off Chateau Belair and landed the picnic party, who proceeded perseveringly to try and reach the summit of the Soufriere. As soon as the cutter had brought the officers on board, we hoisted her up and proceeded at 6 p.m., under steam, north by east on our course to St. Lucia.

From the *Voice* of St. Lucia, written by an officer with reference to St. Vincent after the visit of the Squadron, 1894

Socially, our stay was delightful. From the Administrator downwards we were hospitably received and heartily welcomed. The Club was placed at the disposal of the officers, and balls and dances were given in their honour. Several dances were also given to the petty officers. Two cricket matches were played in the Victoria Park amid great excitement. The lawn tennis courts were in constant use and delightful country rides at one's option. The day before leaving we landed a battalion of "small arm" men who marched past the Administrator Colonel J. H. Sandwith (CB), and an enormous admiring crowd assembled on the parade ground. After marching past first at the "quick" then at the "double" to the music of the mass drum and fife bands of the squadron, the battalion of the seamen performed the review exercise, the marines following with the bayonet exercise. Both of these were exceedingly well carried out.

From *The Guardian* of January 2, 1896
A Fortnight in St. Vincent: A West Indian Holiday

When the arrival of an invitation synchronizes with one's ability to accept it, one feels that one's lot is really a happy one. Such a lot was mine last Easter when, after the toils of term, we packed our portmanteaus and prepared to pay a visit to our friend, the Administrator of St. Vincent. The voyage is barely a twelve-hours run from Barbados. You go on board the mail steamer at five in the afternoon and you wake up at six in the morning in the picturesque little harbour of Kingstown and climb on deck to find a soft breeze blowing off the mountains freshening your faculties after the close and heated atmosphere of the cabin. Right opposite on the shore front as you lie in the harbour are the police barracks and a long row of stores and shops; behind these, half-way up the slope of the hills, which semi-circularly enclose the bay, there peep out here and there from among the forest foliage some well-built houses, the residences of various officials, and there the red-roofed gables of Government House, our destination. Far higher, away to the left, on Battery Point, poised on the extreme edge of the cliff which bounds the harbour, is the old fort, now a signal station; and on the opposite side of the bay a range of black, rocky cliffs terminates the landward vision. Behind in the soft blue of the early morning haze lies the island of Bequia, nine miles to the southward.

The port officer having come on board, we were conducted to the landing stage and put into the buggy waiting for us.

The town, as we drove through it, appeared a cleanly looking, well-laid-out place, possessing wider streets and tidier houses than many other West Indian towns of more than double its size, while the black gravel of crushed lava proved a very welcome change and relief to the eyes after the glaring white coral roads of Barbados. Passing the Cathedral dedicated to St. George, the Roman Catholic chapel and the Wesleyan place of worship, which all stand close together at the western end of the town, we skirted a small open space, dignified with the appellation of Victoria Park, where a new cricket ground was evidently in course of preparation. Then, after winding for some distance alongside the Botanical Gardens, we emerged at their upper end upon the Administrator's house, where a cheery welcome awaited us from our host and hostess, and attempting *chota hazri* [Ed note: a light meal eaten very early in the morning] quenched the pangs of a rising hunger. The view from Government House (and there is only one view, for the forest-clad hills rise abruptly from immediately behind the house) reverses the picture as seen from the harbour, and most lovely it is. And in the evening when the red sun dips into the sea, and the low orange after-glow "lingers in the last-lit west," and the brief tropical twilight rapidly darkens, and the fire-flies flit among the shrubs and glint against the black amphitheatre of forest around the bay, it is hard to find words to paint the enchantment of the scene.

The old fort, with its buildings cunningly constructed in the very sides of the rock, is utilised in various ways by the Government. Part of the former barracks form a poor asylum and another portion of the buildings lower down the cliff are set apart as the "lazaretto".

I accompanied the Administrator one afternoon on a visit of inspection, and climbed to the lookout box of the signalman, whence a different view up the Leeward Coast is obtained, and a glimpse of the inland scenery—ranges of hills tumbled up in charming confusion in one of mother Nature's primaeval volcanic throes.

Perhaps the early mornings were the most enjoyable time of the day, when one climbed the steep path up the hill at the back of the house, cut out from the wild forest, with orchids hanging from the tree trunks and tufts of wild pine and lichen bunching on every bough. Some 30 yards above the house a tennis court of black gravel has been quite recently excavated on the slope by a wondrous feat of engineering skill. Above this, on the verge of the aboriginal greenwood, one could sit in unbroken solitude and read *The Guardian(s)* of the last mail or indulge in quiet daydreams in the almost complete silence, scarcely disturbed by the rustling of the lizards in the grass or the chirping of the crickets in the trees. After breakfast strolls in the Botanical Gardens revealed many new varieties of hibiscus and other tropical flowering shrubs; nor did the enthusiastic curator ever tire of imparting more information upon the cultivation of cocoa, nutmegs and other fruitful trees than I have been able to assimilate or remember. The afternoons were filled up with rides or lawn tennis.

On Sunday the Cathedral claimed our attention. It is a fine, roomy structure, but spoilt by heavy galleries and a towering pulpit out of place midway down the nave.* The people in the gallery immediately behind the preacher can read his manuscript over his shoulder while those in the gallery opposite alone have the privilege of hearing him distinctly. He may indeed preach well, but the greater part of the congregation is not edified. Like most of the large buildings in the Windward Islands, the Cathedral bears the mark of injuries caused by hurricanes. The last severe cyclone was in 1886, when most of the churches in St. Vincent were demolished.** It should be a source of no little satisfaction to the church people of the island that in so short a time their energetic efforts have been so successful as to rebuild and restore the parish churches and chapels to their present condition, for the church in the Windward Islands diocese is disestablished and disendowed and entirely dependent upon its own resources, together with some little aid given by the English so-

---

*This defect has since been remedied. In 1903—when the transept and chancel were improved by the substitution of encaustic tiles for the cement floor through the generosity of the late C. J. Simmons—the pulpit was transferred from the south to the north side of the nave and placed in a better position. The organ also was removed from the north to the south of the transept and improved the position and number of the ladies' choir. The Church Workers Guild which was started about this time deserves much credit for the interest taken in the cleanliness and decorations of the cathedral at all times, and also in the looking after the choir surplices and the altar linen.
**There was a hurricane in 1898 of far greater violence.

cieties. Of late years since the decline in the sugar and arrowroot markets, the struggle has been more than hard to support even a few clergy to minister to the spiritual wants of the population; and year by year it seems to become an increasingly difficult matter to raise the necessary funds. Nor do the English missionary societies appear to adequately realise that the work of sustaining the faith of those who, without the church's influence would undoubtedly relapse into heathenism, has as true a claim to be regarded as real missionary work and to be aided accordingly, as the work of carrying Gospel to those who have never heard it. But, unlike India and Africa, which seem to appropriate almost the whole of the Englishman's interest in missions, the West Indies possess no magical glamour of romance to conjure with. There is only a poverty-stricken church striving to faithfully discharge its duty, and endeavouring in patience and self-denial to supply the bread where otherwise there would be a spiritual famine. One reads with something more than amazement of the success attending the appeals which frequently appear in the English papers from some wealthy London church for so many thousands of pounds to supply it with luxuries, while at the same time the pressing claims of impoverished churches in the colonies are entirely ignored—churches manned by fellow countrymen and struggling for existence, not lacking luxuries but simply bread. Some idea of the spiritual destitution of the church in St. Vincent may be gathered from the fact that, whereas in 1887 ten priests and two deacons were engaged in ministering to the Anglican population, there are now (1894) only six priests, the number of the clergy being reduced by just one-half in seven years.

One parish is 24 miles in length with four churches five miles apart to be served by one priest.

Another parish has an area of over 20 miles, and a scattered population of 7,400 souls. This lack of clergy means in many cases the almost total removal of religious influences from the homes of the poor, and it arises solely from the want of funds to support the much-needed additional curates. There are men enough, willing, zealous, loyal men; but the wherewithal to furnish the hire of which the labourer is worthy cannot be found. The people do their best and undoubtedly deserve more help from external sources. As a rule the stipends of the clergy are provided by an assessment of each parish, the minimum subscription from church members being 6s. per annum. To such members all clerical ministrations are free, save marriages, the fee for which is about 10s. Non-subscribers are charged according to a fixed scale for each ministration: baptisms, 4s.; funerals, 20s.; weddings 22s. Well-to-do members naturally subscribe far more than the minimum, and further sums are derived from the unfortunate system of pew rents.

The picture is sombre-toned in many respects, but it is the picture of a crippled church suddenly called upon to meet unanticipated difficulties and making heroic efforts to maintain its position.

One morning it was decided that we should take a very early ride of seven miles up the Leeward Coast to Layou and then proceed by boat some four miles further to the north to Barrouallie, where we could breakfast with the rector and return home by boat in the evening. The expedition proved an entire success. The early ride was charming. We wound round the mountain sides of deeply indented gullies, fern-covered rocks and sylvan steps on one side, smiling valleys of arrowroot or sugar cane below. Here were mist-en-shrouded peaks towering over our heads, there the far-thrown shadows dreaming on the silent slopes. The road (so called, but frequently little better than a river bed) led us now inland over abrupt acclivities and sudden dips, and now round a rocky headland where the narrow bridle path overhung the "blue pervading sea"* while the morning sun, rising higher every minute, threw magic tints into the shifting mists and flying showers that haunted the higher altitudes around us.

At Layou we found the boat from Kingstown just coming in, our hostess aboard, having timed our ride to the minute. Having telephoned our arrival forward to Barrouallie and backward to Government House, we pushed off in the large, lumbering canoe, which the stalwart Negro boatmen pulled along at the rate of four miles an hour. The villages on the leeward coast are all situated on the seaboard and under the hills. Almost every little bay with its black-sanded beach has its groups of houses and often its little church or chapelry. The parishes are simply long strips of seacoast. On the other side of the island where the cultivable land lies differently, the parishes consist of broad, deep districts penetrating into the interior. Apart from the beautiful scenery and pleasant excursion, that day at Barrouallie was marked cut for recollection by our introduction to a new dish at breakfast, hashed agouti, a native rodent yielding an excellent meat with an unprecedented flavour. The journey home in the evening was a little tedious, as rain fell upon us in the open boat the whole of the way, and we were glad enough when the lights of Kingstown harbour intimated that dinner was within measurable distance

We hoped during our stay to make the ascent of the famous Soufriere in the north of the island and explore the weird solitude of its gaping summit, but this was not practicable. The peculiarity of this volcanic mountain consists in its twin craters, the older and larger of which contains a sulphurous lake of hitherto unfathomable depth. At the last eruption in 1812 the summit

*The vast improvement of the roads will be understood when it is known that motor cars, buses, etc., travel over them from Kingstown frequently to Barrouallie and elsewhere beyond Layou.

of the mountain was blown into the air, and a new crater formed alongside the old one and separated from it only by a narrow neck of rock.* Why nature in her extrusive convulsions preferred to make a new crater instead of using the one ready to hand is a mystery. The terrific force of the eruption may be measured by the fact that some of the volcanic ashes were elevated above the course of the northeast tradewinds into a higher current of air travelling in the opposite direction and were deposited nearly a hundred miles to the east on the island of Barbados, which, for some hours was enveloped in a darkness believed by many of the affrighted natives to be heralding the day of doom. A little heap of this very lava dust collected in Barbados lies before me as I write, and traces of it are even now occasionally met with in turning over the soil in the more remote parts of the island. The oldest of the Negroes still reckon their age from the year of "the dust". Our stay in St. Vincent was shortened by a few days through the arrival of a steamer bound for St. Lucia, which afforded us an opportunity of a direct passage too good to be neglected, for we were anxious to see something of the famous harbour of Castries, whence Rodney had emerged on that memorable day in April 1782, when he saved the English empire by his defeat of the French fleet under De Grasse. Accordingly, we bade our hospitable friends farewell and boarded the *Arabian Prince* of Knott's line of steamships. The passage proved a rough one so that, instead of arriving in Castries harbour about six o'clock in the evening, having left St. Vincent at one, we were delayed until somewhere near midnight. This annoyance, however, was compensated for by the courtesy of the captain and the careful provision made for our comforts, this small boat presenting in this and in some other respects a very favourable contrast to the mail boats of more than three times its size.

The next day we visited the Botanical Gardens, and ascended the Morne Fortune, on the top of which the war office is erecting barracks to accommodate the garrison, which is gradually being removed from Barbados. Time did not allow us to make any expeditions into the interior, for the pleasantest of holidays must have an end. One more night on the sea, and we found ourselves again in Carlisle Bay, with the acquisition of some delightful passages inscribed on memory's page.

T. Herbert Bindley

---

*There was another eruption in 1902.

From a contribution entitled "St. Vincent by Land and Water" published in the *Barbados Herald,* 1895

Saint Vincent is one of the most interesting of the West Indian islands. It charms the tourists with its varied scenes of tropical beauty and to the historian it is full of interest as the place where the aborigines of these sunny Caribbees—the Yellow Caribs—made a desperate struggle for that wild freedom and independence which they enjoyed before Columbus discovered the New World. The following description of it from a tourist's point of view may perhaps be appreciated by those who are in search of some place where a few weeks' vacation may be agreeably spent.

We first sighted the island on a Sunday morning but the weather was cloudy and unpropitious. Frequent showers of rain accompanied by heavy gusts of wind compelled the captain of our vessel to shorten sail, and in the distance the island looked like some huge leviathan afloat on the sullen deep, for the clouds rested in a low line over the land and completely hid from view the summits of mountains and hills.

The weather having improved somewhat we commenced to see the cultivated lands on the windward side of the island, and soon afterwards we passed Milligan Cay and sailed down the channel between St. Vincent and Bequia, picturesque views unfolding themselves as we sped along, especially that landscape which embraces Calliaqua and its beautiful bay, Young's Island and Fort Duvernette, the last named being a ruined fortress perched on the top of a precipitous rock which rises abruptly out of the sea. At 3 p.m. we rounded Cane Garden Point and entered Kingstown which is said to resemble the Bay of Naples. A gentle ripple dimpled the surface of its deep blue water; pelicans and seabirds lazily floated in the air above us. Right ahead lay Kingstown the capital nestled near the shore, and above it towered Mount St. Andrew, a mountain which rises 2,400 feet high, thickly wooded and capped with clouds. The red roofs of the houses contrasted agreeably with the verdure of the various palms and trees, with the dark brown cliffs which shelter the bay and the blue tint of the water. Not far from the dark coloured gravelly beach some schooners and sloops were lying at anchor, while the distant chime of the Sabbath bells fell pleasantly on the ear. It was a scene so peaceful and pretty that it brought to one's mind Coleridge's idea of domestic peace—

Tell me on what holy ground
May Domestic Peace be found!

In a cottaged vale she dwells
List'ning to the Sabbath bells.

The remaining days of our stay at St. Vincent were spent in and about the quiet city of Kingstown. The panorama as seen from Fort Charlotte is very pretty, and to those who pay a flying visit to the island, this view will give them a good idea of the scenery of the colony.

My sketch is now finished, but I must add one word more. We met with some kind friends whom, should I ever meet again, it will be a pleasure to me to say to each—

And there's a hand my trusty fiere!
And gie's a hand o' thine
And we'll tak' a right gud-wellie waught
For auld lang syne.

E. G. S., *a tourist*

———◆◆⚭◆◆———

From *Boston Stamp Book*, 1895

The mountains go sheer down to the sea, the only level spaces being a plain at Georgetown about three miles long and one-half mile wide, and the valley of the Iambou (sic) River, a wonderful cleft or gorge between perpendicular walls of rock, rising perhaps a thousand feet high. At Biabou, Calliaqua, Kingstown, and Chateaubelair are also narrow, level spaces a few hundred yards wide. With these exceptions, the scenery is that of a towering mass of mountains piled up in magnificent confusion, and looking far more like the ideal picture of an artist than an actually existing scene.

When the summit of the Soufriere is wrapped in clouds, as generally is the case, the craters present a very strange and beautiful effect, especially the old crater, that is the one with the lake. For five or ten minutes the clouds will fill the crater to the brim. Then the wind will dive down and roll them out, and the weird lake will suddenly appear in all its uncanny beauty, sometimes yellow-green and sometimes a strange iridescent green, but whatever its colour, being ceaselessly and to all appearance causelessly agitated, and beating its surf against the perpendicular walls of its chasm.

So much for the Soufriere. On the opposite or southern end of the island is the Vigie or "look-out," one of the highest points overhanging the capital, Kingstown, and having on its northern side the strange gorge or canon of the Iambou river. Picture to yourself these mountains—the Soufriere, and the Vigie, the chaotic mass of equally large but unnamed peaks of the Morne-a-Garou between them—all towering share up from the depths of the ocean to heaven with their summits swathed in clouds and their sides covered with a dense virgin tropical forest of from 50 to 150 feet in height, interspersed with narrow and romantic gorges, thronged with waterfalls—picture to yourself, I say, all these beauties, and you will then have some faint conception of St. Vincent, a tropical paradise in the Caribbean sea.

As for the inhabitants of St. Vincent, they are largely Negroes but of a vastly superior character to those in our southern States. They are law-abiding, civil, obliging, and hardworking, owning in many cases, but renting in most, their own little cabins and plantations. They are, in short, an utter contrast to the gambling, ravening and murdering wild beast that so many of their race have become in the "black belt" of the South. The white inhabitants of St. Vincent are kindness, courteousness, and hospitality personified, and I can safely promise anyone who may visit the island will receive a hearty and whole-souled welcome.

This, then is my sketch of St. Vincent, and if any of my readers moved by my loving picture of it should decide to go, see and be enraptured for themselves with the gem of the Caribbean Sea, I will feel myself amply repaid.

Rev. A. S. Hawkesworth, Acting Priest-in-Charge,
Charlotte Parish during 1894

From *Monthly Illustrator*

We hope the name "The Gem of the West Indies," which we have given to St. Vincent, is original, for we should like to enjoy the honour of having been the first to call it by a name so appropriate and one which it so richly deserves.

To this entrancing little haven our thoughts will ever revert with pleasing recollections, and its kind, hospitable people, both white and black, will ever occupy a warm spot in our grateful hearts. We arrived there with nothing to recommend us but the fact that we were strangers, and yet we were received with open arms, and every courtesy and kindness were extended to us by these generous-hearted residents. If we had gone there with the object of enriching every person on the island, and if the accomplishment of that object depended upon the maintenance of our health and comfort, no more solicitude could have been shown us, and from perfect strangers upon whom we had not one particle of claim. Our eyes were indeed open to a phase of human nature which was new to us, and an application of the Golden Rule such as we had in our peregrinations about this selfish, uncharitable world met with only on a very few isolated occasions. And what appealed most touchingly to our gratitude was the kindness of the common poor people who, in their humble way, vied with their more fortunate neighbours in showering upon us evidences of their cordial feeling and of the welcome to their island which they extended us.

How richly it deserves to have the light of prosperity shine upon it as brightly and peacefully as do the grateful rays of the tropical sun which give it its verdure, its beauty, its genial warmth and healthfulness,

St. Vincent is one of the most healthy, if not the healthiest, of the West Indian islands. At an elevation of 600 feet above the sea level, the thermometer ranges from 68 degrees F in the cool season, to 88 degrees in the hot season. The soil is very fertile, being watered by numerous streams and rivulets abounding in small fish called mountain mullet which, *par parentheses,* take the artificial fly like graylings, which they somewhat resemble in taste.

Wm. Benedict Reilly

Tours in the West Indies

This charming island, which contends with Grenada and Dominica for the palm of beauty, is one of the most interesting and also the most woe-begone in the West Indies. Ravaged in turn by French, English and Caribs, it became at last the most English of the true Caribbean Islands, putting Barbados and Antigua apart as being of a totally different type; and even the supporters of the scenery of Dominica and Grenada will admit that the Soufriere of St. Vincent has no rival, while the view of the Leeward Coast from Fort Charlotte, which dominates the town, is very fine.

J. R. Dasent (CB)

From *Columbian Geography*

St. Vincent, the most beautiful and verdant, the Emerald Isle and the peerless link of the Caribbean chain, is of oval shape, with southern and western coasts fantastically fringed by deep indentations, some of which form safe and commodious harbours. It is said that "there is no scenery in Italy nor even in the world, that can surpass, either in beauty or in interest the very lovely approach to the island of St. Vincent along the Windward Coast." The surface bristles with a mass of mountains whose spurs radiate in all directions from the interior to the very beach, where they widen into smiling valleys and charming glens, watered by numerous crystal streams. Lofty peaks and conical pyramids vie with one another in their height and precipitous outlines, and the Soufriere, with its two crater lakes and celebrated for its eruption of 1812, stands in solemn prominence at the head of the heap of rugged highlands. This wonderful mountain forms the grandest natural feature of the island. "Indeed, excepting Etna," says Dr. Davy, "I know of no other mountain more impressive, no one where are better displayed, on one hand the destructive energies of nature in the effects of the volcano, or on the other her restorative and preservative influences in the formation of fertile soils and the growth of a luxuriant vegetation." This active volcano, and the many dead ones which greet the eye in every direction as well as the countless boulders which are strewn on the banks of the rivers, bear ample evidence of the volcanic formation of this enchanting island. The scenery, it need scarcely be observed, is of the wildest grandeur and most magical in its effect. The climate is cool, equable and very healthy. The soil is excellent, especially in the northern wooded portion where it is suitable for the growth of all tropical staples; tea would also find a congenial soil here. The productions and objects of culture are the sugarcane, arrowroot, cacao, groundnuts, spices, annotto seed, cotton, and ground provisions.

The northern part of the island is clothed in dense forest of the largest and most valuable timber trees and cabinet woods. The chief minerals are sulphur, iron-sand and cement; phosphate is found in the island of Balliceaux. Among the animals are the agouti, manicou, mongoose, iguana, and non-venomous snakes; rabbits and deer are plentiful in Balliceaux. The coastal waters swarm with splendid fish, and whale and turtle catching is a lucrative occupation for the men of Bequia.

Vincelonians are handsome, respectable, intelligent, and industrious. There are a few hundred aboriginal Indians, some of whom still speak the language of their forefathers and are under the control of a Headman.[*] They are a fine type, noted for their fearlessness of the sea, hence they make capital boatmen and are usually employed in shipping produce on the dangerous Windward Coast. They do a lot of fishing and are also engaged in basket making, an art in which they greatly excel. The Yellow Caribs, or true aboriginal Indians, were generally found at Sandy Bay on the Windward Coast, while the Black Caribs are usually at Morne Ronde on the Leeward Coast and at a place called Gregg's in the mountains. Education is defective and backward; there are, however, some good schools. Protestantism is the prevailing religion. There are a small number of Catholics.

Kingstown, the capital and chief seat of trade, stands along the shores of a beautiful open roadstead forming a pleasing curve on the southern coast backed by Mount St. Andrew, an elevation of 2,500 feet. The houses are regularly built, the streets well laid out and clean, and the town has a very neat and taking appearance.

Jos. A. DeSuze

———— ◆◆◆ ————

The Caribs

The Caribs and the Indians of Central and South America seem to be of the same stock of people. When and why the Caribs came to these islands we cannot tell with any certainty, but it is likely they were forced by wars to seek shelter here, and perhaps successive immigrations took place, and gradually these islands were occupied in proportion to the attraction of fish and game.

---

*No aboriginal Indians are now in the island.

289

St. Vincent seems to have fascinated them by these very attractions so that they named the island "Hiroon", which means "The Home of the Missed". Then the Caribs settled along the complete coastline, and though fishing and hunting were their general occupation, they must have raised various crops, too, for at a few places their settlements were fairly well inland.

Their progress towards civilization seems to have been very small judging by the evidences we can collect. We have practically no insight into their social customs, and only a small portion of their language was accessible from those living a hundred years ago.

As in North America so in the West Indies, too, the ousted natives have deteriorated instead of advancing alongside their superiors. At present there are very few pure Caribs, for the greater part of those who were left on the island after the deportation to Rattan Island off British Honduras in 1797 after their insurrection with the French against the British, have died out and the remainder have intermarried with the East Indians, Creoles and Negroes and now are indistinguishable from the general population.

There are quite a few monuments to the Caribs in various parts of the island in the shape of carvings on boulders done by them long ago, and many stone implements found where they had occupied. Various places still bear the Carib names of those locations as Marriaqua, Calliaqua, Layou, Wallilabou, Troumaca, etc.

The descendants of the Caribs, though still shy and reserved, are fairly intelligent and hard-working people for they are notorious for their endurance at boat-rowing. Many of them fish and also plant in their reserve lands, some are agricultural labourers and a few are petty artisans.

The stone carvings could be visited by car and the stone implements seen at the public library.

E. O'H. B.

Places of Interest

ST. GEORGE'S CATHEDRAL

Persons desirous of gaining some knowledge regarding the valuable services rendered in connection with memorable events of bygone days should not lose any opportunity of visiting the Cathedral of the Windward Islands Diocese which can be reached in about five minutes from the Kingstown jetty.

The Cathedral is enclosed in spacious grounds and replaces another building which was destroyed by the hurricane in the year 1780. The cost of rebuilding amounted to £47,000 currency. Sir Charles Brisbane, the Governor at the time, obtained a Government contribution of £5,000 sterling out of the purchase money for the Carib lands. The chancel and transepts were added in 1887 under the supervision of Mr. David S. Osment.

The central entrance to it is formed by a paved avenue shaded principally by typical almond trees of considerable age. On the mural tablets and memorials which adorn its walls are recorded significant facts—although concise—sufficient to prove interesting to all who attach some importance to the history of a place. Here and there in the aisle are to be found inscriptions which, like those on the tombs in the yard, afford information of a similar character. A large stone in the floor of the centre aisle is a memorial to Alexander Leith who, during the Carib War of 1795, killed the Carib chief, Chattawae (sic), on Dorsetshire Hill.

The records reveal that "by the Act 6th George IV, c. 88, amended by the 7th George IV, c. 4, His Majesty graciously erected the West India islands into two Sees; the salaries of the Bishop paid out of the 4½ per cent duties were £4,000 each with a provision for a retiring pension of £1,000 after service of 10 years. The sum of £4,300 was placed at the disposal of the Bishop of Barbados for the maintenance of ministers, catechists, and schoolmasters in the Diocese; no minister's salary was to exceed £300.

These episcopal appointments have been of great utility; the clergy have been regulated and a system adopted for conveying general instructions to the Negroes by means of catechists and schoolmasters.

The want of education had been a sore evil in the colonies, but a decided improvement took place under the auspices of the Bishop, and in a few years the parochial schools manifested their utility. The Legislature removed the disabilities attendant on colour, but these concessions would have been of no actual benefit to that race unless they became qualified by education and

291

morals to assume their advanced station in society and to perform the duties required of them.

The completed edifice as it stands today presents an interesting combination of three distinct styles of architecture. The nave and tower are built in the Classic style, and bear resemblance to many of the City of London churches which were designed by Sir Christopher Wren. Since the demolition of the cupola on the tower, however, the tower itself, with its clock and three huge bells, is more reminiscent of the English parish church tower.

The massive transept arch and its companions in the aisles are Norman in design. They present an interesting transition from the classic of the nave to the Gothic of the transepts and chancel. The chancel arch is magnificent in its proportions and simplicity. The upper parts of the walls of the chancel are arcaded, the roof being of the simple barrel type.

The Cathedral church possesses several stained windows of rare beauty. The east window with its three graceful lancets is by Kempe. The magnificent window in the south transept (a recent addition) is a memorial to the late Duke of Clarence and Avondale. It is of Munich glass made to the design of Sir A. Bloomfield. The window in the north transept replaces one of similar design which was destroyed in the hurricane of 1898.

During the last few years many improvements have been carried out, which include the furnishing of chapels in the north transept and south gallery. The reredos at the high altar has been extended and the whole building redecorated throughout.

On April 23rd, 1937, the Canterbury Cross Replica was dedicated and erected in the Cathedral. The inscription in Latin when translated reads, "This Cross is a copy of one made perhaps in Kent in the eighth century. It is set in stone taken from the walls of Christ Church, Canterbury. As the emblem of Salvation and the earnest of friendship it was given to this Cathedral by the Friends of Canterbury Cathedral A.D. 1935."

The Cathedral Church is open all day from 6 a.m. to 6 p.m., and a full round of services is maintained daily.

THE CARNEGIE FREE LIBRARY

The institution was built in 1907-09 from funds given to the Kingstown Board by the late Andrew Carnegie of Skibo Castle, Scotland. The library is maintained chiefly by two annual grants of £100 and £60 provided from the General Revenue of the Colony and funds of the Kingstown Board respectively.

The upper storey is used principally as a lecture hall for intellectual entertainments and occasionally for meetings of recognised associations, and the like. In the lower storey is the Free Reading Room which is opened to the public from 9 a.m. to 9 p.m. daily except on public holidays, and on Sundays from 3 to 6 p.m.

The Committee of Management is comprised of the chairman of the Kingstown Board, two members nominated by the board and two persons nominated by the Government. In 1935 a grant of $1,500.00 was given by the Carnegie Trust Fund of New York.

An interesting collection of Carib Stones, the implements and weapons used by the early inhabitants of St. Vincent, are displayed. Another showcase contains specimens of local products. The local games trophies, won and presented, are also kept on show at the library.

During 1937 over 11,000 volumes were issued from the lending department of the library, which is worked on a subscription basis of 6d. per month for fiction, while other works of literature may be loaned free to registered borrowers. A supply of the leading magazines and newspapers is maintained

---

THE METHODIST CHURCH

The Methodist Church in Kingstown is one of the finest buildings in the island. It is capable of seating 1,600 and has often accommodated on special occasions 2,000 people. It was opened for divine worship on August 1st, 1841, during the ministry of the Rev. John Cullingford. The building suffered considerably during the hurricane of 1898 but was repaired and thoroughly renovated immediately afterwards through the generosity of local Methodists, aided by liberal contributions from England. This arduous task was successfully accomplished by the congregation under the able leadership of the Honourable and Rev. J. H. Darrell. Tablets to the memory of the Revs. J. Cullingford and J. H. Darrell have been placed in the church. In common with other ministers of the Methodist church, they took a prominent part in all that tends to the physical, mental and social well-being of the community as well as its spiritual welfare, their influence being felt beyond the bounds of their own denomination. The Rev. J. H. Darrell enjoyed the unique honour and distinction of being the only Minister of Religion who has had a seat on the Legislative Council. The present Superintendent Minister, the Rev. Herbert H. Cole, has the further distinction of being the only Methodist minister in the Empire who has had a seat as an Official Member of a Legislative Council, he having served for about three years as Acting Inspector of Schools in St. Lucia.

A beautiful stained glass window is to be seen at the back of the mahogany rostrum; a marvellous glass chandelier is a magnificent reminder of the days of candlelight; while a fine organ by Bevington and Sons, London, leads the service of praise.

The present superintendent minister, the Rev. Herbert H. Cole, resides at the Mission House immediately opposite the church and is assisted by the Revs. S. J. Caulton and B. Crosby who reside at Montrose. The Mission House garden has been for many years one of the sights of the town.

ROMAN CATHOLIC CHURCH

A Catholic community has existed in the colony of St. Vincent from time immemorial, and it will be remembered that Christopher Columbus, the great discoverer of the island itself, was a faithful adherent of the Catholic faith. He placed the new acquisition of territory under the protection of St. Vincent because he discovered this island on 22nd January, the festival day of the martyrdom of St. Vincent.

At present three Benedictine monks reside, viz., The Very Rev. Dom Charles Verbeke (OSB, PP), Missionary Rector, Dom Placid Ganteaume (OSB) and Dom Radbodus v. d. Plas (OSB).

Since the year 1918 this mission has been entrusted to the Benedictine Monastery at Mount St. Benedict, Trinidad.

St. Vincent is subject to the Roman Catholic Jurisdiction of the Archdiocese of Port-of-Spain and is honoured every second year by a visitation from the Catholic Archbishop (at present the Right Rev. Dr. Dowling) who resides at Port-of-Spain, Trinidad.

By far the greater number of Catholics reside in Kingstown where they worship in a very artistic chapel dedicated to Our Lady of the Assumption, constructed, it is said, from the design of one of the Pope's Domestic Chapels within the confines of the Vatican at Rome. This very devotional little church is hardly large enough to meet the present requirements of the Catholic population. It has been rebuilt on the site of the one destroyed in 1875, a time it will be remembered of great deluge and hurricane. The rebuilding has been of gradual construction, the steeple and sanctuary being erected by Father Farelly in 1877, whilst the elegant marble altar now standing in the chancel was consecrated in 1882 and is the gift of Mm Joseph DePassos, A. Nieves, Aug. Nieves, and F. Sardine.

The substantial Presbytery adjoining the church was built later in 1891 by the energy and initiative of Father Collins.

Considerable improvements have been made to both church and Presbytery; the latter now known as St. Mary's represents a very artistic edifice since its thorough renovation by Dom Charles Verbeke (OSB, PP).

The Catholic population of St. Vincent is estimated at 5,000, a portion of which is largely scattered throughout the length and breadth of the island. In addition to the Catholic church at Kingstown there are nine minor chapels in which priestly ministration is supplied by one of the monks residing at St. Mary's.

At Bellevue, 1,500 Catholics and a similar number at Mesopotamia have their own respective churches.

There are also chapels at Rylland, Gomea, Escape (Argyle), and Bequia, while at Rosebank, Georgetown and Sandy Bay, mass is offered in temporary buildings.

A large confraternity of those known as The Holy Name Confraternity has a membership of 78 males. For the women of the congregation there exist (1) The Sacred Heart Confraternity (164 members); and (2) The Children of Mary Society (40 members); whilst independently and for both sexes the St. Patrick's and the Mutual Help Societies provide insurance funds in sickness and death for their Catholic memberships.

The Catholic children are educated in two schools viz, at Kingstown and Bellevue. Mr. Compton is the headmaster at Kingstown and Mr. Stephen at the latter place.

St. Mary's is the name assigned to a combination of buildings, the most magnificent in Saint Vincent. The architectural designs are to be seen nowhere else in these smaller islands, if at all in any of the larger ones. A writer declares that "The Monastery with its piazzas, facades, balconies, loggias, and rotundas, with the Romanesque style prevailing, is more like a palace of old Venice than a building to be expected in little St. Vincent...."

Visitors are courteously shown the different artistic work and elegant embellishments which comprise this attractive edifice.

BOTANIC GARDEN

The interesting and beautiful garden is situated about one mile from the landing place in Kingstown in a northwesterly direction and was established as early as 1765 under the control of the Secretary of War. There is an excellent carriage road maintained through the tropical scenery on the way to it. The courteous attention of members of the staff can always be relied upon. Dr. Landsdowne Guilding thus described the garden in the year 1825:

...but the public establishment that reflects the greatest honour on St. Vincent, is its celebrated botanic garden, under the provident and well-directed care of Dr. Anderson. It consists of 30 acres of which no less than 16 are in high cultivation, abounding not only with almost every species of the vegetable world, which the hand of nature has bestowed on these islands for use and beauty, for food and luxury, but also with many valuable exotics from the East Indies and South America. If it be surpassed in this latter respect by the magnificent garden of Mr. East (in Jamaica) it claims at least the honour of seniority, and does infinite credit both to its original founders and present directors.

The success having attracted due attention in England, Dr. G. Young, the first superintendent whose name is recorded, received a gold medal in 1772, and Dr. Anderson a silver medal in 1798 from the Society for the Encouragement of Arts in recognition of the flourishing condition of this garden. The mango and the cinnamon, which were introduced by Lord Rodney in Jamaica in 1782, were sent to this establishment; also some of the original bread fruit plants brought by Captain Bligh from Otaheite (Tahiti) in 1793, and through the zeal and activity of Dr. Anderson two nutmeg trees were procured from Cayenne in 1809. The clove was obtained from Martinique as early as 1787, where it was brought from the East Indies. Great care was bestowed on these spices which became abundant in a few years.

Dr. Anderson was succeeded by Mr. Lockhead, who died in 1815, and whose tomb is in the garden where he laboured. On the death of this superintendent, Mr. Caley was appointed. Under his control the prosperity declined, and in consequence of his demeanor, the War Office dispensed with his services, discontinued the salary and allowances, and directed that any valuable plants which could be removed should be sent to Trinidad. The plants were accordingly transported in May 1823. A few years afterward the Legislature voted £800 currency for the partial maintenance of the garden. This was discontinued in 1828 when £4,500 was voted for the erection of a Government House and three acres of the land were vested in trustees.

Actual cultivation was not however discontinued until 1849; after that period attention was merely paid to the gathering of the exuberant spices and fruit. The great loss sustained by the cyclone in 1886 included a grove of about 29 full-bearing nutmeg trees.

In May 1890 the Botanic Garden was re-established principally for propagating and distributing industrial plants. The area under cultivation was estimated at 14 acres. Mr. Henry Powell of the Royal Gardens Kew, was appointed curator and arrived on the 14th of that month.

Mr. Powell laboured assiduously until May 1904, when he was transferred to British East Africa. During the 14 years that he was in charge, the garden again attained to a high standard of efficiency and was regarded as one of the most beautiful in the West Indies.

Mr. Sands who succeeded him was entrusted also with the Agricultural School, the Experimental Station and Stock Farm attached to it, together with the agricultural oversight of the projects connected with the Land Settlement Scheme and the working of the Government Cotton Ginnery.

The Agricultural School proved of general utility. Among the masters were Mr. C. H. Knowles (BSc) and Mr. W. H. Patterson. They evinced keen and sustained interest in the pupils, a few of whom at the present time occupy responsible positions. The closing of the school is one of the regrettable occurrences in the history of St. Vincent. Many of its sons would have distinguished themselves in the skilled knowledge of agriculture.

The Talipot palm (*Corypha umbraculifera*), which existed in the garden for about 80 years, died in 1923. It flowered in 1922 when its waning vitality was pronounced. Picture postcards and photographs may be obtained if desired. They show it in bloom and in the dual condition of a dying palm with an attractively pretty flowery top.

In commemoration of Their Majesties Coronation and during the function at Government House on 12th May 1937, Mr. A. K. Briant, Superintendent of Agriculture, planted a tree, Queen of Flowering Trees (*Amherstia nobilis*, commonly known as the orchid tree) in an easterly direction of Government House adjacent to the Botanic Gardens.

EDINBORO

The passenger whose destination is Edinboro can, without the assistance of anyone, make his first acquaintance with this holiday resort by looking across the harbour from the starboard side of the incoming ship to a colony of red-roofed bungalows along the shore at Edinboro Bay.

For persons of modest income and those who desire to be within easy reach of Kingstown, Edinboro is the ideal resort. Ten minutes' walk along an oiled and electrically lighted road puts one into the city. Motor car hire is thus reduced to a minimum.

The resident at Edinboro can also see the lights of Kingstown across the harbour and witness the coming and going of all the foreign and coastal seaborne traffic. He therefore enjoys the charms of rural surroundings without losing touch with urban amenities.

At this settlement stood the Commissariat Building, once used as a supply depot for the garrison at Fort Charlotte, which looks down from the adjoining heights separating Ottley Hall and Edinboro. The Commissariat was demolished to make way for the bungalows.

The Fort, now variously used as the colony's charitable institutions and as a light house and signal station, can be reached after half-hour's walk. One can also get there by motor car. Here can be seen a citadel, a dry moat and gun emplacements built in the eighteenth century. The walk to the Fort is the delight of visitors, especially Guianese who are usually charmed with the hills. Visitors from Trinidad have often remarked that a holiday spent at Edinboro costs no more than a holiday of like duration spent "down the islands", that is, the island resort in the Gulf of Para.

Altogether, it might therefore be said that what with its proximity to Kingstown, its up-to-date bungalows at moderate rentals, its lively sea bathing and its delightful setting, Edinboro represents real value for persons wanting a holiday.

FORT CHARLOTTE

Fort Charlotte is situated on a rock about 600 feet above the level of the sea, northwest of Kingstown. It contained barracks for 600 men and had 34 pieces of artillery of different descriptions, besides several out-works for the protection of detached buildings. During the protracted period of hostilities this fortress—a natural vantage ground—was considered the chief defence of the island. A few of the houses are habitable and are in use at the present time. From Kingstown, Fort Charlotte can be reached within 20 minutes, riding or driving, and if by a motor car within 8 minutes. There being a good driving road, every visitor should avail himself of an opportunity to go there.

From this rocky promontory Kingstown, with its semi-circular harbour, can be seen to advantage. Behind the town the lofty mountains with irregular slopes shaped into fantastic forms, are invariably enshrouded with mist and add a sublimity to the panoramic view which is singularly picturesque.

The scenery on the Leeward side is also exceedingly attractive while in a southern direction the Grenadines and islets, resembling the Cyclades of the Grecian Archipelago, present a magnificent picture. Even Grenada can be seen when over that island cumulus (a cloud of a convex or well-rounded upper surface) infinitely reposeful and dignified, serves as a reflector of the slanting rays of the sun, throwing the light necessary to render an island 68 miles away admirably discernible.

There are several other elevations from which Grenada is seen without the aid of the telescope but under identical conditions.

Although St. Lucia cannot be seen from this fort, yet at a short distance from Kingstown travelling in a northwardly direction, that island is nearly always visible and with increased distinctness proportionate to the progress of the journey.

Among the many places from which St. Lucia can be admired may be mentioned the historic fort at Owia, whence the Pitons are distinguished with considerable ease. The scenic effect is strikingly grand, the pleasure is enhanced by the interesting facts of earlier times connected with the various places on the route.

Thus, it will be observed that unlike Grenada and St. Lucia, St. Vincent affords a view of all the islands and dependencies comprised in the Windward Islands Government.

A visitor remarked, "As we fixed our eyes on the landscape which was bathed in the golden glow of the rising sun, we commented on one of the most picturesque forts standing in front of us and also on other beautiful features that could be seen."

FORT COTTAGE

A visitor's remarks:

This cottage is perched like an eagle's nest on the side of a great cliff jutting out to the sea. The road winds up from the little town, a silver streak in a maze of tropical vegetation. There is a bridge near the top of the ascent. It used, I fancy, to be a draw bridge; then a steeper climb round a curve, to the gate of the cottage and a road winds up another 100 yards or so to the summit of this promontory, which is crowned by one of those solid fortresses built in the days when England and France fought for the ownership of the Caribbean Islands and the mastery of the sea.

From the cottage you look down on the harbour at night, with the twinkling lights of Kingstown spread out along the shore or the quiet moonlight playing on the waters: the scene is beautiful.

THE SOUFRIERE

The following paragraphs are extracted from the report of the late Dr. T. Anderson, (MD, BSc, FGS) and Dr. J. S. Flett (MA, DSc, FRSE).

....In the summit of this mountain lies the principal or old crater nearly a mile in diameter from which the eruption took place in 1902. There is likewise a much smaller crater, the so-called "new-crater" which was active in 1812 and may have been formed in that year. These two craters are surrounded to the north by a large crater ring of older date, broken down

299

towards the south, which has been referred to as the Somma Ring, since it bears the same relation to the working cone of the Soufriere as Somma does to Vesuvius. The whole mountain group was formerly known as Morne Garu, but the name has now been appropriated to another mountain about three miles to the south, also formed of volcanic material, but of much older date, which is separated from the Soufriere by a deep depression extending right across the island. The part of this depression on the eastern or windward side of the island is occupied by the Rabaka and other smaller streams and is called the Carib country, while that on the western or Leeward side is drained by the Wallibu and other streams and is here referred to as the Wallibu district. In the 1902 eruption a certain amount of the ejecta overtopped the Somma Ring and descended some of the valleys to the north of it, but by far the greater portion was discharged into the above-mentioned transverse depression. The water from the crater lake was discharged at the beginning of the eruption down the Rabaka and Wallibu Rivers. The former was rendered impassable and thereby cut off escape from the Carib country, where the greater part of the deaths occurred. The solid and gaseous ejecta in the form of the incandescent avalanches and black clouds descended to both sides of the island, and the most important geological phenomena were observed in the Wallibu district....

The upper slopes of the mountain are chiefly formed of beds of tuff like the lower parts but contain perhaps a larger proportion of ejected blocks which naturally fell in greater abundance nearer the crater. They are much cut up into deep ravines, separated by the ridges, the slopes of which are often very steep....

Even in 1902 the new ash, which had never been thick on these slopes, was in great part washed away, and it was only on the ridges and in some of the valley bottoms that any considerable amount of that ash remained. This process, of course, has gone on ever since.

The ash on the ridges still remains, and its surface is consolidated into a thin but hard crust similar to that on the plateaux. This extends generally only to a width of a few feet and often not more than one or two. On each side of the ridge where the ash has been washed away, the old soil has been exposed, and it would doubtless also have been in a great measure removed if it had not been held together by the roots of plants which, as mentioned below, were in many cases not killed. Even when dead, they no doubt held the soil together to a large extent while the new vegetation has been re-establishing itself....

The walls in the greater part of their height are nearly vertical and consist of alternate layers of tuff and compact rock, all dipping outwards from the crater. The latter beds are chiefly lenticular in section and columnar or sub-columnar in structure, the columns being as usual arranged at right angles to the surfaces of cooling. Probably they are chiefly lava flows but some may be intrusive sheets. It was impossible to get near enough to examine their surfaces of contact with adjacent beds. There is a very prominent dyke to the northwest of the crater and a smaller one to the west of it, which cut through

300

several of the massive beds referred to, so that, as intrusive action has undoubtedly occurred, the results might be horizontal sheets as well as vertical dykes. One of the horizontal beds mentioned above situated in the northwest wall of the crater is especially massive. It must be several hundred feet thick and is distinctly columnar....

The profound gorges which score the sides of the volcano give it a picturesqueness which otherwise would have been lacking. When we saw them they were bare and naked, all the green vegetation had disappeared during the eruption; only blackened trunks were left to bear witness to the tropical forest which had once clothed the surface. But though the mountain had lost in beauty and variety of colour, it had gained in interest and impressiveness to the geologist. Every detail of cliff and scar was visible from a distance. The Soufriere had been one of the beauties of the West Indies, and travellers had come from far to gaze on its richly-wooded slopes and to see the marvellous lake which nestled in the crater of its summit.

Magnificent sections are afforded by the sea cliffs on the Leeward side of the Soufriere between Morne Ronde and Quashie Point, and in the deep ravines of the Rozeau Dry River, Larakai and other streams, which descend the mountain slopes. On the windward side also, there are very fine inland cliffs above Overland and Sandy Bay....

The water of the lake was greenish and opalescent, probably from finely-divided particles of precipitated sulphur. It smelt strongly of sulphuretted hydrogen, especially on a hot day (hence the name Soufriere), but was not warm or even tepid, and the adventurous occasionally bathed in the lake. The level of the surface is given on the chart as 1,930 feet, so that the southern wall was 1,100 feet high, and the northern about 1,700 feet. Probably the amount of water varied slightly with the season of the year. There was no outlet, but the excess of rainfall over evaporation leaked away through the bedding planes and joints of the surrounding rock....

The crater lake of the Soufriere is described by all who had the good fortune to see it as having been a thing of beauty. The mists which roll across the mountain top before the steady trade wind too often obscured the view and cheated the traveller of the reward of his arduous climb. But when the clouds lifted and the sun breaking through the veil shone on the pearly-green sheet of water, reflecting from its placid surface the swelling mists above, and set in the sloping verdant crater walls, like an opal surrounded by emeralds, the sight was one the memory of which was cherished for a lifetime....

A trip to the tropics is not complete without a visit to the Soufriere, of which so much is written as to its matchless grandeur as to render needless any extensive description.

Arrangements may be made in Kingstown for conveyance to and from Chateaubelair, in which case the journey may be commenced early in the morn to return the same evening, or proceed by Launch, motor or other boat at 2 p.m. Having obtained permission of the Chief of Police prior to depar-

ture from Kingstown, the Government Rest House can be occupied during the night for a nominal fee.

Guides, whose services are available as attendants, and horses for hire, are easily obtained for moderate sums.

Allowing an hour for the amazement and profound admiration which will be manifested on and about the summit, this expedition can be accomplished within six hours.

The following are extracted from the *New York Herald* by kind permission of Professor Edmund Otis Hovey, Geologist of the American Museum of Natural History, who visited this Island in June, 1908:

At present there is but one well marked crater on the island, that is the famous Soufriere. This has been in eruption at only three periods within historic time,1718, 1812, and 1902-1903. But the Aboriginal Caribs, whom Columbus found here in 1498 on his second voyage, stood in mortal dread of the beautiful mountain, preserving traditions of previous outbreaks and offering valued sacrifices to the goddess dwelling within the crater lake who must be kept in good humour to prevent her destroying the race with fire and burning stones. The recorded eruptions have been violently explosive in character and all have been destructive of human life and property, but adequate accounts of the earlier events are lacking, so that satisfactory comparisons cannot be made between them and the latest. The great crater has always been noted for the beautiful lake within it. This lake has been thrown out at every eruption, and a new crater is said to have been found beside the great one during the outbreak of 1812. Every time, too, the mountain sides were denuded of vegetation and covered with a mantle of varying thickness of ash, cinders and boulders. Apparently the latest eruption, which lasted for eleven months, was the most important of all....

Having visited St. Vincent in May and June, 1902, directly after the eruption began, and again in March, 1903, on both occasions in the interests of the American Museum of Natural History, I became quite familiar with the region and was glad to come again this year in behalf of the same institution for the purpose of making comparisons.

The day after reaching Chateaubelair we started out bright and early for the summit of the mountain, having with us two capable negro men as guides and porters. Passing Richmond Village, we noted that the coating 60 to 70 feet that covered it had become compact and hard, as if it had been there for many times the six years of its actual existence.

The mound looks even more desolate than it did in 1902 and 1903, for the trees then standing have fallen and the walls then visible are now quite inconspicuous. The Richmond estate house on the bluff overlooking the site of the late village likewise resembles an ancient ruin, while the once cultivated fields thereabout, with their new vegetation gaining foothold on the fresh ash, look like virgin land. The sea has encroached greatly on the land here, having cut back more than a hundred yards, apparently into the pile of new ash over the village site. The land at the mouth of the Wallibu River just beyond, has gained, on the contrary, at least 150 yards upon the sea, due to the enormous quantity of ash that the river has brought down from the hillsides in the last six years and deposited along shore. Wallibu Point, like Richmond Point, has been cut back by the sea, but the land again has gained in front of the ruins of Wallibu factory, and the beach is a hundred yards wide outside of the spot where we landed in a boat in May and June, 1902. This was the site of Wallibu Village, but the village and the whole beach, in fact, for two miles was shaken off into deep water by the eruption of May, 1902. The destruction of the old beach has allowed the sea to cut into the points of the old promontories along the coast, but the new ash brought down by the torrents of the rainy season has been distributed along shore and the beach is now widening again....

The revived vegetation, however, is largely in the old volcanic tuff (compacted ash) of the mountain, and it must be said that it is feeble and slow to gain foothold in the really new material. In gullies in the new ash where moisture has remained for long periods, decomposition of the ash has advanced far enough to allow the growth of grass and ferns, while even on the slopes where moisture has not been able to remain so long, moss has established itself more or less abundantly. Even the grass practically ceases at an elevation of about 1,700 feet above the sea, though an occasional bunch may be seen up to the crater rim 1,200 feet higher, and there is moss enough on the mud slopes to produce a greenish appearance at a distance.

The lake filling the bottom of the crater has more than doubled in diameter since I last saw it in 1903, but it still seems smaller than the old crater lake as represented on the British Admiralty chart. In colour the lake has returned to the yellowish-green that prevailed before the eruptions. When I saw it in 1902 and 1903, the lake was a dirty, muddy pool, probably of little depth through which came frequent bursts of steam, fountains of mud and showers of stones. Now, not a sign of steam or other volcanic activity is to be seen, and the surface of the lake is disturbed only by the winds swirling over and into the crater. On the day of our recent visit, a gale of wind was tearing over the mountain top at the rate of 60 to 75 miles an hour, much to our discomfort, and the gusts that reached the little lake produced white capped waves in the lake, which from our distance looked like a miniature storm at sea.

———◆◈◆———

Extract from *The Vincentian* of June 6, 1936:
Scientific Mission of the Royal Society of London
Studying Montserrat Earthquakes

Dr. T. A. Jaggar, Director of the Hawaiian Volcano Observatory, was in Kingstown with Mrs. Jaggar, studying St. Vincent geology. Dr. Jaggar came from Harvard University in May, 1902, on the relief ship *Dixie* and went to Soufriere crater with Hon. D. M. MacDonald.

Dr. Jagger is a member of the mission of four scientists sent to study the needs of Montserrat in the earthquake crisis which has afflicted that Presidency since 1933. The chairman of the mission is Sir Gerald P. Lennox-Conyngham, Lt. Col. of Royal Engineers, head of the Department of Geodesy and Geophysics of Cambridge University, England. Sir Gerald will come to St. Vincent July 6th. The other members of the mission, recently in Montserrat since March, are A. G. MacGregor, (BSc) of the Geological Survey of Scotland, and Dr. C. F. Powell, physicist of the Research Laboratories of Bristol.

Dr. and Mrs. Jaggar arrived on the Lady Nelson June 2, and return to Montserrat June 10, to remain there until June 29. They climbed the Soufriere from Lot Fourteen on June 4, and will examine Wallibou Dry River June 6. Dr. Jaggar is impressed with the fertility of the ash of 1902 and the great forests which have grown up in 34 years. His visit has no relation to any predicting, nor to any apprehension of any sort whatsoever.

He is greatly pleased with the hospitality and interest which has been shown the mission by the governments of the islands and by the owners of agricultural lands. The doing of permanent work of recording land movement will depend in large measure on local interest, and the maps and trails and observatories cannot fail to give St. Vincent new knowledge of its own commercial resources in soil and water and oceanic surroundings.

YOUNG'S ISLAND

"It lies on the deep, where the blue water gleams
A beautiful Island, an Island of Dreams."

Young's Island is a triangular shaped island lying about 200 yards off the southern shores of St. Vincent, rising gradually to an eminence of about 150 ft. above sea level and having an area of nearly 25 acres.

"The Island", as it is popularly termed, is usually approached from the Villa Bay, situated about three miles along the southern coast of St. Vincent and within easy drive of Kingstown. A picturesque landing stage is provided on its northern shore.

On the islet are erected the necessary buildings for a quarantine station. Under the beautiful shady trees on the northern shore stands a mosquito-proof building to serve as a small hospital when required, while on the crest of the Island there is a commodious building containing five bedrooms and one large public room and surrounded by a spacious gallery for use as an observation station. The caretaker's lodge on the northeastern angle completing the trio, adds further charm to the scene.

These buildings are rented out by the Government and form an ideal and popular health resort.

The beauty of the scenery viewed from this islet is magnificent and has been compared to that of the English lake district, while fanned as it is by a continuous and gentle sea breeze, is cool, healthy, and invigorating. Excellent sea bathing is always to be obtained, the water being crystal clear over a bed of snowy white sand.

Many an hour, with good sport, can be spent by lovers of deep sea fishing on the surrounding waters, while at certain periods of the year the ramier, or wild pigeon, in its flight to and from the mainland, forms an excellent diversion for the expert marksman.*

THE LEEWARD DISTRICT

The central range of hills which forms the backbone of the island inclines nearer the sea on the Leeward side than on the windward. This difference imparts to the Leeward district a ruggedness which enhances its beauty but at the same time renders communication difficult and cultivation arduous. Human habitation is here confined practically to the sea coast, with the exception of a village or two in the wider valleys. The larger estates are all within easy reach of the sea, the lands of the interior being in the hands of peasant proprietors who live in the small towns and villages and pay daily visits to their gardens. The Government system of land allotment seems to be in a fair way towards success, and good results are already showing themselves everywhere, especially in the Chauncey-Questelle's settlement and in the Linley Valley. At a glance one perceives a striking contrast in the present condition of the whole of this district as against that of even four years ago. Cultivation has now turned to account large tracts of land that had been mere wilderness. Excellent cotton is produced along the whole of the coast. Arrowroot is also largely grown. The chief products of the interior are cocoa and, in larger quantities, ground provisions. This district is one of the main sources of supply for the vegetable market of Kingstown, whilst a large trade in vegetables is also carried on by sloop with Trinidad and other islands.

It is now possible to drive by motor car from Kingstown to Chateaubelair. The chief means of communication is however by sea in the subsidized launch, motor boat or row boats which vary in length from the little skull

---

*Duvernette islet is adjacent to Young's Island. It is the outer and smaller of the two, conical in shape, 204 feet high, and surmounted by an old fort. These islets are bordered on the east and south sides by a rocky bank extending off 200 yards. There is a narrow 5-fathom channel between them and the mainland.

boat of about eight feet to the large passage boats, the best of which measures 37 feet from bow to stern. Most of these boats are dugouts formed from the trunk of the gomea tree, with a "rising" made of white pine or other foreign wood.

There are three small towns in this district—Layou, 7½ miles from Kingstown; Barrouallie, 12 miles; and Chateaubelair, 21 miles. Barrouallie, the second to Kingstown in population, is the headquarters of the Government revenue department for the district and a port of entry. There is a splendid example of Carib inscriptions on a rock near Layou on the Bellewood Byeway, and another smaller petroglyph in a field of Reversion Estate adjoining the Town of Barrouallie. About half a mile along the coast to the north of Barrouallie is the precipice known as Indian Gallows, a face of rock with a sheer drop of 200 feet into the sea. Legend accounts for the name by describing how Carib husbands were wont to execute unfaithful wives by hurling them over the edge of this cliff to a swift and certain death. A beautiful specimen of basaltic rock is to be found in the Cumberland Valley at Spring Village. The scenery of the entire district is wonderful in its beauty and grandeur. The Buccament Valley Village and the view of the Cumberland Valley from the top of Belle Isle Hill afford a revelation of nature in the enjoyment of her richest endowments.

R. J. Laurie

THE WESTERN GLENS

"The Lord God planted a garden westward." Thus did a traveller paraphrase Genesis when writing of the West Indies. He had experience of many distant lands. And I, who only know England besides the West Indies, can say of Saint Vincent that it has a beauty equal to that of the Old Country—and what more can be said?

There are things in St. Vincent besides its beauty which will surprise or captivate you—its glorious climate, its volcano, its moonlight nights, and its Carib remains, to mention only a few things, but that which will remain is its sheer loveliness. And if you don't believe me, come to Chateaubelair.

It is a somewhat tedious journey certainly, and the means of travel not the fastest, but tell me if it is not worth it for the view as the boat passes Islet and enters Chateaubelair Bay. The green fields (so like England!) sloping up to hills covered with coconut palms which do duty for pines, the warm-tinted cliff to the left, the small town at the water's edge to the right, and over it all, the mountains. And no mere jumble of hills either. Note the massiveness of the round-topped, forest-clad hill above the town. Then turn to the left to that rugged spire of a mountain jutting into the blue of heaven, known as Morne Garu. Were ever two mountains less alike? Yet look further to the left and see the crowning glory of the bay, La Soufriere. The sun is shining on its gaunt bare slopes and on the bank of cloud above it. Often have I seen it at sunset, that bank of cloud giving it all the appearance of being in eruption! Mountains, hills, cliff, green fields and sea—surely such a picture as you would cross half the world to see!

But truly to appreciate the beauties of the district you must walk its paths and climb its hills. So, when you come, come prepared to stay.

If you have a stout heart you should try the Woods Road to Rose Hall. Up the High Street and down a little road to the right, across the river and over the "Plan", then by a path steeply up the hill and so to the main road. As you reach the top, look back, and I'll guarantee you won't want to move for a little while, for here is one of the most impressive views of Chateaubelair and its bay. From this height the Soufriere dominates the scene. The beach is fringed with white, and the cliff on the far side of the bay is reflected in the deep blue of the sea. And looking out beyond the bay those sentinels, the Pitons of St. Lucia, are dimly lined against the blue sky; on your right, the valley running up into the mountains and the clouds, in front, the majestic Soufriere and the mysterious woods of Morne Garu, to your left, the peacefulness of the summer sea.

But walk another 50 feet and so over the saddle of the hill, and there bursts upon you yet another glory, Petit Bordel Valley. Steeply from your feet runs down a field of bananas set in orderly array. At the bottom of the valley are avenues of coconut palms, then come more bananas, this time stretching up hill, then steep cliffs, and well above your head against the sky, peasant lands and plots. To your right, this time, a glimpse of the sea, and to your left, the everlasting hills. A fairy land of every shade of green imaginable, from the blue of the bananas to the amber of the coconuts.

Through this valley lies our way. We pass a small village of mud and thatch, and the tall chimney which reminds us of the days when sugar was king, and then take off our shoes and socks to cross the river. Strangely enough, we did not notice the river from the hillside! Now our way lies along a meadow beside this busy brook, and now, turning away from the river, we begin the serious work of the day, the climb.

The road gets stony. One has the impression of walking through a giant rockery set up on edge. Yet here a cow is feeding, and she stumbles clumsily into the bush to let us pass. By this time we have on our right a sheer cliff of rock, while we look down on our left to the river and the narrow path on its farther bank. Then suddenly the road seems to double on its tracks, and double back again. Now we seem to be clambering over a heap of stones under tropical foliage, and we think it is time to stop and take a breather.

And a good place for it, too. For now we look on Petit Bordel from the other side. Just a patch of cultivation is revealed to us and the road leading up to the old estate house on the hill top. Below, the river tumbles and splashes away to meet the sea. And all this is set in a framework of rock and fern and tree.

But there is another object of interest at this point. Clamber up the cliff to your right and you will come to a "marked stone", a comparatively smooth surface of rock with strange indentations. Mark these indentations with chalk, and strange shapes will stand revealed, faces and bodies such as your child aged five might draw. We are in the presence of one of the permanent memorials of the one-time owners of St. Vincent, the war-like Caribs. They were better artists, however, than these crude marks would lead you to think, as you will agree if you see any of their beautifully finished stone axe heads. But this rock is enough to set us many questions. What was its object? Was it intended to commemorate some savage feat of arms? Was it connected with some religious rite, or was it an essay in art pure and simple, especially simple? Such stones serve to remind us how little we know, how much is still hidden from our eyes.

But we start along the road again, which has taken another turn and climbs more steeply than before up what might best be termed a "corrugation" in the hillside. As we go we obtain an awe-inspiring view of a higher reach of the valley we have just left, a reach where it narrows into a fearsome gorge, down which the river leaps and jumps between its cliffs. But from our vantage point we cannot see (though we can hear) the river. All that presents itself to our eye is a defile of tropical green, hundreds of feet deep, the river hid at the bottom of its green mysteries. Not a break can we see in the primeval forest. As we climb the path the central range of mountains behind it seem to climb the sky to keep us company, and the gorge, majestic though it is, seems to dwarf in its presence.

But—in Vincentian—"What a heat!" A steaminess is hanging over all the woods, our clothes are wet rags clinging to our bodies, the sweat stings on our faces, and our hearts are doing overtime. One more stretch, however, round here, up there and round the corner, and we are at our half-way house, the "Old Works", at the top of the hill. We enter the sombre shade of a row of mahogany trees and look back to the view of the Soufriere. From here we can catch a glimpse of just one corner of Chateaubelair Bay, and now we can see how every hill around the bay leads up and up to the Soufriere and Morne

Garu, while those two mountains over-top all else. The cultivation, which seemed to stretch to the tops of the hills when we were in the valley, is now seen in its true proportion, the untamed mountain woods dominating all. All is silence, and the cadences of the river which still reach us, but serve to intensify a stillness which speaks of overflowing life. A place where one himself should be still, and let the peace and grandeur steal into our own hearts, and thank God that He has kept some places from man's spoliation—and those the wildest.

And now as we press on again, we enter a new world. Nothing could be more striking than the change from the country we have lately passed through. We have finished with the river and the steaming foliage, the woods and narrow gorges. But when we had thought that we had also finished with man's handiwork, we find ourselves in the midst of it again. Now we are in the peasant lands, mostly bare of trees, too much so for their good. A very steep part of the South Downs might look like this were it cultivated and could it grow palms. Some of the trees, such as those with leaves a foot across, also seem out of place. But apart from this, the green of everything, its gentle aspect, the absence of a single angle to any of the hills, the fresh cool breeze, the sea standing up to the sky above the hills, and even an occasional bleat, remind us irresistibly of Sussex or of Dorset. We pass along the edge of "Basin", a hollow as smooth and well-rounded and its sides as steep as its name implies, and join the main road from Troumaca. We are still climbing, but the air and breeze coming ever fresher and cooler invigorate us so that the exertion of the climb is forgotten.

And now we come to the village and find ourselves bestride a ridge 1,200 feet above sea level. A crowd round the water pipe, a host of small boys in shirt tails, a few men and more women make most use of the road. There are half a dozen nice houses and many dozen in terrible squalor. What conditions must be like when the whole family is inside at night and every chink stopped up, one shudders to think. And yet, such is the climate of this village that its health is better than any other place around. Almost the only thing which kills the people is old age! But look around and beyond the village. Every way you look is a panorama fit for Mount Olympus. On one side we look over a maze of wooded hills to the mountains beyond. On the other is the sea, some two and a half miles distant. And to the north the same two sentinels, inescapable, Soufriere and Morne Garu.

What would you like to drink? I can recommend the coconuts and the milk. And after that, and a rest, well, we can talk about returning. If you like we can walk towards the sea to Troumaca and then along the coast road home. Or we can visit the little village even further back known as Jack Hill and then return through the old estate of Palmyra. There are half a dozen variations on the theme, all equally beautiful. Tomorrow of course you may prefer to take things more quietly. Well, we can have a swim at Petit Bordel, or stroll through the lanes of Golden Grove where there are ruins of what must have been the palace home of one of the old-time planters. But there are longer excursions as well, by boat up the wild coast northwards to the Baleine Falls, and by foot to Newfoundland or Tuscany. And of course you could not face your friends if you had to confess that you had visited Chateaubelair but had not climbed the Soufriere! How much they miss who visit St. Vincent and "do" it while their boat is in port!

So once again, when you come, come prepared to stay awhile.

R. A. Marsh

MINERAL SPRINGS

The spring at Belair is about three miles from Kingstown and may be visited by driving in a car whilst admiring the varied cultivation and the landscape within view from the boundaries of Kingstown right on to the spot.

In consequence of the value the Government has attached to this spring, the area of land on which it is situated was reserved when the Authorities at that time dismembered the Estate for Land Settlement purposes. The particular place at which the water rushes upward to the surface of the earth has been enclosed by masonry and is entirely protected.

When the top is open, perhaps to gratify the wishes of visitors, the gurgling sound is audible and attempt to inhale the air emitted from within the enclosure is somewhat suffocating.

It has been said that the water, which is pleasant to the taste, is a saline aperient, rich in muriate and sulphate of soda, well-carbonated and slightly sulphurious. It is exceedingly enjoyable when used with beverages, spirituous or otherwise.

Adjacent to the base of Petit Bonhomme in the Marriaqua Valley, nine miles from Kingstown, there is a similar spring of greater strength, but because of the distance and imperfect road, it is not visited for the purpose of drinking of the spring as in the case of the one at Belair.

The residents at the Belair Settlement use the water there freely as a natural source of supply.

Remarks of E. G. S., a tourist:

At Belair plantation, which is about three miles from Kingstown, is a spring of mineral water. This water is soft and very pleasant to the taste, and when mixed with whisky, gin or other liquors, is still more so. If this spring was situated in Germany, its virtues would be known all over the world by this time. The Spa is well worthy of a visit, and the tourist at the same time has the opportunity of seeing one of the best cultivated plantations in the island.

BEQUIA

Bequia, of course, is one of the islands in that chain, stretching along the Caribbean Sea and known as "The Lost Atlantis". These islands are the crests of what must have been lofty mountains before the continent was submerged long ages ago. The atmosphere of Bequia, though not now so elevated as it was originally, is nevertheless elevating to the human mind and to health.

Coral polyps, as is their way, in making their homes at sea level on the fringes of this submerged peak which sits on the floor of the Atlantic, are slowly but surely adding to the size of Bequia; the sands are being piled up by the sea and held together by grasses on the shore. Let us hope that this continuing growth will not be taken notice of by the Land Tax Commissioners! And so in time, but not in our time I fear, there'll be more of Bequia; well, one can do with more of Bequia!

An oblong stretch of a mixture of soil and rock, some 6 or 7 miles in length and, in parts two in width, fringed by white beaches and bold headlands, lies N.E. and S.W. like a green mound on the vast blue ocean, just 13 degrees north of the equator with the coast of the Spanish Main some 200 miles to the S. of W.

Here can be gathered that welcome feeling of quiet rest, undisturbed by ambition or distress. It seems to be a spot outside of the world and its never-ending strife. The atmosphere is unique—it is a product of years and years of unhurried years.

In that mysterious hour of dawn, when most others are yet asleep, it is somewhat weird to witness the birth of day and the rousing of nature in this remote and secluded spot.

Into the stillness of the Bequia afternoons and sunsets enter many small sounds like minor themes in a symphony. There is the brittle snapping of the logwood pods and the falling of the seeds to the ground; soft rise and fall of wind among leaves, like something that neither comes nor goes, but is just born and dies! The soft whirr of a bird's wings, flying low, is a sudden sound separate from all others. Corn blades moving together with a sighing sound.

311

When night comes only the low voices of the wind and the sea can be heard and perhaps a welcome shower of rain pattering on the roof and lulling one to sleep, to dream if at all, only of an "island of dreams".

Anonymous

Places of Worship

(For S. George's Cathedral see page 289;
For Roman Catholic Church see page 292)

THE METHODIST CHURCH

The Methodist Church in St. Vincent is carried on by the Methodist Missionary Society, of 24 Bishopsgate, London, E.C.2. It is included in the Barbados, Trinidad and Guiana District, which is made up of the Windward Islands, Barbados, Trinidad and Tobago, and British Guiana. Chairman and General Superintendent: Rev. R. W. Charlesworth, 3 Victoria Avenue, Port of Spain; Secretary of the District: Rev. Herbert H. Cole, Mission House, Kingstown, St. Vincent.

There are three circuits in the Island: Kingstown Circuit with churches at Kingstown, Calliaqua, Brighton, Gomea, Hope, Chauncey, Mount Coke, Marriaqua, and Evesham; Georgetown Circuit with churches at Georgetown, Union, South Rivers, Biabou, and Dicksons; and Chateaubelair Circuit with churches at Chateaubelair, Westwood, Barrouallie, Layou, and Spring Village. Services are also held regularly in the Government School at Troumaca. There are three ministers resident in Kingstown, one each at Georgetown and Chateaubelair.

There are twelve Methodist Day Schools in the island managed by the ministers. The number of declared Methodists in the island at the last census was 18,176.

CHURCH OF SCOTLAND

The Church of Scotland in St. Vincent dates from the year 1839. At that time and much later there were many more Scots in the Colony than at the present, but the church continues its work now chiefly among the natives.

In 1902 it was endowed by the late Alexander Porter, Esq, who bequeathed for that purpose £5,000 on condition that only a Scotsman be minister. The organization is under the control of the Colonial Committee of the Church of Scotland who contributes towards the minister's salary in addition to the interest of the endowment, about £100 per annum.

313

In connection with the Church in Kingstown there is Cane Hall mission two miles out.

THE SALVATION ARMY

In the year 1905 Ensign Richard Grant and Lieutenant Patrick Cyrus, both of whom have been described as pioneers, conducted services in premises at Hillsboro Street, Kingstown. At that time Major William Joy was the Divisional Commander in residence at Barbados. The work was carried on successfully, and in 1914 the Army's principal officers purchased land and buildings at Melville and Middle Streets in the city where the services are now regularly conducted. The officer in charge at the present time is Major Henry J. Hogan.

SEVENTH DAY ADVENTISTS

Colporteurs preceded the landing in St. Vincent on 16th October, 1901, the first Seventh Day Adventists missionaries, Elder E. Van Deusen and wife of Michigan, U.S.A. Meetings were held in a rented house in Kingstown for some time. A little chapel was erected at Montrose and dedicated on 12th July, 1903.

There are at present four churches in the island and three companies, also two churches in the Grenadines. Churches: Montrose, Park Hill, Richland Park, Vermont, Bequia, Union Island. Companies: Coull's Hill, Georgetown, Layou.

President—Elder, GORDEN OSS (Trinidad)

District leader—HENRY WISEMAN

Local Elder—JAMES A. WALKER

314

THE GOSPEL HALL

HALIFAX STREET AND MURRAY ROAD

The Brethren held their first services in St. Vincent over forty years ago. The Hall now occupied was purchased in 1903, at which time Mr. Thomas Wales was missionary. Kingstown is the oldest assembly, with others of more recent founding in Georgetown, Stubbs, Brighton, Mesopotamia, and in the islands of Bequia and Union.

NOTE: There are several other places throughout the Colony where persons assemble to pray, sing and in other ways conduct services peculiar to their religious persuasions.

Constitution

The Legislature of St. Vincent, which was created in 1767, originally consisted of a Governor, a nominated Council of twelve members, (which acted in the double capacity of a privy Council and a Legislative Council), and an elected House of Assembly of nineteen members, including two for the Grenadines.

In 1844 an Act was passed extending the qualification and increasing the number of seats by six. Her Majesty graciously assented to this Act and the new Legislature, with a House of Assembly of 25 members, was opened in 1845 by Sir William Struth, who was then administering the Government.

In 1850 an Act was passed which reduced the Assembly to its former number of 19.

The Assembly relapsed into its old habits, and its existence was cut short by the Governor's Proclamation dissolving it on the 15th December, 1855.

The Executive Council Act was further modified in 1868, when the change of constitution from the double to the single Chamber rendered the Act of 1864 inoperative. An Act was then passed leaving it in the hands of the Queen to appoint whom she pleased to the Executive Council.

Doctor Checkley's first idea seems to have been that Crown Colony Government should be substituted for the existing form, and, twice in the early part of the Session of 1866, he gave notice of a resolution to this effect without, however, at the time moving the resolution.

This he did on the 28th of August, when he moved that the proposed change should be submitted to the people at a general election. Doctor Checkley carried his resolution by 7 to 2. This resolution, having been transmitted to the Lieut. Governor, was submitted to the Secretary of State for the Colonies. The general election took place almost immediately after the passing of this resolution. The proposition of a Crown Colony, however, did not appear to find favour with the electors as, though Governor Berkeley alluded to the impending change to Crown Colony Government in his opening speech on the 30th October, Doctor Checkley moved on the following day a resolution in favour of a single Chamber, which was carried by 12 to 5.

This was followed up by the passing in the Assembly, on the 27th November, of a Bill to abolish the existing Constitution and to establish a single Chamber. This Bill was framed upon the principle that the new Chamber should be composed of three official, three nominated, and seven elected members, the House to choose its own President, or Speaker. It will thus be seen that the Assembly contemplated retaining a controlling majority.

317

On the same day on which this Bill was passed, a despatch from the Secretary of State was laid before the Legislature in which Lord Carnavon (referring to the resolution of the House of Assembly of the 28th August that the Island should be made a Crown Colony) said, "Her Majesty's Government will feel it to be their duty, should the Legislature desire it, to assume the responsibility of governing the Colony by the authority of the Crown."

In opening the Legislative Session in 1867, Lieut. Governor Berkeley, referring to the Bill passed on the 27th November of the previous year for altering the Constitution, said, "As from the nature of a measure recently passed for effecting a change in the form of Government of the Colony, it is more than probable that this is the last opportunity I shall have of personally addressing the Legislature of St. Vincent as at present constituted, I cannot conceal my regret that the necessity of any such change should have become apparent, an acknowledgment that conveys with it the admission that there is a lack of ability and independence in the community requisite to administer the affairs of the local Government after a form that has stood the test to which it has been subjected for many years, and which is nearly after the model of that in existence in the mother country. It is true that the line of policy recently pursued has not been progressive, but the question may fairly be asked whether the Government would have been justified in deviating from the beaten track, in the face of an embarrassed exchequer."

On the 2nd April, Governor Berkeley communicated in a message to the Legislature the views of the Imperial Government on the Bill of the 27th November. He informed the Houses that the Secretary of State could not advise the Queen's confirmation of the Bill, unless with such amendments as would give a casting vote in the Legislature to the Crown. Mr. Berkeley's message contained the following passage, "Should you desire to make a change in the constitution of St. Vincent, it can only be on the condition of giving to the Crown a potential voice in the Legislature of the Colony."

A new Legislature comprising 12 members—six elected, three nominated by the Crown and three ex officio with a President appointed by the Governor having a casting vote—met for the first time on 29th January, 1868.

The constitution of 1867 was virtually ended on 22nd September, 1875.

It was not until December, 1877, that the Queen's instructions with regard to it arrived in the Colony, nor until January, 1878, that the Lieut. Governor formally opened, for the first time, the new Council which was in future to legislate for St. Vincent.

From that period a new era commenced in legislation, and while a large amount of useful work has been accomplished, the utmost harmony has marked the proceedings of the Legislature.

318

The Governor of the Windward Islands resides in Grenada but there is an Administrator in St. Vincent. It now consists of an Administrator, Executive Council, and Legislative Council. The Administrator presides over the two Councils in the absence of the Governor of the Windward Islands. In pursuance of an Order in Council dated 21st March, 1924, which came into operation on 1st December, 1924. a partly Elective Legislative Council was constituted, consisting of the Governor, four ex officio members, one nominated unofficial member and three elected members, i.e., one from each of the electoral districts into which the Colony was divided.

Pursuant to an Order in Council dated 27th October, 1936, which came into operation by Proclamation on 18th December, 1936, the nominated and elected members were respectively increased, namely, three ex officio members, three nominated members and five elected members, one for each of the new electoral districts.

Civil Establishment

GOVERNOR'S OFFICE

Governor and Commander-in-Chief of the Windward Islands, His Excellency H. B. Popham, (CMG, MBE)—£2,500—From St. Vincent £375.

Aide-de-Camp and Private Secretary, Lieut. Commander C. D. Milbourne—From St. Vincent £75.

Secretary to Government of Windward Islands, John M. Knight, (MBE)—From St. Vincent £110.

ADMINISTRATOR'S OFFICE

Administrator, Arthur Alban Wright, (CMG)—£1,000 plus £200 duty allowance.

Chief Clerk, S. C. Connell—£250-300 by 10—£50 personal allowance.

Secretary to Administrator, Gordon V. Mancini—£200 to 300 by £10.

Second Clerk, R. Nicholas Jack—£150-200 by 10. Manager Printing Office—£30.

Third Clerk, Dorothy M. Munro—£60-80 by 5.

Fourth Clerk, Freda Grant—£60-80 by 5.

Copyist, Winifred King—£40-50 by 4.

Shorthand Typist, Vacant—£60-80 by 5.

Foreman Printer, J. B. Garraway—£100-150 by 10.

Commissioner of Labour, Vacant—£450.

TREASURY

Treasurer, Collector of Customs and Chief of Excise, Louis Percival Spence —£500. Travelling allowance—£50.

Chief Inland Revenue Officer, V. D. Archer—£250-300 by 10.

First Clerk Treasury, S. F. Leigertwood—£150-200 by 10.

Second Clerk, McD. Smith—£100-150 by 10.

Third Clerk, A. V. Sprott—£100-150 by 10.

Fourth Clerk, G. A. Forde—£60-80 by 5.

Fifth Clerk, H. H. Hamlet—£60-80 by 5.

Sixth Clerk, J. V. Alves—£60-80 by 5.

Seventh Clerk, P. D. O'N. Crichton—£60-80 by 5.

Chief Revenue and Port Officer, A. C. H. Baynes—£200-250 by £10.

First Class Revenue Officer, Barrouallie, E. G. S. Inniss-£150- 200 by 10.

First Class Revenue Officer, Georgetown, J. V. Venner—£150- 200 by 10.

Excise Officer, J. A. McKie—£100-150 by 10.

Second Class Revenue Officer, A. L. Williams—£80-100 by 5.

Second Class Revenue Officer, H. A. Bowman—£80-100 by 5.

Second Class Revenue Officer, J. H. D. Cox—£60-80 by 5.

AUDIT DEPARTMENT

Auditor Windward Islands, J. K. Buchanan—£600.
Audit Clerk, A. L. Dopwell—£200-250 by 10.
Second Audit Clerk, B. A. Richards—£80-103 by 5.
Third Audit Clerk, C. R. Williams—£60-80 by 5.

POST OFFICE

Postmaster, G. Elford Williams--£250-300 by 10.
Chief Clerk, J. A. Matthews--£100-150 by 10.
Second Clerk, A. E. McConnie—£80-100 by 5.
Third Clerk, C. E. Jackson—£60-80 by 5.
Fourth Clerk, Sybil Wall—£40-50 by 4.

JUDICIAL & LEGAL DEPARTMENTS

Chief Justice and Magistrate District 1, G. C. Griffith Williams— £650-700 by 20.
Clerk to Police Magistrate District 1, V. F. Bonadie—£60-80 by 5.
Attorney General, H. A. O'Reilly—£500.
Clerk to Attorney General, J. R. V. B. Cox—£60-80 by 5.
Registrar Supreme Court etc., G. Elmore Edwards—£250-300 by 10.
Clerk to Registrar, A. L. Samuel—£60-80 by 5.
Bailiff Supreme Court, Alvin Seales—£80-100 by 5.
Police Magistrate District 2 and Coroner, Vacant (M. Byron Cox Acting)—£300-350 by 20.
Clerk to Police Magistrate District 2, A. V. King—£80-100 by 5.

POLICE AND PRISONS

Chief of Police, Superintendent of Prisons and Chief Relieving Officer, Major H. Grist—£300-400 by 25.
Sub-Inspector, E. J. Romer Ormiston—£200-300 by 10 plus 50 house allowance.
Senior Sergeant, Frederick John—£110.
2nd Sergeant, James Bramble—£100.
3rd Sergeant, Euston Commissiong—£95.
Chief Warder Prison, Jonathan Joshua—£86-90 by 2.
Matron Female Prison, Elfrida Williams—£40-50 by 4

LOCAL FORCES

Officer in Command, Major H. Grist
Captain, Alban DaSantos
Adjutant, E. J. Romer Ormiston

Lieutenant, Vacant

Second Lieutenants, D. S. Cozier and G. V. Mancini

ST. VINCENT GRENADINES

Medical Officer, District Officer and Magistrate, Dr. K. J. E. McMillan—£120.

Clerical Assistant, A. J. DaSilva—£50 as a clerk; £12 house allowance and £6 duty allowance.

AGRICULTURAL DEPARTMENT

Agricultural Superintendent, Vacant—£450-600 by 25 (C. K. Robinson, Acting)

Field Assistant, L. W. Brown—£100-150 by 5

Foreman Botanic and Experiment Stations and Ranger Government House Lands, R. Vanloo—£60-80 by 5—Free Quarters

Clerical Assistant, Agri. Superintendent, Sydney E. R. Anderson —£40-50 by 4

Cotton Research Officer, Stanley Evelyn—£600

Laboratory Assistant to Research Officer, Nora Grant—£50

Clerical Assistant, Joyce Dean—£50

Instructor for Banana Industry, George Fraser—£150

EDUCATION DEPARTMENT

Headmaster Grammar School, Vacant—£500 (W. M. Lopey, Acting)

First Assistant Master, W. M. Lopey—£250-300 by 10

Second Assistant Master, D. S. Cozier—£200-250 by 10

Third Assistant Master, V. A. Archer—£200-250 by 10

Fourth Assistant Master, V. G. I. DaSilva—£125-175 by 10

Headmistress Girls' High School, L. Smith Moffett—£250- 350 by 10

First Assistant Mistress, Annie Jackson--£100-150 by 10

Second Assistant Mistress, Sheila Wall—£100-150 by 10

Third Assistant Mistress, R. M. Windebank--£100-150 by 10

Fourth Assistant Mistress, Marjorie Pilgrim--£80-100 by 5

PRIMARY EDUCATION.

Inspector of Schools, Clifford G. Palmer—£300-350 by 10

Clerical Assistant, K. V. Jacobs—50

Secretary to Board of Education, R. N. Jack—£12

MEDICAL DEPARTMENT

Senior Medical Officer, J. A. Henderson—£700.

Resident Surgeon Colonial Hospital, Dr. A. Lai Kiow—£400-450 by 20 plus 50 personal allowance

Medical Officer District 1 and Port Health Officer, Dr. H. B. Gregory—£400-450 by 20 plus 28 as P.H.O.

Supernumerary Medical Office, Dr. W. C. G. Murray—£300- 400 by 20

Medical Officer District 2 North, Dr. Reginald Austin—£300-400 by 20

Medical Officer District 2 South and Radiologist, Dr. A. B. Brereton—£400-450 by 20

Medical Officer District 3, Dr. E. D. B. Charles—£400-450 by 20

Medical Officer District 4, Dr. Frank C. Alexis—£400-450 by 20

Medical Officer District 5, Dr. J. W. Gallwey—£400-450 by 20

Medical Officer Southern Grenadines, Dr. K. J. E. McMillan— £300-400 by 20

Nurse Matron, Ivy Freeth—£180-200 by 10

Clerk, Medical Department, M. J. Cropper—£60-80 by 5

Steward & Chief Dispenser Colonial Hospital, E. T. Young— £150-200 by 10, Personal Allowance £25

Second Dispenser, Cyril E. Daisey—£80-100 by 5

Assistant Dispenser, E. Mackie—£60-80 by 5

Laboratory Assistant., M. F. McDowall—£60-80 by 5

Headkeeper Fort Institutions, E. D. Wall—£100-150 by 10

ELECTRICITY DEPARTMENT

Superintendent of Electricity & Telephone Department, J. A. Maloney—£450 plus £40 house allowance

Clerk and Storekeeper, A. D. Duncan—£80-100 by 5

Clerical Assistant, Muriel E. Forde—£40

PUBLIC WORKS DEPARTMENT

Superintendent, Sydney B. Isaacs—£350-400 by 15

Assistant Superintendent of Works, J. P. E. Cropper—£250-300 by £10

Chief Clerk, M. B. Brown £80-100 by 5

Second Clerk, Nellie D. Sprott --£80-100 by 5

Third Clerk, Cynthia B. Isaacs—£60-80 by 5

Foreman Public Works, Joseph Ross—£100-120 by 8, plus £10 duty allowance

Overseer of Crown Lands, Alvin McIntosh—£80-100 by 5

Overseer of Roads, Vivian Durrant-£80-100 by 5

Overseer of Roads, Clairmonte Providence—£80-100 by 5

Overseer of Roads, George Brown- £80-100 by 5

GOVERNMENT COTTON GINNERY

Manager, G. A. Grant—£200

Overseer, C. Bute—£80

Mechanic, Simeon Jack £80

Accountant, R. A. Horne—£100

323

SANITARY DEPARTMENT

Chief Sanitary Inspector, J. L. Chapman—£250-275 by 10. Travelling Allowance £80

District 1, E. G. Williams—£50-60 by 5

District 2 (North), W. A. Providence - £50-60 by 5

District 2 (South), F. A. Trotman—£50-60 by 5

District 3, C. Phills—£50-60 by 5

District 4, A. T. W. Bellingy—£50-60 by 5. Travelling Allowances, £20 each

Councils, Boards, etc.

EXECUTIVE COUNCIL

The Governor, the Administrator, the Attorney General, the Treasurer, Dr. J. A. Henderson, Honourables F. A. Corea, P. W. Verrall, C. B. Sayles (JP).

LEGISLATIVE COUNCIL

The Governor, the Administrator, the Attorney General, the Colonial Treasurer. Nominated Members: Honourables A. M. Punnett, A. M. Fraser (OBE), W. A. Hadley. Elected Members: Geo. A. McIntosh, Kingstown District; N. S. Nanton, North Windward District; A. C. Allen, South Windward District; H. A. Davis, Leeward District; D. C. McIntosh, Grenadines District.

BOARD OF EDUCATION

Rev. H. H. Cole, Chairman; the Senior Medical Officer; the Agricultural Superintendent; the Headmaster, Grammar School; the Headmistress, Girls' High School; the Inspector of Schools, the Right Rev. H. N. Vincent Tonks, the Rev. Father Dom Carlos Verbeke (OSB), Honourable N. S. Nanton, R. M. Anderson, Esq; R. T. Samuel, Esq; Secretary, R. Nicholas Jack.

MEDICAL BOARD

The Senior Medical Officer, the Medical Officer, District 1, the Medical Officer, District 3.

SANITARY AUTHORITY

The Senior Medical Officer, Chairman; the Medical Officer, District 1; the Medical Officer, District 3; the Honourable the Attorney General; the Superintendent of Works, W. M. Grant, Esq, the Honourable G. A. McIntosh, nominated by the Kingstown Board.

KINGSTOWN BOARD

Elected—Honourables Geo. A. McIntosh, H. A. Davis, St. Clair Bonadie, Esq, Henry Bonadie, Esq

Nominated—Honourable L. P. Spence, R. G. Cropper, Esq, R. T. Samuel, Esq, A. G. Hazell, Esq

Warden, Mr. O. C. Cruikshank; Assistant Warden, Mr. O. Iton

ARROWROOT BOARD

Elected—Honourables F. A. Corea, W. A. Hadley, A. M. Punnett, Messrs. Orange Hill Estate Ltd., Stanley deFreitas, A. G. Hazell

Nominated—Colonial Treasurer, Agricultural Supt, R, Minors, Esq

Ecclesiastical

CHURCH OF THE PROVINCE OF THE WEST INDIES
(Anglican)

Bishop of the Windward Islands, The Rt. Rev. H. N. Vincent Tonks
Archdeacon of SS. Vincent and Lucia, The Venerable H. G. Pigott, (M.A.)
Chancellor, His Worship G. Elmore Edwards
Canons, The Venerable H. G. Pigott, M.A.
The Venerable H. T. Shaw, M.A.
The Rev. Canon B. A. Samuel
The Rev. Canon R. J. Laurie, M.A.
The Rev. Canon G. A. I. Frederick, B.A.
The Rev. Canon A. W. Johnson

Parish of SS. George and Andrew, Kingstown

Dean and Rector, The Rt. Rev. H. N. Vincent Tonks
Acting Rector, The Rev. Canon A. W. Johnson
Assistant Priest, The Rev. Canon G. A. I. Frederick, B.A.
Churchwardens , The Honourable H. A. Davis and St. C. McConnie, Esq
Lay Representatives, The Honourable H. A. Davis and St. C. McConnie, Esq

(The Parish Church of S. George was made the Cathedral Church of the Windward Islands in 1884. Other places of worship are S. John's, Belair; S. Mary's, Buccament; The Church School, Lowmans.)

Parish of S. Paul, Calliaqua

Rector, The Rev. A. C. Johnson
Churchwardens, J. H. Walker and D. H. George, Esq
Licensed Reader, J. H. Walker, Esq
Lay Representative, George Stephens, Esq

(Other places of worship are S. Sylvan's, Stubbs; S. Philips, Mesopotamia; S. Matthias', Evesham.)

Parish of Holy Trinity, Georgetown

Acting Rector, The Rev. C. V. Eversley, L.Th.
Churchwardens, W. Thomas and E. Hadley, Esq
Licensed Reader, A. B.Nibbs, Esq
Lay Representative, W. Thomas, Esq

(Other places of worship are S. Peter's, Mount Greenan; S. Matthew's, Biabou; S. John's, Owia; The Church School, Sandy Bay; The Church School, Byera; The Church School, Lowmans; The Mission Room, Greggs.)

Parish of SS. Patrick and David, Barrouallie

Acting Rector, The Rev. E. O. Buxo (LTh)
Licensed Readers, G. M. Sandy, T. W. Clarke and R. A. Brereton, Esq
Lay Representatives, G. M. Sandy and T. W. Clarke, Esq

(Other places of worship are S. David's, Chateaubelair; S. Mary Magdalene's, Coull's Hill; S. James', Layou; All Saints', Rose Bank.)

The Grenadines

Acting Rector, The Rev. Canon A. W. Johnson
Licensed Reader, S. Martin, Esq
Lay Representative, A. Dopwell, Esq

(Places of worship are S. Mary's, Bequia; Christ Church, Canouan; Mission Room, Paget Farm, Bequia; Mission Room, Mustique.)

S. Matthias', Union Island, is served by the Acting Rector of Carriacou, The Rev. I. M. Yerbury.

THE METHODIST CHURCH
Ministers

Kingstown Circuit, Rev. Herbert H. Cole, Superintendent, Mission House, Kingstown
Rev. S. J. Caulton, Montrose
Rev. B. Crosby, Montrose
Georgetown Circuit, Rev. W. Austin Titley, Mission House, Georgetown
Chateaubelair Circuit, Rev. R. A. Marsh, Mission House, Chateaubelair

Education

―――――◆◆∞◆◆―――――

ST. VINCENT, like the rest of the world, has experienced and is still experiencing a renaissance in educational thought and practice.

With remarkable persistence, and in the face of many and real difficulties, she has been trying to keep abreast of the times and has been reconditioning her education system from time to time in the light of modern ideals and local requirements.

A cursory retrospect will reveal the extent of our progress and, incidentally, explain why greater progress has not been made hitherto.

As in the Mother Country, the pioneer work was undertaken by societies, under the auspices of the churches. The Conversion Society and the Society for the Education of the Poor were at work in this colony at the same time, and in a similar capacity as the Royal Lancastrian Association and the British and Foreign School Society were in England; and it is interesting to note that Parliament's first grant to education in England was £20,000 given in 1833, and Government's first grant to education in St. Vincent was £80 given in 1834.

Government did not assume responsibility for the education of the people until 1849, when 27 schools were "aided" with £815 to be distributed among them. The Saint Vincent Grammar School dates from this year. At that time this institution provided education for boys and girls together along the lines of a General Classical and Mathematical curriculum. There were 49 pupils on role in this Grammar School in 1850. They paid £6 per quarter each for tuition fees.

It was just around this time that the first major misfortune put back the hands of the colony's education clock. Cholera and yellow fever broke out (1853), and after being a scourge for a considerable time, left the colony's finance crippled and its population greatly decimated.

The occurrence of this epidemic was all the more deplorable because it checked the laudable efforts of the Education Act of 1853 to establish an enduring system of education". The funds available for education were reduced from £904 in 1854 to £153 in 1855, and for want of financial support, 15 Schools, including the Grammar School, were closed, leaving a total of but 17 Schools in the colony.

Three years after (1857), the colony's first Board of Education was formed. It comprised the Governor (ex officio President), the President and two other members of the Legislative Council, the Speaker, and four other members of the House of Assembly. £700 from the general revenue was to be distributed to the schools by the board thus:

> Church of England Schools, £425
> Wesleyan Schools, £200
> Roman Catholic Schools, £ 75

Things assumed a more promising aspect thenceforth, so promising that we find that the expenditure on education rose from £1,286 in 1874 to £2,100 in 1878, and the Grammar School was re-established. This period of cornucopia for education was mainly the result of the disestablishment of the Anglican Church, which released funds that went to the benefit of the schools; and when the hurricane of September 1898 visited the island, the 17 schools of 1854 had increased to 44, twenty-six of which the hurricane demolished.

It will be seen that the career of our present education system has been one of many ups and downs, but the downs have left more of their depression than the ups their elevation.

After the hurricane, an attempt was made to put the colony back on its feet, and, following the findings of the Royal Commission of 1897, an Agricultural School was opened in October 1900. Many of the schools destroyed by the hurricane were also rebuilt.

The island no sooner started again on its forward march than its progress was again arrested by another natural upheaval, the eruption of the Soufriere volcano in May 1902. In 1903 the number of schools had again fallen to 27, as against 68 in 1880; the Education Grant also dropped.

Up to this time the colony had seen four inspectors of schools. Mr. Edward Ross served 1858-1861. The inspectorate was vacant from 1861 until 1872, when Mr. Thomas Angell Bennett, Immigration Officer, was appointed Inspector of Schools in conjunction with his other duties. After Mr. Bennett came Mr. N. W. Foster in 1877, then Mr. F. H. Watkins in 1883. Mr. F. W. Griffith (1890) preceded Mr. Frederick William Reeves (MA, Cambridge), who came on the scene six years after the eruption. Mr. Reeves made a gigantic attempt to put secondary education on a good footing and to direct the progress of primary education at the same time. The colossal tasks of being headmaster of the newly restarted Grammar School and Inspector of Schools, in charge of 27 primary schools proved too much for even Mr. Reeves, and he gave his health, his life, in the attempt to do above the work of about four men.

During the administration of the Honourable Gideon Murray (now Lord Elibank), a measure of consideration was given to the matter of teachers' salaries, and primary school headmasters heard with joy that it was then possible for them to attain a maximum salary of $26 per month.

The war had its usual stop-action on the active control and interest in education on the part of the authorities.

Under Mr. Popham Lobb's administration various increases in salaries were recommended. Capitation fees and certificate grants were introduced.

In 1922 the Island Scholarship was established, tenable for five years at any university in Europe, Canada or the U.S.A. In 1926 student teacherships were arranged. Funds were set aside to provide a two-year course of training at the Rawle Institute, Barbados, for two pupil teachers on the result of the third year pupil teachers' local examination. The same year saw the Headteachers' Pension Ordinance.

Major Peebles did much during his administration (1929-1933) to better the status of teachers and to lift the prestige of the primary schools.

His Honour, Arthur Francis Grimble (now Governor of the Seychelles), who succeeded Major Peebles, in spite of great administrative difficulties and a somewhat deficient treasury, had many sound schemes in view for the betterment of the education system, but his promotion came before all his schemes materialised.

Such is the cauldron of vicissitudes out of which our education system has emerged, or is just emerging. We have had to encounter tremendous physical, political, natural, and economic difficulties in our struggle upwards, but we are now at a stage where we can hope for a good future for our educational system.

In 1931 Mr. A. I. Mayhew, (CIE), member of the Colonial Office Advisory Committee on Education, and Mr. F. C. Marriot, (CBE, MA), made a searching inquiry into the system of education. The result is the well-known Marriot-Mayhew Report, the recommendations of which would result in a thorough modernisation of the primary and secondary school systems of the West Indies, if the means were to be found for putting these recommendations into operation.

As long as there is education there must be educational problems, for conflict is the very essence of education. The whole civilised world is today faced with educational problems, and St. Vincent is no exception to the rule.

At present the bug-bear is poverty, but the local Handwork Exhibition of April 1937; the good work that is being done in some of the schools under adverse circumstances; the efforts on the part of local teachers to acquire diplomas and certificates; the recent resuscitation of the St. Vincent Teachers' Association; and the general optimism of the teachers, are all indications that "we will be what you are".

Mr. E. C. M. Theobalds, London-trained teacher and Inspector of Schools has done a considerable amount of good and valuable work here, and to him belongs the praise for the infusion of true professional consciousness into the veins of our local teachers. Mr. Theobalds is now on the Inspectorate in Jamaica.

A very pleasing feature has been the selection by Government of competent schoolmasters to act in the absence of Inspectors of Schools. Mr. C. W. Prescod who is at present acting for Mr. Clifford Palmer, (now in England), is the Headmaster of the Georgetown Government School. Mr. Thomas Webster Clarke was the first primary school teacher to act in this capacity, doing so for Mr. E. C. M. Theobalds, when as Inspector he went to England as a Carnegie Scholar.

The most recent demonstration of the progress that primary education is making in the colony is an Education Week, which took place January 10th to 16th, 1938, under the auspices of the St. Vincent Teachers' Association. This effort was a success, and officials and clergy of the colony were represented at the various meetings. His Honour H. A. O'Reilly, Acting Chief Justice, opened and closed this Education Week.

There is hope for the educational system of this colony, for the better staffing of the schools together with the raising of the salaries and qualifications of teachers will surely bring about the materialisation of our dreams.

The number of schools is divided as follows:

> Government schools, 14
> Anglican schools, 9
> Methodist schools, 13
> Roman Catholic schools, 2

Thus, a total of 38

At the end of December 1936, the number of teachers employed was 188.

> Certificated Head Teachers, 36
> Uncertificated Head Teachers, 2
> Certificated Assistant Head Teachers, 37
> Uncertificated Assistant Head Teachers, 6
> Pupil Teachers and Monitors, 107

Eleven of the certificated teachers are trained teachers.

This year (1938) will see the abolition of the monitorial class of teachers.

THE GRAMMAR SCHOOL

The school, which was opened in 1908 under the headmastership of F. W. Reeves, Esq, (MA, Cantab.) with an attendance of 12 boys, made steady and excellent progress under his energetic control. The attendance steadily increased until in 1923 there were 79 names on the roll. Mr. Reeves was also Inspector of Schools until 1924, when the two posts were at last separated. It was more than time that two men should be doing the work of two departments, and the school undoubtedly benefited by the new arrangement.

In 1913 J. E. Blackman, Esq (BA, Dunelm) joined the staff, and in April 1918 Mr. W. M. Lopey, Esq (MA, Dunelm), took Mr. Blackman's place. In 1919 the staff was increased to three, O. D. C. Potter, Esq being appointed as science master, the subject being thus introduced into the curriculum.

In 1913 the school was moved from its quarters in the town to the buildings hitherto occupied by the Agricultural School, which had ceased to exist.

In 1915 the school first took the Cambridge Local Examinations. The attendance at the time was 42. The number of passes increased steadily until in 1926 ten passed the senior examination.

In 1922 the St. Vincent Island Scholarship was instituted, to the value of £250 p.a. Candidates have to be natives or the children of natives of St. Vincent to be receiving their education in the colony, and to be under the age of 20. The award was made on the results of the Senior Cambridge Examination. P. E. McI. Clarke (now Dr. Clarke) had the distinction of being the first winner.

In 1922 an Inter-Schools Tournament in athletics, cricket and football was held in St. Vincent between the Grammar School and St. Mary's College, St. Lucia. In 1925 the Boys' Secondary School, Grenada, took part in the tournament. At first the tournament was held annually, but it has recently been decided that it should be held biennially.

In 1923 the School Debating Society was founded. The society has continued regularly to hold two or three debates a term. In the same year the first school magazine was published. It has been published annually since then.

In 1927 a scout troop was formed with A. V. Sprott, Esq as Scoutmaster.

In 1930 Mr. Reeves retired and, to the deep regret of the whole colony, died a few months later. Mr. Lopey acted as Headmaster until May 1931, when J. S. Clarke, Esq (BA, Harvard), was appointed to the post. 1931 saw two other appointments: Mr. D. S. Cozier succeeded Mr. Potter, and Mr. J. P. Eustace joined the staff as third assistant master. The prefect system was introduced into the school with the object of giving boys a sense of responsibility.

In 1932 the examination for the award of the Island Scholarship was made for the London Matriculation. In 1934 thirteen pupils passed the London Matriculation or the Cambridge School Certificate examination.

In 1933 the numbers reached a new peak of 87, and in 1936 a fourth assistant master was appointed. V. A. A. Archer, Esq (BSA, McGill; MSA,

Toronto), succeeded Mr. Eustace (retired) and V. G. I. DaSilva Esq filled the new post.

In 1933 the Honourable F. A. Corea kindly presented to the school a plot of ground bordering the playing field, thus enabling the ground to be effectively enlarged. A tennis court was laid down the following year, and the ground was considered large enough to play the Fraser-Neckles Cup matches on it.

In 1934 the school, which had previously been divided into two sets, was divided into three houses, called Reeves, Green, and Orange, the object being to make competition keener, particularly in games.

Several changes were made about this time in the curriculum of the school. Agriculture and hygiene were introduced, and physical training became part of the daily timetable. In the top forms science was made alternative with classics. On the appointment of a master with full agricultural qualifications (Mr. Archer), it was decided to make general science compulsory for every boy as an examination subject. This course includes botany, physics, chemistry, soil science, and hygiene. Latin remains in the upper school alternative with extra botany. The other subjects on the curriculum are English, history, geography, mathematics, and French. The junior forms are also taught Scripture and drawing.

The tuition fees have remained the same since the school was started. They are £2 a term, with certain reductions for boys who have brothers or sisters at school and for those who are under 10 years of age. There is now an additional games and library fee of 2/- a term.

In 1936 a school Cadet Corps was formed with 2nd Lieut. Cozier as commanding officer. The corps is a unit of the British National Cadet Association. In the same year the Old Boys' Association was founded with O. D. Brisbane, Esq as its first President and R. N. Jack, Esq, Secretary-Treasurer. There was a membership of 72 at the end of the first year. At an annual meeting held recently, Dr. L. E. Sprott was elected President, Mr. Brisbane's term of office having expired.

GIRLS' HIGH SCHOOL

The Girls' High School was the name given to the private school kept by Miss M. L. Ince when it was taken over by the Government in October 1914. Miss Ince herself was appointed the first Headmistress and Miss M. B. Ince, Assistant Mistress, the number of girls on the register being 31.

In 1915 nine girls passed the Preliminary and Junior Cambridge Local Examinations for the first time.

In 1917 Miss M. B. Ince resigned and Miss Ince was granted a year's leave. The Misses C. C. and M. E. Went of Barbados were appointed to act as Headmistress and Assistant Mistress. But in 1918 Miss Ince resigned and the Misses Went were appointed to the posts of Headmistress and Assistant Mistress. At that time the number of pupils had dropped to 16.

The use of the tennis court in the court house grounds was granted to the pupils and mistresses of the school.

The number of pupils now started steadily to increase until in 1921 it reached 43, and it became necessary to apply for another Assistant. Mrs. A. Jackson was appointed to the post of 2nd Assistant Mistress. That year the Preliminary Cambridge Local Examinations were abolished.

Miss C. C. Went resigned in 1922 and Miss M. E. Went was made Headmistress, Miss Sheila Wall being appointed 2nd Assistant.

In 1925 the girls gave a series of school concerts and the funds derived from them were used to start a school library. This at first was not maintained by Government, but solely by the efforts of the girls and mistresses.

The school having increased to 58 in 1926, the school building was unable to accommodate that number so it was decided to rent Mr. Richards' house opposite to the Girls' High School. This arrangement continued until the next year when the Government decided to build an additional school room to accommodate Forms III & IV.

In 1928 the Internal Exhibition was granted to pupils of the Girls' High School, and that year the first winner of the Government Scholarship for Primary Schools came to the Girls' High School.

The number of pupils continuing to increase, Miss May Jackson was appointed temporary assistant in 1930. The number of pupils on the register was 87.

Miss M. E. Went resigned in 1933 and Mrs. L. S. Moffett (BSc), was appointed Headmistress. Mrs. Windebank was appointed to fill the place of Miss May Jackson who had also resigned. On the arrival of Mrs. Moffett the quarters, which had hitherto been used by the headmistress were converted into classrooms. Latin and botany were now placed on the curriculum.

In July 1934 pupils entered for the London Matriculation for the first time.

In January 1935 the school was moved to Judge's Lodge. A new building was erected. This consisted of four classrooms and lavatories and is connected to the former Judge's Lodge, now the Headmistress's quarters, by a covered concrete path. The lower flat of the Headmistress's quarters is used as an assembly hall and classroom for Form I and the Preparatory Form which was started for little girls and boys. A new mistress, Miss Pilgrim, was appointed to assist with the higher forms.

HOUSES—Grimble, Headmistress and Staff—were substituted for the sets which had hitherto been in existence. Netball and tennis are played by the girls, tournament being held annually among the houses to compete for the tennis Cups and the netball Shield.

The fees of the Girls' High School are the same as those for the Grammar School.

The uniform of the Pupils of the Girls' High School is a blue serge skirt, white middy blouse with a tie of the school colours— blue and silver—black shoes and stockings and a Panama hat with a band of the school colours.

The Old Girls' Association with the Headmistress as President was started in 1931. It offers a scholarship tenable at the Girls' High School for three years and gives help to a few needy old ladies.

ST. VINCENT INTERMEDIATE SCHOOL
Deo Inuante Nitimur

The school was founded in November 1926 by Mr. J. P. Eustace, Second Audit Clerk. The number on roll at its inception was only four. Fighting a single-handed battle, the school weathered many difficulties and today has 115 pupils on roll.

The school is a mixed school in more senses than one. Not only are its pupils of both sexes, but it combines primary and secondary education. The primary aim was to found a school that would bridge the gap between primary and secondary education, and to afford the latter type of education to children whose economic condition may have debarred them from obtaining such an education at the other two Government institutions.

The school has amply justified its existence. Its curriculum is the same as that of the other two secondary schools. The results obtained during the past 12 years compare favourably with the other schools. In 1930 the Administrator, His Honour H. Peebles, was in favour of supporting the school from public funds. Unfortunately, this aid did not meet with the approval of the Legislative Council. This year the attention of Government has again been drawn to the usefulness of the school and Government has kindly voted some assistance. In this, the school has created history being the first private school of its kind to be State-aided.

KINGSTOWN CENTRAL SCHOOL
Palma non sine Pulvere

This school was founded in May 1936 by Mr. B. R. James and caters for boys and girls from five years old and upwards. In the junior department all elementary subjects are taught and pupils are prepared for exhibitions and scholarships tenable at the secondary schools, and in this direction some success has already been gained.

In the senior department, candidates are prepared for the Cambridge Local, the London Matriculation and other recognised examinations.

Number on Roll, 190
Average Attendance for 1937, 140.49

THE GLEN COMMUNITY SCHOOL

This is an interesting educational experiment which is being carried out by the Methodist Missionary Society whose headquarters are at 24 Bishopsgate, London, E.C.2. On an estate of 38 acres, a day school is at present held in buildings of the most modern type. Boys and girls are being educated in the usual subjects of a senior department of a primary school, together with practical agriculture, carpentry, hygiene, cooking, domestic science, needlework, basket-making, and mat-making. The school is modelled on the lines of the Penn Community School, South Carolina At the time of writing, a scheme is under consideration whereby the school will be re-organised and developed as a secondary school with a hostel to accommodate about 150 boarders, so as to bring up the numbers of the scholars to about 250. There will be a resident principal and a specially selected staff, and the curriculum will be enlarged to include scientific as well as practical agriculture, housebuilding, dairying, and stock raising. The scholars will not be trained for the Cambridge Examinations or any similar examinations, but for the practical life of St. Vincent. Visitors are always welcome.

There are a few other private schools in Kingstown that afford fundamental knowledge to a comparatively large number of young children, many of whom, in course of time, enter one or other those schools already described.

Industries

THE ARROWROOT INDUSTRY OF ST. VINCENT

The arrowroot starch industry, in which St. Vincent virtually exercises a world monopoly, dates its development in this island from the abolition of slavery. In the pre-emancipation days, sugar and molasses were the chief products, but after that patches of arrowroot were grown in practically all the gardens of the freed slaves. The cultivation gradually extended and finally ousted sugar cane and cotton from their premier positions. The total production in 1936 amounted to 33,138 barrels of 220 lb. each.

Sowing

The usual time of planting is at the beginning of the rainy season in June. The land is as a rule first ploughed up and the weeds buried under. As St. Vincent soils are very light and sandy, the hoe is the implement employed for this purpose, or more rarely the fork. After the land has been prepared it is marked out for sowing, the hoe being again used and shallow holes made about six to nine inches apart. This operation is known as chipping. Into each hole two bits of rhizome, two or three internodes long, are dropped and lightly covered over with soil.

After Cultivation

Pen manure is usually put on as a mulch soon after supplying at the rate of 15/20 tons per acre. Sometimes the pen manure is spread over the fields before reaping operations and is ploughed into the fields during the subsequent digging of the crop.

Recent experiments indicate that St. Vincent soils are largely deficient in nitrogen and that considerable and profitable increases in yield may be obtained by the application of sulphate of ammonia at the rate of 3 cwt. per acre. This manure, mixed with sand to ensure uniform distribution, is broadcast on the fields when the plants are two to three months old.

Reaping

The arrowroot plant arrives at the flowering stage when about four and a half to five months old and then proceeds to accumulate starch in the rhizomes. The rhizomes are fully mature at about 11 months and the upper portion of the plant dries down. The planting of the crop is so timed that this occurs in the dry season, January to May, whenever possible. Gradually, however, the date of reaping works back into the rainy season and on some of the older fields it may be necessary to reap in October or November; however,

338

that is being discouraged. The greater part of the arrowroot crop is grown on sloping land, and the exposure of large areas of loosened soil results in considerable losses by erosion during the months of October and November when the rainfall is heaviest.

Reaping of the crop merely consists in ploughing up the soil and extracting the rhizomes. As mentioned before, St. Vincent soils are very light and it is quite easy to dig down to a depth of eighteen inches to two feet on good soil with a hoe.

The rhizomes are collected in heaps which are later measured in terms of a standard basket. The average weight of rhizomes in a basket is about 100 lb., and a fair average yield is about 150 baskets per acre. Good fields, however, may yield 200 or 250 baskets per acre. As the rhizomes are taken from the soil, bits (two or three internodes long) of their thin ends (containing least starch) are broken off and dropped into the soil and covered over. These, together with the bits of rhizomes always inadvertently left in the soil, constitute the planting material for the next crop. The rhizomes are then brought to the mill yard by bullock carts, each cart taking a load of 12/15 cwt.

Manufacture

The starch is extracted from the rhizomes by a relatively simple mechanical process. The rhizomes are first dumped into a trough and then passed through a revolving cylindrical washer within which streams of water are constantly playing. From the washer the rhizomes pass on to the grater, a rasping drum that pulps the tissues and so makes possible the separation of starch from the fibres, etc. The pulped mass (bittie) is next thoroughly washed in a copious stream of very pure filtered water over a series of strainers 20 to 120 mesh in ascending order. By this means the starch is separated from the fibrous material as a suspension, and the latter is run on to a long shallow concrete trough (table) which is carefully graded to allow the deposition of all starch granules along the length of the table but separates them from the heavier sand particles and the lighter precipitate of gums, etc.

At the end of a day's run, the starch is dug off the table and stirred up with water to form a thick suspension in the concrete "melting" box. This suspension is then run into settlers or twirling vats where it is given a rotary motion and allowed to settle overnight. Next morning the water is drained off the compact starch layer below. On the top of the more or less pure starch layer, which may be two or more feet in thickness, is a thinner stratum of light starch granules, fibres and gums one or two inches thick and known locally as madungo. This madungo is now usually run over smaller and specially graded tables and the starch extracted, though previously it was all given away to the labourers who used it as a substitute for wheaten flour.

339

The starch is then dug out of the settling vats and placed on coarse mesh wire trays in the drying house. These trays are arranged in tiers with a wooden tray below so that as the starch on the wire above dries and crumbles it falls on to the wooden tray below. When all the starch crumbles readily and is easily shaken off the wire, it is quite dry and is run into bags supplied by the Cooperative Arrowroot Association and transported to the office of this association in Kingstown.

No steam drying is practised and the drying of the starch may require a period of about seven days in good dry weather, though in wet weather the time taken may be 15 days or more. Under the latter conditions, growers are apt to bag starch while it is still a bit moist. The association, therefore, rejects any starch with a moisture content greater than 17.5 per cent.

An average factory in St. Vincent may turn out 16 barrels of 220 lb. each of starch per day. Under good conditions 12 to 14 baskets of rhizomes are required to produce one barrel of starch so that the average yield of starch per acre is about 10/12 barrels. The better estates, however, aim at a yield of 14/16 barrels per acre, and as soon as a field drops below 12, it is thrown out of arrowroot cultivation. Such fields are usually five or six years old, and the rhizomes show signs of deterioration having high percentage of what are known as cigar or long roots. These rhizomes are long and thin with a low starch and high fibre content. When a field is thrown out, it is usually sown in pigeon peas or some other leguminous crop for a year or two and then replanted with arrowroot.

Values And Uses

It is the general impression that arrowroot is used only for invalid foods and for the making of biscuits, but this is quite a mistaken idea. Many really tasty dishes can be made from this product, for cake and pastry making as well as confectionery, chocolates and ice creams. Arrowroot is largely used and it has always been found in the chemists' laboratories where its finest grades are so much used in various preparations.

Cooks find arrowroot invaluable in helping to make the items on the menus appetising and dainty. The fact that arrowroot is so easily digested alone suggests its extreme value to those suffering from that all-too-common complaint indigestion, and it would be wise for all cooks and housewives to have near at hand the little booklet published by the St. Vincent Cooperative Arrowroot Association, St. Vincent, in which is given at great detail the many uses to which arrowroot can be put.

C. B. Sayles
30. 11. 37.

MEMORANDUM ON THE ST. VINCENT
COOPERATIVE ARROWROOT ASSOCIATION

The Association was incorporated under Ordinance No. 15 of 1930 particularly for the purpose of marketing and controlling all arrowroot produced in the colony and intended for export.

A free grant of £3,000 and a loan of £30,000 were made from the Colonial Development Fund through the colonial Government for the financing of the Association. The loan is free of interest for five years, and thereafter interest at the rate of five per centum per annum will be charged. The entire loan is repayable in 20 years or with the option of doing so after 10 years.

Any quantity of arrowroot is received. Any person delivering 50 barrels of arrowroot in the course of any one year is entitled to be registered as a member of the association.

There is a members' roll which is revised annually for the ensuing year.

The arrowroot crop year commences in the month of October in any year and ends on the last day of September in the next calendar year.

The term "barrel" is meant to indicate a quantity of not less than 224 lb. net weight of arrowroot.

In the month of August of each year, a general meeting is held for the purpose of electing 15 delegates from the members. The voting for the election of delegates is done by ballot. Each member is entitled to a vote and to an extra vote in respect of every complete 100 barrels of arrowroot delivered after the first hundred up to a maximum of 10 votes. The 15 delegates meet within a fortnight of their election and elect from amongst the members of the association six members, who need not necessarily be delegates of themselves, to be members of the arrowroot board for the ensuing arrowroot year.

After the six members have been elected to the board, the colonial Government nominates one, but not more than three members to the board, one of which must be a member of the civil service.

The arrowroot board is the controlling body of the association. The person whom the members of the board elect as chairman is ex officio president of the association.

There are at least two general meetings of the association held in each arrowroot year. Other general meetings may be convened upon request in writing of members collectively entitled to not less than one-third of the total number of votes to which all members appearing on the last register of members are entitled.

There is no laid down number of meetings of the board, except that the first meeting shall be within 15 days of the month of October and provided that no period exceeding two months shall elapse between any two meetings.

341

Special meetings of the board may be convened at the request in writing of any three members or any number of members of the association collectively entitled to at least one-fifth of the number of votes to which all the members of the association are entitled on the last register of members.

The board fixes the rates of advances to be paid on the various grades of arrowroot delivered to the association, and the law provides that the advances should not exceed six-tenths of the value of the arrowroot delivered. Small growers, i.e., persons who deliver less than 50 barrels of arrowroot, receive one-quarter as much again as the proportion to be advanced to large growers, who are persons delivering 50 barrels and over of arrowroot.

All arrowroot on delivery to the association is graded by an officer of the association. In case of objections to the grades in which the arrowroot is placed, there is a right of appeal to the board.

There are five grades of arrowroot on which a first advance is made. Any grade below the fifth is termed "ungraded", on which no advance is made but has to await final sale.

Interest at the rate of six per centum per annum is charged on advances, but when each individual grade is sold sufficiently so as to cover the amount advanced on it, the interest charge is stopped.

When the various grades have a substantial balance to their credit after covering the advance, the association usually make an intermediate payment to growers, and when all grades have been entirely sold off, the final payments to growers are made.

In making the final payments, the proceeds of the grades, after deducting the working expenses of the association, are divided pro rata according to weight among all persons who delivered arrowroot for the crop. Each person, whether a member of the association or not, receives the same rate per 100 pounds according to whatever rate the particular grade into which his arrowroot was assigned netted after expenses have been deducted. Therefore, when a final payment is made all persons who delivered arrowroot for a crop receive the same amount proportionally.

COTTON
General

Sea Island Cotton was first grown commercially in St. Vincent in 1903, and fostered by the Imperial Department of Agriculture for the West Indies, soon became one of the major products of the island. As a result of (a) the excellent environment in which it found itself, and (b) the selection and breeding work carried out by officers of the agricultural department and Empire Cotton Growing Corporation, St. Vincent Sea Island Cotton holds the distinction of being the most superfine cotton in the world. This distinction is not a thing of today but runs back many years. During the Great War superfine Sea Island Cotton fetched as high a price as 10/6, being used chiefly in the preparation of gas containers of observation balloons.

The formation of a West Indian Sea Island Cotton Association in 1933 has been of great benefit to the industry. Under its auspices, much is being done to bring to the notice of the public the true value of goods made from genuine Sea Island Cotton, and a trademark has been inaugurated for the protection of the buyers and the safe guarding of the industry. The association is also responsible for the appointment of an entomologist who travels between the cotton growing islands of the West Indies.

Acreage and Yield

In the following table, the area under Sea Island Cotton and the resultant yields for the past decade are given.

Year	Acres.	Weight of Lint (lb.)	No. of bales of 400 lbs
1927-28	3364	328,188	820
1928-29	3386	263,808	660
1929-30	1758	262,382	656
1930-31	3955	605,280	1513
1931-32	1802	209,505	524
1932-33	669	85,852	215
1933-34	1216	99,750	249
1934-35	1464	173,735	434
1935-36	3540	396,960	992
1936-37	5294	417,818	1045
1937-38	4900	˙560,000	˙1400

˙Estimated

According to the Customs' Returns 418,607 lb. of lint were exported, of which 361,401 lb. were white, valued at £32,629, and 57,206 lb. were stained, valued at £1,430. The French market continued to show interest in this product, 59,792 lb. of which being shipped to this destination and the remainder to England.

Prices obtained during the year were excellent and to a large measure compensated for the low yields. A fair proportion of the crop was sold at 24d. c.i.f. Liverpool, after which there was a tendency for the buyers to hold off, and most of the remainder was sold at 23d. Lint for the French market was purchased locally on an f.o.b. basis at an average price of 20d. per lb.

Type Grown

The only type at present in cultivation is the superfine (V. 135) cotton already mentioned as being the best quality in the world.

Its staple length is 2¼ inches and spinning tests conducted by the Fine Spinners and Doublers Association have proved that it is characterised by very great yarn strength and can be spun to even higher counts than 240's.

Season

In 1929 the planting season was changed from June to September in order to obtain for the plant the best climatic conditions for optimum development, that is good rainfall throughout the vegetative period and dry conditions during reaping. Subsequently, representations by growers to the effect that they had too short a planting season have caused a further change; the 1935-36 season opened on 16th August, and from that year planting has been allowed from either the 1st or 16th August as fixed by Government. The change from the June planting has been markedly successful and has vastly improved the quality of the cotton.

The Ginnery

Since 1903 there has been in operation a Government Cotton Ginnery which is a great boon to both estate owners and peasants. Although there are three other ginneries in the colony, a large part of the island's crop is ginned there, and as it is the only factory with a Simon's Patent Heater and machinery for the crushing of seed and expelling of oil; all seed eventually passes to it for treatment. Peasants' seed cotton is purchased at a fixed rate, and at the end of the season when sales have been effected, a bonus is declared and paid. In this way the peasant not only receives ready cash with which to carry on before the selling of his crop, but his interests are well protected. During the last two seasons much has been done to improve the Government Cotton Ginnery and it is an institution of which the colony may well be proud.

The Uses of Cotton and its Byproducts

Lint—Apart from the usual manufactured cotton cloths, new lines of voiles, ladies' stockings, gents' socks, shirtings, handkerchiefs, waterproof overcoats, etc., have been put on the market in London, and much has been done in the way of advertisement at exhibitions like the British Industries Fair and by large interested firms such as Austin Reid which carried out a consistent campaign for the popularising of these goods. That Sea Island Cotton, once given a trial soon establishes itself on its own, is seen from the following quotation made by Sir Philip Cunliffe-Lister (now Lord Swinton) of a remark of the then Prince of Wales: "I am a steady wearer of Sea Island Cotton now on its own merits."

The Wool Industries Research Association has been carrying out tests in the mixing of Sea Island lint with wool to get rid of the shrinking properties of wool and its rough unpleasant feel. The efforts in this direction are being attended with some success.

St. Vincent Superfine Sea Island Cotton is also almost invaluable in the manufacture of certain very fine laces, most of the other cottons not being fine or strong enough.

Sea Island Cotton is used by Dunlop Bros. in the manufacture of tyres, and it will be remembered that when Captain Eyston broke several land speed records not long ago he was using these tyres.

Linters—In St. Vincent these are the short fibres which remain on the seed after ginning and are removed by a second and more intensive ginning process known as delinting. This process is usually conducted at the oil mills in the preparation of the seed for crushing. Linters are bailed in the same way as ordinary cotton. During the World War, a considerable quantity of this material was employed in the manufacture of explosives. In normal times their chemical composition and felting qualities enable them to be used in the manufacture of many articles—stuffing material for cushions, horse collars, mattresses, and upholstery, mixing with wool for hat making and with lamb's wool for fleece-lined underwear, lamp and candle wicks, rope, twine, and carpets, writing paper, also for varnishes, artificial leather, celluloid, artificial silk, and photographic films.

Seed (Oil)— After ginning and delinting, the seed is crushed and oil expressed. This oil by a process of settling and decanting results in (a) crude oil which is refined and sold for cooking purposes, competing in flavour and cooking qualities with most imported oils and (b) "Foots", the residual matter remaining in the settling tanks after the crude oil has been removed. Foots is employed in the local manufacture of a low grade soap which, through its cheapness, is used locally by laundresses; the refined oil can also be employed in the manufacture of paints and varnishes.

345

Seed (Meal and Cake)—The solid matter left on expressing the oil is known as cotton seed meal. This makes an excellent nitrogenous organic fertilizer, and is used to a very great extent by local planters. Cotton seed meal, which has a very high protein content, is also used as a stock feed. Experiments conducted by G. S. Fraps, Chemist of the Texas Agricultural Experiment Station, and others, have demonstrated the fact that used in correct quantities in a mixed diet, cotton seed meal has a very high value as a human food. These experiments have, however, not yet been concluded and so the above statement is at present only of academic interest.

Seed—In the December *Journal of Tropical Agriculture*, Vol. VIII No. 12, it is extracted on page 334, that an economically sound method for manufacturing paper from cotton seed has recently been elaborated in the Hyderabad State in India. In a review of the possibilities of this new industry, K. R. Natarajan estimates that the annual cotton seed crop of India, amounting to about 2 million tons, would be sufficient for the production of 50,000 tons of writing and printing paper, or alternatively would provide all the paper pulp required by the Indian paper making industry.

Stalks—A chemical process for the manufacture of rayon (artificial silk) from cotton stalks has been elaborated in America. This is of great interest in that at present cotton stalks, after harvest, are burnt or destroyed with the object of removing harbourage of certain of the dangerous cotton pests and diseases.

Machinery and Products

The Imperial Department of Agriculture for the West Indies erected the Ginnery in 1903/4 at a cost of £2,000. There are nine roller gins which, on the average, turn out 15.5 bales (400 lbs. each) of lint in a 10-hour day, but as many as 18 bales, that is, 7,200 lbs. of lint have been produced in one day. Two electrically driven hydraulic box presses are operated at a pressure of 2½ tons per sq. inch to pack the lint into square 400 lb. bales for shipment. The seed obtained from ginning is passed through a Simon's Patent Heater at 56° to 58° C. for the purpose of destroying pests and fungi. Very special attention is paid to cotton seed reserved for planting purposes, but all other prime seed is put through the delinting and expressing processes. The raw cotton seed oil is refined into a good quality cooking oil and washing soap is made from the residue. A certain quantity of linters (cotton waste) is exported to Trinidad. The prime cotton seed meal (crushed oil-cake) is all sold locally for manurial and cattle-feeding purposes. All seed obtained from stained seed-cotton is disintegrated and sold as manure.

346

A corn plant is worked in conjunction with the ginnery. It contains a Hess drier with a capacity of 1½ tons at 150° Farenheit, a sheller and a Kelly Duplex Mill fitted with a Rotex sifter.

All the machinery at this factory is driven by two Blackstone oil engines each 30 H.P. and steam for heating purposes is provided by a Robey boiler.

Cooperative Purchase of Peasants' Cotton

Peasants' cotton is purchased at the ginnery on a cooperative system—a fixed sum based on the market value of lint is advanced to peasants on each pound of seed cotton taken to the ginnery. The cotton is ginned, baled and shipped by the department which receives a commission on the proceeds of sale of lint, and after payment of the incidental expenses, the balance of profits is distributed among peasants in the form of a bonus; a half-pound of prime cotton seed meal is also given to every peasant for each pound of white seed-cotton sold. The average advance paid in cash is about 6c. per lb. and the average bonus about 2c. per lb. of seed-cotton.

Corn

The purchase of Indian corn on a cooperative basis has been discontinued but any person paying the moderate charges may have his corn kiln dried and stored on his own account or ground into meal or stock feed as he may desire.

Arrowroot

The quantity of starch exported in 1937 totalled 8,673,117 lb. and is the highest on record, being 1,098,155 lb. greater than the quantity exported in 1936, the largest previously recorded. The chief exports were to the United States of America, which showed a further increase of over three-quarters of a million pounds. There were also slight increases in the exports to the United Kingdom and Canada, and there were indications that a greater interest is being taken in this product in the intercolonial markets.

Stocks have also shown a decline and on 39th September 1937, were nearly 3,000 barrels less than on the same date in 1936.

The propects of the industry are, therefore, very favourable, and there is every indication that the steady increase in exports of the last few years, notably to the United Kingdom and the United States of America, will be continued in 1938.

Sugar

Sugar production in 1937 amounted to 1,278 tons, of which 1,218 tons were dark crystals manufactured at Mt. Bentinck Estate, and the remainder,

60 tons, was muscovado sugar produced at Argyle Estate during a temporary local shortage early in the year. In addition, 32,612.5 proof gallons of rum were distilled at Mt. Bentinck Estate. Exports of sugar in 1937 totalled 500 tons of dark crystals valued at £5,250 to the United Kingdom, so that the total quantity of sugar available for local consumption was only about 700 tons, which proved to be insufficient and consequently sugar was later imported into the colony.

Syrup

Buyers of St. Vincent syrup are of the opinion that the marketing of this product cannot be placed on a really satisfactory basis until uniformity in the quality is assessed. All producers are now agreed on the necessity for blending, but there are great practical difficulties in the way of reconciling conflicting interests, and it is unlikely that complete blending of the total output will be established in the near future. A scheme has been proposed however, which will be put into operation in 1938 whereby a fairly large proportion of the crop will be blended and sold through one organisation. This should go a long way towards establishing some degree of stability in the marketing of St. Vincent syrup.

Bananas

It was estimated that the area under bananas at the end of 1937 was about 1,100 acres or slightly greater than the estimated area at the end of 1936. While the actual increase in the acreage is not great, there was a material improvement in the cultivation. One hundred sixty-eight acres of unsuitable lands have been thrown out of cultivation; 240 acres of selected land have been selected with a greater regard for the requirements of the banana plant.

There was a considerable increase in the production of fruit and the total quantity of fruit sold to the Canadian Banana Company amounted to 75,434 stems valued at £6,366 as compared with 35,550 stems valued at £2,737 during 1936. The percentage counts also showed some improvement and an average 67.38 as against 63.7 in 1936, but the figure is still too low despite the fact that during the year six hands were accepted on only three occasions. This consistent production of fruit with an average count bunch percentage less than 70 would definitely seem to indicate that much of the fruit is being produced under unsuitable conditions. It is anticipated, however, that with better lands coming into production, the grade will show some improvement in 1938.

In 1937 of 9 hands there were 14,773; 8 hands, 24,197; 7 hands, 35,148; 6 hands, 1,316.

Cassava

Owing to the unremunerative prices and to the flourishing state of the arrowroot and cotton industries, practically no attention was devoted to this crop during the period under review, and the acreage under cultivation suffered a further decrease. In consequence, the exports of cassava starch amounted to only 370,885 lbs. valued at £1,932, and part of the exports represented stocks held over from previous years.

It is unlikely that production of cassava starch will be materially increased in the future unless prices show a decided advance. Another factor which may have an important bearing on the cassava industry in St. Vincent is that the Arrowroot Association are making efforts to substitute low grade arrowroot starch for cassava starch in the intercolonial markets, which at present are the most important markets for cassava starch.

During the year, one or two enquiries originating chiefly from Canada were received with regard to this commodity, but invariably the prices offered were too low to attract local producers.

Coconuts

The steady increase in price of copra toward the end of 1936 continued in 1937, and the price touched £25 per ton c.i.f. London early in the year. Thereafter, the price declined and remained around £20 per ton for the first half of the year. In the last six months, prices declined further and did not average better than £16 per ton with poor demand and dull trading. The price of whole nuts did not vary appreciably during the year and was fixed by contract at 816.00 to 818.00 per 1,000 f.o.b. St. Vincent.

Under the circumstances, a large proportion of the nuts obtained from the heaviest pickings in the first half of the year was converted into copra, but later, with the decrease in price of copra, this tendency was markedly reduced.

POSTAL INTELLIGENCE

General Post Office—Kingstown

Branch Post Offices—Edinboro and Sion Hill

District Post Offices—Edinboro, Sion Hill, Arnos Vale, Calliaqua, Stubbs, Mesopotamia, Bridgetown, New Ground, Colonarie, Georgetown, Orange Hill, Questelles, Layou, Barrouallie, Cumberland, Troumaca, Chateaubelair, Bequia, Canouan, Mayreau, Union Island.

Inland Mails

Windward Route: A daily mail service is maintained on the Windward Coast by motor bus leaving Georgetown at 8 a.m. and leaving Kingstown at 2 p.m. Mails are closed 30 minutes before departure of the motor bus. On Wednesdays, mails close at 11.30 a.m.

On public holidays the car does not ply.

Leeward Route: The motor mail launch leaves Kingstown for Chateaubelair at 3 p.m. on Mondays, Tuesdays, Thursdays, and Fridays. On Saturdays, it leaves Kingstown at 3.30 p.m.

On Wednesdays it leaves Kingstown at 1.30 p.m.

It leaves Chateaubelair at 7 a.m. on Mondays, Tuesdays, Wednesdays, Fridays, and Saturdays.

There is no service to Kingstown on Thursdays.

On Sundays and public holidays, the motor mail launch does not ply. Mails are closed for these places and for Layou, Troumaca and Barrouallie at 2 p.m. except on Wednesdays when they are closed at 12 noon. On Mondays, Thursdays and Saturdays they are closed for Cumberland as well.

Grenadines Route: Mails are closed for Bequia daily at 1 p.m. Weekly services are maintained with the St. Vincent Grenadines by auxiliary sloop which leaves St. Vincent every Monday; mails are closed at 9 a.m. It returns every Friday. An auxiliary schooner leaves St. Vincent every Wednesday; mails close at 9 a.m.; it returns every Tuesday.

Rates of Postage

Letters—1 oz., 1d.; every additional ½ ounce, ½d.

Post Cards—Single ½d.

Registration fee—1d.

Newspapers and other printed matter per 4 ozs., ½d.

Parcels Post—Not exceeding 1 lb., 3d.; 1-2 lbs. 5d.; 2-3 lbs., 7d.; 3-4 lbs., 9d., and for every additional lb. not exceeding 11 lbs., 1d.

Inter-Colonial and Foreign Mails

Mails are closed as follows:

For Europe, United States of America, Jamaica, Barbados, St. Lucia, the Northern Islands, St. Thomas, Bermuda, and Canada by the Canadian National Steamships weekly and fortnightly.

Letters and papers posted with a late fee of 2d. in addition to postage, are received up to and within one hour after the time fixed for closing such mails. Money orders, postal orders, parcel post, and registered letter post are closed at noon on the day of the arrival of the steamer.

For Grenada, Carriacou, Trinidad, Demerara, and Colon by the Canadian National Steamships, weekly and fortnightly, and when those steamers connect with one of the Trinidad Line steamers at Grenada, also for Europe, the United States of America, Canada, and Jamaica.

Letters and papers, posted with a late fee of 2d. in addition to postage, are received up to and within one hour after the time fixed for closing such mails. Money orders, postal orders, parcel post, and registered letter post are closed at 3 p.m. on the day preceding the arrival of the steamer.

Mails are also closed for the above-mentioned places by sailing vessel at irregular intervals when opportunity offers.

Rates of Postage

Letters to the United Kingdom and other parts of the British Empire generally, Mandated Territories (except Iraq and Transjordan), Egypt and the British Post Office at Tangier, 1½d. for the first ounce and 1d. for each additional ounce or fraction thereof.

Post cards to the United Kingdom and other places as mentioned in (1), 1d. each.

Letters to the United States of America (including Saint Thomas, Virgin Islands, Puerto Rico, Hawaii, and Alaska) and to places other than those mentioned in (1) ½d. for the first ounce and 1½d. for each additional ounce or fraction thereof.

Postcards to all foreign countries, 1d. each.

Printed papers and books of all places, ½d. per 2 ounces. Literature for the blind, ½d. per 2 lbs.

Commercial papers to all places, 2½d. for the first 10 ounces, and ½d. per 2 ounces thereafter.

Samples to all places, 1d. for the first 4 ounces, and ½d. per 2 ounces thereafter.

Registration fees, 3d.

Acknowledgment of receipt of a registered letter, insured letter, or insured parcel, 3d.

Acknowledgment of payment of a money order in the United Kingdom, 3d.

Parcels post, to United Kingdom, not exceeding 3 lbs. 1/9, exceeding 3 lbs. and not exceeding 7 lbs. 3/3, exceeding 7 lbs. and not exceeding 11 lbs. 4/6, exceeding 11 lbs. and not exceeding 14 lbs. 5/6, exceeding 14 lbs. and not exceeding 18 lbs. 6/6, exceeding 18 lbs. and not exceeding 22 lbs. 7/6. To the Dominion of Canada, Bermuda, British West Indies, British Guiana, British Honduras, and St. Thomas, A.W.I., not exceeding 3 lbs. 1s.; exceeding 3 lbs. and not exceeding 7 lbs. 2s.; exceeding 7 lbs. and not exceeding 11 lbs. 3s.; exceeding 11 lbs. and not exceeding 14 lbs. 4s.; exceeding 14 lbs. and not exceeding 18 lbs. 5s.; exceeding 18 lbs. and not exceeding 22 lbs. 6s. Limit of weight to Canada, 20 lbs.

Other places are subject to higher charges except U.S.A. which is 6d. per lb. up to 22 lbs.

Cash on Delivery Service

The sender shall prepay, by means of postage stamps affixed to the parcel, a special cash on delivery fee calculated as shown in the table below. This fee shall be in every case additional to the ordinary postage and other charges (for express delivery insurance, advice of delivery, and the like).

Trade Charge not exceeding	Fee		Trade Charge not exceeding	Fee	
£	s.	d.	£	s.	d.
1		4½	21	4	6½
2		7	22	4	9
3		9½	23	4	11½
4	1	0	24	5	2
5	1	2½	25	5	4½
6	1	5	26	5	7
7	1	7½	27	5	9½
8	1	0	28	6	0
9	2	0½	29	6	2½
10	2	3	30	6	5
11	2	5½	31	6	7½
12	2	8	32	6	10
13	2	10½	33	7	0½

14	3	1	34	7	3
15	3	3½	35	7	5½
16	3	6	36	7	8
17	3	8½	37	7	10½
18	3	11	38	8	1
19	4	1½	39	8	3½
20	4	4	40	8	6

The sender shall hand the parcel in at the General Post Office, where he shall obtain a certificate of posting, of which the production may be required as a condition of payment of the trade charge money order.

A delivery fee will be charged in certain countries abroad for the delivery service. This fee, particulars of which shall be furnished by the post pffice, shall be collected from the addressee of the parcel, and no deduction in respect of it shall be made from the amount of the trade charge money order.

Delivery

Cash on delivery parcels received in the colony from countries participating in the service shall be delivered from the general post office and notice of their arrival shall be sent to the addressees.

A delivery fee of 4d., in addition to the amount of the trade charge, shall be paid by the addressee in respect of each parcel, and the amount of the trade charge when collected shall be remitted to the sender without deduction.

General Regulations

The sums payable for insurance, including registration, shall:

Not exceeding £12: 8d.

Exceeeding £12 and not exceeding £20: 1/-

The maximum limit of insurance shall be £20.

Rates of postage on air mails prescribed by the Governor

Country of Destination	Air rate (including ordinary postage) per 1/2 ounce or fraction of 1/2 ounce		Country of Destination	Air rate (including ordinary postage) per 1/2 ounce or fraction of 1/2 ounce	
	s	d.			
Antigua		8	French Guiana	1	0½
Argentine	2	4½	Great Britain	1	1
Aruba	1	5	Guadeloupe		9½
Bahamas	2	2½	Guatemala	1	10
Bolivia	2	6½	Haiti	1	4
Brazil	2	1½	Honduras	1	10
British Guiana		8	Jamaica	1	3
British Honduras	1	9	Martinique		9½
Canada	1	1	Mexico	1	10
Canal Zone	1	0½	Nicaragua	1	10
Chile	2	4½	Panama	1	0½
Colombia	1	7	Peru	2	1½
Costa Rica	1	4	Puerto Rico		9½
Cuba	1	4	Salvador	1	10
Curacao	1	5	U.S.A	1	2
Dominican Republic	1	4	Uruguay	2	4½
Dutch Guiana	1	0½	Venezuela	1	0½
Ecuador	1	10	U.S. Virgin Is.		9½
Europe	1	2			

354

Services via London

Colony of Destination	To England by Steamer and Onward by Mail		To New York by Air, Steamer to England and Onward by Air
	First ½ ounce	Each additional ½ ounce	Per ½ ounce
	s. d	s. d	s. d
Australia and New Zealand	1.... ..4½.	1 4	2 4
China	1 9	1 7½	2 8
Dutch East Indies	1 3	1 1½	2 2
Gambia	10½	10	1 10
Gold Coast	7½	7	1 7
Hong Kong	7½	7	1 7
India and Ceylon	7½	7	1 7
Iraq	6	4½	1 5
Kenya, Uganda, Tanganyika, Zanzibar, Northern and South era Rhodesia, South Africa	7½	7	1 7
Madagascar	2 3	2 1½	3 1
Mauritius	7½	7	1 7
Nigeria	7½	7	1 7
Palestine and Egypt	4½	4	1 4
Persia	6	4½	1 5
Portuguese East Africa	1 1	11½	2 0
Portuguese West Africa	11	9½	1.....10
Siam	1 2	1 0½	2 1
Sierra Leone	10½	10	1 10
Straits Settlements and Malay States	7½	7	1 7
Sudan	4½	4	1 4
Syria and Trans-Jordan	6	4½	1 5
European Countries	7	4½	1 6

Letters despatched under these conditions must be clearly endorsed

(1) By steamer to England and onward by air mail, or

(2) By air mail to New York, steamer to England and onward by air mail as the case may be.

Trans Pacific Service

Letters by this route are sent from Trinidad by air to the United States and from San Francisco by air across the Pacific Ocean to the places named.

Letters intended for transmission by this route must bear an air mail label and be marked (just above the address) "BY TRANSPACIFIC ROUTE."

The rates of postage are as follows:

	Per ½ ounce s. d.		Per ½ ounce s. d.
Honolulu	2. ...2	Indochina	4 2
Guam	3.. ..4	Malaya (Straits Settlements)	4 7
Manila (Philippine Islands)	3.. 10	Siam	4 11
Macao (Portuguese Colony)	4 2	India	5 5
Hong Kong	4 2	Dutch East Indies	4 9
China	4 2	Australia and New Zealand	5 2
Japan	4 2		

Money Order Conversion Table

Orders issued in St. Vincent and payable in Canada and the United States		Orders issued in the United States and paid in St. Vincent	
Bank selling rate	Rate of conversion per dollar	Bank buying rate	Rate of conversion per dollar
	s. d.		s. d.
Par	4 2	Par	4 1
Discount not exceeding:			
3 per cent	4 2	Discount not exceeding:	4 0
5 per cent	4 1	1 per cent	3 11
7 per cent	4 0	3 per cent	3 10
9 per cent	3 11	5 per cent	3 9
11 per cent	3 10	7 per cent	3 8
For each additional 2%		9 per cent	3 7
discount deduct	1	11 per cent	
Premium not exceeding:		For each additional 2%	
1 per cent	4 3	discount deduct	1
3 per cent	4 4	Premium not exceeding	
5 per cent	4 5	2 per cent	4 2
7 per cent	4 6	5 per cent	4 3
For each additional 2%		7 per cent	4 4
premium add	1	10 per cent	4 5

If the premium exceeds 10% the rate of conversion shall be prescribed by the Governor.

TELEPHONES

A telephone system practically covers the whole island, the main exchange being situate at Kingstown and subexchanges at Georgetown, Barrouallie and Mesopotamia.

In 1934 the system in Kingstown was converted from magneto to central battery signalling and a new Ericsson board installed consisting of two 100-line panels which can be extended for multiple working, the manual magneto exchange at Mesopotamia was in 1935 replaced by a rural semi-automatic exchange supplied by the G.E.C. of England and of the all relay type, Georgetown and Barrouallie are still magneto.

During the ensuing year an R.S.A.X equipped for 20 lines and two junctions will be fitted at Calliaqua, mainly on account of the electrification of this area and therefore the necessity of reconstructing telephone lines along the transmission route and also to facilitate development.

There are 300 connections including extensions, with a wire mileage of: trunk 64, subscribers 294 (route) and 466 (wire) including 2¼ miles underground route mileage with a wire mileage of 155 miles; in addition 5,000 yards of aerial cable is also erected with a wire mileage of 50 miles.

Private residences, places of business and other premises within the boundaries of any town having a telephone exchange are connected with such exchange on payment of 11 shillings monthly for a wall and 12/- for a desk telephone. A reduction of 20 percent in the charges is made where more telephones than one is rented. Other accommodations are afforded subscribers for nominal amounts.

Premises situated beyond the boundaries of any town having a telephone exchange are also connected with such exchange on the same terms of monthly payment together with the cost of the necessary insulators, wire, and other material required for the connection and for the expenses of erection, the last being calculated at 10 shillings a mile or part thereof; these amounts are payable before the work is undertaken.

Operators at exchanges are on duty to answer calls from subscribers and for the receipt of messages from 6 o'clock a.m. to 10 o'clock p.m. on all days, and from 7 to 10 o'clock a.m. and from 2 to 7 o'clock p.m. Good Friday and Christmas Day. During other hours only calls in respect of business of an urgent nature are attended to.

The fee is at the rate of 6d. for every 20 or fewer number of words in addition to the address, which is transmitted free, and includes the delivery within the boundary of any town.

For the delivery of a message beyond the boundary of a town an additional fee of 6d. is charged for each mile or part of a mile.

A non-renter may communicate with a renter from any exchange for a payment of 3d. for a conversation of not more than five minutes within the area covered by the exchange, 4d. if outside.

A renter may have a message sent from any exchange to a non-renter on payment of a fee for its delivery of 2d. if within the boundary of a town and for 6d. beyond the boundary for each mile or part thereof.

ELECTRICITY

Kingstown and its suburbs are lighted by electricity, while the system extends to Liberty Lodge and Fort Charlotte, a distance of 2 miles on the leeward or western side of St. Vincent, and to Cane Hall and Ratho Mill on the windward or eastern side, a distance of 4 miles. The streets in the town of Calliaqua, three miles from Kingstown on the windward side, are also lighted by electricity.

For the purpose of installing the system, a loan was obtained by the Government from the Colonial Development Committee, and on the 25th May 1931, the actual running of the system commenced when 32 consumers were supplied.

There are three generating units at the power house; 2 Ruston and Hornsby 40 K.W. each and a Belliss and Morcom, 50 K.W.; the voltage used is 230/400 and three phase of 50 cycles.

There is an all-day service obtaining and up to the 14th October 1937; there were 478 consumers on the system.

For domestic purposes there is an all-in domestic rate and the price ranges from 1/- to 2½d. per unit. The price per unit for power purposes ranges from 4d. to 1½ with a fixed charge of 4/2 per month for installed horse power.

Special rates are provided for small consumers and places of public worship. For two lighting points of 30 watts each, the small consumer pays 3/6 per month, and for three points of 30 watts each, 5/- per month. This rate is extended to occupants of houses of an assessed annual rental of £12. 10. 0. and under. The rates extended to all places of public worship are, in respect of all units up to 15, 1/- per unit; over 15 and up to 25, 6d. per unit and over 25, 3d. per unit.

With the amalgamation of both electricity and telephone departments in 1935, the post of chief electrician was abolished and that of Superintendent of Electricity and Telephone Department created.

Institutions

Barclays Bank (Dominion, Colonial And Overseas)
Formerly The Colonial Bank

Incorporated by Royal Charter 1836. Re-incorporated by Act of Parliament 1925, with which are amalgamated.

The National Bank of South Africa Limited and
The Anglo-Egyptian Bank Limited

Head Office: 54, Lombard Street, E.C.3.
London Office for Colonial Banking business—
29 Gracechurch Street, E.C.3.

AUTHORISED CAPITAL 10,000,000
SUBSCRIBED CAPITAL, £6,975.500
PAID-UP CAPITAL, £4,975,500
RESERVE FUND, £2,025,000

Directors

Sir John Caulcutt (KCMG), *Chairman*
William Macnamara Goodenough, *Deputy Chairman*
Arthur Bevington Gillett, *Vice Chairman*

Anthony Charles Barnes (DSO)

The Right Hon. the Earl of Clarendon
(KG, GCMG)

Charles Lyall Dalziel

The Right Hon. Lord Essendon

James Rankine Leisk (CMG)

The Right Hon. Lord Lugard
(GCMG, CB, DSO)

Sir Ernest Oppenheimer (MP)
(Union of South Africa)

Sir Harold Edward Snagge (KBE)

Walter Osborne Stevenson

Herbert Leslie Melville Tritton

General Managers

H. R. Bradfield And J. S. Crossley,

Assistant General Managers

E. O. Holden, F. E. Bettis and D. F. Rigby

Local Director in the West Indies

A. P. G. Austin, Barbados

This Bank is affiliated to Barclays Bank Limited
Head Office: 54 Lombard, Street E.C.3

The Branch of Barclays Bank (Dominion Colonial and Overseas) in St. Vincent, which formerly operated as the Colonial Bank, was opened in 1837. The Colonial Bank was incorporated by Royal Charter in 1836, and established in the succeeding years branches throughout the British West Indies.

Up to 1916, its general banking activities were limited to the West Indies, but in that year the charter was extended and banking business was conducted at other points in the British Empire, as well as in London. In 1917, the charter was further extended which allowed banking business to be conducted at foreign points as well. In 1925, by authority of Act of Parliament, the Colonial Bank was re-incorporated and by amalgamation with the National Bank of South Africa Ltd., and the Anglo Egyptian Bank Ltd. formed Barclays Bank (Dominion Colonial and Overseas). Through this amalgamation the new bank covers extensive territories in South Africa, Egypt, Palestine, East and West Africa, and many other points in the British Empire.

Barclays Bank (Dominion Colonial and Overseas), as is the case with kindred interests such as Barclays Bank (Canada), Barclays Trust Company of Canada, Barclays Bank (France), Ltd., Barclays Bank S.A.I., Rome, The British Linen Bank, and the Union Bank of Manchester, is affiliated to Barclays Bank Ltd. in England, and so through its associations is able to offer a worldwide banking service to its clients.

The facilities afforded by this institution in St. Vincent have been conducive to the progress made in the various agricultural pursuits of the colony. The administration of the business of the bank and the protecting of its interest, although paramount, do not occupy the exclusive attention of the manager, whose vast experience renders him capable of assisting in the affairs of the Government as well as in those of his clients in all stations of life.

The appointments as a justice of the peace and a member of the Executive Council prove the recognition of his ability. The success of the banana industry at its very inception was due to the practical knowledge he possesses. To his foresight must be attributed the absence of difficulty on the part of peasants and others in the financing of their different crops. The Honourable C. B. Sayles (JP), has not failed to identify himself in sports, nor Mrs. Sayles in the application of her rare talent for the furtherance of various efforts for charitable purposes. All members of the staff are always courteous and affable in their demeanour.

Government Savings Bank

Since 1866 a Government Savings Bank has been established at the treasury, Kingstown, but its operations were not extended to the out-districts until

1900, when a branch was opened at Georgetown and Chateaubelair, respectively. In 1911 the branch was transferred from Chateaubelair to Barrouallie.

The bank is opened to the public for the deposit and withdrawal of money daily throughout the year, except on Sundays and holidays, between the hours of 9 a.m. and 3 p.m.; Wednesdays, 9 a.m. to 12 noon.

Deposits are received of one shilling and multiples thereof, not exceeding £200 in any one year up to a maximum of £500.

Interest is allowed at the rate of 2½ per cent per annum on all deposits of £1 and upwards, not exceeding £500.

Married women and minors can make and withdraw deposits in their own names. Deposits are, as a general rule, allowed to be withdrawn on demand, but ten days' delay is prescribed by law.

At 31st December 1937, the total amount to the credit of depositors was £19,957 and £19,120 was invested on deposits in various stocks and shares at 3 to 4 per cent.

There were at 31st December 1937, 887 depositors, sub-divided into 594 at the head bank in Kingstown, and 118, 113 and 62 at the branches of Georgetown, Barrouallie and Union Island, respectively.

The St. Vincent Agricultural Credit & Loan Bank Ltd

In 1909 the St. Vincent Agricultural Credit and Loan Bank, Ltd. was established. The authorised capital of the bank was then 5,000 divided in shares of one dollar each. But at several extraordinary meetings, special resolutions were passed by the shareholders authorising increases in capital to 100,000 shares at one dollar each. At 31st December 1936, the number of shares sold was 46,486, for which there was paid up the subscribed capital of 23,243,00.

The bank is governed by a board of seven directors, two of whom are managing directors. The other five are elected for two years and retire in rotation, their places being filled at the ordinary general meeting held yearly.

During the 29 years of its existence, the bank has been an institution which has so wound itself into the economic life of the community as to become now practically a sine qua non to the large majority of small peasant proprietors, advancing them money to plant their cotton and other crops.

Starting in a small one door room, the bank has now assumed such large proportions that it occupies more than half an entire square at Granby Street.

The balance sheet for 1936 shows that over 42,000 dollars are out at present in loans. The auditing of the bank has for years been done by the Government audit clerk, and this principle which has been put into effect since its inception has created a firm and unwavering confidence in the stability of the bank.

The St. Vincent Chamber of Agriculture & Commerce, Inc.

The Chamber was re-organised in the year 1921 from the Agricultural & Commercial Society and Cotton Growers Association and was incorporated in the year 1926, registered on the 25th day of March in that year.

The objects as set forth in the Memorandum of Association are as follows.

(a) The promotion of the agricultural and commercial interest of the colony, its local, intercolonial, and foreign trade, and its manufactures and industries.

(b) The collection and dissemination of statistical and other information relating to agriculture and commerce, trade, manufactures, and industries.

(c) The offering of suggestions to the Government of the colony on questions of legislature and other measures affecting agriculture, commerce, trade, manufactures, and industries.

(d) The doing of all other such things as may be conducive to the extension of agriculture, commerce, trade, manufactures, and industries, or incidental to the attainment of the above objects.

The business of the chamber is managed by a committee of ten.

The Present Committee

A.G. Hazell, Esq,	President
(Vacant)	Vice-President
W. M. Grant, Esq, Hon.	Secretary and Treasurer

Other members

Honourables A. M. Punnett; F. A. Corea; P. W. Verrail; James Providence, Esq; St. Clair McConnie, Esq; C. K. Robinson, Esq; Agricultural Superintendent, Dr. George MacDonald.

HOSPITALS

In Kingstown is the Colonial Hospital which is situated to the west of the town near the Victoria Park. The hospital consists of three main blocks, one of which was built and is maintained out of a special fund bequeathed by the late Mr. James Graham in 1889. It comprises four private wards and there is, in addition, a smaller block erected in 1936 which houses a self-contained, single-bedded ward erected with funds bequeathed by the late Mr. Conrad Simmons, a bacteriological laboratory, and a radiological clinic. The latter has been built and completely equipped from funds generously provided by Mr. H. L. W. Hayward, a leading planter in St. Vincent. Other buildings in the compound include the operation theatre and an out-patient dispensary in a separate block, a venereal diseases clinic and the nurses' home. The admissions to the hospital reflect the state of health of the colony. They show a low rate for the major diseases usually seen in the tropics, as for example, dysentery and malaria, but a comparatively high rate for more chronic conditions. Admissions during 1937 totalled 1,566 and these are increasing. Separated from the hospital by a road is the building rented for use as a child welfare clinic and the dental clinic. These clinics have all been instituted recently and aim at reducing the wastage due to preventable disease in the island. The following inscriptions in affectionate remembrance of the donors adorn the walls of the building to which they relate:

This Wing was erected in

— 1889 —

From Funds bequeathed for

Charitable purposes in St. Vincent

by the late

JAMES GRAHAM, Esquire

who died 17th May 1877

1937

This Ward is dedicated

In affection and gratitude

to the memory of

CHARLES JAMES

and

CONRAD JOHNSON SIMMONS

Colonists of the Island of

St. Vincent

whose minds were quick to see

and supply the needs of others

In addition to the Colonial Hospital, there are three small casualty hospitals situated respectively at Georgetown, Chateaubelair and Union Island. All these do useful work, and scattered throughout the colony there are 15 dispensaries and a number of medical visiting posts. There have veen some 50,000 attendances at these dispensaries every year.

Fort Institutions

The large stone barracks of Fort Charlotte have been adapted and are used to accommodate mental cases, paupers and those afflicted with leprosy. Each class of case is housed in a separate block, the leper settlement being sited on the extreme promontory of the hill. At Low Point there is an old cantonment that is employed as a sanatorium for early female cases of phthisis.

Between four and five miles away from Kingstown, in a pleasant valley near Calliaqua, a new mental hospital is nearing completion. It is designed and built on modern lines to accommodate 100 patients, and the surrounding area will afford the inmates healthful occupation in agricultural pursuits and in the raising of produce for their consumption. The completion of this modern building will release extra accommodation for paupers, and for early male cases of phthisis (sic) on the Fort site.

The Sanitary Department

The present system of public health administration derives its authority from the Public Health Ordinance, 1927, and the Public Health (Amendment) Ordinance, 1929.

With the proclamation of the 1927 ordinance, a signal advance was made in matters of direction and control. For a colony of the size of St. Vincent, the system of administration by local authorities then in force, was alike cumbersome and ineffective. Vested interest, which in many a larger colony plays such a powerful role in obstructing the enactment and hindering the proper enforcement of legislation, operated unhampered by the restraining influence of an informed public opinion.

The new legislation abolished the local authorities and established a sanitary authority charged with exercising general supervision and control of all sanitary matters in the colony. Executive power was vested in the Chief Medical and Health Officer, now known as the Senior Medical Officer.

Credit for the introduction of this progressive piece of legislation which was stoutly opposed by the advocates of the status quo is due to the late Sir Frederick Seton James (KCMG, KBE), then governor of the Windward Islands, Mr. R. Walter (CMG), who was in charge of the local administration and Dr. Stanley Branch, the colonial surgeon of the day.

In anticipation of the passing of the ordinance, a chief sanitary inspector with the qualification of the Royal Sanitary Institute was appointed. This officer came from the Trinidad service.

As a preliminary to drawing up a programme of sanitary work, and as an indication of the direction in which effort was most needed, the Chief Sanitary Inspector was directed to make a sanitary survey of the colony and to submit a report. The report disclosed conditions which called for early and

364

sustained action and reassured the Government in its determination to put its public health machinery in order.

As a first step, it was necessary to have a trained staff of inspectors, and to this end, the new regime addressed itself. The men then employed were without training and without authority. A statutory notice for the abatement of a nuisance was hardly ever served, nor was a complaint ever lodged. The inspectors were just taken for granted. To the credit of the men it must be said that they applied themselves assiduously to their studies and assumed their new responsibilities with the enthusiasm of reformers.

A campaign against soil pollution was started and hundreds of deep-pit latrines were erected by householders without much ado. Whereas it was the exception to the rule to find a privy on the premises of the average labourer, the reverse is now the position. In and around Kingstown, nearly all the better class premises with sufficient yard space are provided with water closets connected to septic tanks. Such is the porosity of the soil that the system gives little or no trouble.

Kingstown and the small towns were given organised scavenging services under the immediate control of the district sanitary inspectors. Daily house-to-house collection of refuse was instituted and an incinerator erected in each town.

In addition to their inspectorial duties, sanitary inspectors now register all classes of food vendors after half-yearly medical certification. They apply the building regulations and serve notices for the abatement of nuisances and conduct prosecutions. They occupy a position of definite responsibility in the community.

The result of all this has been to influence the lives and habits of the people to a degree which can best be appreciated by persons returning to the colony after long absence. The recent Health Weeks have quickened the critical sense of the populace and made a definite contribution towards the attainment of a "sanitary conscience".

Notwithstanding the absence of a general sewerage system and the presence of housing and water supply problems which call for early attention, it can definitely be said that Kingstown presents an appearance of uniform cleanliness which is a credit to its citizens.

The Georgetown Casualty Hospital

This little institution is an ideal cottage hospital which was opened in the town of Georgetown on the 10th of October 1912 to meet the needs of the residents of Georgetown and the surrounding villages.

It is admirably situated on the seafront of the Windward Coast where fresh air, sunshine and ozone-laden atmosphere are to be had in unlimited quantities and play a great part in the rapid recovery of convalescent patients. The building consists of a two-storey structure which, although small, has everything to be desired in such an institution. On the ground floor there are four rooms comprising an out-patient department, consulting room, dispensary, and steward's quarters. The upper storey is divided into two wards, male and female, clinical laboratory and nurse's quarters. The operating theatre is the feature of the building being constructed on such up-to-date principles as to enable it to be rendered as aseptic as possible. There is a gallery extending all around both storeys of the building.

The present staff: Dr. J. W. Gallwey, medical officer in charge, Ben Richards, dispenser, and Verlaine Jack, nurse.

The Chateaubelair Casualty Hospital

This casualty hospital which was opened in January 1920, and although small, has since its establishment proved most useful to the many needs of the inhabitants of this rural town, Chateaubelair, and the surrounding districts.

The building is divided into two wards, male and female and nurse's quarters. Attached to this institution is a small but convenient operating theatre, a consulting room, mortuary, and an up-to-date dispensary.

The present staff consists of Dr. R. Austin, medical officer in charge, Nurse Madelene Thomas as nurse matron, and Richard John as dispenser-steward.

The Union Island Casualty Hospital

In the year 1936 the building then used as quarters for the district dispenser was converted into a casualty hospital. It is situated on the top of a hill overlooking the Clifton Harbour, Prune Island being in the northeastern direction and Clifton Village toward the west.

At this elevation, fresh air laden with ozone is abundantly pouring in on all sides. It is therefore quite evident that patients will enjoy the best prospects possible for restoration and maintenance of health.

Provision is made in the upper storey for a male ward and a female ward, each measuring about 140 feet square with ample accommodation for two beds in each. On its western side extending the entire length is a gallery 10 feet wide on the level of the upper floor, 10 feet square of which is partitioned for use as a small operating theatre. The lower portion of the building is subdivided for use as a dispensary and as a storeroom. Suitable out-offices are provided. The nurse in charge has accommodation adjacent to the wards to assure easy access to the patients.

This being the first contrivance of its kind in the Grenadines, the inhabitants are exceedingly grateful to His Excellency Sir A. F. Grimble for his sympathetic consideration toward them when Administrator of this colony, and equally so to their much esteemed Dr. R. Austin who successfully urged upon the Administrator the pressing need for such an institution, which is known as The Grimble Casualty Hospital.

The present Staff: Dr. K. J. E. McMillan, medical officer in charge, R. Clouden, dispenser, and Clarice Graham, nurse.

The Thompson Home

This institution was established through the instrumentality of Lady Thompson, wife of the Administrator at the time of the hurricane in 1893. The result of the sad occurrence emphasized the desirability for a suitable place to accommodate destitute ladies in advanced years who had been accustomed to some of the refinements of life.

Contributions amounting to £1,339 17 4 were appropriated to the project. £600 was spent for the purchase of the premises; £330 for making them suitable; and £303 19 3 invested. The balance was reserved for further investments or improvements at the discretion of the committee.

The Thompson Home was formally opened on 11th December 1899 by the late Sir Alfred Maloney (KCMG), at that time Governor of the Windward Islands. During the preceding year, however, accommodation was provided in a rented building from a Government grant of £50 and funds at the disposal of the promoters for the purpose.

The several rooms forming part of the property were all occupied during the past year, and consequently the proceeds from rents supplemented by the annual grant of £15 from the Government were sufficient to defray current expenses.

There are at present nine inmates.

The Trustees are:

A. G. Hazell, Esq; Honourable A. M. Fraser (OBE)

The Committee consists of the following:

367

The wife of the Administrator, *President*
Mrs. J. H. Otway, Vice-President, *Hon. Treasurer and Secretary*

Miss B. Richards, *Hon. Manager*

Miss A. C. McKie	Mrs. F. A. Corea
Mrs. H. N. V. Tonks	Mrs. Agostinho DaSilva
Mrs. C. B. Sayles	Mrs. W. M. Grant
Mrs. E. M. Beach	Miss Muriel Hazel

Miss Millington

Communicants Association

The Communicants' Association of the Cathedral Church of St. George, celebrated its jubilee in October 1906. The object of the association when started was threefold. As its name denotes, it is an association of communicants of the Church of England who joined together (1) to excite one another to the duties of religion, (2) to animate one another to a continual perseverance in piety and goodness, and (3) to impress on one another the rewards of well-doing.

The practical work of the association was comprised in the rules, the chief of which were for the provision of district visitors and a daily meal for the poor. The working members pay six pence monthly, the others one shilling. The number of members varies year by year owing to attendant circumstances. In the secretary's report for 1937 there were 70 on the list. In connection with Their Majesties Coronation, 400 poor persons were supplied with dinner on 13th May 1937 from government funds

The average attendance at the daily meal for the year was 32; and on Christmas Day 200 were provided with a dinner, the same number as in the previous year.

The fund for the maintenance of the soup kitchen depends upon the (1) subscriptions of the members, (2) donations from friends, and (3) a Government grant of £15 per annum.

The list of recipients for 1937 comprised 20 Anglicans, 9 Methodists, 4 Roman Catholics, 5 Salvation Army, 1 Seventh Day Adventist; and the average expense per head per annum was 16s.

The Boy Scouts

Scouting commenced in St. Vincent in 1914, and a charter was granted in Easter of that year legalising the formation of a Boy Scout Association for the island. The movement went on with varying fortunes until 1927, when a visit of scouts from Trinidad in August gave a strong impetus to it. The census returns at 30th September 1937 showed 4 commissioners, O. C. Cruikshank, Esq, Island Commissioner; A. V. Sprott, Esq, District Commissioner for Kingstown; Alban DaSantos, Esq, District Commissioner for Windward; and J. L. Chapman, Esq, District Commissioner for Leeward; and 316 Scouts of all ranks. The officers of the executive committee are J. H. Otway, Esq (OEE), Chairman; W. M. Lopey, Esq (MA), Treasurer; A. J. Archer, Esq, Secretary.

It may be mentioned that the scouts contributed in 1914 to an ambulance bus for use in the Great War; that they sent three scouters to the jamboree at Arrowe Park, England, in 1929; and that they lit beacon fires on heights surrounding Kingstown in celebration of His Majesty's Silver Jubilee in 1935. The association also in 1935 celebrated its coming-of-age by a jamboree which was attended by scouts from the neighbouring islands. The Honourable F. A. Corea has been and still is the association's greatest benefactor.

Patron—His Excellency H. Bradshaw Popham (CMG, MBE)

President—Local Association, His Honour A. A. Wright (CMG)

Vice-President—H. Otway, Esq

2nd Vice-President—Honourable F. A. Corea

Island Commissioner—Captain O. C. Cruikshank

District Commissioner, Kingstown—A. V. Sprott, Esq

District Commissioner, Windward—Captain A. DaSantos

District Commissioner, Leeward—J. L. Chapman, Esq

Local Secretary—A. J. Archer, Esq

Treasurer—W. M. Lopey, Esq

Members, Executive Committee—His Lordship Bishop Tonks; Hon. L. P. Spence; Rev. H. H. Cole; Rev. Fr. Dom Carlos Verbeke; M. Byron Cox, Esq; C. W. Prescod, Esq, Acting Inspector of Schools; J. P. E. Cropper, Esq.

The Girl Guides

Since the inception of Girl Guides in the island, the movement has gone steadily ahead. The first company in St. Vincent was formed in 1928 when Mrs. John Otway was island commissioner. Under her able management the foundations of good guiding were laid. The original company, which is now known as the High School Company, still maintains a high standard of efficiency.

But even prior to that date, to be more strictly accurate, in December 1927, Mrs. Walter, the wife of the Administrator at that time, interested herself in guiding and was in reality the first island commissioner. Miss Sheila

Wall was then captain and Miss Rosamond Orde, lieutenant. During Mrs. Otway's term of office, the number of companies increased to six.

In August 1931, on the resignation of Mrs. Otway, Mrs. Vibert Jackson was appointed island commissioner, and during her term of office a piece of land was purchased and a useful hut built thereon for the Guides headquarters. Mrs. Jackson left the colony in 1935 and Mrs. Hatch acted commissioner until December 1936, when Mrs. Otway was again appointed island commissioner.

The movement at present consists of three Ranger companies, ten Guide Companies and five Brownie Packs and continues to progress satisfactorily.

St. Vincent Grammar School Cadet Corps

Established 2nd term of school year 1936-37
Officer-in-Charge, 2nd Lt. D. S. Cozier (seconded from Vol. Corps)
Committee:
Officer-in-Charge Local Forces
Headmaster Grammar School
Officer-in-Charge Cadet Corps
Mr. V. G. I. DaSilva (Secretary)
Strength 26 (at present). The strength will vary from time to time.

The Corps is a member of the British National Cadet Association and has been affiliated to the St. Vincent Volunteer Corps.

The Old Girls Association

The Old Girls Association of the Girls' High School was inaugurated in 1930 with the object of promoting unity among those who had ceased to be students of an institution which is dear to their hearts.

The two chief aims of the association are the distribution of groceries to aged ladies each Saturday; and the award of a three-year scholarship to the Girls' High School to a child, the financial position of whose parents or guardian would debar her from otherwise attending the Girls' High School.

Up to the present, two scholarship holders have completed their term and a third is now making good progress.

Each year the association holds a reunion which is very much enjoyed as the ladies are very pleased to meet their one-time school companions.

The association is conducted by a president, vice president and a committee; at an annual general meeting all members present are allowed to participate in the proceedings.

The association is now firmly established and its silent work is perhaps its greatest asset.

The membership is satisfactory and is steadily increasing.

The Saint Vincent Grammar School Old Boys Association

The St. Vincent Grammar School Old Boys Association was formed in 1936 with the object of preserving the good name of the St. Vincent Grammar School and of fostering a spirit of friendship between boys of the school past and present. All old boys and all past and present masters of the St. Vincent Grammar School are eligible for membership.

The officers of the association consist of a president, two vice presidents (of whom the Headmaster of the Grammar School shall always be one), and such other vice presidents as may be elected by the association from time to time, and a general secretary-treasurer. The officers are elected annually at a general meeting. Mr. O. D. Brisbane was the first elected president of the association and served as such for two successive years, when he was succeeded in March 1938 by Dr. L. E. Sprott, the present president.

The association, which has been steadily growing in membership, continues to render good and useful service and makes an annual contribution to the Reeves Memorial Scholarship Fund. A beautifully framed portrait of that great educationist, Frederic William Reeves, Esq (MA), late Headmaster of the St. Vincent Grammar School, was recently presented to the school by the association to perpetuate the memory of one who has done so much for the school and for education in this colony.

An annual feature of the association's activities is a reunion held in February each year and taking the form of a banquet to which His Honour the Administrator and Honourable members of the Executive Council are invited.

The St. Vincent Workingmen Cooperative Association Limited

Formed 2nd March, 1936; incorporated 2nd July, 1936

Authorised Share Capital, 824,000.00

Insurance Dept. consists of 9,500 members

The aims and objects are:

1) To protect the workingman in times of trouble, sickness and death;

2) To improve the social and economic condition of the masses;

3) To oppose by all constitutional means any measure that is in its opinion not in the interests of the people.

President, The Honourable Geo. A. McIntosh
Secretary, Mr. James L. Cato

371

The St. Vincent Employers' and Employees' Association

As a result of the unfortunate disturbances of October 21, 1935, a strong feeling of discord arose between the different classes in St. Vincent.

Certain members of the community, actuated by no methods of gain but desirous solely of restoring to St. Vincent her lost good name for friendliness amongst all sections of the community, convened a meeting with a view toward creating an association that would bring together all members of the community regardless of race, colour or creed. The result of this meeting was the formation of the St. Vincent Employers' and Employees' Association on the 1st September 1937. The planters of the island who are the greatest employers of labour readily supported the movement. With two exceptions all the planters are members of this association. The association chose Mr. O. W. Forde, Barrister-at-Law and the owner of the Argyle block of estates, to be its president for two years. Mr. Forde was the founder of the association and received unstinted support from Dr. George MacDonald, Dr. E. Deane, Mr. A. G. Hazell of John H. Hazell Sons & Co. Ltd., Messrs. Alban DaSantos, the owner of Colonarie Estate, Robert M. Anderson, Robert DaBreo, Frank Child, the owner of Grand Sable Estate, James D. Punnett, owner of Cane Hall Estate, W. H. Barnard of the Orange Hill Estates Ltd., Alexander Murdoch Fraser a staunch supporter in the Leeward District and the owner of Rutland Vale Estate. Support was also given by Honourable William Hadley of Union Estate, Messrs. D. A. Richards of Mount Bentinck Estate, Felix DaSantos of Bellevue Estate, George V. Ballantyne, Merchant of Georgetown, Terrence Deare, Roy Punnett of Diamond Estate, the late E. M. Beach of Brighton Estate, and others. The Honourable F. A. Corea who was in England at the inception of the association has given very valuable support and suggestions to the association. The association has increased gradually until its membership now reaches the amount of 2,139. It is expected that its membership will soon reach the 5,000 mark.

The main objects of the association are to create and maintain a better feeling among all classes in the colony of St. Vincent and to provide funds by means of weekly contributions and donations for sick allowances of members and, subject to certain rules, for the payment of $30.00 on the death of any member to his or her heir, executor, administrator or assigns.

Section 29 of the rules provides for a committee of management, who with nine other members elected at a special general meeting for any particular purpose, shall be recognised as an Arbitration Committee before whom any dispute arising amongst members shall be brought for deliberation, the decision in all such matters to be final, and any member disregarding such decision of the Arbitration Committee to be expelled. By virtue of this section it is hoped to smooth out all differences on estates and between all classes of labourers whose employers are members of the association. In the selection of the committee, the greatest judgment will be exercised so as to inspire confidence especially amongst the poorer classes.

The accounts of the association are open to Government inspection at any time between the hours of 10 a.m. and 4 p.m. during each working day.

The association has been registered under The Friendly Societies' Ordinance of 1843.

The Committee of Management comprises the president, Mr. O. W. Forde; the treasurer, Mr. Robert Dabreo; the trustees, Dr. George MacDonald, Mr. A. G. Hazell, The Hon. W. Hadley, Dr. E. Deane, Messrs. R. M. Anderson, Frank Child, Alban DaSantos; and the secretary Mr. O. C. Forde.

The association, while not primarily political, has made and will continue to make to Government suggestions for the general good of all classes in the community. Since the formation of the association, His Excellency the Governor has noted a better feeling amongst the people of St. Vincent and has attributed this to the association.

The Kingstown Club

The Kingstown Club was organized in 1891. The premises, which are eminently suited for the purpose, are situated at James and Middle Streets.

The management of the club devolves on a committee consisting of seven members to be elected annually.

His Excellency the Governor is Patron and the Administrator President; one chairman and vice chairman are elected yearly.

Candidates are elected by ballot and a note of result is recorded. No rejected candidate can again be proposed until the expiration of three months, and a result of a second ballot is final. The entrance fee for members is $10.

The annual subscription is $28.80 payable quarterly, and $14.40 half-yearly for town and country members, respectively.

All active commissioned officers of the Navy and Army are admitted as honorary members during their stay in the colony.

A term of one month is allowed for visitors introduced by members. The committee may, however, extend the period, whereupon the visitors become temporary members and are required to pay in advance a monthly subscription of $3.50. Such temporary membership may be determined by the committee at any time.

Kingstown Tennis Club

The management of the Kingstown Tennis Club is entrusted to a committee of six members consisting of the officers and one other member.

It is provided that the Governor of the colony shall be invited to become Patron of the club during his tenure of office and the officer administering the Government the President thereof during his tenure of office.

Among the classification for membership are included all active commissioned officers of the Navy and Army during their stay in the island and any other person of whom the managing committee may approve.

Any visitor to the colony may be admitted to the club for a period of 14 days on the introduction of a member who shall enter his name in the visitors' book.

Any persons temporarily resident in the colony for more than 14 days who wish to enjoy the privileges of the club may, on being duly proposed and seconded, be admitted as temporary members for a period not exceeding three, months; the committee, however, has power to extend the privilege.

Freemasonry

There is one active Lodge of Freemasons in St. Vincent, namely, "St. George," No. 2616, on the Registry of the Grand Lodge of England. This Lodge was established on 27th May, 1896.

Ancient Order of Foresters

There is one court in the colony, viz: "St. Vincent Morning Star" No. 2298.

Regular meetings are held fortnightly at Granby and James Streets, the property of the court.

The following are the principal objects of the society:

1. For the burial of members their wives or widows;
2. For paying a weekly allowance to members when ill and unable to follow their employment;
3. Granting relief to members in distressed circumstances;
4. Assisting members when compelled to travel in search of employment.

Grand United Order of Oddfellows

There is one lodge for male members in St. Vincent, viz: "St. Vincent" Lodge No. 9111. Dispensated November, 1912.

Regular meetings are held on the 2nd and 4th Mondays in every mouth at the Lodge Hall, Lower Bay Street.

There is also a branch of the Household of Ruth for females: " Alpha" No. 4862. Dispensated 29th December, 1913.

The principal objects of both Societies are the same, viz:

For the burial of members and their children.

For paying a weekly allowance to members when ill and unable to follow their employment.

Granting relief to members in distressed circumstances and assisting members when compelled to travel in search of employment.

Cricket

Cricket is controlled by the St. Vincent Cricket Association of which His Excellency the Governor of the Windward Islands is Patron and His Honour the Administrator is President.

Anyone can become a member of the association on paying the prescribed fee, i.e. 3/- per annum for playing members and 2/- for non-playing members. Lady members of the latter category pay 1/-.

Clubs taking part in the Fraser-Neckles Competition which is played on Victoria Park and the Grammar School ground are provided free of charge with groundsmen, matting for practice and for matches, wicket keeping pads and gloves, ice water on match days, and umpires.

The clubs at present registered with the association are Ramblers, Ex-Grammar School, Grammar School, Workingmen's Association, Endeavour, and Police.

Cricket continues to be the chief outdoor game of the people. The time-honoured custom of country teams paying extended visits to each other's district and engaging in a series of matches, each followed by dancing and merrymaking still continues.

The Cork Cup is the emblem of cricket supremacy in the Windward Islands. Tournaments are played in each colony in turn. Grenada now has the highest number of liens on the cup.

Football

Whereas cricket is played in all parts of the colony, football is hardly seen outside of Kingstown; at the moment, the game is somewhat "under the weather." It lacks organisation and effective leadership. Some attempt at a revival was made last year but it was not attended with much success.

There are, however, four or five clubs of which the Grammar School's is the most active.

St. Vincent Golf Club

A new company, The St. Vincent Golfing and Holiday Resorts Limited, has recently been formed and purchased what is locally referred to as the Ratho Mill Point. A golf course is now being laid out on the very site Lord Elibank selected and used for the purpose. In close proximity the construction of bungalows is already in progress and the erection of an hotel there is under contemplation.

Agricultural Credit Societies

Registered by virtue of the provisions of the Agricultural Credit Societies Ordinance

Clare Valley-Questelles	45 members.
Georgetown	85 members
Three Rivers	49 members

The principal objects are to provide peasant proprietors with the facilities for obtaining money to develop their lands and business through means of a common guarantee and to render absolutely safe all funds invested with such Societies.

Friendly Societies

Anglican—One in Kingstown, "St. George's and St. Andrew's", one in Calliaqua and one in Buccament.

Methodist—One in Chateaubelair and one in Georgetown.

Roman Catholic—Two in Kingstown, "St Patrick's" and " Mutual."

The principal objects are to promote the moral and religious welfare of members and to provide relief during their illness and help at their burial.

There are several guilds and other societies in connection with the religious denominations.

Kingstown—"Provident", "Amicable and Benevolent"

Calliaqua—"Provident"

Park Hill—"Crescent"

Georgetown—"Hand in Hand", "Women Fellowship"

Layou— "Layou Provident", "Providential"

Troumaca—"Temperance"

Chateaubelair—"Provident", "Olive"

Barrouallie—"Provident"Argyle—" Sun."

Marriaqua —"Mutual"

Questelles— "Benevolent"

Union Island —"The Southern Grenadines"

Canouan—"Perseverance"

Bequia—"United Brothers", " Pilgrim Brothers", " Brotherly Love"

Parishes and Districts

Charlotte Parish comprises the lands extending from the northern boundary of the Fancy Estate to the river Iambou and running along the bed of the said river until they reach the high ridge of mountains which runs through the centre of the island of St. Vincent.

St. George's Parish comprises the lands extending from the said river called the Iambou to Kingstown North River where it empties itself into the sea and running up the bed of the last named river until it divides and from thence continuing along the course of the northern branch of the said river to the great ridge of mountains running through the centre of the island of St. Vincent.

St. Andrew's Parish comprises the lands extending from the said river called the Kingstown North River and from the said northern branch thereof unto the high ridge to the northward of Queen's Valley, which divides the said valley from Rutland Valley and running along the said ridge until it meets the great ridge of mountains which runs through the centre of the island of St. Vincent.

St. *Patrick's Parish* extends from the said ridge to the northward of Queen's Valley unto the high ridge to the northward of Cumberland Valley commonly called Byam's Hill, and runs along the said last named ridge until it meets the great ridge of mountains which runs through the centre of the island of St. Vincent.

St. David's Parish extends from the said last mentioned and northern boundary of St. Patrick's Parish unto the northern boundary of Charlotte Parish.

The Grenadines Parish comprises the Island of Bequia and such other of the Islands within this colony commonly called the Grenadines as lie to the northward of the island of Carriacou.

Magisterial Districts

The First District consists of that part of St. George's Parish which lies to the west of the Greathead or Warrawarrou River, and of that part of the Parish of St. Andrew south of the ridge running from Biaha Point to Mt. St. Andrew, separating the Buccament Valley from Clare Valley, etc., the boundaries of which district are shown by a red line drawn on a copy of the Admiralty Chart of St. Vincent, which is recorded in the Registrar's Office at Kingstown in Liber X 5 page 528.

The Second District consists of the whole of the island of St. Vincent (with the exception of the portion comprised in the first Police District).

The Third District consists of the Grenadine Islands included in the Government of St. Vincent.

Medical Districts

No. 1 District—That part of the Parish of St. George, including the Town of Kingstown, which lies to the west of a line from Mount St Andrew to the mouth of Greathead River and that part of the Parish of St. Andrew which lies to the east of a line from Mount St. Andrew to the sea at Ottley Hall works.

No. 2 District, South—That part of the Parish of St. Andrew which is west of the eastern boundary of No. 1 District and that part of St. Patrick's Parish which lies south of a line from Barrouallie to the Central Ridge at the junction of the Parishes of St. Andrew and St. Patrick.

No. 2 District, North—The remainder of the Parish of St. Patrick and the whole of the Parish of St. David.

No. 3 District—That part of the Parish of St. George not included in No. 1 District.

No. 4 District—That part of Charlotte Parish which lies to the south of Byera River.

No. 5 District —The remainder of Charlotte Parish.

No. 6 District—The Grenadine Islands included in the Government of Saint Vincent.

Administrative Districts

Windward District—Includes the whole of Charlotte Parish and such part of the parish of St. George as lies to the east of the high ridge extending from Mount St. Andrew through Dorsetshire Hill to Cane Garden Point.

Leeward District—Includes the whole of the Parishes of St. David, St. Patrick, St. Andrew, and such part of the Parish of St. George as lies to the west of the high ridge extending from Mt. St. Andrew through Dorsetshire Hill to Cane Garden Point.

Electoral Districts for Legislative Councils

Kingstown District—All that district bounded by the highest line of the ridge running from the sea at Byahaut Point to the summit of Mt. St. Andrew, and by the highest line of the ridge running from Mt. St. Andrew to the sea at Cane Garden Point.

Leeward District—All that district in the north, on the Leeward side, included in the whole of the Parishes of St. David and St. Patrick and that part of the Parish of St. Andrew so far south as the highest line of the ridge running from the sea at Byahaut Point to the summit of Mt. St. Andrew.

South Windward District—All that district included in that part of the Parish of St. George not included in the Kingstown Electoral District and all that part of Charlotte Parish south of the highest line of the ridge lying between North Union and South Union and extending inland above Greggs and ending in the Grand Bonhomme.

North Windward District—All that district included in the remaining part of Charlotte Parish.

The Grenadines District—All the islands of the Grenadines included in the Colony of St. Vincent.

Justices Of The Peace

C. O. Hazell, K.C.	Reginald Austin
Ralph Balfour	Donald C. McIntosh
Dr. A. B. Brereton	Dr. K J. E. McMillan
Charles A. Browne	Thomas Osment
Frank Child	C. W. Prescod
A. M. Fraser, O.B.E.	Arnold Morgan Punnett
Edgius Felix DaSantos	Francis Donald Rice
Joseph Milton Gray	Clifford Bertram Sayles
Digby Hadley	

Barristers

C. O. Hazell, K.C.   O. W. Forde

A. A. Richards   N. S. Nanton

Solicitors

M. Byron Cox   R. M. Anderson

A. C. DeBique   E. A. McLeod

Notaries Public

R. M. Anderson   A. A. Richards

O. W. Forde

E. A. McLeod   Stanley deFreitas

Supreme Court Of Judicature
Days of Holding Court

For Criminal Matters—On the 2nd Tuesday in March, July and November.

For Civil Cases without a Jury—On the 3rd Tuesday in every month, except September.

For Civil Cases before a Jury—On the 3rd Tuesday in every month, except September.

For Matters of Summary Jurisdiction—On the 3rd Tuesday in every month, except September.

For Appeals from Magistrates' Decisions—On the 3rd Saturday in every month of the year, except September.

Magisterial Courts
First District

Kingstown Police Court Every Monday and Friday.

Second District

Calliaqua Police Court—The Friday next following the 3rd Tuesday and the 4th Tuesday in every month at 10 a.m.

Mesopotamia Police Court—The Friday next following the 2nd Tuesday and the Thursday next following the 4th Tuesday in every month at 10 a.m.

Colonarie Police Court—The 1st Tuesday in every month at 10 a.m.

Georgetown Police Court—The Friday after the 3rd Tuesday in every month at 10 a.m.

Layou Police Court—The Monday next following the 1st Tuesday in every month at 10 a.m.

Barrouallie Police Court—The Wednesday next following the 2nd Tuesday in every month at 10 a.m.

Chateaubelair Police Court—The 2nd Tuesday in every month at 10 a.m.

Third District

Bequia Police Court—The 2nd Tuesday in every month at 1.30 p.m.

Union Island Police Court—The 3rd Thursday in every month at 10 a.m.

Canouan Police Court—The 3rd Friday in every month at 10 a.m.

Mayreau Police Court—The 3rd Saturday in every month at 10 a.m.

Code of Signals used at Fort Charlotte

B—Red flag with swallow tail—Full rig ship

C—White pennant with red ball—To Leeward

D—Blue pennant with white ball—Schooner

F—Red pennant with white cross—Sloop

G—Yellow and blue pennant—Passing

H—White and Red—square flag—Brigantine

J— Blue, White, and Blue (horizontal)—Brigantine

K—Yellow and Blue—Rig not made out

L—Four-checkered flag—Black and Yellow—3 masted Schooner

N—Sixteen-checkered flag—Blue and White—Fleet or Squadron

P—Blue flag with white square centre—Distress

Q—Yellow flag—Barque

R—Red flag with yellow cross—Under steam

S—White flag with blue centre—Two or more of same rig

T—Red, White and Blue, (perpendicular)—Yacht

V—White flag with red cross from each corner—Royal Mail

W—Blue flag with white and red centres—Foreign Man-of-War.

The Union Jack is used for British ships of war.

The West India Committee

President:

Vice-Presidents: The Duke of Atholl, (KT), (GCVO), (CB), (DSO)

The Rt. Hon. Lord Oliver, (PC), (KCMG), (CB)

Chairman: Lieut.-Colonel Ivan Davson, (OBE), (Td)

Deputy-Chairman: J. Gordon Miller, Esq

Treasurers :—Sir Alfred Sherlock, Thomas Greenwood, Esq

H. J. J. Freeman, Esq	Admiral A. G. Hotham, (CB), (CMG)
C. W. Gurney, Esq	Sir George Huggins, (OBE)
Executive Committee:	T. Harrison Hughes, Esq
A. W. Armour, Esq	B. E. King, Esq (MA), (LLB)
Rolland Beaumont, Esq	R. L. M. Kirkwood, Esq
John Bromley, Esq	The Hon. Dudley G. Leacock
R. Bryson, Esq (OBE)	The Hon. Noel B. Livingston
Evan R. Campbell, Esq	T. H. Naylor, Esq
Harold de Pass, Esq	Lauchlan Rose, Esq (MC)
J. Alan de Pass, Esq	Major Kenneth E. Previte
A. Duckham, Esq	J. H. Scrutton, Esq
Alexander Elder, Esq	The Rt. Hon. Lord Selsdon, (PC), (KBE)
H. Crum Ewing, Esq	
W. G. Freeman. Esq (BSc)	M. Moody Stewart, Esq, (MC)
F. A. Greenaway, Esq	H. A. Trotter, Esq
H. L. Q. Henriques, Esq	R. S. Aucher Warner, Esq, (KC)

Secretary: Sir Algernon Aspinall, (CMG), (CBE), Barrister-at-Law

Assistant Secretary: T. Dowdall Hampson, Esq

The West India Committee, which was established about 1750 and incorporated by Royal Charter of King Edward VII in 1904, is an association of British subjects and firms interested in the agricultural and manufacturing industries and trade of the British West Indies, British Guiana and British Honduras.

Its main object is to promote the interests of such industries and trade and thus to increase the general welfare of those colonies.

Members of the West India Committee have, at 14 Trinity Square, a large room where they may conduct their correspondence, meet friends and read the West Indian newspapers, official gazettes, and London market reports.

In addition there is a well-stocked library of books relating to the West Indies, which to quote Dr. Lowell Ragatz of Washington University is "without question the finest in the world for any one interested in the Antilles".

Agents
John H. Hazell Sons & Co. Ltd

Lloyd's Agency

Harrison Line of Steamers

Aluminum Line

Ocean Dominion S.S. Corp. (Canadian Service)

Bermuda and West Indies Steamship Co.

North British and Mercantile Insurance Co. Ltd.

The Sun Fire Office

The Motor Union Insurance Co., Ltd.

The Goodyear Tire & Rubber Export Co.

General Electric Co. Ltd.

West India Oil Co. S.A.

Petroleum Marketing Co. (West Indies Ltd.)

Hazelhurst & Sons, Ltd. (Soap)

A. & F. Pears (Soap)

British Creameries Ltd. (Lard Compound)

Petters Ltd. (Engines)

Imperial Typewriter Co. Ltd.

Electrolux Ltd. (Refrigerators)

Ailsa Craig Ltd. (Engines)

Jenson and Nicholson Ltd. (Paints)

Bitulac Ltd. (Bituminous Products)

Tunnel Portland Cement Co. Ltd.

Austin Motor Co. Ltd.

White Horse Distillers Ltd.

Gourock Ropework Co. Ltd.

Westminster Tobacco Co. Ltd.

Swift & Co. (Pork Products)

Ardath Tobacco Co. Ltd.

Rankine & Sons Ltd. (Biscuits)

British & Overseas Butter Co. Ltd.

Columbia Phonograph Co.

Crosse & Blackwell Ltd.

John A. Hunter & Co., Ltd.

John Jeffrey & Co., Ltd.

Nugget Polish Co., Ltd.

Willys Export Co. Inc. etc., etc., etc.

Corea & Co. Ltd.

Canadian National Steamships

American Caribbean Line

Royal Netherlands West India Mail

Lake of the Woods Milling Co., Ltd.

United Exporters, Ltd.

West India Oil Co.

Guardian Assurance Co., Ltd.

Petroleum Marketing Co., (West Indies) Ltd.

Dunlop Rubber Co., Ltd.

Nanton, Layne & Co.

Vauxhall and Bedford Vehicles

Hamburg American Line

Whitbread & Co., Ltd.

Pabst Dry Ginger Ale

Jrugens & Co., Ltd.

Wm. Gossages & Sons, Ltd.

James Buchanan & Co., Ltd.

The Murphy Co., Ltd.

DaSilva & Co. Ltd

Steamships and Sailing Craft
J. Bibby & Sons, Ltd.

Peter Dawson, Ltd.
Morris Motors, Ltd.

R. S. Brisbane

The Demerara Mutual Life Assurance
Society, Ltd.

The Bennett College, Ltd.

E. A. McLeod

The Barbados Mutual Royal Insurance
Co., Ltd.

Royal Insurance Co., Ltd.
International General Electric Co. Ltd.

W. J. Abbott

Sun Life Assurance Company of Canada
Marine Insurance
Micheline Tyre Co.
Colgates Palmolive Peet Co.
Compagnie Generale Trans-atlantique (French Line)
Barbados Co-operative Cotton Factory, Ltd.
Pickesgale Saw Mills, Br. Guiana
Humber Fishing & Fish Manure Co.
A.S. Bryden & Sons, Barbados

McConnie, Gill & Co.

RCA Manufacturing Co., Inc. - Radios, Electrolas, Etc.
Opel Motor Cars
Parker Fountain Pen Co., Ltd. - Fountain Pens, Pencils, Quink

H. A. Davis

The Crown Life Assurance Company

Ivan C. Richards

Alliance Assurance Co., Ltd. (Incorporated in England)

H. Jason Jones & Co.

London Assurance Co. Ltd.
St. Lawrence Flour Mills Co.
West Indian Oil Industries Ltd.

St Vincent Trading Company
Standard Brands of New York
Champion Machinery Co. of Joliet Illinois
Ogilvie Flour Mills Co., Ltd.
Baker Perkins Ltd.

Foreign Consuls

Consul-General for Belgium—J. de Neeff, Havana

Consul for France—Monsieur Marie Marc Pelleterat de Borde, Trinidad

Consul for Germany—Paul Urich, Trinidad

Consul for Latvia—Gabriel Descamps, Trinidad

Consul for Netherlands—J. DeVaux, St. Lucia

Consul-General for Norway—Jorgen Brunchorst, Havana.

Consul for Peru —Thomas Hunte, Barbados

Consul for Portugal—Agostinho DaSilva, St. Vincent

Consul for United States of America—Prescott Childs, Barbados

Consul for Venezuela—Señor Pedro Falipe Rojas, Trinidad

Distance Of Highways
(From the Court House, Kingstown)

Windward

	Miles
Bridge over Warrawarrou River	1¾
Calliaqua River	3
Prospect	4
Belvedere palm trees	5½
Diamond Estate	7
Stubbs	7½
Mt. Pleasant House	8
Iambou River	9
Argyle	9½
Escape	10
Peruvian Vale Estate	11
Biabou Estate	12
Bridgetown	12½
The Cedars	14
Union House	15
Sans Souci	16
Mt. Greenan	17

Bellevue	17½
Colonarie Police Station	18
Gorse	19
Byera	19½
Tunnel at Mt. Young	20
Georgetown	22
Langley Park	23
Rabacca Bay	24
Waterloo	24
Orange Hill	26
Tourama Works	27
Overland	28
Sandy Bay	30
Point Espagnol	31¼
Owia Estate	32
Cramacou	33
Fancy Estate	35

Vigie

Fountain	3
Belmont Old Works	6
Four cross roads above Evesham	7½
Mesopotamia	9
Peruvian Vale Estate	11

Leeward

To Lowmans	2
York Valley (Camden Park Works)	2¾
Questelles House	3¼
Chauncey	4
Rillans	4½
Pembroke	5
Cane Grove	5¼
Peniston	5½
Retreat	6
Queensbury	6
Vermont	6½
Turn, north side Buccament Valley	6½
Layou or Rutland Town	7½
Mt. Wynne	11
Peters Hope	11½
Barrouallie or Princes Town	12
Keartons	12½
Wallilabo or Man's Bay	13¼
Belleisle House	15¼

Oushilabou or Cumberland Bay	17½
Coulls Hill	18
Spring Village	18
Troumaca or Suffolk Bay	18¾
Rose Bank	19
Belmont	19
Chateaubelair or Richmond Town	21
Richmond Estate	22
Wallibou House	23
Morne Ronde	24

There is no public road from Morne Ronde to Fancy. The surface is much broken and the distance is about 16 miles.

TAXES, LICENCES, ETC., ABRIDGED

Income Tax

The tax upon chargeable income of a person other than a company:

For every £1 of the chargeable income after deductions:

For every pound of the first £100	£ 4
For every pound of the next £200	6
For every pound of the next £300	1 0
For every pound of the next £400	1 6
For every pound of the next £500	2 9
For every pound of the next £500	3 6
For every pound of the next £500	4 3
For every pound of the next £500	5 0
For every pound of the rest of chargeable income	6 0

The tax upon the chargeable income of a company shall be at the rate of two shillings and sixpence on every pound of chargeable income thereof.

Land And House Tax

Upon houses in the islands of St. Vincent and Union of which the assessed annual rental shall be

Over £2 and not exceeding £3	1/- per house
Over £3 and not exceeding £5	2/- per house
Over£5 and not exceeding £6	2/6 per house
Over £6 and not exceeding £7 10/-	3/4 per house
Over £7 10/-and not exceeding £9	4/- per house
Over £9 and not exceeding £10	5/- per house
Over £10 and not exceeding £12 10/-	6/8 per house

Over £12 10/- and not exceeding £15	10/- per house
Over £15 and not exceeding £20	15/- per house
Over £20 (of the assessed annual rental)	£4%

Port Dues

For every ship at anchor in any port other than ships exempted:

For every steamer	£2 0 0
For every steamer sailing or motor vessel of 100 tons and upwards	10 0 0
For every steamer sailing or motor vessel of 20 tons and under 40	8 0
All others below 20 tons	4 0

Exemptions—His Majesty's ships, ships in service of Govt, of this colony, Ships belonging to the Government of any Foreign State, yachts when sailed exclusively for pleasure, ships in the service of any telegraph company having a station and carrying on business in this colony, and ships employed under contract with His Majesty's Government for the carriage of His Majesty's mails.

Note: In respect of ships registered in this colony and trading between it and other West Indian islands and colonies, only half of the above dues are payable.

Licences

For Sale of Liquor

	£ 3
Class 1—Wholesale licence—Half-yearly	0 0
Class 2—Retail Town licence —Quarterly	
	6
In Kingstown	5 0
In Georgetown	
In Chateaubelair	
In Calliaqua	2
In Barronallie	10 0
In Layou	
	1
Class 3—Retail Country licence—Quarterly	10 0
	1
Class 4—Retail Grenadines licence	10 0
Class 5—Hotel licence—Half-yearly	0 0
Class 6—Refreshment House Licence—Half-yearly	4 0 0
Class 7—Occasional licence—For each day	10 0
Class 8—Bottle Licence—Quarterly	3 0 0

Vehicles, Animals, &c.

	£ 4
Motor Cars not exceeding 1,800 lb. in weight	0 0
Motor Cars not exceeding 1,800 lb. but not exceeding 2,600 lb. in weight	6 0 0
Motor Cars not exceeding 2,609 lb. in weight	8 0 0
	1
Motor Bicycles or tricycles	10 0

Motor Bicycles or tricycles with side car	2 0 0
Motor vehicles used solely as motor hearses, per annum	2 0 0
Every Carriage—For each wheel	5 0
Every Carriage Cart of the gross weight of 400 lb or under	5 0
Every Carriage Cart above the gross weight of 400 lb	
(a) if fitted with pneumatic rubber tires	10 0
(b) of any other kind	15 0
Trailers, motor lorries, vans or omnibuses of less than 2 tons in weight	9 10 0
Trailers, motor lorries, vans or omnibuses of 2 tons but less than three tons in weight	11 10 0
Trailers, motor lorries, vans or omnibuses of 3 tons or over in weight	15 10 0

Notes: (i) Weight means the combined weight of the chassis, body, load, and number of persons to be carried, provided that the weight of each person to be carried shall be taken as 120 lb.

(ii) The owner of any motor vehicle specified above may in every half year take out the licence required and shall pay in respect thereof amounts mentioned under Ordinance No. 9 of 1937.

For the issue of fiscal permits in respect of motor vehicles registered in the colony, each permit	£10 0
Every Coasting Vessel—for every ton of her registered tonnage	1 6
Every Boat—for each foot of measurement from stem to stern	3
Every bicycle, tricycle, velocipede and other similar machine not propelled by mechanical power (except children's cycles used by children under 12 years of age, perambulators and cycles the bond fide property of any visitor to the island provided that such cycles be re-embarked within three months from the day of landing)	5 0
Every bicycle used or kept for letting out on hire	7 6
Every Mare, Gelding, or Mule	10 0
Every Ass	2 6
Every Dog outside Kingstown, except as hereinafter mentioned	3 0
Every Dog inside Kingstown and within half a mile thereof	6 0
Every Stallion three years and over	1 0 0
Every Warehouse for receiving steamers cargo	10 0 0
Other Warehouses	3 0 0

Notes: (i) If the licence is taken out after 30th June, only half the above sum is payable.

(ii Any person usually resident out of the colony and temporarily visiting the colony being in possession and use of any of the animals or articles above in respect of which the licence fee payable equals or exceeds the sum of ten shillings may, in lieu of the usual licence, take out a licence for three months, to be called a visitors' licence, in the same manner and from the same person as the usual licence, paying therefore one quarter of the amount specified for a full year's licence.

Auctioneers, Porters, Insurance Businesses
and Dealers In Motor Vehicles

For every Licence to follow the calling of an Auctioneer	£ 2 0 0
For every Licence to follow the calling of a Porter	1 0
For every Licence which shall be issued in the name of the principal and not the agent, to carry on the business of:	
Life Insurance	5 0 0
Fire	3 0 0
All other Property, Accident or Sickness Insurance	3 0 0
For every Licence to follow the calling of a dealer in motor vehicles	5 0 0

Firearms

To keep firearms and ammunition:	
For every firearm, and ammunition therefor	£ 5 0
For every person authorized by the owner of lands to carry any of his licensed guns and ammunition to. from and on lands belonging to him and to use such guns on these lands only	2 6
To deal in firearms and ammunition or trade as a gunsmith:	
For every licence	1 0 0

Other Licences

Aerated Water Factories—Yearly	£ 2 6
Half-yearly	1 3
Bakehouses—Fee for Registration (annually)	2 6
Boatmen, Kingstown Harbour	1 0
Cocoa, Arrowroot, Nutmegs and Mace—For every licence to purchase or carry on the business of a dealer therein (annually)	2 0 0
Coconuts—For every licence to purchase or carry on the business of a Dealer therein (annually)	2 0 0
Cotton—For every licence to purchase or carry on the business of a Dealer therein (annually)	4 0 0
For every licence solely to purchase or carry on the business of a dealer in Marie Galante cotton and within the Dependencies of Union Island, Canouan and Mayreau	2 10 0
Land Surveyor—Upon grant of licence	5 0 0
Passenger Boats—If granted on or before the 30th June	5 0
If granted after that day	2 6
For a duplicate	0 0 6
Wireless Receiving Apparatus—For every licence to establish (valid for current year) provided that if such licence is granted after the 30th June in any year, there shall be payable in respect thereof a fee of two shillings and sixpence)	0 5 0

390

Stamp Duties

	£ s. d.
Agreements—Agreement or Memorandum of Agreement under hand only where the subject matter thereof shall be of the value of £5 and not exceeding £25	£ 1 0
Exceeding £25 for each additional £25 or part thereof	1 0
Agreement or Memorandum of Agreement for the purchase of or for otherwise dealing with real estate where such purchase or such dealing is to be carried out by subsequent deed	2 0
Agreements not otherwise charged for	0 6
Bills of Exchange and promissory notes payable at sight and up to three days sight or on demand	0 1
Bills of Exchange and promissory notes of any other kind whatsoever (and herein shall be included I. O. U.s and other acknowledgments of indebtedness) drawn or expressed to be payable or actually paid or endorsed or in any manner negotiated within this colony:	
For any sum not exceeding £1	£ 1
For any sum exceeding £1 and not exceeding £10	2
For any sum exceeding £10 and not exceeding £25	3
For any sum exceeding £25 and not exceeding £50	6
For any sum exceeding £50 and not exceeding £75	9
For any sum exceeding £75 and not exceeding £100	1 0
For each additional £25 or part thereof exceeding £100	3
Bills of sale—Absolute	10 0
By way of security	5 0
Of any birth, marriage or death	1
On application for the issue of a Special Marriage Licence by the Governor	1 0 0
On issuing Marriage Licence	1 0 0
The following fees shall be taken by Registrars of Marriages and shall be affixed in stamps:	
On notice of intended Marriage	1 0
On application for certificate of publication of notice of intended marriage	6
On Registration of Marriage before a Registrar of Marriages	1 0
Customs—Ship's Manifest	1 0
Bills of Entry Inwards—Each set	3
Bills of Entry for goods imported into this colony through the post office—each set	1 1/2
Entries for warehousing—each set	3
Shipping Bills—each	1 1/2
Receipt or discharge for the payment of £1 and upwards	1

Fees

For registering any document by which any real estate shall be granted, sold, mortgaged, or incumbered where the consideration money by such document expressed to be paid or secured does not exceed £50	£ 10 0
exceeds £ 50 but does not exceed £ 500	1 0 0
exceeds £ 500 but does not exceed£1,000	1 10 0
exceeds £1,000	2 0 0
For registering any lease or agreement for a lease where the rent reserved does not exceed £10 per annum	5 0
exceeds £10 but does not exceed £100 per annum	10 0
exceeds £100 per annum	1 0 0
For registering of every deed of gift	£10 0
For registering of all copies of wills proved or administration granted	10 0
For registering a power of attorney	1 0 0
For registering every other document required to be registered under this Ordinance and not herein otherwise provided for	10 0
For every search of indexes	2 0
For every inspection of a document	1 0
For every attendance of Registrar in Court to produce any document	10 0
For every copy of a document including certificate per folio of 72 words	6
For every acknowledgment or attestation	2 0
For every search, to be paid by the applicant for the search, if it is a general search	5 0
if it is a particular search	1 0
For a certified copy of any entry given by the Registrar-General, to be paid by the applicant	2 0

Scale Of Charges for the Use of the Quarantine Buildings at Young's Island

For a day only (24 hours)	£ 8 0
For each day after the first up to the sixth	6 0
For a week	2 0 0
For each day after the seventh up to and including the thirteenth	3 0
For a fortnight	3 0 0
For each day after the fourteenth up to and including the day before the completion of a calendar month	3 0
For a month	5 0 0

In addition to the above a fee of four shillings (4/-) to cover the cost of scrubbing will be charged.

For The Isolation Hospital

	£	s	d
For a day only (24 hours)	£	8	0
For each day after the first up to the sixth		6	0
For a week	2	0	0
For each day after the seventh up to and including the thirteenth		3	0
For a fortnight	3	0	0
For each day after the fourteenth up to and including the day before the completion of a calendar month		3	0
For a month	5	0	0

In addition to the above a fee of two shillings and sixpence (2/6) to cover the cost of scrubbing will be charged.

Tariff of Porters' Fares

	£	s	d
For a day's work of 9 hours	£	2	0
For one hour's work or per hour			4
For every parcel not over 10 lb. weight			3
For every parcel over 10 lb. and not over 50 lb.			4
For every parcel over 50 lb. and not over 100 lb.			6

For every parcel over 100 lb. as may be agreed on.
The preceding rates shall be charged for all distances not exceeding one- half mile. For all distances exceeding one-half mile there shall be charged and paid the above rates and one-fourth of the same in addition.

Tariff of Fares for Boats

	£	s	d
For carrying each passenger from any part of the shore between Carpenter's Yard and Bernard's wharf to any vessel lying within the limits of Kingstown Harbour or vice versa or from any one vessel to any other vessel within such limits	£	1	0
Provided that if the same passenger makes the return journey in the same licensed boat the fee to and from will be		1	6
For carrying any letter, message or package between the shore as aforesaid to any vessel as aforesaid or vice versa or from one vessel to another within such limits			6
For each package accompanying a passenger (small parcels carried in a passenger's hand excepted)			4
For each package beyond the first not accompanying a passenger			4
For the use of an entire boat between any of the above points to carry a full complement of passengers and a reasonable quantity of luggage or either		5	0
For waiting, if desired, for any period not exceeding 15 minutes			6
For each subsequent period of waiting of 15 minutes or part thereof			10

Fees Payable in Connection with Motor Cars and Motor Cycles

On the registration of a Motor Car	5 0
On the registration of Cycle	2 6
On the grant of licence to drive a motor car	5 0
In case licence is lost or damaged, for a duplicate licence	1 0

Fares for Hire of Motor Cars

Fares by distance (from 6 a.m to 10 p.m.)
For each mile or part thereof   10d.
For each additional person above two   6d. for the whole distance
Waiting by agreement shall not exceed 1/- for each half-hour
For waiting without agreement the following fares by time
    may be charged in lieu of those by distance:
        10/- per hour for cars carrying up to 4 passengers
        12/6 per hour for carrying over 4 passengers with a minimum
        of one-quarter of an hour free of charge in both cases
From 10 p.m. to 6 a.m. all the above charges to be 50 per cent extra in each case

Fees Payable for the Use of the Motor Ambulance

For conveyance of cases within town of Kingstown to Colonial Hospital	£ 4 0
For conveyance of cases outside the boundary, a charge of 1/6 per mile for the entire distance with a minimum charge of	5 0

Fees Payable to the Port Officer

For every Certificate under section 17	£ 5 0
For visiting a ship between 6 and 9 p.m.	10 0
between 9 p.m. and midnight	15 0
between midnight and 5 a.m.	1 0 0
between 5 a.m. and 6 a.m.	10 0
5 a.m. and 7 a.m. and 9 a.m. and 2 p.m. on Sundays and Public Holidays	10 0

Customs Officers' Fees

For every hour or part of an hour between 5 a.m. and 7.30 a.m. and 5 p.m. and 9 p.m. on Saturdays and 4 p.m. and 9 p.m. on Mondays, Tuesdays, Thursdays and Fridays and between 12 noon and 9 p.m. on Wednesdays	2 6
For every hour or part of an hour between 9 p.m. and 5 a.m.	3 4
For every hour or part of an hour on Sundays and Public Holidays	3 4
For remaining on guard during the night on board of any sailing ship	5 0
For remaining on guard on board of any steamer for any time	

394

not exceeding two hours	5 0
For remaining on guard on board of any steamer for any time exceeding two hours and not exceeding twelve hours	10 0
For attending to enter or clear any ship before or after the prescribed hours, Sundays and Public Holidays excepted	2 6
For attending to enter or clear any ship on Sundays or Public Holidays	3 4

Estate Duty

When the principal value of the Estate			Estate Duty shall be payable at the rate per cent of
Exceeds £100 and does not exceed	£	300	One pound
300		500	One pound five shillings
500		1,000	One pound ten shillings
1,000		3,000	Two pounds
3,000		3,000	Two pounds ten shillings
5,000		10,000	Three pounds
10,000		15,000	Three pounds ten shillings
15,000		20,000	Four pounds
20,000		30,000	Four pounds ten shillings
30,000		40,000	Five pounds
40,000		50,000	Six pounds
50,000		60,000	Seven pounds
60,000		80,000	Eight pounds
80,000 and upwards			Ten pounds (Provided that only one half of the aforesaid rate shall be paid in respect of property, passing on the death of the deceased to the father, mother, wife, husband, children or grandchildren of the deceased)

Reduction in respect of quick succession

Where the second death occurs within one year of the first death	by 50 per cent
Where the second death occurs within two years of the first death	by 40 per cent
Where the second death occurs within three years of the first death	by 30 per cent
Where the second death occurs within four years of the first death	by 20 per cent
Where the second death occurs within five years of the first death	by 10 per cent

Provided that where the value, on which the duty is payable, of the property on the second death exceeds the value, on which the duty was payable, of the property on the first death, the latter value shall be substituted for the former for the purpose of calculating the amount of duty on which the reduction under this section is to be calculated.

Statement of the Assets and Liabilities of the Colony of St. Vincent at 31st December, 1937

LIABILITIES *Deposits*	£	s	d	£	s	d
The Home Fund	305	11	1			
*Savings Bank	19,663	14	2			
Musgrave Prize Fund	73	7	9			
Kingstown Board Reserve Fund for						
redemption of Water Supply Loan 1930	614	12	5			
Simmons Bequest Fund	15	19	5			
Cotton Growers' Association A/c	380	18	7			
Graham Bequest Fund	5,390	12	5			
Hayward X-Ray Fund	44	13	1			
Grenada A/c	343	10	1			
Post Office A/c	65	6	10			
Offices and Laboratory accommodation						
for Cotton Research Officer and other						
Agricultural Officers	381	1	8			
Public Officers' Guarantee Fund	1,445	6	0			
Colonial Development Fund Advances	69	15	11			
Other Deposits	1,371	9	9			
				30,165	19	11
Cotton Factory						
Depreciation Fund	2,548	14	2			
Cotton working A/c	5,438	2	0			
				7,986	16	2
Town Funds						
Calliaqua	7	12	2			
Port Elizabeth	23	9	8			
Chateaubelair	38	2	2			
Georgetown	75	14	8			
Layou	41	9	4			
Barrouallie	17	0	4			
				203	8	4
Special Accounts.						
Permanent Investment Eruption Fund	25,000	0	0			
Revenue Cruiser Depreciation Fund	102	12	1			
Public Property Insurance Fund	5,406	5	11			
Refrigeration Plant Depreciation Fund	516	4	5			
Forward	31,025	2	5	38,356	4	5

*There is also a contingent liability of £233 1 11 in respect of Savings Bank Deposits.

LIABILITIES *(continued)*	£	s	d	£	s	d
Forward	31,025	2	5	38,356	4	5
Electric Light Plant Depreciation Fund	1,065	15	11			
Electric Lighting System Extension to						
Calliaqua Loan A/c		14	4			
Reserve Funds for the redemption of						
the Windward Highway Loans 1919-20	686	3	10			
C. D. F. Loan for Housing Scheme	1,934	15	6			
Land Settlement Loan 1932	2,441	17	7			
Lowmans/Biabou Water Supply Loan 1934	207	10	6			
				37,362	0	1
Surplus						
Colony's Reserve Fund	8,711	13	11			
General Revenue Balance A/c:						
Balance of Surplus and Deficit						
A/c at 1.1.1937	17,824 11 2					
Deduct Surplus and						
Deficit A/c 1937	2,693 2 2					
	15,131 9 0					
Deduct Depreciation of						
Investments 1937	1,192 2 9	13,939	6	3		
				22,651	0	2
				98,639	4	8

ASSETS						
Cash	£	s	d	£	s	d
In Treasury Chest	762	15	5			
In Sub-Accountants' Hands	290	11	4			
In Barclays Bank Current A/c	2,322	5	10			
In Barclays Bank Deposit A/c	11,972	10	5			
Drafts and Remittances	69	16	4			
Crown Agents' Current A/c	891	3	5			
Crown Agents' Joint Colonial Fund	7,000	0	0			
				23,309	2	9
Advances						
Town of Kingstown	49	10	3			
Saint Lucia A/c	128	18	0			
Other Advances	453	18	10			
				632	7	1
Investments						
Colony's Reserve Fund	8,426	2	7			
Permanent Investment Eruption Fund	24,086	11	4			
Savings Bank Fund	19,119	15	5			
Public Officers' Guarantee Fund	1,396	6	7			
Public Officers' Property Insurance Fund	5,406	5	11			
Cotton Factory Depreciation Fund	2,548	14	2			
Graham Bequest Fund	5,473	10	11			
The Home Fund	305	11	10			
Musgrave Prize Fund	73	7	9			
Simmons Bequest Fund	21	16	1			
Refrigeration Plant Depreciation Fund	516	4	5			
Electric Light Plant Depreciation Fund	1,065	15	11			
Revenue Cruiser Depreciation Fund	102	12	1			
Reserve Fund for Land Settlement Loan 1932	2,441	17	7			
Reserve Fund for Kingstown Board Water Supply Loan 1930	614	12	5			
C. D. F. Loan for Housing Scheme	1,934	15	6			
Reserve Fund for Lowmans/Biabou Water Supply Loan 1934	207	10	6			
Reserve Fund for Windward Highway Loans 1919-1920	686	3	10			
				74,427	14	10
				98,369	4	8

Explanatory Notes

The Public Debt at 31st December, 1937, was £95,389 10 8 made up as follows:

	£	s	d
Debenture Holders for Land Settlement Purposes Loan 1932	6,600	0	0(a)
Lowmans/Biabou Water Supply Loan 1934	1,000	0	0(b)
Kingstown Board Water Supply Loan 1930	1,400	0	0(c)
Windward Highway Loans 1919-20	600	10	0(d)
Public Purposes Loan 1937	6,960	10	0(e)
Crown Agents for Electric Light, Telephone and Roads Reconstruction	26,635	11	3 (f)
C. D. F. Loan for St. Vincent Co-operative Arrowroot Association	28,783	10	3
C. D. F. Loan for Roads Improvement	8,312	11	2
C. D. F. Loan for Housing Scheme	6,209	8	9(g)
C. D. F. Loan for Ice and Cold Storage	6,391	16	3
C. D. F. Loan for Public Health	1,506	14	0(h)
C. D. F. Loan for Syrup Investigations	990	0	0
	95,389	10	8

The accumulated Funds for redemption were:

(a) £2,441 17 7
(b)   207 10 6
(c)   614 12 5   General Revenue is responsible only in case of default.
(d)   686   3 10
(e)   376 19 8
(f) 3,535   0 3
(g) 1,934 15 6

(h) The sum of £8 5 4 representing unspent balance of Schemes Nos. 165 and 166 undertaken from this loan from the Colonial Development Fund appears as a liability pending final decision of the Colonial Development Fund Committee in regard to the disposal of same. The Loan has however not been correspondingly reduced.

£9,796 19 9

399

St. Vincent

Comparative Statement of Revenue for the period 1st January to 31st December, 1937

Heads of Revenue	Estimate for the year 1937	Actual Revenue (for the period of the return)			More than estimated			Less than estimated		
	£	£	s	d	£	s	d	£	s	d
Customs										
Import	38,500	38,469	6	9				30	13	3
Export	3,100	3,909	6	8	809	6	8			
Port and Harbour dues										
Tonnage	1,300	1,285	8	10				14	11	2
Port	330	315	16	0				14	4	0
Licences, Excise & Internal Revenue										
Licences—Liquor	850	921	0	0	71	0	0			
Licences—Other	2,725	2,747	3	10	22	3	10			
Excise	4,900	4,909	19	4	9	19	4			
Land and House Tax	6,400	6,455	2	10	55	2	10			
Income Tax	3,800	4,512	13	0	712	13	0			
Other Internal Revenue	4,102	4,408	11	5	306	11	5			
Fees of Court or Office &c.	4,203	3,919	8	5				283	11	7
Post Office	3,338	10,504	15	2	7,166	15	2			
Electricity and Telephones	5,369	5,776	12	7	407	12	7			
Rent of Government Property	250	233	17	10				26	2	2
Interest and Refunds of Loans	3,461	3,620	17	11	159	17	11			
Miscellaneous Receipts	240	507	12	3	267	12	3			
	82,878	92,497	12	10	9,988	15	0	369	2	2
Sales and Leases of Crown Lands	2,300	1,882	0	4				417	19	8
	85,178	94,379	13	2	9,988	15	0	787	1	10
Colonial Development Schemes	451	428	19	5				22	0	7
Total Revenue	85,629	94,808	12	7	9,988	15	0	809	2	5

Comparative Statement of Expenditure for the period
1st January to 31st December, 1937

Heads of Expenditure	Estimate for the year 1937	Actual Expenditure for the period of the return			More than estimated			Less than estimated		
	£	£	s	d	£	s	d	£	s	d
Charge on account of Public Debt	6,716	6,573	17	10	986	3	1	142	2	2
Pensions	4,785	5,771	3	1	80	8	6			
Governor	2,077	2,157	8	6						
Government Office	2,249	2,220	7	4				28	12	8
Treasury, Customs, Port and Excise	4,567	4,548	6	3				18	13	9
Audit Department	634	651	15	2	17	15	2			
Post Office	2,302	2,594	4	11	292	4	11			
Judicial and Legal Departments	3,014	3,125	10	6	111	10	6			
Police and Prisons	7,601	7,224	18	0				376	2	0
Charitable	843	1,015	5	1	172	5	1			
Local Forces	389	270	10	11				118	9	1
St. Vincent Grenadines District	482	495	13	0	13	13	0			
Agricultural Department	3,135	2,841	4	5				293	15	7
Education	12,172	12,158	0	3				13	19	9
Medical Department	16,340	17,095	18	2	755	18	2			
Miscellaneous	4,246	4,790	4	11	544	4	11			
Electricity and Telephones Department	4,296	6,557	4	2	2,261	4	2			
Public Works and Crown Lands	1,980	1,912	6	8						
Public Works Recurrent	5,500	5,731	5	2	231	5	2	67	3	4
Government Cotton Ginnery	200									
Public Works Extraordinary	3,834	9,337	1	0	5,503	1	0			
Government Fruit & Vegetable Bureau										
Total	87,362	97,072	15	0	10,969	13	8	1,058	18	4
Colonial Development Fund Schemes	451	428	19	5				22	0	7
Total Expenditure £	87,813	97,501	14	9	10,969	13	8	1,080	8	11

Dollars and Their Equivalents

S	£	s	d	S	£	s	d	S	£	s	d	S	£	s	d
1=	0	4	2	11=	2	5	10	21=	4	7	6	90=	18	15	0
2=	0	8	4	12=	2	10	0	22=	4	11	8	100=	20	16	8
3=	0	12	6	13=	2	14	2	23=	4	15	10	200=	41	13	4
4=	0	16	8	14=	2	18	4	24=	5	0	0	300=	62	10	0
5=	1	0	10	15=	3	2	6	30=	6	5	0	400=	83	6	8
6=	1	5	0	16=	3	6	8	40=	8	6	8	500=	104	3	4
7=	1	9	2	17=	3	10	10	50=	10	8	4	600=	125	0	0
8=	1	13	4	18=	3	15	0	60=	12	10	0	700=	145	16	8
9=	1	17	6	19=	3	19	2	70=	14	11	8	800=	166	13	4
10=	2	1	8	20=	4	3	4	80=	16	13	4	1,000=	208	6	8

Shillings, Pounds and Their Equivalents

S	£ d	S	£ d	£	S	£	S	£	S
1=	24	11=	2 64	1=	4.80	11=	52.80	25=	120
2=	48	12=	2 88	2=	9.60	12=	57.60	30=	144
3=	72	13=	3 12	3=	14.40	13=	62.40	35=	168
4=	96	14=	3 36	4=	19.20	14=	67.20	40=	192
5=	1 20	15=	3 60	5=	24.00	15=	72.00	50=	240
6=	1 44	16=	3 84	6=	28.80	16=	76.80	60=	288
7=	1 68	17=	4 08	7=	33.60	17=	81.60	70=	336
8=	1 92	18=	4 32	8=	38.40	18=	86.40	80=	384
9=	2 16	19=	4 56	9=	43.20	19=	91.20	90=	432
10=	2 40	20=	4 80	10=	48.00	20=	96.00	100=	480

Percentage Table

From the following table the amount in the £ may be calculated at any rate per cent.

¼%	3-fifths	penny	in the £	5%	1s 0d	in the £	
½%	1 & 1-fifth	pence	do	6%	1s 2 2-5ths	do	
¾%	1 & 4-fifths	do	do	7%	1s 4 4-5ths	do	
1%	2 & 2-fifths	do	do	7½%	1s 6d	do	
1¼%	3	do	do	10%	2s 0d	do	
1½%	3 & 2-fifths	do	do	12½%	2s 6d	do	
1¾%	4 & 1-fifth	do	do	15%	3s 0d	do	
2%	4 & 4-fifths	do	do	20%	4s 0d	do	
2½%	6	do	do	25%	5s 0d	do	
3%	7 & 1-fifth	do	do	33 1/3%	6s 8d	do	
3¾%	9	do	do	50%	10s 0d	do	
4%	9 & 3-fifths	do	do	75%	—15s 0d	do	

Measurements of Land

16 1/2 feet	1 rod		43,560 sq. feet	1 acre
320 rods	1 mile		1 sq. mile	640 acres
66 feet	1 chain		660 feet sq .	10 acres
80 chains	1 mile		208 fr and d8 1/2 in. sq.	1 acre
5,280 feet	1 mile		933 ft and 4 1/2 in. sq.	25 acres

Contents of Fields and Lots

10 rods x 16 rods	1 acre	220 ft. x 198 ft.	1 acre
8 rods x 20 rods	1 acre	440 ft. x 99 ft.	1 acre
5 rods x 32 rods	1 acre	110 ft. x 396 ft	1 acre
4 rods x 40 rods	1 acre	60 ft. x 726 ft.	1 acre
5 yards x 968 yards	1 acre	120 ft. x 363 ft.	1 acre
10 yards x 484 yards	1 acre	240 ft. x 181 1/2 ft.	1 acre
20 yards x 242 yards	1 acre	200 ft. x 108 9-10ths ft.	1/2 acre
40 yards x 121 yards	1 acre	100 ft. x 145 2-10ths ft.	1/3 acre
80 yards x 60 1/2 yards	1 acre	100 ft. x 108 9-10ths ft.	1/4 acre
70 yards x 69 1/2 yards	1 acre		

Weights and Measures

English Money

4 farthings (far)—1 penny (d.)

12 pence—1 shilling (s.)

20 shillings—1 pound (£)

U.S. Money

10 mills (m) 1 cent (ct.)

10 cents 1 dime (d)

10 dimes 1 dollar ($)

Commercial Weight

16 drams (dr.)—1 ounce (oz.)

16 ounces—1 pound (lb.)

2000 pounds—1 ton (T.)

Troy Weight

24 grains (gr.) 1 pennyweight (pwt.)

20 pennyweights 1 ounce (oz.)

12 ounces 1 pound (lb.)

Dry Measure

2 pints (pt.)—1 quart (qt.)

8 quarts—1 peck (pk.)

4 pecks —1 bushel (bu.)

Circular Measure

60 seconds (") 1 minute (min.)

24 hours 1 day (da).

365 1/4 days 1 year (yr.)

Long Measure

12 inches (in.) — 1 foot (ft.)

3 feet— 1 yard (yd.)

16 12 feet — 1 rod (rd.)

320 rd. (5280 ft.) — 1 mile (mi.)

Surveyors' Measure

7.92 inches (in.)—1 link (lk.)

25 links—1 rod (rd.)

100 links (66 ft.)—1 chain (ch.)

80 chains—1 mile (mi.)

Time Measure

60 seconds (sec.)—1 minute (min.)

60 minutes—1 hour (hr.)

24 hours—1 day (da.)

365 1/4 days—1 year (yr.)

Liquid Measure

4 gills (gi.)—1 pint (pt.)

2 pints—1 quart (qt.)

4 quarts—1gallon (gal)

31 1/2 gallons—1 barrel (brl.)

Square Measure

144 square inches—1 square foot

9 square feet—1 square yard

30 1/4 square yards—1 square rod

272 1/4 square feet—1 square rod

160 square rods—1 acre (A.)

640 acres—1 square mile

Cubic Measure

231 cubic inches— 1 gallon

2150.4 cubic inches—1 bushel

1728 cubic inches—1 cubic foot

27 cubic feet—1 cubic yard

128 cubic feet—1 cord (wood)

24 3/4 cubic feet—1 perch (stone)

The City and the Towns

KINGSTOWN, commonly called the principal town of St. Vincent is in reality the City and is crescent-shaped, built on the shore of an excellent bay that is formed by an indentation of the Caribbean Sea. The interior aspect is composed of Mount St. Andrew standing conspicuously in the north, 2,433 feet high, on both sides of which are numerous spurs and minor ranges as irregular in design as they vary in elevation extending westward to the dismantled but majestic Fort Charlotte 600 feet high; thence descending abruptly to "Low Point" about 200 feet and ending at a height of about 50 feet. On the eastern side they extend to Cane Garden about 400 feet high and terminate by a gentle slope to a point of the same name about 20 feet in height.

As the ranges of hills that comprise the landscape correspond naturally with the shape of the bay and City, they contribute to the grandeur peculiar to the picturesqueness of Kingstown and its surroundings.

From Dorsetshire Hill, one of the eminences in an easterly direction, His Late Majesty King George V. once looked with admiration on the city and thus described his impression:

> It commands as from the summit of a natural amphitheatre a sweeping view over the whole of the bay below and of Kingstown with its parallel streets stretching at our feet, and of the two branches of lower hills which embrace it on either side.

The scenery is very beautiful and presents natural features of rare attractiveness. Those who have not ascended our hills or mountains know nothing of the pictorial wealth this little gem of the Lesser Antilles possesses.

Among the buildings of interest in Kingstown is St. George's Cathedral situated at St. George's Place. It is indented about 100 yards from Grenville Street and is approached at the central entrance of its enclosure by a paved walk sheltered by the rich foliage of old almond trees. The cathedral, with its chancel and transept, assumes the shape of a cross and is the largest Anglican church in the Windward Islands Government.

A little beyond is the court house which was presumably built soon after 1798, for in that year resolutions were submitted for its erection and that of the gaol. It is massive, and, being enclosed in spacious grounds with tropical trees, is attractive, yet the general view seems to convey to the mind the gravity of the purposes for which the building is mainly used. The prison walls rise high at the back and to this may also be attributed the solemn feeling which the weird appearance of the locality causes.

405

The City is governed by a board composed of eight members, four of whom are nominated by the Government and four are elected by the ratepayers. The constitution of the present municipality is the result of representation made by the inhabitants who were desirous of obtaining an improved system of town management and consequently asked for a purely elected board to control municipal affairs including finances, levying of rates and all other matters connected with the City. Their entire request was not complied with but a board such as that already described was constituted in 1897.

The vigilance of the sanitary department has been exceedingly effective in the city of Kingstown. Visitors and in transit passengers are often enthusiastic in the expressions of their admiration in respect to its general cleanliness especially when comparisons are made.

Boundaries—The city is bounded on the north by Montrose, Kingstown Park or Paul's and Richmond Hill Estates, on the south by the sea, on the east by lands of Cane Garden to the crossing of the road over the ravine at Kingstown Hill and thence by the highway to Windward and on the west by lands of Montrose and the highway to Fort Charlotte.

Kingstown Bay is generally entered from the southward. Having closed with the south point of St. Vincent which slopes gradually steer along the land at the distance of about ¾ mile, when Young and Duvernette Islets on the northwest side of Calliaqua Bay, and the high land over Kingstown will be seen, and shortly the high bluff of Old Woman Point will come open. Pass Duvernette Islet about ½ mile off and haul in for Cane Garden Point, the southeast extreme of Kingstown Bay, which slopes gently toward the sea.

If bound into the bay in a sailing vessel, haul close around Cane Garden Point, but take care not to be taken aback, and look out for the lofty sails, as the wind is often scant and unsteady and the squalls from the high land are heavy. A vessel may stand over to the western shore without fear, and having tacked, the best anchorage is in 10 fathoms water, dark sand and good holding ground, with the church bearing north (N. 1 deg. E. mag.) about ¼ mile from the shore. If more convenient, a berth will be found farther out in fifteen fathoms, with the church about N. 6 deg. E. (N. 6 deg. E. mag.) and Old Woman Point N. 82 deg. (N. 82 deg. W. mag.).

CALLIAQUA is at a distance of four miles from Kingstown in an easterly direction. On the way to it from Kingstown a magnificent seascape presents itself; an opportunity is sometimes afforded to admire the cultivation of cotton and arrowroot on the Arnos Vale Estate. A glimpse is obtainable of the scenery in a northeasterly direction toward Cane Hall and Fountain Estates where the fringed mountain peaks dominate the valley below. Adjoining the roadside at this portion of the journey which is about midway between Kingstown and Calliaqua, an area of land has been purchased for King George the Fifth Sports Grounds. The bungalows at the palm-fringed beach at the Villa, the Aquatic Club and Young's Island with the land encircling the bay at Calliaqua, when taken as a combined picture can scarcely be compared. Immediately before entering the town of Calliaqua there is to be seen the road leading to the Mental Hospital, the roofs of which can be discerned interspersed among the trees. Bungalows are now being erected at Ratho Mill, about ¼ of a mile from this town where an hotel and golf links now under contemplation will contribute greatly to the economic condition of this locality.

There is an artistic little Anglican church of masonry at Calliaqua; the police station at which the Magistrate holds his court and the Government school house are well suited to their respective purposes. The rectory which is built on an eminence at the eastern extremity affords a panoramic view of the town.

Calliaqua or Tyrrell Bay, immediately east of two islets, Young's Island and Duvernette, is a secure anchorage, but is now only frequented by coasters. Between this bay and Young's Island a reef runs 400 yards off shore to the southward. The bay has a convenient sandy beach for shipping cargo. Two rivulets run into it, and the anchorage is secure.

Boundaries—Starting at the estuary of the Calliaqua River and proceeding thence along the north bank of the said river to the boundary (an open drain) with Glen Estate, which part of the said estate (Glen) is now occupied held or owned by Mr. Charles Layne; thence along the said open drain and on across the Glen and Fair Hall Byeway, and on continuing along the said open drain with lands of Glen Estate now occupied held or owned by Mr. Robert Layne to the lands known or held as Glebe lands; then along the boundary of the said Glebe lands across the Golden Vale Byeway and on continuing with the said lands of the Glebe to a ravine or gully; thence down the said ravine or gully to the sea; thence along the sea coast to the point of departure.

EORGETOWN is the other town in an eastward direction and is at a distance of 22 miles from Kingstown. A portion of the chain of gorgeous mountains by which the island is traversed throughout its entire length can be seen on the journey; and the excellent cultivation of cotton, sugar cane, arrowroot, ground provisions, sometimes ground nuts, cassava, peas, with the varying shades of green, the rich verdure by which the mountain peaks and hills are clothed unite with the view toward the sea, the dashing of wave's against the rocks and the extended white foam on the reefs, to fill any intelligent observer with unspeakable delight.

There are several important and comparatively populous villages on the way at which postal and telephonic communications are established.

Argyle Estate extends to a fascinating bay strewn with pebbles on the seashore. The invigorating breezes flowing unrestrainedly from the sea seem to proclaim on the whispering waves the health lavished as they bathe the rocks and produce the pretty white sprays from which the ozone is filtered on to numerous persons who frequent that place for the life-giving properties dispensed there. The syrup factory is modern and the qualities of the arrowroot and cotton are of a high standard.

The owners of Colonarie and Bellevue Estates like many others have devoted much attention to improved machinery for manufacturing arrowroot; coupled with this effort on their part they have interested themselves in the benefit societies formed for the general assistance of those of slender means. Inhabitants of surrounding villages appreciate their kindness and advice, recognizing as they do the advantages they gain.

There is a Free Public Library of which much use is made and there is a Branch Savings Bank. The benefits derived from the hospital are much appreciated.

The Anglican and Methodist churches are built of masonry and the respective members are numerous.

Boundaries—Starting at the estuary of the Grand Sable North River, thence along the southern bank of the said river to the extreme northwest end of the town with lands acquired by the Government from the Grand Sable Estate (now being used for public purposes); thence along the west side of Jubilee Street in boundary with the said acquired lands, and continuing along the said west side of Jubilee Street with lands of Grand Sable Estate to an iron cannon which marks the south end of Jubilee Street; thence along the road leading to Grand Sable house to a masonry pillar which marks the northwest end of Corbeau Town; thence along the west boundary of Corbeau Town with Grand Sable Estate to a masonry pillar, and continuing along the same boundary to another masonry pillar which marks the southwest end of Corbeau Town; thence along with lands of Grand Sable Estate to a masonry pillar on the east side of the public highway leading into Georgetown; thence along the boundary of Brown's Village with lands of Grand Sable Estate to the sea; thence along the sea coast to the point of departure.

LAYOU is a small town situated on the western or Leeward coast of the island at a distance of about 7½ miles from Kingstown on the shores of a large inlet.

Leaving Kingstown you round Old Woman's Point on which stands the old military hospital, pass a narrow creek with a flat projection of rock, see the buildings of Fort Charlotte towering on the top of a lofty promontory, and soon reach Johnson's Point, fanned by the southwest breeze that sweeps across the channel separating St. Vincent from Bequia. After a few minutes you reach Ottley Hall Bay. Fields of Sea Island Cotton may be seen on Ottley Hall Estate, which is soon left behind, and the long open bay of Camden Park, almost incessantly swept by a gentle land breeze, is reached. Here you see in cultivation fields of cotton, sugar cane and arrowroot.

You now pass a high rocky cliff and see Questelles and Clare Valley, a magnificent rugged stretch of country with beautiful fields of cotton owned by small holders, and the Government school at Questelles nestling amongst the trees on a gentle elevation. Next come the steep slopes and small inlets of Byahaut, some of the slopes covered with the luxuriant foliage of the cotton plant or other tropical cultivation, others with trees and shrubs which seek a place amongst the rocks. Having passed Byahaut Point the beautiful Buccament Valley appears in sight containing the estates of Peniston, Queensberry, Pembroke, and Cane Grove upon which cultivations of sugar cane, cotton, arrowroot, banana, and cocoa are carried on. The mountains overlooking this charming valley are nearly constantly covered with mist. You skirt the shores of the bay, pass a small islet separated from the mainland by a narrow, shallow pass and come to the town of Layou.

There are two places of public worship, the Anglican church and a Methodist chapel. There is a police station where the Magistrate's Court is held. Close by is the estate of Rutland Vale on which sugar cane, cotton, arrowroot, and banana are cultivated and coconut trees flourish.

Boundaries—Commencing from an iron bar marking the most southerly point of the village, known as Jackson's Village in boundary with the lands of the rectory; thence going along the boundary of the Rutland Vale northeast 54 degs. 14 min., a distance of 486 links; thence northwest 325 degs. 25 min. a distance of 504 links; thence northeast 53 degs. 56 min., a distance of 1,213 links to an iron bar on the east bank of the road to Texier; thence along the said bank southeast 112 degs. 44 min., a distance of 495 links; thence northeast 34 degs. 05 min., a distance of 80 links to the centre of a water course; thence along the centre of the said water course in a direction bearing northwest 314 degs. 49 min. to the point of intersection of the eastern boundary of the cemetery; thence along the said boundary of the cemetery in a direction bearing northeast 30 degs. 06 min., a distance of 429 links; thence northwest 58 degs. 44 min., a distance of 133 links to an iron bar on the bank of Rutland Vale Estate road; thence along the bank of the said road until it meets the public highway; thence along the said public highway in a southwesterly direction to the lane or road forming the northeast boundary of lot No. 11 of Jackson's Village; thence along the said lane to the left bank of the Layou

River; thence along the left bank of the Layou River to the seashore; thence along the seashore in a southeasterly direction to the old town boundary of Layou; thence following the old town boundary of Layou to the first point of commencement aforesaid.

Layou Bay—About three miles to the northwest of Old Woman Point is Layou Bay with 20 to 25 fathoms water at 200 yards from the shore. The southeast point is steep-to, and this side of the bay is sandy; the northwest side is rocky, and a small reef extends from the point.

BARROUALLIE is next on the Leeward coast about 12 miles distant from Kingstown and about 4½ miles from Layou.

Leaving the deep inlet of Layou bay you pass a high steep cliff guarding the northwestern extremity of the bay and have a short glimpse of Bambareau, an ideal seaside resort. You journey onward and in quick succession some small indentations with the overlooking hills covered with trees and brushwood fall in the rear, and the long open bay of Mt. Wynne greets the eye with fields of arrowroot and cotton waving on the estate.

The rocky shores of Mt. Wynne Estate are in their turn lost to view and Peters Hope Estate appears with its magnificent chimney, probably the highest in the island, towering in grandeur over the sugar works where modern machinery and electrical appliances have been installed. The excellent quality of the syrup produced there is highly appreciated abroad. Sea Island Cotton is also grown there extensively. Whilst the attention is arrested in gazing on the surrounding scenery you near the high cliff at the southwestern entrance to Barrouallie Bay and soon you reach that town.

There is a pretty Anglican church which was built in 1905 on the same spot where stood a larger church that was destroyed by the hurricane of 1898; but there is not the distinguished bell tower which contributed to the glory of the former building, nor are the beautiful marble tiles that graced the interior of the ruined church to be seen. Near the centre of the town is the Methodist chapel.

There are a police station at which the Magistrate's Court is held, and a branch telephone exchange which is kept at a private residence. The branch office of the Savings Bank which was formerly at Chateaubelair was transferred to Barrouallie in 1911.

The fishing industry in this little town deserves some support to enable those thrifty persons struggling there to develop the production of oil from the black fish. With sufficient advertisement and the desired assistance there might be a remunerative export trade.

Boundaries—The boundaries are fixed northerly, by the ridge bounded with Keartons running to the sea. Easterly below the rock to Reversion down to the road to Peer Hughes with a range of coconut trees, on to the church, down to the school house, crossing a stream with a fence and coconut trees on to the road leading direct from the sea to Reversion Works on by the public road. Bounded southerly by the Glebe, where a pillar is the boundary of Reversion above the road; below the road is a calabash tree with a range of coconut and mango trees down to the sea at Morgan Bay.

Barrouallie Bay lies about 5½ miles to the northwest of Kingstown. Its north side is formed by some remarkable rocks called the Bottle and Glass, which are clear of danger and have a boat channel within them.

Anchorage—If coming from the northward, haul close round these rocks and anchor in 20 fathoms of water, sandy bottom, with the rocks bearing N. 45 degs. W. (N. 44 degs. W. mag.) and the barracks N. 62 degs. E. (N. 62 deg. E. mag.). The bottom on the north side of the bay is foul. The wind is so variable and unsteady under the highland that if intending to remain any tim, it will be better to warp in and drop a second anchor to the eastward in about 12 fathoms. If coming from the southward, the shore may be kept abroad equally close, and the vessel may probably shoot far enough in to drop the inner anchor first. The water being deep so close in, the anchorage is only fit for small vessels.

CHATEAUBELAIR is the other town situated on the western coast of the island about 22 miles from Kingstown and about 10 miles from Barrouallie.

Continuing your voyage from Barrouallie you pass the famous rocks of Bottle and Glass to the north of Barrouallie Bay, in years past a much frequented picnic resort; glide near a steep precipice, skim across Keartons Bay viewing fields of arrowroot and cotton on Keartons Estate, pass another high steep cliff commonly known as Indian Gallows—so-called because of the tragic operations of the early settlers—and reach Wallilabo Bay. Here you see fields of coconut trees, Sea Island Cotton and arrowroot growing on Wallilabo Estate. As you proceed you observe that the mountain spurs that radiate from the main chain that traverses the island from north to south become steeper and more rugged as they terminate for the most part in perpendicular precipices at the water's edge.

As you advance you pass a few creeks on the shores of which are the growing vegetables and arrowroot of a few peasant proprietors, and reach Cumberland Bay where you see fields of arrowroot and cotton growing on the estate. Farther up in the valley are the holdings of several peasants whose principal production are ground provisions. A post office was established at

411

Cumberland in 1912. You proceed viewing the little village of Coulls Hill with its houses scattered on steep hillsides and soon arrive at Troumaca Bay. Here is one of the most thriving villages of the western coast, evidence of the progress of which is borne out by the fact that a post office has been established and a substantial concrete wharf was completed in 1913 at a cost of £145. The bay is very deep, and even when the waters of the neighbouring inlets are so disturbed as to excite some fear, the mariner may cast his anchor in this bay and his ship will ride in safety, the bay being protected by high hills on either side.

You leave the placid waters of Troumaca Bay and may now see St. Lucia looming in the distance. You feast your eyes on the fields of cotton, arrowroot and vegetables of peasants as you go along, passing the village of Rose Bank and reach Petit Bordel Bay with its coconut trees waving their feathery crests on the beach and fields of arrowroot and cotton in the background.

Travelling on you see the very small island known as Islet in front of you. Soon you go through the narrow passage of water that separates Islet from the mainland and behold the town of Chateaubelair lying at the foot of steep and rugged mountains, the far-famed volcano, Soufriere, with the Morne Garou mountain, one of the highest peaks in St. Vincent, appearing in the distance.

Original Boundaries

From the western extremity of the beach, including what is known as Corner Bay, following the high bank in an easterly direction to a point above and including the house of George Bailey; thence in a direct line to the river; thence along the river in a southeasterly direction to the bridge at the public highway; thence along the public highway in a northwesterly direction to the point where the boundary between the Sharpes and Golden Grove Estates strikes the public highway; thence along the boundary between the above mentioned estates to a point in continuation in a direct line in a southerly direction of the existing eastern boundary of the town; thence along a direct line in a northerly direction to a pillar at the back of the church at the termination of the existing eastern boundary of the town; thence along the existing eastern boundary of the town to the pillar at the back of the police station; thence in a direct line to the high bank at the back of and including the houses of Israel and David Connor, respectively; thence following the high bank in a northerly direction to a galba tree at the side of the public highway at the northern end of the town; thence in a direct line to the sea including the house of Thornton Layne.

Alteration of the Boundary by Resolution passed the Legislative Council on 20th July, 1932, in accordance with section 12 (1) of Chapter 212 of the Revisd Edition of the Laws of St. Vincent :

The existing western boundary of the town *i.e.* the Sharpe's River, is hereby abandoned, and the town extended in a southwesterly direction to include all that area of land formerly part of Sharpe's Estate and now subdivided into building lots under the Housing Scheme and bounded as follows, that is to say: Commencing on the south at the western extremity of the Sharpe's Bridge; thence along the Leeward Highway in a southwesterly direction to an iron mark for a distance of 19 chains, 29 links; thence by a line running in a northeasterly direction (bearing 43 degs., 22 min.) to an iron mark for a distance of 5 chains, 65 links; thence by a line running in a northwesterly direction (bearing 328 degs., 27 min.) to an iron mark for a distance of 11 chains, 20 links; thence to a southeasterly direction (bearing 166 degs., 07 min.) for a distance of 6 chains and 74 links to an iron mark on the Sharpe's River.

The following is extracted from the notes of His Late Majesty King George V. when on 12th February, 1880, His Majesty and the lamented Prince Albert Victor visited this Port on H.M.S. *Bacchante*. It is with reference to a picnic party who persevered in ascending the Soufriere mountain on a rainy day.

> *Those who did this were well repaid for their pains when they looked down into the twin crater cauldrons, and saw the sulphurous steam pouring up and mingling with the mist caused by the tradewind as it touched the summit of the mountain, and then both together came swaying this way and that way towards them as they stood for a short time on the edge of the crater, so that they were glad to beat a hasty retreat along the knife-edge of rock, 700 feet in height, and look down on the other side upon the dark mountain tarn, with walls of rock 800 feet in height—a clear mirror in an emerald green frame—which now occupies what was a former crater about two miles in circumference. The sides of this old vent hole are now clothed with foliage instead of fire.*

The following is a description of the Leeward coast by Professor Edmund Otis Hovey, American Geologist, who visited this island in June, 1908

> *We arrived in St. Vincent, at Kingstown, the capital, Monday evening, the fifteenth, and came to Chateaubelair the next afternoon by the mail boat, the* Mizpah, *a 37-foot canoe manned by five rowers and the captain, who acts as steerman, and it has space for sixteen passengers. The trip takes about four hours, but it is a most picturesque and enjoyable journey when the sun remains behind clouds, as it did for us.*

> *The boat hugs the shore all the way, so that one in passing gets the detail of palm, tree fern and other wild plants, arrowroot, cotton, sugar cane*

fields, and estate houses, mills and cabins, while rocky cliffs stand out in bold relief; and narrow valleys invite the nature lover to visit the forest clad mountains that terminate them in the middle of the island. Every ridge that reaches the coast, and there are many of them, reveals the geological history of the island through the action of the sea, which has cut back into the land, leaving terminal bluffs. These show that hundreds, if not thousands, of volcanic eruptions have taken place from several centres within the area of the island, pouring out streams of lava and tremendous clouds of ashes and cinders, which have made an irregular pile about fifteen thousand feet high, counting from its real base, the bottom of the sea. Before it was occupied by human beings, this enormous volcanic pile suffered several changes of level, due to movements of the earth's crust, and a great amount of material has been washed from the surface by rains and carried away from the coast by the waves and currents of the sea. The chemical composition of the lava is such that the ash beds and even the solid rocks have decomposed with comparative rapidity and have furnished soils of remarkable fertility, even for the tropics.

Chateaubelair, the largest, affords anchorage at about 400 yards off its eastern shore in 13 or 14 fathoms of water, with the north point of the bay bearing N. 3 deg. E. (N. 3 deg, E. mag.) the west point S. 79 deg. W. (S. 80 deg. W. mag.) and the town S. 17 deg. W. (S. 18 deg. mag.).

In the middle of the bay there is no bottom with 50 fathoms nor on the west side with 30 fathoms, at 100 yards from the shore.

Chateaubelair is separated from the little bay southward of it by Chateaubelair Island, which is about ¼ mile in length with a rock 7 feet high close off its southern point. Southward of this rock is a narrow passage carrying 6 fathoms water, which is used by boats and sometimes by droghers.

Current and Tides—The main current, within a distance of five miles off St. Vincent, was always found setting to the northward, but within a mile of the coast tidal influence is felt; ½ mile southward of Calliaqua, Cane Garden, and Johnson Points, the ebb stream runs west and northwest about two knots, and the flood to the southward and southeast one knot, at springs, the streams apparently turning at high and low water by the shore, but subject to great irregularities from wind and current. The tide sweeps round Kingstown Bay, the flood to the westward, the ebb to the eastward, sometimes attaining a velocity of nearly two knots.

The wardens who are appointed yearly by the Administrator in respect to each town associate themselves with the Government Officer, described as the Superintendent of Public Works, who is *ex officio* a warden of every town.

The Grenadines

THE GRENADINES form a chain of about 100 islands, cays and rocks, 60 miles long north and south, lying between St. Vincent and Grenada. They are like pearls distributed at irregular distances by Nature's own sweet and cunning hand perhaps to afford the peculiar charm each possesses. The beauty they present is not merely the creature of fancy because the opinion invariably expressed is that it increases on examination. Persons who flew over describe them as "lilies in a pond". Those to the northward of Carriacou are dependencies of St. Vincent; such as are seen from Fort Charlotte and other elevations present an attractive picture. Although there are no rivers and rain is not always plentiful, yet the soil is exceedingly fertile; there are several ponds from which water is obtained mainly for domestic purposes. The continuous sea breeze sustains the salubrity of the climate to which also the healthy condition and longevity of the inhabitants bear testimony.

The value of the salubrious climate of the Grenadines cannot be exaggerated, encircled as they are by the never slumbering sea and fanned by its continuous breezes, the invigoration of health is abundantly ensured.

BEQUIA, the largest of the islands, contains 4,422 acres and is nine miles from St. Vincent.

The ambitious wardens of the town of Bequia considered The Harbour inappropriate as the name of a town. His Honour the Administrator having no objection, with becoming ceremony on Friday 18th June 1937, the name of Her Royal Highness Princess Elizabeth was assigned to that town namely, Port Elizabeth, in commemoration of Their Majesties' Coronation.

A telegram from the Secretary of State for the colonies dated 10th July 1937, conveyed the information that "His Majesty has been pleased to give retrospective approval to the naming of the chief town of the island of Bequia after Princess Elizabeth."

Admiralty Bay is beautiful and commodious, large vessels may be hove down and repaired with perfect safety. It is encircled by land sloping down on each side, terminating at respective distances, seemingly designed to effectuate the safety afforded by this enclosure.

This bay situated on the western side of Bequia, is about one mile deep. In the inner part near the head, which is narrowed by shallows on either side, a vessel would be well sheltered from all winds except from the southwest, and when blowing from this direction, which is an exceedingly rare occurrence, would in a measure be protected from the sea, as it would be broken in passing over the Belmont Shallow and the two banks projecting from the north side of the bay. The inner part of the bay is not of much extent but deep enough for any vessel, and the channel to it between Belmont Shallow, bordering the shore of the bay on the south on the opposite bank, is clear, distinct, and traceable from its darker colour and deeper appearance.

This part of the bay could only be entered by a large vessel under steam or by warping; the water is quite smooth, and small vessels work in.

The Sea Island Cotton produced there continues to be of an exceptionally good quality. Building and repairing of vessels and boats comprise additional occupation to that afforded by agriculture. At some distance within the harbour bar, the little town nestles at the foot of verdant hills that rise here and there in conical shapes. There is a neat Anglican church. A new rectory of masonry has been built where the old wooden structure once stood. There is a Roman Catholic church at Reform; the Seventh Day Adventists and Brethren also have their places of worship.

The sea bathing at Toney Gibbons, Belmont, Reform, and elsewhere is indeed as delightful as it is invigorating yet the special feature at the Spring Estate, unknown elsewhere, is the variation of the temperature of the sea; the warmth can be regulated for those of impaired health by selecting the hour of the day for the bathe. The significance of this will be greatly recognized by the convalescent.

There are places of residence now let to hire: two at Toney Gibbons and two at Belmont. Others will soon be erected at different localities so that the accommodation for visitors will present no difficulty.

Boundaries of Port Elizabeth—From a silk cotton tree at the southwest-corner of the bay to a locust tree, both trees on the Union Land and measuring from tree to tree 306 feet; from the locust tree in a straight line to that part of the back street opposite the northeast corner of the wall enclosing the church yard and 41 feet from the said corner.

From this part of the back street to its termination in Thomas Hill Road; from this termination of the back street to the northeast corner of Barkhurst Farrell's house on the Reform Estate; from the northeast corner of Barkhurst Farrell's house in a straight line westerly to a road called Reform road; from this road to the east side of the Reform Cattle Mill; from thence to sea beach and along the beach to the silk cotton tree first named above.

The silk cotton tree is 22 feet from high water mark and 265 feet from the southwest corner of wall enclosing church yard.

MSTIQUE is 18 miles from St. Vincent, eastward of Bequia, is 2½ miles in length and one in breadth; it contains 1,257 acres and at its southern end is 475 feet high.

No description of this little island can convey to the mind of the reader an idea of its actual appearance; the soil is peculiarly fertile and the excellent pastures are like lawns, most pleasing to behold. The glorious fresh air that blows almost everywhere on the island is an assurance of its healthfulness. It is the recognized health resort of the proprietor and ample provision is therefore made for family accommodation. The building is substantial and suitably furnished; arrangements for the hire of which may be made with the proprietor who is willing to assist in obtaining whatever the visitor may require.

The channel between the Mustiques has 7 fathoms water, and is clear of danger with the exception of the reefs extending 300 yards from Petit Cay and the southwest end of Mustique; as also the 1½ fathom shoal, on which the sea breaks, lying east, distant ½ mile from the south end of the island.

In anchoring in Grand Bay on the west side of the island, a vessel should pass west and northward of the Montezuma Shoal and enter between it and the north point of the bay, or make short tacks in the south part of the bay.

The east of the island is skirted by reefs, and off it is Rabbit Islet with the Brooks, 60 feet high, and other rocks; but as there is no anchorage a vessel should avoid this side of the island.

BALLICEAUX (a corruption of belles oiseaux) and Battawia are two smaller islets near to Mustique, to which the former the Caribs were removed from St. Vincent prior to their transportation to Honduras on 11th March 1797.

It is 1¼ miles in length, ¼ to ½ mile in breadth, and 430 feet high. A five fathom bank extends off its western side, on the edge of which with caution a vessel may anchor, but the water is never smooth although there is no danger for vessels with small draft. There are two shallow patches close in on the northwest and reef uncovered on the southwest side of the island.

At the north end of the island is Cactus Cay, 63 feet high, and at a ¼ mile north of it is Black Rock, 41 feet high, with a two fathom shoal between.

CANOUAN is of an irregular outline to the south of Bequia, 25 miles from St. Vincent; 3¼ miles in length north and south, its northern part 1½ miles in breadth, where it rises to a peak 853 feet above the sea, but the middle is not so high, or in one place more than ¼ mile across and contains 1,694 acres. The southern part projects westward and forms on that side Charlestown Bay, where there is anchorage. The island is more or less bordered by reefs, and on the southeast and south sides they extend off to about ½ mile.

The beautiful little Anglican church, partially destroyed in 1921, has not yet been completely restored. An elegant chapel has been erected there by the Roman Catholic body. There is a remarkable reef of basaltic rock on the east side of the island that forms a carenage, about twelve feet deep toward the land, and on the outer side of the wall, if it may be so termed, it is perpendicular and of unfathomable depth. In the elevated mountain adjoining, called the Marquis de Cazeau's Hill, strong indications of iron ore are visible, and in the clay formation in the valleys, hexagonal crystals are sometimes found. The following is from a report of the Director of the Museum of Practical Geology, London, on minerals and rocks from Canouan.

There are three specimens which might possibly prove to be of economic value—one of Galena and two of Iron-ore. If the Magnetite occurs in large masses in an easily accessible locality it should be analyzed, as probably a valuable source of iron.

Both the northwest and southwest points of the island are bold and may be passed at the distance of 200 yards; but it is not advisable to go so near the northwest point in a sailing vessel, as the peak checks the wind and causes flaws and eddies, but this will not occur near the southwest point. A large vessel should anchor in Charlestown Bay in 17 fathoms water, sand, with the north points in line N. 9 degs. E. (N. 9 degs E. mag.) and the southwest point S. 51 degs. W. (S. 51 degs. W. mag.). Small vessels may anchor close inshore. Within the 15 fathom line of soundings the water shoals suddenly.

To the northward of Friendship Point, the southeast extreme of the island, there is secure anchorage for small vessels inside a sandy cay and the reef. It should be approached from the southwest with smooth water. If the wind be fresh, a vessel should not attempt to pass Friendship Point, as it fronts the channel formed by an open space in the reef east of it, or to enter by this channel; and as this anchorage could only be resorted to on any particular occasion, a person with local knowledge should be obtained. Anchorage will also be found westward of Dove Cays.

About 2/3 mile N. 67 deg. W. (N. 67 deg. W. mag.) of the northwest point of Canouan is a small bank with 6½ fathoms of water in it. Vessels of large draft should avoid it, as with the heavy swell and the doubt that always exists as to whether the shallowest water is absolutely known, it will be more prudent.

MAYREAU the largest of a group comprising the Catholic Islet and Rocks, and Tobago Cays and reefs, is next in the same direction about 37 miles from St. Vincent. It is about 1½ miles in length, nearly a mile in extreme breadth, 347 feet high and contains 600 acres.

This is a pretty little island with scenery quite as attractive as the others in the chain. Roman Catholics are in the ascendency and theirs is the only place of worship.

Catholic Islet and Rocks are about one mile northwest of Mayreau; the islet is 166 feet, and the rocks, at about ¼ mile to the southwest of it, 77 feet high; the passage between them has 6 fathoms water and may be taken with a fair wind in cases of necessity.

At 400 yards northwest of the North Catholic Rocks is a shoal with 3½ fathoms water on it, which must be avoided. A rock 8 feet above water and a small sand cay, called Dry Shingle, are connected to the islet on the east side at the distance of ¼ mile by a bank that encircles it. Between Mayreau and the Dry Shingle is a good channel nearly 600 yards in width and with 5 fathoms water for vessels from the northward for Mayreau anchorage.

Anchorage—Good anchorage in 6 or 7 fathoms water may be had on a bank extending about ¾ mile westward from Mayreau. The best and most roomy berth for leaving with any wind is near the edge of the bank with the middle of the island tearing N. 68 deg. E. (N. 67 deg. E. mag.), but as the trade wind is almost always between northeast and southeast, a vessel may anchor much closer in out of the swell, taking care, however, to avoid a 3-foot shoal at 300 yards off the middle point of the island. The northwest point of Canouan, well open of the northwest point of Mayreau, leads to the westward of the shoal; the two points in line lead on it.

In working for this anchorage, keep on the parallel of Mayreau and do not open the channel between it and Union Island unless the tide is setting to the northward.

On the east side of Mayreau is a secure anchorage for small vessels in from 6 to 9 fathoms water, under cover of the extensive reefs that surround the side of the island. The passage in is from the southward between the reefs on the east and those skirting the shore of the island.

UNION ISLAND is 40 miles from St. Vincent and therefore farther to the south than any of the Grenadines under this Government, being southwest of Mayreau. It contains 2,600 acres and is more or less skirted by reefs that connect to it Frigate Islet, standing at a distance of about 2/3 of a mile on the south, and Red Islet, 140 feet high close to it on the east. About 1/3 of a mile from its north side there is a small sandy cay.

Since the island was acquired by the Government in June 1910, remarkable progress has been made from every point of view.

There are two churches, Anglican and Roman Catholic; the Seventh Day Adventists and Brethren also have their places of worship.

The good work performed there by Dr. R. Austin and Mrs. Austin has earned the abiding gratitude of the people. The hospital erected there through the doctor's instrumentality is of great utility.

Clifton is the port of entry at which place there are established a post office with branch Money Office Department, a Branch Savings Bank and telephonic communication to other parts of the Dependency.

Chatham Bay, on the west side, affords fair anchorage for large vessels in 17 fathoms water, sand; but care should be taken not to go far into the bay, as there is a small shoal with 6 feet water on it about ¼ mile from the shore, and a little inside the depth of 10 fathoms. Small vessels may anchor farther in on the north side of the bay. There are no dangers in entering the bay, which should be from the northward on the port tack. Give the northwest point of the island a berth of about 300 yards and pass close to a remarkably small islet, 52 feet high, at the north point of the bay, and when abreast it, with good way on, shorten sail and the vessel will shoot into the anchorage. Temporary anchorage may be had to the southwest of Frigate Islet in 8 fathoms of water, if wishing to communicate with the villages on the southeast side of the island. Small vessels may go close to Frigate Islet into two or three fathoms.

Clifton Cove, at the east end of the island, is a secure smooth anchorage for small vessels, close to the northeast of a large house. The channel into it is close to the reef which protects the anchorage.

The following is a description by His Late Majesty King George V. extracted from Notes in connection with the cruise on H.M.S. *Bacchante* in 1880:

> *February 5th...at 10 a.m. tacked in order to fetch up to Chatham Bay, Union Island, another of the Grenadines, with far loftier cliffs and more wood-clad than Carriacou, where we anchored in nineteen fathoms at 11.30 a.m. These islands of grey and red rock resemble the Cyclades of the Grecian Archipelago, or the islets in the Inland Sea of Japan....*

The smaller islets are principally used for rearing small stocks and as fishing grounds for the inhabitants of the larger islands.

Agriculture is the chief employment of these robust islanders. At certain months of the year, however, several of the males migrate to Trinidad. These stalwart men generally engage themselves as sailors, others find fishing a lucrative pastime. Numbers of turtle are taken both by nets and on the shore, conchs, and fish of different descriptions swarm the creeks and adjoining banks.

Nowhere in the West Indies can sea bathing be better indulged in than at the Grenadines, their pearly-white sandy beaches render the water attractively transparent.

The auxiliary schooner under contract and the Government sloop have been useful to some extent, but they cannot supply the service that will afford the accommodation and other facilities for enhancing the extensive development of trade and passenger traffic.

An enterprising person or company may profitably establish the salt industry at Canouan, Mayreau and Union Island. Nature is offering prosperity to any progressive man.

ITTLE ST. VINCENT which is 275 feet high is also comprised within this Government. It is situated 3 1/3 miles northeast of the north point of Carriacou and 1/3 of a mile south of Little Martinique. On the northwest side are two sand banks three feet above water, about ¾ mile distant; from the easternmost, a reef, uncovered, sweeps round the whole eastern side of the island.

List of Officers

Who have administered the Government of St. Vincent since its cession to Great Britain in 1763

Governors, Lieutenant Governors and Administrators from 1763 to 1838

Governors
St. Vincent, Grenada, Dominica and Tobago

1763	—	Brigadier General Robert Melville
1771 Mar.		Brigadier General Wm. Leyborne
1776	—	Valentine Morris
1783 Mar.		Edmund Lincol
1787 April, ..		. James Seton.
1798 Mar., ..		William Bentinck.
1806		Sir George Beckwith (KCB)
1808 Nov.		Sir Charles Brisbane (KT)
1831 Jan.		Rt. Hon. Sir George Fitzgerald Hill (Bart)

Barbados, St. Vincent, Grenada and Tobago, also St. Lucia (1838)

1833 Jan.	Major General Sir Lionel Smith(KCB)
1836 Oct.	Sir Evan J. Murray MacGregor (Bart)
1842 Feb.	Rt. Hon. Sir Charles Edward Grey
1846 Dec,	Lieut-Colonel William Reid (CB)
1848 —	Sir W. McB. G. Colebrooke
1856 —	Francis Hincks.
1862 —	James Walker (CB)
1869 —	Rawson W. Rawson (CB)
1875 —	J. Pope Hennessy (CMG)
1876 Dec.	Captain G. C. Strahan (CMG)
1880 July	A. F. Gore (CMG)
1882 Jan.	William Robinson (CMG)

Windward Islands—Grenada, St. Lucia and St. Vincent

1885 May	Sir Walter J. Seudall (KCMG)
1889 Oct.	The Hon. Sir Walter F. Hely-Hutchinson (KCMG)
1893 Aug.	Sir Charles Bruce (KCMG)
1897 Jan.	Sir Alfred Maloney (KCMG)

1900 Dec.	Sir R. B. Llewelyn (KCMG)
906 Sep.	Sir Ralph Williams (KCMG)
1909 May	Sir James Hayes Sadler (KCMG, CB)
1914 Dec.	Sir George B. Haddon-Smith (KCMG)
1924, Feb.	Sir Frederick Seton James (KCMG, KB)
1930 Sep.	Sir Thomas A. V. Best (KCMG, KBE)
1935 Feb.	Sir Selwyn MacGregor Grier (KCMG)
1937 May	H. B. Popham (CMG, MBE)

Lieutenant-Governors

1771 Sep.	Ulysses Fitz-Maurice
1799 May	Drewry Ottley, *President*
1805 Sep.	Robert Paul, *President*
1829 Nov.	Sir William John Struth (KT), *President*
1833 May	Sir George Tyler, (RN)
1842 Jan.	Colonel Sir Richard Doherty (KT)
1845 Oct.	Sir John Campbell (Bart)
1853 Jan.	Richard Graves MacDonnell (CB)
1854 Dec.	Edward John Eyre
1862 May	Anthony Musgrave
1864 Sep.	George Berkeley
1871 June	William Hepburn Renuie
1875 Feb.	George Dundas
1880 Aug.	William Robinson (CMG)

Administrators

1888 April	R. B. Llewelyn
1889 July	Captain I. C. Maling (CMG)
1893 July	Col. J. H. Sandwith (CB)
1895 March	H. L Thompson (CMG)
1901 May	Edward John Cameron, C.M.G.
1909 May	The Hon. C. Gideon Murray
1915 June	R. Popham Lobb (now Nicholson) (CMG)
1923 April	R. Walter (CMG)
1929 April	Major H.W. Peebles (CMG, DSO, CMG)
1933 July	A. F. Grimble (CMG, now KCM.)
1936 June	A. A, Wright (CMG)

MEDICAL OFFICERS

Senior Medical Officer	}	Dr. J. A. Henderson
Medical Officer, District 1 and Medical) Superintendent, Fort Institution and Port Health Officer	}	Dr. H. B. Gregory.
Resident Surgeon, Colonial Hospital and Opthalmologist	}	Dr. A. Lai Kiow
Medical Officer, District 2 North and Medical Officer in Charge, Chateaubelair, Dr. Reginald Austin. Casualty Hospital	}	Dr. Reginald Austin
Medical Officer, District 2 South, Pembroke, and Radiologist	}	Dr. A. B. Bereton
Medical Officer, District 3, Belair, and Medical Superintendent, Mental Hospital, Villa	}	Dr. E. D. B. Charles
Medical Officer, District 4, The Cedars	}	Dr. F. C. Alexis
Medical Officer, District 5, Georgetown, and Medical Officer in Charge of Casualty Hospital, Georgetown	}	Dr. J. W Gallwey.
Medical Officer District 6, Grenadines and Medical Officer in Charge of Casualty Hospital at Union Island; also District Officer and Magistrate Southern Grenadines	}	Dr. W. J. McMillan.
Supernumerary Medical Officer	}	Dr. W. C. J. Murray
Private Practitioners Dr. G. A. MacDonald Dr. Robert A. Bonello	}	Richmond Hill Villa Bungalows

DENTISTS

Dr. Edward Deane | Dr. Frank M. Ellis | Dr. Louis E. Sprott

DISPENSERS

Steward and Chief DisDispenser, Colonial Hospital	}	Eustace T. Young.
2nd Dispenser, Colonial Hospital	}	Cyril E. Daisey
Assistant Dispenser, Colonial Hospital and Dispenser, Dental and V. D. Clinics	}	Eardley McKie
Laboratory Assistant and Assistant at X-Ray Clinic	}	Milton F. McDowall

Dispenser, Lay Superintendent Mental Hospital, Villa	}	Eric Wall
Dispenser, Mental Hospital, Villa	}	Robert E. Paynter
Dispenser Steward, Fort Institution	}	Samuel A. Davy
Dispenser, District 2 North, Chateaubelair Hospital Hospital	}	Richard S. John
Dispenser, District 2 South, Layou	}	Alexander M. Anderson
Dispenser, District 3, Belair	}	Robert James.
Dispenser, District 4, Cedars	}	Edwin R. Pollard (Acg)
Dispenser, District 5, Georgetown Hospital	}	Benjamin A. Richards
Dispenser, District 5, Sandy Bay	}	J. A. Rose.
Dispenser, District 6, Bequia Grenadines	}	Samuel A. Norris
Dispenser, District 6, Union Island Hospital, Grenadines	}	Robert A. Clouden

Private Druggists

N. B. Cropper	Kingstown
W. C. Forde	Kingstown
G. A. McIntosh	Kingstown
David K. Dennie	Kingstown
Robert Ellis	Georgetown
Charles Fraser	Kingstown
Charles H. Findlay	Kingstown
Charles Alexander	Chauncy Village
John Prince	Kingstown
Gladstone King	Richmond Hill

425

List of Chief Justices and Assistant Justices of Saint Vincent| from the year 1786 to 1938

PERIOD OF OFFICE	NAME	POSITION
1786	Henry Sharpe	Chief Justice
1786-1790	Jonas Akers	Senior Asst. Justice
1786	Drewry Ottley	Asst. Justice
1786	George Lowman	Asst. Justice
1787-1805	Drewry Ottley	Chief Justice
1787	William Bannatyne	Asst. Justice
1790	John Findlater	Asst. Justice
1797-1799	Henry Haffey	Asst. Justice
1797	George Sharpe	Asst. Justice
1797-1816	Daniel MacDowall	Asst. Justice
1798	George Lowman	Chief Justice (Ag.)
1798-1802	John Guilding	Asst. Justice
1799	Robert Elmes Henville	Chief Justice (Ag.)
1799-1804	David Miller	Asst. Justice
1807-1811	William Taylor	Chief Justice
1810-1815	John Grant	Asst. Justice
1811-1819	Edward Sharpe	Chief Justice
1813-1814	Warner Ottley	Asst. Justice
1815	Joseph Richard Durham	Asst. Justice
1818-1829	John Dalzell	Asst. Justice
1818-1827	Richard Arrindell	Asst. Justice
1821-1825	Edward Caines	Asst. Justice
1821-1826	William Wylly	Chief Justice
1827	John Dalzell	Chief Justice (Ag.)
1827-1829	John Henry Hobson	Chief Justice
1828	Johnson Littledale	Asst. Justice
1829-1832	Joseph Billinghurst	Asst. Justice
1831-1846	John Peterson	Chief Justice
1841-1864	John Loving Hazell	Asst. Justice
1846-1866	Henry Edward Sharpe	Chief Justice
1850	George Colquhoun Grant	Asst. Justice
1851	Charles A. Bukeley	Asst. Justice
1852-1856	William Laborde	Asst. Justice
1860-1862	John M. Grant	Asst. Justice
1861-1877	William Edwin Hughes	Asst. Justice

Period of Office	Name	Position
1862-1874	G. Van Heyningen	Asst. Justice
1865-1874	Robert Checkley	Asst. Justice
1866	John King	Chief Justice
1867-1896	George Trafford	Chief Justice
1875	John D'Oyly	Asst. Justice
1866-1875	Richard A. St. Hill	Asst. Justice
1896	Leslie Thornton	Chief Justice (Ag.)
1896-1898	G. P. St. Aubyn	Chief Justice (Ag.)
1898-1901	James Bayldon Walker	Chief Justice
1901-1902	Ormond Hazell	Chief Justice (Ag)
1903-1906	Percy Musgrave Cresswell Sheriff	Chief Justice
1907-1912	Walter Sidney Shaw (later Sir Walter &c).	Chief Justice
1908	Malcolm Edward Horne Martin	Chief Justice (Ag)
1912-1914	Robert Blair Roden	Chief Justice
1915-1919	Anthony DeFreitas (now Sir Anthony &c. KT)	Chief Justice
1919-1923	Samuel Joyce Thomas (now Sir Samuel &c. KT)	Chief Justice
1923-1926	James Stanley Rae (now Sir James KT)	Chief Justice
1926-1928	Neville Turton	Chief Justice (Ag)
1928-1930	Willoughby Bullock	Chief Justice
1928	N. Julian Paterson	Chief Justice (Ag)
1930	James Henry Jarrett	Chief Justice (Ag)
1931-1933	Ransley S. Thacker	Chief Justice
1933-1934	Harold John Hughes	Chief Justice (Ag)
1934	Charles Claye Ross	Chief Justice (Ag)
1935-1938	George Cyril Griffith Williams	Chief Justice
1938	H. A. O. O'Reilly	Chief Justice (Ag)

EXTRACT FROM EMPIRE DAY CATECHISM

Q. What is your relation to the British Empire?

A. I am a subject of King George the Sixth, and a citizen of the British Empire.

Q. What is the full title of King George the Sixth?

A. His Most Excellent Majesty GEORGE VI. by the Grace of GOD, of Great Britain, Ireland and the British Dominions beyond the Seas, King, Defender of the Faith, Emperor of India.

Q. What do you mean by the British Empire?

A. That portion of the Earth's land surface which is subject to the authority of King George the Sixth.

Q. The inhabitants of the Earth vary in race, and in the colour of their skins. The principal colours are white, copper, yellow and black. Amongst how many of these races and colours are the subjects of King George to be found?

A. Amongst all.*

Q. How is the British Empire governed?

A. Different portions are governed in different ways. Some portions like the United Kingdom, the Canadian Dominion, the Australian Commonwealth, New Zealand, Cape Colony, Natal, and Newfoundland, are self-governing; others are partly self-governed and partly governed by Officials appointed by the British Government; and others again like India, are governed by Officials appointed by the Home Government; but all acknowledge allegiance to the King Emperor.

Q. What are the duties of British subjects towards their Sovereign?

A. To honour and obey him.

Q. Why is it the duty of British subjects to honour and obey the King?

A. Because King George VI. represents the Majesty and Honour of the Empire, and because, as a constitutional Sovereign, he has sworn to uphold the laws, and to govern his subjects with justice and equity.

Q. What are the duties of a Citizen of the British Empire?

---

*Of the total (498,370,000) only about 70,000,000 are white people and they include people of British stock, Dutchmen, Frenchmen and Spaniards. About 430,000,000 include 360,000,000 natives of Indian and Ceylon.
The black races number 40,000,000; Arabs and Malays both number 6,000,000; there are 1,000,000 Chinese and 1,000,000 Polynesians, and about 100,000 Red Indians in Canada. Just as most of the races of mankind are represented in the British Empire so are most of the religious faiths. The Hindu religion with 210,000,000 adherents is the largest body. Mohammedans second with 100,000,000 and Christians third numbering 80,000,000.—[Ed.]

A. To be the loyal friend of all fellow subjects of the King-Emperor; so to live as never to bring reproach by word or deed on the Empire of which he is a Citizen. To prepare himself by every means in his power to advance the welfare of his fellow Citizen, whether in peace or war, whatever may be their class, creed or colour.

Q. Why should a Citizen of the British Empire owe duties to the State?

A. Because Citizens of the British Empire enjoy privileges, and an amount of personal liberty and freedom greater than those enjoyed by the Citizens of any other State in the world, and therefore owe loyalty and gratitude to the Empire which protects them in the enjoyment of their privileges, liberty, and freedom.

Q. What is the "Empire Day" movement?

A. An effort throughout the King-Emperor's Dominions to remind all British subjects of the virtues which make a good Citizen, such as loyalty, patriotism, courage, endurance, respect for, and obedience to lawful authority, and to encourage self-sacrifice for the public good; to teach all, and especially the young, the sacredness of the Trust committed to them; and to inspire them with determination to do their duty.

Q. What are the "Watchwords" of the Empire Day Movement?

A. "Responsibility, Duty, Sympathy, Self-sacrifice."

Q. What is the "Motto" of the Empire Day Movement?

A. "One King, One Flag, One Fleet, One Empire."

Q. What is the name of the British National Flag?

A. The "Union Jack."

List of Birds

Merula gymnopthalma—Yam Bird. Yellow-eyed Grieve. 8½ inches. Dull olive brown, lighter below; naked skin about eye yellow.

Merula nigrirostris—Grieve. 9 inches. Brown, lighter below.

Myiadestes sibilans—Soufriere Bird. 7 1/4 inches. Nearly black, underparts gray, throat and belly orange rufous. White markings on inner nibs of tail and wing feathers.

Margarops montanus—Spotted Grieve. 9 1/2 inches. Brown, belly white. Dull white markings on wings, tail feathers tipped with white, and white edgings to breast feathers.

Mimus gilvus—Mocking Bird. 8 3/4 inches. Gray white below. Tips of tail feathers and markings on wings, white.

Thryothorus musicus—Wall Bird. Wren. 5 inches. Rusty brown, narrow black lines across wing and tail feathers. White below.

Cartharopega bishovi—Lesser Soufriere Bird. 5 1/2 inches. Black, and band across breast, black. Circle about eye, throat and belly, white.

Seiurus aurocapillus—Oven Bird (U.S.). 5 1/2 inches. Olive green, lighter below. Centre of crown, dull orange with a black line on each side.

Seiurus naevius—Water Thrush (U.S.). 5 inches. Brown above, underparts and line over eye, white.

Certhiola saccharina—Mistletoe-bird. 4 inches. Dark-slaty above, underparts and back bright yellow. White line over eye and white patch on wing.

Certhiola atrata—St. Vincent Blackbird. 4 inches. Black.

Progne dominicensie—West Indian Martin. 7 inches. Steel blue, middle of breast and belly, white.

Petrochelidon fulva—Eave Swallow. 4 3/4 inches. Black, and top of head bluish black. Forehead and lower back, dark rufous brown. Underparts light brownish and white.

Vireo calidris—Lady Bird. 5 3/4 inches. Olive green, lighter below, top of head grayish. Dark stripes through eye and light stripe over it.

Euphonia flavifrons—Blue Head. 4 1/2 inches. Bright green, lighter and duller below. Top of head bright blue, forehead orange.

Calliste versicolor—Golden Tanager. 6 inches. Bright red-gold, appearing yellow, red, or green in different lights. Top of head chestnut, wings and tail dark green. Female—Same, but back green, and top head pale chestnut.

Loxigilla nochs—Red Throat. Sparrow. 4 1/2 inches. Black. Throat and line over eye, chestnut. Female—Dull brown above, gray below.

Tiaris bicolor—Green Bird. 4 inches. Olive green. Breast, throat and forehead black. Female—Olive green, light below.

Quiscalus luminosus—Bequia Sweet. 10 1/2 inches. Black. Female—grayish.

Elainea martinica—Topknot. Flycatcher. 6 1/2 inches. Brownish olive. Throat and breast, grayish; belly yellow, dirty white in middle line.

Myiarchus oberi—Loggerhead. 7 3/4 inches. Brown above, upper breast gray; lower breast and belly sulphur yellow.

Tyrannus rostratus—Pipiri, 9 inches. Gray, white below; wings and tail dark brown.

Chaetura brachyura—Chimney Swift Swallow. 4 1/4 inches. Very dark-brown, tail and lower back gray. Never perches on branches of trees or wires; roosts in hollow trees or chimneys.

Eulampis Jugularis—Red-throated Hummingbird. 4 1/4 inches. Black. Wings and tail green, throat and breast metallic red. Known by its large size.

Eulampis holosericeus—Emerald-throated Hummingbird. 4 1/2 inches. Green, brightest on throat; blue patch on lower breast.

Bellona cristata—Crested Hummingbird. 2 3/4 inches. Dull green above, brown below; head with pointed metallic green crest. Female—dull green, gray below; no crest.

Crotophaga ani—Tick Bird. 12 1/4 inches. Black beak very much arched.

Coccyzus minor—Cuckoo Manioc. 12 inches. Gray above, buff below; white tips to tail feathers.

Ceryle alcyon—Kingfisher. 9 inches. Blue-gray above speckled with white; white below with blue band across breast; head with large crest. Female—additional band on breast and sides, chestnut.

Amazona guildingi—St. Vincent Parrot. 19 inches. Yellow-brown above, reddish-brown below; head blue, forehead white; wide band of yellow and orange on wing. Tail orange at base, yellow at tip, with wide band of blue across middle.

Strix nigrescens - Owl Jumbie Bird. 12 inches. Mottled brown, face reddish, buffy beneath, with small round black spots. Tail banded light and dark brownish. Ends of face feathers (ruff) dark red-brown. Iris chocolate, bill white.

Buteo latissimus—Chicken Hawk, Broad-winged Hawk (U.S.). 14 inches. Mottled brown above, light brown below with dark markings on breast.

Urubitinga anthracina—Black Hawk. 24 inches. Slaty black, tail banded with white.

Falco perigrinus anatum—Duck Hawk. 19 inches. Slaty gray above, dirty white below, with brown markings on breast. A powerful hawk of great quickness and velocity on the wing. Seen about cliffs.

Columba corensis—Ramier. 13 1/2 inches. Slaty gray, head reddish-brown.

Zenaida zenaida — Mountain Dove. 10 inches. Brown above, lighter purplish brown below. Blue streak below ear. Feet red.

Zenaida martinicana—Seaside Dove. 10 inches. Brown above, dull bluish-*white below. Lower back chestnut. Dark-blue line on cheek.*

Columbigallina passerina—Ground Dove. 6 1/4 inches. Dull brown; spots of metallic purple on wings.

Ortalda ruficauda—Cocorico, Chachalaca (Mexico and United States), Guacharaca (Venezuela). Guan. 24 inches. Olive brown, head grayish.

Eupsychortyx sonninii—Quail. 7 ½ inches. Above, mottled reddish-brown, buff, and black; tail slaty; breast, mottled grayish; rest of underparts chestnut brown. Face white; crest and throat buff brown.

Ardea herodias—Gray Gaulding. Great Blue Heron (United States). Mainly slaty gray, lighter below and streaked with white. Readily known by its great size.

Ardea candidissima—Large White Gaulding. White. Known by its large size.

Ardea caerulea—Blue Gaulding. Little Blue Heron (United States). Rather small, slaty blue, neck reddish. Young, white.

Butorides virescens—Gaulding. Green Bittern (United States). Small, grayish green, neck reddish, with white stripe down front.

Porzana Carolina—Sora Rail. Size of quail. Olive brown above, streaked with buff and greenish. Gray below; face black. Lives among mangrove roots and about branches.

Gallinula galeata—Red Seal Coot. Water Fowl. Florida Gallinule (U.S).

Ionornis martinica—Purple Gallinule. Larger than preceding; green and dull purple; seal, white. Rare.

Fulica americana—White Seal Coot. Coot (U.S.). Larger than two preceding; dull gray; white patch under tail.

Anas boschas—Mallard (U.S. and England). Large Duck (Grenada). Large. Light brownish-gray, head bright green; breast chestnut, white collar about neck; belly dirty white. A few feathers just above tail curled up, and forwards. Female—Yellow-brown streaked with lighter.

Querquendula discors—Blue-winged Teal. Distinguished by small size and by having small blue feathers on wing.

Fregata aquila—Man-o-War Bird. Frigate Bird. Known by very large size, deeply forked tail, and long narrow wings. Colour glossy black; young with white on breast.

Pelecanus fuscus—Brown Pelican. Very large and heavy. Long beak, with pouch beneath it, brown.

Sula sula—Booby. Large, but considerably smaller than preceding. Brown above, breast gray. Lower breast and belly, white. Bill yellow.

Sula piscator —White Booby. Same size as preceding. White, with outer large feathers of wing and most of small feathers, dark gray.

Phaethon aethercus—Long Tail Tropic Bird (U.S). Size of Chicken Hawk. White; black markings on wings. Middle tail feathers very long. Including these, the bird measures about 30 inches.

Lanis atricella—Laughing Gull. Black-headed Gull. Somewhat larger than preceding. Light gray above, white below. Head dark gray.

Sterna maxima—Royal Tern. Larger than Tropic Bird. Tail deeply forked. Gray above, white below. Top of head black, with slight crest.

Sterna anosthaetus—Bridle Tern. Top of head black. Back dark gray, lighter toward neck. White below. Forehead and line over eye white. Tail forked. Smaller than the Royal Tern.

Sterna fuliginosa— Sooty Tern. Hurricane Bird. Size and general appearance of preceding, but uniform dark brown above, not lighter toward neck. White below, tail forked.

Sterna dougalli—Roseate Tern. Small. Light gray above; white, with a tinge of pink below. Top of breast black. Tail very deeply forked.

Anons Stolidus—Noddy Mwen. Size of Roseate Tern. Brown. Top of head light gray. Tail not forked.

Oceanites oceanicus—Wilson's Petrel. Size of West Indian Martin, (No. 12), Black; lower back white.

Puffinus auduboni—Diablotin. Somewhat smaller than Tropic Bird (No. 55). Dark brown above, white below. Skims about near surface of water; nests in holes.

Charadrins dominions—Golden Plover.

Squatarola helvetica—Black-billed Plover. White -tailed Plover. Loggerhead.

Aegialitis semipalmata—Ring-neck Plover.

Arenoria interpres—Turnstone (U.S. and England). Calico Bird, Rock Plover. Sandy Plover.

Hiniantopus mexicanus—Black Neck Stilt.

Gallinago delicata—Snipe.

Macrorhamphus scolopaceus—Dowitchu. Duckleg. Duck Bill (Barbados).

Micropalama himantopus—Stilt Sandpiper Cue (Barbados).

Erennetes pusillus—Semipalmated Sandpiper. Small Sandpiper (Grenada). Grass Nit (Barbados).

Tringa minutilla —Least Sandpiper. Cockroach Nit (Barbados).

Tringa maculata—Pectoral Sandpiper. October Chirps (Barbados). Grassbird (Grenada).

Tringa fuscicollis—Red-necked Sandpiper. Gray Nit (Barbados).

Calidris arenaria—Sanderling. Sandy Snipe (Barbados).

Symphemia semipalmata—Willet. White-tailed Curlew (Barbados).

Totanus melanoleucus—Greater Yellow Legs. Pica (Grenada and Barbados).

Totanus flavipes—Lesser Yellow Legs. Longlegs (Barbados).

Totanus solitarius—Solitary Sandpiper. Black-back (Barbados).

Actitis macularius—Spotted Sandpiper. Nit. Spotted Wag (Barbados).

Bartramia longicauda—Upland Plover. Cotton-tree Plover (Barbados).

Numenius hudsonicus—Hudsonian Curlew. Large Curlew. Crookbill Curlew.

Mumenius borealis—Curlew, Chittering Curlew (Barbados).

The foregoing is a list of birds which occur in the colony of St. Vincent, that is, the species inhabiting the island of St. Vincent and the Grenadines as far as, but not including, Carriacou, prepared by Mr. Austin H. Clarke, of Harvard University. "West Indian Bulletin" 1905.

In his description of the birds of St. Vincent (published 1878) Frederick A. Ober, Esq, who was engaged for the Smithsonian Institution, Washington, U.S.A., wrote as follows :

Myiadestes: Soufriere Bird

The almost mythical existence of this bird had rendered it an object of search for half a century. Its weird notes, so melodious and thrillingly solemn, could be heard issuing from the ravines and gorges seaming the sides of the Soufriere Mountain; but the bird ever remained invisible. It is but natural that it should excite great interest and that much importance should be attached to the capture of so rare a bird.

Upon investigation, I found that the statements regarding its secluded habits were in no wise exaggerated.

It was only by camping on the mountain in the "cave" overlooking the crater, that I at last succeeded in taking it. During five days' residence in the cave aforesaid, and in my search through the ravines and gullies of the surrounding woods, 1 captured but five, and these were only brought to bag by the use of a call taught me by the Indians.

Though I regret being obliged to destroy the pleasing fiction of its invisibility, it gives me pleasure to announce its capture. And though I may be able to give its specific name, I will not, but will allow the statement that it is peculiar to this island to remain unchallenged—for the present.

It occurs in greater number, perhaps, than is generally supposed.

BIRDS AND FISH PROTECTED
(ORDINANCE NO. 11. OF 1901)

Any person who kills, wounds, or takes any of the following birds or the eggs or nest thereof, or who has in his possession any such bird killed, wounded, or taken, or any part thereof or the eggs or nest of any such bird, is liable to a fine of five pounds.

Birds Protected unconditionally

Black Hawk

Cuckoo-Manioc—Rain Bird

Flycatcher
  Grey
  Large Blue
  Small Green
  White

House Wren

Humming Bird, Crested—Doctor Bird
  Green Throated
  Ruby Throated

Kingfisher

Lesser Soufriere Bird—Bishop's Warbler

Mistletoe Bird—Yellow Breast

Mocking Bird

Molasses Bird

Parrot

Pipperie, Crested
  Hawk Beater

Redbreast

Redstart

Soufriere Bird

Tanager

Tick Bird

Trembleur

Any person who kills, wounds, or takes any of the following birds, or takes the eggs, or nest of any such bird, or who has in his possession any such bird killed, wounded or taken or any part thereof or the eggs or nest of any such bird during the period *from 1st March to 31st July* in any year is liable to a penalty of five pounds.

Birds Protected conditionally

Cocorico

Wild Pigeon or Rainier

Mountain Dove or Tourterelle

Ground Dove or Ortolon

Every other Species of Wild Quail

The Governor in Council may however by writing under his hand for such time and subject to conditions, authorise any person for scientific purposes to kill or take any bird or the eggs or nest thereof.

435

Protection of Turtle and Oysters

Any person who kills, wounds, or takes or who has in his possession any turtle, or who takes or has in his possession any oysters in the period *from 1st May to 31st August* in any year, is liable to a fine of five pounds.

Any person who takes or destroys any turtle or turtle eggs *on land* or who has in his possession any such turtle or turtle eggs, or who takes, kills, sells or purchases a turtle *of less than 20 lbs. weight,* is liable to a fine of five pounds.

Public Services etc.
of Government Officers

Alexis, Frank C.—Born 2nd January 1913. Educated, Grenada Boys Secondary School, 1922-1929; Skerry's College, Edinburgh, Scotland, Session 1929-30; Royal College of Surgeons—Edinburgh 1930-1935; Grenada. Acting Medical Officer District 4, Sept. to Nov. 1936; Acting Medical Officer District 3. Jan. to April, 1937; St. Vincent: Medical Officer District 2 South, May to Nov. 1937; Medical Officer, District 4, Dec. 1937. Qualifications: (LRCP and S) Edinburgh; (LRFP, S) Glasgow.

Alves, J. Vincent—Born 17th June 1915. Appointed Assistant Teacher Canouan, 1st January 1935. Transferred to the Treasury as clerical assistant 11th October 1937. Appointed 5th class clerk (6th clerk) Treasury 1st February 1938. Acting 3rd clerk Audit Office from 1st May 1938.

Anderson, Sydney Eileen Rosalie—Attended at Miss F. Flintof's Private School for elementary studies, then at the Girl's High School, 1926-36, obtained Junior Certificate Cambridge University, (local Examination) 1930, School Certificate 1933. Matriculation Certificate 1936. Acting Clerical Assistant Agricultural Department 1936, confirmed 1937.

Anderson, Joyce Emmeline—Attended at Miss F. Flintof's Private School and Kingstown Anglican School for elementary Studies, then at the Girls' High School, 1929-36, obtained Junior Certificate Cambridge University (local Examination) 1932, School Certificate 1934. Matriculation Certificate 1936. Acting Clerical Assistant Registrar's Office since 1936.

Archer, Victor Alfred Alleyne—Born 9th June, 1905. Educated St. Mary's College, St. Lucia; Junior Honours, Senior Honours, London Matriculation; Imperial College of Tropical Agriculture 1925-26. Student Assistant, Sugar Chemistry, Govt. Lab., Barbados 1927-28. McGill University (BSA) 1931; University of Toronto (MSA) 1933; Associate of Canadian Institute of Chemistry 1933. Appointed a Master Grammar School, St. Vincent, 9th May 1936.

Austin, Reginald—Born 1902. Educated at the Cedros Government School and Queen's Royal College, Trinidad. Obtained Junior and School Certificates, also Certificate in Chemistry. Entered Skerry's College Edinburgh, Scotland in 1923 and Edinburgh University 1924. When a student, was appointed Clinical Assistant to Dr. J. Comrie, one of the consulting Physicians at the Royal Infirmary, Edinburgh. Engaged in practical work at Coombe Hospital, Dublin. Represented Chinese Students at the Students Council in 1927; Vice-President of the Chinese Students Association and Member of Sino-Scottish Society 1928-29.

Graduated in 1929. Clinical Assistant to Venereal Disease Department, Edinburgh Royal Infirmary and City Corporation, 1930, under Lieut.-Colonel David Lees, (DSO, FRCS, MA, DPH), etc. Assistant Surgeon, Colonial Hospital, Port-of-Spain, Trinidad, 1931-32; Acting Resident Surgeon, Victoria Hospital St. Lucia 1933 and of Colonial Hospital St. Vincent 1933-34. Medical and District Officer St. Vincent Grenadines, August 1934; Medical Officer District 2 (North) 1936.

Baynes, Alfred Cecil Hartington—Born 2nd Dec. 1902. Obtained a Government Exhibition in 1917 to the Grammar School for 4 years; Junior Cambridge Certificate 1919 and School Certificate 1921; Clerical Assistant, Agricultural Dept. 1st Sept. 1921; Clerk to the Magistrate, Second District, 1st Nov. 1921; Second Class Revenue Officer, Georgetown 22nd Dec. 1924; Second Class Revenue Officer, Kingstown 1st Sept. 1927; Acting Excise Officer in charge of Spirit Warehouse 1st Feb to 29th Feb. 1928; Third Class Clerk (Third Clerk) Treasury Department 1st Jan. 1932; Acting Second Class Clerk (First Clerk) Treasury Department 1st July to 30th Sept. 1932; Acting Third Class Clerk (Second Clerk) Treasury Department 11th June to 19th July 1934; Acting District Officer and Magistrate Southern Grenadines 20th July to 26th August 1934; Acting Second Class Clerk (First Clerk) Treasury Department 8th June to 22nd June 1935; Acting First Class Revenue and Excise Officer, Leeward District 6th July to 15th December 1936; Acting Chief Excise Officer &c. 16th Dec. 1936 to 15th June 1937; Chief Revenue and Port Officer, Kingstown, 1st Feb. 1938.

Bowman, Hugh Sinclair Alfonzo—Born 9th May, 1905. Educated at St. Vincent Grammar School from January 1918 to July 1923. 16th August, 1923, Clerk to District Officer and Magistrate Southern Grenadines; 15th April, 1931, Second Class Revenue Officer; 10th June, 1934, Acting Excise Officer, Kingstown, and Admeasurer of Shipping to 20th October, 1934; 1st August, 1935, Acting First Class Revenue and Excise Officer, Georgetown, to 31st October, 1935 ; 3rd Dec., 1935, Acting First Class Revenue and Excise Officer, Georgetown, to 29th March, 1936; 12th Nov., 1936, Acting First Class Revenue and Excise Officer, Georgetown, to 30th April, 1937; 24th Dec., 1937, Acting First Class Revenue and Excise Officer, Georgetown, to 19th January, 1933; Acting Revenue and Excise Officer, Kingstown, 1938.

Brereton, Ardon Beresford—Born 24th February, 1905. Educated at St. Vincent Grammar School 1918 to 1924. Won the St. Vincent Island Scholarship 1924 and proceeded to University of Edinburgh, August 1925. Qualified at Edinburgh July 1930 and acted clinical clerk in Venereal Disease wards until Oct 1930. Supernumerary Medical Officer,

Dominica, from July to Dec. 1931, during which period acted as Resident Surgeon, Roseau Hospital and Medical Officer District "A". January 1932 appointed a J. P. and M. O. District 2 North and Town Warden, Chateaubelair, St. Vincent. March 1935 appointed M. O. District 2 South and Town Warden of Layou, St. Vincent. 1936 proceeded to England on study leave and obtained (DMR & E) (Diploma in Medical Radiology and Electrology) at University of Cambridge in Oct. 1937. Nov. 1937 appointed Radiologist, Colonial Hospital, St. Vincent, along with duties as M. O. District 2 South.

Brereton, Thomas—Born 1908. Educated Government Primary Schools and St. Vincent Grammar School 1922-1926. Cambridge Junior Certificate 1926; Cambridge School Certificate 1928; Local Sanitary Inspector's Diploma 1929. Joined the Sanitary Department 1929; Acting Chief Sanitary Inspector 1932, 1934 and 1935; Acting Fifth class clerk, Medical Department and Land and House Tax Bailiff 1938; Warden, Kingstown Board 1938.

Brown, Maurice Bartholomew—Born 27th March 1908. Won Kingstown Board Scholarship in 1920 at which time was pupil at Kingstown Anglican School. Entered Grammar School in September 1920. Passed Cambridge Junior and School Certificate examinations in 1924 and 1926 respectively. Appointed Clerk, Police Magistrate 2nd District 1st April 1929; Fourth class clerk (chief clerk and storekeeper) Public Works &c. Department 7th December 1936.

Bute, Francis Horatio—Born 15th April 1877. Appointed Temporary 2nd class Revenue Officer, Treasury Dept. February to September 1924; Temporary Land and House Tax Bailiff, Sept. 1924 to March 1925; Temporary 2nd class Revenue Officer, Treasury Dept. March to April 1925; acting Land and House Tax Bailiff April to June 1925; Temporary 2nd class Revenue Officer, Treasury Dept. June 1925 to April 1926; acting Tax Officer April to Nov. 1926; acting 2nd class Revenue Officer, Dec. 1926 to Aug. 1927; Overseer of Roads, Public Works etc. Dept. Sept. 1927; Land and House Tax Bailiff January 1936.

Chapman, John L.—Born 29th January 1893. Certificated Primary School Teacher, Trinidad; Company Sgt.-Major (BWIR) 1919; Mentioned in Despatches; Certificate Royal Sanitary Inspector; Chief Sanitary Inspector, St. Vincent 1926; Acting Inspector of Schools, St. Vincent 1930; Sgt.-Major Volunteer Force; District Commissioner Boy Scouts Association; Secretary Sanitary Authority; carried out sanitary survey, St. Vincent 1927; assisted in organising Sanitary Department and training Sanitary Inspectors; Member of Managing Committee of Cricket

Association and of Sports Association; Secretary Reeves Memorial Scholarship Committee.

Charles, E. D. B.—Born 10th December, 1899. Educated at Grenada Boys Secondary School and at the University of McGill, Canada. Medical welter weight Boxing Champion 1921; Degrees obtained: (MD, CM, LMCC). St. Vincent Medical Officer District 4 (The Cedars) 1926-31; District 2 South, 1931-32; Acting Resident Surgeon, Colonial Hospital 1932-33; Medical Officer, District 2 South 1933-35; District 3 (Belair) 1937. Medical Superintendent, Mental Hospital 1938. Member of Medical Board from 1935.

Connell, Sybbleboyle Cowley—Entered Government Service 5th August 1902, as a Supernumerary in the Government Office, second clerk, Registrar's Office, 1st April 1903; clerk to Chief Justice and Magistrate First District, Nov. 1903; Second clerk to Registrar Supreme Court, 17th Feb. 1910; Secretary Graham Bequest Committee, 4th June 1910; Acting second clerk Govt. Office, 16th Nov. 1910 to 3rd Aug. 1911; Appointed second clerk Govt. Office 4th Aug. 1911; Appointed Secretary, Education Board 14th January 1912; Acting chief clerk, Govt. Office 1912, 1913, 1915; Acting Inspector of Schools 1917; Appointed 2nd clerk Govt. Office, St. Lucia 1919; chief clerk, Attorney General St. Vincent 1927; Acting Registrar Supreme Court from 1927-1928, also Registrar, Births & Deaths; Secretary to Income Tax commissioners 1928; Acting chief clerk, Govt. Office 1928; Acting Magistrate 2nd District 1929; Acting Magistrate 1st District 1929: Acting Registrar Supreme Court 1929; Acting Magistrate 2nd District for the purpose of holding preliminary enquiries 1929; Acting Magistrate Second District 16th Jan. 1930. Special grade clerk (chief clerk) Govt. Office, clerk of Councils and Medical Registrar 1931.

Cox, James Hamilton Dudley—Educated at St. Vincent Grammar School 1923 to 1929. Obtained Junior Certificate Cambridge University 1926 and School Certificate 1929. Appointed clerk, Govt. Fruit and Vegetable Bureau 1931, 5th class clerk (clerk to Police Magistrate) 1931; Acted as 6th clerk Treasury 1935-1936 then as 5th class; as 4th class in 1938; 4th clerk in 1938, (2nd class Revenue Officer) Treasury Department 1938.

Cox, Julian Rey Vincent Byron—Born 1918. Attended the St. Vincent Grammar School from September 1929 to June 1936. Obtained Junior Cambridge Certificate in 1933; School Certificate in 1935; London Matriculation Certificate in 1936; clerical Assistant to the Medical Officer, District Officer and Magistrate, St. Vincent Grenadines July 1936; Fifth class clerk (clerk to the Attorney General) Judicial Department Jan. 1937.

Cozier, D. S.—Educated Harrison College, Barbados Sept. 1921 to Sept. 1928; Imperial College, Trinidad Oct. 1928 to June 1929; Acting Science Master Harrison College, Barbados Sept. 1929 to Dec. 1930; Science Master (now 2nd Assistant) Grammar School, St. Vincent Jan. 1931. Certificate—London Matriculation.

Cropper, James P. E.—Educated at St. Vincent Grammar School, obtaining School Certificate in 1926, Won Island Scholarship for that year and proceeded to Montreal, Canada, to study at McGill University. Graduated in 1931 with a (BSc) (in Electrical Engineering) and in 1933 with (BEng) (in Civil Engineering). Entered Government Service in April 1935 as Assistant Superintendent of Works and Roads and Crown Surveyor.

Cropper, Joyce—Educated at Girls' High School, obtained Junior and Senior Cambridge Certificates. Appointed Clerical Assistant Registrar's Office 1930; Copyist Govt. Office 1931; Fifth class clerk (clerk) Medical Department, 1933.

DaSilva, A. J.—Entered the St. Vincent Grammar School 1929. Obtained Junior Cambridge Certificate 1932, School Certificate 1934 and London Matriculation Certificate 1936. Acted as Assistant Teacher at Chateaubelair 1931; transferred to Kingstown Anglican School in the same capacity in the same year; accepted an appointment as Grading Officer at the Arrowroot Association Department; clerical Assistant to Medical and District Officer, Southern Grenadines, and transferred to Customs Department in 1938.

Dopwell, Ainsley Leverett—Born 1899. Educated at Grammar School, St. Vincent, where he obtained Senior Cambridge Local Certificate with exemption from London Matriculation 1917; clerical assistant to Agricultural Supt. 1st May 1918; clerk to District Officer and Magistrate Southern Grenadines 1st July 1919; 2nd clerk General Post Office 1st March 1920; acted 2nd clerk to Attorney General and Registrar 21st June 1920; resumed as 2nd clerk General Post Office 6th May 1921; 2nd class Revenue Officer, Customs, 1st Sept. 1923; acted 1st class Revenue and Excise Officer, Barrouallie and Leeward District 11th Oct. 1924; resumed as 2nd class Revenue Officer, Customs 9th Nov. 1924; acted District Officer Southern Grenadines 10th July 1927; resumed as 2nd class Revenue Officer Customs 2nd Sept. 1927; chief clerk, General Post Office 25th July, 1930; Audit clerk St. Vincent, 3rd Oct. 1933.

Duncan, Alphonse Donelan—Born 6th Jan. 1905. Educated at St. Mary's College, St. Lucia and St. Vincent Grammar School. Officer-in-Training Agricultural Dept. 1st Feb. 1929; selected to represent St. Vincent at the

World Jamboree held in Arrowe Park, Birkenhead, England, July 1929; acted Foreman Agricultural Experiment Station 15th Dec. 1929; acted clerk, Govt. Fruit and Vegetable Bureau 1st March 1930; appointed clerk, Govt. Fruit and Vegetable Bureau, and Secretary to the Advisory Board, Govt. Fruit and Vegetable Bureau 1st Jan. 1932; clerk Govt. Ice and Cold Storage Plant 1st Jan. 1933; Temporary clerk, Public Works, etc. Dept. 1st Jan. 1934; clerk and storekeeper, Electricity etc. Dept. 29th Jan. 1934.

Durrant, Vivian Hartley—Born 6th June, 1908; Educated at St. Vincent Grammar School; Overseer of Roads, Public Works, &c. Department, 1st February, 1929.

Edwards, George Elmore—Born 15th June 1896. Educated at the Grenada Grammar School, and at Harrison's College, Barbados. Called to the Bar at the Middle Temple on 2nd July, 1919. Actual period of study from May 1917 to December 1918, when 2nd class Honours were secured in the Final Exam. Practised in Grenada, St. Vincent, British Guiana, and again in Grenada. Elected Member of the Grenada Legislative Council April 1928 to May 1933 when resigned voluntarily. Senior Elected Member thereof April 1931 to May 1933, Member of the Executive Council of Grenada June 1932 to May 1933, when resigned voluntarily. One of the West Indies Delegates to the Colonial Office in 1932 on the question of larger representation etc., *inter alia, for* these colonies. Joined the Service on the 6th June 1936 as Registrar of the Supreme Court of St. Vincent. Acted as Police Magistrate, 1st District in conjunction with substantive duties from 18th May to 13th October 1937, and also from 3rd December 1937 to the present time. Appointed Police Magistrate 2nd District as from 1st May 1938, but appointed to act as Police Magistrate 1st District and as Registrar of the Supreme Court of St. Vincent on the said 1st May 1938, until further notice.

Garraway, J. B.—Entered Govt. Printing Office (Grenada) 1906; transferred to St. Vincent as Third compositor and Binder '08; Second compositor and Binder '09; First compositor and Binder '12; Diploma of Merit for Bookbinding from Imperial Department of Agriculture for the West Indies '20; Foreman Printer '30.

Gallwey, J. W.—Graduated (MD, CM) May 1924 Queen's University, Kingston, Ont. Canada; Asst. Anaesthetist, Victoria Hospital, Winnipeg, Canada, June to October 1924; Diploma (LMCC) (Licentiate Medical Council of Canada) Oct. 1924; Licentiate in Medicine and Surgery, Nova Scotia, Canada, Nov. 1924. In practice, Sydney, Cape Breton Island N.S. *Locum Tenens* from Oct. 1924 to July 1925. In practice (private practice) Moser River, N.S. Feb. 1925 to June 1927. Entered St. Vincent Medical Service June 1927.

Grant, George Alexander—Born 5th March 1909. Educated at the Boys' Grammar School, St. Vincent, 1919-28, Cambridge School Certificate with exemption from the London Matriculation, *Proxime Accessit* St. Vincent Island Scholarship, '28; appointed clerk and storekeeper, Electricity Department 1st April '31; clerk Public Works and Crown Lands Department 29th Jan. '34; acting Manager, Govt. Cotton Ginnery 7th Dec. '36. Confirmed 1st Jan. '37.

Gregory. Henry Bascom—Educated Harrison College, Barbados, McGill University, Montreal, Canada; Degrees: (MD, CM, McGill University) (LMS, Nova Scotia). Appointed Medical Officer, District 2 (North) 20th March '20, acting Medical Officer District 2 (South) in conjunction with substantive duties, Aug. to Sept., acting Resident Surgeon and Medical Superintendent Fort Institutions Oct. to Nov. 1920; acting Medical Officer District 2 (South) in conjunction with substantive duties Jan. to April, Medical Officer District 2 (South) April, District 3, July, Kingstown District and portion of District 1, Aug. '21; Medical Officer District 2 (South), (North) April. District 3, acting Resident Surgeon, Colonial Hospital Nov. '22; Medical Officer District 3, '23, acting Medical Officer, District 4 with other duties June '23 to Sept., '24. Again in"25; Medical Officer, District 1, '28, Medical Officer, District 3, 1st July, '31, acting Medical Officer, District 4 in conjunction with duties from Nov. '26 to Dec. '32, again in '33 (but portion) acting Chief Medical and Health Officer, Port Health Officer, Kingstown and Medical Superintendent Fort Institutions March to Oct. '35, Medical Officer District 1, Oct. to Dec. '36, acting Senior Medical Officer in conjunction with substantive duties Dec. '36 to Jan. '37, acting Resident Surgeon in conjunction with duties April '37 to Nov. '37, Acting Senior Medical Officer in conjunction with portion of duties of Medical Officer, District 1, to Feb. '38, acting Resident Surgeon in conjunction with portion of substantive duties to the present time.

Grist, Henry George—Educated Alderham School, Herts. Artists' Rifles Volunteers, February 1899; commissioned 7th (Militia) Battalion Royal Fusiliers December 1899; served in South African War; Regular Army Reserve of Officers 1912-31; Lieutenant 1912-15; Captain 1915-18; Major 1918-31; served with British Expeditionary Force in France 1915-19; Acting Lieutenant-Colonel while in command of the 13th (S) Battalion Northumberland Fusiliers 1916; appointed Staff Captain, Abbeville Area 1918; Released from Service July 1919; appointed Chief of Police etc., St. Vincent 1924.

Isaacs, Sydney Baber (MBE)—Born 22nd August 1883. Educated at St. Vincent Grammar School. Clerk to the Superintendent of Crown Lands and Land Commissioner 22nd Sept. 1902; Third clerk, Treasury Dept. 22rd July '07; Manager Govt. Cotton Ginnery 1st Nov.'10; Windward Warden, Public Works, etc. Dept. and Assistant Tax Officer 1st Sept. 1924; acting Officer-in-charge of Public Works, Crown Lands and Telephone Dept. in conjunction with substantive duties 27th Feb. to 27th July 1925; acting Superintendent of Works, in conjunction with substantive duties 13th Jan. to 1st Feb. 1927; acting Leeward Warden, in conjunction with substantive duties 23rd April to 19th Sept. 1927; Assistant Supt. of Works and Assistant Tax Officer (the offices of Windward and Leeward Wardens abolished) 20th Sept. 1927; acting Superintendent of Works, in conjunction with substantive duties 22nd Sept. 1927 to 16th Sept. 1928; again from 24th Dec. 1930 to 4th Jan. 1931; acting District Officer St. Vincent Grenadines, 8th July 1933 to 19th July 1934; acting Superintendent of Works, in conjunction with substantive duties 20th July to 14th August 1934; Superintendent of Works 15th August 1934; acting Supt. of Electricity etc. Dept. in conjunction with substantive duties 13th July 1937 to 7th Feb 1938; Appointed a Member of the Civil Division of the Order of the British Empire 1st Jan. 1938.

Jack, R. Nicholas—Born 9th April 1905. Educated at Evesham Wesleyan School 1910-1918; Saint Vincent Grammar School 1918-1922 (winner of Govt. Scholarship from Primary Schools 1918); passed the Preliminary, Junior, and Senior Cambridge Examinations in 1920, 1921 and 1922, respectively. Entered the Govt. Service in August 1922 as clerical Assistant at the Govt. Cotton Ginnery; served at the Govt. Cotton Ginnery for 7 months, the Public Works Dept. for 2 years 5 months and the Govt. Office for 12 years 10 months. Present appointment, Second clerk, Govt. Office and Superintendent of the Govt. Printing Office (also Secretary to the Graham Bequest Committee, the Road Board and the Board of Education).

Jackson, Carl Eduard—Born 20th July 1912. Educated at St. Vincent Grammar School 1924-1932. Obtained Preliminary C. O. P. Junior Cambridge, School Certificate. Entered Govt. Service July 1st, 1935 as clerical Assistant to Registrar; acted as Assistant Master, Grammar School on two occasions. Last appointment: clerk to Magistrate, District 2. Present appointment: 3rd clerk, Post Office.

Jackson, Annie—Educated in British Guiana. Assistant Librarian Free Public Library, Georgetown, British Guiana. Entered Public Service of St. Vincent as Assistant Mistress, Girls' High School April 1921; 1st Assistant Mistress, Jan. 1923; Island Secretary, Girl Guides Association April 1929; acted Headmistress Sept. to Dec. 1928; May to Sept. 1933; July 1937 to Feb. 1938.

444

Jacobs, Kathleen V.—Kingstown Board Scholarship winner to Girls' High School 1926, Cambridge School Certificate 1930. Acted clerical Assistant, General Post Office from 1st April to 31st July 1931; Temporary appointment Fifth class clerk (Third clerk) Public Works &c. Dept. from 1st Sept to 31st Dec. 1932; acted Librarian Free Public Library from 1st March to 31st May 1933; acted as Fourth class clerk (Second clerk) Public Works &c. Dept from 23rd August to 22nd Oct. 1933; appointed clerical Assistant, Registry from 25th Sept. 1933; temporary appointment clerical Assistant, Electricity Dept. from 16th August to 20th Oct. 1934; appointed clerical Assistant, Electricity Dept. on 1st April, 1935; appointed clerical Assistant to Inspector of Schools on 7th Dec. 1936.

Lopey, William Marcus—Born 27th Sept. 1894; Educated Parry School, Barbados; Island Scholar 1913 Codrington College, (BA) '16, (MA) '30. Asst. Master, St. Mary's College, St. Lucia, Jan. '17 to March '18; appointed Asst. I. S. and Asst. Master, Grammar School St. Vincent 1st April '18; Asst. Master only Grammar School from Oct. '24; acted Inspector of Schools and Headmaster Gram. School 29th Oct. '19 to Jan. '20; acted Inspector of Schools Aug. to Sept. '22 and Sept. to Dec. '25; acted Headmaster Gram. School June to July '28, Nov. '29 to May '31, June to Sept. '33 and Sept. '37 to May '38. Member of the Committee of Management of the Public Library Jan. '25 to Dec. '30; Member of the Education Board Jan. '26 to Dec. '28.

McConnie, Ada Elaine—Educated St. Vincent Girls' High School; clerical Assistant, Registrar's Office 1926; Fifth clerk Treasury '28; Fourth clerk, Treasury '30; acting Third clerk, Treasury Dept. 11th to 31st May '31, from 1st July to 1st Oct. '32, and from 10th June to 19th July, '34; acting 2nd clerk Treasury from 20th July to 26th August '34; Third clerk General Post Office 7th Dec. '36; 2nd clerk General Post Office 1st Feb. 1938.

McDowall, Dorothy J.—Educated at St. Vincent Girls' High School, Cambridge School Certificate 1931. Appointed Librarian Carnegie Public Library 1st January 1934 on six months probation. Appointment confirmed 1st July 1934.

McIntosh, Alvin—Born 7th October 1913. Obtained primary education in St. Vincent. Attended Queen's Royal College, Trinidad from Sept. 1928 to July 1931 and Granger's Institute, Trinidad as Student in Surveying Sept. 1931 to March 1934. Acting Road Overseer, Public Works Dept. St. Vincent 6th Jan. 1936; appointed as Overseer of Crown Lands 1st **April 1936.**

Maloney, James —Assoc. (IEE). Born 2nd Sept. 1890. Educated Presentation Brothers School, Cork, and Godalming Grammar School, Royal Navy

1906-1920. Served Great War 1914-18, awarded Distinguished Service Medal October 1917 for services action Straits of Otrants, May 1917; Post Office Engineering Dept. Northern Ireland 1920-23; Post Office Engineering Dept. Nigeria 1923-31; Supt. Telephone St. Vincent 1931-36; Supt. Electricity and Telephone Dept. St. Vincent 1936.

Mancini, Gordon V.—Born 31st August 1913. Educated Grenada Boys' Secondary School, School Certificate '30; joined Civil Service Grenada 1st April '32; served in Treasury and Secretariat; transferred to St. Vincent as Secretary to the Administrator 13th March '37.

Matthews, Joseph Adolphus—Born 9th March 1901. Primary School scholar '14, Educated St. Vincent Grammar School Sept. '14 to July '19, Cambridge Senior Certificate; clerical Assistant to the Agricultural Superintendent 1st Feb. '20; clerk to the District Officer Southern Grenadines 1st March '20; second clerk Audit Dept. 1st Jan. '21; acting Audit clerk 1st Nov. '24 to 31st Jan. '25, 15th to 17th June, '25; second clerk, General Post Office 1st July '25; acting chief clerk General Post Office 1st Jan. to 19th Sept. '29; acting chief clerk General Post Office 1st June to 24th July '30; provisionally chief clerk and storekeeper Public Works &c. Dept. 25th July '30; Third class clerk (chief clerk and storekeeper) Public Works &c. Dept. 1st Feb. '31; acting chief clerk General Post Office 11th Jan. to 20th Nov. '34; acting Colonial Postmaster 1st Nov. '34 to 2nd Nov. '36; Third class clerk (chief clerk), General Post Office 15th Feb. '36.

Milbourne, Charles Delves—Educated at Heidleberg College (Germany), King's School, Canterbury, and the Training ship H.M.S. "Conway". Entered the Navy in 1914, served with the Grand Fleet '15-'17 in H.M.S. "King George V". Flag ship of the 2nd Battle squadron, and for the remainder of the War in destroyers at home and in the Mediterranean. After completing professional courses was appointed to H.M.S. "Foxglove," in'20 First Lieutenant and to H.M.S. "Ciraler" in '22. After serving 2 commissions in China retired from the Navy in '23.

Moffett, Laura Gertrude Smith—Born Omagh, Co. Tyrone, Ireland. Married Arthur James Moffett, (MRCVS) (England). Educated High School Galway, Ireland, National University, Ireland. Qualifications: Inter-Exam, in Arts late Royal University, Ireland, Bachelor of Science, National University, Ireland, special course in Geography, Cambridge University, special course in Botany, Manchester University, Member Teachers' Registration Council, Member Association of Headmistresses. Science and Geography Mistress West Norfolk and King's Lynn High School for Girls, Senior Geography and Assistant Mathematics Mistress, Royal School for Daughters of Officers of the Army, Bath; Science and Mathematics Mistress, and Senior Mistress with post of Special

Responsibility, Cavendish High School, Buxton, Derbyshire; Principal, Shide House, Newport, Isle of Wight, Science and Geography Mistress, Queen's College, Barbados B.W.I., Headmistress, High School for Girls, St. Vincent B.W.I..

Murray, Wm. C. G.—Born 20th Nov. 1911. Educated St. Vincent Grammar School '21-'30; studied Medicine at Edinburgh University '31-'35; graduated (MB, CHB. Edin.), July '36; appointed Supernumerary Medical Officer, St. Lucia, Sept. '36, also acted Resident Surgeon, D.M.O. 5 and D.M.O. 4; transferred to St. Vincent as Supernumerary M.O. Aug. '37; acted D.M.O. 5, and 2 south, and D.M.O. 1.

Norris, C. M.—Educated at St. Vincent Grammar School. Certificate London Matriculation 1934; appointed as Fifth class clerk, (second class Revenue Officer, Georgetown), Treasury &c. Department 1st June 193; seconded for duty at Treasury, Kingstown, until 15th June 1937.

O'Reilly, Harry Allan Oswald—Born 12th February 1893. Civil Service St. Lucia 1909-19, Mercantile business '19-'22, Law studies '22, completed between Dec. '22 and June '24. Distinctions: First class Honours in Roman Law, Constitutional Law and Legal History, Criminal Law, Real Property and Conveyancing and Bar Finals. Prize winner: Constitutional Law and Legal History. Honourable mention: Barstow scholarship. Engaged in private practice in Trinidad; Deputy Registrar General, Trinidad '34; acted as Police Magistrate in Trinidad on several occasions; Attorney General etc. St. Vincent '36; acting Chief Justice of St. Vincent '38.

Ormiston, Eric Joseph Romer—Born London 1900. Educated Mr. Percy Roberts' Private School. Joined Army 10th London Regiment '15; transferred to 1st Battalion Rifle Brigade '19; appointed Local Purchase Officer, Attached Indian Supply and Transport '20. Served in Iraq and India. Joined the British Gendarmerie in Palestine '23; transferred to Palestine Police '26; appointed Sergeant Major of Police, Drill and Musketry Instructor to Volunteer Force, Deputy Inspector Weights and Measures and Assistant to Superintendent of Prison St. Vincent '36; appointed Sub-Inspector of Police '37; Lieutenant and Adjutant of the St. Vincent Volunteers; Censor of Cinematograph Films, and Examiner for Motor Drivers licences.

Palmer, Arthur Clifford Gentle (DICTA)—Born 10th Feb. 1906. (Previous service in Grenada, '30-37), Inspector of Schools Feb. '37; Member of the Committee for the Censorship of Cinematograph films, March '37; chairman Board of Education July to August '37, Student, Trustees, Carnegie Corporation, '37.

Pilgrim, Marjorie—Born in Barbados. Educated Queen's College, Barbados. Obtained Junior Cambridge 1930; School Certificate 1931; London Matriculation 1932; London Intermediate Arts 1934. Appointed Third Assistant Mistress, Girls' High School 1935.

Popham, Sir Henry Bradshaw—Born 1st August 1881. Educated at Tonbridge, England. Joined the Somerset Light Infantry in 1900; served in the South African War and obtained two Medals; rendered service in the West African Frontier Force from '06 to '10; joined the Colonial Administrative Service (Gold Coast) '10; Political Officer, Togoland '14 to '20; Senior Assistant Colonial Secretary '21; Provincial Commissioner and member of Gold Coast Legislature '22 to '23; invalided from service '23; served on the staff of the Wembley Exhibition '24 to '25; Commissioner in Cyprus '25; Administrator of Dominica '33 to '37; Governor and Commander-in-Chief of the Windward Islands '37; (MBE) in '18; (CMG) in '35; (KCMG) in '38. Author of various Articles etc. on West African affairs.

Prescod, Christopher Wilberforce—Born 2nd June, 1885. Holder Prelim., Junior and Senior Honour Certificates of the College of Preceptors, St. Vincent First Class Teacher's Certificate, Full Certificate of Proficiency in Pitman's Shorthand and Pitman's Shorthand Teacher's Diploma. Served as a Pupil Teacher at the Georgetown Government School for a few years, and in 1905 appointed Assistant Teacher of that School. Appointed Head Teacher of the Evesham Wesleyan School in '07 and of the Georgetown Government School in '13. In '22 appointed Town Warden of the Town of Georgetown; '28 appointed a Justice of the Peace. In '33 appointed President of the St. Vincent Teachers' Association and member of the Board of Education; '37 Acting Inspector of Schools.

Richards, Robert Bertram Alexander—Educated at St. Vincent Grammar School 1919-26. Obtained Junior Cambridge Certificate in '23 and Cambridge Senior in '26. Third clerk Public Works &c. Dept. 1st Feb. '27; second clerk, Audit Dept. 17th March '27; second clerk to Oct. '29 to Attorney General etc. June '28; acting clerk to Police Magistrate, first district, Sept. '28; acting second clerk Audit Dept. Nov. to Dec. '29; acting chief clerk to Attorney General etc. 5th to 16th Jan. '31; first class clerk (clerk to Magistrate, first district) Judicial etc. Dept. April '31; acting first class clerk (chief clerk to Attorney General etc.) Judicial etc. Dept. Jan. '32; Presiding Examiner for London Matriculation Examination June '32; acting fourth class clerk, (second clerk) Audit Dept. July '32 to Jan. '33; fifth class clerk (second clerk to Attorney General etc.) Judicial etc. Dept. Sept. '32; acting fourth class clerk (second clerk) Audit Dept. 9th to 12th Feb. '33; acting first class clerk (chief clerk to Attorney General etc.) Judicial etc. Dept. 11th April '34 to 17th April '34; and Police Magistrate for Preliminary Inquiries, acting first class clerk (chief clerk to Attorney General etc.) Judicial etc. Dept. Aug. to Oct. '35; fourth class clerk (second clerk) Audit Dept. 1st Jan. '37; Presiding Examiner for London Matriculation Examination Jan. '37; Presiding Examiner for London Intermediate Examination June '37.

Robinson, Copeland Kenrick—Born 1st July 1907. Educated Queens Royal College, Trinidad, Sept. 17-July '25 ; Employed as Field Assistant, Botany Dept., Imperial College of Tropical Agriculture, Aug. '25-Sept. '27; Diploma Course: Imperial College of Tropical Agriculture, Oct. '27-June '30; Field Assistant Froghopper Investigation Committee, Trinidad, June '30-Nov. '32; Scientific Officer St. Vincent Co-operative Arrowroot Association, Nov. '32-Oct., '34 ; Agricultural Assistant Department of Agriculture, and Scientific Officer, Co-operative Arrowroot Association, St. Vincent, Nov,, '34-Aug. '37; acting Agricultural Superintendent, St. Vincent, Aug. '37-Jan '38 ; Agricultural Superintendent, St. Vincent, Jan. '38.

Rochfort-Wade, Thomas Gustavus—Born 3rd June 1901. Headmaster, St. Vincent Grammar School; Educated King William's College, Isle of Man; St. Columba's College, Dublin; Trinity College, Dublin University; The Theological College, Ely. Degrees: Master in Arts, Dublin University (MA) 1930; Fellow of the Royal Geographical Society, (FRGS) '30; Fellow of the Commercial Science Assn. (FComScA) '27; Member, Commercial Teacher's Assn. (MCT) '28; Member, Royal Society of Teachers (MRS) '29. Ordained Deacon '24; Priest '26; Chaplain to the Forces '26-'27; Licensed to officiate as a Priest in the Windward Islands; Captain, The Prince of Wales's Volunteers (South Lancs), Regular Army Reserve of Officers. Service in St. Lucia: Headmaster, Grammar School, '28-'31; Inspector of Schools and Head of the Education Dept. '30-38; Chairman of the Board of Education '36-'38; Member of the Governing Body of the Secondary Schools '30-'38; Chairman of Govt. Committee to consider establishment of an Industrial School '37; Nominated Official Member St. Lucia Legislative Council '30-'36 (Seniority retained by permission while in St. Lucia from '36); Officer Commanding St. Lucia Volunteer Force 7th July '31 to 1st July '38; Member St. Lucia Sanitary Authority, '36; British Social Hygiene Congress '38; attended as St. Lucia Govt. Representative, '38; Acting A.D.C. to H. E. the Acting Governor, on various occasions; Justice of the Peace from May '36. Military Representative of St. Lucia for H. M. Coronation, '37; Jubilee and Coronation Medals. Scouts, 25 years service District Commissioner Isle of Ely, '23-'26 Wood Badge, '20 Medal of Merit, '32 County Commissioner, St. Lucia, '29-'32; Hon.

Commissioner, St. Lucia, '32-38; attended YALE University, U.S.A., as a Govt. nominated representative for a Post-Graduate Seminar in Education, in '34; Credits obtained: Grade A. 6 Semester Honours.

Samuel, Alfred Laborde—Educated St. Vincent Grammar School. Entered 1920. Passed Junior Local Examination (University of Cambridge) '25, passed School Certificate Examination (University of Cambridge) '27, acting 5th clerk Treasury &c. Dept., 6th Jan. '30; Fifth clerk, Treasury etc., Dept. 1st July '30; acting 2nd class Revenue Officer, Treasury etc. Dept., 12th Dec. '30 to 2nd Jan. '31; acting 3rd clerk Treasury etc. Dept. 1st June to 6th Aug. '31; acting second clerk Treasury etc. 7th Aug. to 6th Nov. '31; acting 3rd clerk Treasury etc. Dept. 7th to 20th Nov. '31; fifth class clerk (third clerk) Govt. Office 1st Jan. '32; acting second class Revenue Officer Treasury etc. Dept. Jan. '32; fifth class clerk (clerk to Magistrate First District, Judicial &c. Dept., Sept. '22; fifth class clerk (clerk to Registrar, Judicial &c. Dept., Jan. '37; also Registrar of Births and Deaths for the First District.

Seales, David Alvin—1st May 1937, Acting Assistant Bailiff, Supreme Court; 9th June to 29th June '37, Acting Senior Bailiff, Supreme Court; 21st July to 1st November '37, Acting Senior Bailiff, Supreme Court; 16th October '37, Assistant Bailiff, Supreme Court (confirmed); 2nd Nov.,'37, Senior Bailiff, Supreme Court.

Smith, Duncan McDonald—Born 18th December 1900. Educated at the St. Vincent Grammar School from Sept. '14 to July '19. Holder of the Cambridge Local Junior and Senior Certificates. Copyist Govt. Office 1st August, '19; acting Crown Lands clerk, 24th May to 24 Nov. '20; second clerk to Attorney General 1st Jan. '21; acting 2nd clerk Public Works Dept. 1st Jan. to 4th May '21; second clerk Public Works Dept. 1st Dec. '21; acting chief clerk and storekeeper Public Works Dept. 6th to 31st Dec. '24, 7th to 24th August '37, 17th Nov. '27 to 31st Dec.,'28; chief clerk and storekeeper Public Works Dept. 1st Jan.,'29; provisionally second clerk, Treasury, 1st August, '30; acting cashier, Treasury, 15th August to 14th November, '30; acting chief clerk and storekeeper, Public Works Dept. 12th December '30 to 1st January '31; acting First clerk, Treasury, 10th June to 24th October '34; second clerk Treasury, Aug. 30.

Sprott, Aubrey Vincent—Born 28th October 1905. Educated at St. Vincent Grammar School (1914-24). Holds Cambridge School Certificates with exemptions from London Matriculation Examinations. Entered Govt. Service 22nd Dec. 1924 as clerk to Police Magistrate 2nd District; appointed clerk to Chief Justice and Magistrate, First District 1st Aug. 1926; acted Assistant Master St. Vincent Grammar School on three occasions, from 14th June to 10th July 1928, from 16th Nov. to 14th

Dec. 1929 and from 13th Jan. to 14th April 1931; Private Secretary to the Acting Administrator, in conjunction with substantive duties of clerk to Chief Justice etc. 4th Aug. to 23rd Dec. 1928; Secretary to Board "to enquire into the duties and present remuneration of the Medical Officers in St. Vincent and make recommendations for the improvement of the Medical Service" 25th March 1931; appointed Fourth class clerk (2nd clerk) Public Works etc. Dept. 15th April 1931; appointed 2nd clerk General Post Office 1st Aug. 1931, acting in this Department as chief clerk for short periods in 1931 and 1933 and again from 20th Nov. 1934 to 2nd Nov. 1936 and from 5th June to 5th Dec. 1937; Secretary to Relief and Unemployment Board 14th Aug. 1936; appointed Third class clerk (3rd clerk and cashier) Treasury etc. Dept. 1st Feb. 1938; Secretary to recently appointed Committee of Management King George the Fifth Sports Grounds. Is Secretary to the Anglican Church Parochial Council; a member of the Reeves' Memorial Scholarship Committee; member of the Management Committee of the St. Vincent Sports Association and of the Executive Committee of the St. Vincent Grammar School Old Boys' Association. A Boy Scout for 12 years; at present holds the position of Assistant Commissioner (Kingstown District) of the local Boy Scouts Association and is a holder of the Wood Badge. In July 1929 had the distinction of taking charge of the St. Vincent Contingent of three Scouters to the World Jamboree at Arrowe Park, England; and in August 1935 visited the United States on the invitation of the Boy Scouts of America. Holder of the Royal Humane Society's Bronze Medal and the Silver Cross of the Boy Scouts Association for saving life from drowning in 1926.

Vanloo, Robert Vivian—Born 3rd October 1904. Officer in Training, Agricultural Department, 1st Nov. '27; Foreman, Botanic Station; Inspector, Cotton Stainer Control and Ranger Government House Lands, 1st March '28; Foreman Botanic and Experimental Stations, 16th October '31.

Wall, Eric Douglas—Pursued a course of studies in Pharmacy at Colonial Hospital in 1927. Entered service as Assistant Overseer Pauper, Leper and Lunatic Asylum Jan. 1929; Dispenser District 4 May 1929; Dispenser District 3 Jan. 1930; Dispenser Fort Institutions Jan. 1933; Nov. 1933 visited Trinidad and gained insight in the workings of their Institutions; Feb. 1934 Dispenser District 4; April 1934 escorted a mental case to England; June 1935 appointed acting Head Keeper Fort Institutions; Jan. 1936 appointed Head Keeper Fort Institutions; May 1938 appointed Lay Superintendent Mental Hospital, Villa.

Wall, Sheila Sutherland—Entered Girls' High School as first holder of the Kingstown Board Scholarship 1918. Appointed Laboratory Assistant,

Cotton Research Officer, Aug. '21; entered the Government Service as 2nd clerk to the Attorney General, April '22; present appointment Jan. '23; Matriculated University of London, '34 ; Captain of 1st St. Vincent Company, '28 and during the years '33-'36 as District Commissioner was active in promoting the Guide Movement in the Island. 2nd Assistant Mistress, Girls' High School.

Wall, Sybil Seaten—Clerical Assistant, General Post Office, 4th April 1934; acting 3rd clerk General Post Office 1st Jan. to 26th Feb. '29; acting 2nd clerk G.P.O. 27th Feb. to 21st March '29; acting 3rd clerk G.P.O. 22nd March to 31st July '29, and from 28th April to 31st May '30; acting 2nd clerk G.P.O. 1st June to 12th Sept. '30; acting 3rd clerk G.P.O. 13th Sept. '30 to 31st July '31, 3rd Oct. '33 to 11th Jan. '34 ; 20th Nov. '34 to 7th Aug. '35 ; acting 2nd clerk, G.P.O. 8th Aug. to 20th Oct. '35; acting 3rd clerk, G.P.O. 21st Oct. '35 to 8th Feb. '36; 12th June to 2nd Nov. '36; 5th June to 5th Dec. '37; fifth class clerk (4th clerk) G.P.O. 1st Jan. '38.

Williams, G. C. Griffith—Educated Bromsgrove School, Emmanuel College, Cambridge, (BA), (LLB), 1920, (MA), 1924. Called to the Bar at Middle Temple 1921. Served in France with R.F.A. Wounded 1917. In Chambers in Temple 1921-22. Private practice in Straits Settlements and Johore 1922-31; Chief Justice and Police Magistrate, 1st District, St. Vincent Feb. 1935.

Williams, George Emmanuel Elford—Educated St. Augustine's College, Ramsgate, Kent. University Tutorial College, Red Lion Square, London. Young Officer's Company, Ripon, Yorks. Appointments: Lieutenant, North Staffordshire Regiment 1915-1918; Sub-Inspector of Police and Adjutant, Local Forces, St. Vincent 1925-35; Acting Chief of Police and Commandant, Local Forces, St. Lucia 3rd June 1935 to 31st December 1935; Colonial Postmaster, St. Vincent 1936.

Williams, A. C.—Entered the Grammar School Sept. 1931, took Junior Cambridge Certificate July 1934, Senior Cambridge Certificate July 1936, worked at the Govt. Cotton Ginnery from January 1937-March 1938; called to Treasury Dept. in April 1938 and transferred later in same month to the Customs.

Wright, Arthur Alban, (CMG)—(1937), (BA—B) 1887; ed. St. Edmund's Schl., Canterbury; open exhibnr. St. John's College, Oxford, 1906; Lieut., 3rd Bn. Bedfordshire Regt. (S.R.), '09; 2nd cls. hons. schl., mod. hist., Oxford, '10; (BA), '10; cadet, Fiji, '12; ag. sub-inspr., constab., '12; passed cadet, '14; 2nd grade dist. comsnr., '15 ; dist. comsnr., Nadi, '15 ; ditto, Colo East, '16 ; on mily. duty, '17; 2nd lieut,, 5th Bn. Rifle Brigade, '17; on active serv., France, '17; dist. comnr., Macuata, '20; ditto (1st grade), Nadroga and prov. comsnr., Nadroga and Colo West, '22; ditto,

Colo North, '23; ag. asst. col. sec., Jan. '27; asst. col. sec., Jan. '28; nom. mem., leg. Coun., '29; 1st asst. col. sec., Jan. '31; sec. for native affrs., Mar. '32; mem., exec, and leg. couns.; ag. col. sec. in '32, '33, '34 and '35; gov's, dep. on several occasions, '32-'35 ; ag. gov., Mar-Aug., '35; admstr. and col. sec., St. Vincent, June '36; admstr. St. Lucia, July '38.

Young, Eustace T.—Pupil Teacher of Georgetown Anglican School. Nov. 1894 to Sept. '98; 2nd class Pupil Teacher's Certificate, '96; entered Colonial Hospital Dispensary, as Learner of Pharmacy, March '99; qualified and obtained certificate as Druggist and also appointed Dispenser at Buccament during Influenza Epidemic, May 1900; July 1900 Dispenser to Pauper and Leper Asylums; March 1901 Dispenser, Chateaubelair (acting); April, '01 Dispenser Pauper and Leper Asylums; Sept. '01 Dispenser, Chateaubelair; Jan. '03 2nd Dispenser, Colonial Hospital; June to August '03 specially appointed Dispenser to Union Island during the epidemic of Variola Varicella there. August, '03 resumed duties as 2nd Dispenser, Colonial Hospital; Feb. 8th to 29th, '04 acted as Chief Dispenser, Colonial Hospital, again from June to July '04; Oct. '07 Steward and Chief Dispenser, Colonial Hospital; May 6th, '35 obtained Their Majesties Silver Jubilee Medal.

To the Glory of GOD
and in memory of the Sons of St. Vincent
who gave their lives for King and Country
in the Great War.

1914 — 1918
Roll of Honour
Officers, Non-Commissioned Officers
and Men who were killed in action or who died
from wounds inflicted, accident occurring
or disease contracted while on active service
during the Great War.

Capt, B. Snagg,
Lt. J. H. Browne,
Lt. L. Gresham,
Lt. R. M. Hughes,
Lt. C. D. Proudfoot,
2nd Lt. W. B. W. Durrant,
2nd Lt. S. E. Hadley,
2nd Lt. H. Lewis,
Sgt. W. Hazell,
Lt. Cpl. A. C. R. Jackson,
Private T. Alexander,
Private A. Ashton,
Private C. Austin,
Private B. Ballantyne,
Private L. Baptiste,
Private H. Boyd,
Private B. Brown,
Private J. Brown,
Private R. Browne,
Private T. Cato,
Private S. Charles,
Private T. Charles,
Private W. Charles,
Private C. Clarke,
Private G. Cyrus,
Private C. Doyle,
Private A. Durrant,
Private N. Edwards,
Private C. Gabriel,

Private D. Gabriel,
Private G. Gill,
Private H. A. G. Hadley,
Private C. Hall,
Private M. Hercules,
Private A. Jack,
Private J. Jacobs,
Private C. Jarvis,
Private W. John,
Private W. Laidlow,
Private A. McKie,
Private D. Marksman,
Private J. Marks,
Private N. Martin,
Private J. Nash,
Private A. Neverson,
Private C. Phillips,
Private J. Robinson,
Private P. Simmons,
Private L. Spencer,
Private N. Spencer,
Private W. Stapleton,
Private F. Thomas,
Private L. Thomas,
Private A. Vincent,
Private E. Webb,
Private E. Williams,
Private E. Williams,
Private I. Young.

John H. Hazell Sons & Co., Ltd. Directors and Staff

Directors
A. G. Hazell, Honourable | P. W. Verrall, H. G. Hazell | A. L. Gunn, Secretary

Accountants
Charles G. Layne | Lawrence Gonsalves | Miss Stacy McDowall, Assist. Accountant

Steamship & Customs Dept.
E. A. Banfield | R. W. Gunn | A. Lawrence.

Cashiers
C. L. Sprott | Miss Cecily McDowall | Miss Enid McDowall

Hardware & Lumber Dept.
Samuel Neverson |A. Joseph | James Corner|C. McKie | G. Wallace

Grocery & Liquor Dept.
R. A. Brown | H. Medford | F. M. Banfield | George Mills

V. Bonadie | L. Gibson | O. Eustace | M. McDowall.

Corea & Co. Ltd Directors and Staff

Managing Director
Honourable F. A. Corea

Director
N.A. Duncan | Chas. H. Findlay, Secretary

Chas J. Dopwell, Bookkeeper
E.D. Gillizeau, Steamship Clerk
E.A.H. Lawrence, Asst. Steamship Clerk
Frederick Clarke, Asst. Bookkeeper & Secy, Aquatic Club
DeVere James, Cashier
Miss E. McIntosh, Miss A. Fraser, Miss N Paynter, Stenographers
Gordon Collymore, Customs Clerk

Clerks
Rudolph Baynes, George Walker, Montgomery Daisley, Herbert Samuel,
Lorraine Llewelyn, Peter Da Silva, C.C. Lawrence, J.M. Saunders, H.A. Sutherland

C.L. McDowall, Warehouse Clerk
Miss S. Soso, Telephone Operator

APPENDIX

CHRONOLOGY

1493	Jan. 22, St. Vincent discovered.
1596	Ship *Darling* touched at St. Vincent-
1627	St. Vincent granted to Lord Carlisle.
1643	M. de Bretigny landed at St. Vincent.
1655	Du Parquet sends from Martinique 150 men to destroy Caribs. They ravage the Island and return.
1660	Mar. 31, Peace between French and English. St. Vincent neutral.
1672	St. Vincent granted to Lord Willoughby. Lord Willoughby Governor. Sir Jonathan Atkins, Governor.
1675	Slave ship wrecked on Bequia.
1680	Sir Richard Dutton, Governor.
1685	Colonel Edwin Stede, Governor.
1719	Major Pauline and French Force land to assist Red Caribs. Retire at peace with both tribes.
1722	St. Vincent granted to Duke of Montague. Capt. Uring, Deputy Governor. Vessels sent to commence settlement.
1723	Capt. Brathwaite lands but finds settlement impracticable.
1730	St. Vincent declared neutral by French and English.
1735	Black Caribs 6,000, Red Caribs 4,000. Both tribes always at war.
1748	Neutrality confirmed by Treaty of Aix-la-Chapelle.
1756	War between France and England.
1762	St. Vincent taken by General Monckton from French.
1763	Feb. 10, St. Vincent ceded to England. Many French sell property and leave Island. General Melville, Governor.
1764	Botanic Garden established. 20,538 acres sold for £162,851- 11. 7. Duke of Montague's claim to the Island declared invalid.
1767	First Legislation.
1768	Carib lands ordered to be surveyed and sold—hence dissatisfaction. A land question and Carib War.
1769	Commissioners cease surveying until King's pleasure known-
1771	Commissioners propose exchange of lands with Caribs. They refuse and deny allegiance to King George. Hostilities between Caribs and Settlers. General Leybourne Leybourne, Governor. Ulysses Fitz-maurice, Lt.-Governor.

1772	Gold Medal from Society of Arts sent to Dr. G. Young of Botanic Garden for its flourishing state. Troops under General Dalrymple arrive to aid against Caribs.
1773	Caribs reduced, and laid down their arms. Policy of Government condemned by Parliament. Treaty made with Caribs. English loss, 150 killed and wounded, 110 by climate, 428 on sick list.
1774	Grant of 4,000 acres of land to General Monckton.
1775	General Leybourne, Governor of St. Vincent, Tobago, Dominica, Grenada, died 16th April.
1776	Valentine Morris, Governor of St. Vincent alone.
1778	Grant of 662 acres of land, (Wallibou) to Col. Etherington.
1779	Dissensions between Governor and people. Assembly dissolved. Caribs and French act in concert. Island taken by French.
1780	Oct. 10, Tremendous Hurricane. Church of Kingstown and houses blown down. Two French Frigates destroyed. Admiral Rodney attempted but failed to retake St. Vincent.
1782	Nov. 9, Grant of 20,000 acres of land to Madame Swinburne by Louis of France signed at Versailles.
1783	Peace with France, and St. Vincent restored to England. Edmund Lincoln appointed Governor.
1787	James Seton appointed Governor. First Methodists in St. Vincent. £6,500 paid Madame Swinburne for her grant. 22nd April, Interment of the body of Wilfred Collingwood with military honours.
1789	St. Vincent exports 6,400 hogsheads of Sugar.
1791	Sir W. Young's visit to the Island, of which he wrote a diary.
1793	Breadfruit introduced by Capt. Bligh who left 300 plants. Mr. Lamb, a Wesleyan Missionary, imprisoned for preaching to Negroes. War with France.
1794	French intrigues with Caribs.
1795	Mar. 10, Insurrection in St. Vincent.
	April 6, 46th Regiment arrived.
	April 10, Caribs driven from camp.
	June 8, Colonel Leighton seizes Vigie.
	Sep. 18, Colonel Leighton retires on Kingstown from Mount Young. Colonel Ritchie with supplies for Vigie worsted.
	Sept. 29, General Irvin and 3 regiments arrived. Vigie abandoned.
	Oct. 1, He is foiled at Vigie, but enemy retire. Vigie and country to north occupied.
1796	Jan. 8, British camp at Colonarie surprised.
	June 8, Sir R. Abercromby and 3 regiments arrived.
	June 10, French defeated and war closed.
1797	Mar. 11, Caribs surrendered and transported to Ruattan.
1798	William Bentinck, Governor. Methodists increase to 1,000.
1799	St Vincent exports 12,120 hogsheads of Sugar.
1800	Produce of St. Vincent 16,518 hogsheads of Sugar.
1801	Produce of St. Vincent 17,908 hogsheads of Sugar.

1802	June 11, H W Bentinck arrived.
1804	Magazine door at Fort Charlotte forced open by lightning. Sir George Beckwith appointed Governor; he did, not arrive, however, at St. Vincent till 1806.
1805	St. Vincent exports 17,200 hogsheads of Sugar.
1806	Sir Geo. Beckwith, Governor.
1808	Sir Geo. Beckwith promoted to Barbados. Sir Charles Brisbane appointed Governor. Arrived in St. Vincent 1809.
1812	April 27, Eruption of Soufriere commenced.
1815	Mar. 22, W. Lockhead, Superintendent Botanic Garden died.
1816	From prudential motives, consequent on an insurrection in Barbados, St. Vincent put under Martial Law.
1817	The Newspaper *The Royal Gazette and Weekly Advertiser* first published.
1819	Severe Hurricane.
1820	Sept. 16, The Church in Kingstown consecrated.
1823	Plants from Botanic Garden removed to Trinidad.
1824	Major Champion shot by sentry at Fort Charlotte.
1825	Windward and Leeward Islands created an Episcopal See. Dr. Colridge, Bishop.
1829	Nov., Sir Charles Brisbane died.
1831	Jan. 16, Sir G. Fitzgerald Hill, Bart., Governor. Aug. 11, Great Hurricane.
1833	St Vincent, Barbados, Grenada, and Tobago, one General Government, a Governor in Chief resident at Barbados. May 4, Sir. G. Tyler (RN), Lieut-Governor.
1834	Apprenticeship of slaves established.
1836	The Newspaper *The St. Vincent Chronicle* first published.
1838	Aug. 1, Unconditional emancipation of slaves.
1839	Church of Scotland organised in St. Vincent.
1840	The Newspapers *The New Era* and *The St. Vincent Mirror* published.
1842	Jan. 3, Sir Richard Doherty, Lieutenant-Governor.
1843	Increase of Assembly from 19 to 25 members.
1845	New Legislature opened by Sir Wm. J. Struth, President. Oct. 15, Sir John Campbell, Bart., Lieutenant-Governor arrived.
1846	Portuguese labourers first introduced from Madeira. *The Carriacou Observer and Grenadines Journal* published.
1849	Outbreak of small pox, and deaths of several hundred people. Introduction of liberated Africans.
1850	Assembly reduced to 19.
1852	Dec., Outbreak of yellow fever.
1853	Jan. 10, R. G. MacDonnell (CB), Lieutenant-Governor arrived. Jan. 13, Sir J. Campbell Lieutenant-Governor, died of yellow fever.
1854	Imperial Troops withdrawn. Forts and buildings given to Colonial Government. Incumbered Estates Act passed. Cholera broke out, numerous deaths.

	Dec. 29, Edward J. Eyre, Lieutenant-Governor arrived. Report of Sir John Campbell, Lieutenant-Governor on the general improvement of native population.
1856	Executive Council of ten created, 5 from Legislative Council and 5 from Assembly. Fire at Fort Charlotte. Delegates from Legislature sent to Barbados to confer with Sir F. Hincks.
1858	The Newspaper *St. Vincent Guardian* first published.
1859	Administrative Committee of 3 members—1 from Legislative Council, 2 from Assembly—established for five years. Circuit Court of Appeal for the Windward Islands inaugurated.
1860	Post Office transferred to local control.
1861	Anthony Musgrave, Administrator arrived.
1862	Anthony Musgrave, appointed Lieutenant-Governor.
	Sept. 30th Seditious riots. Martial Law proclaimed. The Newspaper *St. Vincent Witness* first published.
1864	April 8, Constitutional change regarding the Executive Council. Sept. 6, George Berkeley, Lieutenant-Governor arrived.
1866	Oct. 29, Great fire, Kingstown. Ordnance buildings burnt.
1867	Oct. 17, Constitution Act proclaimed. A single chamber created of 12 members—6 elected 3 ex officio, 3 nominated. Franchise—freehold of £10, a leasehold of £20 or an income of £50.
1868	Troops re-stationed in Colony on payment of £4,000 per annum. Council Act modified. *The St. Vincent Government Gazette* first published.
1871	April 9, Census taken: population 35,688.
	June 3, W. H. Rennie, Lieutenant-Governor, arrived.
1872	Fire in Kingstown.
1873	Troops again removed. Disestablishment of Church. *The St. Patrick and St. David's Parish Magazine* first published. Its title was changed to *St. Vincent Church Magazine.*
1875	Feb. 2, George Dundas, Lieutenant-Governor, arrived. Aug. 5, Political constitution altered, Sept. 9, Great Flood.
1876	Dec. 6, Confirmation by Queen of constitution Act of 1875. *The Mail News and Advertiser* and the *St. Vincent Gazette and Planters Magazine* were published.
1878	Jan. 26, Legislative Council under new constitution opened by Lt.-Governor.
1879	Legislature voted £50 toward "The Alice Memorial Fund" for the extension and support of an Institution at Darmstadt. Masquerade: Riot in Kingstown.
1880	Feb. 7, Visit of Prince George.
	Mar. 16, George Dundas (CMG), Lieutenant-Governor died.
	Mar. 17, Major Strahan (CMG), Governor-in-Chief arrived from Barbados on H.M.S. *Griffon*. Military funeral of Lieutenant-Governor George Dundas (CMG), and the administration of the Holy Communion.
	May 20, Cornerstone of Chancel and Transept, Cathedral, laid. Salary of Lieutenant-Governor ceased to be paid from Imperial Funds.

1881   Feb. 1, Kingstown cemetery opened.

1883   April 7, Royal Commissioners arrived on H.M.S. *Dido*. April 17-19,
        Exhibition, in connection with International Forestry Exhibition, Edin-
        burgh.

1885   Her Majesty's Government decided not to press union of Grenada, St.
        Vincent, St. Lucia and Tobago.

1886   Feb. 2 & 3, Exhibition in connection with Colonial and Indian Exhibition,
        London.

        Aug. 16, Terrific Cyclone.

        Aug. 29, Total Eclipse of the Sun; expedition sent to W.I. Petition submit-
        ted for constitution similar to Jamaica's. The Newspaper *The Sentinel*
        first published.

1887   Jan. 12, Presentation by Mrs. Sendall of 84 diplomas and commemorative
        medals awarded by H.R.H. the Prince of Wales in connection with
        Colonial and Indian Exhibition, London.

        March 6, Consecration of Chancel and Transept. Celebration of Her Majes-
        ty's Jubilee.

        Aug. 21, Address from the Legislative Council; special service at St.
        George's Cathedral attended by His Excellency the Governor, members
        of the Councils and Public Officers. Parade Ground designated "Victoria
        Park". Dinner to the poor and inmates of the Hospital and Asylums.

1888   June 9, King Ja Ja arrived on H.M.S. *Icarus*.

1889   Jan. 1, Tobago separated from Windward Islands Govt. Colonial Silver
        Wedding gift to Their Royal Highnesses the Prince and Princess of
        Wales.

        June 1, Graham Wing at Colonial Hospital opened.

        Nov. 24, Sir W. Sendall (KCMG), left Windward Islands.

        Nov. 29, Sir W. Hely-Hutchinson arrived Windward Islands.

1890   Botanic Garden re-established. Oct. 29, Exhibition re Jamaica Exhibition
        of 1891.

1891   Feb. 28, King Ja Ja left on H.M.S. *Pylades*.

        Nov. 19, Introduction of Chief Justice Ordinance met with disapproval.
        H.M.S. *Buzzard* arrived 19th Nov. to allay the excitement. Ordinance
        withdrawn.

        Oct. 1, Streets of Kingstown lighted. *The Sentry* superseded *The Sentinel*.

1892   Jan. 20, Special funeral service at St. George's Cathedral, to correspond
        with that in London, of the lamented Prince Albert Victor.

        Aug. 2, Telephonic communication established.

1893   Mar., Public Library opened. June 30, Sir W. Hely-Hutchinson and Capt.
        I. Maling left. July 4, His Honour J. H. Sandwith arrived. Sept. 12,
        Terrific thunderstorm damage by lightning.

1894   Nov. 16, His Honour J. H. Sandwith left.

        Dec. 24, Fire at Dalrymple's Store.

1895   Feb. 25, Cricket on Victoria Park against First English Cricketers in W. I.
        Local Representatives victorious.

        Mar. 12, His Honour H. L. Thompson arrived.

Apr. 20, Barbados—Lucas to Ross—My last cable to you, one of sincere thanks for many kind attentions shewn me during our visit to the West Indies, which attentions have considerable enhanced the pleasure of our tour. May I ask one further favour by your transmitting the following farewell message to the Captains and Secretaries of the Cricket Clubs appended?—Barbados, Antigua, St. Kitts, St. Lucia, St. Vincent, Grenada, Trinidad, Georgetown, Demerara, Jamaica. We leave to-day your hospitable shores with many regrets; one and all will retain a lasting remembrance of the most delightful sojourn of the first English Cricket Team the West Indies associated with, a lively desire for a speedy return. We sail for the Old Country with a full appreciation of the merit of your cricket, the excellence of your grounds, the perfection of your climate, and warmth of your hospitality. *"Au revoir."*

Sep. 6, Thunderstorm. Telephone exchange damaged by lightning.

1896   Oct. 28, Flood causing extensive damage to property and loss of several lives.

1897   Feb. 11, Arrival of Royal Commissioners on H.M.S. Talbot.

Feb. 15, Cricket Match; Lord Hawke's team defeated local Cricketers.

June, Sir A, Moloney (KCMG), arrived, Windward Islands.

June 20, Thanksgiving services at St. George's Cathedral in celebration, 60th anniversary, Her Majesty's Accession.

June 21, Holiday, royal salute etc. and doles to the poor.

Dec. 14, First election of the Kingstown Board.

1898   Sept. 11, Disastrous hurricane.

Dec. 31, Hurricane Relief Fund amounted to £28,187 16. 11. The Woman's Guild of the Church of Scotland organized. Newspaper *The Rambler* published.

1899   Mar. 12, Memorial service at St. George's Cathedral, consequent on the death in England on Feb. 26 of His Lordship Bishop Bree.

May 17-18, Synod of the Diocese of the Windward Islands held in St. George's Cathedral.

1900   Contributions collected for sufferers at Leeward Islands exceeded £130.

Feb. 16, First installment of £200 to Soldiers' Widows and Orphans Funds remitted.

April 1, Building at Richmond Hill destroyed by fire.

May 16, Installation of His Lordship Bishop Swaby.

July 22, Branch Savings Bank, G'town and Chateaubelair. Dec. 4, Sir A. Maloney (KCMG), left Windward Islands. *The St. Vincent Times* first published.

1901   Jan. 23, Sorrowful intelligence of death of Her Majesty Queen Victoria received.

Jan. 26, Proclamation accession, King Edward VII.

Feb. 2, Memorial services in Churches and Chapels consequent on the death of Her Majesty the Queen.

May 14, His Honour E. J. Cameron arrived.

Aug 20, South-westerly gale. Considerable damage to sailing craft and the jetty in Kingstown.

1902 May 7, Eruption of the Soufriere commenced. Sent 3 electric discharges and magnificent flames from Soufriere.

1903 Feb. 24, Mr. Alexander Porter died at Kingstown Park.

1904 April 6, Ginning commenced at Govt. Cotton Factory.

1905 Mar. 14, Cricket match against Lord Brackley's team.
Sept. 12, Proposed union, Grenada & St. Vincent published.
Nov, 8, Audience protest against constitution, Legislature.
Nov. 15, Demonstration, protest against union with Grenada.

1906 May 15, Fire at Diamond Estate.

1907 Jan. 16, Sir R. C. Williams arrived Windward Islands.
Sept. 9, First *Illustrated Handbook of St. Vincent* published.
Sep. 11, Foundation stone of Free Public Library laid.
Oct. 29, The Kingstown Cotton Factory commenced ginning.

1908 July 30, Proclamation published directing that the Doubloon shall cease to be Legal Tender in the West India Colonies.
Aug. 25, F. W. Reeves, Esq. (MA Cantab), selected as Headmaster, Secondary School and Inspector of Schools. The School was opened in the latter part of Sep.

1909 Feb. 1, Free Public Library formally opened.
Apr. 28, His Hon. E. J. Cameron (CMG),, left for St. Lucia.
May 26, His Hon. The Honourable C. Gideon Murray arrived.
Oct. 13, Sir J. Hayes Sadler arrived Windward Islands.

1910 Jan. 1, Formal opening new jetty in Kingstown.
Jan. 13, *Guide book to St. Vincent* published.
Feb. 27, Arrival of Royal Commissioners.
May 7, Intelligence, death of King Edward VII received.
May 9, Accession of King George V proclaimed.
May 20, Day of mourning. Official service re death of King Edward VII held at St. George's Cathedral.
June 9, Union Island purchased by Government.

1911 Feb. 6-11, Business of Wesleyan Methodist Synod conducted.
Mar. 30-April 1, Synod of the Diocese of the Windward Islands held in the Cathedral.
May 8, The Girls' High School was formally opened by His Honour the Administrator.
June 20, Formal opening of water-service in Barrouallie.
June 22, Celebration of Coronation of Their Majesties the King and Queen.

1912 March 25, Members of the Legislative Council recorded appreciation of services rendered by His Honour W. S. Shaw, Chief Justice. An honorarium of £50 voted for the revision of the laws which he successfully accomplished.
April 4, Ceremony on the occasion of opening of new jetty at Georgetown by His Honour the Honourable C. G. Murray.

April 25, The first West Indian Needlework Exhibition was held at the Free Public Library.

May 3, First general meeting of the St. Vincent Trained Nurses Association was held at the Court House. June 1, The Office of Treasurer was separated from that of Administrator.

1913   Jan. 14, "The Customs Preferential Duties Ordinance 1913" passed the Legislature.

Aug. 4, The water-service and new jetty at town of Layou formally opened.

1914   Feb. 18, Trial trip to Georgetown of the two 5-Seat Touring Cars imported by the Government for the Windward Mails and Passenger Service.

March, St. Vincent Needlework Industry was awarded the prize for best piece of West Indian work at the West Indian Art and Needlework Exhibition held at Trinidad. The Coverlet for which the prize was given was purchased there and presented to Her Highness Princess Marie Louise of Schleswig Holstein. £45. 16. 2 was received here for articles sold.

Apr. 1, Mail Car Service, Kingstown to Georgetown.

Aug., The Martinez Gold Medal awarded to the Permanent Exhibition Committee St. Vincent for best display of Cotton at Tropical Products International Exhibition.

Nov., Subscriptions amounted to £400 to supplement £2,000 voted by Legislative Council for National Relief Fund in connection with war; in addition to 274 barrels of Arrowroot.

Nov. 22, Sir John Roche Dasent (CB) died at his residence, Ascot Heath House, England.

1915   Feb. 22, The Honourable Mrs. Murray, wife of the Administrator, presented with diamond star and Address. On 25th with selected samples of needle-work.

Mar. 9, White Kid Gloves presented to His Honour A. C. Vincent Prior in accordance with time-honoured custom there being no case for trial at the Supreme Court of Judicature in its Criminal Jurisdiction.

1915   Mar. 20, John Gregg Windsor Hazell died.

Mar. 21, St. Vincent No. 1 (Kingstown) Troop of Boy Scouts assembled at Police Barracks to make their Scout Pledge.

May 19, His Honour the Honourable C. Gideon Murray presented with a farewell Address at the Carnegie Library by Members of the Kingstown Board.

May 19, The Fountain erected at the Botanical Gardens in memory of the late John Gregg Windsor Hazell was formally opened by His Honour the Honourable C. Gideon Murray.

May, His Honour The Honourable C. Gideon Murray left the Colony for the position of Administrator of St. Lucia.

June 15, His Honour Reginald Popham Lobb (CMG),, arrived.

Sep. 19, Departure of St. Vincent's First Contingent.

Sep., His Honour the Administrator presented Her Royal Highness Princess Mary's Souvenirs to the Defence Force—Volunteers and Felice.

Oct., Machinery shelling and kiln drying corn successfully installed.

Oct. 5, Telegram from Secretary of State for Colonies "have pleasure to announce safe arrival Grenada and St. Vincent Contingents. His Majesty's Government desire to take this opportunity of conveying their hearty thanks and congratulations to these Colonies on the efforts which are being so successfully made to render effective aid in the common cause."

Nov., Mr. Leon McIntosh Clarke represented St. Vincent at Intercolonial Boy Scouts Tournament British Guiana. Mr. Alexander Smith won Silver Cup given by British Cotton Growing Association for display of Sea Island. Cotton at International Tropical Products Exhibition, held at Islington.

1916   Mar., Major Denzil Branch, a Vincentian, decorated, the Military Cress.

March 17, First Speech Day for Girls' High School.

May 5, His Excellency Sir George Haddon-Smith arrived.

Nov. 16, His Lordship Eishop Swaby died at Barbados.

Dec., The second St. Vincent Active Service. Contingent embarked.

1917   Mar. 27, Kingstown Board provided two annual scholarships—one to Grammar School and one to Girls' High School. Donations of £100 to Queen Alexandria's Field Force Fund and £100 to the War Work of the British and Foreign Sailors Society from St. Vincent Arrowroot Growers and Exporters Association.

Mar., Subscriptions to Surgical Dressings for Red Cross Hospitals Society amounted to £202.56.

1918   Aug., £210. 4. 4 collected for West Indian Flag Day Fund.

May 9, Telegram received announcing retirement of His Honour the Honourable C. Gideon Murray from Colonial Service.

Sep. 13, Fire in Kingstown, London Electric Theatre and E. Pistana's Grocery destroyed.

Nov. 11, Telegram, "Armistice with Germany signed at 5 o'clock this morning."

Nov. 12, Telegram to Secretary of State for Colonies "His Majesty's loyal subjects of the Windward Islands beg to request you to tender to His Majesty their respectful congratulations on the victorious cessation of hostilities which has been achieved by the gallantry of His Majesty's forces and the unity and steadfastness of the people of the British Empire and also on the resolute conduct of the War by His Majesty's Government whereby the honour and integrity of our great Empire has been protected and maintained." *-Hadden Smith*.

St. Vincent Arrowroot Growers and Exporters Association contributed £200 to the British Red Cross Fund and £100 for relief of Sufferers from explosion at Halifax.

Nov. 1, Dr. Irvine McDowall of St. Vincent with the B.W.I.R., in France was promoted from Lieutenant-Surgeon to Captain. St. Vincent Arrowroot Growers and Exporters Association contributed £100 to the West Indies Fund for Sailors.

1919   Feb. 25. St. Vincent Representative Government Association was formed.

March 12, Mass meeting at Kingstown under the auspices of the St. Vincent Representative Government Association.

March 22, His Honour Mr, Anthony De Freitas, Chief Justice, invested with cross of the O.B.E.

May 24, S.S. *Ajax* conveyed St. Vincent Contingents of the B.W.I.R., who returned from the War.

June 13, Other men of the St. Vincent Contingent arrived on the S.S. *Chaleur* having been transhipped from S.S. *Ortega* at Barbados.

June 27, Six invalided men of the local Contingent of the B.W.I.R. arrived on the S.S. *Chignecto*.

July 19, Bank Holiday for participating in Peace Celebrations throughout the Empire.

Aug. 8, Rev. Caspar Alleyne Downie instituted and inducted.

Aug. 11, Andrew Carnegie a philanthropist for whose gift of a library Vincentians are grateful, died of bronchial pneumonia at his Summer House at Lenox, Mass., after an illness of three days.

Aug. 21, Troopship *Pannonia* brought additional men who served with the B.W.I.R.

Oct., Newspaper *Vincentian* first published.

Oct. 16, Samuel Joyce Thomas, Chief Justice, arrived.

1919   Nov. 22, Government Motor Boat *St. Vincent* made its maiden trip to Barrouallie.

1920   Feb. 12, Miss Annie Mackie invested with the Insignia of the O.B.E.

June 30, Minor Industries and Industrial Exhibition held at the Court House.

Aug. 25, Special Service held at St. George's Cathedral on the occasion of the handing over for safe custody of the Flag and Shield (photograph) presented by the League of Empire.

Sep. 6, Celebration of Centenary of St. George's Cathedral.

1921   March 1, Medical Officer Carriacou ceased to be Medical Officer, District 6 (St. Vincent Southern Grenadines).

March 10. Publication of Secretary of State for the Colonies' telegram announcing the expedition to West Indies from London School of Tropical Medicine chiefly for study of Filariasis.

Sep. 8, Hurricane. Considerable damage; also at Trinidad, Grenada and the Grenadines. Relief Committees appointed. In St. Vincent 923 houses damaged, 375 destroyed; in the Grenadines 258 and 305 respectively.

1922   Jan. 11, The Honourable Edward Wood (MP), accompanied by the Honourable W. Ormsby-Gore (MP), and Mr. A. Wiseman of the Colonial Office arrived.

May 11, Letter received from Princess Mary expressing thanks for Casket of native wood and Address re Her Highness' marriage to Lord Lascelles.

May 26, His Majesty the King approved of the appointment of His Honour J. Stanley Rae to be Chief Justice.

Oct. 24, Message received from Captain of H.M.S. *Repulse* thanking people of St. Vincent and Grenadines for hospitality.

1923   May 24, Messages of Their Majesties the King and Queen on Empire Day to the children of the Elementary Schools.

June 2, His Majesty The King was pleased to approve of the bestowal of the Imperial Service Order on the Honourable W. C. Hutchinson.

Oct. 27, Publication of despatches relating to Mr. Wood's observation regarding association of Windward Islands and Trinidad.

1924   War Memorial Committee appointed by His Honour the Administrator.

Feb., Sir George Haddon Smith, Governor, etc., Windward Islands, retires.

March 10, First visit of United States Flying boat which conveyed His Excellency Lieutenant-Colonel W. B. Davidson-Housten (CMG), the Acting Governor of the Windward Islands.

1924   July, His Excellency Sir Frederick Seton James (KBE, CMG), Governor, etc., Windward Islands arrived at Grenada.

Dec. 2, Proclamation published relating to acquisition of land for public purpose—Wireless Station.

Dec. 13, Correspondence published relating to ill-treatment of British West Indian Labourers in Cuba.

1925   Jan. 21, Wireless Station at Cane Garden completed; greetings exchanged with England and Barbados.

March 4, Nomination of candidates for three seats in New Constitution of Legislative Council.

April, War Memorial Fund—£467. 18. 4 including £250 from Government of St. Vincent.

April 20, The Seventh Day Adventists Denomination declared to be a Religious Denomination for purpose of the Marriage Ordinance.

May 13, First session, newly constituted Legislative Council.

May 20, The Honourble James Elliott Sprott (MLC), died.

Nov. 11, Unveiling of War Memorial

1926   March 13, White Kid Gloves presented to His Honour S. J. Thomas, there being no criminal offences for trial. His Excellency Robert Walter (CMG), Acting Governor, etc., left the Colony. His Honour J. S. Rae, Chief Justice, assumed the administration.

July 9, New Code of Regulations for Primary Schools laid before Legislative Council.

Oct. 11, Ordinance to provide pensionable allowance to Head Teachers of Primary Schools published.

Nov. 10, Motor Launch *Phyllis* owned by Mr. Grafton Hazell was launched from Carpenter's Yard where it was built.

1927   Feb. 21, Message of felicitations sent to Barbados on the occasion of Tercentenary celebrations.

April 8, Leoning Amphibian Planes arrived, namely, New York, San Francisco, San Antonio and St. Louis; a photograph was taken of the

467

handing over of the mails by Major Darque to Mr. F. V. Jacobs, Chief Clerk, Post Office, in the presence of Ebenezer Evans, Senior Postman.

1928   May 23, Announcement made of the gift of "Bentinck Ledge" by Conrad Johnson Simmons to the Government.

May 23, New Legislative Council formally opened.

July 31, First appearance of Girl Guides; they marched from their Headquarters to Government House where they were received by Mrs. Walter, Commissioner, and other ladies of the Girl Guide Local Association.

1929   Feb. 1, Lord Beaverbrook's first visit to St. Vincent. Several other distinguished tourists also arrived on S.S. *Laconia*.

April 3, Major H. W. Peebles (DSO, OBE), Administrator, arrived. Gratitude expressed to Mr. Agostinho DaSilva for his untiring efforts to obtain contributions toward the building fund.

July 7, Thanksgiving Service throughout the Colony for recovery of His late Majesty King George V.

Oct. 5, Leeward District deluged by flood causing considerable damage to property including livestock.

Dec., Diocese of Windward Islands separated from that of Barbados.

1930   Feb. 21, Installation of Water Service at Troumaca.

May 1, Enthronement at St. George's Cathedral of His Lordship A. P. Berkely as first Bishop of Windward Islands Diocese.

May 23, His Excellency Sir F. S. James (KCMG), Governor, etc., left for England.

May, His Honour J. H. Jarrett, assumed the administration of the Government.

July 26, Disastrous fire at Orange Hill Estate.

Aug. 1, Frederick William Reeves (MA), died at Grenada, His indefatigable zeal for the advancement of education in St. Vincent and the advantages already accrued will ever be remembered.

Aug. 16, Government Dispensary established at Sandy Bay.

Aug. 28, Conrad Johnson Simmons died. He was a Barrister-at-law, served as a member of the Councils etc. A distinguished Vincentian.

Sep. 19, Alexander Smith, one of the oldest and largest proprietors of the Colony died.

Sep., His Lordship A. P. Berkely, Bishop of the Windward Islands, resigned.

Oct. 23, His Excellency Thomas Alexander Vans Best Governor, etc., arrived, sailed same day for St. Lucia.

Nov. 10, Vincent Hadley a prominent proprietor of St. Vincent died at Trinidad.

Nov., An appeal for contribution to establish Reeves' Memorial Scholarship Fund put into motion.

Nov., His Lordship Vibert Jackson, Archdeacon of Grenada, nominated Bishop of the Windward Islands.

Dec. 3, Handing over and opening to traffic of new Bridge over North River, Kingstown.

1931	Jan. 16, His Honour R.S. Thacker, Chief Justice, arrived.
	May 5, Election day for members of Legislative Council.
	May 20, Formal opening of Legislative Council.
	May 25, Kingstown Power Station commenced to operate.
	June 11, Address of welcome presented to Rt. Reverend Bishop Vibert Jackson (DD).
	Dec. 18, Education Commissioners arrived.
1932	July 24, Rev. Gordon V. Hazelwood, a native of St. Vincent, ordained at St. George's Cathedral.
	Nov. 27, Court "Morning Star" celebrate 88th Anniversary.
	Dec. 9, Closer Union Commission met at Council Chamber.
1933	Jan. 11, Third Annual Teachers' Conference opened by His Honour J. H. Otway, at Georgetown.
	Jan. 28, Farewell Address presented to His Honour Major H. W. Peebles (DSO, OBE), by Kingstown Board.
	Apr. 5, The Honourable A. M. Fraser invested with Insignia of the O.B.E.
	July 6, His Honour Arthur Francis Grimble, Administrator, arrived.
	July, His Excellency Sir Thomas Vans Best left the Colony. His Excellency Charles William Doorly, C.B.E., Governor, etc. (Acting) Windward Islands.
1934	Apr. 28, Dr. P. J. Kelly, Medical Commissioner, arrived. Mr. O. W. Forde, Barrister-at-Law, a native of St. Vincent appointed to act as Attorney General.
	June, Banana Association entered into first contract.
	July 5, St. Vincent Turf Club held meeting at Diamond.
	July, Miss Alice McGhee (MA), a visitor from U.S.A., gives interesting address at Public Library.
	Aug. 5, Mr. C. C. Ross, appointed Attorney General.
	Aug., Mr. T. Webster Clarke appointed to act as Inspector of Schools.
	Aug. 14, Mr. W. E. Dolly, Superintendent of Public Works, died.
	Oct., Eye Clinic opened at Colonial Hospital.
1935	Feb. 2, First Health Week at Union Island observed.
	Feb. 22, His Honour G. C. Griffith Williams, Chief Justice arrived.
	Feb. 25, His Excellency Sir Selwyn McGregor Grier took prescribed oaths as Governor, etc., Windward Islands.
	May 6, Jubilee Stamps on sale at Post Office.
	May. His late Majesty's Silver Jubilee celebrated.
	June, The Hon. J. H. Otway, Colonial Treasurer, awarded the O.B.E., (Civil Division).
	June 29, Comprehensive Report on the introduction and progress of the Banana Industry published. It was written by The Honourable C. B. Sayles the first Chairman of the Association whose enthusiasm and wide experience contributed greatly to success achieved.
	Oct. 8-11, Health Week at Bequia observed.
	Oct. 21, Disturbance in Kingstown, Riot Act read.

Nov. 9, *Vincentian* announced that Henry Langlie Wilmot Hayward, Esq., a native of St. Vincent, generously presented X-Ray Equipment for use at the Colonial Hospital. Dec., Mr. H. A. O'Reilly appointed Attorney General.

1936   Jan. 20, His Majesty King George V. died. Proclamation of accession of King Edward VIII read. Resolution of sympathy on death of His Majesty King George V.

Jan. 28, Requiem Mass at St. George's Cathedral for late King.

Feb. 11, Sir Edward Davson (Bart., KCMG), and Lady Davson arrived.

Feb. 17, Sir John and Lady Maffey arrived.

March 5, His Honour Arthur Francis Grimble (CMG), and family left on S.S. *Inanda*.

March 9, Pair of White Kid Gloves presented to His Honour G. C. Griffith Williams (MA), Chief Justice, signifying no cases for Criminal Sessions.

April 16. Anglican Synod for election of a Bishop held at Cathedral Vestry. No election.

May 5. His Honour A. Alban Wright, Administrator, formally opened the "Grimble's Village" in the vicinity of Rose Hall.

May 9, Notice relating to establishment of Infant Welfare Centre published.

June 17, At Synod in Grenada The Venerable H. N. Vincent Tonks, Archdeacon of Grenada, elected Bishop of the Windward Islands.

July 5-11, Health Week at Georgetown observed.

Aug. New School at Sandy Bay opened.

Oct. 25-30, Health Week at Barrouallie observed.

Nov. 16, His Excellency Sir Selwyn MacGregor Grier (KCMG), laid corner stone of new Mental Hospital.

Nov. 17, Education Commissioners arrived.

Dec. 10, His Lordship H. N. V. Tonks, inducted, installed and enthroned.

Dec. 12. Ex-King Edward VIII abdicated. Accession of King George VI proclaimed.

1937   Jan. 10, Celebration of 105th Anniversary of Methodism. His Majesty the King was pleased to confer the title of C.M.G. upon His Honour A. A. Wright, Administrator.

April 6, His Excellency Sir Selwyn MacGregor Grier (KCMG), opened new Legislative Council.

April, Lieutenant H. J. Hughes appointed to represent the St. Vincent Volunteer Force at the Coronation of Their Majesties the King and Queen.

April, Miss Mabel Sprott, Lieutenant, was selected by the St. Vincent Girl Guide Association as their representative at the Coronation of Their Majesties the King and Queen. Miss Zita K. Chapman a Guide of the First St. Vincent Company also a representative at the Guides Camp for attending the Coronation of Their Majesties the King and Queen.

May, Alfred Gregg Hazeell, Esq. appointed to represent St. Vincent at the Coronation of Their Majesties the King and Queen.

May 26, His Excellency H. B. Popham (CMG, MBE), Governor, etc.,

Windward Islands.

June 9, His Honour A. Alban Wright (CMG), holds Levee at Court House in honour of birthday of His Majesty the King.

June 18, Town of Bequia designated Port Elizabeth with becoming ceremony.

Aug. 2 & 4, Intercolonial Athletic Sports on Victoria Park.

Aug. 6, Sir Edward Davson (Bart., KCMG), died at his home, Eaton Place, England, at the age of 62 years.

Sept., C. W. Prescod Esq. (JP), Head Teacher, Georgetown Government School, appointed to act as Inspector of Schools.

Oct. 16, A man was electrocuted at Cane Hall Estate by lightning during thunderstorm.

Oct. 20, The Honourable Marcus Garvey (DCL), of world-wide fame—a passenger in transit—delivered interesting address to large audience at Carnegie Library.

Oct. 27, The Honourable Marcus Garvey on his return voyage again landed. He delivered another enthusiastic address when there was insufficient room in the Library to accommodate all those who attended. Again he emphasized the fact that the people must gain intelligence and avoid indolence.

Oct. 28, Annual General Meeting of Boy Scout Local Association held at Carnegie Library under the Presidency of His Honour A. Alban Wright, Administrator, when a revival Scout Campaign was launched.

ROBERT MOWBRAY ANDERSON (1870-1962)

Excerpts from
Pioneers in Nation-Building in a Caribbean Mini-State
by Sir Rupert John
©1979, United Nations Institute for Training and Research.

R. M. Anderson was born in Kingstown on 30 August 1870, the child of John Mowbray Anderson and his wife, Jane Walker Anderson (née Campbell). At the time of Robert's birth, his father was then a very active, hardworking stevedore.... Later, he ceased being a stevedore and set himself up in business as a ships' chandler, supplying the various ships that called with fruit and vegetables.

Jane Anderson was a very gentle soul, very much attached to her church, and brought up her son in "the fear and admonition of the Lord." It was not surprising, therefore, that early in his life, Robert Anderson followed closely in his mother's footsteps and became a full member of the Anglican Church, one of the church choir and a server. He was also a member of the Church Lads Brigade and was instrumental in organizing an orchestra among its members.

The educational opportunities available to Robert Anderson were no better than those open to any other black Vincentian boy of his day.... He was sent by his parents to the Anglican Primary School in Kingstown, where he remained until he was fifteen.... (Subsequently) he sought employment in the Government Printing Office and on February 6, 1886 entered that department as an apprentice.

His work provided an excellent continuation of his education and he benefited tremendously from the experience. His progress was so conspicuously outstanding that by the year 1894 he attained the position of Chief Government Printer.

Anderson exhibited such competence and versatility as Chief Government Printer that when the perplexing post of Steward of the Colonial Hospital, which called for a man of dynamism, intelligence and initiative became vacant, he was offered the position on promotion and accepted it. He assumed duties in August 1901 and remained in the post until November, 1904 when he was appointed Clerk to the Registrar of the Supreme Court and Registrar of Births, Marriages and Deaths for the First District of the Colony. At the same time, he was appointed temporary Assistant Landing Waiter (Customs Officer) for special excise duties.... In addition to the various appointments he received that year, he was also selected in August of that year to be a member of a committee to inquire into the administration of poor relief.

Though his employment in the public service of the Colony required, and received from him, his closest application and attention, Robert Anderson found the time to produce in 1907, with the permission of the Government, the first ever illustrated handbook of St. Vincent.

The reception of the first edition of the (handbook) was gratifying. In the preface to the second edition which appeared in 1909 Robert Anderson observed:

> It has been gratifying to note the warm appreciation accorded to the first issue, testified by many kind letters received and favourable references made to it by the press. Thus encouraged to perform the task he had undertaken, he hopes that the support it deserves will continue to be extended to the Handbook, and the benefit to the colony anticipated from its publication will in time be obtained

The third edition of this useful book was published in 1911, the fourth in 1914 and the fifth in 1938, by which time he had already retired from the Government Service.

During Anderson's service at the Registry as Clerk to the Registrar and Registrar of Births and Deaths for the First District, he pursued the study of law with a view to becoming a Solicitor. This he fully accomplished, and after passing the prescribed examinations and fulfilling the other requirements, he was duly admitted to practice as a Solicitor of the Colony on July 12, 1927.

For the greater part of exactly thirty-five years that he was destined to live after his admission, he conducted a busy practice as a Solicitor, advising his clients, preparing their documents and appearing for them in the courts. Yet he found time to employ himself in many other useful fields designed for the general uplift of the community of which he was such a devoted and industrious member.

Having qualified to practice as a solicitor, Anderson retired from the Civil Service. But despite a heavy schedule of legal work, he nevertheless undertook other duties. At that time, the newspaper called *The Sentry,* formerly owned and published by Joseph Elliot Sprott, was in dire need of an editor, following the death in May 1925 of the owner and publisher. Anderson was approached on the matter and willingly accepted the responsibility, for production of the weekly paper. *The Sentry* continued to flourish under his management.

It was not long before he found himself involved in the operation of another newspaper. *The Vincentian,* which had its first publication in October 1919, now needed new management. R. M. Anderson seemed to be the logical person and he gladly assumed the responsibility. Subsequently, *The Sentry* was incorporated into *The Vincentian*.

Anderson was an enthusiastic music lover. He taught vocal as well as instrumental music and encouraged his pupils to learn to play any musical instrument that came within reach of their fingers. He was one of the founding members of the St. Vincent Music Council and the first local secretary for the examinations conducted by the United Kingdom Trinity College of Music.

R. M. Anderson insisted on the use of proper, grammatical English by those around him, and himself set the example of his own impeccable orthodoxy in English usage. It may truly be said of him that he was "a well of English pure and undefiled." So impatient was he of faulty and slovenly speech, and so insistent on proper pronunciation and correct grammar, that he published a pamphlet entitled "Blunders and Blemishes", setting out common errors in English and explaining how they could be remedied.

He was an avid reader and delved deeply into the English classics. He loved Dickens, Kingsley, Scott and Thackeray. Byron, Shelley, Tennyson and Wordsworth were to him real and genuine friends with whom he lived and moved.

His ideas concerning the spoken and written word were very similar to those relating to dress. His dress was as conventionally English as was his language. I knew Robert Anderson fairly well for many years before his death on the 12th July 1962, and I cannot recall ever having seen him outside his home dressed in any other manner than in a spotless white shirt with turned up collar, commonly called 'opera,' dark tie and dark suit, topped with a black Homburg. You could see the reflection of your face from the sheen on his black boots. He disliked slovenly dress no less than he abhorred slovenly speech. I believe he would have given a very good account of himself in an English contest to determine the best dressed gentleman.

The Vincentian under his management clearly manifested the editor's Anglophilia as well as his veneration for the colonial administration. Anderson simply loved the English.

Though he could by no stretch of the imagination be branded an "agitator", a term so often used by colonial administrators to describe anyone in the colonies who clamoured for an improved constitution, yet he was one of St. Vincent's delegates to the West Indian Conference held in Dominica in 1932. The other delegate was Ebenezer Duncan, and together they sailed on 25 October for Dominica where the Conference produced some memorable results, including constitutional reform for St. Vincent, which came into effect in 1937.

For many years he was a Justice of the Peace and an Official Attestor. In 1946 His Majesty King George VI was graciously pleased to approve the award to him of the honour of Member of the Most Excellent Order of the British Empire (MBE) in His Majesty's Birthday Honours.

One might think that in a life so busily engaged in the various activities already mentioned Robert Anderson would have found time for almost nothing else. That was not so. He was an active member of the St. Vincent's Court Morning Star No. 2298 of the Ancient Order of Foresters, as well as a member of the Grand United Order of Odd Follows. He loved cricket and was for many years an enthusiastic cricketer. He also played tennis and was a member of the Kingstown Tennis Club.

R. M. Anderson was a public-spirited, devoted Vincentian whose dedication to duty and to the things he valued might well be emulated by every young Vincentian desirous of playing his part in the progress of his homeland. He was always willing to help where there was a need and loved knowledge in all its manifold forms. Such knowledge he desired not for personal aggrandizement but for sharing with others that together they might lift the general standard of their community. He was a sound and sensible man whose life has meant much to many.

So, we honour the memory of Robert Mowbray Anderson, a light and inspiration to all Vincentians. He will ever be remembered by generations yet unborn by those footprints so indelibly impressed upon the sands of time. He has received for himself praise that will never die and a fitting monument in the hearts of all Vincentians.

Made in the USA
Columbia, SC
06 May 2022